A Garland Series

CLASSICS OF

ENGLISH LEGAL HISTORY

IN THE MODERN ERA

One Hundred and Forty-Two
Rare and Important Titles
Reproduced in Facsimile
in One Hundred and Eleven Volumes

Selected by

David S. Berkowitz
Samuel E. Thorne

William Hawkins

A TREATISE OF THE PLEAS OF THE CROWN

in two volumes
Vol. I

Garland Publishing, Inc.
New York & London • 1978

Bibliographical note:
This facsimile has been made
from a copy in the British Library
(1471.K.21)

*The volumes in this series are printed on
acid-free, 250-year-life paper.*

Library of Congress Cataloging in Publication Data

Hawkins, William, 1673-1746.
A treatise of the pleas of the crown.

(Classics of English legal history in the modern era)
Reprint of the 1716-21 ed. printed by E. Nutt for
J. Walthoe, London.
Includes index.
1. Pleas of the crown. I. Title. II. Series.
KD7869.H39 1979 345'.41'072 77-86642
ISBN 0-8240-3079-6

Printed in the United States of America

A

TREATISE

OF THE

PLEAS

OF THE

CROWN:

OR A

SYSTEM of the Principal Matters relating to that SUBJECT, digested under their proper Heads.

BOOK I.

By *WILLIAM HAWKINS*,
of the *Inner-Temple*, Esq;.

In the *SAVOY*,

Printed by Eliz. Nutt, (Executrix of J. Nutt, Assignee of *Edward Sayer*, Esq;) for J. Walthoe in the *Middle-Temple-Cloysters*; and J. Walthoe, *jun.* against the *Royal-Exchange* in *Cornhill*. 1716.

To the Right Honourable,

THOMAS Lord *PARKER*,

Baron of *MACCLESFIELD*,

Lord Chief Justice of *ENGLAND*.

My LORD,

THE following Treatise containing that Part of the Law, which is peculiarly under the Administration of the Chief Justice of *England*, I presum'd, in regard to the Subject of it, to think of presenting it to your Lordship, which your Goodness having been pleased to permit, it is with the less Uneasiness that I venture to make it Publick; for I could not hope to introduce it into the World with greater Advantage than under your Protection.

This was the real Ground of my Ambition, to dedicate it to your Lordship, and not to give my self an Opportunity of publishing how much I honour those wonderful Talents, that have raised You to so high a Station: A private Character indeed may be set forth to Advantage, and many Virtues in it be made known by an Address of this Nature, which might otherwise have lain for ever concealed: But your Lordship's is Publick and Conspicuous, and can appear no where with so much Lustre as when you sit in Judgment, where that vast Genius you are bless'd with, shines forth to all the World, adorn'd with all the Improvements that Humane Art can furnish, and supported with the greatest Courage and Integrity.

And nothing less, My Lord, could give You that Command of all the Variety of Business which comes before You, and that Facility with which You dispatch it: The most intricate Points of Law, that have for Ages lain in Confusion and Obscurity, when they fall under your Lordship's Consideration, receive such Light, are stated and explain'd with such exact Method, and such Propriety and Beauty of Expression, that the most Polite Compositions appear not

more

more Elegant, nor the most Demonstrative more Convincing: This, My Lord, is the agreeable Part of the Exercise of your Authority, being no Violence to that general Humanity which You delight to shew to all Mankind: But the Duties of your Office require You sometimes to put on another Character, and to shew the awful Face of Justice, to curb the Rage of an unruly People, and to fright them into their Duty by the Terrours of the Law; and 'tis with Pleasure all good Men see your Lordship pursue the prevailing Vices of the Age with such Zeal and Indignation, that Crimes no longer appear less odious for being fashionable, nor are the more secure from Punishment for being popular.

These, My Lord, are Blessings which the whole Nation shares in, and have an Influence upon all Parts of the civil Administration: But we, who have the Honour to attend your Lordship at the Bar, are in a more particular Manner to acknowledge our Obligations, for that Candour and Condescension with which You treat us: The Encouragement You give to our weak Endeavours no less engages our Affections, than your comprehensive Knowledge and clear and accurate Judgment command our Reverence and Esteem.

Such Goodness charms all that approach and feel it; and it was with universal Joy we saw your Lordship's Firmness to the present Establishment, and great Services to your Country, distinguished lately by an Accession of Honour from his Majesty, whose Wisdom in conferring his Favours has eminently appeared, by the many signal Benefits the Nation has received from those who have the Honour to serve Him. I am with the greatest Respect,

MY LORD,

Your Lordship's

Most obliged,

And most Humble Servant,

William Hawkins.

THE

PREFACE.

NOTHING is more common than to hear those who have taken only a superficial View of the Crown-Law, charge it with numberless Hardships and undistinguishing Rigour; whereas those who have more fully examin'd it, agree, that it wants nothing to make it admir'd, for Clemency and Equity, as well as Justice, but to be understood: It is so agreeable to Reason, that even those who suffer by it, cannot charge it with Injustice; so adapted to the common Good, as to suffer no Folly to go unpunished, which that requires to be restrained; and yet so tender of the Infirmities of Humane Nature, as never to refuse an Indulgence where the Safety of the Publick will bear it; it gives the Prince no Power, but of doing Good; and restrains the People from no Liberty, but of doing Evil.

It would be needless therefore to say any Thing of the Usefulness of this Treatise, could I be so happy as any Way to come up to the Design of it, which was, to vindicate the Justice and Reasonableness of the Laws concerning criminal Matters, and to reduce them into as clear a Method, and explain them in as familiar a Manner, as the Nature of the Thing will bear.

Had any of those great Men, who formerly have written on this Subject, gone through the whole Law relating to it, all farther Attempts of this Kind had been unnecessary. The Treatise published under the Name of Sir Matthew Hale, is indeed very useful, and written in a clear Method, and with great Learning and Judgment; but is certainly very imperfect in the Whole, and seems to be only a Model or Plan of a Work of this Kind, which is said to have been intended by him.

Sir Edw. Coke's *third Institute is also a Treatise of great Learning, and not unworthy of the Hand that produc'd it; but yet it seems by no Means a compleat Work, many considerable Heads being either wholly omitted in it, or barely touched upon.*

The Treatise of Sir Will. Staundforde *seems to be writ with great Judgment, but he takes in a very small Compass, scarce mentioning any Offences under Felonies.*

As for the Treatises of Lambard, Crompton, Pulton, *and* Dalton, *they having an Eye chiefly to the Direction of Justices of Peace; and, treating of the Crown-Law no farther than as it concerns them, are far from being compleat Systems of it.*

Upon the whole, I apprehended that none of the Authors before mentioned were so perfect, but that, by reducing all the Laws relating to this Subject, under one general Scheme, they might generally be understood with much less Difficulty than they have hitherto been. This 'twas induc'd me to write on this Subject, and I hope to finish the Whole in two Books, proposing in this First to show the Nature of criminal Offences; and in the Second, the Manner of bringing Offenders to Punishment.

AN

AN
ANALYSIS
OF THE
First BOOK
OF THE
Pleas of the CROWN.

ALL Persons whatsoever are liable to be punish'd as Criminal Offenders, unless they can excuse themselves, either,

1. In respect of their want of Reason: Or,
2. In respect of their Subjection to the Power of others. ch. 1.

Offences considered in relation to the Persons against whom they are committed, are either,

1. Such as are more immediately against God: Or,
2. Such as are more immediately against Man.

Offences more immediately against God are either by Common Law or by Statute.

Those at Common Law are either capital or not capital.

The capital are of three kinds.

1. Heresy, ch. 2.
2. Witchcraft, ch. 3.
3. Sodomy, ch. 4.

Those not capital are either by Common Law or Statute.

Those by Common Law are of five kinds.

1. Blasphemies against God, ch. 5. sect. 1.
2. Scoffing at the Scriptures, ch. 5. sect. 2.
4. Impostures in Religion, ch. 5. sect. 3.
4. Open Lewdness grosly scandalous, ch. 5. sect. 4.
5. Seditious Words against the established Religion, ch. 5. sect. 6.

Those by Statute are two-fold.

1. Such as are against Religion in general.
2. Such as are against the established Church.

Those against Religion in general are of four kinds.

1. Profanations of the Lord's Day, ch. 6. sect. 1, 2, 3.
2. Profane Swearing and Cursing, ch. 6. sect. 4.
3. Drunkenness, ch. 6. sect. 5.
4. Reviling the Lord's Supper, ch. 6. sect. 6.

Those against the established Church are three-fold.

1. Such as concern all Persons in general.
2. Such as more immediately relate to those of the Popish Religion.
3. Such as more immediately regard Protestant Dissenters, ch. 16.

Those which concern all Persons in general, are either,

1. Against the Common Prayer, ch. 7. Or,
2. In accepting or holding an Office without due Conformity to the Church, ch. 8. Or,

3. In

3. In Teaching School without conforming to the Church, ch. 9. Or,

4. In not coming to Church, ch. 10, 11.

Thoſe relating more immediately to Perſons of the Popiſh Religion are of four kinds,

1. Popiſh Recuſancy, ch. 12.

2. The Offence of ſaying or hearing of Maſs, or other Popiſh Service, ch. 13.

3. The Offence of not making a Declaration againſt Popery, ch. 14.

4. The Offence of promoting or encouraging the Popiſh Religion; either,

1. In giving or receiving Popiſh Education, ch, 15. ſect. 1,2,3. Or,

2. In profeſſing the Popiſh Religion, ch. 15, from ſect. 4. to ſect. 15. Or,

3. In buying or ſelling Popiſh Books, ch. 15. ſect. 15.

Offences more immediately againſt Man, are either more immediately againſt the King, or more immediately againſt the Subject.

Thoſe more immediately againſt the King, are either capital or not capital.

The capital are either,

1. High Treaſon: Or,

2. Felonies.

High Treaſon is either,

1. Such as is within 25 *E.* 3. and other Statutes grounded upon it, and explaining it: Or,

2. Such as depends upon ſubſequent Statutes.

Of Treaſon within 25 *Ed.* 3. there are four Species.

1. That which immediately concerns the King, his Wife or Children, ch. 17. ſect. 3, 4, *&c.*

2. That which concerns his Office in the Adminiſtration of Juſtice, ch. 17. ſect. 46.

3. That which concerns his Seal, ch. 17. ſect. 48.

4. That which concerns his Coin, ch. 17. ſect. 54.

Of High Treaſon depending on ſubſequent Statutes, there are three ſpecies.

1. Offences in upholding or favouring the Power of the Pope.

2. Offences againſt the Proteſtant Succeſſion, ch. 17. ſect. 85.

3. Offences in liſting Men without the King's Licence, ch. 17. ſect. 86.

Of Offences in upholding or favouring the Power of the Pope, there are five Species.

1. Extolling the Pope's Power, ch. 17. ſect. 72.

2. Putting in Ure Popiſh Bulls, ch. 17. ſect. 75.

3. Perverting others, or being perverted to Popery, ch. 17. ſect. 76.

4. Receiving Popiſh Orders or Education in Popiſh Seminaries, and not ſubmitting, *&c.* ch. 17. ſect. 79.

5. Refuſing a ſecond Tender of the Oaths, ch. 17. ſect. 84.

Felonies more immediately againſt the King are of five kinds.

1. Offences relating to the Coin or Bullion.

2. Offences againſt the King's Council, ch. 18. ſ. 8.

3. The Offence of paſſing beyond Sea to ſerve a Foreign Prince, ch. 18. ſect. 10.

4. The Offence of imbezilling the King's Armour, ch. 18. ſect. 12.

5. The Offence of relieving a Popiſh Prieſt, ch. 18. ſect. 14.

Of Felony relating to the Coin or Bullion, there are three Species.

1. The Offence of debaſing it, ch. 18. ſect. 1.

2. The Offence of unlawfully diminiſhing it, ch. 18. ſect. 2.

3. The Offence of endeavouring by extraordinary Means to encreaſe it, ch. 18. ſect. 7.

Of Offences more immediately againſt the King, not capital, there are two kinds.

1. *Præmunire.*

2. Miſpriſion.

Offences coming under the notion of *Præmunire*, are either,

1. Againſt the Prerogative of the Crown: Or,

2. Againſt the Authority of the King and Parliament, ch. 19. ſect. 44.

Of Offences of this kind againſt the Prerogative of the Crown, there are nine Species.

1. Making uſe of Papal Bulls, ch. 19. ſect. 12.

2. Derogating from the King's Common Law-Courts, ch. 19. ſect. 14.

3. Appealing to *Rome* from any of the King's Courts, ch. 19. ſect. 20.

4. Exerciſing the Juriſdiction of a Suffragan, without the Appointment of the Biſhop of the Dioceſe, ch. 19. ſect. 21.

5. Re

5. Refusing to elect or consecrate the Person nominated by the King to a Bishoprick, ch. 19. sect. 22.
6. Maintaining the Pope's Power, ch. 19. sect. 23.
7. Bringing in *Agnus Dei*, ch. 19. sect. 24.
8. Contributing to the Maintainance of a Popish Seminary, ch. 19. sect. 26.
9. Refusing the Oaths, ch. 19. sect. 27.

Misprisions more immediately against the King are either Negative or Positive.

The Negative is commonly called Misprision of Treason, ch. 20.

Positive Misprisions of this kind, either amount to Misprision of Treason, or do not.

Of such Misprisions, amounting to Misprisions of Treason, there is only one Species; forgeing foreign Coin not currant here, ch. 20. sect. 7.

Of such Misprisions not amounting to Misprision of Treason, there are four kinds.

1. Contempts against the King's Palace or Courts of Justice, ch. 21.
2. Contempts against his Prerogative, ch. 22.
3. Contempts against his Person or Government, ch. 23.
4. Contempts against his Title, ch. 24.

Of Contempts against the King's Prerogative, there are three Species.

1. Refusing to assist him for the Good of the Publick, ch. 22. sect. 2.
2. Preferring the Interests of a Foreign Prince to that of our own, ch. 22. sect. 3.
3. Disobeying the King's lawful Commands or Prohibitions, ch. 22. sect. 4.

Of Contempts against the King's Person or Government, there are six kinds.

1. Charging the Government with Oppression or weak Administration, ch. 23. sect. 2.
2. Doing an Act which impliedly encourages Rebellion, ch. 23. sect. 4.
3. Endeavouring to frighten the King into a change of his Measures, ch. 23. sect. 4.
4. Spreading false Rumours concerning the King's Intentions, ch. 23. sect. 5.
5. Charging him with a Breach of his Coronation-Oath, ch. 23. sect. 6.
6. Speaking contemptuously of him, ch. 23. sect. 7.

Of Contempts against the King's Title, there are two kinds.

1. Denying his Title, ch. 24. sect. 1.
2. Refusing to take the Oaths required by Law for the support of his Government.

Of Offences in refusing to take such Oaths, there are two kinds.

1. The Offence of refusing the Oath required by Common Law, ch. 24. sect. 3.
2. The Offence of refusing the Oaths required by Statute.

Of Offences in refusing the Oaths required by Statute, there are two kinds.

1. The Offence of refusing the Oaths of Allegiance and Supremacy, ch. 24. sect. 5.
2. The Offence of refusing the Oath of Abjuration, ch. 24. sect. 6.

Offences more immediately against the Subject are either capital or not capital.

The capital are either by the Common Law or by Statute.

Those by the Common Law are committed either,

1. Against the Life of a Man; or,
2. Against his Goods; or,
3. Against his Habitation; or,
4. Against publick Justice.

Those against the Life of a Man are either,

1. Casual, not being occasion'd by the default or procurement of any Man, ch. 26. Or
2. Such as come under the Notion of Homicide, being occasioned by a Man, ch. 26. sect. 2.

Of Homicides there are two kinds.

1. Such as is committed against a Man's own Life, ch. 27.
2. Such as is committed against the Life of another.

Of Homicide against the Life of another, there are two kinds.

1. Such as amounts not to Felony.
2. Such as amounts to Felony.

Of such Homicide not amounting to Felony there are two kinds.

1. Justifiable.
2. Excusable.

Justifiable Homicide is either of a publick or a private Nature.

That of a publick Nature is of two kinds.

1. Such

ANALYSIS.

1. Such as happens in the due Execution, ch. 28. sect. 4. and
2. Such as happens in the due Advancement, of publick Justice.

Of the later there are two kinds.

1. Such as happens in Criminal. ch. 28. sect. 11. And
2. Such as happens in Civil Causes, ch. 28. sect. 17.

Of justifiable Homicide of a private Nature, there are two kinds.

1. Such as happens in killing a Wrong-Doer, ch. 28. sect. 21.
2. Such as happens in killing an innocent Person, ch. 28. sect. 26.

Of excusable Homicide there are two kinds.

1. Homicide *per infortunium*, ch. 29. sect. 1.
2. Homicide *Se defendendo*, ch. 29. sect. 13.

Homicide against the Life of another, amounting to Felony, is either with or without Malice.

That which is without Malice is called Manslaughter or Chancemedley, ch. 30.

Of such Homicide with Malice there are two kinds.

1. Murder, ch. 31.
2. Petit Treason, ch. 32.

Of Murder there are two kinds.

1. Such as is done with express Malice.
2. Such as is done with implied Malice.

Of Murder done with express Malice, there are three kinds.

1. Such as happens in Duelling, ch. 31. sect. 21.
2. Such as happens in killing another without any Provocation; or but upon a slight one, ch. 31. sect. 32.
3. Such as happens in killing one whom the Person killing intended to hurt in a less Degree, ch. 31. sect. 38.

Murder done with implied Malice, generally happens in the following Instances.

1. Where the principal Intention is to commit another Felony, ch. 31. sect. 41.
2. Where the principal Design is to commit a bare breach of the Peace, not intended against the Person of him who happens to be slain, ch. 31 sect. 46.
3. Where the chief Motive is to assist a third Person, ch. 31. sect. 49.
4. Where the direct Design is to escape from an Arrest, ch. 31. sect. 55.
5. Where the principal Purpose is to usurp an illegal Authority, ch. 31. sect. 59.
6. Where no Mischief is intended at all, ch. 31. sect. 61.

Of Petit Treason there are three kinds, ch. 32.

1. Where a Servant kills his Master.
2. Where a Wife kills her Husband.
3. Where an Ecclesiastical Person kills his Prelate.

Of capital Offences at Common Law against the Goods of another, there are two kinds.

1. Simple Larceny.
2. Mix'd Larceny.

Of simple Larceny there are also two kinds.

1. Grand Larceny, ch. 32. sect. 1.
2. Petit Larceny, ch. 32. sect. 31.

Mix'd Larceny is either from the Person of a Man, or from his House, ch. 36.

Of mix'd Larceny from the Person there are two kinds.

1. Robbery, ch. 34.
2. Larceny from the Person, ch. 35.

Also there is another Offence of this Nature call'd Piracy, ch. 37.

Capital Offences at Common Law against the Habitation of a Man are of two kinds.

1. Burglary, ch. 38.
2. Arson, ch. 39.

Offences more immediately against the Subject made capital by Statute, are such as are committed.

1. Against Women, (and of these there are two kinds.
    1. Rape.
    2. Forcible Marriage.)
2. Against the Rights of Marriage, ch. 43.
3. Against the Members of a Man's Body, ch. 44.
4. Against Records, ch. 45.
5. Against Cattle, ch. 46.
6. By Purveyors, ch. 47.
7. By Soldiers and Mariners, ch. 48.
8. By Hunters, ch. 49.

9. By

9. By Forgers of false Deeds, ch. 50.
10. By Gaolers, ch. 51.
11. By Transporters of Sheep or Wool, ch. 52.
12. By Servants, ch. 53.
13. By *Egyptians*, ch. 54.
14. By cutters of Pow-dike, ch. 55.
15. By Trespassers on the Borders, and Rioters, ch. 56.
16. By Bankrupts, ch. 57.
17. By Counterfeiters of Bank-Notes, Exchequer-Bills, Stamps, South-Sea Bonds, Lottery-Orders, &c. ch. 58.

Offences more immediately against the Subject not capital, are of two kinds.

1. Misprision of Felony, ch. 59.
2. Other inferiour Offences.

Such inferiour Offences are of two kinds.

1. Such as amount to an actual Disturbance of the Peace.
2. Such as do not amount to such a Disturbance.

For the prevention of the former of these kinds of Offences, the Law has provided two Remedies.

1. By Surety for keeping the Peace, ch. 60.
2. By Surety for the good Behaviour, ch. 61.

Of the abovementioned Offences amounting to the actual Disturbance of the Peace, there are two kinds.

1. Such as may be committed by one or two Persons.
2. Such as require a greater Number.

Of those which may be committed by one or two Persons there are four kinds.

1. Assaults, ch. 62. sect. 1.
2. Batteries, 62. sect. 2.
3. Affrays, ch. 63.
4. Forcible Entries and Detainers, ch. 64.

Of those which require a greater Number of Persons, there are three kinds.

1. Riots, ch. 65. sect. 1.
2. Routs, ch. 65. sect. 8.
3. Unlawful Assemblies, ch. 65. sect. 9.

Of such inferiour Offences not amounting to an actual Disturbance of the Peace, there are two kinds.

1. Such as are committed by Officers.
2. Such as are committed by common Persons without any relation to an Office.

Of Offences of this Nature committed by Officers, there are three Species.

1. Neglect or breach of Duty, ch. 66.
2. Bribery, ch. 67.
3. Extortion, ch. 68.

Of Offences of this Nature, committed by private Persons, without any relation to any Office, there are two kinds.

1. Such as are infamous and grosly scandalous, proceeding from Principles of down-right Dishonesty, Malice or Faction.
2. Such as are of an inferiour Nature, and neither infamous nor grosly scandalous.

Of Offences of the first sort, there are six Species.

1. Perjury, ch. 69.
2. Forgery, ch. 70.
3. Cheats, ch. 71.
4. Conspiracy, ch. 72.
5. Libels, 73.
6. Keeping of a Bawdy-house, ch. 74.

Of Offences of the latter sort there are two kinds.

1. Such as more immediately affect the Publick.
2. Such as more immediately affect the Interests of particular Persons.

Of those which more immediately affect the Publick, there are four kinds.

1. Common Nusances, ch. 75.
2. Monopolies, ch. 79.
3. Forestaling, Ingrossing, and Regrating, ch. 80.
4. Barratry, ch. 81.

The most remarkable kinds of common Nusances are,

1. Such as relate to Highways.
2. Such as relate to Publick Houses, ch. 78.

Those which relate to Highways come under a two-fold Consideration.

1. As they relate to Highways in general, ch. 76.
2. As they relate to Bridges in particular, ch. 77.

Of

ANATYLIS.

Of the Offences above-mentioned more immediately affecting the Interests of particular Persons, there are three kinds.

1. Usury, ch. 82.
2. Maintenance.
3. Buying or selling a pretended Title, ch. 86.

Maintenance is Two fold.

1. *Ruralis*, ch. 63. sect. 2.
2. *Curialis*, ch. 83. sect. 3.

Of Maintenance *Curialis*, there are three Species.

1. General Maintenance, ch. 83. sect. 4.
2. Champerty, ch. 84.
3. Embracery, ch. 85.

A N

AN ACCOUNT OF THE AUTHORS Referred to in this BOOK.

	A.
Aleyn	*Aleyn's Reports.*
And. 1, 2.	*Anderson's Reports, first and second Part.*
Ass. 1, 2, 3, 4, &c.	*The Book of Assizes in the Reign of King Edward the third, for the first, second, third, fourth Years, &c.*
	B.
Barrow	*Barrow's Supremacy.*
Benloe	*Benloe's Reports.*
Brac. Bracton	*Bracton, De legibus & consuetudinibus Angliæ.*
Bridg.	*Bridgman's Reports.*
Bro.	*Brook's Abridgment.*
Bul. 1, 2, 3.	*Bulstrode's Reports, the first, second and third Part.*
	C.
Caw. Cawley	*Cawley's Laws against Recusants.*
Co. 1, 2, &c.	*Sir Edward Coke's Reports, the first and second Part, &c.*
Co. Litt	*Sir Edward Coke's Commentary upon Littleton.*
Cro. E.	*Croke's Reports for the Reign of Queen Elizabeth.*
Cro. Ja.	*Croke's Reports for the Reign of King James the first.*
Cro. Ca.	*Croke's Reports for the Reign of King Charles the first.*
Crom.	*Crompton's Office of a Justice of Peace; printed in the Year 1606.*
	D
Dalis.	*Dalison's Reports.*
Dal.	*Dalton's Country Justice, printed in the Year 1655.*
Danv. Abr. 1, 2.	*D'Anvers's Abridgment, first and second Part.*
Dav. Davis	*Davis's Reports.*
Dy. Dyer	*Dyer's Reports.*
	F.
F. N. B.	*Fitzherbert's Natura Brevium.*
Fitz.	*Fitzherbert's Abridgment.*
	G.
Gibs. Gibson	*Gibson's Codex Juris Ecclesiastici Anglicani.*

An Account, &c.

H.	
H. P. C.	*Hale's Pleas of the Crown.*
Hard.	*Hardress's Reports.*
Hetl.	*Hetley's Reports.*
Hob.	*Hobart's Reports.*
Hutt.	*Hutton's Reports.*
J.	
1 Jon. Sir Wm. Jon.	*Sir William Jones's Reports.*
2 Jon.	*Sir Thomas Jones's Reports.*
1 Inſ.	*Coke upon Littleton.*
2 Inſ.	*The ſecond Part of Coke's Inſtitutes.*
3 Inſ.	*The third Part of Coke's Inſtitutes.*
4 Inſ.	*The fourth Part of Coke's Inſtitutes.*
K.	
Keb. 1, 2, 3.	*Keble's Reports, the firſt, ſecond and third Part.*
Kell.	*Kellewey's Reports.*
Kelynge	*Kelynge's Reports.*
Kitch.	*Kitchin, of Courts-Leet and Courts-Baron.*
L.	
Lam. Lamb.	*Lambard's Office of Juſtices of Peace, printed in the Year 1614.*
Lane	*Lane's Reports.*
Latch.	*Latch's Reports.*
Leon. 1, 2. 3.	*Leonard's Reports, the firſt, ſecond and third Part.*
Lev. 1, 2.	*Levinz's Reports, the firſt and ſecond Part.*
Litt.	*Littleton's Reports.*
M.	
Mar.	*March's Reports.*
Mod. 1, 2. 3, &c.	*Modern Reports, the firſt, ſecond and third Part, &c.*
Mo.	*Moore's Reports.*
N.	
Noy	*Noy's Reports.*
O.	
Ow. Owen.	*Owen's Reports.*
Pal. Palm.	*Palmer's Reports.*
Parſons	*Parſons againſt Sir Edward Coke's fifth Inſtitute.*
Pl. Com.	*Plowden's Commentaries.*
Po. Poph.	*Popham's Reports.*
Pult.	*Pulton, De Pace Regis & Regni.*
R.	
Ray. Raym.	*Raymond's Reports.*
Reg.	*Regiſter.*
R. A. Rol. Ab. 1, 2.	*Rolle's Abridgment, the firſt and ſecond Part.*
R. R. Rol. Re. 1, 2.	*Rolle's Reports, the firſt and ſecond Part.*
Ruſhw. Coll.	*Ruſhworth's Collections.*
S.	
Saun. 1, 2.	*Saunder's Reports, the firſt and ſecond Part.*
Sav.	*Savil's Reports.*
Selden's Janus Anglorum	*Jani Anglorum facies altera by Mr. Selden, tranſlated into Engliſh by Redman Weſtcot, and printed in the Year 1682.*
Selden's Epinomis	*England's Epinomis by Mr. Selden, printed in the Year 1682.*
Sid. Syd. 1, 2.	*Siderfin's Reports, the firſt and ſecond Part.*
V.	
Vaugh.	*Vaughan's Reports.*
Vent. 1, 2.	*Ventris's Reports, the firſt and ſecond Part.*
W.	
Watſ. Watſon	*Watſon's Compleat Incumbent, Folio Edition.*
Win. Winch	*Winch's Reports.*
Wood's Inſ.	*Wood's new Inſtitute of the Imperial or Civil Law.*
Y.	
Year Books.	
Yel.	*Yelverton's Reports.*

A

A TREATISE OF THE PLEAS OF THE CROWN.

BOOK I.

CHAP. I.

Of the Persons who may be guilty of criminal Offences.

THE Guilt of offending againſt any Law whatſoever, neceſſarily ſuppoſing a wilful Diſobedience thereof, can never juſtly be imputed to thoſe who are either uncapable of underſtanding it, or of conforming themſelves to it: Therefore, before I come to the ſeveral kinds of Offences, I ſhall ſhew what Degrees of Diſcretion and Freedom are neceſſarily required in the Commiſſion of them; for the better Underſtanding whereof, I ſhall conſider what Offenders are excuſable,

1. In reſpect of their Want of Reaſon;
2. In reſpect of their Subjection to the Power of others.

Sect. 1. As to the firſt Point it is to be obſerv'd, [a] That thoſe who are under a natural Diſability of diſtinguiſhing between Good and Evil, as Infants under the Age of Diſcretion, Ideots and Lunaticks, are not puniſhable by any criminal Proſecution whatſoever.

[a] H.P.C. 10. 43, 65. Pult. 122. b. Dalt. ca. 95. Bro. Coron. 6, 61, 136, 170, 217. 3 H. 7. 1. b.

Sect. 2. Indeed it was [b] anciently holden, in Reſpect of that high Regard which the Law has for the Safety of the King's Perſon, That a Madman might be puniſh'd as a Traitor, for killing or offering to kill the King; but this is [c] contradicted by the later Opinions.

[b] 4 Co. 124. b. 2 Rol. Rep. 324.

[c] 3 Inſt. 46. 6. H. P. C. 10. 43. Co. Litt. 247.

Sect. 3. And it ſeems agreed at this [d] Day, That if one who has committed a capital Offence, become *Non Compos* before Conviction, he ſhall not be arraigned; and if after Conviction, that he ſhall not be executed.

[d] H. P. C. 10. 3 Inſt. 4. 6. 1 And. 107, 109. 26 Aſſ. Pl. 27. Sav. 50, 57.

Sect. 4. But by 12 *Annæ*, 23. which ſeems to be agreeable to the [e] ancient Common Law, a dangerous Madman may be kept in Priſon till he recover his Senſes; and by the Common Law, if it be doubtful whether a Criminal, who at his Trial is in [f] appearance a Lunatick, be ſuch in Truth or not, it ſhall be tried by an Inqueſt of Office, to be returned by the Sheriff of the County wherein the Court ſits; and if it be found by them that the Party only feigns himſelf mad, [g] and he ſtill refuſe to anſwer, he ſhall be dealt with as one who ſtands mute.

[e] 26 Aſſ. Pl. 27. Bro. Coron. 101.

[f] 1 And. 107. Sav. 50.

[g] H.P.C. 226. Sav. 56.

Sect. 5. And if one who wants Diſcretion commit a [h] Treſpaſs againſt the Perſon or Poſſeſſion of another, he ſhall be compelled in a civil Action to give Satisfaction for the Damage.

[h] 2 R.A. 547. Pl. 4. Ho. 134.

Sect. 6. And he who is guilty of any Crime whatever, thro' his [i] voluntary Drunkenneſs, ſhall be puniſhed for it as much as if he had been ſober.

35 H. 6. 11. b. Co. Lit. 247. b. Bro. Coron. 6. Dalt. ca. 95.

Sect. 7. Alſo he who incites a Madman to do a Murther or other Crime is a [k] principal Offender, and as much puniſhable as if he had done it himſelf.

[i] Co. Lit 247.

[k] H. P. C. 43, 44. Keyl. 53. Dalt. ca. 95.

Sect. 8. And if it appear by the Circumſtances, that an Infant under the Age of Diſcretion could [l] diſtinguiſh between Good and Evil, as if one of the Age of nine or ten Years kill another, and hide the Body, or make Excuſes, or hide himſelf, he may be convicted and condemned, and forfeit, *&c.* as much as if he were of full Age. But in ſuch a Caſe the Judges will in Prudence reſpite the Execution in order to get a Pardon: And it is ſaid, That if an Infant apparently wanting Diſcretion, be indicted and found guilty of Felony, the Juſtices themſelves may diſmiſs him without a Pardon, *&c.*

[l] H. P. C. 43. 12 Aſſ. Pl. 30. 3 H. 7. 1, b. 12. b. Bro. Coron. 74, 133. 3 H. 7. 1. b. 12. b.

As to the ſecond Point, *viz.* How far thoſe are to be excuſed who are under the Power of others:

S. P. C. 16. F. H. P. C. 35. 35 H. 6. 11. b. Bro. Coron. 6, 61.

Sect. 9. 1. A Feme Covert is ſo much favour'd in reſpect of that Power and Authority which her Husband has over her, that ſhe ſhall not ſuffer any Puniſhment for committing a bare [m] Theft in Company with, or by Coercion of, her Husband.

[m] Keyl. 31. S. P. C. 26. c. 142. c. 27 Aſſ. 40. H. P. C. 65.

Sect. 10. Neither ſhall ſhe be deemed acceſſary [n] to a Felony for receiving her Husband who has been guilty of it, as her Husband ſhall be for receiving her.

[n] 3 Inſt. 108. H. P. C. 65.

Sect. 11. But if ſhe commit a Theft of her own voluntary [o] Act, or by the bare command of her Husband; or be guilty of Treaſon, Murther, or Robbery, in Company with, or by Coercion of, her Husband, ſhe is puniſhable as much as if ſhe were Sole.

[o] H. P. C. 65. Dalt. ca. 104.

Sect. 12. Alſo a Wife may be indicted together with her Husband, and condemned to the Pillory with him for keeping a Bawdy-Houſe; for this is an Offence as to the Government of the Houſe, in which the Wife has a prin-

Queen and Williams, Mich. 10 Annæ.

principal Share; and alſo ſuch an Offence as may generally be preſumed to be managed by the Intrigues of her Sex.

Sect. 13. And generally a Feme Covert ſhall anſwer as much as if ſhe were Sole, for any Offence, not capital, againſt the Common Law, or Statute; and (if it be of ſuch a Nature that it may be committed by her alone, without the Concurrence of the Husband,) ſhe may be puniſhed for it without the Husband, by way of Indictment, which being a Proceeding grounded merely on the Breach of the Law, the Husband ſhall not be included in it for an Offence to which he is no way privy; but if a Wife incur the Forfeiture of a penal Statute, the Husband may be made a Party to an Action or Information for the ſame, (as he may be generally to any Suit for a Cauſe of Action given by his Wife,) and ſhall be liable to anſwer what ſhall be recovered thereon.

9 Co. 71. Con. Mo. 813. 1 Sid. 410. 2 Keb. 634. Vide Ho. 93, Noy 103. Savil. 25. 1 Rol. Rep. 93, 94, 233, 234. Cro. Ja. 482. 11 Co. 61. b. 62.

Sect. 14. 2. Neither a Son, nor a Servant, are excuſed the Commiſſion of any Crime, whether capital or not capital, by the Command or Coercion of the Father or Maſter.

3 Keb. 34. H. P. C. 66. Moor 813.

CHAP. II.

Of Hereſy.

OFfences conſidered in Relation to the Perſons againſt whom they are committed, are either,

1. Such as are mote immediately againſt God; or,
2. Such as are more immediately againſt Man.

Offences more immediately againſt God are either by Common Law or by Statute.

Thoſe at Common Law are either capital or not capital. The capital Offences of this Nature are of three Kinds:

1. Hereſy.
2. Witchcraft.
3. Sodomy.

Concerning Hereſy I ſhall conſider,

1. What it is;
2. By whom it is cognizable;
3. How it is puniſhable.

Sect. 1. As to the firſt Point it ſeems, That among Proteſtants Hereſy is taken to be a falſe Opinion repugnant to ſome Point of Doctrine clearly revealed in Scripture, and either abſolutely eſſential to the Chriſtian Faith, or at leaſt of moſt high Importance.

Sect. 2. But it is impoſſible to ſet down all the particular Errors which may properly be called Heretical, concerning which there are, and always have been, ſo many intricate Diſputes; However the 1 *Eliz.* 1. which erected the High-Commiſſion-Court, having reſtrain'd the ſame from adjudging any Points to be Heretical, which have not been determined to be be such either by Scripture, or by some one of the four first General Councils, or by some other Council, by express Words of Scripture, or by the Parliament with the Assent of the Convocation, it has been since generally holden, that these Rules will be good Directions to Ecclesiastical Courts in Relation to Heresy.

3 Inst. 40. H. P. C. 3.

See Bro. Heresy. 2 Roll. Ab. 226.

Sect. 3. As to the second Point, *viz.* By whom Heresy is cognizable, it is certain, That the Convocation may declare what Opinions are Heretical: But it hath been questioned of late, Whether they have Power at this Day to convene and convict the Heretick?

F. N. B. 269. 12 Co. 56, 57. 3 Inst. 40. H. P. C. 5. Gibson 401, 410. 12 Co. 56, 57, 93. 3 Inst. 40.

Sect. 4. However it is agreed, That every Bishop may convict Persons of Heresy, within his own Diocese, and proceed by Church-Censures against those who shall be convicted; but it is said, That no Spiritual Judge, who is not a Bishop, hath this Power; and it has been questioned, Whether a Conviction before the Ordinary were a sufficient Foundation whereon to ground the Writ *de Hæretico comburendo*, as it is agreed that a Conviction before the Convocation was?

Sect. 5. By 24 *H.* 8. 9. the Archbishop of either Province may cite any Person before him for Heresy, if the immediate Ordinary either consent thereto, or do not his Duty in punishing the same.

27 H. 8. 14. b. 5 Co. 58. a. H. P. C. 4. Hob. 236.

Sect. 6. But it is certain, That a Man cannot be proceeded against at the Common Law in a Temporal Court merely for Heresy; yet if in Maintenance of his Errors he set up Conventicles, and raise Factions, which may tend to the Disturbance of the publick Peace, it seemeth that he may in this Respect be fined and imprisoned upon an Indictment, *&c.* at the Common Law.

H. P. C. 4.

Sect. 7. Also a Temporal Judge may incidentally take Knowledge whether a Tenet be Heretical or not; as where one was committed by Force of 2 *H.* 4. 5. for saying, That he was not bound by the Law of God to pay Tithes to the Curate: And another for saying, That though he was excommunicate before Man, yet he was not so before God. The Temporal Courts, on an *Habeas Corpus* in the first Case, and an Action of false Imprisonment in the other, adjudged neither of these Points to be Heresy within that Statute; for the King's Courts will examine all Things which are ordain'd by Statute.

3 Inst. 42. 1 Ro. Re. 110. 2 Bulf. 300.

5 Co. 58. 1 And. 191. 3 Leon. 199. 3 Lev. 314.

Sect. 8. Also in a *Quare impedit*, if the Bishop plead that he refused the Clerk for Heresy, it seems that he must set forth the particular Point, that it may appear to be Heretical to the Court wherein the Action is brought, which having Conusance of the original Cause, must by Consequence have a Power as to all incidental Matters necessary for the Determination of it; and without knowing the very Point alledged against the Clerk, will not be able to give Directions concerning it to the Jury, who (if the Party be dead) are to try the Truth of the Allegation.

Sect. 9. But if a Man be proceeded against as an Heretick in the Spiritual Court *pro salute animæ*, and think himself aggrieved, his proper Remedy seems to be to bring his Appeal to a higher Ecclesiastical Court, and not to move for a Prohibition from a Temporal one, which, as it seems to be agreed, cannot regularly determine or discuss, what shall be called Heresy.

5 Co. 58. a. 27 H. 8. 14, b.

F. N. B. 269. 3 Inst. 43. H. P. C. 5. Doctor and Student, lib. 2. ca. 29. H. P. C. 5.

Sect. 10. As to the third Point, *viz.* How Heresy is punishable; there is no Doubt but that at Common Law one convicted thereof, and refusing to abjure it, or falling into it again after he had abjured it, might be burnt by Force of the Writ *de Hæretico comburendo*, which was grantable out of Chancery upon a Certificate of such Conviction; but it is said, That he for-

forfeited neither Lands nor Goods, because the Proceedings against him were only *pro salute animæ.*

Sect. 11. But at this Day the said Writ *de Hæretico comburendo* is abolished by 29 *Car.* 2. 9. And all the old Statutes, which gave a Power to arrest or imprison Persons for Heresy, or introduced any Forfeiture on that Account, are repealed; yet by the Common Law an obstinate Heretick being excommunicate, is still liable to be imprisoned by Force of the Writ *de Excommunicato capiendo*, till he make Satisfaction to the Church. And by 9 & 10 *Wil.* 3. 32. *If any Person having been educated in, or having made Profession of, the Christian Religion within this Realm, shall be convicted in any of the Courts of* Westminster, *or at the Assizes, of denying any one of the Persons in the Holy Trinity to be God, or of maintaining that there are more Gods than one, or of denying the Truth of the Christian Religion, or the Divine Authority of the Holy Scriptures, he shall for the first Offence be adjudged uncapable of any Office; and for the second, shall be disabled to sue any Action, or to be a Guardian, Executor, or Administrator, or to take by any Legacy or Deed of Gift, or to bear any Office Civil or Military, or Benefice Ecclesiastical, for ever, and shall also suffer Imprisonment for three Years, without Bail or Mainprize, from the Time of such Conviction.*

H. P. C. 4, 5.
12 Co 44.

CHAP. III.

Of Witchcraft.

Sect. 1. OF Offenders of this Nature there are said to be three Kinds, 1. Conjurers, who by Force of certain Magick Words endeavour to raise the Devil, and compel him to execute their Commands. 3 Inst. 44. Dalt. ca. 107.

2. Witches, who by Way of friendly Conference are said to bargain with an evil Spirit to do what they desire of him.

3. Sorcerers or Charmers, who by the Use of certain superstitious Forms of Words, or by Means of Images, or other odd Representations of Persons or Things, &c. are said to produce strange Effects above the ordinary Course of Nature.

Sect. 2. All these were anciently punish'd in the same manner as Hereticks, by the Writ *de Hæretico comburendo* after a Sentence in the Ecclesiastical Court, and a Relapse. And it is said also, That they might be condemned to the Pillory, &c. upon an Indictment at Common Law. 3 Inst. 44. F.N.B. 269. b. H. P. C. 6. S. P. C. 38. g. Cro. Eliz. 571.

Sect. 3. In the Time of King *Edward* the third, one taken with the Head and Face of a dead Man, and a Book of Sorcery, was brought into the King's-Bench: But there being no Indictment against him, he was sworn that from thenceforth he would not be a Sorcerer, and then delivered from Prison, and the Head was burnt at his Charge: But this Method seems to be obsolete at this Day. 45 Ed. 3. 17. b. Bro. Cor. 15. 2 Keb. 719.

Sect. 4. By 1 *Jac.* 1. *cap.* 12 the only Law now in Force against these Offenders, they are divided into two Degrees; and those in the first Degree, and their Accessaries before, shall suffer as Felons without Clergy; and of these there are the four following Species.

1. *Such as shall use any Invocation or Conjuration of any evil Spirit*; and such seem clearly to be within the Law, though no Spirit do actually appear. H. P. C. 6. 3 Inst 45. con.

H. P. C. 6. 3 Inst. 45. 2. *Such as consult, covenant with, entertain, employ, feed, or reward any evil Spirit to any Intent:* And these are agreed to be within the Statute, though nothing farther be done upon such Consultation, *&c.*

H. P. C. 6. 3 Inst. 45. 3. *Such as take up any dead Person's Body or any Part thereof, to be used in any manner of Witchcraft:* And these are also clearly within the Statute, though they do not actually so use it.

H. P. C. 7. 3 Inst. 45. 1 Jon. 143. 4. *Such as exercise any Witchcraft, Inchantment, Charm or Sorcery, whereby any Person shall be killed, destroyed, consumed, or lamed in his or her Body, or any Part thereof:* But none are within this Branch who do not actually effect such Mischief.

Sect. 5. Those in the second Degree, shall for the first Offence suffer a Year's Imprisonment, and the Pillory; and for the second, as Felons without Clergy; and these by the manifest Purport of the Words of the Act, which is very obscurely penned, seem to be divided into the two following Species.

1. *Such as take upon them by Witchcraft, Inchantment, Charm or Sorcery, to tell where Treasure is to be found, or where Things lost or stoln may be found, or to do any Thing to the Intent to provoke any Person to unlawful Love, or to hurt or destroy any Person in his or her Body, though the same be not effected.*

H. P. C. 8. 3 Inst. 46. 2. *Such as shall use any Witchcraft,* &c. *whereby any Cattle or Goods of any Person shall be destroyed, wasted or impaired:* But those who take upon them to do this, are not within the Act unless they actually do it.

CHAP. IV.

Of Sodomy.

12 Co. 36, 37. 3 Inst. 58. *Sect.* 1. ALL unnatural Carnal Copulations, whether with Man or Beast, seem to come under the Notion of Sodomy, which was Felony by the ancient Common Law, and punish'd, according to some Authors, with Burning, according to others, with Burying alive: But at this Day by Force of 25 *H.* 8. 6. *&* 5 *El.* 17. is punished in the same manner as other Felonies which are excluded from the Clergy.

12 Co. 36, 37 3 Inst 58. *Sect.* 2. In every Indictment for this Offence, there must be the Words *Rem habuit veneream & carnaliter cognovit*; and consequently some kind of Penetration, and also of Emission, must be proved; but any the least Degree is sufficient, and Emission is *prima facie,* an Evidence of Penetration.

CHAP. V.

Of Offences against God not Capital at Common Law.

OFfences more immediately against God not Capital, are either by the Common Law or Statute.

Those by the Common Law are,

Sect. 1. I. All Blasphemies against God, as denying his Being or Providence.

Sect. 2.

Sect. 2. II. All profane Scoffing at the Holy Scripture, or exposing any Part thereof to Contempt or Ridicule.

Sect. 3. III. Impostures in Religion, as falsly pretending to extraordinary Commissions from God, and terrifying or abusing the People with false Denunciations of Judgments, *&c.* *See the Case of* James Nailor, *and of the* French *Prophets*, &c. 1 Sid. 168. 1 Keb. 620.

Sect. 4. IV. All open Lewdness grosly scandalous, such as was that of those Persons who exposed themselves naked to the People in a Balcony in *Covent-Garden* with most abominable Circumstances.

Sect. 5. Offences of this Nature, because they tend to subvert all Religion or Morality, which are the Foundation of Government, are punishable by the Temporal Judges with Fine and Imprisonment, and also such corporal infamous Punishment as to the Court in Discretion shall seem meet, according to the Heinousness of the Crime.

Sect 6. V. Seditious Words in Derogation of the Established Religion are indictable, as tending to a Breach of the Peace; as these, Your Religion is a new Religion, and Preaching is but Prattling, and Prayer once a Day is more edifying. 2 R. A. 187. Pl. 1. Cro. Ja. 421.

CHAP. VI.

Of Offences by Statute against Religion in general.

OFFENCES by Statute not Capital more immediately against God, are either,

1. Such as are against Religion in general; or,
2. Such as are against the Established Church.

Those against Religion in general are of several Kinds; as,

Sect 1. I. All Profanations of the Lord's Day; for by 1 *Car.* 1. 1. *There shall be no Assembly of People, out of their own Parishes, on this Day, for any Sports whatsoever; nor any Bull-baiting or Bear-baiting, Interludes, common Plays or other unlawful Exercises and Pastimes, used by any Persons in their own Parishes, on Pain that every Offender shall forfeit* 3 s. *and* 4 d. *to the Use of the Poor*, &c.

Sect. 2. By 29 *Car.* 2. 7. *No Persons whatsoever above fourteen Years old, shall exercise any worldly Labour, Business, or Work of their ordinary Calling on the Lord's Day, (except Works of Necessity and Charity, and the Dressing and Selling of Meat in an Inn and Victualling House, for those who cannot otherwise be provided,) on Pain of forfeiting* 5 s. *And no Person shall publickly cry, or expose to Sale, any Goods whatsoever on this Day, (except Milk, which may be sold before Nine in the Morning, and after Four in the Afternoon,) on Pain of forfeiting the same.* Par. 3.

Sect. 3. *Also no Drover, Horse-courser, Waggoner, Butcher or Higler, shall travel, or come to their Inn on this Day, on Pain of twenty Shillings. And no Person shall use, employ, or travel with any Boat or Barge, without the Allowance of some Justice of Peace*, &c. *on Pain of five Shillings.* But by 11 & 12 Gul. 21. *Forty Watermen may be appointed by the Company of Watermen to ply on the* Thames, &c.

&c. *And by* 9 Ann. 23. *Hackney Coach-Men and Chair-Men are permitted to work within the Bills of Mortality on Sunday.*

Sect. 4. II. All profane Swearing and Cursing; for by 21 *Jac.* 1. 20. and 6 & 7 Gul. 11. *Every Servant, Day-Labourer, Seaman or Soldier, convicted of profane Cursing or Swearing, forfeits one Shilling, and every other Person two Shillings, and shall be registred at Sessions*; and by 13 Car. 2. cap. 9. Artic. 2. *All Persons in the King's Pay at Sea, for profane Oaths,* &c. *shall be punished by Fine and Imprisonment, as the Court-Martial shall think fit.*

Sect. 5. III. Drunkenness, for which by 1 *Jac.* 1. 5. all Persons whatsoever forfeit five Shillings to the Poor; and for which Seamen may by 13 *Car.* 2. 9. be punished by Fine, *&c.* as the Court-Martial shall think fit.

Sect. 6. IV. Reviling the Sacrament of the Lord's Supper with contemptuous Words, *&c.* for which (by 1 *Ed.* 6. 1. which was repealed by 1 *Mar.* 2. and revived by 1 *El.* 1.) the Offender shall be imprisoned, fined, and ransomed.

Sect. 7. I shall not mention the Offences against 2 *&* 3 *Ed.* 6. 19. and 5 *El.* 5. relating to Fasts and Fish-Days, because it is expresly declared, That those Statutes are enacted merely on a political Account, and it is made penal to affirm that any eating of Fish or forbearing of Flesh mentioned therein, is necessary to Salvation, or that it is the Service of God.

CHAP. VII.

Of Offences against the Common Prayer.

OFFENCES against the Established Church are,

1. Such as concern all Persons in general;
2. Such as more immediately relate to those of the Popish Religion;
3. Such as more immediately regard Protestant Dissenters.

Those which concern all Persons in general; are,

1. Against the Common Prayer.
2. In accepting or holding an Office without due Conformity to the Church.
3. In teaching School without conforming to the Church.
4. In not coming to Church.

Sect. 1. And first of Offences against the Common Prayer, as to which it is to be observed, That by 2 *&* 3 *Ed.* 6. 1. and 6 *Ed.* 6. 1. (which were repealed by 1 *Mar.* 2. and revived by 1 *El.* 2.) the Common Prayer Book was first established under severe Penalties, but the same Penalties being repeated and enlarged by 1 *El.* 2. and 13 *&* 14 *Car.* 2. 4. which enacts the use of the same Common Prayer with some Alterations; those Statutes of *Ed.* 6. seem at this Day to be of little Use.

Sect. 2. By 1 El. 2. Par. 4. *If any Parson, Vicar, or other whatsoever Minister, that ought to say the said Common Prayer,* &c. *shall refuse to use it in such Church,* &c. *or other Place where he should use to minister the same, or willfully or obstinately standing in the same, use any other Form, or speak any Thing in Derogation of the said Book, or any Thing therein contain'd, he forfeits for the first Offence one Year's Profit of all his spiritual Promotions, and shall suffer six Months Imprisonment; and for the second Offence shall be deprived,* &c.

In the Construction of this Act it has been resolved,

Sect. 3. I. That under the Words, *Parson, Vicar, or other whatsoever Minister that ought or should say the said Common Prayer,* &c. those Clergymen who have no Cure are included as much as those who have one, and that they are punishable for using any other Form, *&c.* inasmuch as by their Ordination they are oblig'd to officiate in the Offices of the Church, *&c.* and it is said that they are sufficiently shewn to be in Holy Orders by the Word *Clericus* in an Indictment. Dyer 203. Pl. 73, 74.

Sect. 4. II. That this Statute being not only in the Affirmative, but also expresly saving the Jurisdiction of Ecclesiastical Courts, does not restrain them from proceeding against these Offenders in their own Methods, as Disturbers of the Unity and Peace of the Church; and consequently that such Persons may be deprived by the said Courts according to the Course of the Spiritual Law, for the first Offence. 5 Co. Cawdry's Case, 5. b. 6. a. Poph. 59. 2 Rol. Abr. 222, 5.

Sect. 5. Also it is farther enacted, by 1 *El.* 2. Par. 9. *That if any Person shall in Plays, Songs, or other open Words, speak any Thing in derogation, depraving or despising of the said Book,* &c. *Or by open Fact compel, or otherwise procure or maintain any Minister to say any Common Prayer openly,* &c. *in other Form: Or shall by any of the said Means let any Minister to say the said Common Prayer,* &c. *he shall forfeit one hundred Marks for the first Offence, and four hundred for the Second,* &c. (*which if he pay not within six Weeks after Conviction, he shall suffer six Months Imprisonment for the first Offence, and twelve for the second,*) *and for the third Offence shall forfeit all his Goods and Chattels, and shall suffer Imprisonment for Life.*

Sect, 6. It has been made a Question in the Construction of this Clause, Whether if the Party die within six Weeks, the said Forfeiture be not discharged, since by the Act of God the Election of paying it, or suffering Imprisonment in lieu of it, is taken away? Dyer 203.74. 231. 4.

CHAP. VIII.

Of Offences in accepting or holding an Office without due Conformity to the Church.

OFfences in accepting or holding an Office without due Conformity to the Church, are of two Kinds,

1. In not receiving the Sacrament both before and after the Acceptance of an Office.

2. In going to any other Place for religious Worship, than the Church, during the Continuance in an Office.

Sect. 1. As to the first of these Offences, it is enacted by 13 *Car.* 2. Stat. 2. *Cap.* 1. Par. 10, 12. *That no Person shall be placed, elected, or chosen, to any Office or Place of Mayor, Alderman, Recorder, Bailiff, Town-Clerk, Common-Council-Man, or other Office of Magistracy, Place of Trust, or other Imployment*

D re-

relating to the Government of any City, Corporation, Borough, Cinque-Port, or other Port-Town, who shall not have received the Sacrament according to the
5 Mod. 431. *Rites of the Church of* England *within one Year next before such Election; and that every Person so placed or elected shall take the Oaths of Allegiance and Supremacy at the same Time when the Oath for the due Execution of the said Office,* &c. *shall be administred; (and that the same Persons who administer the latter may administer the former,* &c.) *And that in Default hereof every such Election, Placing and Choice, shall be void.*

Sect. 2. Also it is enacted by 25 *Car.* 2. *That all Officers civil and military, (Except those of Inheritance, appointing sufficient Deputies) and all who have any Fee,* &c. *by Patent from the King, (Except such as shall be granted for valuable Consideration for Life or Years, and not relate to any Office or Place of Trust;) and also all who have any Place of Trust, or any Employment in the King's Houshold, shall take the Oaths of Allegiance and Supremacy, and Test, the next Term, (in the King's Bench or Chancery, or Quarter-Sessions;) and receive the Sacrament within three Months, and give in a Certificate thereof proved by two Witnesses to the Court wherein they take the said Oaths. And in case of Neglect shall be disabled to hold the said Offices,* &c. *and forfeit five hundred Pounds, except Fems Covert,* &c.

Sect. 3. Notwithstanding the Words of the first of these Acts are so very strong as to make such Election, *&c.* void, and those of the second to make such Persons disabled in Law to all Intents and Purposes whatsoever, to have, occupy, or enjoy the said Offices, yet it seems to be the better Opinion, that the Acts of one under such a Disability being instated in such an Office, and executing the same without any Objection to his Authority, may be valid as to Strangers; for otherwise not only those who no way infringe this Law, but even those whose Benefit is intended to be advanced by it, might be sufferers for another's Fault to which they are no Way privy; and one Chasm in a Corporation happening thro' the Default of one Head-Officer would perpetually vacate the Acts of all others, whose Authority in respect of their Admission into their Offices, or otherwise, may depend on his.

3 Keb 606, 665,682,721. 2 Jon. 81. 137. 2 Lev. 184. 242.

Sect. 4. By 25 *Car.* 2. Parag. 17. it is expresly provided, *That the said Act shall not extend to Constables, or Church-wardens, or such like inferiour civil Officers, or to a Bailiff of a Manor or Lands, or such like private Officers.*

5 Mod. 431, 432. But it hath been questioned, Whether it extends to the Censor of the College of Physicians?

Sect. 5. As to the second Offence of this Kind, *viz.* that of going to any other Place for religious Worship than the Church, during the Continuance of an Office, it is enacted by 10 *Ann.* 2. Par. 1. *That if any Person who shall have any Office, civil or military, or receive any Pay, Salary, Fee, or Wages, by reason of any Grant from the Crown, or have any Command or Place of Trust from the Crown, or shall be admitted into any Service or Employment in the King's Houshold or Family, or if any Person bearing any Office of Magistracy, or Place of Trust, or other Employment relating to the Government of any City, Corporation, Borough, or Cinque-Port, who by* 13 Car. 2. *Stat.* 2. Cap. 1. *or* 25 Car. 2. 21. *are obliged to receive the Sacrament, according to the Usage of the Church of* England, *shall at any Time after their Admission into any such Office,* &c. *and during their Continuance in the same, knowingly or willingly be present at any Assembly in* England, Wales, *or* Berwick *on* Tweed, *for the Exercise of Religion in other Manner than according to the Church of* England, *at which Assembly there shall be ten Persons besides those of the Family,* &c. *or at any such Meeting where such Liturgy is used, and the King, and such others as shall be lawfully appointed to be prayed for, shall not be prayed for in express Words, &c. he shall forfeit forty Pounds;* and by Par 2,3,4. *every Person convicted of such Offence shall be disabled to hold any Office or Employment whatsoever in* England, &c. *unless he shall after such Conviction conform to the Church of* England *for one Year, without being present at any such Meeting, and receive the Sacrament three Times in the Year, and also make Oath of such his Conformity in some Court in* Westminster, &c. *the next Term after his Admission into any such Office, &c.*

Sect. 5. But by Par. 5. *No Person shall suffer for any Offence against this Act, unless Oath be made thereof within ten Days, and the Offender prosecuted within three Months, and the Offence proved by two Witnesses;* and by Par. 6. *No Person having an Office of Inheritance is within the Act, so as such Person do substitute his sufficient Deputy.*

CHAP. IX.

Of Offences in teaching School without conforming to the Church.

Sect. 1. AS to the Offence of teaching School without conforming to the Church, so far as it concerns all Persons in general, it is enacted by 23 *El.* 1. Par. 6 *&* 7. *That if any Person or Persons, Body Politick or Corporate, shall keep or maintain any School-master who shall not repair to Church according to the Form of the said Statute, or be allowed by the Bishop or Ordinary of the Diocese, (who shall not take any Thing for the said Allowance) they shall forfeit for every Month ten Pounds; and such School-master presuming to teach contrary to the said Act, and being thereof convict, shall be disabled to be a Teacher of Youth, and shall suffer Imprisonment without Bail or Mainprize for one Year.*

Sect. 2. And it is farther enacted by 1 *Jac.* 1. 4. Par. 9. *That no Person shall keep any School, or be a School-master, out of the Universities or Colleges of this Realm, except it be in some publick or free Grammar-School, or in some such Nobleman's or Noblewoman's, or Gentleman's or Gentlewoman's House, as are not Recusants, or where the same School-master shall be specially licenced thereunto by the Archbishop, Bishop, or Guardian of the Spiritualities of that Diocese, upon pain, that as well the School-master, as also the Party that shall retain or maintain any such School master, contrary to the Meaning of the said Statute, shall forfeit each of them, for every Day so wittingly offending, forty Shillings.*

Sect. 3. But it having been doubted whether such Persons as are within the Benefit of 1 *Gul. & Mar.* 18. commonly called *The Toleration Act*, are not exempted from the Penalties of the above mentioned Statutes, it was farther enacted by 12 *Ann.* 7. *That whoever shall keep any publick or private School or Seminary, or teach any Youth as Tutor, or School-master, (unless he instruct them only in Reading, or Writing, Arithmetick, or such mathematical Learning as relates to Navigation, or some mechanical Art, and that in the* English *Tongue; or unless he shall be a Foreigner of a Foreign reformed Church, and teach the Children of such Foreigners only) without having first subscribed that Part of the Declaration in* 13 & 14 Car. 2. *which relates to Conformity to the Liturgy of the Church of* England, *and also having obtained a Licence from the Bishop,* &c. *and shall be thereof convicted in any of the Courts at* Westminster, or *or at the Assizes, or before Justices of Oyer and Terminer, shall be committed to the common Gaol for three Months,* &c.

Sect. 4. Also it is enacted by the said Statute, *That such a Licence shall not be granted to any one who does not produce a Certificate of his having received the Sacrament according to the Church of* England *within one Year next before, and also take the Oaths of Allegiance and Supremacy, and Abjuration, and the Declaration against Transubstantiation*; and it is further enacted, *That if any Person so licenced, shall at any Time after, during his keeping School,* &c. *knowingly resort to any Conventicle,* &c. *for the exercise of Religion, or teach any other Catechism than the Catechism in the Common Prayer, his Licence shall be void, and he shall be liable to the above mentioned Penalty, and be thenceforth incapable of keeping any School, publick or private, or instructing any Youth as Tutor or School-master.*

Sect. 5. *But Tutors in either University, and Persons employed by any Nobleman or Woman, to teach his or her Children, are excepted, so that they qualify themselves according to this Act in every respect, except only that of taking a Licence from the Bishop.*

As to Popish School-masters in particular. See *Chap.* 15. *Sect.* 13.

CHAP. X.

Of Offences in not coming to Church.

FOR the better Understanding of the Offences of not coming to Church, so far as the same relate to all Persons in general, except such as are within the Indulgence of 1 *Will. & Mar.* 18. which is commonly called *The Toleration Act*, I shall consider:

1. How far Persons are punishable for their own Absence from the Church.
2. How far they are punishable for suffering such Absence in others.

And first, In Order to shew how far Persons are punishable for their own Absence, I shall consider the following particulars;

1. What Forfeitures of Money, Lands or Goods, such Offenders incur.
2. In what Manner they are to be proceeded against for those Forfeitures.
3. What other Inconveniencies they are subject unto.
4. By what Means they may be discharged.

As to the first Point, I shall consider,

1. What Forfeitures of Money; and,
2. What Forfeitures of Lands and Goods, such Offenders are liable unto.

And first, The Forfeitures of Money to which they are liable, are threefold;

1. That of twelve Pence for the Absence of one Sunday, or other Holy Day.
2. That of twenty Pounds for the Absence of every Month contained in a Conviction.
3. That of twenty Pounds for the Absence of every Month after a Conviction.

Sect. 1. And first, The Forfeiture of twelve Pence for the Absence of one *Sunday* or other Holy Day, depends upon 1 *El.* 2. by which it is enacted, *That all Persons inhabiting within this Realm, or any other the King's Dominions, shall diligently and faithfully, having no lawful or reasonable Excuse to be absent, endeavour to resort to their Parish Church or Chapel accustomed, or upon reasonable Let thereof, to some usual Place where Common Prayer and such Service of God shall be used, in such Time of Let, upon every Sunday, and other Days ordained and used to be kept as Holy Days, and then and there to abide orderly and soberly, during the Time of the Common Prayer, Preaching, or other Service of God there to be used and ministered, upon pain of Punishment by the Censures of the Church, and also upon Pain that every Person so offending, shall forfeit for every such Offence twelve Pence.*

In the Exposition of this Statute, the following Opinions have been holden.

Sect. 2. I. That the Indictment needs not shew that the Party had no reasonable Excuse for his Absence, or that he is an Inhabitant within this Realm, *&c.* But that the Defendant, if he have any Matter of this kind in his Favour, ought to shew it. 2 Leon. 5. Godbolt 148. See 29 El. 6. Par. 5.

Sect. 3. II. That if the Spiritual Court, proceeding upon this Statute, refuse to allow a reasonable Excuse, they may be prohibited; but that if they proceed wholly on their own Canons, they shall not be at all comptrolled by the Common Law, (unless they act in Derogation from it, as by questioning a Matter not triable by them, as the Bounds of a Parish, *&c.*) for they shall be presumed to be the best Judges of their own Laws. 2 Rol. Rep. 438, 455. 1 Bulst. 159. See Gibs. 358.

Sect. 4. III. That he who misbehaves himself in the Church, or misses either Morning or Evening Prayer, or goes away before the whole Service is over, is as much within the Statute as he who is wholly absent. 1 Rol. Rep. 93. Godbolt. 148. Dal. ca. 45. fol. 106.

Sect. 5. IV. That the Offence in not coming to Church consisting wholly in a Non-feasance, and not supposing any Fact done, but barely the Omission of what ought to be done, needs not be alledged in any certain Place; for properly speaking, it is not committed any where. 1 And, 139. Hob. 251. See 2 Leon. 167.

Sect. 6. Secondly, The Forfeiture of twenty Pounds for the Absence of a whole Month contained in a Conviction, depends upon 13 *El.* 1. Par. 5. by which it is enacted, *That every Person above the Age of sixteen Years, who shall not repair to some Church, Chapel or usual Place of Common Prayer, but forbear the same, contrary to the Tenor of the said Statute of* 1 El. 2. *and being thereof lawfully convicted, shall forfeit to the King for every Month which he or she shall so forbear, twenty Pounds.*

In the Exposition hereof it hath been resolved,

Sect. 7. I. That this Statute by inflicting twenty Pounds for a Month's Absence, dispenses not with the Forfeiture of twelve Pence, given by 1 *El.* 2. for the Absence of one *Sunday*, for both may well stand together, and the twelve Pence is immediately forfeited upon the Absence of each particular Day. 11 Co. 63. b. 1 Rol. Re. 94.

Sect. 8. II. That those Words *being thereof lawfully convicted*, are no more than the Law would have implied, if they had not been expressed, and therefore operate nothing; from whence it follows, That they neither cause the Party to forfeit any Thing by a Conviction unless Judgment be given thereon, nor restrain the Forfeiture to such Offences only as are committed after a previous Conviction, inasmuch as they mean no more than what the Law provides of common Right in every Case, *viz.* That the Party shall forfeit nothing till he be convicted. 11 Co. 57. b. 59. b. 1 R. R. 89, 90, 233, 23[illegible]. Dy. 160. Pl. 40. 3 Bulst. 87.

1 Co. 58. a. b. 60. a. 1 Rol. Rep. 89, 90.

Sect. 9. III. That he who is condemned on Demurrer, or *nihil dicit*, is ſufficiently convicted within the Act; for whoever is adjudged is convict, though it follow not that every one who is convict is adjudged, *&c.*

Cro Ja. 529.

Sect. 10. IV. That one who was ſick for part of the Time contained in an Information upon this Statute, ſhall not be at all excuſed by Reaſon of ſuch Sickneſs, if it be proved that he was a Recuſant both before and after; for it ſhall be intended that he obſtinately forbore during that Time.

Yel. 100. Cro El. 835. 2 Rol. Abr. 521. c. Cawley 61.

Sect. 11. V. That the Time of a Month intended by the Statute, ſhall be computed not by the Kalendar, but by the Number of Days, allowing 28 Days to each, according to the common Rule of expounding Statutes which ſpeak generally of a Month.

* 3 Lev. 333.

Sect. 12. Thirdly, The Forfeiture of twenty Pouuds for the Abſence of every Month after a Conviction, depends upon 29, (or rather * 28) *El.* 6. Par. 2, 3, 4. and 3 *Jac.* 1, 4. Par. 8, 3. by which it is enacted, *That every Offender being convicted of not coming to Church, contrary to the Purport of the Statutes above mentioned, ſhall pay twenty Pounds for every Month after ſuch Conviction, until he ſhall conform himſelf and come to Church.*

Sect. 13. As to the ſecond Branch of this Head, *viz*, What Forfeiture of Lands and Goods ſuch Offenders are liable to, the ſame depends alſo upon 29 *El.* 6. Par. 4. and 3 *Jac.* 1. 4. Par. 8, 9. by which it is enacted *That if the Offender ſhall make Default of Payment of the twenty Pounds, both for every Month contained in the Conviction, and alſo for every Month ſubſequent, during which he ſhall not conform himſelf to the Church, the King ſhall take, ſeize and enjoy all his Goods, and two Parts of his Hereditaments, Leaſes, and Farms, leaving the third Part only of the ſame Hereditaments, Leaſes and Farms, to and for the Maintenance and Relief of the ſame Offender, his Wife,*

See 29 El. 6. Par. 1, 8.

Children, and Family, notwithſtanding any prior Conveyance thereof made by ſuch Offender with Power of Revocation, or to the Uſe of himſelf or his Family. Alſo by the ſaid Statute of 3 Jac. 1. 4. Par. 11. *the King may refuſe the Penalty of twenty Pounds a Month, though it be tendered according to Law, and thereupon ſeize two Parts of all the Hereditaments, Leaſes and Farms, which at the Time of ſuch Seizure ſhall be, or afterwards ſhall come to any ſuch Offender, or to any other to his Uſe or in Truſt for him or at his Diſpoſition, or whereby or in Conſideration whereof he or his Family ſhall be relieved, maintained or kept, leaving unto him his chief Manſion Houſe, as part of his third Part.*

In the Conſtruction of theſe Statutes the following Points have been reſolved.

1 Jones 24, 25. Cawley 171, 172.

Sect. 14. I. That the King by making his Election given him by 3 *Jac.* 1. to ſeize the Offender's Hereditaments, *&c.* waives the Benefit of the twenty Pounds a Month, and the Power of ſeizing the Offender's Goods.

12 Co. 1, 2. 1 Leon. 98. 1 Rol. Re. 7.

Sect. 15. II. That a Recognizance or Bond taken by ſuch Offenders, either in their own Names or in the Names of others to their Uſe, are within the Statute of 29 *El.* for the Words thereof to this Purpoſe are, *That the King ſhall take, ſeize, and enjoy all the Goods,* &c. which in an Act of Parliament will include the whole perſonal Eſtate; and though a Choſe in Action cannot properly be ſaid to be taken or ſeized, yet may it properly enough be ſaid to be enjoyed.

Owen 37. 1 Leon. 97. Cawley 107. a

Sect. 16. III. That no Copyhold Lands are within 29 *El.* (and by the ſame Reaſon it ſeemeth that they are not within 3 *Jac.* 1.) in Reſpect of the Prejudice which would accrue to the Lord by the Loſs of his Services, *&c.*

Sect. 17. IV. That the Profits of the Lands seized by the King by Force of 29 *El.* for the Non-payment of the twenty Pounds a Month, ought not to be applied to the Satisfaction thereof, but that the Lands ought to remain in the King's Hands by way of Pledge, till the whole Forfeiture be paid some other Way; but this Construction of the Statute seeming over severe, it was provided by 3 *Jac.* 1. 4. Par. 5. *That the Profits of the said Lands should go towards the Satisfaction of the twenty Pounds.* Cro. El. 845. 2 Rol.Re. 25. Palm. 41. Sir W. Jon. 24.

Sect. 18. It hath been questioned, Whether an Estate conveyed by another in Trust for a Recusant, be liable to be seized by Force of the said Statute of 29 *El.* because it expresly avoids such Conveyances only as are made by the Recusant himself *to his own Use*, &c. And perhaps if it shall plainly appear, That an Estate is settled *bona fide* in Trust for a Recusant by some Friend of his, upon some other View, and not merely with an Intent to evade the Statute, it may be reasonable to exempt such a Conveyance out of the Meaning of it; however it is clear from the express Words of 3 *Jac.* 1. 4 Par. 11. *That the King, upon his waiving the Forfeiture of the twenty Pounds a Month, may seize two Parts of all the Hereditaments,* &c. *which shall come to any such Offenders, or to others to their Use, or in Trust for them:* Also it is said, That the King may seize an Estate which is granted to a Recusant in Trust for another, and it is certain that the Statute has made no express Provision for the *Cestui que Trust.* Lane 105, 106. Cawley 169. See 12 Co. 1[?]2. Lane 39.

As to the second general Head of this Chapter, *viz.* In what Manner Offenders of this Nature are to be proceeded against for the Forfeitures above mentioned, I shall consider,

1. How they are to be proceeded against for the said Forfeitures of Money, and

2. In what Manner for the said Forfeitures of Lands and Goods.

As to the Prosecution for the said Forfeitures of Money, I shall shew,

1. How they are to be proceeded against for the said Forfeiture of twelve Pence for the Absence of every *Sunday, &c.* and

2. In what Manner for the said Forfeiture of twenty Pounds for the Absence of every Month contained in a Conviction, and

3. In what Manner for the said Forfeiture of twenty Pounds for the Absence of every Month after a Conviction.

Sect. 19. And first, As to the Recovery of the said Forfeiture of twelve Pence for the Absence of every *Sunday*, it was enacted by 1 *El.* 2. *That the same should be levied by the Church-wardens of the Parish where such Offence should be done, to the Use of the Poor of the same Parish, of the Goods, Lands, and Tenements of such Offenders, by way of Distress:* But this being defective in not shewing by whom, or in what Manner such Offenders should be convicted, or by whom the Warrant for levying the said Forfeiture should be granted; it was farther enacted by 3 *Jac.* 1. 4. Par. 27. *That it shall be lawful for any one Justice of the Peace of the Limit, Division, or Liberty wherein the said Party shall dwell, upon the Confession of the Party, or the Oath of one Witness, to call the said Party before him, and if he shall not make a sufficient Excuse and due Proof thereof, to the Satisfaction of the said Justice of Peace, that it shall be lawful for the said Justice of Peace to make a Warrant to the Church-warden of the said Parish where the said Party shall dwell, to levy twelve Pence for every such Default, by Distress and Sale of the Offender's Goods, rendering the Overplus to the said Offender; and that in Default of such Distress, it shall be lawful for the said Justice of Peace to commit every such Offender to Prison, until the said Forfeiture shall be paid, which shall be employed to the*

the Use of the Poor of the Parish wherein the Offender shall be resident or abiding at the Time of the Offence.

Sect. 20. As to the second Point, *viz.* In what Manner the said Offenders are to be proceeded against for the said Forfeiture of twenty Pounds for the Absence of every Month contain'd in a Conviction, I shall consider,

1. In what Manner the same may be recovered at the Suit of the King, and

2. In what Manner at the Suit of an Informer.

And first, as to the Recovery hereof at the King's Suit, I shall consider,

1. In what Manner it may be recovered at the King's Suit by way of Indictment.

2. In what Manner by way of Action or Information.

See 1 Rol. Re. 94. 11 Co. 63. Cawley 66, 67, 82, 83.

Sect. 21. And first, as to the Recovery hereof at the Suit of the King by way of Indictment, it was enacted by 23 *El.* 3. Par. 9. *That the Justices of Oyer, Assize, Gaol-Delivery, and Quarter Sessions of the Peace, might enquire of and determine these Offences, within one Year and a Day:* But by 29 *El.* 6. Par. 2. *It was ordained that all such Convictions should be in the King's Bench, or at the Assizes, or general Goal-Delivery, and not elsewhere:* However by 3 *Jac.* 1. 4. Par 7. the Jurisdiction of the Sessions is revived.

Sect. 22. Also it is farther enacted by 29 *El.* 6. Par. 5. and 3 *Jac.* 1. 4. Par. 7. *That upon an Indictment at the Assizes, Gaol-Delivery, or General Sessions of the Peace, Proclamation shall be made that the Offender render himself to the Sheriff before the next Assizes, Goal-Delivery or Sessions; and that if he shall not then appear of Record, upon such Default recorded, the same shall be a Conviction in Law, as if a Trial by Verdict on the Indictment had been recorded.*

Raym. 434.

Sect. 23. In the Construction hereof it hath been resolved, I. That such a Conviction shall not be look'd on as a Judgment; for the Words are, *It shall be a Conviction in Law, as if a Trial,* &c. *had been recorded:* And consequently that it cannot be reversed by Writ of Error, which cannot be brought on any Record which is not a Judgment, and therefore that the Party has no other Remedy against an insufficient Conviction, but to remove it into the Exchequer, and quash it there. Also upon the same Ground it has been holden, That a Forfeiture due to the King by Force of such a Conviction, shall not be taken to be within the Exception of a general Pardon, which excepts all Forfeitures, *&c.* converted to a Debt by Judgment.

11 Co. 65. a. Vide infra Sect. 42.

Palm. 40, 41. Bridg. 123. 3 Lev. 333.

Sect. 24. II. That if the Proclamation do not pursue the Statute, as if it appoint that the Body shall be rendered at next Sessions, *&c.* whereas by the Statute it ought to order a Render to the Sheriff, and that before the next Sessions, the Conviction is insufficient.

Cawley 164. Poph. 29. Keilw. 180. a.

Sect. 25. III. That an actual personal Appearance of the Defendant at the next Sessions, *&c.* will no way avail him unless the same be entered of Record.

Hob. 205.

Sect. 26. It has been holden, That a Man cannot be convicted by Force of this Statute upon a Default on a Proclamation, *&c.* in the King's Bench, because this Court is not mentioned in the Statute: But perhaps this Opinion may justly be questioned, because the Court of King's Bench being the supreme Court of Assize, and Gaol-Delivery, *&c.* in the County where it sits, it seems that a Statute by giving any Power to the Courts of Assize or Gaol-Delivery, does impliedly give the same to the Court of King's Bench, unless it have some restrictive Words to the contrary.

H. P. C. 156. Cro. Ca. 465. 1 Lev. 179. 2 Mod. 128, 129.

Sect. 27. If the Defendant do appear, there is no doubt but that the Proceedings ought to be according to the common Course of Law upon other Indictments in all Respects, except those which are within the Restraint of 3 *Jac.* 1. 4. Par. 16, 17. by which it is enacted, *That no such Indictment, nor any Proclamation, Outlawry, or other Proceeding thereupon, shall at any Time hereafter be avoided, discharged or reversed, by reason of any Default in Form or lack of Form, or other Defect whatsoever,* (*other than by direct Traverse to the Point of not coming to Church,* &c.) *but the same Indictment* Cro. Ca. 504. *shall stand in Force and be proceeded upon; any such Default of Form, or other Defect whatsoever notwithstanding, unless the Party so indicted shall conform,* &c. Raym. 434.

Sect. 28. However it hath been resolved,

I. That the Party is only restrained from taking Advantage of Defects in the Record it self, and that he may plead any collateral Matter, as a Pardon, or *autrefoits convict*, &c. 11 Co. 59. b. 65. a b. 1 Rol. Re. 95. Cro Jac. 480, 482.

Sect. 29. II. That he may even reverse a Judgment after Verdict for any such Defect in the Record it self, as tends to the King's Prejudice, as the Omission of a *Capiatur*, *&c.* And that he may reverse an Outlawry for any common Defect, upon putting in Bail, and traversing the Indictment as to the Point of not coming to Church, which is very agreeable to the Purport of the whole Clause, the latter Part whereof seems manifestly to qualify the Generality of the former. Cro. Ca. 504, 505. Show. 309. 5 Mod. 141. 3 Keb. 591.

Sect. 30. Secondly, As to the Recovery of the said Forfeiture by way of Action or Information at the King's Suit, it was enacted by 35 *El.* 1. Par. 10. *That all and every the said Pains, Duties, Forfeitures and Payments, shall and may be recovered and levied to her Majesty's Use, by Action of Debt, Bill, Plaint, Information, or otherwise, in any of the Courts commonly called the King's Bench, Common Pleas, or Exchequer, in such Sort and in all Respects, as by the ordinary Course of the Common Laws of this Realm, any other Debt due by any such Person in any other Case should or may be recovered or levied, wherein no Essoign, Protection, or Wager of Law shall be admitted or allowed.*

Sect. 31. It is said, That the principal End of making this Clause, was to enable the Queen to proceed against the Husband for the Recusancy of his Wife, which she could not do by Virtue of any of the former Statutes, by which she had no other way of proceeding but by Indictment, and consequently could not charge the Husband for the Forfeiture of the Wife, because she could not make him a Party to the Suit, as she may by Force of this Statute; However it is said, That on a Conviction of the Wife upon an Indictment, the Lands and Leases which the Husband has in her Right, may be seized by Exchequer-Process. 11 Co. 61. b. 62. a. Vide supra ca. 1. S. 13. Cro. Ja. 482. Bridgm. 122. seems cont.

Sect. 32. As to the second Particular, *viz.* In what manner an Informer may proceed for the Forfeitures aforesaid, it is enacted by 23 *El.* 1. Par. 11. *That all Forfeitures of any Sums of Money limited by that Act, shall be divided into three equal Parts, whereof one Third shall be to the Queen, to her own Use, one other Third to the Queen, for the Relief of the Poor in the Parish where the Offence shall be committed, to be delivered by the Warrant of the principal Officers in the Receipt of the Exchequer, without further Warrant from her Majesty; and the other Third to such Person as will sue for the same in any Court of Record, by Action of Debt, Bill, Plaint, or Information, in which Suit no Essoign,* &c. *shall be allowed: And that every Person which shall forfeit any Sums of Money by Virtue of that Act, and shall not be able, or shall fail to pay the same within three Months after Judgment thereof given, shall be* 2 Leon. 167. & 29. Eliz. 6. Par. 7.

committed to Prison, there to remain until he have paid the said Sums, or conform himself to go to Church, and there do as is aforesaid.

Sect. 33. It has been objected, That this Clause shall not extend to the said Forfeiture of twenty Pounds a Month for not coming to Church, because the same is by the former Part of this Statute given expresly to the Queen, whereas the Forfeitures for saying or hearing Mass, and keeping an unlicenced School-master, are inflicted by the same Statute indefinitely, and not expresly given to any one; from which it is argued, That this latter Clause of Distribution ought only to be apply'd to the said indefinite Clauses, and not to take from the Queen any Part of that which was expresly given her before; yet it has been answered and resolved, That it shall equally extend to all; for the Limitation of the Forfeiture to the Queen is mere Surplus, and no more than the Law would have implied, *& expressio eorum quæ tacite insunt nihil operatur.*

See 3 & 6 Par. 11 Co. 58 a. 1 Rol. Re. 89.

11 Co. 58. a.

1 And. 139, 140.

Sect. 34. Also it has been resolved, That an Informer may sue, not only for the third Part which belongs to him, but for the whole Penalty in the Behalf of himself and the King, and that the Judgment shall be that they shall recover, *&c.*

Sect. 35. Also it has been adjudged, That neither the above mentioned Clause of 29 *El.* 6. which orders, That all Convictions upon 23 *El.* shall be certified into the Exchequer, and also that the Offender shall pay to the Queen twenty Pounds for every Month contained in the Indictment, *&c.* nor the said Clause in the 35 *El.* 1. by which it is enacted, That all the said Pains, *&c.* shall be recovered to the Queen's Use, do take away the Suit of the Informer, against one not proceeded against by the King, or the third Part of the Penalty given him by 23 *Eliz.* For the plain Purport of both these Acts is to further the Punishment of Recusants, and therefore inasmuch as they are in the Affirmative, and consistent with 23 *El.* they shall not be construed to abrogate any Part of it.

Supra Sect. 13.

Supra Sect. 33.

11 Co. 61, 62. 1 Rol. Re. 92. 93.

Sect. 36. Moreover it is manifest that 29 *El.* 6. extends only to the King's Suit by Indictment, for the Word Indictment is mentioned almost in every Clause.

Sect. 37. And it also follows from hence, That the second Paragraph of the said Statute of 29 *El.* which enacts, That Convictions for this Offence shall be only at Assizes, Gaol-Delivery, or the King's Bench, restrains only Convictions upon Indictments, and consequently does not any Way impeach the Jurisdiction of the Common Pleas or Exchequer, as to Informations, *&c.*

Hob. 205. Con. 11. Co. 61. a.

Sect. 38. It seems the better Opinion, (upon comparing all the Books together, which differ much from one another both in stating the Cases, and giving the Reasons of the Judgments relating to this Matter,) that a Conviction at the King's Suit, whether strictly regular or erroneous, will be a good Bar to a Suit by an Informer, because while it stands in Force, it makes the Party liable to the Forfeiture of twenty Pounds a Month, and no one ought to be punished twice for the same Offence: But it hath been resolved that an erroneous, and strongly holden that a regular, Conviction by Proclamation is no Bar to a new Suit by the King, because such a Conviction is of no greater Effect than a Conviction by Verdict, and consequently the King may waive it and begin anew.

11 Co. 49. b. 65. a. 1 Rol. Re. 93. Cro. Jac 481, 482. Noy 117. Lane 60. Palm. 39, 40, 41. 2 Rol. Re. 108. Bridg. 122, 123.

Sect. 39. But it seems very doubtful whether the Conviction of a Feme Covert upon an Indictment be a Bar to an Information against her and her Husband, because the Husband is not liable to pay the Forfeiture recovered upon an Indictment.

Cro. Jac. 481, 482. Bridg. 120, 121, 122. 2 Rol Re. 108. Vide supra. cap. 1. S. 13.

Sect. 40. It seems that the ordinary Method of recovering the said Forfeiture of twenty Pounds for every Month contained in a Conviction, either at the Suit of the King, or of an Informer, may sufficiently appear from what has been already said; but there is an extraordinary Remedy provided by the said Statute of 29 *El.* 6. to enforce the Party to take Care of the Payment of the Forfeiture of the twenty Pounds for every Month contained in an Indictment whereon he shall be convicted, by making his Lands and Goods liable to be seized by the King for the Non-payment thereof into the Exchequer, upon such of the Terms of *Easter* or *Michaelmas*, as shall be next after his Conviction; but this extends not to a Conviction by Way of Action, or Information, as more fully appears from the two next Sections.

Sect. 41. As to the third Point, *viz.* In what Manner the Forfeiture of twenty Pounds for the Absence of every Month after a Conviction is to be recovered, it seems needless to enquire how far it may be recovered by an Action or Information for it at the King's Suit, inasmuch as the said Statutes of 29 *El.* 6. & 3 *Jac.* 1. have made a most effectual Provision for the Payment of it, by expresly enacting, *That every such Offender being once convicted, shall for every Month after such Conviction, without any other Indictment or Conviction, pay into the Exchequer twice in the Year,* viz. *in every* Easter *and* Michaelmas *Term, as much as shall then remain unpaid, after the Rate of twenty Pounds for every Month after a Conviction, and that for a Default herein the King may seize all the Goods, and two Parts of the Hereditaments of such an Offender,* &c.

Sect. 42. But it seemeth that these Clauses extend not to any Conviction upon an Information, or Action, *&c.* but only to a Conviction upon an Indictment, for there is no other Suit referred to besides that of Indictment; also it is said that the said Clauses extend to no Convictions by Verdict or otherwise, unless Judgment be given thereon; because, till then, nothing is forfeited. And from the same Ground it seems to follow, That they would not have extended to a Conviction by Default upon Proclamation, if there had been no other Words in the Statute to this Purpose, than those by which it is enacted, *That such a Default recorded shall be as sufficient a Conviction in Law of the said Offence, whereof the Party standeth indicted, as if upon the same Indictment a Trial by Verdict thereupon had proceeded and been recorded,* which Words of themselves can by no Means make such a Conviction amount to a Judgment after Verdict, without which there can be no Forfeiture upon any other Conviction; and therefore it seemeth that the Forfeiture caused by such a Conviction must depend upon the other Clauses of the said Statutes, and the constant Tenor of our Law Books, which seem to suppose that a Person so convicted shall be liable to the said Forfeitures, as much as one against whom a Judgment is expresly given.

> Cawley 102, 103.
> Vide supra, Sect. 8.
> See 29 El. 6. Par. 6. 3 Jac. 1. 4. Par. 7, 8, 9. Cawley 103, 104.

Sect. 43. As to the second general Branch of this Head, *viz.* In what manner Offenders of this Nature are to be prosecuted for the Forfeiture of Lands or Goods, it appeareth from the 13th, 14th, 15th, 17th, 18th, 40th and 41st Sections of this Chapter, that the King hath his Election either to seize all the Goods and two Parts of the Hereditaments and Leases of the Offender, upon his making Default in the Payment of twenty Pounds, both for every Month contained in an Indictment whereon he shall be convicted, and also for every Month subsequent, or else to refuse the said Penalty of twenty Pounds a Month, and thereupon to seize two Parts of the Hereditaments and Leases of the Offender.

Sect.

Sect. 44. It also appeareth from what has been said in the forty-second Section of this Chapter, that the King hath this Advantage of seizing the Lands and Goods of the Offender upon no other Conviction but such as followeth an Indictment, nor even upon such a Conviction without a Judgment, unless it be caused by a Default upon a Proclamation; therefore I shall add no more to this Head, except these two following Observations:

2 Inst. 573. 8 Co. 169. Plowd. 486.

Sect. 45. I. That the King cannot seize the Lands, till it appears by the Return of an Inquisition to that purpose to be awarded, of what Lands, *&c.* the Offender was seised, because the King's Title to Lands ought always to appear of Record.

Bro. Coro. 2, 14, 25, 45, 47, 55, 60. 1 Rol. Re. 7. 2 Rol. Ab. 184. Pl. 3.

Sect. 46. II. That the King, according to the better Opinion, may seize the Goods, but not grant them over, without such an Inquisition.

Sect. 47. As to the third general Head of this Chapter, *viz.* What Disabilities, and other Inconveniencies, Offenders of this Kind are liable unto, it is enacted by 3 *Jac.* 1. 5. Par. 8. *That no Recusant convict shall practise either the Common or Civil Law, or Physick, or use the Trade of an Apothecary, or be Judge or Minister of any Court, or bear any Office in Camp, Troop, or Company of Soldiers, or in any Ship, or Fortress, but shall be utterly disabled for the same, and forfeit for every such Offence, one hundred Pounds.*

Sect. 48. Also it is farther enacted by the said Statute of 3 *Jac.* 1. 5. Par. 22, *That such Recusants as shall be convicted at the Time of the Death of any Testator, or at the Time of the Granting of any Administration, shall be disabled to be Executors or Administrators; and that no such Persons shall be Guardians to any Child,* &c.

Sect. 49. And it is enacted by 23 *El.* 1. *That every Person forbearing the Church twelve Months, shall on Certificate thereof into the King's Bench by the Ordinary, a Justice of Assize and Gaol-Delivery, or a Justice of Peace of the County where such Offender shall dwell or be, be bound with two sufficient Sureties in the Sum of two hundred Pounds at the least to the Good Behaviour, and so continue bound until such Offender shall conform himself,* &c.

Sect. 50. As to the fourth general Head of this Chapter, *viz.* By what means Offenders of this Nature may be discharged from the said Forfeitures, *&c.* it is enacted by 23 *El.* 1. Par. 10. *That every Person guilty of the above mentioned Offences, who shall before he be thereof indicted, or at his Arraignment or Trial before Judgment, submit and conform himself before the Bishop of the Diocese where he shall be resident, or before the Justices where he shall be indicted, arraigned, or tried, (having not before made like submission at any his Trial, being indicted for his first like Offence,) shall upon his Recognition of such submission in open Assizes, or Sessions of the County where such Person shall be resident, be discharged of all and every the said Offences against the said Statute,* &c.

Sect. 51. Also it is enacted by 29 *El.* 6. Par. 6. *That whensoever any such Offender shall make submission, and become conformable, according to the Form limited by the above mentioned Statute of* 23 El. 1. *or shall fortune to die, that then no Forfeiture of twenty Pounds for any Month, or Seizure of the Lands of the same Offender, from and after such Submission and Conformity, or Death, and full Satisfaction of all the Arrearages of twenty Pounds Monthly, before such Seizure due or payable, shall ensue, or be continued against such Offender so long as the same Person shall continue in coming to Divine Service, according to the Intent of the said Statute.*

Sect. 52. But this Statute being thought not to give sufficient encouragement to such Persons to conform to the Church, because, by the most favourable Construction that could be made, it still obliged them to pay such Debts as were due to the King by force of a Judgment, it was enacted by 1 *Jac.* 1. 4. Par. 2, *That a Recusant conforming himself according to the Meaning of the above mentioned Statutes*, &c. *shall during such Conformity, be discharged of all Penalties, which he might otherwise sustain by reason of his Recusancy.* 1 Rol. Re 94.

Sect. 53. And it hath been resolved that such Conformity may by Force of this Statute be pleaded as well to the Suit of an Informer as to that of the King; and that after Judgment it will be a good Ground for an *Audita Querela* against an Informer; and also may be pleaded against the King before Execution awarded. Raym. 391, 465. 2 Jon. 187. 1 Mod. 213. 1 Rol Re. 95. 2 Bul. 324, 325. Savil. 130.

Sect. 54. However, there seems to be no Remedy for such a Person to get a Restitution of such of the Profits of his Lands as have been actually taken by the King.

Sect. 55. It seemed very doubtful before 1 *Jac.* 1. 4 how far the Lands of an Heir were chargeable with the Forfeitures incurred by his Ancestor in Respect of his Recusancy, but this seems to be for the most Part cleared by the 3d, 4th and 5th Paragraphs of that Statute, by which it is enacted, *That the Heir, if he be no Recusant, or were such, and conform, shall be freed from all Penalties happening upon him by reason of his Ancestor's Recusancy, unless the two Parts of the Lands were seized by the King in the Ancestor's Life, in which Case they shall continue in the King's Hands till the whole Debt shall be levied. But it is farther enacted, That the King shall not extend the other third Part of the Lands for the said Penalty.* Lane 92, 93, 106. Cawley 109, 110.

Sect. 56. It seems by the manifest Purport of this Statute, that the Heir of a Recusant, being also a Recusant himself, has no Remedy, but by conforming, to free his Fee-Simple Lands from any of the Forfeitures incurred by his Ancestor, whether the Lands were seiz'd in the Ancestor's Life or not: However, it is said, that the Land in Fee-Tail, which he claims from such Ancestor, is no way chargeable after the Death of the Ancestor, with any Forfeitures upon a Conviction by Proclamation, (which has no greater Effect than a Verdict recorded,) but only with such as are due upon a Judgment; which, as it is agreed, charge an Heir in Tail by Force of 33 *H.* 8. 39. Par. 29. which makes an Heir chargeable with the Debts of his Ancestor by Judgment, Recognizance, Obligation, or other Specialty; but perhaps the Authority of these Opinions may justly be questioned: For tho' a Conviction by Proclamation amount not to a Judgment, yet surely it cannot be inferiour to an Obligation: And therefore perhaps the Books cited in the Margin are misreported in this particular, and the more proper Distinction may be this; That an Heir in Tail is chargeable only with the Forfeitures for those Months which are contained in the Indictment it self, on which a Judgment is afterwards given, or a Conviction by Proclamation recorded, and not for the Months subsequent to such Conviction, or Proclamation, inasmuch as the first seem to be Debts appearing of Record, the latter not; and the same Distinction seems applicable to such Lands in Tail of an Heir who conforms, as were seized in the Ancestor's Life; but it is clear, that such only of his Lands as were so seized are in any Case liable, whether he claim them in Fee-Simple or Tail. Moore 523. 1 Rol. Re. 94. Cro El. 846. Cawley 109, 110, 150, 151, 152.

CHAP. XI.

Of the Offence of suffering others to be absent from Church.

HAving shewn how far all Persons in general are punishable for their own Absence from the Church, I am now to shew how far they may be punished for the Absence of others; as to which it is enacted by 3 *Jac.* 1. 4. Par. 32, 33, 34. *That whosoever shall retain or keep in his Service, Fee or Livery, or shall willingly maintain, retain, relieve, keep, or harbour, in his House, any Servant, Sojourner, or Stranger, (except a Father or Mother, wanting, without Fraud or Covin, other Habitation, or sufficient Maintenance, and also except a Ward, or Person committed to the Custody of another by Authority,) who shall not go to some Church or Chapel, or usual Place of Common Prayer, to hear Divine Service, but shall forbear the same for the Space of one Month,* &c. *shall for every Month that he shall keep such Servant,* &c. *forfeit ten Pounds.*

CHAP. XII.

Of Popish Recusancy.

AND now we are come to Offences against the Established Church, more immediately relating to those of the Popish Religion, for the better understanding whereof I shall consider:

1. The above mentioned Offence of not coming to Church, so far as it particularly concerns those of this Persuasion.
2. The Offence of saying or hearing Mass, or other Popish Service.
3. The Offence of not making a Declaration against Popery.
4. The Offence of promoting or encouraging the Popish Religion.

And first, As to the said Offence of not coming to Church, so far as it particularly concerns those of the Popish Religion, who in respect hereof are commonly called Popish Recusants, I shall consider;

1. How far such Recusants are punishable in their own Persons.
2. How far they make others liable to be punished.

As to the first of these Points, *viz.* How far such Recusants are punishable in their own Persons, it is to be observed that they are not only liable to all the Forfeitures and Disabilities, and other Inconveniencies mentioned in Chap. 10. but also to many particular Disabilities, Restraints and Forfeitures, and other Inconveniencies, to which no others are liable.

And first, They are put under the following Disabilities,

1. That of bringing an Action.

2. That of presenting to a Church.
3. That of bearing any publick Office, or Charge.
4. That of claiming any Part of a Husband's personal Estate.
5. That of claiming an Estate by Curtesy, or by Way of Dower, after a Marriage against Law.

Secondly, They are put under the following Restraints,

1. From going above five Miles from Home.
2. From coming to Court.
3. From keeping Arms.
4. From coming within ten Miles of *London*.

Thirdly, They are liable to the following Forfeitures,

1. That of two Parts of a Jointure or Dower.
2. That of twenty Pounds for not receiving the Sacrament yearly after Conformity.
3. That of one hundred Pounds for an unlawful Marriage.
4. That of one hundred Pounds for an Omission of lawful Baptism.
5. That of twenty Pounds for an unlawful Burial.

Lastly, They are subject to the following Inconveniencies,

1. That their Houses may be searched for Reliques, whether they be Men or Women.
2. If they be Women and married, that they may be committed, *&c.*

Sect. 1. As to the first of the said Disabilities, *viz.* That of bringing an Action, it is enacted by 3 *Jac.* 1. 5. Par. 11, 12. *That every Popish Recusant convict shall stand to all Intents and Purposes disabled as a Person lawfully excommunicated, and as if such Person had been so denounced and excommunicated according to the Laws of this Realm, until he or she shall conform,* &c. *And that every Person, sued by such Person so disabled, may plead the same in disabling of such Plaintiff, as if he or she were excommunicated by Sentence in the Ecclesiastical Court: Except the Action of such Recusant do concern some Hereditament or Lease, which is not to be seized into the King's Hands, by Force of some Law concerning Recusancy.*

In the Exposition hereof it hath been resolved,

Sect. 2. I. That the Plea of such a Conviction, like all other Pleas in Disability, ought to be pleaded before Imparlance, and also to conclude with a Demand if the Plaintiff shall be answered. Noy 89. Latch. 176, 177. Hetl. 18.

Sect. 3. II. That such Plea ought also to shew before what Justices the Conviction was, that the Court may know where to send for a Certificate thereof if it be denied; and also that the Record it self, or at least a Certificate thereof, ought to be immediately produced, according to the general Rule of the Law, as to all dilatory Pleas grounded upon Records. Noy 89. Latch. 176. 3 Lev. 333, 334.

Sect. 4. III. That if after such a Plea it be certified that the Plaintiff hath conformed, and thereupon the Defendant be ordered to plead in chief, and then the Plaintiff relapse and be convict again, the Defendant cannot plead the same in Disability a second Time. Hetl. 176.

Sect. 5. IV. That it must appear either from the Conviction it self, or by proper Averments, that the Plaintiff is convicted of Popish Recusancy, because no Recusants, except Popish ones, are within the said Clause; however, that this is sufficiently set forth, by alledging that the Plaintiff being *Papalis Recusans*, was indicted and convicted *Secundum formam Statuti, &c.* 3 Lev. 333, 334. 11, 12.

Sect. 6. And some have gone so far as to hold, That all Popish Recusants convict may be taken up by the Writ *De Excommunicato capiendo*, and that they are not to be admitted as competent Witnesses in any Cause; 2 Bul. 155, 156.

Cause; but this seems to be a Construction over severe: For, inasmuch as this, like all other Penal Statutes, ought to be construed strictly, and the Words thereof are no more than, That such Persons shall stand disabled, *&c.* as Persons lawfully excommunicate, *&c.* and the Purport thereof may be fully satisfied by the Disability to bring any Action, it seems to be too rigorous to carry them farther.

Cawley 216.

Sect. 7. As to the second of the said Disabilities, *viz.* That of presenting to a Church, the same being at this Day extended by 12 *Ann.* 2. to all Persons making Profession of the Popish Religion, I shall refer the Reader for the Matters relating to this Head, to Chap. 15, wherein is shewn how penal it is, barely to profess the said Religion; and I shall only take Notice in this Place, that by 1 *Gul. & Mar,* 26. Par. 4. *If the Trustee, Mortgagee, or Grantee of any Avoidance, whereof the Trust shall be for any Popish Recusant convict, shall present without giving Notice in Writing of the Avoidance to the University,* &c. *within three Months after the Avoidance, he forfeits five hundred Pounds.*

Sect. 8. As to the Third of the said Disabilities, *viz.* That of bearing any publick Office or Charge, it is enacted by 3 *Jac.* 1. 5. Par. 9. *That no Popish Recusant convict shall exercise any publick Office, or Charge, in the Commonwealth, but shall be utterly disabled to exercise the same, by himself or his Deputy.*

Sect. 9. It is observable that this Clause is more strongly penned than that which immediately precedes it, relating to all Recusants in general, as to the following Particulars:

1. That this extends to all publick Offices and Charges in general, whereas the former extends only to those which are particularly enumerated.

2. That this expresly disables a Popish Recusant to exercise such an Office by himself or his Deputy, but the other says nothing at all of the Exercise of an Office by a Deputy.

Sect. 10. As to the Fourth of the said Disabilities, *viz.* That of claiming any Part of a Husband's personal Estate, it is enacted by 3 *Jac.* 1. 5. Par. 10. *That every Woman being a Popish Recusant convict, (her Husband not standing convicted of Popish Recusancy) which shall not conform her self and remain conform'd, but shall forbear to repair to some Church or usual place of Common Prayer, and there hear Divine Service and Sermon, if any then be, and receive the Sacrament of the Lord's Supper, according to the Laws of this Realm, by the Space of one whole Year next before the Death of her said Husband, shall not only be disabled to be Executrix or Administratrix of her said Husband, but also to have or demand any Part of her said Husband's Goods or Chattels, by any Law, Custom or Usage whatsoever*; and by 3 *Jac.* 1. 5. Par. 13. *Every Woman is put under the like Disability, being a Popish Recusant, who shall be married otherwise than according to the Church of* England.

Sect. 11. As to the Fifth of the said Disabilities, *viz.* That of claiming an Estate by the Curtesy, or by way of Dower, *&c.* it is enacted by 3 *Jac.* 1. 5. Par. 13. *That every Man who being a Popish Recusant convict, shall be married otherwise than in some open Church or Chapel, and otherwise than according to the Orders of the Church of* England *by a Minister lawfully authorized, shall be disabled to have any Estate, as Tenant by the Courtesy; and that every Woman being a Popish Recusant convict, who shall be married in other Form than as aforesaid, shall be disabled to claim her Dower or Jointure, or Widow's Estate,* &c.

Sect. 12. As to the first of the above mentioned Restraints, *viz.* That from going above five Miles from Home, *&c.* it is enacted by 35 *El.* 2. and 3 *Jac.* 1. 5. Par. 6, 7. *That every Popish Recusant convict shall repair to his*

his Place of Dwelling, &c. *and not remove above five Miles from thence, unless he be urged by Process,* &c. *or have a Licence from the Privy Council,* &c. *or under the Hands and Seals of four Justices of Peace, with the Assent in Writing of the Lieutenant of the County, or of the Bishop,* &c. *(Every Licence of which kind by Justices of Peace, must express both the particular Cause and the Time for which it is given, and ought not to be granted without a previous Oath of some reasonable Cause,) under Pain of forfeiting all his Goods and Hereditaments, (whether Freehold or Copyhold,) for his Life, or of abjuring the Realm, if he be not worth twenty Marks a Year, or forty Pounds in Goods, unless he recant before Conviction, and also continue conformable.* See Cawley 128, 129, &c. 207, 208.

Sect. 13. Note, That the Privy Council may grant such Licence without any Special Cause or Oath, *&c.* but that the Justices of Peace cannot: And it hath been resolved, That in pleading a Licence of Justices of Peace, you must expresly shew that it was made under their Hands and Seals, and also set forth the Cause in particular for which it was granted, and the Time for which it was limited, and that the Party was sworn to the Truth of such Cause, *&c.* Cro. Jac. 352. 1 Rol. Re. 108. Moore 836.

Sect. 14. It is said, That if the same Person be both a Justice of Peace and a Lieutenant, he cannot both join in a Licence as Justice of Peace, and also give his Assent as Lieutenant, but can only act in one Capacity. Cro. Ja. 352. 1 Rol. Re. 108. Moore 836.

Sect. 15. It seems that the Miles shall be computed according to the *English* manner, allowing 5280 Foot, or 1760 Yards to each Mile, and that the same shall be reckoned not by strait Lines as a Bird or Arrow may fly, but according to the nearest and most usual way. Cawley 130, 131. Cro. El. 212.

Sect. 16. As to the Second of the above mentioned Restraints, *viz.* That which relates to the coming to Court, it is enacted by 3 *Jac.* 1. 5. Par. 2. *That no Popish Recusant convict shall come into the Court or House where the King or his Heir apparent shall be, unless he be commanded so to do by the King, upon Pain of one hundred Pounds,* &c. And it is farther enacted by 30 *Car.* 2. St. 2. Par. 5, 6. *That every Popish Recusant convict, who shall come advisedly into, or remain in the Presence of the King or Queen, or shall come into the Court or House where they or any of them reside, shall be disabled to hold or execute any Office or Place of Trust Civil or Military, or to sue in Law or Equity, or to be an Executor, &c. or capable of any Legacy or Deed of Gift, and shall forfeit for every wilful Offence five hundred Pounds, unless such Person do within the Term next after such his coming or remaining, take the Oaths of Allegiance and Supremacy, and make the Declaration against Transubstantiation and the Invocation of Saints,* &c. *in the Court of Chancery.*

Sect. 17. As to the Third of the above mentioned Restraints, *viz.* That which relates to the keeping of Arms, it is enacted by 3 *Jac.* 1, 5. Par. 27, 28, 29. *That all such Armour, Gun-powder, and Munition of whatsoever Kinds, as any Popish Recusant convict shall have in his own House or elsewhere, or in the Possession of any other at his Disposition, shall be taken from him by Warrant of four Justices of Peace at their General or Quarter-Sessions, (except such necessary Weapons as shall be allowed him by the said four Justices for the Defence of his Person or House) and that the said Armour,* &c. *so taken, shall be kept at the Costs of such Recusant, in such Place as the said four Justices at their said Sessions shall appoint: And that if any such Recusant having such Armour,* &c. *or if any other Person who shall have any such Armour,* &c. *to the Use of such Recusant, shall refuse to discover to the said Justices, or any of them, what Armour he hath, or shall let or hinder the Delivery thereof to any of the said Justices, or to any other Person authorized by their Warrant to take the same, that then every Person so offending shall forfeit his said Armour,* &c. *and*

also

also be imprisoned for three Months without Bail, by Warrant from any Justices of Peace of such County. And it is farther enacted, *That notwithstanding the taking away such Armour,* &c. *yet such Recusant shall be charged with the maintaining of the same, and with the providing of a Horse,* &c. *in such Sort as others of his Majesty's Subjects.* Also it is farther enacted by 1 *Will. & Mar.* 15. *That no reputed Papist refusing to make the said Declaration against Popery, mentioned in* 30 Car. *shall keep Arms*; as is set forth more at large, *Chap.* 14. *Sect.* 4.

Sect 18. As to the fourth of the above mentioned Restraints, *viz.* That which relates to the coming within ten Miles of *London*, it is enacted by 3 *Jac.* 1. 5. Par. 4, 5. *That no Popish Recusant, &c. shall remain within the Compass of ten Miles of* London *under Pain of one hundred Pounds, except such Persons as at the Time of the said Act did use some Trade, Mystery, or manual Occupation in* London, &c. *and such as shall have their only Dwelling in* London, &c. Also reputed Papists refusing to make the Declaration mentioned in the precedent Sections, are to be removed from *London, &c.* by Force of 1 *Will. & Mar.* 9. which is set forth more at large in *Cha.* 14. *Sect.* 3.

Sect. 19. As to the first of the above mentioned Forfeitures, *viz.* That of two Parts of a Jointure or Dower, it is enacted by 3 *Jac.* 1. 5. Par, 10. *That every married Woman being a Popish Recusant convict, (her Husband not standing convicted of Popish Recusancy,) who shall not conform her self and remain conformed, but shall forbear to repair to some Church or usual Place of Common Prayer, and there to hear Divine Service and Sermon, if any then be, and receive the Sacrament of the Lord's Supper, according to the Laws of this Realm, within one Year next before the Death of her said Husband, shall forfeit to the King the Profits of two Parts of her Jointure and Dower of any Hereditaments of her said Husband,* &c.

Sect. 20. As to the second of the above mentioned Forfeitures, *viz.* That of twenty Pounds, *&c.* for not receiving the Sacrament yearly after Conformity, it is enacted by 3 *Jac.* 1. 4. Par. 2, 3. *That if any Popish Recusant convict, who hath conformed himself to the Church,* &c. *shall not receive the Sacrament in his own Parish-Church,* &c. *within one Year after his Conformity, he shall forfeit twenty Pounds, and for the second Year forty Pounds, and for every Year after sixty Pounds,* &c.

Sect. 21. As to the third of the above mentioned Forfeitures, *viz.* That of one hundred Pounds for an unlawful Marriage, it is enacted by 3 *Jac.* 1. 5. Par. 13. *That every Popish Recusant convict, who shall be married to a Woman who is no Inheritrix, otherwise than according to the Church of* England, *shall forfeit one hundred Pounds.*

Sect. 22. As to the fourth of the above mentioned Forfeitures, *viz.* That of one hundred Pounds for the Omission of a lawful Baptism, it is enacted by 3 *Jac.* 1. 5. Par. 14. *That every Popish Recusant, who shall not cause his or her Child to be baptized, within one Month after its Birth, by a lawful Minister,* &c. *shall forfeit one hundred Pounds,* &c.

Sect. 23. As to the Fifth of the above mentioned Forfeitures, *viz.* That of twenty Pounds for an unlawful Burial, it is enacted by 3 *Jac.* 1. 5. Par. 15. *That if any Popish Recusant not being excommunicate, shall be buried in any other Place than in the Church or Church-yard, or not according to the Ecclesiastical Laws of this Realm, the Executors,* &c. *of such Recusant, knowing the same, or the Party that causeth him to be so buried, shall forfeit twenty Pounds,* &c.

Sect. 24. As to the Inconvenience to which all such Offenders are liable, *viz.* That of having their Houses searched for Reliques, *&c.* it it is enacted by 3 *Jac.* 1. 5. Par. 26. *That any two Justices of Peace, and all Mayors, Bailiffs and chief Officers of Cities, and Towns Corporate, in their respective Jurisdictions, may search the House and Lodgings of every Popish Recusant convict for Popish Books and Reliques; and that if any Altar, Pix, Beads, Pictures, or such like Popish Relique, or any Popish Book, be found in the Custody of such Person, as in the Opinion of the said Justices,* &c. *shall be unmeet for him or her to have or use, it shall be defaced and burnt, if it be meet to be burnt; and if it be a Crucifix or other Relique of any Price, the same shall be defaced at the General Quarter-Sessions in the County where it shall be found, and then restored to the Owner.*

Sect. 25. As to the Inconvenience to which such Offenders being Fems-Covert are liable, *viz.* that of being committed, it is enacted by 7 *Jac.* 1. 6. Par. 28. *That if any married Woman being a Popish Recusant convict, shall not within three Months after her Conviction, conform her self and repair to Church and receive the Sacrament,* &c. *she may be committed to Prison by one of the Privy Council, or by the Bishop, if she be a Baroness; or if under that Degree, by two Justices of Peace, whereof one to be of the* Quorum, *there to remain till she conform,* &c. *unless the Husband will pay to the King ten Pounds a Month for her Offence, or else the third Part of all his Lands,* &c. *at the Choice of the Husband,* &c.

Sect. 26. And now I am to consider in the second Place, how far such Recusants make others liable to be punished; as to which it is to be observed, That the Husband of a Popish Recusant convict is not only liable to the Forfeiture of ten Pounds a Month for the Absence of any of his Servants from Church, by Force of 1 *Jac.* 1. which is set forth more at large in the foregoing Chapter, *But is also utterly disabled by the ninth Paragraph of the said Statute, to exercise any Publick Office or Charge in the Common wealth by himself or by his Deputy; (except such Husband himself, and his Children which shall be above the Age of nine Years abiding with him, and his Servants in Houshold, shall once every Month at the least, not having any reasonable Excuse to the contrary, repair to some Church or Chapel usual for Divine Service, and there hear Divine Service; and the said Husband, and such his Children and Servants, as are of meet Age, receive the Sacrament of the Lord's Supper, at such Times as are limited by the Laws of this Realm, and do bring up his said Children in the true Religion.)*

Sect. 27. Also it is farther enacted by the said Statute of 3 *Jac.* 1. 5. Par. 26. *That the House of one whose Wife is a Popish Recusant convict, may be searched by any two Justices of Peace,* &c. *for Popish Books,* &c.

CHAP. XIII.

Of Offences in saying or hearing Mass, or other Popish Service.

Sect. 1. As to the Offence in saying or hearing Mass, it is enacted by 23 *El.* 1. Par. 4. *That every Person who shall say or sing Mass, being thereof lawfully convict, shall forfeit two hundred Marks, and be committed to Prison in the next Gaol, there to remain by the Space of one Year, and from thenceforth till he have paid the said Sum of two hundred Marks;*

and

and that every Person, who shall willingly hear Mass, shall forfeit the Sum of one hundred Marks, and suffer a Year's Imprisonment.

Sect. 2. Also it is enacted by 11 & 12 *Will.* 3. 4. Par. 2, 3, 4, 5. *That every Person, who shall apprehend any Popish Bishop, Priest, or Jesuit, and prosecute him to Conviction for saying Mass, or exercising any other Part of the Function of a Popish Bishop or Priest, shall receive one hundred Pounds of the Sheriff, and that every such Popish Bishop,* &c. *(except, being a Foreigner, he be entered in the Secretary's Office, and officiate only in the House of a Foreign Minister,) shall be adjudged to perpetual Imprisonment.*

CHAP. XIV.

Of the Offence of not making a Declaration against Popery.

THE Offence of refusing to make a Declaration against some of the Principal Doctrines of the Popish Religion puts all Persons under the following Restraints;

1. From sitting in Parliament.
2. From holding a Place at Court.
3. From living within ten Miles of *London.*
4. From keeping Arms.

Also it puts them under a Disability of presenting to a Church.

Sect. 1. As to the first of the above mentioned Restraints, *viz* That which relates to the sitting in Parliament, it is enacted by 30 *Car.* 2. Stat. 2. Chap. 1. *That no Peer shall vote or make his Proxy in the House of Peers, or sit there during any Debate; and that no Member of the House of Commons shall vote or sit there during any Debate after the Speaker is chosen, until such Peer or Member shall take the Oaths of Allegiance and Supremacy, and make a Declaration of his Belief that there is no Transubstantiation in the Sacrament of the Lord's Supper; and that the Invocation or Adoration of the Virgin* Mary, *or any other Saint, and the Sacrifice of the Mass, as they are now used in the Church of* Rome, *are Superstitious and Idolatrous,* &c. *on Pain that every such Offender shall be adjudged a Popish Recusant convict, and disabled to hold or execute any Office,* &c. *or from thenceforth to sit or vote in either House of Parliament, to sue in Law or Equity, or to be Guardian, Executor or Administrator, or capable of any Legacy or Deed of Gift, and shall forfeit for every wilful Offence five hundred Pounds.*

Sect. 2. As to the second of the above mentioned Restraints, *viz.* That which relates to the holding a Place at Court, it is enacted by the said Statute of 30 *Ca.* 2. Stat. 2. Par. 9, 12, 13. *That every Person who shall be a sworn Servant to the King, shall take the said Oaths, and make and subscribe the said Declaration in Chancery, the next Term after he shall be so sworn a Servant,* &c. *And that if any such Person neglecting so to do, shall advisedly come into or remain in the Presence of the King or Queen, or shall come into the Court or House where they or any of them reside, he shall suffer all the Penalties expressed in the foregoing Section, unless such Person so coming into*

 the

the King's Presence, &c. *shall first have Licence so to do, by Warrant under the Hands and Seals of six Privy Counsellors, by order of the Privy Council, upon some urgent Occasion therein to be expressed, which such Licence exceed not ten Days, and be first filed,* &c. *in the Petty-Bag Office, for any Body to view without Fee,* &c. *and no Person be licenced for above thirty Days in one Year.*

Sect. 3. As to the third of the above mention'd Restraints, *viz.* That which relates to the living within ten Miles of *London,* it is enacted by 1 *Will. & Mar.* 9. *That every Justice of Peace in* London *and* Westminster, *and within ten Miles thereof, shall cause to be arrested and brought before him all reputed Papists, (except Foreigners, being Merchants, or menial Servants to some Ambassadour or publick Agent, and except all such as used some Trade, Mystery, or some manual Occupation at the Time of the said Act, in* London, &c. *and also except all such Persons as had their Dwelling in* London, &c. *within six Months before the thirteenth of* February 1688. *and no Dwelling elsewhere, and certified their Names to the Sessions before the first of* August 1689.) *and that every such Justice shall tender the said Declaration to every such Person, and that every such Person refusing the same, and afterwards remaining in* London, &c. *or within ten Miles thereof, or being certified to the King's Bench or Quarter-Sessions, at the next Term or Sessions, as having refused to make the said Declaration, and neglecting to make the same in such Court, shall suffer as a a Popish Recusant convict,* &c.

Sect. 4. As to the fourth of the above mentioned Restraints, *viz.* That which relates to the keeping Arms, it is enacted by 1 *Will. & Mar.* 15. *That any two Justices of Peace may and ought to tender the said Declaration, to any Person whom they shall know or suspect, or have Information of, as being a Papist or suspected to be such; and that no such Person so required, and not making and subscribing the said Declaration, or not appearing before the said Justices upon Notice to him given, or left at his usual Abode, by one authorized by Warrant under the Hands and Seals of the said Justices, shall keep any Arms or Ammunition, or Horse above the Value of five Pounds, in his own Possession, or in the Possession of any other Person to his Use, (other than such necessary Weapons, as shall be allowed him by the Quarter-Sessions for the Defence of his House or Person) and that any two Justices of Peace, by Warrant under their Hands and Seals, may authorize any Person in the Day-time, with the Assistance of the Constable or his Deputy or the Tithing-man, to search for all such Arms,* &c. *and Horses, and seize them to the King's Use, and that the said Justices shall deliver the said Arms and Ammunition at the next Quarter-Sessions in open Court; and that whoever shall conceal,* &c. *or shall be aiding to the concealing any such Arms or Horses, shall be committed to the common Gaol by Warrant under the Hands and Seals of any two Justices of Peace, and also forfeit treble the Value; and that those who discover any such Arms or Ammunition, so as the same may be seized, shall have the full Value thereof, to be awarded to them by the Sessions,* &c. *and that such Refusers of the said Declaration,* &c. *shall be discharged whenever they shall make the same.*

Sect. 5. As to the above mentioned Disability of presenting to a Church, it is enacted by 1 *Wil. & Mar.* 26. That whoever shall refuse to make the said Declaration upon such a Tender thereof as is prescribed by the said Act, shall be disabled to present to any Benefice, *&c.* But it seems needless to set forth the Clause of the said Statute relating to this Matter at large in this Place, inasmuch as by 12 *Annæ* 14. All Persons whatsoever making Profession of the Popish Religion are under the like Disability, as will appear from *Ch.* 15. *Sect.* 6, 7, *&c.*

CHAP. XV.

Of Offences in promoting or encouraging the Popish Religion.

OFfences in promoting or encouraging the Popish Religion seem to be reducible to the following Heads;

1. Giving or receiving Popish Education.
2. Professing the Popish Religion.
3. Buying or selling Popish Books.

Sect. 1. The first Offence of this Kind, *viz.* That of giving or receiving Popish Education depends upon several Statutes; and first it is enacted by 1 *Jac.* 1. 4. Par. 6, 7. *That if any Person or Persons under the King's Obedience shall go, or send or cause to be sent, any Child or any other Person under their or any of their Government, beyond the Seas, out of the King's Obedience, to the Intent to enter into, or reside in, or repair to any College,* &c. *of any Popish Order, Profession or Calling, to be instructed, perswaded or strengthened in the Popish Religion, or in any sort to profess the same, every such Person so sending such Child,* &c. *shall forfeit* 100 *l. And every such Person so passing or being sent,* &c. *shall in respect of him or herself only, and not in respect of any of his Heirs or Posterity, be disabled to inherit, purchase, take, have or enjoy, any Profits, Hereditaments, Chattels, Debts, Legacies or Sums of Money,* &c. *whatsoever: And that all Estates, Terms, and other Interests whatsoever to be made, suffered or done, to the Use or Behoof of any such Person, or upon any Trust or Confidence, mediately or immediately, to or for the Benefit or Relief of any such Person, shall be utterly void.*

Sect. 2. And it is farther enacted by 3 *Jac.* 1. 5. Par. 16. *That if the Children of any Subject within this Realm (the said Children not being Soldiers, Mariners, Merchants, or their Apprentices or Factors) shall be sent or go beyond Sea, to prevent their good Education in* England, *or for any other Cause, without the Licence of the King or six of his Privy Council (whereof the Principal Secretary to be one) under their Hands and Seals, that then every such Child shall take no Benefit by any Gift, Conveyance, Descent, Devise or otherwise, of or to any Hereditament or Chattel, till such Child being of the Age of eighteen Years or above, take the Oath of Obedience before some Justice of Peace of the County, Liberty or Limit, where the Parent of such Child did and shall inhabit: And that in the mean Time the next of Kin to such Child, who shall be no Popish Recusant, shall have the said Hereditaments,* &c. *so given,* &c. *until such Child shall conform,* &c. *and take the said Oath and receive the Sacrament; and that after such Conformity,* &c. *he who hath received the Profits of the said Hereditaments,* &c. *shall accompt for the same, and in reasonable Time make Payment thereof, and restore the Value of the said Goods,* &c. *And that whoever shall send such Child over Seas, shall forfeit one hundred Pounds,* which by 11 *&* 12 *Will.* 3. 4. Par. 6. *shall be to the sole Use and Benefit of the Person who shall discover the Offence.*

Sect. 3. Also it is enacted by 3 *Car.* 1. 2. *That if any Person under the Obedience of the King shall go, or shall convey or send, or cause to be sent or conveyed,*

veyed, any Person out of the King's Dominions, into any Parts beyond the Seas, out of the King's Obedience, to the Intent to enter into, or be resident or trained up, in any Priory, Abbey, Nunnery, Popish University, College or School, or House of Jesuits, Priests, or in a private Popish Family, and shall be there by any Popish Person instructed, perswaded or strengthned in the Popish Religion in any sort to profess the same, or shall convey or send, or cause to be conveyed or sent, any Thing towards the Maintenance of any Person so going or sent, and trained and instructed as is aforesaid, or under the Colour of any Charity towards the Relief of any Priory, &c. *or religious House whatsoever; every Person so sending,* &c. *any such Person or Thing, and every Person passing or sent, being thereof convicted,* &c. *shall be disabled to prosecute any Suit in Law or Equity, or to be Executor or Administrator to any Person, or capable of any Legacy or Deed of Gift, or to bear any Office within the Realm. And shall forfeit all his Goods and Chattels, and shall forfeit all his Hereditaments, Offices and Estates of Freehold, during his Life.*

The second Offence of this Kind, *viz.* That of professing the Popish Religion is punished with the following Disabilities,

1. Of taking an Estate in Lands.

2. Of presenting to a Church.

Also it is punished with the following Restraints,

1. From keeping School.

2. From with-holding a competent Maintenance from a Protestant Child.

Sect. 4. As to the first of the above mentioned Disabilities, *viz.* That of taking an Estate in Lands, it is enacted by 11 & 12 *W.* 3. 4. *That every Person educated in or professing the Popish Religion, who shall not within six Months after the Age of eighteen Years, take the Oaths of Allegiance and Supremacy, and subscribe the Declaration against Popery mentioned in* 30 Car. 2. *Stat.* 2. *Chap.* 1. *in the Chancery, or King's Bench, or Quarter-Sessions of the County where such Person shall reside, shall in Respect of himself or herself only, and not in Respect of any of his or her Heirs or Posterity, be disabled to inherit or take by Descent, Devise or Limitation, in Possession, Reversion or Remainder, any Lands, Tenements or Hereditaments, in* England *or* Wales, &c. *And during the Life of such Person, and until he take the said Oaths,* &c. *his next of Kin being a Protestant, shall enjoy the same, without being accomptable for the Profits, but shall not do wilful Waste under pain of forfeiting treble Damages to the Party so disabled: And all Papists, or Persons making Profession of the Popish Religion, are disabled to purchase in their own Names, or the Names of others, to their use or in Trust for them: And all Estates, Terms and other Interests and Profits whatsoever, out of Lands made to their Use, or on any Trust, mediately or immediately, for their Benefit, are void.*

Sect. 5. In the Construction hereof it was resolved by the House of Lords in *Roper*'s Case, That the Devise of the Residue of Money arising from the Sale of an Estate appointed to be sold for Payment of Debts, *&c.* is within the Statute.

Sect. 6. As to the second of the above mentioned Disabilities, *viz.* That of presenting to a Church, which by 3 *Jac.* 1. 5. Par. 18,19,20,21. and 1 *Will.* & *Mar.* 26. did extend only to Popish Recusants convict, and Persons refusing to make the Declaration against Popery, mentioned in 30 *Car.* 2. Stat. 2. It is enacted by 12 *Ann.* 14. *That every Papist, or Person making Profession of the Popish Religion,* &c. *and every Mortgagee, Trustee, or Person any Ways intrusted by or for such Papist,* &c. *with or without Writing, shall be disabled to present to any Benefice, School, or Hospital,* &c. *or or to grant any Avoidance of any Benefice, Prebend or Ecclesiastical Living; and that in all such Cases the Universities shall present.*

Sect. 7. Also by Force of the said Statute, *The Ordinary may tender the Declaration against Transubstantiation to any reputed Papist making a Presentation, and upon a Refusal to take the same, the Presentation shall be void: Also the Ordinary may examine every Presentee upon Oath, Whether the Person who presented him be the true Patron, or only a Trustee? And the Court wherein a* Quare Impedit *shall be brought, may in like Manner examine the Parties, and a Bill may be brought in any Court of Equity to discover such secret Trusts,* &c. *and the Answer of such Persons upon any such Examination or Bill shall be good Evidence against such Patron, in respect of such a Presentation, but not as to any other Purpose.*

Sect. 8. I do not know that any Resolution hath been given on either of the above mentioned Statutes of 1 *Will. & Mar.* or 12 *Ann.* However the Expositions which were made on 3 *Jac.* 1. seeming to be for the most part applicable to these latter Statutes also, I shall take Notice of the principal of them; as,

Sect. 9. I. That where a Presentment is *pro hac vice* vested in the University by reason of the Patron's being a Popish Recusant at the Time when the Church became void, it shall not be devested again by his conforming himself to the Church. (10 Co. 57. b.)

Sect. 10. II. That such a Patron is only disabled to present, and that he continues Patron as to all other Purposes, and therefore that he shall confirm the Leases of the Incumbent, *&c.* (Cawley 230.)

Sect. 11. III. That such a Person by being disabled to grant an Avoidance, is no way hindred from granting the Advowson itself in Fee, or for Life or Years, *bona Fide*, and for good consideration. (1 Jon. 19, 20.)

Sect. 12. IV. That if an Advowson or Avoidance belonging to such a Person come into the King's Hands, by reason of an Outlawry, or Conviction of Recusancy, *&c.* the King, and not the University, shall present. (1 Jon. 20, 21, &c. Hob. 126, 127. Mo. 872.)

Sect. 13. As to the first of the above mentioned Restraints, *viz.* that which relates to the keeping School, it is enacted by the said Statute of 11 & 12 *Will.* 3. 4. Par. 3. *That if any Papist, or Person making Profession of the Popish Religion, shall be convict of keeping School, or taking upon themselves the Education or Government, or Boarding of Youth in any Place within this Realm, or the Dominions thereunto belonging, they shall be adjudged to perpetual Imprisonment.*

Sect. 14. As to the second of the above mentioned Restraints, *viz.* That which relates to the Power of a Popish Parent over his Protestant Child, it is enacted by the said Statute of 11 & 12 *Will.* 3. 4. *That if any Popish Parent, in order to compel a Protestant Child to a Change of Religion, shall refuse to allow such Child a sufficient Maintenance, suitable to the Degree and Ability of such Parent, and to the Age and Education of such Child, the Lord Chancellor upon Complaint may make such Order therein, as shall be agreeable to the Intent of the said Act.*

Sect. 15. The third Offence of this Kind, *viz.* That of selling or buying Popish Books depends upon 3 *Jac.* 1. 5. Par. 25. by which it is enacted, *That no Person shall bring from beyond the Seas, nor shall print, buy or sell any Popish Primers, Ladies Psalters, Manuals, Rosaries, Popish Catechisms, Missals, Breviaries, Portals, Legends and Lives of Saints, containing superstitious Matter, printed or written in any Language whatsoever, nor any other superstitious Books, printed or written in the* English *Tongue, on pain of forfeiting forty Shillings for every Book,* &c. *and the Books to be burnt.*

CHAP. XVI.

Of Offences against the Established Church by Protestant Dissenters.

Sect. 1. BY 31 *El.* 1. *Obstinate Nonconformists were compellable to abjure the Realm, and were also subject to all the Penalties mentioned in the tenth and eleventh Chapters:* But at this Day by 1 *Will. & Mar.* 18. Par. 2. *All Persons dissenting from the Church, (except Papists, and those who shall in Preaching or Writing deny the Doctrine of the Trinity,) are exempted from all Penal Laws relating to Religion, except* 25 Car. 2. *Chap.* 2. *(by which all Officers of Trust are bound to receive the Sacrament according to the Usage of the Church of* England, *and also to take the Oaths of Allegiance and Supremacy, and the Test;) and also except* 30 Car. 2. *Chap.* 1. *Stat.* 2. *(by which the Members of both Houses of Parliament, and all the King's Sworn Servants are bound to make a Declaration against Transubstantiation and the Invocation of Saints, and the Sacrifice of the Mass,) provided such Dissenters take the Oaths of Allegiance and Supremacy, and make the said Declaration against Transubstantiation,* &c. *and come to some Congregation for religious Worship in some Place registred either in the Bishop's Court, or at Sessions, the Doors whereof shall neither be locked, barred, nor bolted.* Par. 17. Vide supra, Ch. 8. Par. 16, 17, 19.

Sect. 2. Also by Par. 8, 9, 10, 11, 12. *Dissenting Teachers are tolerated, if they take the said Oaths,* &c. *at the General or Quarter-Sessions to be held for the Place where such Persons live, and subscribe the twenty nine Articles of the Church of* England, *except those few scrupled ones concerning Church-Government and Infant-Baptism:* And by 10 *Ann.* 2. Par. 7, 8, 9. *They may qualify themselves as well during a Prosecution upon any Penal Statute, as before, and being qualified in one County may officiate in another, upon producing a Certificate and taking the said Oaths,* &c. *if required.*

Sect. 3. Also by the said Statute of 1 *Will. & Mar.* Par. 13, 14, 15. *Those who scruple the taking of any Oath are within the late Indulgence, provided they subscribe the aforesaid Declaration, and also a Declaration of Fidelity to the King, and against the deposing Doctrine and Papal Supremacy; and also profess their Faith in God the Father, and Jesus Christ his eternal Son, the true God, and the Holy Spirit, one God for evermore; and acknowledge the Holy Scriptures of the Old and New Testament to be given by Divine Inspiration.*

CHAP. XVII.

Of High Treason.

OF Offences more immediately against Man, some are more immediately against the King, others more immediately against the Subject.

Offences more immediately against the King are either Capital or not Capital.

The Capital Offences of this Nature are either High Treason or Felonies.

Sect. 1. And first of High Treason, concerning which, before 25 *Ed.* 3. 2. there was great Diversity of Opinions, and many Offences were taken to be included in it, besides those expressed in the said Statute; as the killing of the King's [a] Father or Brother, or even of his [b] Messenger; producing the [c] Pope's Bull of Excommunication, and pleading it in Disability; refusing to accuse a Man in the King's Courts, and [d] summoning him to appear, and defend himself before a foreign Prince, and other such like Acts tending to diminish the Royal Dignity of the Crown.

[a] 3 Inst. 7.
[b] 22 Ass. 49.
[c] 30 Ass. 19. Bro.Trea.14.
[d] 3 Inst. 7. S. P. C. 1. b.

Sect. 2. But all Treasons were settled by the said Statute of 25 *Ed.* 3. 1. which by 1 *Mar.* Sess. 1. Chap. 1. was re-inforced, and again made the only Standard of Treason; and all Statutes between the said Statutes of 25 *Ed.* 3, and 1 *Mar.* which made any Offences High or Petit Treason, or Misprision of Treason, are abrogated, so that no Offence is at this Day to be esteemed High Treason, unless it be either declared to be such by the said Statute of 25 *Ed.* 3. or made such by some Statute since 1 *Mar.* and therefore I shall consider,

1. Such Offences as are High Treason within the said Statute of 25 *Ed* 3. or other Statutes grounded thereon, and explaining the same.

2. Such as are made High Treason by subsequent Statutes.

And first, by the said Statute of 25 *Ed.* 3. there are four Kinds of High Treason.

1. That which immediately concerns the King, his Wife, or Children.

2. That which concerns his Office in the Administration of Justice.

3. That which concerns his Seal.

4. That which concerns his Coin: And these three last are called Interpretative Treasons. H. P. C. 17.

Sect. 3. That of the first Kind is thus declared by the following Words of the said Statute of 25 *Ed.* 3. *Whereas divers Opinions have been before this Time, in what case Treason shall be said, and in what not, the King at the Request of the Lords and of the Commons, hath made a Declaration in the Manner as hereafter followeth; that is to say: When a Man doth compass or imagine the Death of our Lord the King, or of my Lady his Queen, or of their eldest Son and Heir: Or if a Man do violate the King's Companion, or the King's eldest Daughter unmarried, or the Wife of the King's eldest Son and Heir: Or if a Man do levy War against our Lord the King in his Realm, or be adherent to the King's Enemies in his Realm, giving to them Aid and Comfort in the Realm or elsewhere, and thereof be provably attainted of open Deed by the People of their Condition.*

For the Explication of which I shall consider,

1. The Branch relating to the King and his Relations.

2. That concerning the levying of War, and adhering to the King's Enemies, *&c.*

3. That concerning an Overt Act.

As to the Branch relating to the King and his Relations, I shall consider the following Particulars:

1. Who may be guilty.

2. What is the Import of the Words, *Compass or imagine the King's Death.*

3. Who is a King within this Act.

4. What is the Extent of the Clause concerning the King's Relations.

Sect. 4. As to the first Point, *viz.* who may be guilty,

1. I shall take it for granted at this Day, That all Subjects of the Age of Discretion, and of [a] Sane Memory, whether they be [b] Ecclesiastical or Temporal Men or Women, are included within those general Words *When a Man doth compass,* &c.

Sect. 5. II. Also it seems clear, That the Subjects of a foreign Prince coming into *England* and living under the Protection of our King, may, in respect of that local Ligeance which they owe to him, be guilty of High Treason, and indicted, that they *contra Dominum Regem,* (the Words *naturalem Dominum suum,* being omitted) did compass, *&c. contra Ligeantiæ suæ Debitum:* And it is said, That even an Ambassadour commiting a Treason against the King's Life, may be condemned and executed here, and that for other Treasons he shall be sent home.

Sect. 6. [c] But it seemeth that Aliens who in an hostile Manner invade the Kingdom, whether their King were at War or Peace with ours, and whether they come by themselves or in Company with *English* Traitors, cannot be punished as Traitors, but shall be dealt with by Martial Law.

Sect. 7. [d] It hath been resolved, That one born a natural Subject is bound to such an inseparable Allegiance to our King, that howsoever he may endeavour to renounce it, and transfer his Subjection from his natural to a foreign Prince, yet if he practise what in any other Subject would amount to High Treason, he shall suffer as a Traitor.

Sect. 8. As to the second Point, *viz.* the Import of the Words, *Compass or imagine the King's Death,* since the said Statute these Words have been so strictly followed, that where a King has been actually murthered, yet not the Killing him, but the Compassing his Death has in the Indictment been laid as the Treason, and the Killing as an Overt Act thereof.

Sect. 9. And such Compassing the King's Death may be manifested not only by Overt Acts of a direct Conspiracy to take away his Life, but also by such as shew such a Design as cannot be executed without the apparent Peril thereof; as by [e] writing Letters to a foreign Prince, inciting him to invade the Realm; or assembling Men together in order to [f] imprison or [g] depose the King, or to [h] compel him by Force to yield to certain Demands, or to levy War *against* [i] *his Person.*

Sect. 10. But it is possible that it may not be proved by an [k] Act which directly causes the King's Death; as the Glancing of an Arrow did that of *William Rufus,* proving fatal merely thro' an unfortunate Accident, and being accompanied with no unlawful Circumstance.

Sect. 11. As to the third Point, *viz.* Who is a King within this Act, It seems agreed, That [l] every King for the Time being, in actual Possession of the Crown, is a King within the Meaning of this Statute: For there is a Necessity that the Realm should have a King by whom and in whose Name the Laws shall be administred; and the King in Possession being the only Person who either doth or can administer those Laws, must be the only Person who has a Right to that Obedience which is due to him who administers those Laws; and since by Vertue thereof he secures to Us the Safety of our Lives, Liberties and Properties, and all other Advantages of Government, he may justly claim Returns of Duty, Allegiance and Subjection.

[a] See Chap. 1.
[b] See Kellw. 181, 182, &c. 3 Inst. 4.
Calvin's Case 6. Dy. 145. Pl. 62. Bro. Trea. 32. 3 Inst. 4, 5, 10. H. P. C. 10, 15. Hob. 271.
1 Ro. Re 185.
[c] Bro. Treas. 1. 32. H. P. C. 10, 15. Calvin's Case 6. b. 3 Inst. 11. Con. Dalis. 32.
[d] Dy. 300. Pl. 38. Co. Lit. 129. a.
Kelynge 8. *In the Case of the Regicides.*
[e] Dy. 238. Pl. 29. H. P. C. 11. 3 Inst. 14.
[f] 3 Inst. 6, 12. 38. H. P. C. 11.
[g] Kely. 20, 21. H. P. C. 11. *Tho' this was made a Query in* Bro. Treas. 24.
[h] Kelynge 21. Moor 621.
[i] Kelynge 14, 15, 17, 20, 21.
[k] 3 Inst. 6.
[l] H. P. C. 12. 3 Inst. 7. 9 Ed. 4. 1. b.

Sect.

9 Ed. 4. 1. b. Bro. Treas. 10, 32. 3 Inst. 7. H. P. C. 12. Dal. ca. 89. f. 223.

Sect. 12. And this plainly appears even by the prevailing Opinions in the Time of King *Edward* the Fourth, in whose Reign the Distinction between a King *de Jure* and *de Facto* seems first to have begun; and yet it was then laid down as a Principle, and taken for granted in the Arguments of *Bagot*'s Case, That a Treason against *Henry* the Sixth, while he was King, in compassing his Death, was punishable after *Edward* the Fourth came to the Crown, from which it follows, that Allegiance was allowed to have been due to *Henry* the Sixth while he was King, because every Indictment of Treason must lay the Offence, *contra Ligeantia Debitum.*

9 Ed. 4. 1. b. 2. a. Bro Judg. 42. Charter of Pardon 22. 9 Ed. 4. 1, 2, 11.

Sect. 13. It was also settled, That all judicial Acts done by *Henry* the Sixth while he was King, and also all Pardons of Felony and Charters of Denization granted by him, were valid; but that a Pardon made by *Edward* the Fourth, before he was actually King, was void, even after he came to the Crown.

9 Ed. 4. 2. a.

Sect. 14. And by the 11 *H.* 7. Chap. 1. it is declared, *That all Subjects are bound by their Allegiance to serve their Prince and Sovereign Lord for the Time being, in his Wars, for the Defence of him and his Land, against every Rebellion, Power and Might reared against him,* &c. *and that it is against all Laws, Reason and good Conscience, that they should lose or forfeit any Thing for so doing:* And it is enacted, *That from thenceforth no Persons that attend on the King for the Time being, and do him true and faithful Allegiance in his Wars within the Realm or without, shall for the said Deed and true Duty of Allegiance be convict of any Offence.*

Sect. 15. From hence it clearly follows;

I. That every King for the Time being has a Right to the People's Allegiance, because they are bound thereby to defend him in his Wars against every Power whatsoever.

Sect. 16. II. That one out of Possession is so far from having any Right to our Allegiance by Vertue of any other Title which he may set up against the King in Being, that we are bound by the Duty of our Allegiance to resist him.

Kel. 14.

Sect. 17. It is true indeed, that after the Restoration of King *Charles* the Second, it was resolved, That all those who acted against, and kept him out of Possession, in Obedience to the Powers then in Being, were Traitors.

Kel. 14, 15. 1 Keb. 315. 1 Keb. 454.

Sect. 18. But it ought to be considered, that it was first resolved by the same Judges, That King *Charles* the Second was King *de Facto* as well as *de Jure*, from his Father's Death; and it is apparent, that no other Person was in Possession of any Sovereign Power known to our Laws.

3 Inst. 7. H. P. C. 12.

Sect. 19. However, it is a general uncontested Rule, That upon the Death of a King in actual Possession of the Crown, his Heir is a King within the Act before his Coronation; for without a King to execute the Laws, Justice must fail; and therefore it is a Maxim, That the King never dies.

1 Mar. Sess. 3. Ch. 1. H. P. C. 12. 3 Inst. 8.

Sect. 20. A titular King, as the Husband of a Queen Regnant, seems to be within the Words, yet is clearly not within the Meaning of this Law; and *è converso*, a Queen Regnant, is not within the strict Words, and yet she is undoubtedly within the Meaning; for by the Words, *Our Lord the King*, is meant, any Person invested with the Regal Power.

Sect. 21. By 1 *Will. & Mar.* Sess. 2. Chap. 2. Par. 9. *Every Person that shall be reconciled to, or hold Communion with, the Church of* Rome, *or profess the Popish Religion, or marry a Papist, shall be excluded, and be for ever uncapable to inherit, possess, or enjoy the Crown of this Realm,* &c. *And in every such Case the People of this Realm are absolved from their Allegiance,* &c.

Sect. 22. As to the fourth Point, *viz.* The Extent of the Clause concerning the King's Relations, it is to be observed,

1. That no Queen or Princess Dowager is any Way within the Purview of it. 3 Inst. 8, 9. H. P. C. 12.

2. That if the Companion, (by which Word is meant the Wife) of the King or Prince, consent to an Adulterer, she is no less guilty of High Treason than he. 3 Inst. 8, 9. H. P. C. 12.

3. That under the Words, *Their eldest Son and Heir,* the Son of a Queen Regnant is included, and also the second Son after the Death of the first, and perhaps also a collateral Heir apparent, especially if he be declared such by Parliament. 3 Inst. 8, 9. H. P. C. 12.

And now we are come to the second general Branch of this Kind of High Treason, *viz.* That concerning the levying of War, *&c.* and adhering to the King's Enemies, *&c.* in treating whereof I shall consider,

1. What Acts shall be said to amount to a levying of War against the King.

2. What shall be said to be an Adherence to the King's Enemies.

Sect. 23. As to the first Point, it is to be observed, That not only those who directly rebel against the King, and take up Arms in order to dethrone him, but also in many other Cases, those who in a violent and forcible Manner withstand his lawful Authority, or endeavour to reform his Government, are said to levy War against him; and therefore,

Sect. 24. Those that hold a Fort or Castle against the King's Forces, or keep together armed Numbers of Men against the King's express Command, have been adjudged to levy War against him. But those who join themselves to Rebels, *&c.* for fear of Death, and retire as soon as they dare, seem to be no way guilty of this Offence. 3 Inst. 10. H. P. C. 14. Bro. Treas. 24. Dal. ch. 89. fo. 224. Moor 621. H. P. C. 14.

Sect. 25. II. Those also who make an Insurrection in order to redress a publick Grievance, whether it be a real or pretended one, and of their own Authority attempt with force to redress it, are said to levy War against the King, altho' they have no direct Design against his Person, inasmuch as they insolently invade his Prerogative, by attempting to do that by private Authority, which he by publick Justice ought to do, which manifestly tends to a downright Rebellion; as where great Numbers by Force attempt to remove certain Persons from the King; or to lay violent Hands on a Privy Counsellor; or to revenge themselves against a Magistrate for executing his Office; or to bring down the Price of Victuals; or to reform the Law or Religion; or to pull down all Bawdy-houses; or to remove all Inclosures in general, *&c.* But where a Number of Men rise to remove a Grievance to their private Interest, as to pull down a particular Inclosure intrenching upon their Common, *&c.* they are only Rioters. 3 Inst. 9, 10. 2 And. 5. Kelynge 75, &c. Moor 621. Cro. Ca. 583. Poph. 122, 123. 2 And. 4, 5. 3 Inst. 9. H. P. C. 14. Kelynge 76. 1 Sid. 358. 3 And. 66. Pop. 121.

Sect. 26. In a special Verdict, not only those who are expresly found to have been aiding and assisting a rebellious Insurrection, but perhaps also those who are only found to have acted in the Execution of the intended Violence, or to have attended the principal Offender from the Beginning, tho' they be not found to have known the Design of the Rising, shall be adjudged guilty of High Treason; but those who are found only to have suddenly join'd with them in the Streets, and to have flung up their Hats and hallowed with them, are guilty of no greater Offence than a Riot at most. 3 Inst. 9. H. P. C. 14. Kelynge 75. Moore 621, 622.

Dalis. 14, 15. H.P.C. 13, 14. Dy. 98. Pl. 56. Kely. 19, 20. Hetl. 65. 3 Inst. 9.

Sect. 27. However it is certain, That a bare Conspiracy to levy such a War can not amount to Treason unless it be actually levied; yet it hath been resolved that a Conspiracy to levy War against the King's Person may be alledged as an Overt Act of compassing his Death, and that in all Cases, if the Treason be actually compleated, the Conspirators, *&c.* are Traitors as much as the Actors.

3 Inst. 11. 3 Inst. 10. H. P. C. 14. Dalis. 89, 224. H. P. C. 115.

Sect. 28. As to the second Point, (*viz.*) What shall be said to be an Adherence to the King's Enemies, *&c.* this is explained by the Words subsequent, *Giving Aid and Comfort to them*; from which it appears, that any Assistance given to Aliens in open Hostility against the King, as by surrendring a Castle of the King's to them for Reward, or selling them Arms, *&c.* is clearly within this Branch; but it is said that the Succouring a Rebel fled into another Realm is not, because a Rebel is not properly an Enemy, and the Statute is taken strictly.

3 Inst. 12, 13.

Sect. 29. As to the Branch relating to an Overt Act, I shall take it for granted, that some Overt Act must be alledged in every Indictment of High Treason, in compassing the Death of the King, *&c.* but there hath been some Question concerning what shall be said to be such an Overt Act, in treating whereof I shall consider,

1. What Facts amount to such an Overt Act.
2. Whether any Words be sufficient.

H. P. C. 13. 3 Inst. 13, 14. Bro. Treason 24.

Sect. 30. As to the first Point it seems clearly agreed by all, That Conspiring the King's Death, and providing Weapons to effect it, or sending Letters to incite others to procure it, or actually assembling People in order to take the King into their Power, and all other such like notorious Facts, done in pursuance of a treasonable Purpose against the King's Person, may be alledged as Overt Acts to prove the Compassing his Death.

[a] Kelynge 14, 17. [b] Kelynge 20, 21. [c] Kelynge 15, 17. [d] 1 And. 106. [e] Kelynge 22. 2 Rol. Rep. 89, 90.

Sect. 31. It has also been adjudged, That the [a] levying War against the King's Person; or the bare [b] consulting to levy such War; or meeting together and [c] consulting the Means to destroy the King and his Government; or [d] assembling with others and procuring them to attempt the King's Death; or [e] printing treasonable Positions, as that the King is accountable to the People, and that they ought to take the Government into their own Hands, *&c.* or publishing a Book to prove that the King's Government is Antichristian and Heretical, *&c.* may be alledged as Overt Acts to prove the Compassing the King's Death.

2 Rol. Re. 89. Cro. Ca. 125. 2 Rol. Re. 89. *See the Reversal of the Attainder of* Algernoon Sydney.

Sect. 32. As to the second Point, *viz.* Whether any Words are sufficient Overt Acts? it has been holden, That written Words in a Sermon or other Writing may amount to Overt Acts of compassing the King's Death, tho' the same neither actually were, nor ever were intended to be, preached or published; but this Opinion seems to be over severe, for tho' it be true, that *scribere est agere*, yet surely it cannot with any Propriety be said, that to write in such a private Manner *est apertè agere*, and it seems rigorous to make that amount to a malicious Design against the King, which perhaps was only done by Way of Amusement or Diversion.

S. P. C. 2. Kelynge 13. 3 Inst. 14, 140. H. P. C. 13.

Sect. 33. But the great Question is, Whether Words only spoken can amount to an Overt Act of compassing the King's Death? Which having been questioned by some great Men, and denied by others, I dare not be peremptory concerning it.

Sect. 34. However it seems agreed, That Words spoken only in Contempt and Disgrace of the King, and not directly shewing any Purpose to rebel, or any Way to hurt his Person, or disturb his Government, as those which charge him with a personal Vice, as Drunkenness, &c. or a personal Defect, as Want of Wisdom, or Steadiness, &c. shall not be so far strained as to be made Overt Acts of compassing his Death, &c.

> Cro. Ca. 125. Cro. Ca. 117, 125.

Sect. 35. Indeed it has been holden, That to affirm that another has a better Title than the King is High Treason, because it tends to draw People from their Allegiance, and to create a Mutiny, &c. but perhaps this may be questioned, because it cannot certainly appear from such Words, whether the Speaker had a Design against the King's Person or no? However there can be no Doubt, but that such Discourses are highly punishable, as great Misdemeanors, and tending to raise Doubts, and disturb the Government.

> Yelv. 107. 2 Ro. Re. 90. Palm. 426.

Sect. 36. Also the following Words have been adjudged High Treason, If King *Henry* the Eighth will not take back his Wife, he shall not be King, but shall die; —— If the King will arrest me for High Treason I will stab him; —— If I knew that *Perkin Warbeck* was the Son of *Edward* the Fourth, I would take his Part against *Henry* the Seventh.

> 1 Ro.Re.185. 14 H.8. 12. a.

Sect. 37. But however the Laws may stand in relation to such conditional Words, I cannot see any Reason why [a] deliberate Words, which shew a direct Purpose against the King's Life, as these, If I meet the King I will kill him, being spoken maturely and advisedly, should not amount to an Overt Act of compassing or imagining his Death, as it hath been often adjudged that they do.

> [a] 1 Ro. Re. 185. Cro. Ca. 125. 332. 1 Lev. 57. Kelynge 13. 1 Keb. 14. 34. 179. 231. Dalt. Ch. 89. fo. 223, 224. 3 Mod. 53. *See the Precedent cited* Cro. Ca. 118.

Sect. 38. [b] And since the Compassing or Imagining of the King's Death is the Treason, and Words be the most natural Means of expressing the Imagination of the Heart, why should they not be good Evidences of it? Besides it has been often adjudged, That falsly to charge a Man with speaking Treason is actionable, which could not be if no Words could amount to Treason, as in the Arguments of those Cases it is clearly holden that they may, and not so much as made a Question.

> [b] Yelv. 107, 197. Cro. Ja. 276, 405, 413. Hutt. 75. Winch 124. 1 Bulf. 148. 3 Bulf. 225. 1 Ro.Re.444.

Sect. 39. Besides it is certain, That before the 25 *Ed.* 3. Words might amount to Treason; and it is a general Rule, That in doubtful Cases the Reason of the Common Law ought to govern the Construction of a Statute. Also there can be no doubt but that he who by Command or Persuasion induces another to commit a Treason, is himself a Traitor; (for without Question by such Means he would be accessary to a Felony; and it is an uncontroverted Rule, That whatever will make a Man an Accessary in Felony, will make him a Principal in Treason,) and yet he does no Act but by Words.

> S. P. C. 2. b. H. P. C. 215.

Sect. 40. As to Sir *Edward Coke*'s Argument from 3 *H.* 7. 14. which makes the Compassing the King's Death, or that of any of his Council, &c. by the King's Servants, Felony; from whence he infers, that in the Judgment of this Parliament, the Compassing the King's Death by bare Words could not be Treason before; it may be answered, That this Argument extends as well to the King's Servants Compassing his Death by any other Act whatever, as to their doing it by bare Words; for all are equally within the 3 *H.* 7. and yet none will contend, but that the former hath always been Treason.

> 3 Inst. 38.

Sect. 41. As to the Argument that Compassing the King's Death by bare Words cannot amount to Treason, within 25 *Ed.* 3. because many late temporary Acts of Parliament have made it Treason, which would be needless if it were so before; it may be answered, That the principal End of those Statutes was to make it Treason to charge the King with Heresy or Schism, or Usurpation, or to affirm that it was lawful to take up Arms against him, which the *Romanists* were apt to be guilty of at the

> H. P. C. 13.

Vide 2 Ro. Rep. 89, 90. the Beginning of the Reformation, and it may be questioned whether these be Overt Acts of High Treason within 25 *E.* 3.

Sect. 42. Indeed it is recited in the Preamble of 1 *Mar.* Sess. 1. Chap. 1. *That the State of every King consists more assuredly in the Love of the Subject towards their Prince, than in the Dread of Laws made with rigorous Pains; and that Laws made for the Preservation of the Commonwealth without great Penalties are more often obeyed and kept, than Laws made with extream Punishments. And in special such Laws so made, whereby not only the Ignorant but also the Learned, minding Honesty, are often trapped, yea many Times for Words only, without other Fact or Deed done or perpetrated; and thereupon the Queen calls to remembrance, that many, as well honourable Persons, as others of good Reputation, had then of late, (for Words only, without other Opinion, Fact, or Deed,) suffered shameful Death, and expresses her Pleasure, that the Severity of such like extream dangerous and painful Laws shall be abolished.* And then follows the enacting Clause, *That from thenceforth none Act or Offence, being by Act of Parliament or Statute made Treason, Petit Treason, or Misprision of Treason, by Words, Writing, Cyphering, Deeds, or otherwise whatsoever, shall be taken, had, deemed, or adjudged to be High Treason, Petit Treason, or Misprision of Treason, but only such as be declared and expressed to be Treason, Petit Treason, or Misprision of Treason, by* 25 Ed. 3. *Nor that any Pains of Death, Penalty or Forfeiture, in any Ways ensue to any Offender for the doing any Treason,* &c. *other than such as by the said Statute of* 25 Ed. 3. *be ordained; any Statute since the said twenty-fifth Year of* Ed. 3. *or other Declaration to the contrary in any wise notwithstanding.*

Sect. 43. And it must be confessed, That this Statute *primâ Facie* seems very much to favour the Opinion, That no Words whatsoever can of themselves amount to Overt Acts of High Treason, inasmuch as one of the principal Mischiefs intended to be redressed by it seems to be, that Men had often suffered as Traitors for Words only; yet the Force of this Objection will be very much lessened, if we consider, that the principal Purport of the said Statute of 1 *Mar.* seems to be, to make the 25 *Ed.* 3. according to the Intention of the Makers of it, the only Standard of Treason, and to abolish all subsequent Statutes which had made any Offences Treason, which were not contained in the said Statute of 25 *Ed.* 3. but no Way to extenuate the Crimes mentioned in 25 *Ed.* 3. or to take away the Force of any natural Exposition thereof; for the first Part of the Preamble complains of such Laws as not only inflicted Punishments over severe for the Crimes intended to be restrained by them, but were also penned in such a Manner as to be often apt to entrap the wisest by bare Words; but surely this can no Way be applicable to 25 *Ed.* 3. inasmuch as no Punishments can be thought extream for the Crimes therein restrained, and there can be no danger from that Statute of any Man's being punished for unwary or innocent Words, inasmuch as there is no Colour to say, that any Words, as such, are punished within that Statute, but only the most wicked Imagination of the Heart, which may be sometimes proved by the Evidence of Words: And it farther appears from the next Part of the Preamble of the said Statute of 1 *Mar.* that it has an Eye only to such Statutes as are above mentioned, inasmuch as it complains of Persons having suffered shameful Deaths for Words only, without other Opinion, Fact, or Deed, which is very applicable to those many Statutes in the Time of *H.* 8. as 26 *H.* 8. 13. and 35 *H.* 8. 3. and some others, which made bare Words High Treason, many of which were so far from purporting a Design against the King's Life, that they were scarce otherwise Criminal than as they were prohibited by thoſe Statutes; but ſurely this can have no Relation to 25 *Ed.* 3. either in puniſhing a Man for ſuch Imaginations of the Heart as are moſt perverſly wicked, or in ſuffering thoſe Imaginations to be proved upon him from his own Mouth. Alſo it is farther remarkable, That the enacting Clauſe reſtrains only ſuch Offences as are made High Treaſon by Statutes ſubſequent to 25 *Ed.* 3. from being adjudged High Treaſon by Words, Writing, Cyphering *&c.* and ſeems to leave the Offences contained in the ſaid Statute to the ſame Conſtruction which they had before.

Sect. 44. As to the Authority of Sir *Edward Coke* in his third Inſti- 3 Inſt. 14, 140.
tutes it is the leſs to be regarded, becauſe he himſelf was clearly of ano- 1 Ro. Re. 185.
ther Opinion when he was Chief Juſtice.

Sect. 45. Neither does it appear to me, That my Lord Chief Juſtice
Hale was at all of this Opinion; for though in the latter Edition of
his *Treatiſe of the Pleas of the Crown*, it be ſaid, That compaſſing by bare
Words, is not an Overt Act, *&c.* yet in the firſt Edition publiſhed in
the Year 1678. it is twice ſaid, That it hath been adjudged that Words Old Edition,
are an Overt Act. 13, 16.

Sect. 46. The ſecond kind of High Treaſon concerning the King's Office in the Adminiſtration of Juſtice is expreſſed in the Words following: *If a Man ſlay the Chancellor, Treaſurer, or the King's Juſtices of the one Bench or the other, Juſtices in Eyre, or Juſtices of Aſſize, and all other Juſtices aſſigned to hear and determine, being in their Places doing their Offices.*

Sect. 47. It hath been holden, That this Part of the Statute ſhall not H. P. C. 17.
be extended by Equity, to any other high Officers of State beſides theſe 3 Inſt. 18, 38.
expreſly named, nor even to theſe when they are not in actual Execution
of their Offices, nor to any Attempt to kill them, nor even to the actual
wounding of them, unleſs Death enſue. *See the next Chapter.*

Sect. 48. The third Kind of High Treaſon relating to the King's Seal, 3 Inſt. 15.
is ſaid to have been High Treaſon at the Common Law, and is expreſſed S. P. C. 2, 3.
in the following Words, *And if a Man counterfeit the King's Great or Privy
Seal.*

Sect. 49. It hath been holden, That theſe Words extend to the H. P. C. 18.
Aiders and Conſenters to ſuch Counterfeiting, as well as to the Actors. S. P. C. 3. a.

Sect. 50. But not to an Intent or Compaſſing to do it, if it be not 3 Inſt. 15.
actually done. H. P. C. 18.

Sect. 51. Nor to the fixing of the Great Seal to a Patent without a 3 Inſt. 15.
Warrant for ſo doing. H. P. C. 18. Con. Dal.

Sect. 52. [a] Nor to the razing of the Name of one Manor out of a c. 89. f. 225.
Patent, and putting in that of another, nor to any artificial removing of
the true Writing, and adding Matter altogether new: Nor, by the bet- [a] Kelynge 80.
ter Opinion, to the taking off the Wax impreſſed with the Great Seal 3 Inſt. 15. 12 Co. 15,
from a true Patent, and fixing it to a Writing purporting a Grant from the 16, 17.
King. 3 Inſt. 15, 16. 2 Keb. 74.

Sect. 53. [b] Nor to the counterfeiting of the Sign-Manual, or Privy Bro. Treaſ. 3.
Signet, but this is made High Treaſon by 1 *Mar.* 6. 17, 48. 40 Aſſ. 32.

Sect. 54. The fourth kind of High Treaſon concerning the Coin, is 2 H. 4. 25.
expreſſed in theſe Words, *If a Man counterfeits the King's Money, and if a* H. P. C. 18.
Man bring falſe Money into this Realm, counterfeit to the Money of England, Con. S. P. C. 3.
as the Money called Luſhburgh, *or other like to the ſaid Money of* England, Letter B.
knowing the Money to be falſe, to merchandize or make Payment, in deceit of our [b] 1 Ro. Re. 50,
ſaid Lord the King and his People. 51.

In treating hereof I shall consider,

1. The Branch relating to the counterfeiting of the King's Money.
2. That concerning the bringing of false Money into the Realm, *&c.*

In treating of the first Branch I shall shew,

1. What Degree of counterfeiting Money will amount to High Treason.
2. What shall be said to be the King's Money within this Act.

Bro. Treas. 27. H. P. C. 20. 3 Inst. 16. Contra 6 H. 7. 13. 3 H. 7. 10. 2 Inst. 375. 3 Inst. 17. H. P. C. 127. Kelynge 33. Contra Dyer. 296. H. P. C. 19. *3 H. 7. 10. b. H. P. C. 128. Bro. Treas. 19. 3 Inst. 577. 3 Inst. 17. 2 Keb. 36. Dyer. ca. 89.

Sect. 55. As to the Point of counterfeiting, it is said, That those who coin Money without the King's Authority, are guilty of High Treason within this Act, whether they utter it or not; and that those who have the King's Authority to coin Money, are guilty of High Treason if they make it of baser Alloy than they ought; and that those also are guilty of the same Crime, who receive and comfort one who is known by them to be guilty thereof; but that Clippers, *&c.* are not within this Statute.

Sect. 56. *But it seems, That those who barely utter false Money made within the Realm, knowing it to be false, are neither guilty of High Treason, nor of a Misprision thereof, but only of a high Misprision: Yet by 8 *&* 9 *Will.* 3. 26. they are in some Cases made guilty of Felony, for which see the next Chapter.

Sect. 57. As to the second Point, *viz.* What shall be said to be the King's Money? It seems, That such only as is coined by the King's Authority either in Gold or Silver within the Realm, and consequently not brass Farthings, *&c.* shall come under this Denomination.

Sect. 58. But the Mischiefs intended to be remedied by this Statute, having been found by Experience not to have been sufficiently redressed by it as thus restrained, the same have been farther provided for by subsequent Statutes.

Sect. 59. For by 1 *M.* Sess. 2. *Ca.* 6. *Those who forge any Foreign Coin of Gold or Silver, which shall be currant by Consent of the King shall be guilty of High Treason.*

Sect. 60. And by 14. *El.* 3. *Those who forge Money not currant,* &c. *their Aiders and Abetters are guilty of Misprision of Treason.*

Sect. 61. By 5 *El.* 11. *Whoever shall wash, clip, round or file,* And by 18 *El.* 1. *Whoever shall impair, diminish, falsify, scale or lighten, for Lucre or Gain, the proper Money of this Realm, or that of other Realms made currant by Proclamation, shall be deemed as an Offender in Treason, and forfeit all his Chattels absolutely, and his Hereditaments for Life, but without Corruption of Blood or Loss of Dower.*

Sect. 62. By 8 *&* 9 *W.* 3. 25. made perpetual by 7 *Annæ* 25. *Whoever shall knowingly make or mend, or begin to make or mend, buy, sell, or have in his Possession any Mould or Press for coining; or convey such Instruments out of the King's Mint, or mark on the Edges any Coin currant, or counterfeit or colour or gild any Coin resembling the currant Coin of this Kingdom, or any round Blanks of base Metal,* &c. *shall be guilty of High Treason, but without Corruption of Blood or Loss of Dower*; And by 7 *Annæ* 25. *The Prosecution for such making,* &c. *may be at any Time within six Months.*

Sect. 63. And by Par. 5. *Such Instruments may be seized by any Person, and brought before a Justice of Peace, in Order to be produced in Evidence at the Trial of such Offenders; and after they shall be so produced, they shall be defaced and destroyed; and all false Money which shall be so produced shall be cut in Pieces.*

Sect. 64. By 6 *&* 7 *Will.* 3. 17. *Whoever shall apprehend a Coiner or Clipper,* &c. *and prosecute him to Conviction, shall receive of the Sheriff forty Pounds,* &c. *And he who being guilty himself shall discover two or three more, shall have a Pardon.*

As to the second Branch concerning the bringing false Money into the Realm the following Particulars are observable.

Sect. 65. I. That the Money so brought must be counterfeited according to the Similitude of *English* Money: But by 1 & 2. *Phil. & Mar.* 11. *It is made High Treason to bring into the Realm Money counterfeited according to the Similitude of foreign Coin currant here, to the Intent to merchandize therewith.* H P. C. 21. S. P. C. 3.

Sect. 66. II. That it must be brought by one who knows it to be false.

Sect. 67. III. That it must be brought from a foreign Nation, and not from *Ireland*, or other Place subject to the Crown of *England*; for though to some Purposes they be distinct from the Realm of *England*, and consequently Money brought from thence may within the Letter of the Statute be said to be brought into the Realm; yet inasmuch as the counterfeiting is punishable there by the Laws of our King as much as in *England*, the bringing Money from such Places has been construed to be no more within the Act than if they were actually in *England*. 3 H. 7. 10. S. P. C. 3. 3 Inst. 18. H. P. C. 12. Bro. Treas. 19. Dal. 89. f. 225

Sect. 68. IV. That the bare uttering of such Money here by one who brought it not over, is not within this Branch; but by Force of an ancient Statute, if false Money be found in the Hands of a suspicious Person, he may be arrested till he have found his Warrant. 3 Inst. 18. H. P. C. 21,

Sect. 69. That it is not necessary that such false Money be actually paid away or merchandized withal, for the Words are to merchandize or make Payment, *&c.* which only import an Intention to do so, and are fully satisfied whether the Act intended be performed or not: But *Quære*, because both *Coke* and *Hale* seem to hold otherwise; however it is clear, that bringing over Money counterfeited according to the Similitude of foreign Coin is Treason within 1 & 2 *Phil. & Mar.* 11. 3 Inst. 18. H. P. C. 21.

Sect. 70. Also in the said Statute of 25 *Ed.* 3. there is this Clause, *And because that many other like Cases of Treason may happen in Time to come, which a Man cannot think nor declare at this present Time, it is accorded, That if any other Case, supposed Treason, which is not above specified, doth happen before any Justices, the Justices shall tarry without any going to Judgment of the Treason, till the Cause be shewed and declared before the King and his Parliament, whether it ought to be judged Treason or other Felony.*

Sect. 71. By Virtue of this Clause, many Offences which are not High Treason within this Statute, as the Murther of an Ambassador, *&c.* were declared by the Parliament to be High Treason, but these and all other such like Declarations are made void by 1 *Mar.* 1. And it seems that the Parliament have no such Power at this Day by Virtue of the said Clause, inasmuch as the said Statute of 1 *Mar.* expresly enacts, *That no Offence shall be deemed High Treason, but only such as is declared and expressed to be so by* 25 *Ed.* 3. and takes no Notice of the said Clause relating to the Parliament. 3 Inst. 8. 12 Co. 16.

And now we are come to Offences which have been made High Treason since the said Statute of 1 *Mar.* and in treating of these, we shall consider,

1. Offences in upholding or favouring the Power of the Pope.
2. Offences against the Protestant Succession.
3. Offence of listing Men without the King's Licence.

And first, Offences in upholding or favouring the Power of the Pope, seem reducible to the following Heads:

1. Extolling the Pope's Power.
2. Putting in Ure Popish Bulls.
3. Perverting others, or being perverted to Popery.

4. Re-

4. Receiving Popish Orders or Education in Popish Seminaries, and not submitting, *&c.*

5. Refusing a second Tender of the Oaths.

Sect. 72. And first, The Offence of extolling the Pope's Power is made High Treason by 5 *El.* 1. Par. 2 & 10. by which it is enacted, *That if any Person within the Queen's Dominions, shall by Writing, Cyphering, Preaching or Teaching, Deed or Act, advisedly and wittingly hold or stand with, extol or set forth, maintain or defend, the Jurisdiction of the Bishop of* Rome, *heretofore claimed in this Realm, or by any Speech, open Deed or Act, willingly or advisedly attribute any such Authority to the See of* Rome, *he shall be guilty of a* Præmunire *by the first Offence, of High Treason by the second, but without Corruption of Blood or Loss of Dower.*

Sect. 73. It has been holden, That he who knowing the Effect of a Book written beyond Sea, brings it over and secretly tells it; and also, That he who hearing the Contents thereof commends it; and also, That he who knowing its Contents, secretly conveys it to a Friend with an Intent to pervert him, is in Danger of the Statute; and it has been resolved, That he who having read the Book does afterwards in discoursing of it, allow it to be good; and also, That whoever writes or prints such a Book, and after publishes it, is clearly guilty: But it is said, That he who having heard of the Contents, barely buys and reads the Book, is not within the Statute. (Dyer 282.)

Sect. 74. It has also been holden, That if one who is convicted and condemned for an Offence of this Nature, being afterwards demanded by the Judges, Whether he be still of the same Opinion? answer, That he is, he is guilty of High Treason, as having advisedly maintained the Pope's Power a second Time. (Sav. 46 Pl 99.)

Sect. 75. The second Offence of this kind, *viz.* That of putting in Ure a Popish Bull, is made High Treason by 13 *El.* 2. Par. 2 & 3. By which it is enacted, *That if any within the Queen's Dominions shall put in Ure, any Bull or Instrument of Absolution or Reconciliation obtained from the See of* Rome; *or shall take upon him by Colour thereof to absolve or reconcile any Person; or to grant or promise any Absolution or Reconciliation; or shall willingly receive any such Absolution or Reconciliation, or shall obtain from the See of* Rome *any Bull or Writing whatsoever, or publish or any Ways put the same in Ure, he is guilty of High Treason.* And by Par. 4. *Accessaries after the Offence incur a* Præmunire. And by Par. 5, 6. *These who within six Weeks disclose not an Offer of such Bulls,* &c. *to some Privy Counsellor,* &c. *are guilty of a Misprision of Treason.*

Sect. 76. The third Offence of this kind, *viz.* That of perverting others, or being perverted to Popery, is made High Treason by 23 *El.* 1. Par. 2. & 3 *Jac.* 1. 4. Par. 22, 23. by which it is enacted, *That if any one shall pretend to have Power, or shall put in Practice to withdraw a Subject from his natural Obedience to the King, or to withdraw them for that Intent to the* Romish *Religion, or to move to promise any Obedience to any foreign Power, or to do any Overt Act to that Intent, or to reconcile one to the See of* Rome; *and if any Person shall by any Means be willingly withdrawn, or promise Obedience as aforesaid, he is guilty of High Treason.*

Sect 77. But by 3 *Jac.* 1. 4. Par. 24. *If any Person who is reconciled to the See of* Rome *beyond the Seas return into the Realm and submit himself,* &c. *and take the Oaths within six Days after his Return, he is excused.* (See Cawley 187.)

Sect. 78. It seemeth that the bare pretending to such a Power, without any farther Act in endeavouring to perswade Persons from their Allegiance, or the bare endeavouring so to perswade them, without any Pretence of such a Power, is High Treason within these Acts. (Savil. 3. Pl. 9.)

Sect. 79. The fourth Offence of this kind, *viz.* That of receiving Popish Orders or Education, *&c.* is made High Treason by 27 *El.* 2. Par. 3. by which it is enacted, *That if any Ecclesiastick born in the Queen's Dominions, and ordained or professed by Popish Authority, shall remain in the Queen's Dominions, or come from beyond Sea, and not submit to some Bishop or Justice of Peace within three Days, and take the Oaths,* &c. *he shall be guilty of High Treason.*

Sect. 80. And by Par. 5. *If any Subject not being an Ecclesiastick, shall not return from a Popish Seminary within six Months after a Proclamation to that Purpose in* London, *and submit,* &c. *within two Days, he shall be guilty of High Treason, whenever he shall otherwise return.*

Sect. 81. And by Par. 13. *If any Subject shall know that any such Priest is within the Realm, and not discover him to some Justice of Peace,* &c. *within twelve Days, he shall be fined and imprisoned at the Queen's Will; and if any Justice of Peace,* &c. *to whom such Matter shall be discovered, shall not give Information to some of the Privy Council,* &c. *within twenty-eight Days, he shall forfeit two hundred Marks.*

In the Construction of this Statute it hath been resolved,

Sect. 82. I. That in an Indictment grounded on this Statute against a Priest remaining here beyond the Time limited by the Statute, it must be alledged, That he was born in the Realm, *&c.* and also that he was ordained, *&c.* by Authority challenged or pretended from the See of *Rome*; but that there is no need to shew in what Place in particular he was born, or whether he were ordained within the Realm or beyond Sea. Poph. 94.

Sect. 83. II. That one in Popish Orders, being in a Ship in Order to go to *Ireland*, and driven by a Storm into *England*, and immediately apprehended, is not guilty of High Treason within this Act; for his Design of going to *Ireland* was prevented, *& nil efficit conatus, nisi sequatur effectus*; Raym. 377. and he was forced into *England* by the Act of God, and against his Will; neither can he be said to remain here within the Intent of the Statute, because he was compelled to it by Reason of the Prosecution.

Sect. 84. The fifth Offence of this Nature, *viz.* That of refusing a second Tender of the Oaths, is made High Treason by 5 *El.* 1. Par. 11, 12 *&* 20. by which it is enacted, *That if any Person who shall have a Charge, Cure, or Office in the Church, or an Office or Ministry in an Ecclesiastical Court, or if any Person who shall wilfully refuse to observe the Rites of the Church of* England, *after having been admonished by the Ordinary,* &c. *or that shall say or hear private Mass,* &c. *shall refuse a second Tender of the Oaths, he shall be guilty of High Treason, but without Corruption of Blood.* Vid. infra Ch. 19.

Sect. 85. Secondly, Offences against the Protestant Succession made High Treason are twofold:

1. Denying the Power of the Parliament to limit the Succession of the Crown, which is made High Treason, by 4 *Anne* 8. Par. 1. 2. and 6 *Anne* 1, Par. 1, 2. whereby it is enacted, *That whoever shall maliciously, advisedly and directly by Writing or Printing declare, maintain and affirm, That the pretended Prince of* Wales, *or any other, hath any Right or Title to the Crown, otherwise than according to* 1 *W. & M.* ch. 2. or 12 *W.* 3. ch. 2. *or that the Kings of this Realm, by the Authority of Parliament, are not able to make Laws to limit and bind the Crown to the Descent and Government thereof, shall be guilty of High Treason, and that those that maliciously and directly affirm the same by Preaching, Teaching or advised speaking, shall be guilty of a* Præmunire.

2. Endeavouring maliciously, advisedly and directly to hinder any Person who shall be next in Succession, according to 1 *W.& M.* and 12 *W.* 3. which is made High Treason by 1 *Anne* 17.

Sect. 86. 3. The Offence of listing Men without the King's Licence is made High Treason by 12 *Anne* 11. by which it is enacted, *That every Subject shall be guilty of High Treason, who shall in the Kingdom of* Great Britain *or* Ireland, *list or enter himself in the Service of any foreign Prince or Person as a Soldier, or procure another to be so listed, or to go beyond Sea with such Intent without the King's Licence, or in the* French *King's Service even with our King's Licence, until the said* French *King shall have disbanded all his* English *Regiments,* &c. But this Act is to continue but for three Years.

CHAP. XVIII.

Of Felonies more immediately against the King.

FElonies more immediately against the King are of five Kinds:

1. Offences relating to the Coin or Bullion.
2. Offences against the King's Council.
3. The Offence of passing beyond Sea to serve a foreign Prince.
4. Imbezilling the King's Armour.
5. The Offence of relieving a Popish Priest.

Felonies relating to the Coin or Bullion are of three kinds:

1. The Offence of debasing it.
2. The Offence of unlawfully diminishing it.
3. The Offence of endeavouring by extraordinary Means to increase it.

Sect. 1. And first, The Offence of debasing the Coin or Bullion was provided against by many ancient Statutes, which seem to be obsolete at this Day; for the Importation of ill Money was made Felony by 17 *Ed.* 3. 3 Inst. 92, 93. N. 15. (which was never printed,) and so was the Payment of Blanks, (which were made of a base Alloy,) by 2 *H.* 6. 9. and the coining or bringing in Gally Half-pence, Suskins or Dodkins, by 3 *H.* 5. 1. However it is made High Treason to bring in false Money, *&c.* by 25 *Ed.* 3. Supra Ch. 17. and 1 *&* 2 *Ph. & Mar.* 11. And by 8 *&* 9 *Will* 3. 25. Par. 6. *It is made Felony to blanch Copper for Sale, or to mix blanched Copper with Silver, or knowingly to buy or sell, or offer to Sale blanched Copper alone, or mixt with Silver, or knowingly and fraudulently to buy,* &c. *any Mixture which shall be heavier than Silver, and look, and touch, and wear like Standard Gold, but be manifestly worse, or to receive or pay any Counterfeit milled Money,* &c. *at a lower Rate than the same by its Denomination doth import, or was coined or counterfeited for.*

Sect. 2. Secondly, The Offence of diminishing the Coin or Bullion of the Kingdom has been always thought to be of very ill Consequence, as tending to impoverish the Nation, and to embarass Trade, and with an Eye to those Inconveniences it was made Felony by 17 *Ed.* 3. *N.* 15. (which was never printed,) to transport Silver, except Plate carried over by Great Men to serve their Houses; also the Transportation thereof was prohibited by many other Statutes, as 27 *Ed.* 3. 14. 5 *Rich.* 2. 2. 2 *H.* 4. 16. 2 *H.* 6. 6. and 3 *H.* 8. 1. But this general Restraint being found by Experience to be inconvenient to Trade, which by exporting Money to one Market may bring back such Goods, as will more than make up the Loss, from another, it was enacted by 15 *Ca.* 2. 7. *Par.* 12. *That any Person might export any foreign Coin or Bullion without Duty, first making an Entry thereof in the Custom-House.* Poph 149. Hob. 270. 3 Inst. 92, 93.

Sect. 3. But this Licence having been often abused by the Transportation of such Silver, which having been coined into *English* Money or wrought into Plate, was afterwards melted down into the Form of foreign Coin or Bullion, it was, in Order to prevent this Mischief, enacted by 6 & 7 *Will.* 3. 17. Par. 3. *That none shall cast or make Ingots or Bars of Silver in Imitation of* Spanish, *under Pain of five hundred Pounds.* And it is farther enacted by the said Statute, Par. 5. *That no Person shall transport, or cause to be transported, any molten Silver, but only such as shall be marked or stamped at Goldsmith's-Hall,* &c. *nor even that without a Certificate under the Hands of one of the Wardens of the Goldsmiths Company, that Oath hath been made by the Owner or Owners thereof, and likewise by one credible Witness, that the same is lawful Silver, and that no Part thereof was (before the same was molten) the currant Coin of this Realm, nor Clippings thereof, nor Plate wrought within this Kingdom,* &c.

Sect. 4. Also it is farther enacted, Par. 6. *That any Officer of the Custom-House may seize any molten Silver which shall be put on Board any Vessel, without having such Mark or Stamp, and also such Certificate as is above mentioned.*

Sect. 5. And it is farther enacted, Par. 7. *That if any Broker, not being a trading Goldsmith, or Refiner of Silver, shall buy or sell any Bullion or molten Silver, he shall suffer Imprisonment for six Months without Bail.*

Sect 6. Also it is farther enacted, Par. 13, 14. *That if a Doubt shall arise upon Bullion shipped to be exported, whether the same be* English *or Foreign, the Proof shall lie upon the Owner,* &c. *And that if any Person shall enter or ship any Bullion, by the said Act allowed to be exported, other than in the Name of the true Owner, Proprietor or Importer, the Exporter shall forfeit the same, or the full Value thereof.*

Sect. 7. Thirdly, The Endeavours of some Persons in making Use of extraordinary Methods for the producing of Gold and Silver, were found by Experience to be so prejudicial to the Publick, both from the lavish Waste of many valuable Materials, and also from the Ruin of many Families, which had been occasioned by such Useless Expences, that it was thought necessary to put a Check to such Practices by some severe Law, and for that Purpose it was made Felony, by 5 *H.* 4. 4. *to multiply Gold or Silver, or to use the Art or Craft of Multiplication.* And it was holden, That the practising to find out the Philosophers Stone, by which it is imagined that all Metals may be made Gold, was Felony within this Statute: But this Restraint having been found to have no other Effect, upon the unaccountable Vanity of those who fancied such Attempts to be practicable, but only to send them beyond Sea, to try their Experiments with Impunity in other Countries, the Statute of 5 *H.* 4. was at last wholly repealed by 1 *Will.* & *Mar.* 30. Dyer 88. Pl. 105.

Sect. 8.

Sect. 8. As to the second kind of Felonies more immediately against the King, *viz.* those which are against his Council, it is enacted by 3 *H.* 4. 13. *That if any sworn Servant in the Chequer-Roll of the King's Houshold, under the State of a Lord, make any Confederacy, Compassing, Conspiracy or Imagination with any Person to destroy or murther the King, or any Lord of his Realm, or any other Person sworn to the King's Council, he shall be guilty of Felony.*

Sect. 9. And it is farther enacted by 9 *Anne, That if any Person shall attempt to kill, assault, strike or wound any Privy Counsellor in Execution of his Office, he shall suffer as a Felon without Clergy.*

Sect. 10. As to the Third Offence of this kind (*viz.*) That of passing beyond Sea to serve a foreign Prince, it is enacted by 3 *Jac.* 1. 4. Par. 18, 19, 20, 21. *That every Subject, who shall go out of the Realm to serve any foreign Prince or State, or shall pass over the Seas, and there voluntarily serve any such foreign Prince or State, not having before his going taken the Oath of Obedience, shall suffer as a Felon; and that if any Gentleman, or Person of higher Degree, or any Person who hath born any Office or Charge in Camp or Army, shall go out of the Realm to serve such foreign Prince,* &c. *without being bound with two Sureties in a Bond, conditioned that he shall not be reconciled to the See of* Rome, *nor enter into any Conspiracy against the King, he shall be a Felon.*

3 Inst. 80. Dalt. ch. 107. Cawley 182.

Sect. 11. Note, That by 1 *Will. & Mar.* Sess. 1. Chap. 8. this Oath of Obedience is taken away, and the new Oaths of Allegiance and Supremacy enjoined in the Room thereof.

See the next Chapter.

Sect. 12. As to the fourth Offence of this kind, *viz.* That of imbezilling the King's Armour, it is enacted by 31 *El.* 4. *That if any Person, having the Charge or Custody of the King's Armour, Ordnance, or Munition,* &c. *or of any Victuals provided for the victualling of any Soldiers or Mariners,* &c. *shall for Lucre and Gain, or wittingly, advisedly, and of Purpose to hinder or impeach the King's Service, imbezil, purloin, or convey away any of the same Armour,* &c. *to the Value of twenty Shillings, he shall be judged guilty of Felony.*

3 Inst. 78, 79. *Sect.* 13. *But such Offender must be prosecuted within the Year next after the Offence done; neither shall he forfeit his Hereditaments any longer than during his Life; nor shall his Blood be corrupted, or his Wife lose her Dower.*

Sect. 14. As to the fifth Offence of this Kind, *viz.* That of relieving a Popish Priest, it is enacted by 27 *El.* 2. Par. 4. *That whoever shall wittingly and willingly receive, relieve, comfort, aid or maintain any Jesuit, Seminary, or other Popish Priest,* &c. *being at Liberty or out of Hold, knowing him to be such a Jesuit,* &c. *shall for such Offence be adjudged a Felon without Benefit of Clergy.*

Cawley 90, 91.

CHAP. XIX.

Of Præmunire.

OFfences more immediately against the King, not capital, come generally under the Titles of *Præmunire*, Misprision, and Contempts. In treating of *Præmunire* I shall consider,

1. What Offences come under this Notion.
2. How they are punished.

And first, Offences coming under the Notion of *Præmunire*, seem to be reducible to the following general Heads;

1. Offences against the Prerogative of the Crown.
2. Offences against the Authority of the King and Parliament.

Those of the first kind seem to come under the following Particulars;

1. Making Use of Papal Bulls.
2. Derogating from the King's Common Law Courts.
3. Appealing to *Rome* from any of the King's Courts.
4. Exercising the Jurisdiction of a Suffragan without the Appointment of the Bishop of the Diocese.
5. Refusing to elect or consecrate the Person nominated by the King to a Bishoprick.
6. Maintaining the Pope's Power.
7. Bringing in *Agnus Dei*.
8. Contributing to the Maintenance of a Popish Seminary.
9. Refusing the Oaths.

Sect. 1. But inasmuch as these Offences depend chiefly upon Statutes made for the Preservation of the Sovereignty of the Crown from the Incroachments of the See of *Rome*, I shall, in order to shew the Reasonableness of these Laws, take a short View of those Usurpations which made them necessary.

Sect. 2. It is the general Opinion, That Christianity was first planted in this Island by some of the Eastern Church, which is very probable, from the ancient *Britains* observing *Easter* always on the fourteenth Day of the Month, according to the Custom of the East.

Davis 88.con. Selden's Janus Anglorum 27.

Sect. 3. But the *Saxons* being converted about the Year 600. by Persons sent from *Rome*, and wholly devoted to the Interest thereof, it cannot be expected that such an Opportunity of enlarging the Jurisdiction of that See should wholly be neglected.

Sect. 19. * And yet *Saunders*, in his Attempt to answer Sir *Edward Coke*'s fifth Report concerning the King's Ecclesiastical Authority, is scarce able to produce any Instances of the Papal Power in this Kingdom before the *Norman* Conquest. Indeed he tells us, That four or five Persons were made Bishops by the Pope at the first Conversion, but offers not any Example thereof between the Year 669, and the Conquest; and it is certain, That all Bishopricks were then conferred by the King's Delivery of a Ring and a Pastoral Staff.

*Saund. ch. 6. Par. 12, 20, 21, 22, 24, 25, 57, 59. *See Barrow from Page* 258 *to* 262. 1 Ro. Ab. 882. 1 Inst. 134 a. 144. a. Selden's Janus Anglorum 42, 65.

Sect. 5. † Neither is he able to produce any Instance, that looks like an Appeal to *Rome* before the Conquest, except in the Case of two Bishops, and he is forced to own, That even one of these Bishops was deposed by two Kings, and could get no Relief against either of them, notwithstanding the Pope's utmost Application in his Favour.

† Saund. ch. 6. Par. 29, 30, 31, 32, 50, 51, 52, 53, 54, 55, 56. *See Barrow from Page* 242 *to* 258. Selden's Janus Anglorum 59, 67, 68.

Sect. 6. Nor can he shew more than four or five Instances of Exemptions from ordinary Jurisdiction, granted or confirmed by Popes to Religious Houses in those Days, which plainly shews that his Concurrence was not thought necessary; and it appears, That our ancient Kings, of their own Authority, exempted some Abbeys from Episcopal Jurisdiction; and it hath always been a received Rule, even in the Times of Popery, That the Chancellor shall visit a Church of the King's Foundation, notwithstanding it be not specially exempted.

Saund. ch. 6. *from* Par. 37 *to* 48. 1 H. 7. 25. 21 Ed. 3. 60. a, b. 1 Inst. 144. a. F. N. B. 42. a. 27 Ed. 3. 85. a. 6 H. 7. 14. a. 2 Rol. Abr. 230, 231.

Davis 89. *Sect.* 7. But the Pope having favoured and supported *William* the first in his Invasion of the Kingdom, took that Opportunity of enlarging his Incroachments, and in this King's Reign began to send his Legates hither; and prevailed at first with *Henry* the first, and afterwards with King *John*, to give up the Donation of Bishopricks; and in the Time of King *Stephen*, gained the Prerogative of Appeals; and in the Time of *Henry* the second, exempted all Clerks from the Secular Power.

Davis 90, 93. 2 Rol. Rc. 103. Palm. 25, 26. Selden's Janus Anglorum 67.

Sect. 8. Indeed this King did at first strenuously withstand these Innovations, and abolished most of them by the Constitutions of *Clarendon*: But upon the Death of *Becket*, who for having violently opposed the King, was slain by some of his Servants, the Pope got such an Advantage over the King, that he was never after able effectually to execute those Laws.

Selden's Epinomis, cap. 8. Dav. Rep. 91.

Sect. 9. And not long after this, by a general Excommunication of the King and People, for several Years, because they would not suffer an Archbishop to be imposed upon them, King *John* was reduced to such Straits, that he was obliged to surrender his Kingdoms to the Pope, and to receive them again, to hold of him for the Rent of a Thousand Marks.

Sect. 10. And in the following Reign of *Henry* the third, partly from the Profits of our best Church Benefices, which were generally given to *Italians*, and others residing at the Court of *Rome*, and partly from the Taxes imposed by the Pope, there went yearly out of the Kingdom Seventy thousand Pounds Sterling.

2 Inst. 584. Dav. 95.

Sect. 11. The Nation being under this Necessity, was obliged to provide for the Prerogative of the Prince and the Liberties of the People, by many strict Laws. And in the Reign of *Edward* the first, Religious Houses were prohibited, under high Penalties, to send any Thing to their Superiors beyond Seas; and it was declared by Parliament, That the Pope's taking upon him to dispose of *English* Benefices to Aliens was an Incroachment not to be endured; and soon after, these Grievances produced those more severe Laws against the above mentioned Offences of this Nature, the Particulars whereof are before set forth.

2 Inst. 580.

Sect. 12. And first the Offence of making use of Papal Bulls is made a *Præmunire* by many ancient as well as later Statutes; for it is enacted by 25 *Ed* 3. called the Statute of Provisors, *That whoever shall by a Papal Provision disturb any Patron to present to a Benefice*, &c. *shall be fined and imprisoned till he make full Renunciation*, &c. And it is farther enacted by 25 *Ed.* 3. Stat. 5. Chap. 22. *That if any one purchase a Provision of an Abbey or Priory, he shall be out of the King's protection.* And by 38 *Ed.* 3. & 12 *R.* 2. 15. & 13 *R.* 2. Stat. 2. Chap. 2. *That whoever shall accept a Benefice contrary to* 25 Ed. 3. *shall be banished.* And by 13 *R.* 2. Stat. 2. Chap. 3. *That whoever shall bring a Sentence of Excommunication against any Person for executing the said Statute of* 25 Ed. 3. *shall suffer Pain of Life and Member.* And by 16 *R.* 2. 5. *That whoever shall purchase or pursue, or cause to be purchased or pursued, in the Court of* Rome *or elsewhere, any Translations, Processes, Sentences of Excommunication, Bulls, Instruments or other Things contrary to the Tenor of that Statute, which touch the King, against him, his Crown, his Regality and his Realm, or bring them within this Realm, or receive them,* &c. *shall be out of the King's Protection, and their Lands and Tenements, Goods and Chattels forfeited to the King.* And by 2 *H.* 4. 3. *That whoever shall purchase from* Rome *a Provision of Exemption from ordinary Obedience*; and by 2 *H.* 4. 4. *That whoever shall put in Execution Bulls purchased by those of the Order of* Cisteaux *to be discharged of Tithes, shall incur the like Penalty.* Also Offenders of this Nature are farther restrained by 6 *H.* 4. 1. 7 *H.* 4. 8.

See Register 64. 1. 3 Inst. 127.

9 *H.* 4. 8. & 3 *H.* 5. 4. *By which the Statutes above mentioned are enforced and explained.* And it is farther enacted by 23 *H.* 8. 21. Sect. 22. *That whoever shall sue for, or execute any Licence, Dispensation, or Faculty from the See of* Rome; and by 28 *H.* 8. 16. (by which all Bulls, Briefs, *&c.* heretofore obtained from *Rome*, are made void,) *That whoever shall use, alledge, or plead the same in any Court, unless they were confirmed by that Statute, or afterwards by the King, shall incur the like Penalty.* Yet it hath been holden, That the alledging of an ancient Bull in order to induce another principal Matter whereon to ground a Title without claiming any Thing from the Bull it self, is not within this Statute. 2 Lev. 251.

Sect. 13. By 13 *El.* 2. those who purchase any Bull, *&c.* from *Rome*, are guilty of High Treason, But those ancient Statutes still continue in force; and it is in the Election of the Crown to proceed either upon them, or 13 *El.* Also by the said Statute of 13 *El. The Aiders, Comforters, and Maintainers of such Offenders after the Offence, to the Intent to uphold the said usurped Power, incur a* Premunire. Vide supra Chap. 17. Davis 84.

Sect. 14. The second Offence of this Nature, *viz.* That of derogating from the King's Common Law Courts, is said to have been a High Offence at Common Law, and is made a *Præmunire* by many ancient Statutes; for by 27 *Ed.* 3. 1. & 38 *Ed.* 3. of Provisors, *If any Subject draw any out of the Realm in Plea, whereof the Cognizance pertains to the King's Court, or of Things whereof Judgments be given in the King's Court, or sue in any other Court to defeat or impeach the Judgments given in the King's Court, he shall be warned to appear,* &c. *in proper Person, at a Day containing the space of two Months; at which if he appear not, he and his Proctors,* &c. *shall be put out of the King's Protection, his Lands and Chattels forfeited, his Body imprisoned and ransomed at the King's Will,* &c. 2 Rol. Abr. 176. O 3. 177. P. 1. 3. 3 Inst. 125. Bro. Præmunire 3.

Sect. 15. And by 16 *Rich.* 2. 5. *Both those who shall pursue or cause to be pursued in the Court of* Rome *or elsewhere, any Processes or Instruments or other Things whatsoever which touch the King, against him, his Crown, and Regality or his Realm, and also those who shall bring, receive, notify or execute them, and their Abettors,* &c. *shall be put out of the King's Protection,* &c.

Sect. 16. In the Construction of these Statutes it was holden, That certain Commissioners of Sewers for summoning one before them who had got a Judgment at Law, and imprisoning him till he would release it, were guilty of a *Præmunire.* 2 Bulst. 199. 3 Inst. 125. Cro. Ja. 336.

Sect. 17. Also there have been formerly many strong Opinions, That ‖ Suits in Equity to relieve against a Judgment at Law are within these Statutes; especially if the End thereof be to controvert the very Point determined at Law, or to seek Relief after Judgment in a Case wherein the Law may relieve, as against excessiveness of Damages, *&c.* But it seems to be generally agreed at this Day, That no such Suit is within the Intention of the said Statutes. ‖ 3 Inst. 123, 124. See 4 H. 4. Ch. 23. 2 Chan. Cases 97. Dy. 201. Pl. 64, 301. a. 1 Lev. 241, 242. Hard. 125. 1 Danv. Abr. 764. Pl. 2. 1 Sid. 463. 1 Mod. 59. 3 Keb. 221.

Sect. 18. It hath been said, That * Suits in the Admiralty or Ecclesiastical Courts within the Realm are within 16 *R.* 2. 5. (by Force of those Words, *or elsewhere,*) if they concern Matters, the Cognizance whereof belongs to the Common Law; as where a Bishop deprives an Incumbent of a Donative, or excommunicates a Man for hunting in his Parks, *&c.* * 3 Inst. 120, 121, 122. Bro. Præmun. 5, 12, 16, 31. 15 H. 7. 9. a. 12 Co. 37.

Sect. 19. But it seemeth, That a Suit in those Courts for a Matter which appears not by the Libel it self, but only by the Defendant's Plea, or other Matter subsequent, to be of temporal Cognizance, (as where a Plaintiff libels for Tithes, and the Defendant pleads that they were severed from the nine Parts, by which they became a Lay Fee,) is not within 2 Rol. A. 177. Pl. 2. Mod. 838. 12. Co. 37. Cro. Jac. 134.

within the Statute, because it appears not that either the Plaintiff or the Judge knew that they were severed.

Sect. 20. The third Offence of this Nature, (*viz.*) That of appealing to *Rome* from any of the King's Courts, is made a *Præmunire* by 24 *H.* 8. 12. *and* 25 *H.* 8. 19. by which it is enacted, *That all such Appeals as formerly were made to* Rome, *shall from henceforth be made to the High Court of Chancery.*

Sect. 21. The fourth Offence of this Nature, (*viz.*) That of exercising the Jurisdiction of a Suffragan, without the Appointment of the Bishop of the Diocese, is made a *Præmunire* by 26 *H.* 8. 14. which sets forth at large for what Towns such Suffragans may be nominated by the King, and also how they may be nominated, consecrated and commissioned.

Sect. 22. The fifth Offence of this Nature, (*viz.*) That of refusing to elect or consecrate the Person nominated by the King to a Bishoprick, is made a *Præmunire* by 25 *H.* 8. 28. by which it is enacted, *That if any Dean and Chapter refuse to elect the Person named in the King's Letter for a Bishoprick within twelve Days, and to certify such Election to the King within twenty Days after the Licence shall come to their Hands, or if any Archbishop or Bishop after such Election (or Nomination by the King in default thereof certified unto them by the King) shall refuse to confirm and consecrate the Person so signified to them, they incur a* Præmunire.

See Chap. 17. *Sect.* 23. The sixth Offence of this Nature, (*viz.*) That of maintaining the Pope's Power, is made a *Præmunire* upon the first Conviction, and High Treason upon the second.

Sect. 24. The seventh Offence of this Nature, (*viz.*) That of bringing in *Agnus Dei*, is made a *Præmunire* by 13 *El.* 2. Par. 7, 8. by which it is enacted, *That if any one shall bring into the Realm,* &c. *any* Agnus Dei, Cawley 52, 53. *Crosses, Pictures, Beads, or such like superstitious Things pretended to be hallowed by the Bishop of* Rome, &c. *and shall deliver or offer the same to any Subject to be worn or used in any wise; or if any one shall receive the same to such Intent,* Cawley 54. *and not clear himself by discovering the Offender,* &c. *he shall incur a* Præmunire.

Sect. 25. *And so shall a Justice of Peace in the same County, who having any Offence in that Act declared unto him, shall not declare it to a Privy Counsellor, within sixteen Days.*

Sect. 26. The eighth Offence of this Nature, (*viz.*) That of contributing to the Maintenance of a Popish Seminary, is made a *Præmunire* by 27 *El.* 2. Par. 6.

Sect. 27. The ninth Offence of this Nature, (*viz.*) That of refusing the Oaths, is made a *Præmunire* by several Statutes, for by 1 *El.* 1. Par. 19. it is enacted, *That all Ecclesiastical Persons, and all Ecclesiastical and Temporal Officers, and all Persons having the King's Fees or Wages*; and by Par. 26. *That all Persons taking Orders, or any Degree in any University within the Realm, shall take the Oath of Supremacy under Pain of losing their Benefices and Offices.* And it is farther enacted by 5 *El.* 1. Par. 5. *That all the Persons above mentioned, who are required by the said Statute of* 1 El. 1. *to take the said Oath, and all School-masters publick and private, Barristers, Attorneys, Sheriffs, and Officers belonging to the Common or any other Law, or to the Crown, or to any Court whatsoever, shall take the said Oath in open Court before they shall be admitted to any such Vocation or Office,* &c. *And if they belong not to any Court, That then they shall take the same before such Person as shall admit them to such Vocation,* &c. *or before Commissioners appointed under the Great Seal,* &c. And it is farther enacted, Par 6. *That any Bishop may tender the said Oath to any spiritual Person within his Diocese, as well in Places exempt as others*; and by

Par. 7. *That Commissioners may be appointed by the Lord Chancellor to tender the same to such Persons as by their Commission they shall be authorized to tender it unto*; and by Par. 8. *That if any Person, compellable by either of the said Acts, or appointed by such Commissioners to take the said Oath, shall refuse to take it on a Tender thereof, he shall incur a* Præmunire. And by Par. 9. *That such Refusal shall be certified within forty Days before the King in his Court of King's Bench, by those who have Authority to tender the said Oath, under the Penalty of one hundred Pounds; and that the Sheriff of the County wherein the said Court shall sit may impanel a Jury who shall inquire of such Refusal in such Manner as if it had happened in the same County.*

In the Construction of these Statutes it hath been resolved:

Sect. 28. I. That the Obligation to take the said Oath continued after the Death of Queen *Elizabeth*, tho' the Statutes say nothing of her Successors; and the like Resolution also has been made in Relation to the Oaths appointed by subsequent Statutes. Raym. 212. 1 Vent. 171.

Sect. 29. II. That in a Commission authorizing Persons to tender the said Oath, a general Description of the Persons to whom it shall be tendered is sufficient, without naming them particularly by their Names. Raym. 445.

Sect. 30. III. That if the Person who tendered the Oath as Bishop, was not a Bishop at that Time, the Defendant may give it in Evidence upon the general Issue. Dy. 234. Pl. 15.

Sect. 31. IV. That the said Oath must in Substance be taken in the very Words expressed in the Acts, and can not be qualified with any Reserve whatever: Yet it hath been resolved, that to use the Words [In Conscience] instead of [In my Conscience,] or [Sea of *Rome*,] instead of [See of *Rome*,] makes no material Variance. 1 Bulst. 197, 198. 1 Vent. 172, 173.

Sect. 32. V. That a Certificate of a Refusal of the said Oath made to the Judges of the said Court of the King's Bench by Name, and not to the King in his said Court, is sufficient within the Meaning of the Statute. Raym. 445.

Sect. 33. VI. That an Ecclesiastical Person is well described in such a Certificate by the Addition of *Legum Doctor, & Sacris Ordinibus constitutus*, without adding *Clericus*, &c. Dy. 234. Pl. 15.

Sect. 34. VII. That such a Certificate being entered of Record, as brought into Court such a Day and Year *per* A. B. *Cancellar'* of such a Bishop is good, without entering that it was so brought *per Mandatum Episcopi.* Dy. 234. Pl. 15.

Sect. 35. VIII. That the Trial must be by a Jury of the County wherein the Oaths were refused; for the Statute only authorizes an Indictment by a Jury of the County, wherein the Court sits. Dy. 234. Pl. 15.

Sect. 36. IX. That any Misrecital of the very Words of the Oath, in an Indictment for not taking it, is erroneous. *See the Books above cited.*

Sect. 37. By 3 *Jac.* 1. 4. Par. 13, 14. *Any Bishop, or two Justices of Peace, whereof one is to be of the* Quorum, *might tender the Oath of Obedience therein prescribed, to any Person above the Age of eighteen Years, being under the Degree of Nobility, and convicted or indicted of Recusancy, or not having received the Sacrament twice in the Year past, and also to any suspected Stranger who shall not purge himself upon Oath; and shall certify the Names of such as take the said Oath to the next Quarter-Sessions, and commit those who refuse it till the next Assizes or Sessions, where the same shall be again tendered; and if the said Persons, or any other Persons whatsoever of the Age of eighteen Years, other than Noblemen or Noblewomen, shall there refuse to take it, they incur a* Præmunire, *unless they be Femes Covert, who shall be committed till they take it.*

Sect. 38. By Par. 41. *The Lords of the Council in like manner may tender the said Oath to any Nobleman or Woman, of the Age of eighteen Years, who refusing the same incur a* Præmunire, *Femes Covert excepted.*

Sect. 39. By 7 *Jac.* 1. 6. Par. 2. *All Persons whatsoever, as well Ecclesiastical as Temporal, of what Estate, Dignity, Pre-eminence, Sex, Quality or Degree soever he or she shall be, above the Age of eighteen Years, being in that Act mentioned and intended, shall take the said Oath; and any Privy Counsellor or Bishop, may require any Baron or Baroness, of the Age of eighteen Years, and any two Justices of the Peace, whereof one to be of the* Quorum, *may require any other Person of that Age to take it. And if any Person of or above the said Age or Degree shall be presented,* &c. *for not coming to Church,* &c. *then three of the Privy Council, whereof the Lord Chancellor,* &c. *to be one, shall require such Person to take the said Oath. And if any Person whatsoever, of the said Age and under the said Degree, shall be presented,* &c. *for not coming to Church,* &c. *or if the Minister,* &c. *shall complain to any Justice of Peace,* &c. *and the Justice shall find Cause of Suspicion, then any one Justice of Peace shall require such Person to take the said Oath,* &c. *And all such Persons refusing a Tender of the said Oath, shall be bound over to the Assizes or Sessions, where if they refuse again, they incur a* Præmunire: And Par. 27. *All such Refusers are disabled to execute any publick Place of Judicature, or bear any other Office, (being no Office of Inheritance or ministerial Function,) or to practise the Common or Civil Law, Physick or Surgery, or the Art of an Apothecary.*

See Cawley 246, &c.

Sect. 40. In the Construction of these Statutes it hath been resolved, That the Justices of Peace, *&c.* may send their Warrant to bring such Persons before them, but that they cannot authorize the Constable to break open the Doors to take them.

12 Co. 130, 131.

Sect. 41. But by 1 *Will. & Mar. the Oaths of Supremacy and Obedience prescribed by these Acts were abrogated, and the following Oath and Declaration substituted in their Room.*

I A. B. *do sincerely promise and swear, That I will be faithful and bear true Allegiance to his Majesty King* George:

I A. B. *do swear, That I do from my Heart abhor, detest and abjure, as impious and heretical, that damnable Doctrine and Position, that Princes excommunicated or deprived by the Pope, or any Authority of the See of* Rome, *may be deposed or murdered by their Subjects, or any other whatsoever:*

And I do declare, That no foreign Prince, Person, Prelate, State, or Potentate, hath or ought to have, any Jurisdiction, Power, Superiority, Pre-eminence or Authority Ecclesiastical or Spiritual, within this Realm:

Sect. 42. And by Par. 3, 4, 5. *All Persons who are required to take, or authorized to tender, the said abrogated Oaths, or either of them, are in like manner required and authorized to take and tender the said Oath and Declaration, under the same Penalties,* &c. See Chap. 24.

Sect. 43. By 7 *Will.* 3. 24. *Serjeants at Law, Counsellors, Attorneys, Solicitors, Proctors, Clerks or Notaries, practising as such in any Court whatsoever, without taking the said Oaths and subscribing the said Declaration, incur a* Præmunire.

Sect. 44. And now I am in the second Place to consider those Offences against the Authority of King and Parliament, which come under the Notion of *Præmunire*, as to which it is enacted by 6 *Ann.* 7. *That if any Person shall maliciously and directly, by Preaching, Teaching, or advised Speaking, declare, maintain and affirm, that the pretended Prince of* Wales, *hath any Right or Title to the Crown of these Realms, or that any other Person or Persons hath or have any Right or Title to the same, otherwise than according to* 1 Will. & Mar. 2. *and* 12 Will. 2. *and the Acts then lately made in* England *and* Scotland, *mutually for the Union of the two Kingdoms; or that the Kings or Queens of this Realm, with the Authority of Parliament, are not able to make Laws to limit the Crown and the Descent,* &c. *thereof, shall incur a* Præmunire.

Sect. 45. As to the second general Point of this Chapter, *viz.* In what manner Offences of this Nature are punished, it is to be observed, That most of the Statutes of *Præmunire* refer the Punishment to 16 *Rich.* 2. 5. which enacts, That those who offend against the Purport thereof *shall be put out of the King's Protection, and their Lands and Tenements, Goods and Chattels forfeited to our Lord the King: And that they be attached by their Bodies if they may be found, and brought before the King and his Council, there to answer to the Cases aforesaid, or that Process be made against them by* Præmunire facias, *in manner as is ordained in other Statutes of Provisors.*

Sect. 46. Inasmuch as this Statute expresly saith, that such Offenders shall be put out of the King's Protection, and also the Statute of 25 *Ed.* 3. Stat. 5. Chap. 22. had farther added, *That any one might do with a Purchaser of the Provisions therein prohibited as with the King's Enemy, and that he who should offend against such an one in Body, Lands, or Goods, should be excused*, it was formerly holden, That a Person attainted in a *Præmunire* might lawfully be slain by any one, as being the King's Enemy and out of the Protection of the Laws, but the later Opinions seem to have disapproved of this Severity; however it is expresly enacted by 5 *El.* 1. Par. 21, 22. *That it shall not be lawful to kill any Person attainted in* Præmunire, *saving such Pains of Death or other Hurt or Punishment, as heretofore might, without danger of Law, be done upon any Person that shall send or bring into the Realm, or within the same shall execute, any Process,* &c. *from the See of* Rome. 1 Inst. 130. 12 Co. 68. 3 Inst. 128. Bro.Cor. 197.

Sect. 47. But howsoever the Law may stand in Relation to such Persons as are within the Exception of this Act, it is certain that no Person whatsoever attainted of any *Præmunire* can bring an Action for any Injury whatsoever; and that no one knowing him to be guilty can with Safety give him Aid, Comfort, or Relief. 1 Inst. 130. See 1 El. 1. Par. 39.

Sect. 48. But it hath been resolved, That those general Words in the Statute 16 *Rich.* 2. 5. That all the Lands and Tenements shall be forfeited, extend not to Land entailed, after the Death of the Offender. 1 Inst. 130. 3 Inst. 126. 2 Lev. 169.

Sect. 49. Also it hath been resolved, That a Statute, by appointing that an Offender shall incur the Penalty and Danger mentioned in the 16 *Rich.* 2. 5. does not confine the Prosecution for the Offence to the particular Process thereby given. 1 Vent. 173.

CHAP. XX.

Of Misprision of Treason.

Sect. 1. THE Word Misprision has not any certain Signification, but is generally applied to all such high Offences as are under the Degree of Capital, and nearly bordering thereupon; and it is said that a Misprision is contained in every Treason or Felony whatsoever, 2 R. 3. 10. b. S. P. C. 37. b. Bro.Cor. 174. Treas. 25, 31.

ever, and that one who is guilty of Felony or Treason may be proceeded against for a Misprision only, if the King please.

Offences of this Kind are generally said to be twofold;

1. Negative, which consist in the Omission of something which ought to be done.
2. Positive, which consist in some Misdemeanour actually committed.

Sect. 2. The negative Misprision more immediately against the King is commonly called Misprision of Treason, which is an Offence consisting in the bare Knowledge and Concealment of High Treason, (whether it
H. P. C. 127. be such by 25 *Ed.* 3. or subsequent Statutes,) without any Degree of Assent thereto; and this is declared to be a Misprision only by 1 & 2
Bract. 118. b. S. P. C. 37. b. 3 Inst. 36. *Mar.* 10. But at Law any delay in discovering High Treason, whatever Excuses the Party might have for it, was deemed an Assent to it, and consequently High Treason.

Sect. 3. And at this Day, if the Concealment of High Treason be accompanied with any Circumstances which shew an Approbation thereof,
H. P. C. 127. Kely. 17, 21. it amounts to High Treason; as if one, having Notice before-hand that Persons design'd to meet in order to conspire against the Government, go into their Company and hear their treasonable Consultation and conceal it; or if one, who has been once accidentally in such Company, and heard such Discourse, meet the same Company a second Time, and hear such like Discourse, and conceal it.

3 H. 7. 10. H. P. C. 127. 3 Inst. 138. 11 Co. 81, 82. Con. Dy. 296. Pl. 21. *Sect.* 4. Also whoever receives and comforts a Traitor, knowing him to be such, whether by counterfeiting of Coin, or otherwise, is himself a principal Traitor; for such a Receipt of a Felon makes the Receiver an Accessary to the Felony, and whatever makes an Accessary in Felony, makes a Principal in Treason.

Sect. 5. Neither can a Person, who has knowledge of a Treason, se-
Kely. 22. H. P. C. 127. S. P. C. 37. b. cure himself by discovering that there will be a Rising in general, without disclosing the very Persons intending to rise; nor even by discovering of these to a private Person who is no Magistrate.

Kely. 22. *Sect.* 6. But it seems that one who is only told in general that there will be a Rising, without knowing any of the Persons, or particulars of the Design, is not bound to make any Discovery at all.

Sect. 7. There is one positive Misprision which is made Misprision of Treason, by 14 *El.* 3. by which it is enacted, that those who forge foreign Coin, not currant here, are guilty of Misprision of Treason, *&c.*

CHAP. XXI.

Of Contempts against the King's Courts.

OTher positive Misprisions more immediately against the King seem reducible to the following Heads:

1. Contempts against his Palace or Courts of Justice.
2. Contempts against his Prerogative.

3. Contempts against his Person or Government.
4. Contempts against his Title.

Sect. 1. And first, Contempts against the King's Palace, *&c.* have always been look'd upon as very high Misprisions, and by the ancient Law before the Conquest, Fighting in the King's Palace was a capital Offence; and by 33 *H.* 8. 12. Par. 7. Malitious Striking in the King's Palace, whereby any Blood shall be shed, is punishable with the Loss of Hand, perpetual Imprisonment, and Fine at the King's Pleasure.

3 Inst. 140. Poph. 206.

Sect. 2. But it seems probable from the Construction of this whole Act, and the general Tenor of the Law-Books, That Striking in a Palace, wherein the King is not at the Time actually resident, is not within the Statute; and it is said that the Instance which is given in the third Institute to the contrary, is not warranted by the Record.

See the first Paragraph of the Act. S. P. C 38 a. Bro. Pain. 16. Dal. cap 90. 6 Mod. 75, 76.

Sect. 3. However it is certain, That by the Common Law which continues to this Day, Striking in *Westminster-Hall*, where the King is only present, as represented by his Judges, and by their Administration distributing Justice to his People, is more penal than any Striking in another Place in his actual Presence; for the latter is not punished with the Loss of Hand, unless some Blood be drawn, nor even then with the Loss of Lands or Goods: But if a Person draw his Sword on any Judge, in the Presence of the Court of King's Bench, Chancery, Common Pleas, or Exchequer, or before the Justices of Assize, or Oyer and Terminer, whether he strike or not, or strike a Juror, or any other Person, with or without a Weapon, he shall lose his Hand and his Goods, and the Profits of his Lands during Life, and suffer perpetual Imprisonment, [a] if the Indictment lay the Offence as done *coram Domino Rege.*

3 Inst. 140. 2 Inst. 549. 3 Inst. 140. S. P. C. 38. a. Dal. ch. 90. Cro. El. 405. 41 Ass. 25. 22 E. 3. 18. a. Dy. 188. Pl. 11. Dalis. 23. 2 Rol. Ab. 76. Pl. 2, 3. H. P. C. 131, 132. 1 Keb. 751. 11 Co. 71.

Sect. 4. [b] Neither can one who is guilty of such Offence excuse the same, by shewing that the Person so struck by him gave the first Assault.

[a] Owen 126. Cro. Eliz 405.

Sect. 5. [c] Also he who rescues a Prisoner from any of the Courts abovementioned, without striking a Blow, shall forfeit his Goods and the Profits of his Lands, and suffer Imprisonment during Life, but not lose his Hand, because he did not strike.

[b] 1 Levin. 106. 6 Mod. 172. Noy 104. Cro. Ja. 367. [c] 22 E. 3. 13. a.

Sect. 6. [d] And he who makes an Affray in the Palace-Yard near the said Courts, but out of their View, shall be imprisoned during the King's Pleasure, and severely fined, but not lose his Hand.

3 Inst. 141. con. H. P. C. 131. [d] Cro El. 405. Cro. Ca. 373. Sir W. Jon. 345. Owen 120.

Sect. 7. And not only those who are guilty of such an actual Violence, but also those who disturb such Courts by threatening or reproachful Words to any Judge sitting in them, are guilty of a high Misprision; and in the Time of *Edward* the First, one *William de Bruce*, who, upon hearing Judgment given against him in the Exchequer, said to the Chief Baron, *Roger, Roger, Thou hast had thy Will of me, which of a long Time thou hast sought, and I will remember it,* was for these Words imprisoned during the King's Pleasure, and ordered to walk from the King's Bench to the Exchequer, bareheaded and ungirt, and to ask forgiveness, *&c.* And in the Time of *Charles* the First, one *Harrison*, for rushing into the Court of Common Pleas, and saying to Justice *Hutton* sitting there, *I do accuse Mr. Justice* Hutton *of High Treason,* was fined five thousand Pounds and imprisoned during the King's Pleasure, and ordered to go to all the Courts of *Westminster-Hall* with a Paper on his Head shewing his Offence, and to make his Submission, *&c.* And these Cases are the more remarkable, because in the first, the Offender was of a very honourable Family, and in the second, a Bachelor of Divinity, and yet condemned to such corporal Punishment,

3 Inst. 142. Moor 819. Cro. Ca. 503, 504. Hutt. 131. Poph. 135.

nishment, the lowest of which is in Judgment of Law higher than the greatest Fine whatever.

Hob. 220. Moore 563. *Sect.* 8. Also all who reflect on the Justice or Honour of those High Courts seem to be indictable and highly finable; as if one charge an Exemplification under the great Seal to be contrary to the Original.

1 Lev. 107. 1 Keb. 558. *Sect.* 9. Also he who gives another the Lie in *Westminster-Hall*, sitting the Courts, shall be bound to his good Behaviour.

3 Inst. 141. *Sect.* 10. And he who makes an Affray in the Presence of any of the King's inferiour Courts of Justice, is highly finable, but not punishable with Loss of Hand, *&c.*

Sect. 11. And he who speaks contemptuous and reproachful Words to the Judge of such a Court in Execution of his Office is [a] immediately finable by such Judge, or, as some say, may be [b] indicted, *&c.* as [c] if one give the Lie to a Judge of a Court-Leet in the Face of the Court, or being [d] admonished by him to pull off his Hat, say, *I do not value what you can do*, or tell him in the Face of the Court that he is [e] forsworn, or call [f] him Fool, *&c.* or [g] say, *If I can not have Justice here, I will have it elsewhere.*

[a] Cro. E. 78. 2 R. A. 78. Pl. 4, 6. [b] 1 Sid. 144. con. 2 Rol. Ab. 78 Pl. 4. [c] Owen 113. Moore 470. Cro. El. 581. [d] Raym. 68. 1 Keb. 451, 465. [e] 2 Rol. Ab. 78. Pl. 4. [f] Cro. El 78. Moore 247. [g] 1 Sid. 144. 1 Keb. 508.

Sect. 12. And it was formerly [h] holden that a Man might be indicted for a Slander of the Justice of the Nation, by reflecting on a Sentence given in any Court Ecclesiastical or Temporal, whether directly, as where one said that such a Sentence given by the High Commission-Court, was against Law; or obliquely, as where one said that such a Sentence was just, but that the Testimonies on which it was founded were false, or the *Affidavits* equivocating.

[h] 2 Rol. Ab. 78. Pl. 3. 1 Rol Re. 245. Hob. 202. Moore 819.

Sect. 13. But it seems the better Opinion at this Day, That a Man can not be indicted for any scandalous or contemptuous Words spoken of or to such Officers, not being in the actual Execution of their Office; for such an Offence seems rather to proceed from ill Breeding than a Contempt of the Government; and tho' it may be a Cause to bind a Man to his Good Behaviour, yet it does not seem to be of such Consequence as to be a sufficient Ground of a publick Prosecution, as for an Offence against the common Peace, *&c.* And agreeably hereto it hath been resolved, That a Man shall not be indicted for saying, [i] *That whenever a Burgess of such a Town puts on his Gown, Satan enters into him*; or, [k] *That the Mayor and Aldermen of such a Town are as great Villains as any that rob on the Highway*; or, [l] *That the Justices of Peace understand no more of the Statutes of Excise than this Jug, nor one of twenty of the Parliament-Men who made them*; or, [m] *That such a Justice of Peace is a Fool, an Ass, and a Coxcomb, for making such a Warrant, and understands no more Law than a Slick-hill*; or, [n] *That he is not fit to be a Justice of Peace; for that he will do right or wrong according as his Affections lead him*; or, [o] *That such an Order is a Numscul Order, and that the Justice deserves to be hanged who made it*; or, [p] *That such a Justice of Peace is a forsworn Wretch, and that he will fling his Purse at him*; or for [q] saying to a Mayor of a Town, *You, Mr. Mayor, I do not care a Fart for you; You, Mr. Mayor, are a Rogue and a Rascal.*

[i] 1 Mod. 35. 2 Keb. 594. [k] 5 Mod. 203. [l] 2 Keb. 494. 5 Mod. 204. [m] *Queen and* Wrightson. [n] *Queen and* Soley. [o] *Queen and* Legasley. [p] *Queen and* Broxham. [q] 6 Mod. 124.

Sect. 14. And not only those who disturb the Administration of Justice by direct Contempts offered to the King's Courts, but also all such as are guilty of any injurious Treatment of those Persons who are under the more immediate Protection of those Courts, are highly punishable by Fine and Imprisonment; as if a Man assault or threaten his Adversary for suing him, or a Counsellor or Attorney for being employed against him, or a Juror for giving a Verdict against him, or a Gaoler for keeping a Prisoner in safe Custody.

3 Inst 142. H. P. C. 131. 2 Rol. Ab 76. D. 2.

Sect. 15. Also all who endeavour to stifle the Truth, and prevent the due Execution of Justice, are highly punishable, as those who being examined before the Privy Council concerning their Knowledge of a Crime whereof a third Person is accused, disclose what passed in such Examination, in order to suppress a farther Discovery; and also all those who dissuade, or but endeavour to dissuade, a Witness from giving Evidence against a Person indicted, *&c.* or who advise a Prisoner to stand mute on his Arraignment, *&c.* And it was anciently holden, that if one of the Grand Inquest discover to any Persons indicted the Evidence against them, he is an Accessary to the Offence, whether Treason or Felony; and at this Day it is agreed, that he is guilty of a high Misprision, punishable by Fine and Imprisonment.

Hob. 271. Raym. 376. *Trial per Pais* 164. H. P. C. 131. 2 Rol. Ab. 77. F. 2. S. P. C. 11. A. 35. B. 27 Aff. 63. Bro. Cor. 113. H. P. C. 131. 3 Inst. 22. 106. *See* 3 Leon 207.

CHAP. XXII.

Of Contempts against the King's Prerogative.

Sect. 1. Contempts against the King's Prerogative are of so various a Nature that they can not well be reduced to any certain Heads; however, the Principal of them seem to come under the following Particulars:

1. Refusing to assist the King for the Good of the Publick.
2. Preferring the Interests of a foreign Prince to that of our own.
3. Disobeying the King's lawful Commands or Prohibitions.

Sect. 2. First therefore, It is a high Offence for any Subject to deny the King that Assistance for the Good of the Publick, either in his Councils or Wars, which by the Law he is bound to give him; as for a Peer not to [a] come to the Parliament at the Day of Summons, or to [b] depart from thence without the King's Licence; or for a [c] Privy Counsellor to refuse to give his Advice on an Affair of State; or for any [d] private Subject to refuse to serve the King in Person, if he be able, or to find another if he be not able, in the Defence of the Realm, against Rebels and foreign Invaders; or, as some say, to refuse to serve the King for Pay in his Wars abroad.

[a] Moore 778. Pl. 1080. Noy 102. [b] S P. C. 38 A Fitz Coro. 161. [c] 2 Rol. Ab. 211. A. 1. [d] 2 Rol. A. 165. X. 166. Bro. Tenure 44. 73. *See* 1 Ed. 3. ch. 5. 18 Ed. 3. ch. 7. 25 Ed. 3. ch. 8. 4 H. 4. ch. 13. 11 H. 7. ch. 1 & 18.

Sect. 3. Secondly, It is so high an Offence to prefer the Interests of a foreign Prince to that of our own, that it is criminal to do any Thing which may but incline a Man so to do; as to receive a Pension from a foreign Prince without the Leave of our King.

3 Inst. 144.

Sect. 4. Thirdly, It is also a high Crime to disobey the King's lawful Commands or Prohibitions; as by obstinately refusing Obedience to his Writs; or contemning a Summons from his Council to appear before them; or not answering such Questions in relation to a Matter wherein the Interest of the State is concerned, as shall be proposed by the Privy Council; or not returning from beyond Sea upon the King's Letters to that Purpose; (for which the Offender's Lands shall be seized till he return, and when he does return he shall be fined,) or assembling at a Tur-

Cro. Ca. 153. Cro. Ca. 257. Hob. 235. 12 Co. 94. Dy. 176. Pl. 30, 31, 128. Pl. 61, 75. b. Moore 109, 779. Lane 43 3 Inst. 179. Savil. 7, 8.

2 Rol. Ab. 208. O. F. N. B. 85. 1 Chan. Cases 116. 3 Inst. 178.

Turnament against the King's exprefs Prohibition; or going beyond Sea against the King's Will exprefly fignified, either by the Writ *Ne exeas Regnum*, (which may be directed as well to a Layman as to a Clergyman, and on the Suggeftion of a private as well as of a publick Matter,) or under the Great or Privy Seal or Signet, or by Proclamation.

CHAP. XXIII.

Of Contempts against the King's Person or Government.

Sect. 1. ALL Contempts againft the King's Perfon or Government are very highly criminal, and punifhable with Fine and Imprifonment, and fometimes with the Pillory, by the Difcretion of the Judges, upon Confideration of all the Circumftances of the Cafe; but inafmuch as it is generally obvious to common Senfe, in what Cafes and to what degree a Man is guilty of this Offence, and it would be endlefs to enumerate all the Particulars, I fhall content my felf with glancing at fome of the moft general Heads; as,

Cro. Ca. 168. 2 Keb. 336.

Sect. 2. I. The charging the Government with Oppreffion or weak Adminiftration; as by faying, *That Merchants are fcrewed up here in* England *more than in* Turkey; or, *That it is a good World when beggarly Priefts are made Lords*, &c.

5 Mod. 363.

Sect. 3. II. The doing an Act which impliedly encourages Rebellion; as by abfolving Perfons at the Gallows, who being condemned for High Treafon, fhew no fign of Repentance, but perfift in juftifying the Fact.

Cro. Ja. 37. Moore 756. Noy 101.

Sect. 4. III. Endeavouring to frighten the King into a Change of his Meafures with threats of the Uneafinefs of his Subjects; as by fubfcribing a Petition to him, in which it is intimated, that if it be denied many Thoufands will be difcontented, *&c.*

Cro. Ja. 38.

Sect. 5. IV. Spreading falfe Rumours concerning the King's Intentions; as that he defigns to grant a Toleration to Papifts, *&c.*

Noy 105.

Sect. 6. V. Charging him with a Breach of his Coronation Oath.

See Cro. Ca. 117, &c.

Sect. 7. VI. Speaking contemptuoufly of him; as by curfing him, *&c.* or giving out that he wants Wifdom, Valour or Steadinefs; or in general, doing any Thing which may leffen him in the Efteem of his Subjects, and weaken his Government, or raife Jealoufies between him and his People.

CHAP.

CHAP. XXIV.

Of Contempts against the King's Title.

CONtempts against the King's Title are of two Kinds,

1. Denying his Title.
2. Refusing to take the Oaths required by Law for the Support of his Government.

Sect. 1. The first Offence of this Kind, *viz.* That of denying the King's Title, hath by some been carried so high as to be adjudged an Overt Act of Compassing his Death; however, it is certainly most highly criminal, and punishable with Fine and Imprisonment, and also such infamous corporal Punishment as to the Discretion of the Court shall seem proper, according to the Heinousness of the Crime and the Circumstances of the Parties; as if a Man in Writing or Discourse shall maintain that the King is an Usurper, or that another hath a better Title to the Crown, *&c.* for such like Insinuations manifestly tend to raise Tumults and Disorders in the State, and to alienate the Affections of the People from the Prince, and incline them to favour the Pretensions of another; and it is highly presumptuous for private Persons to intermeddle with Matters of so high a Nature; and it will be impossible to preserve the Peace of a Government, unless Subjects will quietly submit themselves to those whom Providence has placed over them, and prefer the publick Good to their own private Inclinations and Opinions: For otherwise, whenever the Title to the Crown shall happen to be contested, it will be impossible to end the Difference without perpetual civil Broils and Dissensions, and the Prince who prevails will be tempted to esteem those of the contrary Party rather as Enemies than Subjects, if he finds them ready and desirous to lay hold of all Opportunities to disturb his Government, and shake off their forc'd Obedience. And since there is no Tribunal but that of Heaven to which Princes can appeal for the Decision of their Titles, when that seems so far to have declared in Favour of one as to give him quiet Possession of the Throne, the publick Peace, which is the End of all Government, requires a dutiful Submission to him; and it is the highest Madness to give up that Ease and Security which we may enjoy from a peaceful Obedience, in exchange for that Disorder, Uncertainty, and Bloodshed, which cannot but be expected from an attempt to wrest the Scepter out of the Hands of our Prince; and it is the highest Ingratitude to make no other return but Disloyalty and Rebellion, for all the Happiness we can enjoy under a just Administration; and it is the greatest of Absurdities to think that the Good of the Community, for the sake of which all Government was instituted, ought not to be preferred before the disputed Title of a particular Person or Family: All we can desire from Government is the secure Enjoyment of what we may call our own, and whether this or that Competitor to the Crown be the Instrument of this Happiness to us, seems little to concern us. Let the Title of one out of Possession of the Throne be never so plausible, it must have its original Foundation

Yelv. 107. 2 Rol. Rc. 90. Palm. 424.

from some positive Law; which, when it cannot take Effect without involving a Nation in Discord and Confusion, the avoiding whereof is the very End of all Laws, it must give way to the publick Necessity of the State; for there can be no human Institution whatsoever but must be limited by this implicit Reserve from the first Principles of Reason, that where-ever the Execution of it shall be absolutely inconsistent with the Happiness of the People for whose sake it was ordained, it ought so far to be suspended.

Sect. 2. For this and many other such like Reasons, the Law has always had a most tender Regard for the Security of the Prince in Possession of the Crown, and as it has made it High Treason to compass his Death, *&c.* as appears from Chap. 17. Sect. 11, *&c.* so hath it also made it highly Penal in any inferiour Degree to disturb or disquiet his Government.

As to the second kind of Offences of this Nature, *viz.* That of refusing to take the Oaths required by Law for the Support of the King's Government; I shall consider,

1. The Offence of refusing the Oaths required for this Purpose by the Common Law.

2. The Offence of refusing the Oaths required by Statute.

Finch *of Law* 241, 242. *Sect.* 3. As to the first particular, it seems to be a high Contempt at the Common Law to refuse to take the Oath of Allegiance to the King, which all Laymen above the Age of twelve Years are bound to take at the Torn or Court-Leet, *&c.* and surely nothing can be more unreasonable than to deny the King, whose Government we are happy under, all proper Assurances of our Fidelity to him; for how can we expect to enjoy the Privileges of Subjects from one to whom we refuse to acknowledge our selves Subjects, or hope for Protection from one whom we provoke to esteem us as his Enemies, or blame that Government for treating us as Malecontents, to which we give so just a Cause to suspect our Fidelity? If we consult the Law of God, that will tell us, *That the Powers that be are ordained of God*; If we will hear the Voice of Reason, that will convince us, that not only the Peace and Safety of the Community, but also our own Preservation requires us to pay a dutiful Obedience to those who govern us; and can we think it unlawful to engage our selves to do what it is our Duty to do? If we will consult the Practice of all Nations, that will shew us, that even Conquest, which is the weakest of all Titles, has always been esteemed to give the Conqueror such a Right to the Obedience of the Conquered, that upon his taking them into his Protection, they have in all Ages been ready to promise a reciprocal Obedience; and if we will consult our own Laws, we shall find them to direct us to pay our Allegiance to the King who governs us, as has been fully proved in the Chapter of High Treason.

Sect. 4. As to the second Kind of Offences of this Nature, *viz.* That of refusing the Oaths required by the Statute for the Support of the Government, I shall consider;

1. The Offence of refusing the Oaths of Allegiance and Supremacy.

2. The Offence of refusing the Oath of Abjuration.

Sect. 5. As to the first of these Offences, *viz.* That of refusing the Oaths of Allegiance and Supremacy, which since the Reformation of Religion have been thought necessary to be required from all Persons, especially from those who are intrusted with any Office, in order to secure our Princes from the Intrigues of Popes, who have often taken upon them to dispense with Oaths of Allegiance made to such Princes whom they are pleased to call Hereticks, and to perswade the People that they may lawfully depose those who have so far incurred the Displeasure of the Bishop of *Rome*, as to be excommunicated by him, it having been shewn already in Chap. 8. under what Penalties Officers are bound to take the said Oaths, and in Chap. 19. S. 27. *&c.* how far all Persons whatsoever are compellable to take them under Pain of incurring a *Præmunire*, I shall only take Notice in this Place, of the Method of Proceeding on 1 *Will. & Mar.* 8. by which it is enacted, *That Persons refusing the said Oaths being tendered to them by Persons lawfully authorized to tender the same, shall be committed by the Persons making such a Tender for three Months, unless they shall pay such Sum not exceeding* 40 *s. as the Persons who shall make such Tender shall require of them, and if they refuse again at the End of the three Months, that they shall be imprisoned six Months, or pay a Sum not above ten nor under five Pounds, and also find Sureties for their good Behaviour and Appearance at the next Assizes, where if they refuse the said Oaths they shall be incapable of any Office, and continue bound to their good Behaviour, and if they refuse the Declaration mentioned in* 30 Ca. 2. *they shall suffer as Popish Recusants convict.*

Sect. 5. It seems to be the Intention of this Statute, to give the Government an Election to proceed either on the mild Method therein prescribed, or the more severe one appointed by the former Laws, according to the Circumstances of the Case, and Quality of the Offender, *&c.*

Sect. 6. As to the second Offence of this Kind, *viz.* That of refusing the Oath of Abjuration, the same depends on those Laws which the Nation has been of late under a Necessity of establishing, by adding a new Limitation to the Law relating to the Succession of the Crown, excluding all Papists from a Possibility of inheriting it; who, if they be true to their Engagements to their own Religion, cannot but be false to those they may make to ours, and can never be expected to execute those Laws, which they cannot but think void, as being repugnant to the Laws of God; or to defend that Faith which they think damnable, or to observe those Oaths which seem to them to have been ordained for the Support of Irreligion. And from these Considerations they have been disabled from inheriting the Crown, it seeming of absolute Necessity in our present Circumstances for the good of the Community, to make such an Alteration in the Law, which like all other humane Laws depending merely on the Policy of Man, seems to have nothing in it so sacred as to oblige the People unalterably to abide by it to the Hazard of their common Safety, Peace and Happiness, for the sake whereof it was at first ordained: For surely, there cannot be so much Danger to the common Good from such an Alteration, as must needs follow from the Government of a Prince, whose Conscience is under the Influence of those who are implacable Enemies to the Religion of his Country, and who thinks himself bound by his Duty to God and his Church, to promote that Interest which his People think themselves under the like Obligations to oppose: From which unhappy Circumstances nothing can be expected but endless Factions and Discords, and irreconcileable Jealousies and Distrusts between Prince and People, which if they break not into an open Rupture, will at least be attended with such Convulsions and Uneasinesses, as render a State of Government scarce one Degree more secure than a State of Anarchy and Confusion.

Sect. 7. For the remedying of such like Inconveniences, it having been thought proper to exclude all Papists from the Crown, it was likewise thought expedient to secure the present Settlement, by obliging all Officers, *&c.* to take the Oath of Abjuration, as to which it is enacted by 13 and 14 *Will.* 3. 6. and 1 *Georg.* 13. *That all Persons who shall be admitted,*

&c.

&c. *into any Office Civil or Military, (not being an Office of Inheritance, executed by a lawful Deputy) or shall receive any Pay, Salary, Fee or Wages, by Reason of any Patent or Grant from the King, or that have a Command or Place of Trust under the King,* &c. *or shall be admitted into any Service or Imployment in the King's Houshold or Family, or of his Royal Highness* George *Prince of* Wales, *or her Royal Highness the Princess of* Wales, *or their Issue, and all Ecclesiastical Persons, Heads or Governors, of what Denomination soever, and all other Members of Colleges and Halls in any University that shall be of the Foundation, or enjoy any Exhibition, being of, or as soon as they shall attain, the Age of eighteen Years, and all Persons teaching or reading to Pupils in any University or elsewhere, and all School-masters and Ushers, and all Preachers and Teachers of separate Congregations, High or Chief Constables, and every Person who shall act as Serjeant at Law, Counsellor at Law, Barraster, Advocate, Attorney, Sollicitor, Proctor, Clerk, or Notary, by practising in any Manner as such, in any Court or Courts whatsoever within that Part of* Great Britain *called* England, *shall within three Months after they shall be admitted into, or enter upon any such Preferment, Benefice, Office, or Place, or come into such Capacity, or take upon them such Practice, Imployment or Business, take and subscribe the Oaths of Allegiance, Supremacy and Abjuration, at one of the Courts at* Westminster, *or at the General Quarter-Sessions of the Peace where they shall reside, or otherwise they shall be* ipso facto *adjudged incapable, and disabled in Law, to have, occupy, or enjoy the said Offices,* &c. *and if they shall by themselves, or Deputy or Trustee, execute any the said Offices,* &c. *and shall be thereof convict,* &c. *they shall be disabled to prosecute any Suit at Law or Equity, or to be Guardians, Executors, or Administrators, or capable of any Legacy or Deed of Gift, or to be in any Office within this Realm, or to vote at any Election for Members of Parliament, and shall forfeit five hundred Pounds,* &c.

Sect. 9. And it is farther enacted by the said Statute, *That any two Justices of Peace, or any other Person or Persons who shall be by the King for that Purpose specially appointed by order in the Privy Council, or by Commission under the Great Seal, may administer and tender the said Oaths to any Person whatsoever, whom they shall suspect to be dangerous or disaffected; and that if any Person to whom the said Oaths shall be so tendered, shall neglect or refuse to take the same, or if any Person being summoned by the said Justices,* &c. *in order to take the said Oaths, either in proper Person, or by Notice left at his Place of Abode with one of the Family, shall neglect or refuse to appear,* &c. *such Refusal shall be certified at Sessions,* &c. *and from thence to the King's-Bench or Chancery,* &c. *and every such Person so neglecting to take the said Oaths, shall be adjudged a Popish Recusant convict,* &c.

Sect. 10. And it is farther enacted by the said Statute, *That if any Member of either University shall neglect to take and subscribe the said Oaths according to the Intent of the said Act, or to produce a Certificate thereof, under the Hand of some proper Officer of the respective Court, and cause the same to be entered in the Register of the proper College or Hall, within one Month after his having taken and subscribed the said Oaths; and if the Persons in whom the Right of Election of such Member shall be, do neglect to elect some fitting Person in his stead within twelve Months,* &c. *that then the King may, under the Great Seal or Sign Manual, nominate some fitting Person qualified according to the local Statutes of such College,* &c. *and if the Head of any College,* &c. *shall neglect to admit such Nominee by the Space of ten Days after such Admission shall be demanded of him, that then the local Visitor shall admit the said Nominee; and if such Visitor shall neglect or refuse to admit such Person within the Space of one Month after the same shall be demanded, that then the Court of King's-*

Bench may issue a Writ of Mandamus *to such Visitor to admit such Nominee*, &c.

Sect. 11. And it is farther enacted by the said Statute, *That no Peer shall vote or make his Proxy, or sit in the House of Peers during any Debate, and that no Member of the House of Commons shall vote or sit during any Debate in the said House, after the Speaker is chosen, until he shall have taken the said Oaths*, &c. *under Pain of the Disabilities and Forfeitures above mentioned*, &c.

CHAP. XXV.

Of Felony.

OFfences more immediately against the Subject, are either Capital or not Capital.

The Capital are either by the Common Law or by Statute.

Sect. 1. Those by the Common Law come generally under the Title of Felony, which, *ex vi Termini*, signifies *quodlibet crimen felleo animo perpetratum*, and can be expressed by no Periphrasis, or Word equivalent, without the Word *Felonicè*. 1 Inst. 391.

Sect. 2. Felony is said to be included in High Treason, and consequently a Pardon of Felony discharges an Indictment of High Treason, if it want the Word *Proditoriè*. H. P. C. 11. 3 H. 7. 10. a. 3 Inst. 15.

Sect. 3. It is always accompanied with an evil Intention, and therefore shall not be imputed to a mere Mistake or Mis-animadversion, as where Persons break open a Door in order to execute a Warrant, which will not justify such a Proceeding; *Affectio enim tua nomen imponit operi tuo; item crimen non contrahitur nisi nocendi voluntas intercedat.* But the bare Intention to commit a Felony is so very criminal, That at the Common Law it was punishable as Felony where it missed its Effect through some Accident, no way lessening the Guilt of the Offender; but it seems agreed at this Day, That Felony shall not be imputed to a bare Intention to commit it, yet it is certain that the Party may be very severely fined for such an Intention. Brac. lib. 2. ca. 4. S.P.C. 17. a. 27. b. 1 Lev. 146. 1 Sid. 230, 231. 5 Mod. 206.

CHAP. XXVI.

Of casual Death and of Deodands.

OF capital Offences at Common Law more immediately against the Subject, there are three principal Kinds:

1. Such as are committed against his Life.
2. Such as are against his Goods.
3. Such as are against his Habitation.

Sect. 1. There is another mix'd kind of Capital Offences, which consists in the Hinderance of the due Process of publick Justice, which I shall consider in the second Book, wherein I shall treat of the Means of bringing Offenders to their due Punishment.

Bract. lib. 3. cap. 4. *Sect.* 2. Offences against the Life of a Man come under the general Name of Homicide, which in our Law signifies the killing of a Man by a Man.

Sect. 3. But before I treat hereof, it may not be improper to consider the killing of a Man merely *per Infortunium*, occasioned by some Animal or Thing without Life, without the Default or Procurement of another Man, as where one is killed by a Fall from a Horse or Cart, *&c.* which, though it be not properly Homicide, nor punishable as a Crime, yet it is taken Notice of by the Law as far as the Nature of the Thing will bear, in order to raise the greater Abhorrence of Murder, and the Crom. 31. a. unhappy Instrument or Occasion of such Death is called a Deodand and forfeited to the King, in order to be disposed of in pious Uses by the King's Almoner; as also are all such Weapons whereby one Man kills another.

S. P. C. 21. a. 3 Inst. 58. H. P. C. 34. Pult. 125. a. Dal. cap. 97. *Sect.* 4. It seems clearly settled, That a Horse, *&c.* killing an Infant within the Age of Discretion, are as much forfeited as if he were of Age: But formerly it was holden, That a Horse or Cart, by a Fall from which an Infant was slain, were not forfeited, perhaps for this Reason, because the Misfortune might rather seem owing to the Indiscretion of the 2 Keb. 719, 806. Infant than any Default in the Horse, *&c.* But this Distinction has not been allowed, of late; for the Law does not ground the Forfeiture on any Default in the Things forfeited, since it extends it to Things without Life to which its plain, that no manner of Fault can be imputed.

S. P. C. 20 b. Pult. 124 b. 1 Sid. 206, 207 1 Lev. 136. Raym. 97. *Sect.* 5. Also by the Opinion of our ancient Authors, Things fix'd to a Freehold, as the Wheel of a Mill, a Bell hanging in a Steeple, *&c.* may be Deodands, but by the later Resolutions they cannot, unless they were severed before the Accident happened.

6 Mod. 187. 1 Keb. 723, 745. S. P. C. 21. Pult. 125. a. 3 Inst. 58. H. P. C. 33. Cro Jac. 483. 2 Rol. Re. 23. Popham 136. *Sect.* 6. However, as it is agreed by all, a Ship in salt Water, whether in the open Sea or within the Body of a County, from which a Man falls and is drowned, is not forfeited, because Persons at Sea are continually exposed to so many Perils, that the Law imputes such Misfortunes happening there, rather to them than to the Ship; also it seems clear, That when a Man riding on a Horse over a River is drowned through the Violence of the Stream, the Horse is not forfeited, because not that, but the Waters caused his Death: But it is said, That a Ship by a Fall from which a Man is drowned in the fresh Water shall be forfeited, but not S. P. C. 20. b. 21. 3 Inst. 58. Pult. 125. See S. P. C. 20. b. & Quære. Pult. 124. b. the Merchandize therein, because they no way contribute to his Death. And by the same Reason it seems, That if a Man riding on the Shafts of a Waggon fall to the Ground and break his Neck, the Horses and Waggon only are forfeited, and not the Loading, because it no Way contributed to his Death; for which Cause, where a Thing not in Motion causes a Man's Death, that Part thereof only which is the immediate Cause is forfeited. As where one climbing upon the Wheel of a Cart while it stands still, falls from it and dies of the Fall, the Wheel only is forfeited: But if he had been killed by a Bruise from one of the Wheels being in Motion, the Loading also would have been forfeited, because the Weight thereof made the Hurt the greater; and it is a general Rule, That where-ever the Thing which is the Occasion of a Man's Death is in Motion at the Time, not only that Part thereof which immediately wounds him, but all Things which move together with it, and

help to make the Wound more dangerous are forfeited also; for the Rule is, *Omnia quæque movent ad Mortem sunt Deodanda.*

Sect. 7. In all these Cases, if the Party wounded die not of his Wound within a Year and a Day after he received it, there shall be nothing forfeited, for the Law does not look on such a Wound as the Cause of a Man's Death, after which he lives so long: But if the Party die within that Time, the Forfeiture shall have Relation to the Wound given, and cannot be saved by any Alienation or other Act whatsoever in the mean Time. H. P. C. 55. S. P. C. 21. b. Dalt. ca. 97. Pl. Com. 260. Kellw. 68. b.

Sect. 8. However, nothing can be forfeited as a Deodand, nor seized as such, till it be found by the Coroner's Inquest to have caused a Man's Death; but after such Inquisition, the Sheriff is answerable for the Value of it, and may levy the same on the Town where it fell, and therefore the Inquest ought to find the Value of it. 5 Co. 110. b. Co. Li. 115. a. Dal. cap. 97. S. P. C. 21. a. Pult. 125. a.

CHAP. XXVII.

Of Felo de se.

HOmicide properly so called, is either against a Man's own Life or that of another.

In treating of Homicide against a Man's own Life, I shall consider:

1. In what Cases a Man shall be said to be a *Felo de se.*
2. What he shall forfeit for this Offence.

Sect. 1. As to the first Point, I shall take it for granted, That in this as well as in all other Felonies, the Offender ought to be of the Age of Discretion, and *Compos Mentis*, and therefore that an Infant killing himself under the Age of Discretion, or a Lunatick during his Lunacy, cannot be a *Felo de se.* Crom. 30. a. b. 31. a. H. P. C. 28. Dal. cap. 92. 3 Inst. 54.

Sect. 2. But here I cannot but take Notice of a strange Notion, which has unaccountably prevailed of late, That every one who kills himself must be *Non compos* of Course; for it is said to be impossible, That a Man in his Senses should do a Thing so contrary to Nature and all Sense and Reason. 3 Mod. 100

Sect. 3. If this Argument be good, Self-Murder can be no Crime, for a Madman can be guilty of none: But it is wonderful that the Repugancy to Nature and Reason, which is the highest Aggravation of this Offence, should be thought to make it impossible to be any Crime at all, which cannot but be the necessary Consequence of this Position, That none but a Madman can be guilty of it. May it not with as much Reason be argued, That the Murder of a Child or of a Parent is against Nature and Reason, and consequently that no Man in his Senses can commit it? But has a Man therefore no Use of his Reason, because he acts against right Reason? Why may not the Passions of Grief and Discontent tempt a Man knowingly to act against the Principles of Nature and Reason in this Case, as those of Love, Hatred and Revenge, and such like, are too well known to do in others?

Sect. 4.

Sect. 4. However our Laws have always had such an Abhorrence of this Crime, That not only he who kills himself with a deliberate and direct Purpose of so doing, but also in some Cases he who maliciously attempts to kill another, and in Pursuance of such Attempt unwillingly kills himself, shall be adjudged in the Eye of the Law a *Felo de se*; for where-ever Death is caused by an Act done with a murderous Intent, it makes the Offender a Murderer; and therefore if *A.* discharge a Gun at *B.* with an Intent to kill him, and the Gun break and kill *A.* or if *A.* strike *B.* to the Ground, and then hastily falling upon him wound himself with a Knife which *B.* happens to have in his Hand and die, in both these Cases *A.* is *Felo de se*, for he is the only Agent.

Dal. cap. 92. 44 E. 3. 44. 44 Ass. 55. Bro. Cor. 12, 14. Dalt. cap. 92.

Sect. 5. But if *B.* being so assaulted, had been driven to the Wall, and holden up a Pitch-fork or Knife, standing in his Defence, and *A.* had hastily run upon the same and been slain, *B.* should be judged to kill him in his own Defence. And for the same Reason perhaps in the Case above, if *B.* after he had fallen to the Ground, had holden up his Knife or Sword in his Defence, and *A.* had fallen thereon and been slain, *B.* should be judged to kill him *se defendendo*; for here *B.* exerts his Strength in his own Defence, and by so doing occasions the mortal Wound received by *A.*

S. P. C. 16. a. 20. H.P.C. 28, 29. Pult. 119. b. Crom. 28. Con. 3 Inst. 54. *But the Case there is not rightly stated as it is in the Books.*

Sect. 6. He who kills another upon his Desire or Command, is in the Judgment of the Law as much a Murderer, as if he had done it merely of his own Head, and the Person killed is not looked upon as a *Felo de se*, inasmuch as his Assent was merely void, as being against the Laws of God and Man: But where two Persons agree to die together, and one of them at the Perswasion of the other buys Ratsbane, and mixes it in a Potion, and both drink of it, and he who bought and made the Potion, survives by using proper Remedies, and the other dies, perhaps it is the better Opinion, That he who dies shall be adjudged a *Felo de se*, because all that happened was originally owing to his own wicked Purpose, and the other only put it in his Power to execute it in that particular Manner.

Kellw. 136. a. Moore 754. Pl. 1041.

Sect. 7. [a] As to the second Point, *viz.* What such an Offender shall forfeit, it seems clear, that he shall forfeit all Chattels Real or Personal, which he hath in his own Right, and also all such Chattels Real whereof he is possessed either jointly with his Wife, or in her Right; and also all Bonds and other Personal Things in Action belonging solely to himself; and also all Personal Things in Action, and, as some say, entire Chattels in Possession, to which he was intituled jointly with another, on any Account except that of Merchandize: But it is said, That he shall forfeit a Moiety only of such joint Chattels as may be severed, and nothing at all of what he was possessed of as Executor or Administrator.

[a] S. P. C. 189. F. G. 262, 263. H. P. C. 29. Plow. Com. 262, 263. S P.C. 188. a. Crom. 31. a. 3 Inst. 55. 19 H. 6. 47. a. 8 E. 4. 24. b. Raym. 7. Plow. Com. 243, 259, 323 b.

Sect. 8. [b] However the Blood of a *Felo de se* is not corrupted, nor his Lands of Inheritance forfeited, nor his Wife barred of her Dower.

[b] Plow. Com. 261. b. 262 a.

Sect. 9. [c] Also no Part of the Personal Estate is vested in the King, before the Self-Murder is found by some Inquisition; and consequently the Forfeiture thereof is saved by a Pardon of the Offence before such Finding.

[c] 5 Co. 110. b. 3 Inst. 54. 1 Saund. 368. 1 Sid. 150, 162. 2 Mod. 53. 3 Mod. 100. 241, 242. Con. 1 Lev 8. 1 Keb. 67, 68.

Sect. 10. [d] But if there be no such Pardon, the whole is forfeited immediately after such Inquisition, from the Time such mortal Wound was given, and all intermediate Alienations are avoided.

[d] Plow. Com. 260. H. P. C. 29. 5 Co. 110.

Sect. 11. [e] And such Inquisitions ought to be by the Coroner *super visum Corporis*, if the Body can be found; and an Inquisition so taken, as some say, cannot be traversed.

[e] H. P. C. 29. 3 Inst. 55.

Sect. 13. But if the Body cannot be found, so that the Coroner, who has Authority only *super visum Corporis*, cannot proceed, the Inquiry may be by Justices of Peace, (who by their Commission have a general Power to inquire of all Felonies,) or in the King's-Bench, if the Felony were committed in the County where the said Court sits; and such Inquisitions are traversable by the Executor, *&c.* 3 Inst. 55. H. P. C. 29. 2 Lev. 141.

Sect. 14. Also all Inquisitions of this Offence being in the Nature of Indictments, ought particularly and certainly to set forth the Circumstances of the Fact; and in the Conclusion add, That the Party in such manner murdered himself.

Sect. 15. Therefore if either the Premisses be insufficient, as if it be found that the Party flung himself into the Water, *& sic seipsum emergit*, which is Nonsence, (because *emergo* signifies only to rise out of the Water,) or if there be wanting the proper Conclusion, *& sic seipsum murdravit*, the Inquisition is not good. 3 Lev. 140. 3 Mod. 100. 2 Lev. 152.

Sect. 16. Yet if it be full in Substance, the Coroner may be served with a Rule to amend a Defect in Form. 1 Sid. 225, 259 3 Mod. 101. 1 Keb. 907.

CHAP. XXVIII.

Of Justifiable Homicide.

HOmicide against the Life of another either amounts to Felony, or does not.

That which amounts not to Felony, is either justifiable and causes no Forfeiture at all, or excusable and causes the Forfeiture of the Party's Goods.

And first of Justifiable Homicide, concerning which I shall premise these general Rules:

Sect. 1. I. It must be owing to some unavoidable Necessity, to which the Person who kills another must be reduced without any manner of Fault in himself. Vid. Sect. 22.

Sect. 2. II. There must be no Malice coloured under Pretence of Necessity; for where-ever a Person who kills another, acts in Truth upon Malice, and takes Occasion from the Appearance of Necessity to execute his own private Revenge, he is guilty of Murder. 2 Rol. Rep. 120, 121. Kelynge 28. H. P. C. 38. Bract. lib. 3. cap. 4. 21 Ed. 1. de Malefactor' in Parcis.

Sect. 3. III. According to the Opinion of the old [a] Books, (which in this respect seem to be contradicted by [b] others more modern,) it seems, That one may set forth a Fact, amounting to Justifiable Homicide, in a Special Plea to an Indictment or Appeal of Murder; and that the same being found true, he shall be dismissed, without being arraigned or enforced to Plead Not guilty. And indeed it seems extreamly hard, That a Sheriff or Judge who condemn or execute a Criminal, *&c.* should be forced on a frivolous Prosecution to hold up their Hands at the Bar for it, *&c.* But it is agreed, That no one can plead a Fact amounting to Homicide *se defendendo*, or by Misadventure, but that in such a Case the Defendant must plead Not guilty, and give the Special Matter in Evidence: [a] 22 Ass. 55. 27 Ass. 41. 37 H. 6. 20, 21. a. Bro. Appeal, 5, 129. Bro. Coro. 57, 87, 89. b. [b] 35 H. 6. 11. b. 58. Bro. Appeal. 122.

T

2 Inst. 316. 1 Inst. 283. H. P. C. 38. Bro. Coro. 1.

dence: And it is alſo agreed, That where a Special Fact, amounting to juſtifiable Homicide, is found by the Jury, the Party is to be diſmiſſed, without being obliged to purchaſe any Pardon, *&c.*

H P. C. 38.

Juſtifiable Homicide is either of a publick or a private Nature.

That of a publick Nature, is ſuch as is occaſioned by the due Execution or Advancement of publick Juſtice.

That of a private Nature is ſuch as happens in the juſt Defence of a Man's Perſon, Houſe, or Goods.

And firſt, I ſhall conſider juſtifiable Homicide in the due Execution of publick Juſtice, as to which the following Rules muſt be obſerved:

Dalt cap 98. 10 Co. 76. 22 E. 4. 33 a. H. P. C. 35.

Sect. 4. I. The Judgment by Virtue whereof any Perſon is put to Death, muſt be given by one who has Juriſdiction in the Cauſe; for otherwiſe both Judge and Officer may be guilty of Felony.

Sect. 5. And therefore if the Court of Common Pleas give Judgment on an Appeal of Death, or Juſtices of Peace on an Indictment of Treaſon, and award Execution, which is executed, both the Judges who give, and the Officers who execute, the Sentence, are guilty of Felony, becauſe theſe Courts having no more Juriſdiction over theſe Crimes than mere private Perſons, their Proceedings thereon are merely void, and without any Foundation.

H. P. C. 35. Dalt. cap. 98

Sect. 6. But if the Juſtices of Peace, on an Indictment of Treſpaſs, arraign a Man of Felony, and condemn him, and he be executed, the Juſtices only are guilty of Felony, and not the Officers who execute their Sentence; for the Juſtices had a Juriſdiction over the Offence, and their Proceedings were irregular and erroneous only, but not void.

Sect. 7. II. The Judgment muſt be executed by the lawful Officer.

[a] 1 Inſt. 128. b. 2 Aſſ. pl. 3. S. P. C. 13. a. 11 H. 4. 12. a. Plow. Com. 306. b. 3 Inſt. 131.

Sect. 8. [a] Indeed it was formerly holden, That any one might as lawfully kill a Perſon attainted of Treaſon or Felony, as a Wolf or other wild Beaſt; and anciently a Perſon condemned in an Appeal of Death, was delivered to the Relations of the Deceaſed in order to be executed by them.

[b] 27 Aſſ. 41. Bro. Appeal. 69. Coro. 67, 197. 1 Inſt. 128. b Dalt. cap. 98 H. P. C 35.

Sect. 9. [b] But at this Day, as it ſeems agreed, if the Judge, who gives the Sentence of Death, and, *à fortiori*, if any private Perſon execute the ſame, or if the proper Officer himſelf do it without a lawful Command, they are guilty of Felony.

[c] 35 H. 6. 58 b. Bro. Appeal. 5. S P. C. 13. H. P. C. 36, 272.

Sect. 10. [c] III. The Execution muſt be purſuant of, and warranted by, the Judgment, otherwiſe it is without Authority; and conſequently if a Sheriff behead a Man where it is no Part of the Sentence to cut off the Head, he is guilty of Felony.

And now we are come to Juſtifiable Homicide in the due Advancement of publick Juſtice, which I ſhall conſider:

1. In Relation to criminal,
2. In Relation to civil Cauſes.

And firſt, Homicide in the Advancement of publick Juſtice in criminal Cauſes may be juſtified in ſeveral Caſes; as,

22 Aſſ. 55. Bro. Cor. 87, 89. S. P. C. 13. 3 Inſt. 221. Dal. cap. 98. H P. C. 36. Crom. 30.

Sect. 11. I. If a Perſon having actually committed a Felony will not ſuffer himſelf to be arreſted, but ſtand on his own Defence, or fly, ſo that he cannot poſſibly be apprehended alive by thoſe who purſue him, whether private Perſons or publick Officers, with or without a Warrant from a Magiſtrate, he may be lawfully ſlain by them.

Sect. 12. II. If an innocent Person be indicted of a Felony, where, in Truth, no Felony was committed, and will not suffer himself to be arrested by the Officer who has a Warrant to that Purpose, he may lawfully be killed by him, if he cannot otherwise be taken; for there is a Charge against him upon Record to which at his Peril he is bound to answer. *See the Authorities above cited.*

Sect. 13. III. If a Criminal, endeavouring to break the Gaol, assault his Gaoler, he may be lawfully killed by him in the Affray.

Sect. 14. IV. If those who are engaged in a Riot, or a Forcible Entry, or Detainer, stand in their Defence and continue the Force in Opposition to the Command of a Justice of Peace, *&c.* or resist such Justice endeavouring to arrest them, the killing of them may be justified; and so perhaps may the killing of dangerous Rioters by any private Persons, who cannot otherwise suppress them, or defend themselves from them, inasmuch as every private Person seems to be authorized by the Law to arm himself for the Purposes aforesaid. Crom. 30. b. 158 b. H. P. C. 37. Poph. 121.

Sect. 15. V. If Trespassers in a Forest, Chace, Park, or Warren, or any inclosed Ground wherein Deer are kept, will not render themselves to the Keepers, upon an Hue and Cry made to stand to the King's Peace, but fly from, or defend themselves against them, they may be slain by Force of the Statute *de Malefactoribus in Parcis*, and 3 and 4 *Will. & Mar.* 10. S. P. C. 13. b. Crom. 30 b. Dyer 326. Pl. 3.

Sect. 16. VI. If either of the Parties fighting in a Combat allowed by Law, for the Trial of some Special Cases, be slain, he who kills him is justified, and the Death of the other is imputed to the just Judgment of God, who is presumed to give the Victory to him who fights in Maintenance of the Truth. Dalt. cap. 98. Plow. Com. 9. b. 3 Inst. 221. 37 H. 6. 21. a.

Secondly, Homicide in the Advancement of Justice in civil Causes, may also be justified in some Cases.

Sect. 17. [a] As where a Sheriff, *&c.* attempting to make a lawful Arrest in a civil Action, or to retake one who has been arrested and made his Escape, is resisted by the Party, and unavoidably kills him in the Affray. [a] 1 Rol. Re. 189. H. P. C. 37. 3 Inst. 56. Crom. 24. a. Dalt. cap 98.

Sect. 18. [b] And in such Case the Officer is not bound to give back, but may stand his Ground and attack the Party. [b] H. P. C. 37.

Sect. 19. But no private Person of his own Authority can arrest a Man for a civil Matter, as he may for Felony, *&c.* Crom. 30. b.

Sect. 20. Neither can the Sheriff himself lawfully kill those who barely fly from the Execution of any civil Process. H. P. C. 37.

And now I am to consider Justifiable Homicide of a private Nature, in the just Defence of a Man's Person, House or Goods, in treating whereof I shall shew,

1. In what Cases the killing of a Wrong-doer may be justified by Reason of such Defence.
2. Where the killing of an innocent Person may be so justified.

Sect. 21. And first the killing of a Wrong-doer in the making of such Defence, may be justified in many Cases; as where a Man kills one who assaults him in the High way to rob or murder him; or the Owner of a House, or any of his Servants, or Lodgers, *&c.* kill one who attempts to burn it, or to commit in it Murder, Robbery, or other Felony; or a Woman kills one who attempts to ravish her; or a Servant coming suddenly and finding his Master robbed and slain, falls upon the Murderer immediately and kills him; for he does it in the Height of his Sur- 24 H. 8. c. 5. Dalt. cap 98. H. P. C. 32. S. P. C. 14. Bro. Coro. 100, 102. Cro. Ca. 544. 26 Ass. 23. Bro. Cor. 100. Crom. 26 b.

Surprize, and under just Apprehensions of the like Attempt upon himself: But in other Circumstances he could not have justified the killing of such an one, but ought to have apprehended him, *&c.*

Sect. 22. Neither shall a Man in any Case justify the killing another Crom. 27. b. H. P. C. 56. by a Pretence of Necessity, unless he were himself wholly without Fault in bringing that Necessity upon himself; for if a Man, in Defence of an Injury done by himself, kill any Person whatsoever, he is guilty of Manslaughter at least; as where divers Rioters wrongfully detain a House by Force, and kill those who attack it from without, and endeavour to burn it.

Sect. 23. Neither can a Man justify the killing another in Defence of H.P.C.40,57. Cro. Ca. 538. Dalt. cap. 98. his House or Goods, or even of his Person, from a bare private Trespass; and therefore he that kills another, who claiming a Title to his House, attempts to enter it by Force and shoots at it, or that breaks open his Windows in order to arrest him, or that persists in breaking his Hedges after he is forbidden, is guilty of Manslaughter; and he who in his own Defence kills another that assaults him in his House in the Day-time, and plainly appears to intend to beat him only, is guilty of Homicide *se defendendo*, for which he forfeits his Goods, but is pardoned of Course; Pult. 119. a. H. P. C. 40. Crom. 28. a. 3 Inst. 138. Poph. 121. yet it seems, That a private Person, and, *à fortiori*, an Officer of Justice, who happens unavoidably to kill another in endeavouring to defend himself from, or suppress dangerous Rioters, may justifie the Fact, inasmuch as he only does his Duty in aid of the publick Justice.

Sect. 24. And I can see no Reason why a Person, who without Provocation, is assaulted by another in any Place whatsoever, in such a Manner N.Bendlo.47. 1 And. 41. as plainly shews an Intent to murder him, as by discharging a Pistol, or pushing at him with a drawn Sword, *&c.* may not justify killing such an Assailant, as much as if he had attempted to rob him: For is not he who attempts to murder me more injurious than he who barely attempts to rob me? And can it be more justifiable to fight for my Goods than for my Life? And it is not only highly agreeable to Reason, that a Man in such Circumstances may lawfully kill another, but it seems also to be Crom. 27. b. 28. b. Dalt. cap. 98. S. P. C. 15. a. 3 Inst. 57. confirmed by the general Tenor of our Law-Books, which speaking of Homicide *se defendendo*, suppose it done in some Quarrel or Affray; from whence it seems reasonable to conclude, That where the Law judges a Man guilty of Homicide *se defendendo*, there must be some precedent Quarrel, in which both Parties always are, or at least may justly be sup- Bacon 33. posed to have been, in some Fault, so that the Necessity to which a Man is at length reduced to kill another is in some Measure presumed to have been owing to himself: For it cannot be imagined, That the Law, which is founded on the highest Reason, will adjudge a Man to forfeit all his Goods, and put him to the Necessity of purchasing his Pardon, without some Appearance of a Fault. And though it may be said, That there is none in Chance-medley, and yet that the Party's Goods are also forfeited by that. I answer, That Chance-medley may be intended to proceed from some Negligence, or at least want of sufficient Caution in the Party, who is so unfortunate as to commit it, so that he doth not seem to be altogether faultless. Besides, one of the Reasons S. P. C. 15. Dalt. cap. 98. given in our Law-Books for which Homicide *se defendendo* forfeits Goods, is because thereby a true Man is killed; but it seems absurd, That he who apparently attempts to murder another, which is the most heinous of all Felonies, should be esteemed such, when those who attempt other Felonies, which seem to be much less criminal, are allowed to be killed as downright Villains, not deserving the Protection or Regard of the Law.

Sect. 25. However, perhaps in all these Cases, there ought to be a Distinction between an Assault in the Highway and an Assault in a Town; for in the first Case it is said, That the Person assaulted may justifie killing the other without giving back at all: But that in the second Case, he ought to retreat as far as he can without apparently hazarding his Life, in respect of the Probability of getting Assistance. N Bendlo. 47. Crom. 27. b. 28. a. Dal cap. 98. H. P. C. 42.

II. Also the killing of an innocent Person in the Defence of a Man's self, is said to be justifiable in some special Cases, as,

Sect. 26. I. If two be shipwreck'd together, and one of them get upon a Plank to save himself, and the other also, having no other Means to save his Life, get upon the same Plank, and finding it not able to support them both, thrust the other from it, whereby he is drowned, it seems that he who thus preserves his own Life at the Expence of that of another, may justifie the Fact by the inevitable Necessity of the Case. Dal. cap. 98.

Sect. 27. II. If a Man be awakened in the Night with an Alarm that Thieves are in his House, and searching for them in the dark with his Sword drawn, happen to kill a Person lying hid in Part of the House, who in Truth had no ill Design, and was brought thither by a Servant in order to assist in cleaning the House, it seemeth that he may justifie the Fact, inasmuch as it hath not the Appearance of a Fault. Cro. Car. 538. March. 5.

CHAP. XXIX.

Of Excusable Homicide.

EXcusable Homicide is either *per infortunium*, or *se defendendo*.

In treating of which, I shall first shew the Nature of each of them distinctly, and then consider those Properties wherein they both agree.

Sect. 1. And first of Homicide *per Infortunium*, or by Misadventure, which is where a Man in doing a lawful Act, without any Intent of Hurt, unfortunately chances to kill another; as, 3 Inst. 56. H. P. C. 31.

Sect. 2. I. Where a Labourer being at Work with a Hatchet, the Head thereof flies off, and kills one who stands by. 6 Ed. 4. 7. b. Bro. Coro. 59. 148.

Sect. 3. II. Where a third Person whips a Horse on which a Man is riding, whereupon he springs out, and runs over a Child and kills him, in which Case the Rider is guilty of Homicide *per infortunium*; and he who gave the Blow, of Manslaughter. H P. C. 58, 59.

Sect. 4. III. Where a Workman, having first given loud Warning to all Persons to stand clear, flings down a Piece of Timber from a private House standing out of the Road, and thereby kills one who happens to be underneath: (But if any Person fling down such a Piece of Timber idly in Play, or even a Workman fling it down in the Streets of a Town, where the Danger is apparent in respect of the number of People continually passing by, he is guilty of Manslaughter.) Kelynge 40. Bract. lib. 3. cap. 4. Dalt. ca. 96. H. P. C. 31. Bro. Coro. 229.

Sect. 5. IV. Where a Schoolmaster in correcting his Scholar, or a Father his Son, or a Master his Servant, or an Officer in whipping a Criminal condemned to such Punishment, happens to occasion his Death; (yet if such Persons in their Correction, be so barbarous as to exceed all Bounds of Moderation, and thereby cause the Party's Death, they are guilty of Manslaughter at the least; and if they make use of Bract. lib. 1. ca. 4. H. P. C. 31. Crom. 28. b. Dalt. cap. 96. Kellw. 136.

Kelynge 65. Vide 5 Mod. 287, 288, &c.

an Inſtrument improper for Correction, and apparently indangering the Party's Life, as an iron Bar, or Sword, *&c.* or kick him to the Ground, and then ſtamp on his Belly and kill him, they are guilty of Murder.)

Kellw. 108. Bro Cor. 148. Vid Kelynge 41.

Sect. 6. V. Where one lawfully uſing an innocent Diverſion, as ſhooting at Butts, or at a Bird, *&c.* by the glancing of an Arrow, or ſuch like Accident, kills another.

Kellw. 108, 136. Crom. 29 a. 11 H. 7. 23. a.

Sect. 7. VI. Where a Perſon happens to kill another in playing a Match of Foot-ball, Wreſtling, or ſuch like Sports which are attended with no apparent Danger of Life, and intended only for the Trial, Exerciſe, and Improvement, of the Strength, Courage, and Activity of the Parties.

a 11 H 7. 23. a. 3 Inſt. 160. Kellw. 108, 136 H. P. C. 31.

Sect. 8. [a] VII. Where one kills another in fighting at Barriers or Tilting by the King's Command, which by the better Opinion, ſecures him from being guilty of Felony, by Reaſon of any ſuch unfortunate Accident.

Dalt. cap. 96. Hob. 134 Cromp 29 a. Con Bro. Cor. 22. b H P C. 31. H P. C. 32. c H. P. C. 58.

Sect. 9. [b] But if a Perſon kill another by ſhooting at a Deer, *&c.* in a third Perſon's Park, in the doing whereof he is a Treſpaſſer; or by ſhooting off a Gun, or throwing Stones in a City or Highway, or other Place where Men uſually reſort; or [c] by throwing Stones at another wantonly in Play, which is a dangerous Sport, and has not the leaſt Appearance of any good Intent; or by doing any other ſuch idle Action as cannot but indanger the bodily Hurt of ſome one or other; or by tilting or playing at Hand-ſword without the King's Command; or by parrying with naked Swords covered with Buttons at the Points, or with Swords in the Scabbards, or ſuch like raſh Sports, which cannot be uſed without the manifeſt Hazard of Life, he is guilty of Manſlaughter.

Con. Hob. 134. Dalt. cap. 98. H. P. C. 57. Aleyn 12.

H.P.C. 52, 57. Kelynge 117.

Sect. 10. And if a Man happen to kill another in the Execution of a malicious and deliberate Purpoſe to do him a perſonal Hurt, by wounding or beating him; or in the wilful Commiſſion of any unlawful Act, which neceſſarily tends to raiſe Tumults and Quarrels, and conſequently cannot but be attended with the Danger of perſonal Hurt to ſome one or other; as by committing a Riot, robbing a Park, *&c.* he ſhall be adjudged guilty of Murder.

3 Inſt. 56. Kelynge 117. Supra Ch. 27. Sect 4. H. P. C 52.

Sect. 11. And *à fortiori*, he ſhall come under the ſame Conſtruction, who in the Purſuance of a deliberate Intention to commit a Felony, chances to kill a Man, as by ſhooting at tame Fowl, with an Intent to ſteal them, *&c.* for ſuch Perſons are by no Means favoured, and they muſt at their Peril take care of the Conſequence of their Actions; and it is a general Rule, That where-ever a Man intending to commit one Felony, happens to commit another, he is as much guilty as if he had intended the Felony which he actually commits.

H. P. C. 32. 44. 3 Inſt. 57. Dal. cap. 93. 11 H. 7. 23. a. Bro. Coro. 229. Dalt. cap. 97.

Sect. 12. Neither ſhall he be adjudged guilty of a leſs Crime who kills another, in doing ſuch a wilful Act as ſhews him to be as dangerous as a wild Beaſt, and an Enemy to Mankind in general; as by going deliberately with a Horſe uſed to ſtrike, or diſcharging a Gun, among a Multitude of People, or throwing a great Stone or Piece of Timber from a Houſe into a Street, through which he knows that many are paſſing; and it is no Excuſe that he intended no Harm to any one in particular, or that he meant to do it only for Sport, or to frighten the People, *&c.*

Vide ſupra. Ch. 28. S. 23. 24. H.P.C 40, 41. S. P. C. 15.

Sect. 13. And now I am to conſider Homicide *ſe defendendo*, which ſeems to be where one who has no other poſſible Means of preſerving his Life from one who combats with him on a ſudden Quarrel, or of defending his Perſon from one who attempts to beat him, (eſpecially if ſuch

Attempt be made upon him in his own House,) kills the Person by whom he is reduced to such an inevitable Necessity.

Sect. 14. And not only he who on an Assault retreats to a Wall, or some such Streight, beyond which he can go no farther, before he kills the other, is judged by the Law to act upon unavoidable Necessity: But also he who being assaulted in such a Manner, and in such a Place, that he cannot go back without manifestly indangering his Life, kills the other without retreating at all.

Bro. Coro. 125. 43 Ass. 31. Pult. 119. a. sect. 14. 3 Inst. 56. H. P. C. 41.

Sect. 15. And notwithstanding a Person who retreats from an Assault to the Wall, give the other divers Wounds in his Retreat, yet if he give him no mortal one till he get thither, and then kill him, he is guilty of Homicide *se defendendo* only.

H. P. C. 41. Crom. 28. S. P. C. 15. a. Pult. 119. b. sect. 14.

Sect. 16. And an Officer who kills one that resists him in the Execution of his Office, and even a private Person that kills one who feloniously assaults him in the Highway, may justify the Fact without ever giving back at all.

H. P. C. 41. 3 Inst. 56. Crom. 28. a. Vide supra. Ch. 28. S. 18.

Sect. 17. According to some good Opinions, even he who gives another the first Blow on a sudden Quarrel, if he afterwards do what he can to avoid killing him, is not guilty of Felony; yet such a Person seems to be too much favoured by this Opinion, inasmuch as the Necessity to which he is at last reduced, was at the first so much owing to his own Fault. And it is now agreed, That if a Man strike another upon Malice Prepense, and then fly to the Wall, and there kill him in his own Defence, he is guilty of Murder.

S. P. C. 15. a. Crom. 28. a. Dalt. cap. 98. Kelynge 58. H. P. C. 42. Dalt. cap. 98.

Sect. 18. Thus far of each kind of excusable Homicide distinctly considered, and now I am to consider those Properties wherein they both agree.

Sect. 19. And first it seems clear, That neither of these Homicides are Felonies, because they are not accompanied with a felonious Intent, which is necessary in every Felony.

3 Inst. 56. 2 Inst. 149.

Sect. 20. And from hence it seems plainly to follow, That they were never punishable with Loss of Life: And the same also farther appears from the Writ *de Odio & Atia*, by Vertue whereof, if any Person committed for killing another, were found guilty of either of these Homicides, and no other Crime, he might be bailed; and indeed it seems to be against natural Justice to condemn a Man to Death, for what is owing rather to his Misfortune than his Fault.

Vide infra S. 24.

Sect. 21. It is true indeed, That some of our best Authors have argued from the Statute of *Marlbridge*, ch. 26. which enacts, That *Murdrum de cætero non adjudicetur, ubi Infortunium tantummodo adjudicatum est, &c.* that before this Statute Homicides by Misadventure, or *se defendendo*, were adjudged Murder, and consequently punished by Death.

2 Inst. 56. S. P. C. 16. C.

Sect. 22. But to this it may be answered, That Murder in those Days, signified only the private killing of a Man by one who was neither seen nor heard by any Witness, for which the Offender, if found, was to be tried by Ordeal, and if he could not be found, the Town in which the Fact was done, was to be amerced sixty six Marks, unless it could be proved that the Person killed was an *Englishman*; for otherwise it was presumed that he was a *Dane* or *Norman*, who in those Days were often privately made away by the *English*. And it being a Doubt whether Homicide by Misadventure, *&c.* were to be esteemed Murder in this Sense, it seems to have been the chief Intent of the Makers of this Statute to settle this Question.

Bract. 134. b. Kelynge 121. Bract. 135. a.

Sect.

H.P.C. 98, 99. 2 Inst. 315. Dalt. cap. 98.

Sect. 23. II. However it is certain, That notwithstanding neither of these Offences be Felonies, yet a Person guilty of them is not bailable by Justices of Peace, but must be committed till the next coming of the Justices of Eyre or Gaol-Delivery.

Regist. 133 b. 3 Inst. 42, 315. 9 Co. 56.

Sect. 24. Indeed anciently a Person committed for the Death of a Man, might sue out the Writ *de Odio & Atia*, which by *Magna Charta* 26. is grantable without Fee; and if thereon, by an Inquest taken by the Sheriff, he were found to have done the Fact by Misadventure or *se defendendo*, he might be mainprized by twelve Men, upon the Writ *de ponendo in Ballium*. But such Writs and Enquiries were taken away by the Statute of *Gloucester*, 9 and 28 *Ed.* 3. 9. And though perhaps they were again revived by 42 *Ed.* 3. 1. which makes all Statutes, contrary to *Magna Charta*, void; yet at this Day they seem to be obsolete, and indeed useless, inasmuch as the Party may probably be sooner delivered in the usual Course, by the coming of the Justices of Gaol-Delivery.

S.P.C. 77, G. 2 Inst. 43, 315. 9 Co. 56. Co. Bail and Mainprize, c. 10.

Vide supra. Ch. 28. S. 3.

III. It is also agreed, That no one can excuse the killing another, by setting forth in a special Plea, that he did it by Misadventure or *se defendendo*, but that he must plead Not guilty, and give the special Matter in Evidence. And that where-ever a Person is found guilty of such Homicide, either upon a special Indictment for the same, or by a Verdict setting forth the Circumstances of the Case on a general Indictment of Murder or Homicide, he shall be discharged out of Prison upon Bail and forfeit his Goods: But that upon removing the Record by *Certiorari* into Chancery, he shall have his Pardon of Course, without staying for any Warrant from the King to that Purpose.

4 H. 7. 2. a. Kellw. 53 a. 108. b. 2 Inst. 316. S. P. C 15 b. 16. b. Dalt. cap. 96, 98. F. N. B. 246. C. H.

CHAP. XXX.

Of Manslaughter.

HOmicide against the Life of another, amounting to Felony, is either with or without Malice.

3 Inst. 55, 57. Dalt. cap 94. H.P.C. 56, 57.

Sect. 1. That which is without Malice is called Manslaughter, or sometimes Chance-medley, by which we understand such killing as happens either on a sudden Quarrel, or in the Commission of an unlawful Act, without any deliberate Intention of doing any Mischief at all.

H. P. C. 217.

Sect. 2. And from hence it follows, That there can be no Accessaries to this Offence before the Fact, because it must be done without Premeditation.

Sect. 3. But the Learning relating to this Head being for the most part co-incident with that of others, it will be superfluous to enlarge on it here; and therefore I shall refer the Reader to other Chapters for the particular Cases, as to the following Chapter of Murder, from Section 21 to 32. for those concerning Duelling; and to the said Chapter, Sections 47, 48, 49. and to Chapter 28. Sections 14, 15. for such as happen in a Riot, *&c.* and to Chapter 29 from Section 6 to Section 13. for such as fall out in the Execution of a rash, unlawful Action.

Sect. 4. But there is a particular kind of Manslaughter proper to be considered here, from which the Benefit of the Clergy is taken away by 1 *Jac.* 1, 8. *Where any Person shall stab or thrust any Person or Persons that hath not then any Weapon drawn, or that hath not then first striken, the Party which shall so stab or thrust, so as the Person or Persons so stabbed or thrust, shall thereof die within the Space of six Months then next following, although it cannot be proved that the same was done of Malice fore-thought.*

Sect. 5. It is generally holden, That this Statute is but declarative of the Common Law, and in the Construction thereof, the following Points have been resolved. 1 Bulst. 87. Kelynge 55.

Sect. 6. I. That where-ever a Person who happens to kill another, was struck by him in the Quarrel before he gave the mortal Wound, he is out of the Statute, though he himself gave the first Blow. 1 Jon. 240. Vide 3 Lev. 266.

Sect. 7. II. That he only who actually gives the Stroke, and not any of those who may be said to do it by Construction of Law, as being present, and aiding and abetting the Fact, are within the Statute; from whence it follows, That if it cannot be proved by whom the Stroke was given, none can be found guilty within the Statute. H. P. C. 58. Aleyn 44.

Sect 8. III. That the Killing of a Man with a Hammer, or such like Instrument, which cannot come properly under the Words Thrust, or Stab, is not a Killing within the Statute; but it seems that the discharging a Pistol, or throwing a Pot, or other dangerous Weapon at the Party, is within the Equity of the Words, *having a Weapon drawn*; for Penal Statutes are construed strictly against the Subject, and favourably and equitably for him. 1 Jones 432. 3 Lev. 266.

Sect. 9. IV. That there is no need to lay the Conclusion of the Indictment *contra formam Statuti*, because the Statute makes no new Offence, but only takes away the Privilege of the Clergy from an old one, and leaves it to the Judgment of the Common Law; from whence it follows, That a Person indicted on the Statute, may be found guilty of Manslaughter generally. Also from the same Ground it hath been resolved, That if both an Indictment lay, and a Verdict also find, a Fact to be *contra formam Statuti*, which cannot possibly be so, as that *A.* and *B.* aided and abetted *C. contra formam Statuti*, yet neither such Indictment nor Verdict are void, but *A.* and *B.* shall be dealt with in the same Manner as they should have been, if those Words *contra formam Statuti* had been wholly omitted, because the Substance of the Indictment being found, they may be rejected as Surplus and Senseless: And, *à fortiori*, therefore it is certain, that they shall do no Hurt to an Indictment or Verdict containing a Fact which may be within the Statute. H. P. C. 58. H. P. C. 58, 266. Aleyn 47. Cro. Jac. 283.

Sect. 10. V. That as these Words *contra formam Statuti*, do not vitiate an Indictment which would be good without them; so also, That they will not supply a Defect in a vitious one, which does not specially pursue the Statute. H. P. C. 58.

CHAP. XXXI.

Of Murder.

HOmicide against the Life of another amounting to Felony with Malice, is either Murder or Petit Treason.

Brac. 134. b. 135. a. Kelynge 121. &c. Brac. 121. a.

Sect. 1. And first of Murder, which anciently signified only the private killing of a Man, for which by Force of a Law introduced by King *Canutus* for the Preservation of his *Danes*, the Town or Hundred where the Fact were done, was to be amerced to the King, unless they could prove that the person slain were an *Englishman*, (which Proof was called *Englescbire*,) or could produce the Offender, *&c.* And in those Days, the open wilful killing of a Man through Anger or Malice, *&c.* was not called Murder, but voluntary Homicide.

S. P. C. 18. b. 19. a.

Sect. 2. But the said Law concerning *Englescbire* having been abolished by 14 *Ed.* 3. 4. the Killing of any *Englishman* or Foreigner through Malice prepense, whether committed openly or secretly, was by Degrees called Murder; and 13 *Ric.* 2. 1. which restrains the King's Pardon in certain Cases, does in the Preamble, under the general Name of Murder, include all such Homicide as shall not be pardoned without special Words; and in the Body of the Act expresses the same by Murder, or Killing by Await, Assault, or Malice prepensed. And doubtless the Makers of 23 *H.* 8. *cap.* 1. which excluded all wilful Murder of Malice prepense from the Benefit of the Clergy, intended to include open, as well as private, Homicide within the Word Murder.

Sect. 3. By Murder therefore at this Day we understand, the wilful killing of any Subject whatsoever, through Malice fore-thought, whether the Person slain be an *Englishman* or Foreigner.

And for the better understanding hereof, I shall examine the following Particulars:

1. In what Cases a Man may be said to kill another.
2. In what Places such Killing is within the Cognizance of the Law.
3. Who are such Persons by killing of whom a Man may commit Murder.
4. What Killing shall be adjudged to be Malice prepense, or Murder.

3 Inst. 48. H. P. C. 53. Palm. 548.

Sect. 4. As to the first Point, *viz.* In what Cases a Man may be said to kill another; not only he who by a Wound or Blow, or by Poisoning, Strangling, or Famishing, *&c.* directly causes another's Death, but also in many Cases, he who by wilfully and deliberately doing a Thing which apparently endangers another's Life, thereby occasions his Death, shall be adjudged to kill him.

Crom. 24 b. Pult. 122. a. b. Dalt. cap 93.

Sect. 5. And such was the Case of him who carried his sick Father, against his Will, in a cold frosty Season, from one Town to another, by Reason whereof he died.

Sect. 6. Such also was the Case of the Harlot, who being delivered of a Child, left it in an Orchard covered only with Leaves, in which Condition it was struck by a Kite, and died thereof. Crom. 24 b. Dal. cap. 93.

Sect. 7. And in some Cases a Man shall be said, in the Judgment of the Law, to kill one who is in Truth actually killed by another, or by himself; as where one by Duress [a] of Imprisonment compels a Man to accuse an innocent Person, who on his Evidence is condemned and executed; or where one incites a [b] Madman to kill himself or another; or where one lays [c] Poison with an Intent to kill one Man, which is afterwards accidentally taken by another, who dies thereof. [a] S.P.C. 36.c. 3 Inst. 91. [b] Dal. cap. 93. Supra Ch. 1. S. 7. [c] Plow. Com. 474.

Sect. 8. Also he who wilfully neglects to prevent a Mischief, which he may, and ought to provide against, is, as some have said, in Judgment of the Law, the actual Cause of the Damage which ensues; and therefore if a Man have an Ox or Horse, which he knows to be mischievous, by being used to gore or strike at those who come near them, and do not tie them up, but leave them to their Liberty, and they afterwards kill a Man, according to some Opinions, the Owner may be indicted, as having himself feloniously killed him; and this is agreeable to the *Mosaical* Law. However, as it is agreed by all, such a Person is certainly guilty of a very gross Misdemeanour. 9 Co. 81. Fitz. Corone 311. S. P. C. 17. a. Crom. 24. b. Dalt. cap. 93. Pult. 122. b. H. P. C. 53. Exodus c. 21. v. 29.

Sect. 9. Also it is agreed, That no Person shall be adjudged by any Act whatever to kill another, who doth not die thereof within a Year and a Day after; in the Computation whereof, the whole Day on which the Hurt was done shall be reckoned the first. H. P. C. 55. Pult. 123. a. Dalt. cap. 93. S. P. C. 21. d.

Sect. 10. But if a Person hurt by another, die thereof within a Year and a Day, it is no Excuse for the other that he might have recovered, if he had not neglected to take care of himself. 3 Inst. 53. Kelynge 26. 1 Keb. 17.

Sect. 11. As to the second Point, *viz.* In what Places such killing is within the Conusance of the Law, it seems, That the Killing of one who is both wounded and dies out of the Realm, or wounded out of the Realm and dies here, cannot be determined at common Law, because it cannot be tried by a Jury of the Neighbourhood where the Fact was done. But it is agreed, That the Death of one who is both wounded and dies beyond Sea, and it is said by some, That the Death of him who dies here of a Wound given there, may be heard and determined before the Constable and Marshal, according to the Civil Law, if the King please to appoint a Constable. And it seemeth also to be clear, That such a Fact being examined by the Privy Council, may by Force of 33 *H.* 8. 23. be tried (in Relation to the principal Offenders, but not as to the Accessaries) before Commissioners appointed by the King in any County in *England.* 3 Inst. 48. 2 Inst. 51. Co. Lit. 75. S.P.C. 65. a. Bro. Appeal. 153. Cro. Car. 247. 1 And. 195.

Sect. 12. A Murder at Sea was anciently cognizable only by the Civil Law, but now by Force of 27 *H.* 8. 4. and 28 *H.* 8. 15. it may be tried and determined before the King's Commissioners in any County of *England* according to the Course of the Common Law; yet the Killing of one who dies at Land of a Wound received at Sea, is neither determinable at Common Law, nor by Force of either of these Statutes; but it seems, that it may be tried by the Constable and Marshal, or before Commissioners appointed in Pursuance of the aforesaid Statute of 33 *H.* 8. 23. 3 Inst. 48, 49. 1 Leon 270. H. P. C. 54. 3 Inst. 48.

Sect. 13. It is said by some, That the Death of one who died in one County, of a Wound given in another, was not indictable at all at Common Law, because the Offence was not compleat in either County, and the Jury could enquire only of what happened in their own County. But it hath been holden by others, That if the Corps were carried into the 3 Inst. 48, 49. Bro. Coro. 140, 141, 143. Indictm. 13, 45. S. P. C. 90. c. 6 H. 7. 10. a.

Finch. Law 431. S. P. C. 182. c. Bro. Appeal. 3, 80, 83, 85, 149

the County where the Stroke was given, the whole might be enquired of by a Jury of the same County: And it is agreed, That an Appeal might be brought in either County, and the Fact tried by a Jury returned jointly from each: And at this Day by Force of 2 and 3 *Ed.* 6. 24. the whole is triable by a Jury of the County wherein the Death shall happen, on an Indictment found, or Appeal brought, in the same County.

Cro. Car. 247. 1 Jon. 255. 1 Lev. 118. Latch. 12. 118

Sect. 14. Also by Force of 26 *H.* 8. 6. a Murder in *Wales* may be enquired of in an adjoining *English* County, but Appeals must still be brought in the proper County.

3 Inst. 50.

Sect. 15. As to the third Point, *viz.* Who are such Persons by killing of whom a Man may commit Murder; it is agreed, That the malicious Killing of any Person, whatsoever Nation or Religion he be of, or of whatsoever Crime attainted, is Murder.

Bract. 121. S. P. C. 21. Bro. Coro. 91. H. P. C. 53. 3 Inst. 50. 3 Ass. 2. Bro. Coro. 68. Dalt. cap 93.

Sect. 16. And it was anciently holden, That the causing of an Abortion by giving a Potion to, or striking, a Woman big with Child, was Murder: But at this Day, it is said to be a great Misprision only, and not Murder, unless the Child be born alive, and die thereof, in which Case it seems clearly to be Murder, notwithstanding some Opinions to the contrary. And in this Respect also, the Common Law seems to be agreeable to the *Mosaical*, which as to the Purpose is thus expressed, *If Men strive and hurt a Woman with Child, so that her Fruit depart from her, and yet no Mischief follow, he shall be surely punished, according as the Woman's Husband will lay upon him, and he shall pay as the Judges determine; And if any Mischief follow, then thou shalt give Life for Life.*

Exodus c. 21. v. 22, 23.

Dyer 186. 3 Inst. 51.

Sect. 17. It seems also agreed, That where one counsels a Woman to kill her Child when it shall be born, who afterwards does kill it in Pursuance of such Advice, he is an Accessary to the Murder.

Kelynge 127.

Sect. 18. As to the fourth Point, *viz.* What Killing shall be adjudged of Malice prepense or Murder; it is to be observed, That any formed Design of doing Mischief may be called Malice; and therefore that not such Killing only as proceeds from premeditated Hatred or Revenge against the Person killed, but also in many other Cases, such as is accompanied with those Circumstances that shew the Heart to be perversly wicked, is adjudged to be of Malice prepense, and consequently Murder.

Kelynge 130.

Sect. 19. And according to this Notion, I shall consider,

Such Murder as is occasioned through an express Purpose to do some personal Injury to him who is slain in particular, which seems to be most properly called express Malice.

Kelynge 129. 130.

2. Such as happens in the Execution of an unlawful Action, principally intended for some other Purpose, and not to do a personal Injury to him in particular who is slain, in which Case the Malice seems to be most properly said to be implied.

Sect. 20. As to Murder in the first Sense, such Acts as shew a direct and deliberate Intent to kill another, as Poisoning, Stabbing, and such like, are so clearly Murder, that I know not any Questions relating thereto worth explaining: But the Cases which have born Dispute, have generally happened in the following Instances;

1. In Duelling.
2. In killing another without any Provocation, or but upon a slight one.
3. In killing one whom the Person killing intended to hurt in a less Degree.

1 Bulst. 86, 87.

Sect. 21. As to the first Instance of this Kind, it seems agreed, That where-ever two Persons in cool Blood meet and fight on a precedent Quar-

rel,

rel, and one of them is killed, the other is guilty of Murder, and cannot help himself by alledging that he was [a] first struck by the Deceased; or that he had often [b] declined to meet him, and was prevailed upon to do it by his Importunity; or that it was his only Intent to vindicate his Reputation; or that he meant not to kill, but only to disarm, his Adversary: For since he deliberately engaged in an Act highly unlawful, in Defiance of the Laws, he must at his Peril abide the Consequences thereof. [a] 2 Bulst. 147. Crom. 22 b. [b] 1 Rol. Rep. 360. 3 Bulst. 171. H. P. C. 48.

Sect. 22. And from hence it clearly follows, That if two Persons quarrel over Night, and appoint to fight the next Day; or quarrel in the Morning, and agree to fight in the Afternoon; or such a considerable Time after, by which, in common Intendment, it must be presumed that the Blood was cooled, and then they meet and fight, and one kill the other, he is guilty of Murder. 3 Inst. 51. H. P. C. 48. Kelynge 56. 1 Lev. 180.

Sect. 23. And where-ever it appears from the whole Circumstances of the Case, That he who kills another on a sudden Quarrel, was Master of his Temper at the Time, he is guilty of Murder; as if after the Quarrel he fall into other Discourse and talk calmly thereon; or perhaps if he have so much Consideration, as to say, That the Place wherein the Quarrel happens, is not convenient for Fighting; or that if he should fight at present, he should have the Disadvantage by reason of the Height of his Shoes, *&c.* Kelynge 56. 1 Sid. 177. 1 Lev. 180.

Sect. 24. And if *A.* on a Quarrel with *B.* tell him that he will not strike him, but that he will give *B.* a Pot of Ale to strike him, and and thereupon *B.* strike, and *A.* kill him, he is guilty of Murder; for he shall not elude the Justice of the Law by such a Pretence to cover his Malice. H. P. C. 48.

Sect. 25. In like Manner if *B.* challenge *A.* and *A.* refuse to meet him, but in order to evade the Law, tell *B.* that he shall go the next Day to such a Town about his Business, and accordingly *B.* meet him the next Day in the Road to the same Town, and assault him, whereupon they fight, and *A.* kills *B.* he is in my Opinion guilty of Murder, unless it appear by the whole Circumstances that he gave *B.* such Information accidentally, and not with a Design to give him an Opportunity of Fighting. Con. Crom. 22. b. H. P. C. 48.

Sect. 26. And at this Day it seems to be settled, That if a Man assault another with Malice prepense, and after be driven by him to the Wall, and kill him there in his own Defence, he is guilty of Murder, in respect of his first Intent. Crom. 22. b. Palt. 119. b. Dalt. cap 93. H. P. C. 47. Kelynge 58, 129.

Sect. 27. And it hath been adjudged, That even upon a sudden Quarrel, if a Man be so far provoked by any bare Words or Gestures of another, as to make a Push at him with a Sword, or to strike at him with any other such Weapon as manifestly indangers his Life, before the other's Sword is drawn, and thereupon a Fight ensue, and he who made such Assault kill the other, he is guilty of Murder; because that by assaulting the other in such an outrageous Manner, without giving him an Opportunity to defend himself, he shewed that he intended not to fight with him, but to kill him, which violent Revenge is no more excused by such a slight Provocation, than if there had been none at all. Crom. 23. a. b. Dalt. cap. 93. Kelyn. 61. and Mawgridge's Case.

Sect. 28. But it is said, That if he who draws upon another in a sudden Quarrel, make no Pass at him till his Sword is drawn, and then fight with him, and kill him, he is guilty of Manslaughter only, because that by neglecting the Opportunity of killing the other before he was on Kelynge 55, 61, 131.

his Guard, and in a Condition to defend himſelf, with like Hazard to both, he ſhew'd that his Intent was not ſo much to kill, as to combat with the other, in Compliance with thoſe common Notions of Honour, which prevailing over Reaſon, during the Time that a Man is under the Tranſports of a ſudden Paſſion, ſo far mitigate his Offence in Fighting, That it ſhall not be adjudged to be of Malice prepenſe.

2 Rol. Re. 461.

Sect. 29. And if two happen to fall out upon a ſudden, and preſently agree to fight, and each of them fetch a Weapon, and go into the Field, and there one kill the other, he is guilty of Manſlaughter only, becauſe he did it in the Heat of Blood.

H. P. C. 48. 3 Inſt. 51.

Sect. 30. And ſuch an Indulgence is ſhewn to the Frailties of humane Nature, That where two Perſons who have formerly fought on Malice, are afterwards to all Appearance reconciled, and fight again on a freſh Quarrel, it ſhall not be preſumed that they were moved by the old Grudge, unleſs it appear by the whole Circumſtances of the Fact.

Crom. 23. a. Dalt. cap. 93. H. P. C. 49. 1 Rol. Rep. 360. 3 Bulſt. 171.

Sect. 31. But the Law ſo far abhors all Duelling in cold Blood, That not only the Principal who actually kills the other, but alſo his Seconds are guilty of Murder, whether they fought or not; and ſome have gone ſo far as to hold, That the Seconds of the Perſon killed are alſo equally guilty, in Reſpect of that Countenance which they give to their Principals in the Execution of their Purpoſe, by accompanying them therein, and being ready to bear a Part with them: But perhaps the contrary Opinion is the more plauſible; for it ſeems too ſevere a Conſtruction to make a Man by ſuch Reaſoning the Murderer of his Friend, to whom he was ſo far from intending any Miſchief, that he was ready to hazard his own Life in his Quarrel.

H. P. C. 51. Dalt. cap 93. H. P. C. 51.

Sect. 32. And now I am to conſider the ſecond Inſtance of this kind, *viz.* Such Murder as happens in killing another without any Provocation, or but upon a ſlight one; as to which it is to be obſerved, That where-ever it appears that a Man killed another, it ſhall be intended, *prima facie,* that he did it maliciouſly, unleſs he can make out the contrary, by ſhewing that he did it on a ſudden Provocation, *&c.*

Kelynge 27

Sect. 33. Alſo it ſeems to be agreed, That no [a] Breach of a Man's Word or Promiſe, no Treſpaſs either to [b] Lands or Goods, no Affront by bare [c] Words or Geſtures, however falſe or malicious it may be, and aggravated with the moſt provoking Circumſtances, will excuſe him from being guilty of Murder, who is ſo far tranſported thereby, as immediately to attack the Perſon who offends him, in ſuch a Manner as maniſeſtly endangers his Life, without giving him Time to put himſelf upon his Guard, if he kills him in Purſuance of ſuch Aſſault, whether the Perſon ſlain did at all fight in his Defence or not; for ſo baſe and cruel a Revenge cannot have too ſevere a Conſtruction.

[a] Kelynge 135. 2 Rol. Rep. 460, 461. [b] Kelynge 131, &c. Dalt. cap. 93. [c] Cro. El. 779. Noy. 171. 1 Sid. 277. 1 Levin. 180. Hob. 121. Con. 1 Jon. 432. a.

Sect. 34. But if a Perſon ſo provoked, had beaten the other only in ſuch a Manner, that it might plainly appear that he meant not to kill, but only chaſtiſe him; or if he had reſtrained himſelf till the other had put himſelf on his Guard, and then in fighting with him had killed him, he had been guilty of Manſlaughter only.

Kelynge 131. Kelynge 55, 61, 131.

Sect. 35. And of the like Offence ſhall he be adjudged guilty, who ſeeing two Perſons fighting together on a private Quarrel, whether ſudden or malicious, takes Part with one of them, and kills the other.

Kelynge 61, 136. Cro. Jac. 296. 12 Co. 87.

Sect. 36. Neither can he be thought guilty of a greater Crime, who [a] finding a Man in Bed with his Wife, or being actually [b] ſtruck by him, or pulled by the Noſe, or fillipped upon the Forehead, immediately kills him;

[a] Kelynge 137. Raym. 212. 2 Keb. 829. [b] Kelynge 135.

him; or [c] who happens to kill another in a Contention for the Wall; or [d] in the Defence of his Perſon from an unlawful Arreſt; or [e] in the Defence of his Houſe from thoſe who claiming a Title to it, attempt forcibly to enter it, and to that Purpoſe ſhoot at it, &c. or in [f] the Defence of his Poſſeſſion of a Room in a Publick Houſe, from thoſe who attempt to turn him out of it, and thereupon draw their Swords upon him; in which Caſe the killing the Aſſailant hath been holden by ſome to be juſtifiable: But it is certain, That it can amount to no more than Manſlaughter.

[c] H. P. C. 57. 3 Inſt. 55. [d] Kelynge 137. [e] H. P. C. 57. Crom. 27. a. [f] Kelynge 51.

Sect. 37. Nor was he judged criminal in a higher Degree, who ſeeing his Son's Noſe bloody, and being told by him, That he had been beaten by ſuch a Boy, ran three Quarters of a Mile, and having found the Boy, beat him with a ſmall Cudgel, whereof he afterwards died.

H. P. C. 48. Cro. Jac. 296. 12 Co. 87.

Sect. 38. And now we are come to the third Inſtance of this kind, *viz.* Such Murder as happens in killing one whom the Perſon killing, intended to hurt in a leſs Degree; as to which it is to be obſerved, That where-ever a Perſon in cool Blood by way of Revenge, unlawfully and deliberately beats another in ſuch a Manner, that he afterwards dies thereof, he is guilty of Murder, however unwilling he might have been to have gone ſo far.

Kelyn. Mawgridge's Caſe. H. P. C. 49. 50, 51, 52.

Sect. 39. Alſo it ſeems, That he who upon a ſudden Provocation executeth his Revenge in ſuch a cruel Manner, as ſhews a cool and deliberate Intent to do Miſchief, is guilty of Murder, if Death enſue; as where the Keeper of a Park finding a Boy ſtealing Wood, tied him to a Horſe's Tail and beat him, whereupon the Horſe ran away and killed him.

Cro. Car. 131. 1 Jon. 198. Palm. 545. H. P. C. 49.

Sect. 40. And now I am to conſider the ſecond general Branch of this Head, *viz.* In what Caſes ſuch killing ſhall be adjudged Murder, which happens in the Execution of an unlawful Action, principally intended for ſome other Purpoſe, and not to do a perſonal Injury to him in particular who happens to be ſlain; and this I ſhall conſider in the following Inſtances:

1. Where the principal Intention is to commit another Felony.
2. Where the principal Deſign is to commit a bare Breach of the Peace, not intended againſt the Perſon of him who happens to be ſlain.
3. Where the chief Motive is to aſſiſt a third Perſon.
4. Where the direct Deſign is to eſcape from an Arreſt.
5. Where the principal Purpoſe is to uſurp an illegal Authority.
6. Where no Miſchief is intended at all.

Sect. 41. As to the firſt Particular, *viz.* Such killing as happens in the Execution of an unlawful Action, whereof the principal Intention was to commit another Felony; it ſeems agreed, That where-ever a Man happens to kill another in the Execution of a deliberate Purpoſe to commit any Felony, he is guilty of Murder; as where a Perſon ſhooting at tame Fowl, with an Intent to ſteal them, accidentally kills a Man; or where one ſets upon a Man to rob him, and kills him in making Reſiſtance; or where a Perſon ſhooting at, or fighting with one Man, with a Deſign to murder him, miſſes him and kills another.

H. P. C. 50. Kelynge 117. H. P. C. 46, 50. Dalt. cap. 93. Moore 87.

Sect. 42. And not only in such Cases where the very Act of a Person having such a felonious Intent, is the immediate Cause of a third Person's Death, but also where it any Way occasionally causes such a Misfortune, Pl.Crom.474. it makes him guilty of Murder; and such was the Case of the Husband, who gave a poisoned Apple to his Wife, who eat not enough of it to kill her, but innocently, and against the Husband's Will and Perswasion, gave Part of it to a Child who died thereof; such also was the Case of 9 Co. 81. the Wife who mixed Ratsbane in a Potion sent by an Apothecary to her Husband, which did not kill him, but afterwards killed the Apothecary, who to vindicate his Reputation tasted it himself, having first stirred it about. Neither is it material in this Case, That the stirring of the Potion might make the Operation of the Poison more forcible than otherwise it would have been; for inasmuch as such a murderous Intention, which of it self perhaps in strictness might justly be made punishable with Death, proves now in the Event the Cause of the King's losing a Subject, it shall be as severely punished as if it had had the intended Effect, the missing whereof is not owing to any want of Malice, but of Power.

Pl.Crom.474. 9 Co. 81.b. *Sect.* 43. But if one happen to be poisoned by Ratsbane laid in order to destroy Vermine, the Person by whom he is so killed is guilty of Homicide *per infortunium* only, because his Intentions were wholly innocent.

H. P. C. 50. *Sect.* 44. Also if a third Person accidentally happen to be kill'd by one engaged in a Combat with another upon a sudden Quarrel, it seems that he who kills him is guilty of Manslaughter only; but it hath been H. P. C. 45. 3 Inst. 52. Dal cap. 93. Savil. 67. Kelynge 66. 22 Ass. 71. H. P. C. 50. 4 Co. 40. b. 9 Co 68. Crom.25.a.b. adjudged, That if a Justice of Peace, Constable, or Watchman, or even a private Person, be killed in endeavouring to part those whom he sees fighting, the Person by whom he is killed, is guilty of Murder; and that he cannot excuse himself by alledging that what he did was in a sudden Affray in the Heat of Blood, and through the Violence of Passion; for he who carries his Resentments so high, as not only to execute his Revenge against those who have affronted him, but even against such as have no otherwise offended him but by doing their Duty, and endeavouring to restrain him from breaking through his, shews such an obstinate Contempt of the Laws, that he is no more to be favoured, than if he had acted in cool Blood.

Kelynge 66. *Sect.* 45. Yet it hath been resolved, That if the third Person slain in such a sudden Affray, do not give Notice for what Purpose he comes, by commanding the Parties in the King's Name to keep the Peace, or otherwise manifestly shewing his Intention to be not to take Part in the Quarrel, but to appease it, he who kills him is guilty of Manslaughter only, for he might suspect that he came to side with his Adversary.

Sect. 46. As to the second Instance of this kind, *viz.* Such killing as happens in the Execution of an unlawful Action, where the principal Design is to commit a bare Breach of the Peace, not intended against the Person of him who happens to be slain; it seems clear, That where divers Persons resolving generally to resist all Opposers in the Commission of any Breach of the Peace, and to execute it in such a Manner as natu- Savil. 67. Moore 86. Palm. 35. Crom. 24.b. 25.a. H. P. C. 47. 5 Mod. 289. Dyer 128. Pl. 60. S. P. C. 17.b. rally tends to raise Tumults and Affrays, as by committing a violent Desseisin with great Numbers of People, hunting in a Park, *&c.* and in so doing happen to kill a Man, they are all guilty of Murder; for they must at their Peril abide the Event of their Actions, who wilfully engage in such bold Disturbances of the Publick Peace, in open Opposition to, and Defiance of, the Justice of the Nation.

Sect. 47. Yet where divers Rioters having forcible Possession of a House, afterwards killed the Person whom they had ejected, as he was endeavouring in the Night forcibly to regain the Possession, and to fire the House, they were adjudged guilty of Manslaughter only, notwithstanding they did the Fact in Maintenance of a deliberate Injury, perhaps for this Reason, because the Person slain was so much in Fault himself. Crom. 28 b. H. P. C. 56.

Sect. 48. But if in such, or any other, Quarrel, whether it were sudden or premeditated, a Justice of Peace, Constable, or Watchman, or even a private Person, be slain in endeavouring to keep the Peace and suppress the Affray, he who kills him is guilty of Murder; for notwithstanding it was not his primary Intention to commit a Felony, yet inasmuch as he persists in a less Offence with so much Obstinacy as to go on in it to the Hazard of the Lives of those who no otherwise offend him, but by doing their Duty in Maintenance of the Law, which therefore affords them its more immediate Protection, he seems to be in this Respect equally criminal, as if his Intention had been to commit a Felony. H. P. C. 45. Dalt. cap. 93. 3 Inst. 52. Kelynge 66. 22 Ass. 71. 4 Co. 40. b. 9 Co. 68. Crom. 25.

Sect. 49. As to the third Instance of this kind, *viz.* such Killing, as happens in the Execution of an unlawful Action, the principal Motive whereof was to assist a third Person, it seems clear, That if a Master maliciously intending to kill another take his Servants with him, without acquainting them with his Purpose, and meet his Adversary and fight with him, and the Servants seeing their Master engaged take part with him, and kill the other, they are guilty of Manslaughter only, but the Master of Murder. Pl. Crom. 100, 101. a. Crom. 23. Dalt. cap. 93. H. P. C. 51, 52.

Sect. 50. And therefore it follows, *à fortiori*, That if a Man's Servant, or Friend, or even a Stranger, coming suddenly, see him fighting with another and side with him, and kill the other; or seeing his Sword broken send him another, wherewith he kills the other, he is guilty of Manslaughter only. Crom. 26. b. H. P. C. 57. Dalt. cap 94. 1 Rol. Rep. 407, 408. 3 Bulst. 206. H. P. C. 52.

Sect. 51. Yet in this very Case if the Person killed were a Bailiff, or other Officer of Justice, resisted by the Master, *&c.* in the due Execution of his Duty, such Friend or Servant, *&c.* are guilty of Murder, whether they knew that the Person slain were an Officer or not. Kelynge 67, 86, 87.

Sect. 52. But perhaps it may be objected, That in this last Case there seems to be no more Malice than in the former; and such third Person being wholly ignorant that the Party killed was an Officer, seems to be no more in Fault than if he had been a private Person.

Sect. 54. To this it may be answered, That all Fighting is highly unlawful, and that he who on a sudden seeing Persons engaged in it, is so far from endeavouring to part them, as every good Subject ought, that he takes part with one Side, and fights in the Quarrel, without knowing the Cause of it, shews a high Contempt of the Laws, and a Readiness to break through them on a small Occasion, and must at his Peril take heed what he does; and consequently might perhaps in strict Justice be adjudged in the foregoing Cases to act with Malice, which doth not always signify a particular ill Will against the Person killed, as appears by many of the above mentioned Cases; and though such Person be favoured in respect of the suddenness of the Occasion where both the Quarrel and the Persons are private, yet he must not expect such Indulgence, where the Fight, in which he so rashly ingages, was begun in open Opposition to the Justice of the Nation, and a Person happens to be killed thereby who engaged in Maintenance thereof, and on that Account is under its more particular Care; and may justly challenge, that his Op- 1 Sid. 160. Noy. 50. Plow. Com. 100.

Oppofers be made Examples to deter others from joining in fuch unwarrantable Quarrels.

Kelynge 60, 137. Crom. 27. a. Dent's *Case lately adjudged.* *Sect.* 54. But if a Man feeing another arrefted and reftrained from his Liberty, under Colour of a Prefs-Warrant or Civil Procefs, *&c.* by thofe who in Truth have no fuch Authority, happen to kill fuch Trefpaffers in refcuing the Perfon oppreffed, he fhall be adjudged guilty of Manflaughter only, notwithftanding the injured Perfon fubmitted to them, and endeavoured not to refcue himfelf, and the Perfon who refcued him, did not know that he was illegally arrefted; for fince in the Event it appears, that the Perfons flain were Trefpaffers, covering their Violence with a fhew of Juftice, he who kills them is indulged by the Law, which in thefe Cafes judges by the Event, which thofe who engage in fuch unlawful Actions muft abide at their Peril.

Sect. 55. As to the fourth Inftance of this kind, *viz.* Such Killing as happens in the Execution of an unlawful Action, whereof the direct Defign was to efcape from an Arreft, it feems to be agreed, That whoever kills a Sheriff, or any of his Officers, in the lawful Execution of a Civil Procefs, as on arrefting a Perfon upon a *Capias*, *&c.* is guilty of Murder. (Dal. cap. 93. H. P. C. 45. Crom. 24. a.)

9 Co. 68. Cro. Jac. 280. 9 Co. 66. Cro. Jac. 280. 6 Co. 68. b. 69. a. Cro. Jac. 486. 9 Co. 69. *Sect.* 56. Neither is it any Excufe to fuch a Perfon that the Procefs was erroneous, (for it is not void by being fo,) or that the Arreft was in the Night, or that the Officer did not tell him for what caufe he arrefted him, and out of what Court, (which is not neceffary when prevented by the Party's Refiftance;) or that the Officer did not fhew his Warrant, which he is not bound to do at all, if he be a Bailiff commonly known, nor without a Demand, if he be a fpecial one.

Yet the Killing of an Officer in fome Cafes will be Manflaughter only, as,

Cro. Car. 372. 1 Jon. 346. 12 Co. 49. *Sect.* 57. I. Where the Warrant by which he acts gives him no Authority to arreft the Party; as where a Bailiff arrefts *J. S.* a Baronet, who never was knighted, by force of a Warrant to arreft *J. S.* Knight.

Sect. 58. II. Where a good Warrant is executed in an unlawful Manner; as if a Bailiff be killed in breaking open a Door or Window to arreft a Man; or perhaps if he arreft one on a *Sunday* fince 29 *Ca.* 2. 7. by which all fuch arrefts are made unlawful. (H. P. C. 45.)

Sect. 59. As to the fifth Inftance of this kind, *viz.* Such Killing as happens in the Execution of an unlawful Action, whereof the principal Purpofe was to ufurp an illegal Authority, it feems clear, That if Perfons take upon them to put others to Death, either by Vertue of a new Commiffion wholly unknown to our Laws, or by Vertue of any known Jurifdiction, which clearly extends not to Cafes of this Nature; as if the Court of Common Pleas caufe a Man to be executed for Treafon or Felony; or the Court Martial, in Time of Peace, put a Man to Death by the Martial Law, both the Judges and Officers are guilty of Murder. (Supra Ch. 28 S. 5. H. P. C. 46.)

Sect. 60. But where Perfons act by Vertue of a Commiffion, which if it were ftrictly regular would undoubtedly give them full Authority, but happens to be defective only in fome Point of Form, it feems that they are no way criminal.

Sect. 61. As to the fixth Inftance of this kind, *viz.* Such Killing as happens in the Execution of an unlawful Action, where no Mifchief was intended at all, it is faid, That if a Perfon happen to occafion the Death of another, in advifedly doing any idle wanton Action, which cannot but be attended with the manifeft Danger of fome other; as by riding with a Horfe (Vide fupra Ch. 29 S. 12.)

Horse known to be used to kick among a Multitude of People, by which he means no more than to divert himself by putting them into a Fright, he is guilty of Murther.

Sect. 63. Also it has been anciently holden, That if a Person not duly authorized to be a Physician or Surgeon, undertake a Cure, and the Patient die under his Hand, he is guilty of Felony; but inasmuch as the Books wherein this Opinion is holden were written before the Statute of 23 *H.* 8. which first excluded such felonious Killing, as may be called willful Murther of Malice prepense, from the Benefit of Clergy, it may be well questioned, whether such Killing shall be said to be of Malice prepense, within the Intent of that Statute; however it is certainly highly rash and presumptuous for unskilfull Persons to undertake Matters of this Nature; and indeed the Law can not be well too severe in this Case, in order to deter ignorant People from endeavouring to get a Livelihood by such Practice, which can not be followed without the manifest Hazard of the Lives of those who have to do with them: But surely the charitable endeavours of those Gentlemen who study to qualify themselves to give Advice of this Kind, in order to assist their poor Neighbours, can by no Means deserve so severe a Construction from their happening to fall into some Mistakes in their Prescriptions, from which the most learned and experienced can not always be secure.

S P.C. 16. b. Pult. 22. b. Crom. 27. 43 Ed. 3. 33. b. Fitz. Coron. 163.

See Dal. ch. 93.

For other particulars relating to this Head, see the Chapter of Principals and Accessaries, *in the Second Book.*

CHAP. XXXII.

Of Petit Treason.

Sect. 1. AT Common Law not only the Offences specified in 25 *Ed.* 3. but many others also were esteemed Petit Treasons, which are not so at this Day; as [a] Piracy by a Subject; [b] Discovery of the King's Counsel by one of the Grand Jury; an [c] Attempt by a Wife to kill her Husband, *&c.* But by 25 *Ed.* 3. no Offence shall be adjudged Petit Treason, except in the following Instances:

3 Inst. 20, 21. [a] 40 Ass. Pl. 35. [b] 27 Ass. 63. 3 Inst. 22. Dalt. ca. 91. [c] S P.C. 10. b.

1. Where a Servant kills his Master.
2. Where a Wife kills her Husband.
3. Where an Ecclesiastical Man, secular, or religious, kills his Prelate to whom he owes Obedience.

Sect. 2. And this Statute has been so strictly construed, that no other Case whatsoever, which cannot be brought within the Meaning of these Words, however it may be in its own Nature more heinous, shall, by Parity of Reason, be expounded to be within the Equity of them; and therefore the Murther of a Father by a Son shall not be punished as Petit Treason, unless the Son may by a reasonable Construction come under the word Servant, by serving the Father for Meat, Drink, Clothes, or Wages, in which case he shall be indicted by the Name of a Servant.

Dalis. 14. 3 Inst. 20. H. P. C. 24. Dalt. ca. 91. Crom. 91. b.

Sect.

Bro. Treaſ. 8, 12. Plow. Com. 86. 19 H. 6. 47. b. 3 Inſt. 20.

Sect. 3. Yet the Murther of a Miſtreſs, or of a Maſter's Wife, has been adjudged Petit Treaſon within this Statute, for notwithſtanding the Perſons ſlain can in neither of theſe caſes, in good Grammar, come under the word Maſter, yet they are clearly within the meaning thereof, being uſed here to ſignify any Perſon to whom another ſtands related as a Servant.

33 Aſſ. 7. Bro. Coro. 116. S. P. C. 10. Plow. Com. 260. a. 1 Co. 99. b.

Sect. 4. Alſo the Murther of a Perſon by one who was his Servant, upon Malice conceived during the Service, tho' it be not within the expreſs Words, is within the meaning of them, inaſmuch as it is but the Execution of the treaſonable Intention of the Party while he was a Servant.

H. P. C. 24. S. P. C. 10. N. 3 Inſt. 20.

Sect. 5. Alſo the Procuring, Aiding, or Abetting, of any of theſe Offences, is clearly puniſhable within the meaning of this Act, in the ſame manner as it was before; for the plain Intent of the Statute is only to reſtrain the Judges from proceeding againſt other Crimes as Petit Treaſons, but no way to alter the Law as to theſe.

H. P. C. 24. H. P. C. 24. Daliſ. 16. Dalt. ca. 91. Crom. 19, 20. Dy. 254. Pl. 103. Bro. Coro. 119. 40 Aſſ. 25. H. P. C. 215. 3 Inſt. 139. Crom. 19. b. Dy. 128. Pl. 37. Moore 91. Pl. 227. Daliſ. 16. Dy. 332. Pl. 25. Daliſ. 16.

Sect. 6. And therefore it ſeems agreed, That Perſons accuſed of Petit Treaſon ſhall be conſtrued to be either not guilty at all, or Principal or Acceſſary, according to the known Rules of Law in other Caſes; and from hence it follows, That if the Fact appear to have been done upon a ſudden falling out, or in the Party's neceſſary Self-defence, *&c.* it cannot be Petit Treaſon: For inaſmuch as all Petit Treaſon implies Murther, and is the higheſt Degree thereof, where-ever the Circumſtances do not make the Offence Murther, they can not make it Petit Treaſon; and *vice verſâ*, generally where-ever the Circumſtances are ſuch as will make the Killing of a Stranger by a Stranger Murther, they make the Killing of a Huſband, or Maſter, *&c.* Petit Treaſon: Yet it hath been adjudged, That if a Wife, or Servant, procure a Stranger to kill the Huſband, or Maſter, in the Abſence of ſuch Wife, or Servant, neither the Procurer nor Actor are guilty of Petit Treaſon, but of Murther only; becauſe it is an allowed Maxim, That the Offence of an Acceſſary can never be of a higher Kind than that of the Principal; but it ſeems clear, That if the Wife or Servant be either actually preſent, when the Crime is done, or preſent only in Judgment of Law, as being in the ſame Houſe, but not in the ſame Room, (in which caſe the Hopes of their immediate Aſſiſtance encourages and imboldens the Murtherer to commit the Fact, which otherwiſe perhaps he would not have dared to do, and makes them guilty in the ſame Degree as if they had actually ſtood by with their Swords drawn, ready to ſecond the Villany,) ſuch Wife, or Servant, being Principals as much as the Stranger, are guilty of Petit Treaſon, and the Stranger of Murther; but it is ſaid, That if a Wife procure a Servant to kill the Huſband, both are guilty of Petit Treaſon: And even if a Stranger procure a Wife, or Servant, to kill the Huſband, or Maſter, it ſeems that he may be indicted as acceſſary to Petit Treaſon.

CHAP. XXXIII.

Of Simple Larceny.

AND now we are come to Offences againſt the Goods of another, which are generally called Larcenies, from the *Latin* word *Latrocinium*, of which there are two Kinds:

1. Simple Larceny.
2. Mix'd Larceny.

Simple Larceny is alſo of two Kinds,

1. Grand Larceny.
2. Petit Larceny.

Sect. 1. Simple Grand Larceny is a felonious and fraudulent taking, H. P. C. 60
and carrying away, by any Perſon, of the mere perſonal Goods of ano- Dal. ca. 101.
ther, not from the Perſon, nor out of his Houſe, above the Value of
twelve Pence.

For the better Explication of which Definition, I ſhall in order conſider the ſeveral Parts of it; as,

1. What ſhall be ſaid to be a felonious, and fraudulent taking.
2. What ſhall be ſaid to be a carrying away.
3. By whom the Offence may be committed.
4. What are ſuch Goods, the Taking whereof may be felonious.
5. How far ſuch Goods ought to belong to another.
6. Of what Value they muſt be.

Sect. 2. As to the firſt particular, *viz.* what ſhall be ſaid to be a fe- Kelynge 24.
lonious and fraudulent Taking, it is to be obſerved, That all Felony in- Bro. Coro. 45,
cludes Treſpaſs, and that every Indictment of Larceny muſt have the 48, 58, 137,
words *Felonicè cepit*, as well as *aſportavit*, from whence it follows, That if 160. H. P. C. 61.
the Party be guilty of no Treſpaſs in taking the Goods, he cannot be
guilty of Felony in carrying them away.

Sect. 3. And from this Ground it hath been holden, That one who 3 Inſt. 103.
finds ſuch Goods as I have loſt, and converts them to his own Uſe *Ani-* H. P. C. 61.
mo furandi, is no Felon; and, *à fortiori*, therefore it muſt follow, That one
who has the actual Poſſeſſion of my Goods by my Delivery, for a ſpe-
cial Purpoſe, as a Carrier who receives them in order to carry them to a 13 Ed. 4. 9, 10.
certain Place, or a Tailor who has them in order to make me a Suit of S. P. C. 25. a.
Clothes, or a Friend who is intruſted with them to keep for my Uſe, can- 3 Inſt. 108.
not be ſaid to ſteal them, by imbeziling of them afterwards.

Sect. 4. And herein our Law differs from the Civil, which, agreeably S. P. C. 25.
to the *Moſaical* Law, having no capital Puniſhment for bare Thefts, deals *See* Exod. 22.
with Offences of this Kind as ſuch, as in ſtrict Juſtice moſt certainly it
may; but our Law, which puniſhes all Theft with Death, if the Thing
ſtoln be above the Value of twelve Pence, and with corporal Puniſh-
ment if under, rather chuſes to deal with them as civil than criminal Of-
fences, perhaps for this Reaſon in the above mentioned Caſe concerning
Goods loſt, becauſe the Party is not much aggrieved where nothing is
taken but what he had loſt before; and for this Cauſe in the other Caſes,

concerning the imbeziling of Goods delivered to another by the Owner, because the Party being intrusted with the whole Possession, it may be presumed that both the Offender and his Offence are known, and consequently the Person injured is supposed to have a Remedy by Action against him, from which consideration some have made it Part of the Definition of Larceny, that it be committed without the Knowledge of the Owner, and it seems rigorous to have Recourse to severe Laws, where probably more gentle ones will be effectual.

Dalt. ch. 101.

Sect. 5. And agreeably hereto it has been resolved, That even those who have the Possession of Goods by the Delivery of the Party, may be guilty of Felony by taking away Part thereof with an intent to steal it; as if a Carrier open a Pack and take out part of the Goods, or a Weaver who has received Silk to work, or a Miller who has Corn to grind, take out part with an Intent to steal it, in which cases it may not only be said that such Possession of a part distinct from the whole was gained by Wrong, and not delivered by the Owner, but also that it was obtained basely, fraudulently, and clandestinely, in Hopes to prevent its being discovered at all, or fix'd upon any one when discovered.

13 Ed 4 9, 10. S. P. C. 25. A. Dal. ca. 102. Kelynge 35. 1 Rol. Ab. 73. Pl. 16.

Sect. 6. Also it seems generally agreed, That one who has the bare Charge, or the special Use of Goods, but not the Possession of them, as a Shepherd who looks after my Sheep, or a Butler who takes care of my Plate, or a Servant who keeps a Key to my Chamber, or a Guest who has a piece of Plate set before him in an Inn, may be guilty of Felony, in fraudulently taking away the same; for in all these cases the Offence may as properly come under the word *Cepit*, the Injury to the Owner is as great, and the Fraud as secret, and the Villany more base, than if it had been done by a Stranger.

3 H. 7. 12. b 21 H. 7. 14 b. Bro. Coro. 58. 137. S P. C. 25. A. Dalt. ca. 102. Moore 246. Poph. 84.

Sect. 7. Also it seems clear, That if a Carrier, after he has brought the Goods to the Place appointed, take them away again secretly *animo furandi*, he is guilty of Felony, because the Possession which he received from the Owner being determined, his second Taking is in all Respects the same as if he were a mere Stranger.

H. P. C. 62. 3 Inst. 107. Bro. Coro. 160. S. P. C 25.

Sect. 8. And not only he who first lays his Hands on my Goods himself, but in many cases he who receives them from another, may be guilty of feloniously taking them; as if a Person intending to steal my Horse, take out a Replevin, and thereby have the Horse delivered to him by the Sheriff; or if one intending to rifle my Goods, get Possession from the Sheriff, by vertue of a Judgment obtained, without any the least Colour of Title, upon false Affidavits, *&c.* in which cases the making Use of legal Process is so far from extenuating that it highly aggravates the Offence, by the Abuse put on the Law, in making it serve the purposes of Oppression and Injustice.

3 Inst. 108. H. P. C. 63. Kelynge 43. 1 Sid. 254. Raym. 276.

Sect. 9. Also he who steals my Goods from *J. S.* who had stoln them before, may be indicted, or appealed, as having stoln them from me, because in Judgment of Law, the Possession as well as Property always continued in me. And for this cause, he who steals my Goods in the County of *B*, and carries them to the County of *C*, may be indicted or appealed in the County of *C*, as well as that of *B*, because the Possession still continuing in me, every Moment's Continuance of the Trespass is as much a Wrong to it, and may come under the word *Cepit*, as much as the first Taking. Yet a Pirate carrying the Goods whereof he robbed me at Sea, into any County, can not be indicted for Felony there, because the original Taking was not such a Felony whereof the Common Law takes conusance.

13 E. 4. 3. b. H. P. C. 64. 69 184. S P. C 61. 182. Bro. Appeal. 84, 100. Coro. 171. 3 Inst. 113.

Sect. 10. It seems not to have been clearly settled before 3 & 4 *Will. & Mar.* 9. whether a Lodger, who stole the Furniture of his Lodgings, were indictable as a Felon, inasmuch as he had a kind of special Property in the Goods, and was to pay the greater Rent in consideration of them; but if it had appeared clearly, from the whole Circumstances of the Case, that the first Intention of the Party in coming to the House was not to have the conveniency of Lodging in it, but only, under the Colour thereof, to have the better Opportunity of rifling it, and to elude the Justice of the Law, by endeavouring to keep out of the Letter of it, by gaining a Possession of the Goods with the Consent of the Owner, I can not see any good Reason why such a Person should not be esteemed as much a Felon as a mere Stranger, inasmuch as his whole Design was to defraud the Law, and the Consent of the Owner was grounded on a Supposition of his coming as a Lodger, and could never have been gained if the Truth had appeared, which the Party shall get no Advantage by falsifying: And it brings a Contempt upon the Justice of the Nation to suffer its Laws to be evaded by such little Contrivances: However this Question is now settled by the said Statute, which hath enacted and declared, *That if any Person or Persons shall take away with an Intent to steal, imbezil or purloin, any Chattel, Bedding, or Furniture, which by Contract or Agreement he or they are to use, or shall be let to him or them to use, in or with such Lodging, such taking, imbeziling, or purloining, shall be to all Intents and Purposes taken, reputed, and adjudged to be Larceny and Felony, and the Offender shall suffer as in case of Felony.* Kelynge 24, 81. Shower 50, 57.

Sect. 11. It is recited by 21 *H.* 8. 7. *That before the Time of the said Statute, divers, as well Noblemen, as other the King's Subjects, had, upon Confidence and Trust, delivered unto their Servants their Caskets, and other Jewels, Money, Goods and Chattels, safely to keep, to the use of their said Masters or Mistresses, and after such Delivery the said Servants had withdrawn themselves and gone away from their said Masters or Mistresses, with the said Caskets, Jewels, Money, goods and Chattels, or part thereof, to the Intent to steal the same, and defraud their said Masters or Mistresses thereof, and sometime being with their said Masters and Mistresses, had converted the said Jewels, Money, and other Chattels, or part thereof, to their own Use, which misbehaviour so done, was doubtful in the Common Law, whether it were Felony or not; and by reason thereof the aforesaid Servants had been in great Boldness to commit such or the like Offences.* And thereupon it is enacted, *That all and singular such Servants, (being of the Age of eighteen Years, and not Apprentices,) to whom any such Caskets, Jewels, Money, Goods or Chattels by his or their said Masters or Mistresses shall from thenceforth so be delivered to keep, That if any such Servant or Servants withdraw him or them from their said Masters or Mistresses, and go away with the said Caskets, Jewels, Money, Goods or Chattels, or any part thereof, to the Intent to steal the same, and defrand his or their said Masters or Mistresses thereof, contrary to the Trust and Confidence to him or them put, by his or their said Masters and Mistresses, or else being in the Service of his said Master or Mistress, without Assent or Commandment of his Master or Mistress he imbezil the same Caskets, Jewels, Money, Goods or Chattels, or any part thereof, or otherwise convert the same to his own Use, with like purpose to steal it, That if the said Caskets, Jewels, Money, Goods, or Chattels, that any such Servant shall so go away with, or which he shall imbezil with purpose to steal it, as is aforesaid, be of the Value of 40 s. or above, That then the same false, fraudulent, and untrue Act and Demeanour, from thenceforth, shall be deemed and adjudged Felony,* &c.

In the Construction of this Statute the following Opinions have been holden,

Dal. ca. 102. H. P. C. 63. *Sect.* 12. I. That it extends only to such as were Servants to the Owner of the Goods, both at the Time when they were delivered, and also at the Time when they were stoln.

Sect. 13. II. That it is strictly confined to such Goods as are delivered to keep, and therefore that a Receiver, who having received his Master's Rents, runs away with them, or a Servant who being intrusted to sell Goods, or to receive Money due on a Bond, sells the Goods, *&c.* and departs with the Money, is not within the Statute; but that a Servant who receives his Master's Goods from another Servant to keep for the Master, is as much guilty as if he had received them from the Master's own Hands, because such a Delivery is looked upon as a Delivery by the Master.

Dy. 5. Pl. 2, 3. H. P. C. 62, 63. 3 Inst. 105. Dal. ca. 102. Dy. 5. Pl. 3.

H. P. C. 63. Dal. ca. 102. Dy. 5. *Sect.* 14. III. That it includes not the wasting or consuming of Goods howsoever wilful it may be: nor the taking away of an Obligation, or any other bare *Chose* in Action.

Sect. 15. IV. That it extends not to the Taking of such Things whereof the actual Property is not in the Master at the Time; and therefore, That if a Servant having Money, or Corn, *&c.* delivered to him, melt down the Money of his own Head without the command of his Master, into a piece of Plate, or turn the Corn into Malt, and then run away with them, that he is not within the Statute, because the Property of these Things is so far changed by altering them in such a manner that they can not be known again, and the Master can not afterwards take them without a Trespass; but it is agreed, That if a Servant make a Suit of Clothes of Cloth, or a Pair of Shoes of Leather, delivered to him by the Master, and then run away with them, that he is within the Statute, because the Property is no way altered; and even in the first Case, whether the very Taking of the Plate, or Malt, be within the Statute or not, yet I can see no reason why the whole Act of the Servant taken together, should not be looked upon as a Conversion of the Master's Goods to his own Use, with an Intent to steal them, which brings it within the express Letter of the Statute: And it has been resolved, That a Servant who changes his Master's Money from Silver to Gold, and then runs away with it, *&c.* is within the Statute, and I can see no good Distinction between that and the present Case.

1 H. 7. 16. a. Crom. 50. Dal. ca. 102. See Crom. 50. Dal. ca. 102.

Sect. 16. The Benefit of the Clergy was taken away from all Felonies within this Statute, by 27 *H.* 8. 17. and restored by 1 *Ed.* 6. 12. but taken away again by 12 *Annæ* 7. from all such as shall be committed in a Dwelling-house, or Out-house.

Sect. 17. By 7 *Jac.* 1. 7. *If any Sorter, Kember, Carder, or Spinster of Wool, or Weaver of Yarn made of such Wool, shall imbezil any Wool or Yarn delivered to him to be wrought, and shall be thereof convict before two Justices of Peace, according to the Method prescribed by that Statute, he shall be whipped,* &c.

Sect. 18. As to the second particular, *viz.* What shall be said to be such a carrying away of the Thing stoln, as will bring the Case within the word *Asportavit*, which is necessary in every Indictment of Larceny, it seems that any the least removing of the Thing taken from the Place where it was before, is sufficient for this Purpose, tho' it be not quite carried off; and upon this Ground the Guest, who, having taken off the Sheets from his Bed with an Intent to steal them, carried them into the Hall, and was apprehended before he could get out of the House, was adjudged guilty of Larceny; so also was he who having taken a Horse in

3 Inst. 108. 27 Ass. 39. S. P. C. 26 a. Lib. Coro. 107. 3 Inst. 109. Dal. ca. 102.

a Close with an Intent to steal him, was apprehended before he could get him out of the Close; neither is he less guilty who pulls off the Wool from another's Sheep, or strips their Skins, with an Intent to steal them; or he who intending to steal Plate, takes it out of a Trunk wherein it was, and lays it on the Floor, and is surprized before he can carry it off.

Dalt. 21. Crom. 36. a. Kelynge 31.

Sect. 19. As to the third particular, *viz.* By whom Larceny may be committed, It is certain that a Feme Covert may be guilty thereof by stealing the Goods of a Stranger, but not by stealing her Husband's, because a Husband and Wife are considered but as one Person in Law; and the Husband by endowing his Wife at the Marriage with all his worldly Goods, gives her a kind of Interest in them; for which cause, even a Stranger can not commit Larceny in taking the Goods of the Husband by the Delivery of the Wife; as he may by taking away the Wife by Force and against her Will, together with the Goods of the Husband.

Pult. 127. H. P. C. 65. Bro. Co. 142. Dal. ca. 104. 13 Ass. 5. 18 Ed. 3. 32. a. Bro. Coro. 77. S. P. C. 94. B. Dal. ca. 104. Crom. 35.

Sect. 20. It is said to be no Felony for one reduced to extream Necessity, to take so much of another's Victuals as will save him from starving, but if such his Necessity be owing to his Unthriftiness, surely it is far from being any Excuse.

Dalt. ca. 99. Crom 33. a. *See* Proverbs ch. 6. v. 30.

As to the fourth Point, *viz.* What are such Goods, the stealing whereof may amount to Felony, the following particulars are to be observed.

Sect. 21. I. They ought to be no way annexed to the Freehold, and therefore it is no Larceny, but a bare Trespass, to steal Corn, or Grass, growing, or Apples on a Tree, or Lead on a Church, or House, but it is Larceny to take them, being severed from the Freehold, whether by the Owner, or even by the Thief himself, if he sever them at one Time and then come again at another Time and take them: And the general Reason of this Distinction between Chattels fix'd to a Freehold and those lying loose, perhaps may be this; because the former, not being to be removed without Trouble and Difficulty, are not so liable to be stoln, and therefore need not to be secured by so severe Laws as the others require.

12 Ass. 32. Bro. Coro. 77. 1 Mod. 89. H. P. C. 66. Crom. 37. a. 18 H. 8. 2. S. P. C. 25. b.

Sect. 22. II. They ought to have some Worth in themselves, and not to derive their whole Value from the Relation they bear to some other Thing, which can not be stoln, as Paper or Parchment on which are written Assurances concerning Lands, or Obligations, or Covenants, or other Securities for a Debt, or other *Chose* in *Action*: And the Reason wherefore there can be no Felony in taking away any such Thing seems to be, because, generally speaking, they being of no manner of use to any but the Owner, are not supposed to be so much in danger of being stoln, and therefore need not to be provided for in so strict a manner as those Things which are of a known Price, and every Body's Money; and for the like Reason it is no Felony to take away a Villain, or an Infant in Ward, *&c.*

H. P. C. 66, 67. 3 Inst. 109. Bro. Coro. 155. S. P. C. 25. b. Crom. 27. b. H. P. C. 66 S. P. C. 25 Bro. Coro. 155.

Sect. 23. III. They ought not to be Things of a base Nature, as Dogs, Cats, Bears, Foxes, Monkeys, Ferrets, and the like, which, howsoever they may be valued by the Owner, shall never be so highly regarded by the Law, that for their sakes a Man shall die; as he may for stealing a Hawk, known by him to be reclaimed, not only by Force of the Statute of 37 *Ed.* 3. 19. but also at Common Law, in respect of that very high Value which was formerly set upon that Bird.

H. P. C. 66. 3 Inst. 109. 7 Co. 18 a. 3 H. 8 3. b. Crom 36. a. b. Dalt. ca. 103.

Sect. 24. As to the fifth Point, *viz.* How far the Goods taken away ought to belong to another; it seems agreed, That the taking of Goods where-

Bro Coro. 190.

H P. C. 67. 22 Ass. Pl 99. 3 Inst. 108. S. P. C. 25. b. Dalt. ca. 103.

whereof no one had a Property at the Time, can not be Felony; and therefore, That he who takes away Treasure-trove, or a Wreck, Waif, or Stray, before they have been seized by the Persons who have a Right thereto, is not guilty of Felony, and shall be only punished by Fine, *&c.*

3 Inst. 109. H P. C. 67. Owen 20.

Sect. 25. Neither shall he who takes Fish in a River, or other great Water, wherein they are at their natural Liberty, be guilty of Felony, as he may be who takes them out of a Trunk or Pond, *&c.*

7 Co. 18. 22 Ass. 95. 22 H 6. 59. b. 18 Ed. 4. 8. a. Bro. Coro 92, 155, 164. Dalt, ca. 92. S. P. C. 25. b. 3 Inst. 109, 110. 18 H. 8. 2. a, b.

Sect. 26. Upon the like Ground it seems clear, That a Man can not commit Felony by taking Deer, Hares, or Conies, in a Forest, Chase, or Warren, or old Pigeons being out of the House, *&c.* But it is agreed, That one may commit Larceny in taking such or any other Creatures *feræ Naturæ*, if they be fit for Food, and reduced to tameness, and known by him to be so; and it seems the most plausible Opinion, That it is Felony to steal wild Pigeons in a Dove-house shut up, or Hares or Deer in a House, or even in a Park, inclosed in such a manner that the Owner may take them whenever he pleases, without the least Danger of their escaping, in which Case they are as much in his Power as Fish in a Pond, or young Pigeons, or Hawks in a Nest, *&c.* in taking of which, for the like reason, it seems to be agreed, that Felony may be committed.

H. P. C. 68. 7 Co. 17, 18. Dalt. ca. 103. H. P. C. 68. 3 Inst. 109. *seem contrary.*

Sect. 27. Also it seems clear, That one may commit Felony by taking away Swans marked or pinioned, or those which are unmarked, if they be kept in a Pond or private River; neither can I see why it is not as much Felony to steal the Eggs of such Swans or Hawks, as it is to steal their young Ones, unless it be because 11 *H.* 7. 17. has appointed a less Punishment for this Offence.

H P. C. 68. 3 Inst. 109.

Sect. 28. However, there is no doubt but that the taking of Domestick Beasts, as Horses, Mares, Colts, *&c.* or of any Creatures whatsoever, which are *domitæ Naturæ*, and fit for Food, as Ducks, Hens, Geese, Turkeys, Peacocks, or their Eggs, or young Ones, may be Felony.

S. P. C. 25, 95. A. Dy. 99. Pl. 61. Dal. ca. 103. H P. C. 67. 7 Ed 4. 14 b. 15. a. S. P. C. 95. H. Dal. ca. 103. 3 Inst. 110. Bro. Indictm. 33. [a] 3 Inst. 110. 12 Co. 113. H. P. C. 67. Con. Dal. ca. 103.

Sect. 29. Also it is said, That there may be Felony in taking Goods the Owner whereof is unknown, in which case the King shall have the Goods, and the Offender shall be indicted for taking *Bona cujusdam Hominis ignoti*; and it seems, That in some cases the Law will rather feign a Property, where in strictness there is none, than suffer an Offender to escape; and therefore it is said, That he who takes away the Goods of a Chapel, or Abbey, in Time of Vacation, may be indicted in the first Case, for stealing *Bona Capellæ*, being in the Custody of such and such, and in the second, for stealing *Bona Domus & Ecclesiæ*, *&c.* and *à fortiori* therefore it follows, That he who steals Goods belonging to a Parish-Church, may be indicted for stealing *Bona Parochianorum*; and it hath been adjudged, That he who takes off a [a] Shrowd from a dead Corps, may be indicted as having stoln it from him who was the Owner thereof when it was put on, for a dead Man can have no Property.

[b] 7 H 6. 43. a. 5 H. 7. 18. b. Bro. Coro. 45, 160. S. P. C. 26. A. 3 Inst. 110. Dalt. ca. 103. [c] H. P. C. 67. Kellew. 70. b.

Sect. 30. And there is a special Case wherein it is said, That a Man may commit Larceny by taking of Things, whereof the absolute Property is in himself; as if *A.* [b] deliver Goods to *B.* being a Tailor, or Carrier, *&c.* and afterwards, with an Intent to make him answer for them, fraudulently and secretly take them away; for *B.* had a special Kind of Property in the Goods so delivered to him, in respect whereof, if a [c] Stranger had stoln them, he might have been indicted generally, as having stoln *B.*'s Goods, and the Injury is altogether as great, and the Fraud as base, where they are taken away by the very Owner.

Sect. 31. As to the sixth [d] Point, *viz.* of what Value the Goods stoln must be, if they be but of the Value of 12 *d.* or under, the Offence can be but Petit Larceny. [d] 22 Aff. 39. Bro Coro. 84, 85. S P. C. 24. H. K.

2 Rol. Re. 78. Dal. ca. 101. 2 Inst. 189. Kelynge 68. H. P. C. 69, 70.

Sect. 32. Yet [e] if two Persons, or more, together, steal Goods above the Value of twelve Pence, every one of them is guilty of Grand Larceny, for each Person is as much an Offender as if he had been alone. [e] S.P.C. 24. K. Dal. ca. 101. H. P. C. 70. Crom. 36. a.

Sect. 33. Also it [f] seems the currant Opinion of all the old Books, That if one at several Times steal several Parcels of Goods, each under the Value of twelve Pence, but amounting in the whole to more, from the same Person, and be found guilty thereof on the same Indictment, he shall have Judgment of Death as for Grand Larceny, but this Severity is seldom practised. [f] S. P. C. 24. I. K. Crom. 36. a. Dal. ca. 101. H. P. C. 70. 2 Keb. 519.

In what Cases simple Larceny is excluded from the Benefit of the Clergy will be shewn hereafter in the second Book, in the Chapter concerning Clergy.

Sect. 34. And now we are come to Petit Larceny, which seems to agree with Grand Larceny in all the particulars above-mentioned, except only the Value of the Goods; so that where-ever an Offence would amount to Grand Larceny, if the Thing stoln were above the Value of twelve Pence, it is Petit Larceny, if it be but of that Value, or under. H. P. C. 69.

Sect. 35. And if one be indicted for stealing Goods to the Value of ten Shillings, and the Jury find specially that he is guilty, but that the Goods are worth but ten Pence, he shall not have Judgment of Death, but only as for Petit Larceny. Bro. Coro. 84, 184. S. P. C. 24. L. Dal. ca. 101. Crom. 36. a. Hetl. 66.

Sect. 36. It seems that all Petit Larceny is Felony, and consequently requires the word *Felonicè*, in an Indictment for it; yet it is certain, That it is not punished with the Loss of Life, or Lands, but only with the Forfeiture of Goods and Chattels, and whipping, or other corporal Punishment. 7 H. 8. 23. Bro. Coro. 2, 219. Appeal. 72, 143. H. P. C. 70. Con. S. P. C. 24. b. Dal. ca. 101.

CHAP. XXXIV.

Of Robbery.

Sect. 1. MIXT or complicated Larceny is such as hath a farther Degree of Guilt in it, as being a Taking from the Person of a Man, or from his House.

Sect. 2. Larceny from the Person of a Man either puts him in Fear, and then it is called Robbery; or does not put him in Fear, and then it is called barely, Larceny from the Person.

Sect. 3. Robbery is a felonious and violent taking away from the Person of another, Goods or Money to any Value, putting him in Fear. H. P. C. 71. 3 Inst. 68.

In

In the Explication whereof, I shall consider the following Particulars:

1. What Taking away will satisfy the Word *Cepit* in an Indictment for this Offence.
2. What shall be said to be a Taking away from the Person.
3. What kind of Taking shall be said to be violent.
4. In what Respects Robbery differs from other Larcenies.

H. P. C. 72. 44 E. 3. 14. b. 4 H. 4. 3. a. Dalt. cap. 100. S. P. C. 27. f. Crom. 34. a. 3 Inst. 68. Fitz. Cor. 464.

Sect. 4. As to the first Point, *viz.* What Taking away will satisfy the Word *Cepit* in an Indictment for Robbery; it seems clear, That he who receives my Money by my Delivery, either whilst I am under the Terror of his Assault, or afterwards while I think my self bound in Conscience to give it him by an Oath to that Purpose, which in my Fear I was compelled by him to take, may in the Eye of the Law, as properly be said to take it from me, as he who actually takes it out of my Pocket with his own Hands.

3 Inst. 69. H. P. C. 72.

Sect. 5. Neither can he, who has once actually compleated the Offence, by taking my Goods in such a Manner into his Possession, afterwards purge it by any Re-delivery, *&c.*

S. P. C. 27. g. Crom. 34. 3 Inst. 69. Dalt. cap. 100. H. P. C. 71, 72.

Sect. 6. But he who only attacks me in order to rob me, but does not take my Goods into his Possession, though he go so far as to cut off the Girdle of my Purse, by Reason whereof it falls to the Ground, is not guilty of Robbery; but highly punishable by Fine and Imprisonment, *&c.* for so enormous a Breach of the Peace.

Crom. 34. a. b. 1 And. 116. Pudsey's Case. Crom. 34. Dalt. cap. 100. H. P. C. 72.

Sect. 7. Yet in some Cases a Man may be said to rob me, where in Truth he never actually had any of my Goods in his Possession; as where I am robbed by several in one Gang, and one of them only takes my Money, in which Case, in Judgment of Law, every one of the Company shall be said to take it, in respect of that Encouragment which they give to one another through the Hopes of mutual Assistance in their Enterprize: Nay, though they miss of their first intended Prize, and one of them afterwards ride from the rest, and rob a third Person in the same High-way out of their View, and then return to them, all are guilty of Robbery; for they came together with an Intent to rob, and to assist one another in so doing.

S. P. C. 27. d. Crom. 34, 35. Dalt. cap. 100. 3 Inst. 69. H. P. C. 73. Sty. Rep. 156.

Sect. 8. As to the second Point, *viz.* What shall be said to be a Taking away from the Person; not only the Taking away a Horse from a Man where on he is actually riding, or Money out of his Pocket, but also the Taking of any Thing from him openly and before his Face, which is under his immediate and personal Care and Protection, may properly enough be said to be a Taking from the Person: And therefore he who having first assaulted me takes away my Horse standing by me, or having put me in Fear, drives my Cattle in my Presence out of my Pasture, or takes up my Purse which in my Fright I cast into a Bush, or my Hat which fell from my Head, or robs my Servant of my Money before my Face, may be indicted as having taken such Things from my Person.

H. P. C. 71, 72. Crom. 34 b. Dal. cap. 100.

Sect. 9. As to the third Point, *viz.* What kind of Taking shall be said to be violent; where-ever a Person assaults another with such Circumstances of Terror as put him into Fear, and causes him by Reason of such Fear to part with his Money, the Taking thereof is adjudged Robbery, whether there were any Weapon drawn or not, or whether the Person assaulted delivered his Money upon the other's Command, or afterwards gave it him upon his ceasing to use Force, and begging an Alms; for he was put into Fear by his Assault, and gives him his Money to get rid of him.

Sect. 10. And some have gone so far as to hold, That if a Man, meeting another going with his Goods to Market in order to sell them, compell him to sell them to him against his Will, he is guilty of Robbery, though he give for them more than they are worth: But perhaps this Opinion is too severe, because the Grievance to the Party seems rather to proceed from the Perverseness of his Humour, than from any real Injury done to him; and there seems to be no such Enormity in the Intention of the Wrong-doer, as is implied in the Notion of Felony. Crom. 34 b. 35. Dalt.cap.100

Sect. 11. However it is certain, That the Claim of Property, in the Thing taken away, without any Colour, is no manner of Excuse. H. P. C. *first Edition* 62.

As to the fourth Point, *viz.* In what respects Robbery differs from other Larcenies.

Sect. 12. I. No other Larceny shall have Judgment of Death, unless the Thing stoln be above the Value of twelve Pence; but Robbery shall have such Judgment, how small soever the Value may be of the Thing taken away. S. P. C. 27. a. Crom. 33. b. Dal. cap 100. H. P. C. 74.

Sect. 13. II. Other Larcenies, whether from the Person or not, shall not be supposed to be done with Violence or Terror, but Robbery is always laid as done on an Assault with Violence, and putting the Party in Fear, which is properly thus expressed in an Indictment, —— *à Persona* J. S. *violenter & felonice cepit & asportavit in magnum prædicti* J. S. *Terrorem.* H. P. C. 74. 3 Inst. 68. Kelynge 70.

Sect. 14. III. But they all agree in this, That the Offenders had the Benefit of the Clergy at the Common Law, but many of them are at this Day excluded in many Cases by Statute; for which see the Chapter in the second Book concerning Clergy.

CHAP. XXXV.

Of Larceny from the Person.

Sect. 1. Larceny from the Person of a Man without putting him in Fear, is either done privily without his Knowledge, (in which Case it is excluded from the Benefit of the Clergy by 8 *El.* 4.) or openly and avowedly before his Face; as if one take off my Hat from my Head, and run away with it, or come into my Shop and cheapen Goods, and run away with them without paying for them, which is agreed not to be Robbery, and as it seems is more properly indictable as a Trespass than Felony, unless the Offender were either unknown, or immediately fled the Country if he were known; otherwise I have a Remedy against him in the ordinary Course of Civil Justice; and it seems rigorous to make such Offences capital, which probably may sufficiently be provided against by more gentle Methods. Dy. 224. Pl. 30. 2Rol.Re.154. H. P. C. 73, 74, 75. Crom. 34. b. Dalt.cap.100. Raym. 275, 276.

Sect. 2. However it is certain, That all open Larcenies from the Person are within the Benefit of the Clergy, except such as are committed in a Dwelling House, *&c.* to the Value of forty Shillings, from which it is taken away by 12 *Anne.*

Sect. 3. Also a private Larceny from the Person shall have the Benefit
H. P. C. 75. of the Clergy, unless it be laid in the Indictment as done *clam* and *secretè*, &c. in exact Pursuance of the Words of 8 *El.* 4.

H. P. C. 75. Dalt. cap. 100. *Sect.* 4. And no such Larceny shall have Judgment of Death but only as of Petit Larceny, if the Jury find the Offender guilty under the Value of twelve Pence; for the Statute does not alter the Nature of the Offence, or make that capital which was not so before, but only leaves the Offender to the Judgment of the Common Law.

CHAP. XXXVI.

Of Larceny from the House.

Sect. 1. THE other Branch of complicated Larceny, is that which is
H. P. C. 76. from the Habitation of a Man, which though it seem to have a higher Degree of Guilt than simple Larceny, yet I do not find it distinguished from it by the Common Law, either as to the Circumstances above mentioned which are requisite to constitute the Offence, or as to the Punishment.

Sect. 2. However it is at this Day excluded from the Benefit of the Clergy in many Cases by several Acts of Parliament, which I shall particularly consider in the second Book in the Chapter concerning Clergy.

CHAP. XXXVII.

Of Piracy.

Sect. 1. TO what has been said concerning such Larcenies as are Felonies by the Common Law, it may not be improper to add somewhat concerning Piracy and Depredation at Sea, which is a capital Offence by the Civil Law.

40 Ass. 25. 3 Inst. 115. S. P. C. 10. 0. H. P. C. 77. 28 H. 8. c. 15. 3 Inst. 112. H. P. C. 77. *Sect.* 2. It is said, That before 25 *Ed.* 3. this Offence was punished at Common Law as Petit Treason, if committed by a Subject, and as Felony, if committed by a Foreigner: However it seems agreed, that after that Statute by which all Treason is confined to the Particulars therein set down, it was cognizable only by the Civil Law.

3 Inst. 112. *Sect.* 3. But this proving very inconvenient, because by that Law no Offender shall have Judgment of Death, without his own Confession, or direct Proof by Eye-Witnesses, it was enacted by 28 *H.* 8. 15. *That all Felonies and Robberies,* &c. *upon the Sea, or in any Haven, River, Creek, or Place, where the Admiral or Admirals have or pretend to have Power, Authority or Jurisdiction, shall be inquired, tried, heard, determined and judged in such Shires and Places in the Realm, as shall be limited by the King's Commission or Commissions to be directed for the same, in like Form and Condition, as if any such Offence or Offences had been commited or done in or upon the Land, and such Commissions shall be had under the King's Great Seal, directed to the Admiral or Admirals, or*

to

to his or their Lieutenant, Deputy and Deputies, and to three or four such other substantial Persons, as shall be named or appointed by the Lord Chancellor of England *for the Time being, from Time to Time, and as oft as Need shall require, to hear and determine such Offences, after the common Course of the Laws of this Land used for Felonies and Robberies,* &c. *done and committed upon the Land within this Realm.*

Sect. 4. And it is farther enacted by the said Statute, *That if any Person or Persons happen to be indicted for any such Offence done, or hereafter to be done, upon the Seas, or in any other Place above limited, that then such Order, Process, Judgment and Execution, shall be used, had, done and made, to and against every such Person and Persons so being indicted, as against Felons,* &c. *for any Felony,* &c. *upon the Land, by the Laws of the Land is accustomed.*

Sect. 5 And it is farther enacted by the said Statute, *That such as shall be convict of any such Offence by Verdict, Confession, or Process by Authority of any such Commission, shall have and suffer such Pains of Death, Losses of Lands, Goods and Chattels, as if they had been attainted and convicted of such Offence done upon the Land, and also that they shall be excluded from the Benefit of the Clergy.*

In the Exposition of this Act it has been holden,

Sect. 6. I. That it does not alter the Nature of the Offence, so as to make that which was before a Felony only by the Civil Law, now become a Felony by the Common Law; for the Offence must still be alledged as done upon the Sea, and is no Way cognisable by the Common Law, but only by Vertue of this Statute, which by ordaining that in some Respects it shall have the like Trial and Punishment, as are used for Felony at Common Law, shall not be carried so far as to make it also agree with it in other particulars which are not mentioned: And from hence it follows, That this Offence remains as before of a special Nature, and that it shall not be included in a general Pardon of all Felonies, which, as it was before this Statute, to be expounded of no Felonies which are such only by the Civil Law, shall continue still to have the same Construction. 3 Inst. 112, 113. H. P. C. 77. Moore 756. 3 Inst. 112. Co. Lit. 391. H. P. C. 77.

Sect. 7. From the same Ground also it follows, That no Persons shall, in Respect of this Statute, be construed to be, or punished as, Accessaries to Piracy before or after, as they might have been if it had been made a Felony by the Statute, whereby all those would incidentally have been made Accessaries in the like Cases, in which they would have been Accessaries to a Felony at Common Law; And from hence it follows, That Accessaries to Piracy, being neither expresly named in the Statute, nor by Construction included in it, remain as they were before, and were triable by the Civil Law, if their Offence were committed on the Sea, but if on the Land, by no Law until 11 and 12 *Wil.* 3. 7. for 2 and 3 *E.* 6. 24. which provides against Accessaries in one County to a Felony in another, extends not to Accessaries to an Offence committed in no County, but on the Sea; but by the said Statute of 11 and 12 *Wil.* they are triable in like Manner as the Principals are by the Statute of 28 *H.* 8. 3 Inst. 112. H. P. C. 77. 215.

Sect. 8. From the same Ground also it follows, That an Attainder for this Offence corrupts not the Blood, inasmuch as the Statute only says that the Offender shall suffer such Pains of Death, *&c.* as if he were attainted of a Felony at Common Law; but says not that the Blood shall be corrupted, *&c.* 3 Inst. 112. H. P. C. 77.

Sect. 9. Yet it has been resolved, That an Offender standing mute on an Arraignment by Force of this Statute, shall have Judgment of Pain *Fort & dure*; for the Words of the Statute are, *That a Commission shall be* 3 Inst. 114. Dyer 241. Pl. 49.

directed, &c. to hear and determine such Offences after the common Course of the Laws of this Land, &c.

Sect. 10. II. It has been holden, That the Indictment for this Offence must alledge the Fact to be done upon the Sea, and must have both the Words *Felonicè* and *Piraticè*: And that no Offence is punishable by Vertue of this Act as Piracy, which would not have been Felony if done on the Land, and consequently that the Taking of an Enemy's Ship by an Enemy, is not within the Statute.

3 Inst. 112. S.P.C. 114.a. 1Rol.Re. 175.

Sect. 11. III. It is agreed, That this Statute extends not to Offences done in Creeks or Ports within the Body of a County, because they are, and always were, cognizable by the Common Law.

Moore 756. 1Rol.Re. 175. H. P. C. 77. 3 Inst. 113.

Sect. 12. It is enacted by 11 and 12 *Wil.* 3. 7. which was continued by 1 *Georg.* 25. for five Years, and from thence to the End of the next Sessions of Parliament, *That all Piracies, Felonies and Robberies committed in or upon the Sea, or in any Place where the Admiral has Jurisdiction, may be tried and determined at Sea or upon the Land, in any of his Majesty's Islands, or Plantations, &c. to be appointed by the King's Commission under the Great Seal, or the Seal of the Admiralty, directed to any of the Admirals, &c. and such Persons and Officers by Name, or for the Time being, as his Majesty shall think fit, who shall have Power jointly or severally, by Warrant under Hand and Seal of any of them, to commit any Person against whom Information of any such Offences shall be given upon Oath, and to call a Court of Admiralty, which shall consist of seven Persons at the least, and shall proceed in the Trial of the said Offenders, according to such Directions as are set forth at large in the said Statute.*

Sect. 13. And it is farther enacted by the said Statute, Par. 8. *That if any of his Majesty's natural born Subjects or Denizens of this Kingdom, shall commit any Piracy or Robbery, or any Act of Hostility, against others his Majesty's Subjects, upon the Sea, under Colour of any Commission from any foreign Prince or State, or Pretence of Authority from any Person whatsoever, such Offender and Offenders, and every of them, shall be deemed, adjudged, and taken to be Pirates, Felons and Robbers; and they and every of them being duly convicted thereof, according to this Act, or the aforesaid Statute of King* Henry *the Eighth, shall have and suffer such Pains of Death, Loss of Lands, Goods and Chattels, as Pirates, Felons and Robbers upon the Seas ought to have and suffer.*

Sect. 14. And it is farther enacted by the said Statute, *That if any Commander or Master of any Ship, or any Seaman or Mariner, shall in any Place where the Admiral hath Jurisdiction, betray his Trust and turn Pirate, Enemy or Rebel, and piratically and feloniously run away with his or their Ship or Ships, or any Barge, Boat, Ordnance, Ammunition, Goods or Merchandizes, or yield them up voluntarily to any Pirate, or bring any seducing Message from any Pirate, Enemy or Rebel, or consult, combine, or confederate with, or attempt or endeavour to corrupt, any Commander, Master, Officer or Mariner to yield up or run away with any Ship, Goods or Merchandize, or turn Pirate, or go over to Pirates, or if any Person shall lay violent Hands on his Commander, whereby to hinder him from fighting in Defence of his Ship and Goods committed to his Trust, or that shall confine his Master, or make or endeavour to make a Revolt in his Ship, shall be adjudged to be a Pirate, Felon, and Robber; and being convicted thereof, according to the Direction of this Act shall have and suffer Pains of Death, Loss of Lands, Goods and Chattels, as Pirates, Felons and Robbers upon the Seas ought to have and suffer.*

Sect. 15. And it is farther enacted by the said Statute, *That all and every Person and Persons whatsoever, who shall either on the Land or upon the Seas, wittingly or knowingly set forth any Pirate, or aid and assist, or maintain, procure, command, counsel, or advise any Person or Persons whatsoever, to do or commit any Piracies or Robberies upon the Seas; and such Person or Persons shall thereupon do or commit any such Piracy or Robbery, then all and every such Person or Persons whatsoever, so as aforesaid, setting forth any Pirate, or aiding or assisting, maintaining, procuring, commanding, counselling or advising the same, either on the Land or upon the Sea, shall be adjudged to be Accessary to such Piracy and Robbery done and committed:* And further, *That after any Piracy or Robbery is or shall be commited by any Pirate or Robber whatsoever, every Person or Persons, who, knowing that such Pirate or Robber has done or committed such Piracy and Robbery, shall on the Land or upon the Sea receive, entertain, or conceal any such Pirate or Robber, or receive or take into his Custody, any Ship, Vessel, Goods or Chattels, which have been by any such Pirate or Robber piratically and feloniously taken, shall be, by this Statute likewise adjudged to be, accessary to such Piracy and Robbery: And that all such Accessaries to such Piracies and Robberies, shall be enquired of, tried, heard, determined and adjudged according to the common Course of the Law, according to the said Statute of* 28 H. 8. *as the Principals of such Piracies and Robberies may be, and no otherwise; and being thereupon attainted, shall suffer such Pains of Death, Loss of Lands, Goods and Chattels, and in like manner as the Principals of such Piracies, Robberies and Felonies, ought to suffer according to the said Statute of* H. 8. *which is declared to be in full Force, any Thing in this last Act to the contrary notwithstanding.*

CHAP. XXXVIII.

Of Burglary.

AND now we are come to Offences against the Habitation of a Man, which are of two kinds:

1. Burglary.
2. Arson.

Sect. 1. Burglary is a Felony at the Common Law, in breaking and entering the Mansion House of another, or (as some say,) the Walls or Gates of a walled Town in the Night, to the Intent to commit some Felony within the same, whether the felonious Intent be executed or not. H. P. C. 79. 22 Ass. 95. Bro. Cor. 93. 3 Inst. 63. S. P. C. 30. a. Dalt. cap. 99. Crom. 31. a.

For the better Understanding whereof, I shall consider the following Particulars:

1. What shall be accounted Night-time for this Purpose.
2. Whether there must be both an actual Entry and Breaking.
3. What Breaking is sufficient.
4. What Entry.
5. In what Place this Offence may be committed.
6. What Degree of Guilt is required in the principal Intention.

Sect. 2. As to the first Point, *viz.* What shall be accounted Night-Time for this Purpose; there are some Opinions, That Burglary may be committed at any Time after Sun-set, and before Sun-rising; but it seems the much better Opinion, That the Word *Noctanter*, which is precisely necessary Dalt. cap. 99. S. P. C. 30. a. Crom. 33. a. H. P. C. 79. 3 Inst. 63. Savil 47. Crom. 32. a. 7 Co. 6.

neceſſary in every Indictment; for this Offence cannot be ſatisfied in a legal Senſe, if it appear upon the Evidence, that there was ſo much Day-light at the Time, that a Man's Countenance might be diſcerned thereby.

Dalt. cap 99. Crom 32. a. Dyer 99 a. S. P. C. 30. a. 3 Inſt. 64. H. P. C. 80.

Sect. 3. As to the ſecond Point, *viz.* Whether there muſt be both an actual Entry and Breaking; notwithſtanding ſome looſe Opinions to the contrary, there ſeems to be no good Cauſe to doubt but that both are required to compleat this Offence, for the Words *fregit* and *intravit*, being both of them preciſely neceſſary in the Indictment, both muſt be ſatisfied: And *à fortiori*, therefore there can be no Burglary where there is neither of them; as if on a bare Aſſault upon a Houſe, the Owner fling out his Money.

Con. Dalt. cap 99. Crom. 31. b.

3 Inſt. 64. H. P. C. 80.

Sect. 4. As to the third Point, *viz.* What Breaking is ſufficient; it ſeems agreed, That ſuch a Breaking as is implied by Law in every unlawful Entry on the Poſſeſſion of another, whether it lie open or be incloſed, and will maintain a common Indictment, or Action of Treſpaſs *Quare clauſum fregit*, will not ſatisfy the Words *Felonicè & Burglariter fregit*, except in ſome ſpecial Caſes, in which it is accompanied with ſuch Circumſtances as make it as heinous as an actual Breaking: And from hence it follows, That if one enter into a Houſe by a Door which he finds open, or through a Hole which was made there before, and ſteal Goods, *&c.* or draw any Thing out of a Houſe through a Door or Window which were open before, or enter into a Houſe by the Doors open in the Daytime, and lie there till Night, and then rob and go away, without breaking any Part of the Houſe, he is not guilty of Burglary. But it is certain, That he would have been guilty thereof if he had opened the Window, or unlocked the Door, or broken a Hole in the Wall, and then had entered, *&c.* or if having entered by a Door which he found open, or having lain in the Houſe by the Owner's Conſent, he had but unlatched a Chamber-Door; or if he had come down by the Chimney: (in which Caſe though it might be ſaid, That the Houſe was open there, and ſo not actually broken; yet it was as much incloſed as the Nature of the Thing would bear.) And according to ſome Opinions, he would have been in like manner guilty, if upon an Aſſault made by him upon the Houſe, with an Intent to rob it, the Owner had opened the Door in order to drive him off, and thereupon he had entered: (in which Caſe, as ſome ſay, the opening of the Door by the Owner, being occaſioned by the felonious Attempt of the other, is as much imputable to him as if it had been actually done by his own Hands.)

H. P. C. 80. 82. Con. Dal 99. Crom. 34. a. H. P. C. 81. Dalt. cap. 99. 1 And. 115. H. P. C. 80. Dalt cap 99. Savil. 47. Dal. cap. 99. Kelynge 67. H. P. C. 81, 82. Hutt. 20. Crom. 32 a. Con. 1. And. 115.

Sect. 5. And it has alſo been reſolved, That where divers Perſons came to a Houſe with an Intent to rob it, and knocked at the Door, pretending to have Buſineſs with the Owner, and being by that Means let in, rifled the Houſe, they were guilty of Burglary: Alſo it hath been adjudged, That thoſe were no leſs guilty, who, having a Deſign to rob a Houſe, took Lodgings in it, and then fell on the Landlord and robbed him; for the Law will not endure to have its Juſtice defrauded by ſuch Evaſions. And for the like Reaſon, *à fortiori*, it has been reſolved, That where Perſons, intending to rob a Houſe, raiſed a Hue and Cry, and prevailed with a Conſtable to make a Search in the Houſe, and having got in by that Means, with the Owner's Conſent, bound the Conſtable, and robbed the Inhabitants, they were guilty of Burglary; for there cannot be a greater Affront to publick Juſtice, than to make Uſe of legal Proceſs as a Stale for ſuch villainous Purpoſes; and therefore the whole Act is eſteemed tortious *ab initio*.

Kelynge 42. Kelynge 63, Crom. 32. b. Dalt. cap 99. H. P. C. 81.

3 *Sect.*

Sect. 6. It is recited by 12 *Annæ* 7. *That there had been ſome Doubt, Whether the entring into a Manſion-Houſe, without breaking the ſame, with an Intent to commit ſome Felony, and breaking the ſaid Houſe in the Night-time to get out, were Burglary*: And thereupon it is declared and enacted, *That if any Perſon ſhall enter into the Manſion or Dwelling-Houſe of another by Day or by Night, without breaking the ſame, with an Intent to commit Felony, or being in ſuch a Houſe, ſhall commit any Felony, and ſhall in the Night-time break the ſaid Houſe to get out of the ſame, ſuch Perſon is, and ſhall be taken to be, guilty of Burglary, and ouſted of the Benefit of Clergy, in the ſame Manner as if ſuch Perſon had broken and entered the ſaid Houſe in the Night-time, with an Intent to commit Felony there.*

Sect 7. As to the fourth Point, *viz.* What Entry is ſufficient to this Purpoſe; it ſeems agreed, That any the leaſt Entry, either with the whole, or but with Part of the Body, or with any Inſtrument, or Weapon, will ſatisfy the Word *Intravit* in an Indictment of Burglary; as if one do but put his Foot over a Threſhold, or his Hand, or a Hook, or Piſtol, within a Window, or turn the Key of a Door which is locked on the Inſide, or diſcharge a loaded Gun into a Houſe, *&c.*

Dalt. cap. 99. H. P. C. 81. 1 And. 115. Crom. 31, 32. Crom. 32. a. Con 1 And. 115.

Sect. 8. Nay, it is certain, That in ſome Caſes one may be guilty of Burglary, who never made any actual Entry at all; as where divers come to commit a Burglary together, and ſome ſtand to watch in adjacent Places, and the others enter, and rob, *&c.* for in all ſuch Caſes, the Act of one is in Judgment of Law the Act of all.

Crom. 32. a. H P C. 80, 81.

Sect. 9. And upon the like Ground, I can ſee no Reaſon why a Servant, who, confederating with a Rogue, lets him in to rob a Houſe, *&c.* ſhould not be guilty of Burglary as much as he; for it is clear, That if the Servant were out of the Houſe, the Entry of the other would be adjudged to be his alſo; and what Difference is there, when he is in the Houſe?

Con. H. P. C. 81. Dalt. cap 99.

Sect. 10. As to the fifth Point, *viz.* In what Place this Offence may be committed, it ſeems to be the currant Opinion at this Day, That it can be only in a Dwelling-Houſe, and that the Indictment for it muſt neceſſarily alledge the Fact *in Domo manſionali*. And Sir *Edward Coke* ſeems to ſay, That the Breaking a Church, *&c.* is therefore Burglary, becauſe the Church is the Manſion-Houſe of God: But I can find nothing in the more ancient Authors to countenance this Nicety; for the general Tenor of the old Books ſeems to be, That Burglary may be committed in breaking Houſes, or Churches, or the Walls, or Gates of a Town. And *Staundforde* and *Anderſon* mention Precedents of Indictments of Burglary *in Domo*, without adding *Manſionali*: However, the conſtant Courſe of late Precedents and Opinions makes it certainly a very dangerous, if not an incurable, Fault, to omit the Word *Manſionalis* in an Indictment of Burglary in a Houſe; and therefore without Queſtion, it ought always to be inſerted where the Truth of the Caſe will bear it. But ſure it cannot be neceſſary or proper to have any ſuch Word in an Indictment of Burglary in a Church, which by all the Books above cited, ſeems to be taken as a diſtinct Burglary from that in a Houſe.

4 Co. 40. a. 3 Inſt. 64, 67. H. P. C. 82, 86. 3 Inſt. 64. H. P. C. 82. Bract. 144. b. Bro. Coro 93. 22 Aſſ 39, 95. Dalt. cap. 99. 27 Aſſ. 38. 1 And. 302. S. P. C. 30. Dalt. cap 99

Sect. 11. However it is agreed by all, That a Houſe wherein a Man dwells but for Part of the Year, or a Houſe which one has hired to live in, and brought Part of his Goods into, but has not yet lodged in; or a Chamber in one of the Inns of Court wherein a Perſon uſually lodges, or a Houſe which a Man's Wife hires without his Privity, and lives in by her ſelf without him, may be called his Dwelling-Houſe; and will ſufficiently ſatisfy the Words *Domus manſionalis* in the Indictment, whether any Perſon were actually therein, or not, at the Time of the Offence.

Crom. 33. b. Dalt. cap. 99. H. P. C. 82. Moore 660. Pl. 903. 4 Co. 40. a. Cro. Car. 474. 1 Jon. 394. H. P. C. 82. Kelynge 54. Poph. 52. 3 Inſt. 64.

Sect.

3 Inst. 64. Dalt. cap 99. Bro. Cor. 180. Crom. 32. b. H. P. C. 82.

Sect. 12. Also all Out-Buildings, as Barns, Stables, Dairy-Houses, *&c.* adjoining to a House, are looked upon as Part thereof, and consequently Burglary may be committed in them; but if they be removed at any Distance from the House, it seems that it has not been usual of late to proceed against Offences therein as Burglaries.

Kelynge 27, 52, 83. Con. Kelynge 83. Vide supra Sect. 11. Crom. 33. a. Dalt. cap 99. Co. Lit. 48. b. H. P. C. 83.

Sect. 13. If several Persons dwell in one House as Servants, Guests, or Tenants at Will, or otherwise having no fix'd and certain Interest in any Part thereof, and a Burglary be committed in any of their Apartments; it seems clear, that the Indictment shall lay the Offence in the Mansion-House of the Proprietor, *&c.* But if one hire a distinct Apartment in a House for his Lodging for a certain Time, and a Burglary be committed therein, I can see no good Reason why the Indictment may not lay the Offence in *Domo mansionali* of such Lodger; for it seems to be agreed, That an Indictment for a Burglary committed in a Chamber in one of the Inns of Court, may lay the Offence *in Domo mansionali* of the Owner of the Chamber; and why may not such an Apartment, with as much Propriety, be called the Mansion-House of him that takes it, during the Time that he has a certain Interest in it? For so long as it is severed by the Lease, it seems in the Eye of the Law to be as distinct from the other Parts of the House, as if the Person who rents it, had a Freehold or Inheritance in it. And as to the Objection, That he goes into the House by the same Door with the other Inhabitants, and therefore is but an Inmate, and the whole ought to be considered but as one House; I answer, That he must have some Way to his Appartment as incident to his Interest in it, and that such Way lying through a Door which is common to him with others, doth not make the Apartment it self in any Respect less his own, than a Way through a Door belonging to himself only would have done.

Kelynge 83.

Sect. 14. And if the Law be so in this Case, it seems to me very reasonable also, That if such a Lodger take also a Cellar in the said House, a Burglary committed in such Cellar, may be alledged *in Domo mansionali* of the Lodger, whether the Cellar had any Communication with the House or not; for since it seems to be agreed, That a Barn or Stable, or other Out-Building near to a House, shall be looked on as Part thereof, why should not such a Cellar have the like Estimation? *Sed Quære*, for *Kelynge* seems to incline to a different Opinion.

Sect. 15. However it is agreed by all, That if one hire a Part of a House to lodge in, which is actually divided from the rest, and have a Door of its own to the Street, a Burglary therein may be alledged *in Domo mansionali* of such Person.

H. P. C. 83.

Sect. 16. But if he had taken it as a Shop or Work-house for his Use in the Day-time only, it seems that a Felony therein cannot be alledged in a Mansion-House; not of him that lets it, because it is severed by the Lease from that Part of the House which belongs to him, nor of him to whom it is let, because he takes it not to lodge in.

H. P. C. 82, 83. 22 Ass. 95. Bro. Coro. 93. S. P. C. 30. Dalt. cap. 99. Crom. 31.

Sect. 17. From what has been said it clearly appears, That no Burglary can be committed by breaking into any Ground inclosed, or Booth, or Tent, *&c.* for there seems to be no Colour from any Authority ancient or modern, to make any Offence Burglary that is not done either against some House, or Church, or the Walls, or Gates of some Town.

Dy. 99. Pl. 58. Dalis 22. 3 Inst. 65.

Sect. 18. As to the sixth Point, *viz.* What Degree of Guilt is required in the principal Intention of the Offender, it seems clear, That there can be no Burglary but where the Indictment both expresly alledges, and the Verdict also finds, an Intention to commit some Felony; for if it appear

 that

that the Offender meant only to commit a Trespass, as to beat the Party, *&c.* he is not guilty of Burglary. However, it seems much the better Opinion, That an Intention to commit a Rape, or such other Crime which is made Felony by Statute, and was a Trespass only at Common Law, will make a Man guilty of Burglary, as much as if such Offence were a Felony at Common Law, because where-ever a Statute makes any Offence Felony, it incidentally gives it all the Properties of a Felony at Common Law. Kelynge 30. H.P.C.83,84. Crom.32.a.b. Con. Dalt. cap 99. H. P. C. 215. Infra Ch. 46. Sect. 3.

CHAP. XXXIX.

Of Arson.

ARSON is a Felony at Common Law, in maliciously and voluntarily burning the House of another by Night or by Day. Bro. Coro. 135, 155. S. P. C. 36. 3 Inst. 66. Dal. cap 105. 2 Inst. 188. 11 Co. 29.

For the better Explication whereof I shall consider:

1. What is such a House in which Arson may be committed.
2. Whether this Offence may be committed in the Offender's own House.
3. How much of the House ought to be burnt.
4. With what Degrees of Malice.

Sect. 1. As to the first Point, *viz.* What is such a House in which Arson may be committed; it seems agreed, That not only a Mansion-House, and the principal Parts thereof, but also any other House, and the Out-buildings, as Barns, and Stables, adjoining thereto; and also Barns full of Corn, whether they be adjoining to any House or not, are so far secured by Law, that the malicious burning of them is Arson; and it is said, That in an Indictment they are well expressed by the Word *Domus*, without adding *Mansionalis*. 3 Inst. 67. 4 Co. 20. Dal. ca. 105. 11 H 7. 1. Bro. Coro. 226 S. P. C. 36. H. P. C. 86.

Sect. 2. But it seems that at this Day the Burning of the Frame of a House, or of a Stack of Corn, *&c.* is not accounted Arson, because it cannot come under the Word *Domus*, which seems at present to be thought necessary in every Indictment of Arson; yet it is said, That anciently the Burning a Stack of Corn was accounted Arson. And at this Day by 43 *El.* 13. *it is Felony without the Benefit of the Clergy, wilfully and of Malice to burn or cause to be burned, or aid, procure, or consent to the Burning of, any Barn, Stack of Corn, or Grain, in the Counties of* Northumberland, Cumberland, Westmorland *and* Durham. And by 22 and 23 *Ca.* 2. 7. *it is Felony, in the Night-time, maliciously, unlawfully, and willingly to burn or cause to be burned any Stacks or Ricks of Corn, Hay, or Grain, Barns, or other Houses, or Buildings, or Kilns, in any Place whatsoever: But the Offender may avoid Judgment of Death by chusing Transportation, and may be proceeded against by any three Justices of Peace, according to the Method prescribed by the Statute*, which is set forth more at large in Chap. 46. H P C 86. 3 Inst 67. 3 Inst. 67. Britt. fo. 16. S. P. C. 36. Dal. cap. 105.

Sect. 3. As to the second Point, *viz.* Whether Arson may be committed in the Offender's own House, it seems clearly agreed, That one seized in Fee, or but possessed for Years, of a House standing by it self at 1 Jon. 351. Cro. C. 377.

a Distance from all others, cannot commit Felony in burning the same: Also it seems the much stronger Opinion, That a Man so seized or possessed of a House in a Town, who burns his own with an Intent to burn his Neighbour's, but in the Event burns his own only, is not guilty of Arson; for by the general Tenor of the Books speaking of this Offence, it seems to be supposed to be done in the House of another, and not of the Offender; neither shall any Act, which is only a Crime in Respect of the Injury which it does, or may do, to another, be made a Felony by Reason of an Intention thereby to commit a Felony, if such Intention be not executed: However this is certainly an Offence highly punishable, in Regard of the Malice thereof, and the great Danger to the Publick which attends it, and the Offender may be severely fined and imprisoned during the King's Pleasure, and set on the Pillory, and bound to his good Behaviour during Life.

3 Inst. 67. Dalt. cap. 105. Cro. Ca. 338. 1 Inst. 351. H. P. C. 85. Kelynge. 29.

Sect. 4. As to the third Point, *viz.* How much of such House ought to be burnt, it seems to be clearly agreed, That neither a bare Intention to burn a House, nor even an actual Attempt to do it by putting a Fire to Part of a House, will amount to Felony, if no Part of it be burnt; for the Indictment must have the Words *Incendit & combussit*: But it is certain, That if any Part of the House be burnt, the Offender is guilty of Felony, notwithstanding the Fire afterwards be put out, or go out of it self.

H. P. C. 85. Dal. cap 105. 3 Inst. 66.

Sect. 5. As to the fourth Point, *viz.* With what Degrees of Malice such House ought to be burnt; it seems clear, That if the Fire happened through Negligence or Mischance, it cannot make him, who is the unfortunate Cause of it, guilty of Arson; for the Indictment must alledge the Offence to have been done *Voluntariè ex malitiâ suâ praecogitatâ & felonicè.* Yet if one maliciously intending only to burn the House of *A.* happen thereby to burn the House of *B.* it is certain that he may be indicted as having maliciously burned the House of *B.* for where a felonious Design against one Man misses its Aim, and takes Effect upon another, it shall have the like Construction as if it had been levelled against him who suffers by it.

3 Inst. 67. H. P. C. 85. Plow. Com 475.

CHAP. XL.

Of Felonies by Statute.

OFfences more immediately against the Subject, made capital by Statute, and not reduced to any of the foregoing Heads, are such as are committed;

1. Against Women.
2. Against the Rights of Marriage.
3. Against the Members of a Man's Body.
4. Against Records.
5. Against Cattle.
6. By Purveyors.
7. By Soldiers and Mariners.
8. By Hunters.

9. By Forgers of falſe Deeds.
10. By Gaolers.
11. By Tranſporters of Sheep or Wool.
12. By Servants.
13. By Egyptians.
14. By Cutters of Pow-dike.
15. By Treſpaſſers on the Borders, and Rioters.
16. By Bankrupts.
17. By Counterfeiters of Bank-Notes, Exchequer-Bills, Stamps, South-Sea Bonds, Lottery-Orders, *&c.*

In treating hereof, I ſhall firſt conſider ſuch Points as relate to them all in general, and then deſcend to each Crime in particular, in the Order before ſet down.

As to what relates to them all in general, I will ſhew,

1. Where an Offence ſhall be ſaid to be made Felony by Statute.
2. What is incidentally implied in every ſuch Statute.

Sect. 1. As to the firſt Point it ſeems clear, That not only thoſe Crimes which are made Felonies in expreſs Words, but alſo all thoſe which are decreed to have or undergo, Judgment of Life and Member by any Statute, become Felonies thereby, whether the Word Felony were omitted or mentioned. Bro. Coro. 204. 3 Inſt. 91. 2 Inſt. 434. Co. Lit. 391.

Sect. 2. But an Offence ſhall never be made Felony by the Conſtruction of any doubtful and ambiguous Words of a Statute, and therefore, if it be only prohibited under Pain of forfeiting all that a Man has, or of forfeiting Body and Goods, or of being at the King's Will for Body, Land, and Goods, it ſhall amount to no more than a high Miſdemeanour, puniſhable by Impriſonment, *&c.* Co. Lit. 391. Hob. 270. 3 Inſt. 146.

Sect. 3. Alſo where a Statute makes a ſecond Offence Felony, or ſubject to a heavier Puniſhment than the firſt; it is always implied, That ſuch ſecond Offence ought to be committed after a Conviction for the firſt; From whence it follows, That if it be not ſo laid in the Indictment, it ſhall be puniſhed but as the firſt Offence; for the gentler Method ſhall firſt be tried, which perhaps may prove effectual. H. P. C. 8. 2 Bulſt. 349. Dy. 323. Pl. 31. 1 Leon 295.

Sect. 4. As to the ſecond Point, *viz.* What is incidentally implied in every Statute making an Offence Felony; it ſeems clear, That every ſuch Statute does by neceſſary Conſequence ſubject the Offender to the like Attainder and Forfeiture, *&c.* and alſo does require the like Conſtruction, as to thoſe who ſhall be accounted Acceſſaries before or after, and to all other Intents and Purpoſes, as is incident to a Felony at Common Law. 3 Inſt. 47, 59, 90. H. P. C. 215. Daliſ. 11, 22.

Sect. 5. Yet where ſuch a Statute ſaves the Corruption of Blood, it impliedly ſaves the Deſcent of the Land of the Offender to his Heir: Alſo where it ſaves the Land to the Heir, it prevents the Corruption of Blood ſo far; and it is ſaid, That in both Caſes it ſaves the Wife's Dower, becauſe where-ever an Heir takes as Heir, he ſhall not avoid a Title of Dower in Reſpect of the ſame Inheritance. But notwithſtanding ſuch a ſaving the Land ſhall be forfeited for the Life of the Offender. 3 Inſt. 47. H. P. C. 8. 3 Inſt. 47.

Sect. 6. If one commit an Offence which is made Felony by Statute, and then the Statute be repealed, he cannot be puniſhed as a Felon in Reſpect of that Statute. Bro. Coro. 203.

CHAP.

CHAP. XLI.

Of Rape.

OFFENCES againſt Women made Felonies by Statute are of two Kinds.

1. Rape.
2. Forcible Marriage.

In treating of Rape, I ſhall conſider,

1. What ſhall be called a Rape.
2. How it is puniſhed.

Co. Lit. 190. 3 Inſt. 60. 2 Inſt. 180. 12 Co. 37. 3 Inſt. 59, 60. H. P. C. 117. Ruſhworth Collect. Part 2. Vol. I. 94. 3 Inſt. 59.

Sect. 1. As to the firſt Point, It ſeems that Rape is an Offence in having unlawful and carnal Knowledge of a Woman, by Force and againſt her Will: But it is ſaid, That no Aſſault upon a Woman in order to raviſh her, howſoever ſhameleſs and outrageous it may be, if it proceed not to ſome Degree of Penetration, and alſo of Emiſſion, can amount to a Rape; however it is ſaid, That Emiſſion is, *primâ facie*, an Evidence of Penetration.

Dal. ca. 105. Bro. Parliament 55. 5 Ed. 4. 6. a. Ruſhworth Coll. Part 2. Vol. 1. 100. Bract. 147. S. P. C. 24. Bract. 148. Finch. 204. Dal. cap. 107.

Sect. 2. Offences of this Nature are not any way mitigated, by ſhewing that the Woman at laſt yielded to the Violence, if ſuch her Conſent was forced by Fear of Death, or of Dureſs; nor is it any Excuſe, that ſhe conſented after the Fact, or that ſhe was a common Strumpet; for ſhe is ſtill under the Protection of the Law, and may be forced. But it was anciently ſaid, to be no Rape to force a Man's own Concubine. Alſo it hath been ſaid by ſome to be no Rape to force a Woman who conceives at the Time; for it is ſaid, That if ſhe had not conſented, ſhe could not have conceived: But this Opinion ſeems very queſtionable, not only becauſe the previous Violence is no way extenuated by ſuch a ſubſequent Conſent, but alſo becauſe if it were neceſſary to ſhew that the Woman did not conceive, this Offender could not be tried till ſuch Time as it might appear whether ſhe did or not, and likewiſe becauſe the Philoſophy of this Notion may very well be doubted of.

Ruſhworth Coll. Part 2. Vol 1. 100. Bract. 147. a. Dalt ca. 107. Cromp 100. a Dy. 304. Pl. 51.

Sect. 3. It is a ſtrong, but not a concluſive Preſumption againſt a Woman, That ſhe made no Complaint in a reaſonable Time after the Fact.

Sect. 4. It was a Queſtion before 18 *El.* 7. Whether a Rape could be committed on a Child of the Age of ſix or ſeven Years, but by that Statute, *whoſoever ſhall unlawfully and carnally know and abuſe any Woman Child under the Age of ten Years, ſhall ſuffer as a Felon without Clergy.*

Co Ca 332

Sect. 5. Upon an Indictment for this Offence, it is no way material whether ſuch Child conſented, or were forced; yet it muſt be proved, That the Offender entered into her Body, *&c.*

Dalt. ca. 107.

Sect. 6. All who are preſent and actually aſſiſt a Man to commit a Rape, may be indicted as principal Offenders, whether they be Men or Women.

Sect. 7. As to the second Point, *viz.* How Rape is punished, it is said, that of old Time it was Felony, and consequently punishable with Death, especially if the Party ravished were a Virgin, unless such Virgin would accept of the Offender for her Husband, in which Case she might save his Life by marrying him. But afterwards it was looked upon as a great Misdemeanour only, but not Felony; and the Offender was punished with the Loss of his Eyes and Testicles: And by the Statute of *Westm.* 1. 13. It was reduced to a Trespass, subjecting the Offender to two Years Imprisonment, and a Fine at the King's Will. But the smallness of the Punishment proving a great Encouragement to the Offence, it was made Felony again, by the Statute of *Westminster* 2. 34. and by 18 *El.* 7. it is excluded from the Benefit of the Clergy.

Bract. 147, 148. S. P. C. 21. b. 22, 23. 2 Inst. 181. Dalt. cap. 99. Crom. 32. con. Co. Li. 123. b. Fleta lib. 1. cap. 40. 3 Inst. 180.

CHAP. XLII.

Of Forcible Marriage.

Sect. 1. THE marrying a Woman of Substance by Force, and other Offences of the like Nature, were made Felonies by 3 *H* 7. 2. which was enacted in the following Words:

Sect. 2. *Where Women, as well Maidens as Widows and Wives, having Substances, some in Goods moveable, and some in Lands and Tenements, and some being Heirs Apparent unto their Ancestors, for the Lucre of such Substances, be oftentimes taken by Mis-doers, contrary to their Will, and after married to such Mis-doers, or to other by their Assent, or defiled, to the great Displeasure of God, and contrary to the King's Laws, and Disparagement of the said Women, and utter Heaviness and Discomfort of their Friends, and to the evil Ensample of all other: It is therefore ordained, established, and enacted by our Sovereign Lord the King, by the Advice of the Lords Spiritual and Temporal, and the Commons in the said Parliament assembled, and by Authority of the same, That what Person or Persons from henceforth that taketh any Woman (so) against her Will unlawfully, that is to say, Maid, Widow, or Wife, that such Taking, Procuring, and Abetting to the same, and also receiving wittingly the same Woman so taken against her Will, and knowing the same, be Felony: And that such Mis-doers, Takers, and Procurators to the same, and Receitors, knowing the said Offence in Form aforesaid, be henceforth reputed and judged as principal Felons: Provided alway, that this Act extend not to any Person taking any Woman, only claiming her as his Ward or Bond-Woman.*

Sect. 3. And by 39 *El.* 9. *All Persons who shall be Principals, or Procurers or Accessaries before such Offence committed, are excluded from the Benefit of the Clergy.*

In the Construction of the said Statute of 3 *H.* 7. 2. the following Points have been resolved.

Sect. 4. I. That the Indictment must expresly set forth, both that the Woman taken away had Land or Goods, or was Heir Apparent, and also that she was married or defiled, because no other Case is within the Preamble of the Statute to which the enacting Clause clearly refers; for it does not say, That what Person, *&c.* that taketh any Woman against her Will, but what Person that taketh any Woman *so* against her Will.

Hob. 183. Cro. Ca. 485. Dalis. 22. 1 And. 115. 3 Inst. 61. H. P. C. 118. Savil 59. 12 Co. 20, 110.

Sect. 5. II. That the Indictment ought also to alledge, That the taking was for Lucre, because the Words of the Preamble are so, but that it needs not set forth, That it was with an Intention to marry or defile the Party, because the Words of the Statute neither require such an Intention, nor does the Want thereof any Way lessen the Injury.

Hob. 182. Cro. Ca. 485, 489.

Sect. 6. III. That it is no manner of Excuse, That the Woman at first was taken away with her own Consent, because if she afterwards refuse to continue with the Offender, and be forced against her Will, she may from that Time as properly be said to be taken against her Will, as if she had never given any Consent at all; for till the Force was put upon her, she was in her own Power.

Hob. 182. Cro. Ca. 485.

Sect. 7. IV. That it is not material whether a Woman so taken away, be at last married, or defiled, with her own Consent or not, if she were under the Force at the Time, because the Offender is in both Cases equally within the Words of the Statute, and shall not be construed to be out of the Meaning of it, for having prevailed over the Weakness of a Woman, whom by so base Means he got into his Power.

Cro. Ca. 493. 3 Keb. 193.

Sect. 8. V. That those who after the Fact receive the Offender, but not the Woman, are not Principals within this Statute, because the Words are, *receiving wittingly the same Woman so taken*, &c. but it seems clearly, That they are Accessaries after the Offence, according to the known Rules of Common Law.

3 Inst. 61. Dalis. 22. S. P. C. 44.

Sect. 9. VI. That those who are only privy to the Marriage, but no way Parties to the Forcible Taking away, or consenting thereto, are not within the Statute.

Cro. Ca. 482. H. P. C. 119.

Sect. 10. VII. That where a Woman is taken by Force in the County of *A.* and married in the County of *B.* the Offender may be indicted and found guilty in the County of *B.* because the continuing of the Force there amounts to a Forcible Taking within the Statute.

Cro. Ca. 488. Hob. 183. H. P. C. 119.

CHAP. XLIII.

Of Offences against the Rights of Marriage,

Cro. El. 94.

Sect. 1. OFfences against the Rights of Marriage, at Common Law, are looked upon as Spiritual Offences, and punishable only by the Ecclesiastical Law, but one of them is made Felony, but not excluded from the Benefit of the Clergy, by 1 *Jac.* 1. 11. by which it is enacted, *That if any Person or Persons, within his Majesty's Dominions of* England *and* Wales, *being married, do marry any Person or Persons, the former Husband or Wife being alive, that then every such Offence shall be Felony, and the Person and Persons so offending, shall suffer Death as in Cases of Felony. And the Party and Parties so offending, shall receive such and the like Proceeding, Trial, and Execution, in such County, where such Person or Persons shall be apprehended, as if the Offence had been committed in such County, where such Person or Persons shall be taken or apprehended.*

Sect. 2. But it is provided by the said Statute, *That nothing therein contained, shall extend to any Person or Persons whose Husband or Wife shall be continually remaining beyond the Seas by the Space of seven Years together, or whose*

Husband or Wife shall absent him or her self the one from the other, by the Space of seven Years together in any Parts within his Majesty's Dominions, the one of them not knowing the other to be living within that Time.

Sect. 3. And it is farther provided, *That the said Statute shall not extend to any Person or Persons who shall be at the Time of such Marriage divorced by Sentence in the Ecclesiastical Court, or to any Person or Persons where the former Marriage shall be by Sentence in the Ecclesiastical Court declared to be void and of no effect: Nor to any Person or Persons, for, or by Reason of, any former Marriage had or made within Age of Consent.*

Sect. 4. Also it is farther provided, *That no Attainder for this Offence shall make or work any Corruption of Blood, Loss of Dower, or Disinherison of Heir or Heirs.*

In the Construction of this Statute it has been holden,

Sect. 5. I. That not only those who are divorced *à vinculo Matrimonii*, but also those who are divorced only *à Mensâ & Thoro Causâ Adulterii* or *Sævitiæ*, are within the Exception in this Statute, notwithstanding there be not the Word *Divortiamus*, but only the Word *Separamus*, in the Sentence; because the Statute, being penal, shall be construed favourably, and such Separations are taken for Divorces in common Understanding. 3 Inst. 89. H. P. C. 122. Kelynge 27. Cro. Ca. 461, 462. *This is made a Query.*

Sect. 6. II. Where either of the Parties were within the Age of Consent at the Time of the first Marriage, that not only such Person as was within such Age, but also the other who was above it, is within the Exception of the Statute, because the Power of disagreeing to such Marriage is equal on both Sides. 3 Inst. 89. H. P. C. 121. 1 Rol. Ab. 340. Pl. 13, 141. Pl. 14, 15, 16, 17. Co. Lit. 79.

Sect. 7. III. That if the first Marriage were beyond Sea, and the later in *England*, the Party may be indicted for it here, because it is the later Marriage that makes the Offence; but if the first Marriage were in *England*, and the later beyond Sea, it is said that the Offender cannot be indicted here; *sed quære* why not? for the Words of the Statute are, *That the Parties so offending shall receive such and the like Proceeding, Trial, and Execution, in such County where such Person or Persons shall be apprehended, as if the Offence had been committed in such County, where such Person or Persons shall be taken or apprehended.* 1 Sid. 171. Kelynge 80.

CHAP. XLIV.

Of Offences against the Members of a Man's Body.

IN treating of Offences against the Members of a Man's Body, I shall consider,

1. What Offences of this Nature are esteemed Mahims.
2. How they are punished by the Common Law.
3. How they are punished by Statute.

Sect. 1. As to the first Point, it seems that such a Hurt of any Part of a Man's Body, whereby he is rendered less able in Fighting, either to defend himself or annoy his Adversary, is properly Mahim. Fleta, lib. c. 40 Brit. 48. Bract. 144. b. 145. S. P. C. 38. b. Co. Lit. 126, 128. 3 Inst. 62, 118.

Sect.

25 Ed. 3. 94. *See the Authors above cited.* *Sect.* 2. And therefore the cutting off, or disabling, or weakening a Man's Hand, or Finger, or striking out his Eye or Fore-tooth, or castrating him, are said to be Mahims, but the cutting off his Ear, or Nose, *&c.* are not esteemed Mahims, because they do not weaken, but only disfigure him.

Bract. 144. b. Fleta, lib. 1. cap. 40. S. P. C. 37. a. 3 Inst 62, 118. H. P. C. 133. *Sect.* 3. As to the second Point, *viz.* How such Offences are to be punished, it is to be observed, that all Mahim is Felony; and it is said, That anciently Castration was punished with Death, and other Mahims with the Loss of Member for Member; but afterwards no Mahim was punished in any Case with the Loss of Life or Member, but only with Fine and Imprisonment.

S e 5 H. 4. c. 5. *Sect.* 4. As to the third Point, *viz.* How such Offences are punished by Statute, it is enacted by 22 and 23 *Ca.* 2. cap. 1. *That if any Person shall on Purpose and of Malice fore-thought, and by lying in wait, unlawfully cut out, or disable, the Tongue, put out an Eye, slit the Nose, cut off a Nose, or Lip, or cut off or disable any Limb, or Member, of any Subject of his Majesty, with Intention in so doing to maim or Disfigure, in any the Manners before mentioned, such his Majesty's Subject, That then and in every such Case the Person or Persons, so offending, their Counsellors, Aiders and Abettors, knowing of, and privy to the Offence as aforesaid, shall be and are by the said Statute declared to be Felons, and shall suffer Death as in Cases of Felony without Benefit of Clergy.*

Sect. 5. But it is provided by the said Statute, *That no Attainder of such Felony shall extend to corrupt the Blood, or forfeit the Dower of the Wife, or the Lands, Goods or Chattels of the Offender.*

CHAP. XLV.

Of Offences against Records.

Sect. 1. AT Common Law the imbezilling, defacing, or altering any Record, without due Authority, was an Offence highly punishable by Fine and Imprisonment, *&c.* and in many Cases it was made Felony by the following Clause of 8 *H.* 6. 12. (3 Inst. 71, 72.)

Sect. 2. *It is ordained, That if any Record or Parcel of the same, Writ, Retorn, Panel, Process, or Warrant of Attorney, in the King's Courts of Chancery, Exchequer, the one Bench or the other, or in his Treasury, be willingly stoln, taken away, withdrawn, or avoided, by any Clerk, or by other Person, because whereof any Judgment shall be reversed: That such Stealer, Taker-away, Withdrawer, or Avoider, their Procurators, Counsellors, and Abettors, thereof indicted, and by Process thereupon made, thereof duly convict by their own Confession, or by Inquest to be taken of lawful Men, (whereof the one half shall be of the Men of any Court of the same Courts, and the other half of other) shall be judged for Felons, and shall incur the Pain of Felony: And that the Judges of the said Courts, of the one Bench or of the other, have Power to hear and determine such Defaults before them, and thereof to make due Punishment, as afore is said.*

3 Inst. 71. In the Construction of this Clause, it hath been holden:

Sect. 3. I. That it extends only to the Courts which are expresly named; and to the Court of Chancery, so far only as it proceeds according to the Course of the Common Law.

Sect. 2. II. That it extends not to such Offence by the Judges of any Court; for whereas it begins with expresly naming Clerks which are inferior to them, it shall not be intended to include them under the general Words following; however by 8 *R.* 2. 4. *Judges as well as Clerks are to pay a Fine to the King, and make Satisfaction to the Party for falsly entering Pleas, or rasing Rolls, or changing Verdicts to the Disherison of any one*; And they are highly punishable at Common Law for other Offences of like Nature, as for inserting a Bill of Indictment not found by the Jury among those which were found, and such like. And Justice *Ingham* in the Reign of *Edward* the first was fined eight hundred Marks for rasing a Fine of thirteen Shillings and four Pence, set on a poor Man, and making it six Shillings and eight Pence. 3 Inst. 72. 2 R. 3, 10. 3 Mod. 66. Bro.Cor. 174. Tregs 31. Con. Bro. Presentment 23. Indictment 14, 50. 3 Inst. 72.

Sect. 5. III. That not only such an Alteration whereby a Judgment is actually reversed, but also such whereby it is reversible, whether it were made before or after the Judgment was given, or whether it be or be not afterwards amended by the Court, is within this Act; for those Words in the Statute *whereby any Judgment shall be reversed*, are taken to have the same Purport, as if it were said, whereby any Judgment shall be annulled, or lose its Force or Effect; for it is plain, That the Statute cannot intend that the Judgment must be actually reversed by Writ of Error, because it speaks of stealing or carrying away, or avoiding of Records, which makes it impossible that the Judgment should be reversed at all, because no Writ of Error can remove a Judgment which appears not. And it has been holden, That if *A. B.* be outlawed by the Name of *A. C.* and afterwards the Record be rased, and *A. B.* inserted, the Offence is within the Statute, because the Record against *A. C.* is annulled, and the Judgment prevented, which might have been given on a Writ of Error for this Defect. 2 Rol. Re. 81. 2 R. 3. 10. S. P. C. 36. b. 3 Inst. 72. 11 Rep. 34. b.

Sect. 6. IV. If the Felony were committed partly in one County, and partly in another, but not so as to amount to a compleat Offence within the Statute in either, That the Party cannot be indicted for a Felony, because the Counties cannot join in an Indictment, and that which is done in one cannot be found in another, but that he may be indicted for a Misprision in either County. 2 R. 3 10. b. 11.] S. P. C. 36. 3 Inst. 73.

Sect. 7. V. That the Act, by making those who are Accessary before the Fact principal Felons, does not mean any way to favour those who are Accessary after, but to leave them to the general Construction of the Law. 3 Inst. 72. Con. S. P. C. 44. d.

Sect. 8. VI. That by the last Clause of the Act, the Justices of either Bench have a Concurrent Authority, and that they which shall first enquire shall proceed; and that if the Offence were committed in the County where the Benches sit, they need no other Commission; but if it were done in another County, that they must have a special Commission: And if in *London*, that they shall have a Commission in which the Mayor shall be omitted, for the Charters of the City which require that he shall be a Principal in every Commission, extend not to such Causes which are specially limited to particular Judges. 3 Inst. 73. 3 Inst. 72. 2 R. 3. 11. a

Sect. 9. By 21 *Jac.* 1. 26. *It is made Felony without the Benefit of Clergy, but not so as to corrupt the Blood, to acknowledge or procure to be acknowledged, any Fine, Recovery, Deed enrolled, Statute, Recognizance, Bail, or Judgment in the Name of any other Person or Persons not privy or consenting to the same.*

Sect. 10. In the Construction hereof it has been holden, That if a Man personate another in the County of *A.* in putting in Bail before a Judge, and the Bail be filed in the County of *B.* the Trial shall be in the County of *A.* 2 Jon. 64.

Sect. 11. Also it is enacted by 4 & 5 *Will. & Mar.* 4. *That any Person or Persons who shall before any Commissioner authorized to take Bail, by vertue of the said Statute, in Actions depending in the Courts of King's Bench, Common Pleas, or Exchequer, represent, or personate any other Person or Persons, whereby the Person or Persons so represented and personated, may be liable to the Payment of any Sum or Sums of Money, or Debt, or Damages, to be recovered in the same Suit or Action, wherein such Person or Persons are represented and personated, as if they had really acknowledged and entered into the same, being lawfully convicted thereof, shall be adjudged Felony.*

CHAP. XLVI.

Of Offences relating to Cattle.

BY 22 & 23 *Car.* 2. 7. it is made Felony, *Malitiously, unlawfully, and willingly, to kill or destroy any Horses, Sheep, or other Cattle of any Person or Persons whatsoever in the Night-time, but Liberty is given to the Offender to avoid Judgment of Death, by chusing Judgment of Transportation for seven Years; and any three Justices of Peace for the County, Division, City, Town-corporate, or Place, whereof one to be of the* Quorum, *are authorised to enquire as well by the Oaths of twelve lawful Men, of the same County, as by Examination of Witnesses upon Oath, or by any lawful Ways or Means, which to them shall seem meet, of the said Offences, and in Order thereunto to issue out Warrants, as well for the summoning of Jurors, as for the apprehending of all Persons, who shall or may be suspected thereof, and to take their Examination touching the same, as also to cause all such other Persons as to them shall seem likely to make Discovery thereof, to appear before them, and to give Information upon Oath concerning their Knowledge of the Premisses, so as no Person so to be examined shall in any wise be proceeded against for any Offence concerning which he shall be so examined as a Witness, and shall upon such his Examination make a true Discovery of: And if any Person who shall be thought likely to make such Discovery, being summoned by the said Justices, refuse to appear, or to be examined as a Witness, he may be committed by the said Justices to the County-Gaol, till he shall submit to be examined. Provided, That no Person shall be questioned for any Offence against the said Statute, unless he be proceeded against within six Months after the Offence committed.*

CHAP. XLVII.

Of Offences by Purveyors.

Sect. 1. ANciently the King's Court was supplied with Necessaries from the ancient Demesnes of the Crown, which were manured for that purpose, and in respect thereof the Tenants of those Lands had many privileges, which they still enjoy; but this Method being found to be

2 Inst. 543.

be troublesome and inconvenient, was by Degrees disused, and afterwards the King used to appoint certain Officers to buy in Provisions for his Houshould, who were called Purveyors, and claimed many Privileges by the Prerogative of the Crown, and seem to have had the Pre-emption of all such Victuals as were bought by any one to sell again. Noy 101.

Sect. 2. By *Magna Charta*, chap. 21. *The King shall not take the Timber of any Person against his Will, and by many subsequent Statutes, several Offences of Purveyors were made Felonies, as if they took Things above the Value of twelve Pence, against the Will of the Owner, without Warrant, or without such Appraisement as was directed by those Statutes, or without paying for them,* &c. 28 E. 1. ch. 2. 36 E. 3 ch. 2, 3, 4, 5, 6. 5 E. 3. ch. 2. 2 Inst. 82. Dalt. ca. 107. Crom. 48. 1 Bulf. 96, 97.

Sect. 3. But these Laws having been found by Experience not to have sufficiently provided against the Oppressions of *Persons imployed for making Provisions for the King's Houshold, Carriages, and other Purveyance for his Majesty*, and several Counties having found themselves obliged to submit to sundry Rates and Taxes, and Compositions to redeem themselves from such Vexations and Oppressions, as it is recited by 12 *Car.* 2. 24. Par. 12. it was enacted by the said Statute, *That from thenceforth no Sum or Sums of Money, or other Thing shall be taken, raised, taxed, rated, imposed, paid, or levied, for or in regard of any Provision, Carriages, or Purveyance for his Majesty, his Heirs or Successors.* See Mo. 762, 770, 778. Noy 101.

Sect. 4. And it is farther enacted by the said Statute Par. 13. *That no Person or Persons by any Warrant, Commission, or Authority under the great Seal, or otherwise by Colour of buying or making Provision or Purveyance for his Majesty, or any Queen of* England *for the Time being, or of any the Children of any King or Queen of* England *for the Time being, or that shall be, or for his, their, or any of their Houshold, shall take any Timber, Fuel, Cattle, Corn, Grain, Malt, Hay, Straw, Victual, Cart, Carriage, or other Thing whatsoever, of any the Subjects of his Majesty, his Heirs, or Successors, without the free and full Consent of the Owner or Owners thereof, had and obtained without Menace or Enforcement; nor shall summon, warn, take, use, or require any the said Subjects to furnish or find any Horses, Oxen, or Cattle, Carts, Ploughs, Wains, or other Carriages, for the use of his Majesty, his Heirs or Successors, or of any Queen of* England, *or of any Child, or Children of any of the Kings or Queens of* England *for the Time being, for the carrying the Goods of his Majesty, his Heirs or Successors, or the said Queens, or Children, or any of them, without such full and free Consent as aforesaid, any Law, Statute, Custom, or Usage to the contrary notwithstanding.*

Sect. 5. And it is further enacted Par. 14. *That no Pre-emption shall be allowed or claimed in the behalf of his Majesty, or of any of his Heirs or Successors, or of any of the Queens of* England, *or of any of the Children of the Royal Family for the Time being, in Market or out of Market, but that it be free to all and every the Subjects of his Majesty, to sell, dispose, or employ his said Goods to any other Person or Persons, as him listeth, any pretence of making Provision or Purveyance of Victual, Carriages, or other Thing for his Majesty, his Heirs or Successors, or of the said Queens, or Children, or any pretence of Pre-emption in their, or any of their Behalfs notwithstanding. And if any Person or Persons shall make Provision or Purveyance for his Majesty, his Heirs or Successors, or any the Queens, or Children aforesaid, or impress, or take any such Carriages, or other Things aforesaid, on any pretence or colour of any Warrant aforesaid, under the Great Seal, or otherwise, contrary to the Intent hereof, it shall be lawful for the Justices of Peace, or such two, or one of them as dwell near, and to the Constables of such Parish or Village where such occasion shall happen, at the Request of the Party grieved; to commit or cause to be committed, the Party or Parties so doing and offending, to Gaol, till the next Sessions, there to be indicted and proceeded against for the same,* &c.

Sect.

Sect. 6. But this absolute and universal Restraint of all Kinds of Purveyance having been found by Experience inconvenient, it was enacted by 13 & 14 *Car.* 2. 20. which has been often continued by subsequent Statutes, That the Officers of the Navy may press Carriages for the use of his Majesty's Navy and Ordnance, according to the Regulations prescribed by that Statute, and the like was enacted by 1 *Jac.* 2. 10. in relation to the King's Royal Progresses, *&c.*

CHAP. XLVIII.

Of Offences by Soldiers and Mariners.

Offences by Soldiers or Mariners, made Felony by Statute, are of three Kinds:

1. Wandering without a Testimonial.
2. Departing from the King's Service without Licence.
3. Destroying a Ship.

Sect. 1. The first of these Offences depends upon 39 *El.* 17. by which it is recited, *That divers licentious Persons, contemning both Laws, Magistrates, and Religion, had used to wander up and down in all Parts of the Realm, under the Name of Soldiers and Mariners, abusing the Title of that honourable Profession, to countenance their wicked Behaviours, and that such Persons had used to assemble themselves weaponed in the Highways, and elsewhere in Troops, to the great Terror and Astonishment of her Majesty's true Subjects, the Impeachment of her Laws, and the Disturbance of the Peace and Tranquility of this Realm: And that many hainous Outrages, Robberies, and horrible Murders had been daily committed by such dissolute Persons*; and thereupon it is enacted, *That all idle and wandering Soldiers or Mariners, or idle Persons which shall be wandering as Soldiers or Mariners, shall settle themselves in some Service, Labour, or other lawful course of Life, without wandering, or otherwise repair to the Places where they were born, or to their Dwelling-Places, if they have any, and there remain, betaking themselves to some lawful Trade or course of Life, as aforesaid; upon pain, That all Persons offending contrary to this Act, shall suffer as in case of Felony, without Clergy.*

Sect. 2. And it is farther enacted, *That every idle and wandering Soldier or Mariner, which, coming from his Captain from the Seas, or from beyond the Seas, shall not have a Testimonial under the Hand of some one Justice of the Peace, of, or near, the Place where he landed, setting down therein the Place and Time, where and when he landed, and the Place of his Dwelling or Birth, unto which he is to pass as aforesaid, and a convenient Time therein limited for his Passage, or having such Testimonial, shall wilfully exceed the Time therein limited, above fourteen Days: And also, as well every such idle and wandering Soldier or Mariner, as every other idle Person wandering, as Soldier or Mariner, which shall at any Time hereafter forge or counterfeit any such Testimonal, or have with him or them any such Testimonial forged, or counterfeited as aforesaid, knowing the same to be counterfeited or forged, in all these cases every such Act or Acts to be Felony, and the Offenders to suffer as aforesaid, without any Benefit of Clergy.*

I Sect.

Sect. 3. And it is farther enacted, *That it shall be lawful for the Justices of Assizes, Justices of Gaol-Delivery, and the Justices of Peace of every County, and all Justices of Peace in Towns-corporate, having Authority to hear and determine Felonies, to hear and determine all such Offences in their general Sessions, and to execute the Offenders, which shall be convicted before them, as in Cases of Felony is accustomed, except some honest Freeholder,* &c. *will take such Offender into his Service for one whole Year, and also be bound by Recognizance of ten Pounds, to keep the said Person for one whole Year, and bring him to the next Sessions for the Peace and Gaol-Delivery next ensuing after the said Year; and if any such Person so retained, depart within the Year, without the Licence of him that so retained him, then, to be indicted, tried, and judged as a Felon, and not to have the Benefit of the Clergy.*

Sect. 4. But it is provided by the said Statute, *That if any such idle and wandering Person as aforesaid shall happen to fall sick by the Way, so that by reason of his Weakness he can not travel to his Journey's End within the Time limited within his Testimonial, no such Person to be within the Danger of this Statute, so as he settle himself in some lawful course of Life, as aforesaid, or repair, as aforesaid, to the Place where he was born, or was last abiding, within convenient Time after the Recovery of his Sickness, and there remain as aforesaid.*

Sect. 5. And it is farther provided by the said Statute, *That if such Soldier or Mariner repairing to his Place of Birth,* &c. *can not get work, he shall be set to work by two Justices of Peace,* &c.

Sect. 6. And it is farther provided, *That if such Soldier or Mariner resort to some Justice of the Peace next adjoining to his Place of Landing, or to such his direct Way home, and make known unto the said Justice his Poverty; that the said Justice, upon perfect Notice thereof had, may licence the same Soldier or Mariner to pass the next and direct Way to the Place where he is to repair, and to limit him so much Time only, as shall be necessary for his travel thither; and that in such case his Licence being so made, and he pursuing the Form of such his Licence, shall and may, for his necessary Relief in his Travel, ask and take the Relief that any Person shall willingly give him.*

Sect. 7. The second Offence of this Kind, *viz.* That of departing from the King's Service without Licence, depends upon several Statutes, for it was enacted by 18 *H.* 6. 19. *that Soldiers retained in the manner prescribed by that Act, departing from their Captains without Licence, shall be guilty of Felony;* but this Statute is now of little use, because the Method of retaining Soldiers therein referred to, is disused. 3 Inst. 86. 6 Co. 27. Co. Lit. 71. Dal. ca. 107. Cro. Ca. 71. Hutt. 134.

Sect. 8. However, by 7 *H.* 7. 1. and 3 *H.* 8. 5. still in force, *If any Soldier, being no Captain, immediately retained with the King, who shall be in Wages and retained, or take any Prest, to serve the King upon the Sea, or upon the Land beyond the Sea, depart out of the King's Service, without Licence of his Captain, he shall suffer as a Felon, without the Benefit of the Clergy. And all Justices of Peace in every Shire in* England, *where any such Offenders be taken, have Power to enquire of the said Offences, and the same to hear and determine, as they may do of Felony, Trespasses, and of other Offences expressed in the King's Commission to them made, as though the said Offences were done in the same Shire.* 3 Inst. 86. Dalt. ca. 107. 2 And. 151. 3 Mod 124. *See also the other Books above cited.*

Sect. 9. And by 2 *Ed.* 6. 2. *If any Soldier, serving the King in his Wars, in any his Dominions, or on the Seas, or beyond the Seas, or in Scot*land, *depart without Licence of the Lieutenant, or Admiral, or Captain,* &c. *with Booty, or otherwise, being in the Enemy's Country, or elsewhere in the King's Service, or out of any Garrison where he shall be appointed to serve, he shall be adjudged a Felon, and excluded from his Clergy; and the Justices of eve-* 3 Inst. 86. 6 Co. 67.

ry Shire where such Offender shall be taken, may enquire of and determine the Offence, &c.

Sect. 10. The third Offence of this Kind, *viz.* That of destroying a Ship depends upon 22 & 23 *Car.* 2. 11. and 1 *Annæ* 9. by which it is enacted, *That if any Captain, Master, Mariner, or other Officer, belonging to any Ship, shall wilfully cast away, burn, or otherwise destroy the Ship to which he belongeth, or procure the same to be done, to the Prejudice of the Owner or Owners thereof, or of any Merchant or Merchants that shall load Goods thereon, he shall suffer as a Felon, without the Benefit of the Clergy, and if the Offence were committed in the Admiral's Jurisdiction, shall be tried in the Manner prescribed by* 28 H. 8. 15.

CHAP. XLIX.

Of Felonies by Hunters.

3 Inst. 76.77. Dal. ca. 29.

IT is recited by 1 *H.* 7. 7. *That many great Outrages, Murthers, Insurrections and Rebellions had often been occasion'd by Persons in great Numbers, with painted Faces, Visors, and otherwise disguised, and riotously, and in manner of War arrayed, and hunting as well by Night as by Day*; and thereupon it is enacted, *That as often as Information shall be made of any such unlawful Huntings by Night, or with painted Faces, to any of the King's Council, or to any Justice of Peace of the County, of any Person suspected thereof, any of the same Council, or Justices, to whom such Information shall be made, may make a Warrant to arrest such Person, and may also examine him of the said Hunting, and of the said Doers in that Behalf; and if the same Person wilfully conceal the said Huntings, or any Person with him defective therein, that then the same Concealment be Felony; and if he then confess the Truth, and all that he shall be examined of, and knoweth in that behalf, that then the said Offences of Huntings be against the King but Trespass finable, by reason of the same Confession, at the next general Sessions of the Peace to be holden in the same County, by the King's Justices of the same Sessions, there to be sessed. And if any rescous or disobedience be made to any Person, having Authority to do Execution or Justice, by any such Warrant, by any Person, the which so should be arrested, so that the Execution of the same Warrant thereby be not had, that then the same Rescous and Disobedience, be Felony, inquirable and determinable as aforesaid; and if any Person or Persons shall be convict of any such Huntings, with painted Faces, Visors, or otherwise disguised, to the Intent they should not be known, or of unlawful Hunting in Time of Night, that then the same Person or Persons so convict, to have like Punition, as he or they should have, if he or they were convict of Felony.*

CHAP. L.

Of Felonies by Forgers of False Deeds.

BY 5 *El.* chap. 14. *If a Man be convict or condemned of forging or publishing a forged Deed, and after such Conviction or Condemnation, do commit the like Offence, he is made guilty of Felony, and excluded from the Benefit of Clergy*; as shall more fully be shewn in the Chapter of *Forgery*.

CHAP. LI.

Of Felonies by Gaolers.

BY 14 *E.* 3. 10. *If any Keeper of a Prison, or Under-Keeper, by too great Duress of Imprisonment, and by Pain, make any Prisoner that he hath in his Ward, to become an Appellor against his Will, he is guilty of Felony:* And it is said to be no Way material, whether the Approvement be true or false, or whether the Appellee be acquitted or condemned; but at Law this Offence was esteemed a Misprision only, unless the Appellee were hanged, by reason of the Appeal. S. P. C. 36. C. 3 Inst. 91.

CHAP. LII.

Of Felonies by Transporters of Sheep or Wool.

Sect. 1. BY some old Statutes, and 13 & 14 *Car.* 2. 18. the Exportation of Wool was made Felony; but by 7 & 8 *W.* 3. 28. it is reduced to a Misdemeanour only, and it is subjected to severe Penalties by many late Statutes. 3 Inst. 95, 96. 1 W. & M. Sess. 1. cap. 32. 7 & 8 W. 3. cap. 28. 9 & 10 W. 3. cap. 40. 11 & 12 W. 3. cap. 10.

Sect. 2. It is enacted by 8 *El.* 3. *That no Person or Persons shall bring, deliver, send, receive, or take, or procure to be brought, delivered, sent, or received, into any Ship or Bottom, any Rams, Sheep, or Lambs, or any manner of other Kind of Sheep, being alive, to be carried and conveyed out of this Realm of* England. Wales, *or* Ireland, *or out of any of the King's Dominions, on Pain that every such Person or Persons, their Aiders, Abettors, Procurers and Comforters, shall for the first Offence forfeit all his Goods for ever, whereof the one Moiety shall be to the King, the other Moiety to him that will sue for the same:* And further, *That every such Offender shall suffer Imprisonment by the Space of one whole Year, without Bail or Mainprize, and at the Year's end, shall in some open Market-Town, in the fulness of the Market, on the Market-Day, have his left Hand cut off, and that to be nailed up, in the openest Place of such Market;*

and that every Person or Persons estsoons offending against this Statute, shall be adjudged a Felon, &c.

CHAP. LIII.

Of Felonies by Servants.

IT is recited by 33 *H.* 6. 1. *That divers Houshold-Servants, as well of Lords, as of other Persons of good Degree, had then of late, shortly after the Death of their said Lords and Masters, violently, and riotously, taken and spoiled the Goods which were of their said Lords and Masters at the Time of their Death, and the same distributed among themselves*; and thereupon it is enacted, *That after Information made to the Chancellor by the Executors of any such Person, or two of them, of such Riot, Taking, and Spoil; the Chancellor, by the Advice of the two Chief Justices, and Chief Baron, or two of them, may make out Writs to such Sheriffs as shall be thought necessary, commanding them to make such Proclamation, as by the said Statute is directed, for the Offenders to appear in the King's Bench at such a Day, whereupon, if they make Default, they shall be attainted of Felony; but if they appear, they shall be committed or bailed, till they have answered the said Executors in such Actions, which the said Executors will declare against them, or any of them, for the Riot, Taking, and Spoiling aforesaid.*

CHAP. LIV.

Of Felonies by Egyptians.

BY 1 & 2 *Ph. & Mar.* 4. *All outlandish Persons, called* Egyptians, *being of the Age of thirteen Years, who shall be transported into this Realm of* England *or* Wales, *and continue within the same by the Space of one Month*; and by 5 *El.* 20. *All Persons being of the Age of fourteen Years, who shall be seen or found within this Realm of* England *or* Wales, *in any Company or Fellowship of Vagabonds, commonly called, or calling themselves,* Egyptians, *or counterfeiting, transforming, or disguising themselves by their Apparel, Speech, or other Behaviour, like unto such Vagabonds, commonly called, or calling themselves,* Egyptians, *and shall continue and remain in the same, either at one Time, or at several Times, by the Space of one Month, shall suffer as Felons, without the Benefit of the Clergy.*

CHAP. LV.

Of Felonies by Cutters of Pow-dike.

IT is recited by 22 *H.* 8. 11. which was repealed by 1 *Ed.* 6. and revived by 2 and 3 *Ph.* and *Mar.* 19. *That divers Persons had maliciously at sundry Times cut down and broken up, divers Parts of the Dike, called the new* Pow-dike *in* Marshland, *in the County of* Norfolk, *and the broken Dike, otherwise called* Oldfelde-Dike *by* Marshland, *in the Isle of* Ely, *in the County of* Cambridge : *By Reason whereof the Ground within the Country of* Marshland *in the Counties aforesaid, had been many Times drowned; and the Inhabitants had not only been put to great Charges and Expences, but also had lost much Cattle, and also many People had been drowned in their Beds*: And thereupon it is enacted, *That every such perverse and malicious cutting down, and breaking up of, any Part or Parts of the said Dikes, or of any other Bank, being parcel of the Rind and uttermost Part of the said Country of* Marshland, *by any Person or Persons, otherwise than in working upon the said Bank or Dikes, for the repairing, fortifying, and amending of the same, shall be adjudged Felony, and that the Justices of Peace of the said Counties of* Norfolk *and* Cambridge, *within the said Isle, shall have full Power at their Sessions to cause Enquiry to be made of every such Offence, to award like Process, Judgment, and Execution, as they have used to do upon other Felonies, being Felony at Common Law.*

CHAP. LVI.

Of Felonies by Trespassers on the Borders, and Rioters.

IT is recited by 43 *El.* 13. *That then of late Years many of the Queen's Subjects dwelling in the Counties of* Cumberland, Westmorland, *and the Bishoprick of* Durham, *had been taken, some from their own Houses, and other in travelling on the High-way, or otherwise, and been carried away as Prisoners, and kept barbarously, and cruelly, until they had been redeemed by great Ransomes; and also, that then of late Time there had been many Incursions, Robberies, and burning and spoiling of Towns, Villages, and Houses, within the said Counties, so that divers of the Queen's Subjects, in the said Counties, had been enforced to pay a certain Rate of Money, Corn, Cattle, or other Consideration, commonly called Black-mail, to divers inhabiting upon or near the Borders, being Men of Name, and friended and allied with divers in those Parts, who were commonly known to be great Robbers, and Spoil-Takers, within the said Counties, to the End thereby to be by them protected from the Danger of such as used to rob and steal in those Parts*; and thereupon it is enacted, *That whosoever shall at any Time hereafter without good and lawful Warrant or Authority, take any of her Majesty's Subjects against his or their Will or Wills, and carry them out of the same Counties, or detain, force, or imprison him, or them, as Prisoners, or against his or their Wills, to ransom them, or to make a Prey or Spoil of his or their Person, or Goods, upon deadly Feud or otherwise: Or whosoever shall be privy, consenting, aiding, or assisting unto any such Taking, Detaining, or Carrying away, or procure the Taking, Detaining or Carrying away, of any such Person or Persons, Prisoners as aforesaid: Or whosoever shall take, receive, or carry, to the Use of himself, or wittingly to the Use of any other, any Money, Corn, Cattle, or other Consideration, commonly called Black-maile, for the protecting, or defending of him or them, or his or their Lands, Tenements, Goods, or Chattels, from such Thefts, Spoils, and Robberies, as is aforesaid: Or whosoever shall give any such Money, Corn, Cattle, or other Consideration, called Black-maile, for such Protection as is aforesaid, and shall be of the said several Offences, or of any of them, indicted and lawfully convicted, or shall stand mute, or shall challenge peremptorily above the Number of twenty, before the Justices of Assizes, Justices of Gaol-Delivery, Justices of Oyer and Terminer, or Justices of Peace, within any of the said Counties, at some of their General Sessions within some of the said Counties to be holden, shall be reputed, adjudged, and taken to be as Felons, and shall suffer Pains of Death, without any Benefit of Clergy,* &c.

Notorious Rioters in some Cases, are made guilty of Felony by 1 *Georg.* 1. 5. as is shewn at large in the Chapter of Riots.

For the Suppression of Thieves and Robbers called Moss-Troopers, see 13 and 14 *Ca.* 2. 22. which is continued by 12 *Anna* for eleven Years, and from thence to the End of the first Sessions of the next Parliament.

CHAP. LVII.

Of Felonies by Bankrupts.

Sect. 1. IT is enacted by 4 *Anna* 17. which was continued by 7 *Anna* for seven Years, and from thence to the End of the next Session, *That if any Person or Persons who after the 24th of* June 1706, *shall become Bankrupt, and against whom a Commission of Bankrupt shall be awarded, shall not within thirty Days next after Notice thereof in Writing, left at the usual Place of Abode of such Person or Persons, and Notice given in the Gazette, that such Commission is issued, and of the Time and Place of meeting of the Commissioners, surrender him, her, or themselves to the said Commissioners or some of them, and submit to be examined, from Time to Time, upon Oath, by and before the said Commissioners, or the major Part of them, and in all Things conform to the several Statutes which had then been made concerning Bankrupts, and also upon such Examination fully, and truly disclose and discover, how, and in what manner, and to whom, and upon what Consideration, he, she, or they, hath or have disposed, assigned, or transferred, any of his, her, or their Goods, Wares, Merchandizes, Money, or other Effects, or Estate, and all Books, Papers, and Writings, relating thereunto, of which he, she, or they were possessed, or in or to which he, she, or they were any way interested, or intituled, or which any Person or Persons, had, hath, or have had, in Trust for him, her or them, or for his, her, or their Use, at any Time before or after the issuing out of the said Commission, and also deliver up unto the said Commissioners, or the major Part of the Commissioners by the said Commission authorized, all such Part of his, her, or their, the said Bankrupts Goods, Wares, Merchandizes, Effects and Estate, and all Books, Papers, and Writings, relating thereunto, as at the Time of such Examination shall be in his, her, or their Possession, Custody, or Power, (his, her, or their Wives and Childrens necessary wearing Apparel*

 only

only excepted,) then he, she, or they, the said Bankrupt, in Case of any Default, or wilful Omission therein, or in any the Premisses, and being thereof lawfully convicted by Indictment or Information, shall suffer as a Felon, without the Benefit of Clergy.

Sect. 2. But it is provided by the said Statute, *That the Lord Chancellor may enlarge the Time for such Persons surrendering themselves, and discovering their Estates, for any Time as he shall think fit, not exceeding sixty Days, so as such Order for so enlarging the Time, be made five Days before the Time on which such Persons were so to surrender themselves,* &c.

Sect. 3. And it is farther enacted by 5 *Annæ* 22. *That if any Person or Persons who shall become Bankrupt, or any other Person or Persons, by or with his, her, or their Order, Consent, or Privity, shall after the 25th of* April 1707. *remove, carry away, conceal, destroy, or imbezil any of the Goods, Wares, Merchandizes, Moneys, or Effects, whereof he, she, or they, or any Person or Persons in Trust for him, her, or them, is, or are possessed, or entituled unto, to the Value of twenty Pounds or upwards, or any Books of Accompts, Bonds, Bills, Notes, Papers, or Writings relating thereunto, with Intent to defraud his, her, or their Creditors, every such Person and Persons so becoming Bankrupt, and being thereof lawfully convicted, shall suffer as a Felon without Benefit of Clergy.*

Vide 3. George c. 12. & 5. Geo. c. 24.

CHAP. LVIII.

Of Felony by Counterfeiters of Bank-Notes, Exchequer-Bills, Stamps, South-Sea Bonds, Lottery-Orders, &c.

Sect. 1. AND first as to Counterfeiters of Bank-Notes, it is enacted by 8 and 9 *Will.* 3. 19. Par. 36. *That the forging or counterfeiting the Common Seal of the Governor and Company of the Bank of* England, *or of any sealed Bank-Bill, made or given out in the Name of the said Governor and Company, for the Payment of any Sum of Money, or of any Bank-Note of any Sort whatsoever, signed for the said Governor and Company of the Bank of* England, *or the altering or rasing any Endorsment on any Bank-Bill, or Note of any Sort, shall be adjudged to be Felony without Benefit of Clergy.*

Sect. 2. Secondly, As to Counterfeiters of Exchequer-Bills, it is enacted by 7 and 8 *Wil.* 3. 31. Par. 78. *That if any Person or Persons shall forge or counterfeit any such Bill of Credit, as by the said Statute the Commissioners of the Treasury were authorized to issue out, or tender in Payment any forged or counterfeited Bill of Credit, or demand Money thereupon at the Exchequer, (knowing the Bill so tendered, or whereupon the Money shall be so demanded, to be actually forged or counterfeited) and with Intention to defraud his Majesty, or any other Person or Persons, every such Person or Persons so offending shall be adjudged a Felon.*

Sect. 3. And the like was enacted by 8 and 9 *Wil.* 3. 23. in relation to the Exchequer-Bills issued out by Authority of that Statute, and the Offenders are excluded from the Benefit of the Clergy, as appears from *Washington*; but this Part of the Statute is omitted out of the last Volume of the Statutes at large. Washington's Abr. 515.

Sect. 4. And it is farther enacted by 5 *Annæ* 13. Par. 22. *That if any Person or Persons shall forge or counterfeit any Exchequer-Bill, to be issued by Vertue of that Statute, or any Endorsement thereon, or tender in Payment any such*

such forged or counterfeit Exchequer-Bill, or with such counterfeit Endorsment, or demand to have the same exchanged for ready Money by the Governor and Company of the Bank of England *or their Successors, (knowing the Bill so tendered or demanded to be exchanged, or the Endorsment thereon, to be forged or counterfeit) and with Intention to defraud her Majesty, her Heirs or Successors, or the said Governor and Company, or their Successors, or any Person or Persons, Body Politick or Corporate, then every such Person or Persons so offending, (being thereof lawfully convicted,) shall be adjudged a Felon, and suffer as in Cases of Felony, without Benefit of Clergy.*

Sect. 5. And the like is enacted by 7 *Annæ* 7. and also by 9 *Annæ* 7. and by 1 *Georg.* 12. in Relation to Exchequer-Bills made forth in Pursuance of those Acts.

Sect. 6. As to Counterfeiters of Stamps, it is enacted by 9 and 10 *Will.* 3. 25. Par. 59. *That if any Person or Persons whatsoever shall counterfeit or forge any Stamp or Mark to resemble any Stamp or Mark which shall be provided, made or used in Pursuance of that Act, or shall counterfeit or resemble the Impression of the same, upon any Vellum, Parchment or Paper, thereby to defraud his Majesty, his Heirs or Successors, of any of the said Duties upon Vellum, Parchment or Paper, or shall utter, vend, or sell Vellum, Parchment or Paper, with such counterfeit Mark or Marks thereupon, knowing such Mark or Marks to be counterfeit, that the Person so offending being thereof convicted in due Form of Law, shall be judged a Felon, and shall suffer Death, as in Cases of Felony, without the Benefit of Clergy.*

Sect. 7. And the like is enacted by 10 *Annæ* 19. in Relation to the Stamps to be provided in Pursuance of that Act, with this Addition, *That those who shall privately and fraudulently use any Stamps or Marks thereby to defraud her Majesty of any Duty upon Vellum, Parchment or Paper by the said Act granted, shall be adjudged in like manner guilty.*

And the like is enacted by 10 *Annæ*, 26. and by 12 *Annæ* 9. and also by 12 *Annæ* 19. In Relation to the Stamps or Marks to be provided in Pursuance of those Statutes.

Sect. 8. As to Counterfeiters of South-Sea Bonds, it is enacted by 9 *Annæ* 21. *That if any Person or Persons shall forge or counterfeit the common Seal of the South-Sea Company, or shall forge, counterfeit or alter any Bond or Obligation under the common Seal of the said Company, or shall offer to dispose of, or pay away any such forged, counterfeited, or altered Bond, (knowing the same to be such,) or shall demand the Money therein contained, or pretended to be due thereon, or any Part thereof, of the said Company, or any of their Officers, knowing the same to be forged, counterfeited, or altered, with Intent to defraud the said Company, or any other Person or Persons, every such Offender shall suffer as a Felon without the Benefit of the Clergy.*

Sect. 9. As to Counterfeiters of Lottery-Orders, it is enacted by 12 *Annæ* 2. *That if any Person or Persons shall forge or counterfeit any Lottery-Order, made in Pursuance of* 9 Annæ 6. *or* 23. *or* 10 Annæ 19 *or* 26. *or alter the Number or principal Sum of any such Order, or counterfeit the Hand of any Person to such Order, thereby to procure a fraudulent Assignment, or sell any such Order, knowing the same to be forged or counterfeit, or knowing that the Name of the Owner is forged, in order to procure such fraudulent Assignment; then all and every such Person or Persons being therefore convict, shall suffer as in Cases of Felony, without Benefit of Clergy.*

 CHAP.

CHAP. LIX.

Of Misprision of Felony.

Offences more immediately against the Subject, not capital, are either Misprision of Felony, or other inferior Offences.

Sect. 1. It is said, That every Felony includes Misprision of Felony, and may be proceeded against as a Misprision only if the King please, as hath been shewn already in Chapter 20. Bro. Treaf. 25 2 Ric. 3. 10. S. P. C. 32.d.

Sect. 2. But generally Misprision of Felony, is taken for a Concealment of Felony, or a procuring of the Concealment thereof, whether it be Felony by the Common Law, or by Statute. H. P. C. 129. S. P. C. 37.c. 3 Inst. 139.

Sect. 3. For this Offence every common Person is punishable by Fine and Imprisonment at Common Law. And by the Statute of *Westm.* 1. 9. *If the Sheriff, Coroner, or any other Bailiff within a Franchise or without, for Reward or for Prayer, or for Fear, or for any manner of Affinity, conceal, consent, or procure to conceal the Felonies done in their Liberties; or otherwise will not attach nor arrest such Felons (there as they may) or otherwise will not do their Office, for Favour borne to such Mis-doers, and be attainted thereof, they shall have one Year's Imprisonment, and after make a grievous Fine at the King's Pleasure if they have wherewith; and if they have not whereof, they shall have Imprisonment of three Years.* Bro. Treaf. 25. 3 Inst. 173.

Sect. 4. By 3 *H.* 7. 1. *The Justices of the Peace of every Shire of this Realm, for the Time being, may take by their Discretion an Inquest, whereof every Man shall have Lands and Tenements to the yearly Value of forty Shillings at the least, to enquire of the Concealments of other Inquests taken before them, and afore other, of such Matters and Offences as are to be enquired and presented afore Justices of Peace, whereof Complaint shall be made by Bill or by Bills, as well within Franchise as without. And if any such Concealment be found of any Inquest, as is afore rehearsed, had or made within the Year after the same Concealment, every Person of the same Inquest to be amerced for the Concealment, by Discretion of the same Justices of the Peace, the said Amerciaments to be sessed in plain Sessions.*

Sect. 5. To this Title of Misprision of Felony, That of Theftbote seems not improperly reducible, which is where one not only knows of a Felony, but takes his Goods again, or other amends, not to prosecute. S. P. C. 40.b. 3 Inst. 134. H. P. C. 130.

Sect. 6. This Offence is very nearly allied to Felony, and is said to have been anciently punished as such: But at this Day, it is punishable only with Ransom and Imprisonment, unless it were accompanied with some Degree of Maintenance given to the Felon, which makes the Party an Accessary after the Fact. S. P. C. 40.b. Fitz. Coro. 353. 3 Inst. 134.

Sect. 7. But the bare Taking of one's own Goods again, which have been stoln, is no Offence at all, unless some Favour be shewn to the Thief. Bro. Cor. 122. 42 Ass. Pl. 5. H. P. C. 130. Cro. El 486. 1 Rol. Ab. 67. Pl. 27.

CHAP. LX.

Of Surety of the Peace.

INferior Offences more immediately against the Subject, not capital, either amount to an actual Disturbance of the Peace, or do not.

And first, I shall consider such Offences of this kind, as amount to an actual Disturbance of the Peace: But before I descend to the several kinds thereof, it may not be improper first to shew what Security may be had against the Breach of the Peace before it happens; and in order hereto, I shall examine how the Peace may be secured.

1. By Surety for keeping the Peace.
2. By Surety for the good Behaviour.

As to Surety for keeping the Peace, I shall consider the following Particulars:

1. In what Cases it ought to be taken *ex Officio.*
2. At whose Request it ought to be granted.
3. Against whom it ought to be granted.
4. For what Cause it is grantable.
5. In what manner it is grantable by the Courts of Chancery and King's Bench.
6. In what manner it is grantable by a Justice of Peace.
7. In what manner the Process for it ought to be executed.
8. How such Process may be superseded.
9. What ought to be the Form of a Recognizance for this Purpose.
10. How such a Recognizance may be discharged.
11. How such a Recognizance ought to be certified and proceeded upon.
12. How it may be forfeited.

Dalt. cap. 67. fol. 158, 159. Lamb 77, 78. 9 Ed. 4. 3. a. Bro. Peace 7, 8. Crom. 135, 142.

Sect. 1. As to the first Point, *viz.* In what Cases Surety of the Peace ought or be taken *ex Officio*, it seems, That any Justice of Peace may, according to his Discretion, bind all those to the Peace, who in his Presence shall make any Affray, or shall threaten to kill or beat any Person, or shall contend together with hot Words, or shall go about with unusual Weapons or Attendants, to the Terror of the People; and also all such Persons as shall be known by him to be common Barrators; and also all those who shall be brought before him by a Constable for a Breach of the Peace in the Presence of such Constable; and all such Persons who, having been before bound to keep the Peace, shall be convicted of having forfeited their Recognizance.

Dalt. cap. 67. 21 E. 4. 40. Crom. 142 b. Dalt. cap. 67.

Dalt. cap. 68. Lamb 78, 79. Crom. 133. b. 134.

Sect. 2. As to the second Point, *viz.* At whose Request the Surety of the Peace ought to be granted; it seems agreed at this Day, That all Persons whatsoever, under the King's Protection, being of sane Memory, whether they be natural and good Subjects, or Aliens, or attainted of Treason, *&c.* have a Right to demand Surety of the Peace.

Dalt. cap. 68. Lamb. 80.

Sect. 3. But it has been questioned, whether Jews or Pagans, or Persons attainted of *Præmunire*, have a Right to it or not.

Sect.

Sect. 4. However it is certain, That a Wife may demand it against her Husband threatening to beat her outrageously, and that a Husband also may have it against his Wife. Dalt. cap. 68. Lamb. 78. Crom. 133. b. 3 Lev. 128.

Sect. 5. As to the third Point, *viz.* Against whom the Surety of the Peace ought to be granted, there seems to be no Doubt but that it ought upon a just Cause of Complaint to be granted by any Justice of Peace against any Person whatsoever, under the Degree of Nobility, being of sane Memory, whether he be a Magistrate or private Person, and whether he be of full Age or under Age, *&c.* But Infants and Femes Covert ought to find Security by their Friends, and not to be bound themselves; and the safest Way of proceeding against a Peer is by Complaint to the Court of Chancery or King's Bench. F.N.B. 80.f. Dalt. cap. 68. Lamb. 81, 82. Cromp. 134, 135. *See the Books above cited.*

Sect. 6. As to the fourth Point, *viz.* For what Cause the Surety of the Peace is grantable; it seems clear, That where-ever a Person has just Cause to fear that another will burn his House, or do him a corporal Hurt, as by killing or beating him, or that he will procure others to do him such Mischief, he may demand the Surety of the Peace against such Person; and that every Justice of Peace is bound to grant it, upon the Party's giving him Satisfaction upon Oath, that he is actually under such Fear; and that he has just Cause to be so, by Reason of the other's having threatened to beat him, or lain in wait for that Purpose; and that he does not require it out of Malice, or for Vexation. Dalt cap. 67. Lamb. 82. Cromp. 135.

Sect. 7. It seems also the better Opinion, That he who is threatened to be imprisoned by another, has a Right to demand the Surety of the Peace; for every unlawful Imprisonment is an Assault and Wrong to the Person of a Man: And the Objection, That one wrongfully imprisoned may recover Damages in an Action, *&c.* and therefore needs not the Surety of the Peace, is as strong in the Case of Battery as Imprisonment, and yet there is no doubt, but that one threatened to be beaten may demand the Surety of the Peace. Dalt. cap. 67. Lamb. 82, 83. Con. 17 Ed. 4. 4. Bro. Peace 22. Cromp. 135. a.

Sect. 8. As to the fifth Point, *viz.* In what manner such Surety is grantable by the Courts of Chancery and King's Bench, it is enacted by 21 Jac. 1. 8. *That all Process for the Peace or good Behaviour to be granted or awarded out of the same Courts, or either of them, against any Person or Persons whatsoever, at the Suit of, or by the Prosecution of any Person or Persons whatsoever, shall be void and of none Effect, unless such Process shall be so granted or awarded, upon Motion first made before the Judge or Judges of the same Courts respectively, (sitting in open Court, and upon Declaration in Writing upon their corporal Oaths, to be then exhibited unto them by the Parties which shall desire such Process,) of the Causes for which such Process shall be granted or awarded, by or out of the said Courts respectively, and unless that such Motion and Declaration be mentioned to be made upon the back of a Writ, the said Writings there to be entered and remain of Record: And that if it shall afterwards appear unto the said Courts, or either of them respectively, that the Causes express'd in such Writings, or any of them be untrue, That then the Judge or Judges of the said Courts, or either of them respectively, shall and may award such Costs and Damages unto the Parties grieved, for their, or any of their wrongful Vexations in that Behalf, as they shall think fit: And that the Party or Parties so offending, shall and may be committed to Prison by such Judge or Judges, until he or they pay the said Costs and Damages.*

Sect. 9. As to the sixth Point, *viz.* In what manner such Surety is grantable by a Justice of Peace, it seemeth certain, That if the Person to be bound be in the Presence of the Justice, he may be immediately com- 14 H. 7. 8, 9, 10. 9 Ed. 4. 3. a. Bro. Mainp. 39. 2 Rol. Re. 146

committed, unleſs he offer Sureties; and from hence it follows, *à fortiori*, That he may be commanded by Word of Mouth to find Sureties, and committed for his Diſobedience; but it is ſaid, That if he be abſent, he ought to be brought by Warrant before ſome Juſtice of Peace, in order to find Sureties, and that ſuch Warrant ought to be under Seal, and to ſhew the Cauſe for which it is granted, and at whoſe Suit, and that it may be directed to any indifferent Perſon.

Lamb 85, &c. Dalt. cap. 69.

Sect. 10. As to the ſeventh Point, *viz.* In what Manner the Proceſs for the Peace ought to be executed, it ſeems needleſs to give a particular Account of the Execution of the Writ of *Supplicavit*, becauſe I do not find that it is much in Uſe at this Day, and therefore I ſhall refer the Reader for this purpoſe to *Fitzherbert*'s *Natura Brevium*, fol. 80, *&c.* But as to the Execution of the Warrant of a Juſtice, the following Rules are to be obſerved.

Lamb. 89.

Sect. 11. I. It can be executed only by the Perſons to whom it is directed, or ſome of them, unleſs it be directed to the Sheriff, who may either by Parol, or by Precept in writing, authorize an Officer ſworn and known, to ſerve it, but can not impower any other Perſon without a Precept in writing.

Sect. 12. II. If the Warrant be made in the common Form, directing the Officer to cauſe the Party complained of to come before ſome Juſtice of Peace, to find ſufficient Surety, *&c.* and if he ſhall refuſe ſo to do, to convey him immediately to Priſon, without expecting any further Warrant, until he ſhall willingly do the ſame, *&c.* the Officer who ſerves it, before he makes any Arreſt, ought firſt to require the Party to go with him, and find Sureties according to the Purport of the Warrant, but upon his Refuſal to do either, he may carry him to the Gaol by Force of the ſame Warrant, without more.

Long Quinto. 5 Ed. 4. 12. b. 13. a. Bro Falſe Impriſ. 18. Dalt. ca. 69. Lamb 90, 91. Crom. 235. 5 Co. 59. b.

Sect. 13. III. If the Warrant ſpecially direct, that the Party ſhall be brought before the Juſtice who made it, the Officer ought not to carry him before any other: But if the Warrant be general, to bring him before any Juſtice of Peace, *&c.* the Officer has the Election to bring him before what Juſtice he pleaſes, and may carry him to Priſon for refuſing to find Surety before ſuch Juſtice.

5 Co. 59. Dal. ca. 69. Bro. Falſe Impriſon. 11. 21 H. 7. 21. a. Lamb. 94, 95.

Sect. 14. As to the eighth Point, *viz.* How ſuch Proceſs may be ſuperſeded, it is ſaid, That if one who fears that the Surety of the Peace will be demanded againſt him, find Sureties before any Juſtice of the Peace of the ſame County, either before or after a Warrant is iſſued againſt him, he may have a *Superſedeas* from ſuch Juſtice, which ſhall diſcharge him from Arreſt from any other Juſtice, at the Suit of the ſame Party, for whoſe Security he has given ſuch Surety: Alſo it is ſaid, That an Appearance upon a Recognizance for the Peace may be ſuperſeded, by finding Sureties in the Chancery or King's Bench, and purchaſing a Writ teſtifying the ſame. But this Practice having often been abuſed by turbulent Perſons, who deſervedly fearing to be bound to the Peace or good Behaviour, by Juſtices of Peace, would procure themſelves to be bound thereto in the ſaid Courts, upon inſufficient Sureties, or upon the colourable Proſecution of ſome Perſon who would be ready at all Times to releaſe them at their Pleaſure, whereupon Writs of *Superſedeas* had been often directed to Juſtices of Peace, commanding them to forbear to arreſt the Parties for ſuch Cauſes, by reaſon whereof ſuch turbulent Perſons uſed to miſdemean themſelves among their Neighbours with Impunity, as it is recited by 21 *Jac.* 1. 8. it is thereupon enacted by the ſaid Statute, *That all Writs of* Superſedeas, *to be granted out of either of the ſaid Courts,*

Dalt. ca. 69. Lamb. 112, 113. See 2 Roll. A. 492 F.

I *ſhall*

shall be void, unless such Process be granted upon Motion in open Court first made, &c. *upon such sufficient Sureties, as shall appear unto the Judge or Judges of the same Court respectively, upon Oath, to be assessed at five Pounds Lands, or ten Pounds in Goods, in the Subsidy Book, at the least; which Oaths, and the Names of such Sureties, with the Places of their Abode, and where they stand so assessed in the subsidy Books, shall be entered, and remain of Record in the same Courts: And unless it shall also first appear unto the said Judge or Judges, from whom such* Supersedeas *is desired, That the Process of the Peace, or good Behaviour, is prosecuted against him or them, desiring such* Supersedeas, bonâ fide, *by some Party grieved, in that Court, out of which such* Supersedeas *is desired to be so awarded and directed.*

Sect. 15. As to the ninth Point, *viz.* What ought to be the Form of such a Recognizance: If it be taken in Pursuance of a Writ of *Supplicavit*, it must be wholly governed by the Directions of such Writ; but if it be taken before a Justice of Peace, upon a Complaint below, it seems that it may be regulated by the Discretion of such Justice, both as to the Number and sufficiency of the Sureties, and the Largeness of the Sum, and the Continuance of the Time, for which the Party shall be bound; and it hath been said, That a Recognizance to keep the Peace as to *A. B.* for a Year, or for Life, or without expressing any certain Time, (in which Case it shall be intended to be for Life,) or without fixing any Time or Place for the Party's Appearance, or without binding him to keep the Peace against all the King's People in general, is good.

Lamb. 100, 101. Dal. ca. 70.

Sect. 16. However, it seems to be the safest Way to bind the Party to appear at the next Sessions of the Peace, and in the mean Time to keep the Peace as to the King, and all his Liege People, especially as to the Party, according to the common Form of the Precedents.

Lamb. 105. Dal. ca. 124.

Sect 17. As to the tenth Point, *viz.* How such a Recognizance may be discharged, it seems agreed, That it may be discharged by the Demise of the [a] King in whose Reign it was taken, or of the [b] principal Party who was bound thereby, if it were not forfeited before; also it hath been holden, That it may be discharged by the Release of the Party at whose Complaint it was taken, being certified together with it, but this may justly be questioned, because the Recognizance is not to the Subject but to the King, and consequently can not be discharged by the Subject, who is not a Party to it; however, such a Release will be a good Inducement to the Court, to which such a Recognizance shall be certified, to discharge it; and so also will the Non-Appearance of the Party at whose complaint it was taken, in order to pray the Continuance of it; and yet it is said, That the Sessions in that case may, in their Discretion, refuse to discharge it; however, it is certain that such a Recognizance can not be pardoned, or released by the King, before it is broken, because the Subject has a Kind of Interest in it; and it is said, That the Sureties are not discharged by their Death, but that their Executors, *&c.* continue bound as their Testators, *&c.* were.

[a] Bro. Peace 15. 1 H. 7. 2. [b] 15 H. 7. 2. b. 13. A. 21 Ed. 4. 70. b. Dalt. ch. 71. [c] Lamb. 110, &c. Crom 139. b. 169. a. Bro. Peace 17. Crom. 144. b. 1 H. 7. 10. b. 11 H. 7. 12. a. 11 H. 4. 43. a. Bro Peace 17.

Sect. 18. As to the eleventh Point, *viz.* How such a Recognizance ought to be certified, and proceeded upon: If it be taken by Force of a Writ of *Supplicavit*, it needs not be certified till the Justice receive a Writ of *Certiorari* to that purpose; but if it be taken upon a Complaint below, it must be certified, sent, or brought to the next Sessions of the Peace by Force of 3 *H.* 7. 1. that the Party so bound may be called; and by the same Statute, *if the Party then make Default, the same Default shall be then recorded, and the same Recognizance with the Record of the Default, shall be*

Lamb. 111, 112, &c. Dal. ca. 70.

Hill. 1 Geor. *between the King and* Combs. *agreed.*

be certified into the Chancery, King's Bench or Exchequer: However, if the Party have any Excuse for his not appearing, it seems that the Sessions is not bound peremptorily to record his Default, but may equitably consider of the Reasonableness of such Excuse; and it is said, That the Sessions can not in any Case proceed against the Party for a Forfeiture of his Recognizance, either in respect of his not appearing, or breaking the Peace, but that the Recognizance in such Case ought to be removed into some of the King's Courts of *Westminster-Hall*, who shall proceed thereon by *Scire Facias* upon such Recognizance, and not by Indictment, *&c.*

Dal. ch. 71. Raym. 169 1 Roll. A. 900. Pl. 4.

3 Bulst. 120.

Sect. 19. It seemeth, that in a *Scire Facias* upon such a Recognizance, it is sufficient to lay the Fact alledged for a Breach thereof, as having been done *contra pacem*, without using the words *Vi & Armis.*

Bro Peace 20. Dalt. ch. 72. Lamb. 127, 128.

Sect. 20. As to the twelfth Point, *viz.* How such a Recognizance may be forfeited, there is no Doubt but that it may be forfeited by any actual Violence to the Person of another, whether it be done by the Party himself, or by others thro' his Procurement, as Manslaughter, Rape, Robbery, unlawful Imprisonment, *&c.*

Lamb 115, &c. Dalt ch. 72. 2 H 7 2. b. *seems otherwise* 18 Ed. 4. 28. a. 22 Ed 4. 35. b. Cro. Ca. 498, 499. *See the Books cited in the Section following, and* 2 R. A. 545. Pl. 2, 3, 4, 5, 6, 7. 8. 547. E 3.

Sect. 21. Also it has been holden, That it may be forfeited by any Treason against the Person of the King, and also by any unlawful Assembly *in Terrorem Populi*, and even by Words directly tending to a Breach of the Peace, as by challenging one to fight, or, in his Presence, threatning to beat him, *&c.*

Cro. El. 86. Mo. 249. 2 Rol. Re. 199, 227. Palm. 126.

Sect. 22. However, it seems that it shall not be forfeited by bare Words of Heat and Choler, as the calling a Man Knave, Teller of Lies, Rascal, or Drunkard; for tho' such Words may provoke a cholerick Man to break the Peace, yet they do not directly challenge him to it, nor does it appear that the Speaker designed to carry his Resentment any farther; and it hath been said, That even a Recognizance for the good Behaviour, shall not be forfeited for such Words, from whence it follows, *à fortiori*, That a Recognizance for the Peace shall not.

Sect. 23. Also there are some actual Assaults on the Person of another, which do not amount to a Forfeiture of such a Recognizance; as if an [a] Officer, having a Warrant against one who will not suffer himself to be arrested, beat or wound him in the Attempt to take him; or if a [b] Parent in a reasonable Manner chastise his Child, or a Master his Servant, [c] being actually in his Service at the Time; or a [d] Schoolmaster his Scholar, or a [e] Gaoler his Prisoner, or even a [f] Husband his Wife; or if [g] one confine a Friend who is mad, and bind, and beat him, *&c.* in such a Manner as is proper in such Circumstances; or if a Man [h] force a Sword from one who offers to kill another therewith; or if a Man gently lay his Hands on another and thereby stay him from inciting a Dog against a third Person; or if [i] I beat one (without [k] wounding him, or throwing at him a dangerous Weapon) who wrongfully endeavours with Violence to dispossess me of my Land, or Goods, and will not desist upon my laying my Hands gently on him, and disturbing him; or if a Man beat, [l] or, as some say, wound, or maim one who makes an Assault upon his Person, or that of his [m] Wife, Parent, Child, or Master;

[a] 2 Ed. 4 6. 21 H 7. 39. [b] Dalt ca. 72. Crom. 136. b. [c] 38 H 6. 25. [d] H. P. C. 31. 21 Ed 4. 6. [e] Dal. ca. 72. [f] Crom. 28. b. 136. b. F. N B. 80. F. Herley 149. [g] 22 Ass. 56. 2 R. A 546. C. 22 Ed. 4. 5. a. b. [h] Cro. Ja. 134. 2 R A. 546. Pl. 35, 59. E. [i] 3 H. 4. 6. b. 9. a. 19 H. 6 31 b. 10 E. 4. 6. b. 11 Ed. 4. 28. b. Kellew 92. a. Yelv. 172. 2 R. A. 547. E. 1, 2. 548. Pl. 2, 3, 4, 5. 6, 7. 549. P. 9, 10, 11. Pult. 5, 6. Crom. 137. a. Dal. ca. 72. [k] 2 R. A. 548. Pl. 4, 8. [l] 41 Ass. 21. 27 Ed 3. 94. a. 25 Ed. 3. 42. a. 8 H. 4 8. a. b 9 Ed. 4. 48 b. 12 Ed. 4. 6. a. Bro. de Tort. Demesne 57. 1 Sid. 246. Kelyn. 128. 2 R A 547. F. Pl. 1, 2, 3, 4. 1 Keb. 884, 921. 2 Inst 316 [m] 35 H. 6. 50. b. 51. a. 19 H. 6. 31. a. b. 66. a. 12 Ed 4. 6. a. Crom. 136. b. Dal. ca. 72. 2 R. A 546. D. 1, 2, 3.

eſpecially, if it appear that he did all he could to avoid fighting before he gave the Wound; or if a Man [n] fight with or beat one who attempts to kill any Stranger; or if a Man even [o] threaten to kill one who puts him in Fear of Death in ſuch a Place where he can not ſafely fly from him; or if one [p] impriſon thoſe whom he ſees fighting, till the Heat be over.

[n] 12 H. 8. 2 b. [o] 32 H. 6. 18. b. 10 Ed. 4. 6. b. [p] 2 Rol. Ab. 559 E. 22 E. 4. 45. b. [q] 2 R. A. 546. D. 2.

Sect. 24. According to ſome Opinions, a [q] Maſter ſhall not forfeit ſuch a Recognizance for beating another in defence of his Servant, but it is ſaid, That a [r] Servant is liable to ſuch Forfeiture for beating another in Defence of his Maſter's Son, tho' he were commanded by the Maſter ſo to do, becauſe he is not a Servant to the Son; and for the like Reaſon it is ſaid, That a [ſ] Tenant ſhall incur the like Forfeiture for beating another in Defence of his Landlord, *&c.*

19 H. 6. 31. b. 66. a. Dal. ca. 72. Crom. 136. b. Con. 9 Ed. 4. 48. b. [r] 9 Ed. 4. 48. b. Bro. Treſp. 189. [ſ] Dalt. ch. 72.

Sect. 25. But it ſeems agreed, That no one ſhall forfeit ſuch a Recognizance by a bare Treſpaſs on another's Lands, or Goods, unleſs it be accompanied with ſome Violence to the Perſon.

Lamb. 129. Crom. 136. b. Dalt. ca. 72. Cro. El. 86.

Sect. 26. And it ſeems to be the better Opinion, That a Man is in no Danger of ſuch a Forfeiture from any Hurt done to another, by playing at Cudgels, or ſuch like Sport, by Conſent, becauſe the Intent of the Parties ſeems no way unlawful, but rather commendable, and tending mutually to promote Activity and Courage; yet it is ſaid, That he who wounds another in fighting with naked Swords, does in Strictneſs forfeit ſuch a Recognizance, becauſe no Conſent can make ſo dangerous a Diverſion lawful.

Moore 249. Dalt. ca. 22. Bro. Coron. 229. Fitz. B. 224.

Sect. 27. But it ſeemeth, That a Man ſhall not forfeit ſuch Recognizance, by a Hurt done to another merely thro' Negligence, or Miſchance; as where one Soldier hurts another by diſcharging a Gun in Exerciſe, without ſufficient Caution; for notwithſtanding ſuch Perſon muſt, in a Civil Action, give the other Satisfaction for the Damage occaſioned by his Want of Care, yet he ſeems not to have offended againſt the Purport of ſuch a Recognizance, unleſs he be guilty of ſome wilfull Breach of the Peace.

Ho. 134. 2 R. A. 548. G.

CHAP. LXI.

Of Surety for the Good Behaviour.

AND now we are come to Surety for the Good Behaviour, which being of great Affinity with Surety of the Peace, both as to the Manner in which it is to be taken, ſuperſeded, and diſcharged, *&c.* ſeems not to require a particular Conſideration, ſave only as to the following Points,

1. For what Misbehaviours it is to be required.
2. For what it ſhall be forfeited.

Sect. 1. As to the firſt Point, it is to be obſerved, That by 34 *Ed.* 3. 1. *Juſtices of Peace are impowered to reſtrain Offenders, Rioters, and all other Barrators, and to purſue, arreſt, take, and chaſtiſe them, according to their Treſpaſs, or Offence; and to cauſe them to be impriſoned, and duly puniſhed according to to the Laws and Customs of the Realm, and according to that which to them shall seem best to do by their Discretions, and good Advisement, and also to inform them, and to enquire of all those that have been Pillors and Robbers in the Parts beyond the Sea, and be now come again, and go wandering, and will not labour as they were wont in Times past; and to take and arrest all those, that they may find by Indictment or by Suspicion, and to put them in Prison, and to take of all them that be not of good Fame, where they shall be found, sufficient Surety and Mainprize of their Good Behaviour towards the King and his People, and the other duly to punish, to the Intent that the People be not by such Rioters troubled nor endamaged, nor the Peace blemished, nor Merchants, nor other passing by the Highways of the Realm disturbed, nor put in the Peril which may happen of such Offenders.*

4 Inst. 181. 2 H. 7. 2. b. 3. a. Lamb. 115, 116, 117. Dalt. ca. 75.

Sect. 2. In the Construction hereof there seem to have been some Opinions, that the Statute, speaking of those that be not of good Fame, means only such as are defamed, and justly suspected that they intend to break the Peace, and that it does not any Way extend to those who are guilty of other Misbehaviours not relating to the Peace; but this seems much too narrow a Construction, since the above mentioned Expression of Persons of evil Fame, in common Understanding, as properly includes Persons of scandalous Behaviour in other Respects, as those who by their quarrelsome Behaviour give just Suspicion of their Readiness to break the Peace; and accordingly it seems to have been always the better Opinion, That a Man may be bound to his Good Behaviour for many Causes of Scandal which give him a bad Fame, as being contrary to good Manners only; as for [a] haunting Bawdy-houses with Women of bad Fame; or for [b] keeping bad Women in his own House; or for speaking Words of Contempt of an inferiour [c] Magistrate, as a Justice of Peace, or Mayor of a Town, *&c.* tho' he be not then in the actual Execution of his Office, or of an inferiour Officer of Justice, as a Constable, and such like, being in the actual Execution of his Office.

[a] 13 H. 7. 10. b. [b] Crom. 140 a. [c] Cro. El. 78. 1 Levin. 52, 53, 107. Con. Cro. El. 689. Palm. 130.

1 Rol. Rep. 227, 228. 3 Bulf. 139, 140. Cro. Ca. 498, 499. Cro. El 86. Moore 249. 2 Rol. Re. 199, 227. Palm. 126.

Sect. 3. However, it seems the better Opinion, That no one ought to be bound to the Good Behaviour for any rash, quarrelsome, or unmannerly Words, unless they either directly tend to a Breach of the Peace, or to scandalize the Government, by abusing those who are intrusted by it with the Administration of Justice, or to deter an Officer from doing his Duty; and therefore it seems, That he who barely calls another Rogue, or Rascal, or Teller of Lies, or Drunkard, *&c.* ought not for such Cause to be bound to the Good Behaviour.

Dalt. 75. 1 Rol. Re. 150.

Sect. 4. However, I can not find any certain precise Rules for the Direction of the Magistrate in this Respect, and therefore am inclined to think, that he has a discretionary Power to take such Surety of all those whom he shall have just Cause to suspect to be dangerous, quarrelsome, or scandalous, as of those who sleep in the Day, and go abroad in the Night, and of such as keep suspicious Company, and of such as are generally suspected to be Robbers, *&c.* and of Eves-Droppers, and common Drunkards, and all other Persons, whose Misbehaviour may reasonably be intended to bring them within the Meaning of the Statute, as Persons of evil Fame, who, being described by an Expression of so great Latitude, seem in a great Measure to be left to the Judgment of the Magistrate.

Palm. 129, 130.

Sect. 5. As to the second Point, *viz.* For what Misbehaviours such a Recognizance shall be forfeited, it is laid down as a general Rule in the Argument of *Stamp* and *Hide*'s Case, That whatever will be a good Cause to bind a Man to his Good Behaviour, will forfeit a Recognizance

3 for

for it, yet this is since denied in *Heyward's* Case; and indeed does by no Means seem to be maintainable, because the Statute in ordering Persons of evil Fame to be bound in this Manner, seems in many Cases chiefly to regard the Prevention of that mischief which they may justly be suspected to be likely to do; and in that Respect requires them to secure the Publick from that Danger which may probably be apprehended from their future Behaviour, whether any actual Crime can be proved upon them, or not; and it would be extremely hard in such Cases to make Persons forfeit their Recognizance, who yet may justly be compellable to give one, as those who keep suspicious Company, or those who spend much Money idly, without having any visible Means of getting it honestly, or those who lie under a general Suspicion of being Rogues, *&c.* Cro. Ca. 499. 13 H. 7. 10. b. Dalt. ca. 75.

Sect. 6. However, it seems that such a Recognizance shall not only be forfeited for such actual Breaches of the Peace, for which a Recognizance for the Peace may be forfeited, but also for some others, for which such a Recognizance can not be forfeited; as for going armed with great Numbers to the Terror of the People, or speaking Words tending to Sedition, *&c.* and also for all such actual Misbehaviours which are intended to be prevented by such a Recognizance, but not for barely giving Cause of Suspicion of what perhaps may never actually happen. 2 H. 7. 2. b. Cro. Ca. 499.

CHAP. LXII.

Of Assaults and Batteries.

AND now I am come to consider the several Kinds of actual Disturbances of the Peace, and these are; either,

1. Such as may be committed by one or two Persons.
2. Such as require a greater Number.

Those which may be committed by one or two Persons, are,

1. Assaults and Batteries.
2. Affrays.
3. Forcible Entries and Detainers.

As to Assaults and Batteries, I shall consider the following particulars:

1. What shall be said to be an Assault.
2. What shall be said to be a Battery.
3. In what Cases they may be justified.
4. In what Manner they are to be punished.

Sect. 1. As to the first Point, it seems that an Assault is an Attempt, or Offer, with Force and Violence, to do a corporal Hurt to another; as by striking at him with, or without, a Weapon, or presenting a Gun at him, at such a Distance to which the Gun will carry, or pointing a Pitch-fork at him, standing within the Reach of it, or by holding up Pulton 4. a. 6 Mod. 173, 174. 2 R. A. 545, 10, 11.

1 Keb 921. 40 Ed. 3. 40 a. 42 Ed. 3. 7. a. 45 Ed 3. 24. b. 25. a. 22 Aff. 60. 2 R. A. 545. Pl. 1, 2, 3, 4, 5, 6, 7, 8 22 Aff. Pl 11. Pult. 3. Lamb. 126. one's Fist at him, or by any other such like Act done in an angry threatening Manner; and from hence it clearly follows, That one charged with an Assault and Battery, may be found guilty of the former, and yet acquitted of the later. But notwithstanding the many ancient Opinions to the contrary, it seems agreed at this Day, that no Words whatsoever can amount to an Assault.

Sect. 2. As to the second Point, *viz.* What shall be said to be a Battery, It seems that any Injury whatsoever, be it never so small, being actually done to the Person of a Man, in an angry, or revengeful, or rude, or insolent, Manner, as by Spitting in his Face, or any Way touching him in Anger, or violently justling him out of the Way, are Batteries in the Eye of the Law: But it is said to be no Battery to lay one's Hand gently on another whom an Officer has a Warrant to arrest, and to tell the Officer that this is the Man he wants. 6 Mod. 149, 172. 2 R. A. 546. Pl. 1, 2.

Sect. 3. As to the third Point, *viz.* In what Cases an Assault and Battery may be justified, this is so fully set forth already in the Chapter of *Surety of the Peace*, that there seems to be no need of any farther Consideration thereof in this Place; and therefore I shall only add, That where a Man in his own Defence beats another who first assaults him, *&c.* he may take an Advantage thereof upon an Indictment, as well as upon an Action; but with this Difference, that in the first Case he may give it in Evidence upon the Plea of Not guilty, and in the later he must plead it specially. 6 Mod. 172.

Sect. 4. As to the fourth Point, *viz.* How unlawful Assaults and Batteries are punished, there is no doubt but that the Wrong doer is Subject, both to an Action at the Suit of the Party, wherein he shall render Damages, *&c.* and also to an Indictment at the Suit of the King, wherein he shall be fined according to the Heinousness of the Offence.

CHAP. LXIII.

Of Affrays.

IN treating of Affrays, I shall consider,

1. What shall be said to be an Affray.
2. How far it may be suppressed by a private Person.
3. How far by a Constable.
4. How far by a Justice of Peace.
5. In what Manner the several Kinds of Affrays may be punished.

Sect. 1. As to the first Point, it is said, That the word Affray is derived from the *French* word *Effraier*, to terrify, and that in a legal Sense it is taken for a publick Offence, to the Terror of the People, from whence it seems clearly to follow, That there may be an Assault which will not amount to an Affray; as where it happens in a private Place, out of the hearing or seeing of any, except the Parties concerned; in which Case it cannot be said to be to the Terror of the People; and for this 3 Inst. 158. Dalt. ca. 8. Lamb. 125, 126.

this Cause such a private Assault seems not to be inquirable in a Court-Leet, as all Affrays certainly are, as being common Nusances. 4 H. 6. 10. a. 8 Ed. 4. 5. b.

Sect. 2. Also it is said, That no quarrelsome or threatening Words whatsoever shall amount to an Affray; and that no one can justify laying his Hands on those who shall barely quarrel with angry Words, without coming to blows; yet it seemeth, That the Constable may, at the Request of the Party threatened, carry the Person who threatens to beat him before a Justice of Peace, in Order to find Sureties. H. P. C. 135. 23 E. 4. 45. b. Dal. ch. 8. Lamb. Constable 14.

Sect. 3. Also it is certain, That it is a very high Offence to challenge another, either by Word or Letter, to fight a Duel, or to be the Messenger of such a Challenge, or even barely to endeavour to provoke another to send a Challenge, or to fight, as by dispersing Letters to that purpose, full of Reflections, and insinuating a Desire to fight, *&c.* Poph. 158. 3 Inst. 158. 1 Sid. 186. 1 Keb. 694. Hob. 120, 215. 2 Rol. Ab. 78.

Sect. 4 But granting that no bare Words, in the Judgment of Law, carry in them so much Terror as to amount to an Affray; yet it seems certain, That in some Cases there may be an Affray where there is no actual Violence; as where a Man arms himself with dangerous and unusual Weapons, in such a Manner as will naturally cause a Terror to the People, which is said to have been always an Offence at Common Law, and is strictly prohibited by many Statutes: For by 2 *Ed.* 3. 3. it is enacted, *That no Man, great nor small, of what Condition soever he be, except the King's Servants, in his Presence, and his Ministers in executing of the King's Precepts, or of their Office, and such as be in their Company assisting them, and also upon a Cry made for Arms to keep the Peace, and the same in such Places where such Acts happen, be so hardy to come before the King's Justices, or other of the King's Ministers doing their Office, with Force and Arms, nor bring no Force in Affray of Peace, nor to go nor ride armed by Night nor by Day, in Fairs, Markets, nor in the Presence of the Justices or other Ministers, nor in no part elsewhere, upon pain to forfeit their Armour to the King, and their Bodies to prison, at the King's Pleasure. And that the King's Justices in their Presence, Sheriffs, and other Ministers in their Bailiwicks, Lords of Franchises, and their Bailiffs in the same, and Mayors and Bailiffs of Cities and Boroughs, within the same Cities and Boroughs, and Borough-holders, Constables and Wardens of the Peace within their Wards, shall have Power to execute this Act: And that the Justices assigned, at their coming down into the Country, shall have Power to enquire how such Officers and Lords have exercised their Offices in this Case, and to punish them whom they find, that have not done that which pertained to their Office*; and this Statute is farther enforced by 7 *Rich.* 2. 13. and 20 *Rich.* 2. 1. Lamb. 126. 3 Inst. 160. 76 D. 2 Rol. Ab. 78. Pl 4. H. P. C. 137.

And in the Exposition of it, the following Points have been holden:

Sect. 5. I. That any Justice of Peace, or other Person, who is impowered to execute this Statute, may proceed thereon, either *ex Officio*, or by Force of a Writ out of Chancery formed upon the Statute, and that if he find any Person in Arms contrary to the Form of the Statute, he may seize the Arms, and commit the Offender to Prison; and that he ought also to make a Record of his whole Proceeding, and certify the same into the Chancery, where he proceeds by Force of the said Writ, or into the Exchequer, where he proceeds *ex Officio*. F. N. B. 249. 3 Inst. 161. Dal. ch. 21. Lamb. 168, &c. Dalis. 23. 2 Bulst. 330.

Sect. 6. II. That where a Justice of Peace, *&c.* proceeds upon the said Writ, he may not only imprison those whom he shall find offending against the Statute in his own View, but also those who shall be found by an Inquest taken before him, to have offended in such Manner in his Absence; and I do not see why he may not do the same where he proceeds *ex Officio*; for seeing the said Writ hath no other Foundation but the Cro. El. 294. Con. Lamb. 170.

the ſaid Statute, and is the moſt authentick Explication thereof, it ſeemeth that the Rules therein preſcribed, ſhould be the beſt Direction for all Proceedings upon that Statute.

Cro. El. 294.

Sect. 7. III That the Under-Sheriff may execute the ſaid Writ, being directed to the Sheriff, if it name him only by the Name of his Office, and not by his proper Name, and do not expreſly command him to act in his proper Perſon.

24 Ed. 3. 33. a. b. 21 H. 7. 39. a. 3 Inſt. 161, 162. Con. 2. Rol. 78. d. 21 H. 7. 39. a. 3 Inſt. 162.

Sect. 8. IV That a Man cannot excuſe the wearing ſuch Armour in Publick, by alledging that ſuch a one threatened him, and that he wears it for the Safety of his Perſon from his Aſſault; but it hath been reſolved, That no one ſhall incur the Penalty of the ſaid Statute for aſſembling his Neighbours and Friends in his own Houſe, againſt thoſe who threaten to do him any Violence therein, becauſe a Man's Houſe is as his Caſtle.

3 Mod. 117, 118. 2 Bulſt. 330. Crom. 64. a.

Sect. 9. V. That no wearing of Arms is within the meaning of this Statute, unleſs it be accompanied with ſuch Circumſtances as are apt to terrify the People; from whence it ſeems clearly to follow, That Perſons of Quality are in no Danger of Offending againſt this Statute by wearing common Weapons, or having their uſual Number of Attendants with them, for their Ornament or Defence, in ſuch Places, and upon ſuch Occaſions, in which it is the common Faſhion to make uſe of them, without cauſing the leaſt Suſpicion of an Intention to commit any Act of Violence or Diſturbance of the Peace. And from the ſame Ground it alſo follows, That Perſons armed with privy Coats of Mail to the Intent to defend themſelves againſt their Adverſaries, are not within the Meaning of this Statute, becauſe they do nothing *in terrorem Populi.*

Poph. 121, 122.

Sect. 10. VI. That no Perſon is within the Intention of the ſaid Statute, who arms himſelf to ſuppreſs Rioters, Rebels, or Enemies, and endeavours to ſuppreſs or reſiſt ſuch Diſturbers of the Peace or Quiet of the Realm; for Perſons who ſo arm themſelves, ſeem to be exempted out of the general Words of the ſaid Statute, by that Part of the Exception in the beginning thereof, which ſeems to allow all Perſons to arm themſelves upon a Cry made for Arms to keep the Peace, in ſuch Places where ſuch Acts happen.

Lamb. 131. 3 Inſt. 158. H. P. C. 131. 2 Inſt. 52. 22 E. 4. 44. b. Dalt. cap. 8. Lamb. 131. 3 Inſt. 138. Con. Lamb. 131. Dalt. cap. 8.

Sect. 11. As to the ſecond Point, *viz.* How far an Affray may be ſuppreſſed by a private Perſon, it ſeems agreed, That any one who ſees others fighting, may lawfully part them, and alſo ſtay them till the Heat be over, and then deliver them to the Conſtable, who may impriſon them till they find Surety for the Peace; alſo it is ſaid, That any private Perſon may ſtop thoſe whom he ſhall ſee coming to join either Party; and from hence it ſeems clearly to follow, That if a Man receive a Hurt from either Party in thus endeavouring to preſerve the Peace, he ſhall have his Remedy by an Action againſt him; alſo upon the ſame Ground it ſeems equally reaſonable, That if he unavoidably happen to hurt either Party, in thus doing what the Law both allows and commends, he may well juſtify it, inaſmuch as he is no Way in Fault; and the Damage done to the other, was occaſioned by a laudable Intention to do him a Kindneſs.

Lamb. 131. Dalt. cap. 8. 3 Inſt. 158. Bro. Faux Impriſonment 35, 44. H. P. C. 135. 10 H. 7. 20. 2 Inſt. 52.

Sect. 12. However it ſeems clear, That if either Party be dangerouſly wounded in ſuch an Affray, and a Stander-by, endeavouring to arreſt the other, be not able to take him without hurting, or even wounding him, yet he is no Way liable to be puniſhed for the ſame, inaſmuch as he is bound under Pain of Fine and Impriſonment, to arreſt ſuch an Offender, and either detain him till it appear whether the Party will live or die, or carry him before a Juſtice of Peace, by whom he either is to be bailed or committed, *&c.*

Sect.

3

Sect. 13. As to the third Point, *viz.* How far an Affray may be suppressed by a Constable; it seems agreed, That a Constable is not only impower'd, as all private Persons are, to part an Affray which happens in his Presence, but is also bound at his Peril to use his best Endeavours to this Purpose, and not only to do his utmost himself, but also to demand the Assistance of others, which if they refuse to give him, they are punishable with Fine and Imprisonment.

3 Inst. 158. H. P. C. 135. Lamb. 132, 133. Dalt. cap. 8. 3 H. 7. 10. b.

Sect. 14. And it is said, That if a Constable see Persons either actually engaged in an Affray, as by Striking, or offering to strike, or drawing their Weapons, *&c.* or upon the very Point of entering upon an Affray, as where one shall threaten to kill, wound, or beat another, he may either carry the Offender before a Justice of Peace, to the End that such Justice may compel him to find Sureties for the Peace, *&c.* or he may imprison him of his own Authority for a reasonable Time, till the Heat shall be over, and also afterwards detain him till he find such Surety by Obligation: But it seems, That he has no Power to imprison such an Offender in any other manner, or for any other Purpose; for he cannot justify the committing an Affrayer to Gaol till he shall be punished for his Offence: And it is said, That he ought not to lay Hands on those, who barely contend with hot Words, without any Threats of personal Hurt, and that all which he can do in such a Case, is to command them under Pain of Imprisonment to avoid Fighting.

Lamb 132, 133. Dalt. ca. 1, 8. H. P. C. 136. Dalt. cap. 1, 8. Bro. Surety, 23. 36. Moore 284. Pl. 436. 3 H. 4. 9. a. 22 Ed. 4. 35. b. 10 Ed. 4. 18. 5 H. 7. 6. a. Savil. 97, 98.

Sect. 15. But he is so far intrusted with a Power over all actual Affrays, that though he himself is a Sufferer by them, and therefore liable to be objected against, as likely to be partial in his own Cause, yet he may suppress them; and therefore, if an Assault be made upon him, he may not only defend himself, but also imprison the Offender, in the same manner as if he were no way a Party.

5 H. 7. 6. a. H. P. C. 136. 1 Rol. Re. 238. 2 Bulst. 329.

Sect. 16. And if an Affray be in a House, the Constable may break open the Doors to preserve the Peace; and if the Affrayers fly to a House, and he follow with fresh Suit, he may break open the Doors to take them.

13 Ed. 4. 9. a. 7 Ed. 3. 12. b. Dalt. cap. 8, 67. Lamb 133, 134.

Sect. 17. But it is said, That a Constable hath no Power to arrest a Man for an Affray done out of his own View, without a Warrant from a Justice of Peace, unless a Felony were done or likely to be done; for it is the proper Business of a Constable to preserve the Peace, not to punish the Breach of it; nor does it follow from his having Power to compel those to find Sureties who break the Peace in his Presence, that he has the same Power over those who break it in his Absence, inasmuch as in such Case it is most proper to be done by those who may examine the whole Circumstances of the Matter upon Oath, which a Constable cannot do; yet it is said, That he may carry those before a Justice of Peace, who were arrested by such as were present at an Affray, and delivered by them into his Hands.

H. P. C. 135. Cro. El. 375. Owen 105. H. P. C. 136. H. P. C. 92. Lamb, 131. Dalt. cap. 8.

Sect. 18. As to the fourth Point, *viz.* In what manner an Affray may be suppressed by a Justice of Peace; there is no doubt, but that he may and must do all such Things to that Purpose, which a private Man or Constable, are either enabled, or required by the Law to do: But it is said, That he cannot without a Warrant authorize the Arrest of any Person for an Affray out of his View; yet it seems clear, that in such Case he may make his Warrant to bring the Offender before him, in order to compel him to find Sureties for the Peace.

H. P. C. 136. Dalt. cap. 8. Bro. false Imprisonment 6. 12, 33. 14 H. 8. 7. Moore 468. Pl. 551.

Sect. 19. Alſo it ſeems, That a Juſtice of Peace has a greater Power over one who hath dangerouſly wounded another in an Affray, than either a private Perſon or a Conſtable; for there does not ſeem to be any good Authority, that theſe have any Power at all to take Sureties of ſuch an Offender: but it ſeems certain, That a Juſtice of Peace has a diſcretionary Power either to commit him or to bail him, till the Year and Day be paſt; but it is ſaid, that he ought to be very cautious how he takes Bail, if the Wound be dangerous; for that if the Party die, and the Offender appear not, he is in Danger of being ſeverely fined, if he ſhall appear upon the whole Circumſtances of the Caſe to have been too favourable.

See 38 Ed. 3. 6. b. 7. a. 22 Aſſ. 56. 5 Mod. 84.

H. P. C. 36. Dalt. cap. 8. Poph. 153.

Sect. 20. As to the fifth Point, *viz.* In what manner the ſeveral kinds of Affrays are to be puniſhed, it ſufficiently appears from the foregoing Part of this Chapter, how ſuch Affrays as are accompanied with Force and Arms, are to be dealt with upon the Statute of *Northampton*; and therefore I ſhall only examine in this Place, what Penalties other Affrays are liable unto, as to which it is to be obſerved, That all Affrays in general are puniſhable by Fine and Impriſonment, the Meaſure of which is to be regulated by the Diſcretion of the Judges according to the Circumſtances of the Caſe, which very much vary the Nature of this Crime, and in ſome Caſes make it ſo inconſiderable as ſcarce to deſerve to be taken Notice of; and in others, make it an Offence of a very heinous Nature, as in the following Inſtances;

1. In Reſpect of the dangerous Tendency thereof.
2. In Reſpect of the Perſons againſt whom it is committed.
3. In Reſpect of the Place wherein it happens.

Sect. 21. And firſt, An Affray may receive an Aggravation from the dangerous Tendency thereof, as where Perſons cooly and deliberately engage in a Duel, which cannot but be attended with the apparent Danger of Murder, and is not only an open Defiance of the Law, but carries with it a direct Contempt of the Juſtice of the Nation, as putting Men under a Neceſſity of righting themſelves; upon which Conſiderations, Perſons convicted of barely ſending a Challenge, have been adjudged to pay a Fine of one hundred Pounds, and to be impriſoned for one Month without Bail, and alſo to make a publick Acknowledgment of their Offence, and to be bound to their good Behaviour.

Poph 153. 3 Inſt. 158.

1 Sid. 186. 1 Keb. 694.

Moore 563, Pl. 763.

Sect. 22. Secondly, An Affray may receive another Aggravation from the Perſons againſt whom it is committed; as where the Officers of Juſtice are violently diſturbed in the due Execution of their Office, as by the Reſcous of a Perſon legally arreſted, or the bare Attempt to make ſuch a Reſcous; for all the Miniſters of the Law are under its more immediate Protection.

Sect. 23. Thirdly, An Affray may receive a farther Aggravation from the Place wherein it is committed, and upon this Reſpect all Affrays in the King's Courts are ſo ſeverely puniſhed, as hath been ſhewn already in Chapter 21, and upon the ſame Account alſo, all Affrays in a Church or Church-yard, have been always eſteemed very heinous Offences, as being great Indignities to the Divine Majeſty, to whoſe Worſhip and Service ſuch Places are immediately dedicated. And upon this Conſideration, all irreverent Behaviour in theſe Places hath been eſteemed ſo criminal by the Makers of our Laws, that they have not only ſeverely puniſhed ſuch Diſturbances in them which are puniſhable where-ever they happen, as all actual Affrays, *&c.* but alſo ſuch, which if they happen elſewhere,

12 Co 101, 1 Keb 296, 491. 1 Mod. 186 188

are not punishable at all; as bare quarrelsome Words, and even such which would be commendable if done in another Place; as Arrests by Vertue of legal Process: But for the better Understanding hereof, I shall consider the several Statutes made for this Purpose.

Sect. 24. And first, It is enacted by 5 and 6 *Ed.* 6. 4. *That if any Person whatsoever, shall by Words only quarrel, chide, or brawl, in any Church or Church-yard, that then it shall be lawful unto the Ordinary of the Place where the same Offence shall be done, and proved by two lawful Witnesses, to suspend every Person so offending; that is to say, if he be a Layman,* ab ingressu Ecclesiæ, *and if he be a Clerk, from the Ministration of his Office, for so long Time as the same Ordinary shall by his Discretion think meet and convenient, according to the Fault.*

Sect. 25. And it is farther enacted by the said Statute, *That if any Person shall smite or lay any violent Hands upon any other, either in any Church or Church-yard; that then,* ipso Facto, *every Person so offending shall be deemed excommunicate, and be excluded from the Fellowship and Company of Christ's Congregation.*

Sect. 26. And it is also farther enacted by the said Statute, *That if any Person shall maliciously strike any Person with any Weapon in any Church or Church-yard, or shall draw any Weapon in any Church or Church-yard, to the Intent to strike another with the same Weapon; that then every Person so offending, and thereof being convicted by Verdict of twelve Men, or by his own Confession, or by two lawful Witnesses, before the Justices of Assize, Justices of Oyer and Terminer, or Justices of Peace in their Sessions, by Force of this Act, shall be adjudged by the same Justices before whom such Person shall be convicted, to have one of his Ears cut off,* &c. *and besides that every such Person to be, and stand* ipso Facto *excommunicated, as aforesaid.*

And in the Exposition hereof it hath been holden;

Sect. 27. I. That notwithstanding the Words of the Statute be expressed, That he who smites another in the Church, *&c.* shall, *ipso Facto,* be deemed excommunicate; yet there ought either to be a precedent Conviction at Law, which must be transmitted to the Ordinary, or else the Excommunication must be declared in the Spiritual Court upon a proper Proof of the Offence there; for it is implied in every Penal Law, that no one shall incur the Penalty thereof, till he be found guilty upon a lawful Trial; also it must be intended in the Construction of this Statute, That the Excommunication ought to appear judicially, for otherwise there could be no Absolution. Dyer 275. Pl 48. Cro Ja. 462. 1 Vent. 146. Lit. 149. Hett. 86. Cro. El. 919.

Sect. 27. II. That he who strikes another in a Church, *&c.* can no way excuse himself, by shewing that the other assaulted him. Cro. Ja. 367.

Sect. 28. III. That Church wardens, or perhaps private Persons, who whip Boys for playing in the Church, or pull off the Hats of those who obstinately refuse to take them off themselves, or gently lay their Hands on those who disturb the Performance of any Part of divine Service, and turn them out of the Church, are not within the meaning of the Statute. 1 Saund. 13, 14. 1 Sid. 301. 3 Keb. 124. 1 Mod. 168.

Sect. 29. Also it is enacted by 1 *Ma.* Sess. 2. cap. 3. *That if any Person or Persons, of their own Power and Authority, shall willingly and of Purpose by open and overt Word, Fact, Act, or Deed, maliciously or contemptuously molest, let, disturb, vex or trouble, or by any other unlawful Ways and Means, disquiet, or misuse, any Preacher who shall be licenced, allowed, or authorized to preach by the Queen's Highness, or by any Archbishop, or Bishop of this Realm, or by any other lawful Ordinary, or by any of the Universities of* Oxford *and* Cambridge, *or otherwise lawfully authorized or charged, by Reason of his or their Cure, Benefice,*

fice, or other Spiritual Promotion or Charge, in any of his, or their open Sermon, &c. *or if any Person or Persons shall maliciously, willingly, or of purpose, molest, let, disturb, vex, disquiet, or otherwise trouble any Parson, Vicar, Parish-Priest, or Curate, or any lawful Priest, preparing, saying, doing, singing, ministring or celebrating the Mass, or other such divine Service, Sacraments, or Sacramentals, as was most commonly frequented and used in the last Year of the Reign of the late Sovereign Lord King* Henry *the eight, or that at any Time hereafter should be allowed, set forth, or authorized by the Queen's Majesty; or if any Person or Persons shall unlawfully, contemptuously, or maliciously, of their own Power or authority, pull down, deface, spoil, or otherwise break any Altar or Altars, or any Crucifix, or Cross, in any Church, Chapel, or Church-yard; every such Offender and Offenders, his or their Aiders, Procurers, or Abettors, may be apprehended by any Constable, or Church-warden of the Place where such Offence shall be committed, or by any other Officer or Person then being present at the Time of the said Offence; and being so apprehended, shall be brought before some Justice of Peace by whom they shall be committed forthwith, and within six Days the Matter shall be examined by the same, together with some other Justices; and on Proof by two Witnesses or Confession, the Offender shall be committed for three Months, and also till the next Quarter-Sessions, where if they repent, they shall be discharged upon giving Sureties for their good Behaviour for a Year, and if they do not repent they shall be committed till they do.*

2 Jon. 159. Con. Aleyn 50. 2 Bulst. 51.

Sect. 30. It hath been resolved, That the Disturbance of a Minister in saying the present Common Prayer is within this Statute; for the express mention of such Divine Service, as should afterwards be authorized by Queen *Mary*, doth implicitly include such also as should be authorized by her Successors; for since the King never dies, a Prerogative given generally to one, goes of Course to others.

Sect. 31. Also it is enacted by 1 *Will.* and *Mar.* 18. Par. 19. *That if any Person shall willingly and of Purpose, maliciously or contemptuously come into any Cathedral or Parish Church, Chapel, or other Congregation permitted by the said Act, and disquiet or disturb the same, or misuse any Preacher or Teacher, such Persons, upon Proof before any Justice of Peace, by two or more sufficient Witnesses, shall find two Sureties to be bound by Recognizance in the penal Sum of fifty Pounds, and on Default of such Sureties shall be committed to Prison, there to remain till the next General or Quarter-Sessions, and upon Conviction of the said Offence at the said General or Quarter-Sessions, shall suffer the Pain and Penalty of twenty Pounds.*

CHAP. LXIV.

Of Forcible Entries and Detainers.

Lamb. 135. Dalt. cap. 76. Crom. 70. a. b.

Sect. 1. IT seems that at the Common Law a Man disseised of any Lands, or Tenements, (if he could not prevail by fair Means,) might lawfully regain the Possession thereof by Force, unless he were put to a Necessity of bringing his Action, by having neglected to re-enter in due Time: And it seems certain, That even at this Day, he who is wrongfully dispossessed of his Goods, may justify the re-taking of them by Force from the Wrong-doer, if he refuse to re-deliver them; for the Violence which happens through the Resistance of the wrongful Possessor,

Kellw. 92. Yelv. 172.

being originally owing to his own Fault, gives him no just Cause of Complaint, inasmuch as he might have prevented it by doing as he ought.

Sect. 2. But this Indulgence of the Common Law, in suffering Persons to regain the Lands, they were unlawfully deprived of, having been found by Experience to be very prejudicial to the publick Peace, by giving an Opportunity to powerful Men, under the Pretence of feigned Titles, forcibly to eject their weaker Neighbours, and also by Force to retain their wrongful Possessions, it was thought necessary by many severe Laws to restrain all Persons from the use of such violent Methods of doing themselves Justice.

Sect. 3. However, even at this Day, in an Action of Forcible Entry grounded on those Laws, if the Defendant make himself a Title which is found for him, he shall be dismissed without any Inquiry concerning the Force; for howsoever he may be punishable at the King's Suit, for doing what is prohibited by Statute, as a Contemner of the Laws, and Disturber of the Peace, yet he shall not be liable to pay any Damages for it to the Plaintiff, whose Injustice gave him the Provocation in that Manner to right himself. 17 H. 7. 17. a. b. 21 H. 6. 39. b. F N B. 249. d. Bro. Force 5, 11, 29.

Sect. 4. Since therefore Offences of this Nature are made such, not by the Common Law, but by Statute; I shall for the better Understanding thereof, consider the several Statutes relating to this Subject.

Sect. 5. And first, I find it agreed, That by 2 *Ed.* 3. which is commonly called the Statute of *Northampton*; if there be any Use made of Arms to strike a Terror into the Persons upon whom a Forcible Entry is made, any Justice of Peace or other Officer, who is within the Purview of that Statute, may both seize the Arms for the King's Use, and also imprison the Offenders, but not restore the Party injured to his Possession; but the said Statute having been fully set forth in the foregoing Chapter, I shall proceed to those Statutes which more directly relate to this Matter. 3 Inst. 161. Crom. 162. a. Dalt. cap. 80.

Sect. 6. And first it is enacted by 5 *Rich.* 2. 7. in the following Words, *And also the King defendeth, That none from henceforth make any Entry into any Lands and Tenements, but in Case where Entry is given by the Law; and in such Case not with strong Hand, nor with Multitude of People, but only in peaceable and easy Manner. And if any Man from henceforth do to the contrary, and thereof be duly convict, he shall be punished by Imprisonment of his Body, and thereof ransomed at the King's Will.*

Sect. 7. But this Statute being found by Experience not sufficiently to have provided against the Mischief intended to be redressed by it, inasmuch as it gave no speedy Remedy to the Party injured, against the Wrong-doer, but left him to the common Course of proceeding by way of Indictment or Action, and made no Provision at all against Forcible Detainers, it was thought necessary to supply these Defects by other additional Laws; and to this Purpose it was farther enacted by 15 *Rich.* 2. ch. 2. *That the said Statute and all others made against Forcible Entries, &c. shall be fully executed; and farther, That at all Times that such forcible Entries shall be made, and Complaint thereof cometh to the Justices of Peace, or to any of them, that the same Justices or Justice take sufficient Power of the County, and go to the Place where the Force is made; and if they find any that hold such Place forcibly, after such Entry made, they shall be taken and put in the next Gaol, there to abide convict by the Record of the same Justices or Justice, until they have made Fine and Ransom to the King. And that all the People of the County, as well the Sheriff as others, shall be attendant upon the same Justices, to go and assist the same Justices to arrest such Offenders, upon Pain of Imprisonment, and to make Fine to the King: And in the same manner it shall be done of them that make such Forcible Entries in Benefices or Offices of Holy Church.*

8 Co. 121. a. Dalt. cap. 22. Lamb. 151. Dalt. cap. 22. [a] B. R. Hill. 1708. Kellw. 41. a. Crom. 195. b. 196. Dalt. cap. 22. Moore 848.

Sect. 8. In the Exposition of this Statute it hath been holden, That one Justice of Peace may make a Record of such a forcible Holding, and that such Record is not traversable, because the Justice of Peace in making thereof, acts not as a Minister, but as a Judge: Also it hath [a] lately been solemnly resolved in Colonel *Leighton*'s Case, That the same Justice may assess the Fine for this Offence; but it is said, That such Justice of Peace hath no Power to commit the Offender to Gaol, unless he do it immediately upon the Fact, or unless the Offender shall afterwards refuse to find Sureties for his good Behaviour. Also it was holden by the Court in *Leighton's* Case above mentioned, That if a Person against whom a Complaint shall be made as having been guilty of a Forcible Entry, shall either traverse the Entry or the Force, the Justice may summon a Jury for the Trial of such Traverse, for it is impossible to determine it upon View; and if the Justice have no Power to try it, it would be easy for any one to elude the Statute by the Tender of such a Traverse, and therefore by a necessary Construction, the Justice must needs have this Power as incidental to what is expresly given him.

Sect. 9. But this Statute being likewise very defective in many Respects, as in not giving any Remedy against those who were guilty of a Forcible Detainer after a peaceful Entry; nor even against those who were guilty of both a Forcible Entry and Forcible Detainer, if they were removed before the coming of a Justice of Peace; and in not giving the Justices of the Peace any Power to restore the Party injured by such Force to his Possession; and also in not fixing any Pain on the Sheriff for not obeying the Precepts of the Justices in the Execution of the said Statutes; it was farther enacted by 8 *H.* 6. 9. *That from henceforth where any doth make any Forcible Entry in Lands and Tenements, or other Possessions, or them hold forcibly, after Complaint thereof made within the same County where such Entry is made, to the Justices of the Peace, or to one of them, by the Party grieved, that the Justices or Justice so warned, within a convenient Time, shall cause, or one of them shall cause, the said Statute duly to be executed, and that at the Costs of the Party so grieved.*

Sect. 10. And it is farther enacted by the said Statute, *That though such Persons making such Entries be present, or else departed before the coming of the said Justices or Justice, notwithstanding the same Justices or Justice in some good Town next to the Tenements so entered, or in some other convenient Place, according to their Discretion, shall have, and either of them shall have, Authority and Power to enquire by the People of the same County, as well of them that make such Forcible Entries in Lands and Tenements, as of them which the same hold with Force. And if it be found before any of them, that any doth contrary to this Statute, then the said Justices or Justice shall cause to reseize the Lands and Tenements so entered or holden as afore, and shall put the Party so put out, in full Possession of the same Lands and Tenements, so entered or holden as before.*

Sect. 11. And it is farther enacted by the said Statute, *That when the said Justices or Justice make such Inquiries as before, they shall make, or one of them shall make, their Warrants and Precepts to be directed to the Sheriff of the same County, commanding him of the King's Behalf, to cause to come before them, and every of them, sufficient and indifferent Persons, dwelling next about the Lands so entered as before, to enquire of such Entries, whereof every Man which shall be impanelled to enquire in this Behalf, shall have Land or Tenement of the yearly*

Value of fourty Shillings by the Year at the least, above Reprizes, and that the Sheriff return Issues upon every of them at the Day of the first Precept returnable, twenty Shillings, and at the second Day forty Shillings, and at the third Time an hundred Shillings, and at every Day after the double. And if any Sheriff or Bailiff within a Franchise having Return of the King's Writ, be slack, and make not Execution duly of the said Precepts to him directed to make such Enquiries, that he shall forfeit to the King twenty Pounds for every Default, and moreover shall make Fine and Ransom to the King. And that as well the Justices or Justice aforesaid, as the Justices of Assizes, shall have Power to hear and determine such Defaults of the said Sheriffs and Bailiffs, at the Suit of the King, or of the Party grieved, &c.

Sect. 12. And it is farther enacted by the said Statute, *That Mayors, Justices or Justice of Peace, Sheriffs and Bailiffs of Cities, Towns and Boroughs having Franchise, have in the said Cities, Towns, and Boroughs, like Power to remove such Entries, and in other Articles aforesaid, rising within the same, as the Justices of Peace, and Sheriffs in Counties and Countries aforesaid have.*

Sect. 13. But it is provided by the said Statute, *That they who keep their Possessions with Force in any Lands and Tenements, whereof they or their Ancestors, or they whose Estate they have in such Lands and Tenements, have continued their Possessions in the same by three Years or more, be not endamaged by Force of this Statute.*

Sect. 14. And the said Proviso was farther enforced and explained by 31 *El.* 11. by which it is declared and enacted, *That no Restitution upon any Indictment of Forcible Entry, or holding with Force, be made to any Person, if the Person so indicted, hath had the Occupation, or been in quiet Possession, for the Space of three whole Years together, next before the Day of such Indictment so found, and his Estate therein not ended; which the Party indicted may alledge for stay of Restitution, and Restitution to stay till that be tried, if the other will deny or traverse the same: And if the same Allegation be tried against the same Person so indicted, he is to pay such Costs and Damages to the other Party, as shall be assessed by the Judges or Justices before whom the same shall be tried; the same Costs and Damages to be recovered and levied, as is usual for Costs and Damages contained in Judgments upon other Actions.*

Sect. 15. In the Construction of these Statutes it was holden, That if a Lessee for Years or Copyholder were ousted, and the Lessor or Lord disseized, and such Ouster as well as Disseisin were found in an Indictment of Forcible Entry, the Court might in their Discretion award a Restitution of Possession to such Lessee or Copyholder, which was by necessary Consequence a Reseisin of the Freehold also, whether the Lessor or Lord had desired or opposed it: But it was a great Question, Whether a Lessee for Years or a Copyholder, being ousted by the Lessor or Lord, could have a Restitution of their Possession within the Equity of 8 *H.* 6. the Words whereof as to this Purpose are, that the Justice shall re-seize the Lands, *&c.* by which it seems to be implied, That the Party must be ousted of such an Estate therein, whereof he may be said to be seized, which must be a Freehold at least. (Crom. 161. b. 166. b. Yelv. 81. Con. 1 Leon. 327. Lamb. 155. Crom. 71. Dalt. cap. 77. Savil 68. Pl. 141.)

Sect. 16. But to remove this Doubt, it is enacted by 21 *Ja.* 1. 15. *That such Judges, Justices, or Justice of the Peace, as by reason of any Act or Acts of Parliament then in force, were authorized and enabled upon Enquiry, to give Restitution of Possession unto Tenants, of any Estate of Freehold, of their Lands or Tenements, which shall be entered upon with Force, or from them withholden by Force, shall by Reason of that Act have the like, and the same Authority and Ability from thenceforth (upon Indictment of such Forcible Entries, or forcible with-holding before them duly found) to give like Restitution of Possession*

session unto Tenants for Term of Years, Tenants by Copy of Court-Roll, Guardians by Knights-Service, Tenants by Elegit, *Statute-Merchant, and Staple of Lands or Tenements, by them so holden, which shall be entered upon by Force, or holden from them by Force.*

Sect. 17. But it hath been holden, That a Tenant by the Verge is not within this Statute, because he is not within the express Words; *sed Quare*, for since such Person hath no other Evidence of his Title, but by the Copy of Court-Roll, he seems at least to be within the Meaning, if not within the Words, of the Statute; however it seems clear, That if a Lessor eject his Lessee for Years, and afterwards be forcibly put out of Possession again by such Lessee, he hath no Remedy for a Restitution by Force of any of the above mentioned Statutes, for he cannot have it by 8 *H.* 6. because he always continued seized of the Freehold, and clearly he is not within 21 *Jac.* 1. 15.

Latch 182. See Co. Litt. 61. Crom. 71. a. 166. b. Dal. ch. 77.

Sect. 18. However there seems to be no doubt, but that a Justice of Peace, *&c.* may, in either of the said Cases, remove the Force, and commit the Offender, *&c.*

Lamb. 155. Crom. 71. a. Dal. ch. 77. 2 Keb. 495.

Sect. 19. Having thus set forth the several Statutes relating to this Subject, together with the Mischiefs which occasioned them, and the several Defects of each of them, I shall, for the better Understanding of them all in general, proceed to examine the following Particulars:

1. What shall be esteemed an Entry within these Statutes.
2. What Entry is to be adjudged forcible.
3. What Detainer.
4. In respect of what Kind of Possessions one may be guilty of such forcible Entry or Detainer.
5. What Persons may be guilty thereof.
6. What ought to be the Form of a Record grounded upon these Statutes.
7. Of what Kind of Possessions a Restitution is to be awarded.
8. To whom such Restitution ought to be made.
9. By whom, and in what Manner, it is to be awarded and given.
10. In what Cases it may be barred by the Continuance of a Possession for three Years.
11. For what other Causes it may be stayed.
12. How it may be superseded before it is executed.
13. How it may be set aside after it is executed.

Sect. 20. As to the first Point, *viz.* What shall be esteemed an Entry within these Statutes, it seems certain, That if one who pretends a Title to Lands, barely go over them, either with, or without a great Number of Attendants, armed or unarmed, in his Way to the Church, or Market, or for such like purpose, without doing any Act, which either expresly or impliedly amounts to a Claim of such Lands, he can not be said to make an Entry thereinto within the Meaning of these Statutes.

Crom. 70. b. Dal. ch. 77.

Sect. 21. Yet in such Case, if he make an actual Claim with any Circumstances of Force or Terror, he seems to be guilty of a forcible Entry within 1 *&* 15 *Ric.* 2. whether his Adversary actually quit his Possession or not.

Crom. 69. Dal. ch. 77. Con. Cro. Ca. 486.

Sect. 22. Also all those who accompany a Man when he makes a forcible Entry, shall be adjudged to enter with him, within the Intent of these Laws, whether they actually came upon the Lands, or not.

Crom. 69. a. Dal. ch. 77.

Sect. 23. So also shall those who having an Estate in Land by a defeasible Title, continue with Force in the Possession thereof, after a Claim made by one who had a Right of Entry thereto. Crom. 69. b. Dal. ch. 77. Co. Lit. 256, 257.

Sect. 24. But he who barely agrees to a forcible Entry made to his Use, without his Knowledge or Privity, shall not be adjudged to make an Entry within these Statutes, because he no way concurred in, or promoted the Force. Crom. 69. a. Dal. ch. 77. 2 H. 7. 16. b.

Sect. 25. As to the second Point, *viz.* What Entry is to be adjudged forcible, it seems clear, That it ought to be accompanied with some Circumstances of actual Violence or Terror; and therefore, That an Entry which hath no other Force than such as is implied by the Law, in every Trespass whatsoever, is not within these Statutes. Lamb. 140, &c. Dalt. ch. 77. Co. Litt. 257. b.

And therefore, for the better Understanding hereof, I shall consider;

1. In Respect of what Acts of Violence an Entry may be adjudged forcible.

2. In Respect of what Circumstances of Terror.

Sect. 26. As to the first of these particulars, it seems to be agreed, That an Entry may be said to be forcible, not only in Respect of a Violence actually done to the Person of a Man, as by beating him if he refuse to relinquish his Possession, but also in Respect of any other Kind of Violence in the Manner of the Entry, as by breaking open the Doors of a House, whether any Person be in it at the same Time or not, especially if it be a Dwelling-house, and perhaps also by any Act of Outrage after the Entry, as by carrying away the Party's Goods, *&c.* which being found in an Assize of Novel Disseisin, will make the Defendant a Disseisor with Force, and subject him to fine and imprisonment: And according to some Opinions, an Entry may be said to be forcible from the bare drawing up of a Latch, or pulling back the Bolt of a Door; but surely such inconsiderable Circumstances as these, which commonly pass between Neighbour and Neighbour, without any Offence at all, can never bring a Man within the Meaning of these Statutes, which speak of Entries with strong Hand, or Multitude of People; and it hath been holden, That an Entry into a House through a Window, or by opening a Door with a Key, is not forcible: And it is said, That if one find a Man out of his House, and forcibly with-hold him from returning to it, and send Persons to take peaceable Possession thereof, in the Party's Absence, yet he is not guilty of a forcible Entry, inasmuch as he did no Violence to the House, but only to the Person of the other: But perhaps this Opinion may justly be questioned, because though the Force be not actually done upon the Land, nor in the very Act of the Entry, yet since it is used with an immediate Intent to make such Entry, and is the only Cause that it met with no Opposition, surely it cannot be said, that the Entry is without Force, which, whether it be upon, or off the Land, seems equally within the Statute. H. P. C. 116. 2 Rol. Re. 2. Noy 136. 30 Ass. 50. 11 H. 4. 16. b. 17. a. 2 Inst. 235, 236. Dal. ch. 77. Crom. 70. a. b. Moore 656. Pl. 899. Noy 137. Dalt. ch. 77. H. P. C. 138. Lamb. 143. 2 Rol. Re. 2. Lamb. 143. Dal. ch. 77.

Sect. 27. As to the second Particular, *viz.* In respect of what Circumstances of Terror an Entry may be adjudged forcible; it is to be observed, That where-ever a Man, either by his Behaviour or Speech, at the Time of his Entry, gives those who are in Possession of the Tenements which he claims, just cause to fear, that he will do them some bodily Hurt, if they will not give way to him, his Entry is esteemed forcible, whether he cause such a Terror, by carrying with him such an unusual H. P. C. 128. Lamb. 142, &c. Dal. ca. 77.

10 H. 7. 12. a. Crom. 69. Pl. 14, 24.

See the Books above cited.

Number of Servants, or by arming himſelf in ſuch a Manner, as plainly intimates a Deſign to back his Pretenſions by Force, or by actually threatening to kill, maim, or beat thoſe who ſhall continue in Poſſeſſion, or by giving out ſuch Speeches as plainly imply a Purpoſe of uſing Force againſt thoſe who ſhall make any Reſiſtance, as if one ſay that he will keep his Poſſeſſion in ſpite of all Men, *&c.*

Bro. Dureſs. 12, 16. 1 Inſt. 253. b. Dal. ca. 77.

Sect. 28. But it ſeemeth that no Entry ſhall be judged forcible from any threatening to ſpoil another's Goods, or to deſtroy his Cattle, or to do him any other ſuch like Damage which is not perſonal.

Lamb. 143.

Sect. 29. However it is clear, That it may be committed by a ſingle Perſon, as well as by twenty.

H. P. C. 138.

Sect. 30. As to the third Point, *viz.* What Detainer is to be adjudged forcible, it ſeemeth certain, That the ſame Circumſtances of Violence or Terror, which will make an Entry forcible, will make a Detainer forcible alſo; from whence it ſeems to follow, That whoever keeps in his Houſe an unuſual Number of People, or unuſual Weapons, or threatens to do ſome bodily Hurt to the former Poſſeſſor, if he dare return, ſhall be adjudged guilty of a forcible Detainer; and it hath been ſaid, That he alſo ſhall come under the like Conſtruction, who places Men at a Diſtance from the Houſe, in order to aſſault any one who ſhall attempt to make an Entry into it; and that he alſo is in like Manner guilty who ſhuts his Doors againſt a Juſtice of Peace coming to view the Force, and obſtinately refuſes to let him come in: But it is ſaid, That a Man ought not to be adjudged guilty of this Offence, for barely refuſing to go out of a Houſe, and continuing therein in deſpight of another.

Lamb. 145. Crom. 70. H. P. C. 139. Dal. ca. 77.

Crom. 70. b. Lamb. 145.

Crom. 70. b. Lamb. 145.

Crom. 73. Dal. ca. 77.

Sect. 31. As to the fourth Point, *viz.* In reſpect of what Kind of Poſſeſſions one may be guilty of a forcible Entry or Detainer within theſe Statutes, it ſeems clear, That one may come within the Danger thereof by a Force done to Eccleſiaſtical Poſſeſſions, as [a] Churches, [b] Vicaridge-Houſes, *&c.* as much as if the ſame were done to any temporal Inheritance; alſo it hath been holden for a general Rule, That one may be indicted for a forcible Entry into any ſuch incorporeal Hereditament, for which a [c] Writ of Entry will lie, either by the Common Law, as for [d] Rent, or by Statute, as for [e] Tithes, *&c.* but I do not find any good Authority, That ſuch an Indictment will lie for a [f] Common or [g] Office; but it ſeems agreed, That an Indictment of forcible Detainer lies againſt any one, whether he be the Tertenant, or a Stranger, who ſhall forcibly diſturb the lawful [h] Proprietor in the Enjoyment of any of the above mentioned Poſſeſſions; as by violently reſiſting a Lord in his Diſtreſs for a Rent, or by menacing a Commoner with bodily Hurt, if he dare put in his Beaſts into the Common, *&c.* yet it ſeems clear, That no one can come within the Danger of theſe Statutes by a Violence offered to another in reſpect of a Way, or ſuch like Eaſement, which is no Poſſeſſion. Alſo it ſeemeth, That a Man cannot be convicted upon View, by Force of 15 *Ric.* 2. 2. of a forcible Detainer of any ſuch Tenement, wherein he cannot be ſaid to have made a precedent forcible Entry, becauſe that Statute gives the Juſtices a Juriſdiction of no other forcible Detainer, but what follows a forcible Entry.

[a] 1 Sid. 101. 1 Levin. 90. 1 Keb. 438. [b] Cro. Ja. 41. [c] Cro. Ca. 201. [d] 20 H. 6. 11. a. 22 H. 6. 33. a. Bro. Force 7. Cro. Ca. 201. [e] Cro. Ca. 201. [f] See Cro. Ca. 486. See Dal. ca. 77. [g] Cro. Ja. 18. [h] Crom. 69, 70. Lamb. 144. Dal. ca. 77.

1 Mod. 73. 2 Keb. 709.

Vide infra Sect. 40.

Sect. 32. As to the fifth Point, *viz.* Who may be guilty of a forcible Entry or Detainer within theſe Statutes; it ſeems clear, That no one can come within the Intention thereof by any Force whatſoever done by him in entering into a Tenement, whereof he himſelf had the ſole and lawful Poſſeſſion, both at and before the Time of ſuch Entry; as by breaking open the Doors of his own Dwelling-house, or of a Castle, which is his own Inheritance, but forcibly detained from him by one who claims the bare Custody of it; or by forcibly entering into the Land in the Possession of his own Lessee at Will. *Sed Quære.*

> Moore 785. Cro. Ja. 18. 2 Keb. 495.

Sect. 33. But it seems clear, That a Jointenant, or Tenant in Common, may offend against the Purport of these Statutes, either by forcibly ejecting, or forcibly holding out his Companion, for tho' the Entry of such a Tenant be lawful *per my & per tout*, so that he cannot in any Case be punished in an Action of Trespass at the Common Law, yet the Lawfulness of his Entry no Way excuses the Violence, or lessens the Injury done to his Companion, and consequently an Indictment of forcible Entry into a Moiety of a Manor, *&c.* is good.

> 8 Ed. 4. 9. 1. 19. 2. 10 H. 7. 27. 2. Latch. 214. Palm. 419.

Sect. 34. Also if a Man have been in Possession of Land for never so long a Time, by a defeasible Title, and another who hath a Right of Entry thereunto, make a Claim, and yet such wrongful Possessor still continue his Occupation with Force and Arms, he is punishable for a forcible Entry and Detainer against the Purport of these Statutes, because all the Estate whereof he was seized before such Claim, was wholly defeated by it, and his Continuance in Possession afterwards amounted in the Judgment of Law to a new Entry.

> Co. Lit. 256, 257. Crom. 69. b. Lamb. 160, 161. Dal. ch. 77.

Sect. 35. It is said, That an Infant or Feme Covert may be guilty within the Intention of these Statutes, in respect of such actual Violence as shall be done by them in Person, but not in respect of what shall be done by others at their Command, because all such Commands of theirs are void: Also it is said, That a Feme Covert may be imprisoned for such Offence, but that an Infant ought not, because he shall not be subject to corporal Punishment, by Force of the general Words of any Statute, wherein he is not expressly named.

> Dal. ch. 77. Crom. 69. Co. Lit. 357. b. Bro. Imprison. 43, 45, 75, 101.

As to the sixth Point, *viz.* What ought to be the Form of a Record grounded upon these Statutes, it hath been resolved.

Sect. 36. First, That it is sufficient in the Caption of such an Indictment, to say, That it was taken before *A. B. & C. D. Justiciariis ad pacem Domini Regis conservandam assignatis*, without shewing that they had Authority to hear and determine Felonies and Trespasses, for the Statute enables all Justices of Peace, as such, to take such Indictments.

> Palm. 277. Cro. Ja. 633.

Sect. 37. Secondly, It hath also been resolved, That the Tenement in which the Force was committed, must be described with convenient certainty, for otherwise the Defendant will neither know the special Charge to which he is to make his Defence, neither will the Justices or Sheriff know how to restore the injured Party to his Possession; and from hence it follows, That an Indictment of a forcible Entry into a [a] Tenement, (which may signify any Thing whatsoever, [b] wherein a Man may have an Estate of Freehold,) or into a House [c] or Tenement, or into two Closes of Meadow [d] or Pasture, or into a Rood [e] or half a Rood of Land, or into [f] certain Lands belonging to such a House, or into such a House, without shewing in what [g] Town it lies, or into a [h] Tenement with the Appurtenances called Trupenny in *D.* is not good. But it hath been resolved, That an Indictment for a forcible Entry *in* [i] *Domum Mansionalem sive Messuagium* is good, for these are Words equipollent: Also that such an Indictment for an Entry into a [k] Close, called Serjeant *Hern*'s Close, without adding the Number of Acres, is good, for here is as much Certainty as is required in an Ejectment; and it hath

> Dal. ch. 81.
> [a] Dal. 15. 2 Rol. Re. 46. 2 Rol. Ab. 80. Pl. 6. 3 Leon. 102. [b] Co. Lit. 6. a. [c] 2 Rol. Ab. 40. Pl. 4, 5. 1 Rol. Re. 334. Cro. Ja. 633. Palm. 277. [d] 2 Rol. Ab. 81. Pl. 4. [e] 1 Bulst. 201. [f] 2 Leon. 186. 3 Leon. 102.

Bro. forcib. Ent. 23. [g] 2 Leon. 186. [h] 2 Rol. Ab. 80. Pl. 7. [i] Cro. Ja. 633. Palm. 277. [k] Cro. El. 458. 2 Rol. Ab. 80. Pl. 8.

been

been adjudged, That ſuch Indictment may be void as to ſuch Part thereof only which is uncertain, and good for ſo much as is certain, and therefore, that an Indictment for a forcible Entry into a Houſe, and certain Acres of Land thereto belonging, may be quaſhed as to the Land, and ſtand good as to the Houſe.

2 Leon. 186. 3 Leon. 102.

Sect. 38. Thirdly, It hath been alſo reſolved, That an Indictment, on 5 or 15 *Rich.* 2. needs not ſhew who had the Freehold at the Time of the Force, becauſe thoſe Statutes ſeem equally to puniſh all Force of this Kind, without any Way regarding what Eſtate the Party had on whom it was made; yet it ſeems, That ſuch an Indictment ought to ſhew that ſuch Entry was made on the Poſſeſſion of ſome Perſon, who had ſome Eſtate in the Tenements, either as a Freeholder or Leſſee for Years, *&c.* for otherwiſe it doth not appear, that ſuch Entry was made injurious to any one; but it is ſaid, That an Indictment on 8 *H.* 6. muſt ſhew, that the Place wherein the Force was committed was the Freehold of the Party grieved at the Time of ſuch Force; and therefore, That it is not ſufficient to ſay that the Defendant with ſtrong Hand, *&c.* entered into ſuch a Houſe, *exiſtens liberum Tenementum J. S. &c.* without ſaying, *adtunc exiſtens liberum Tenementum J. S.* for otherwiſe it may be intended, that it was his Freehold at the Time of the Indictment only, and not at the Time of the Force; and according to the general Opinion, an Indictment on that Statute cannot warrant an Award of Reſtitution, unleſs it find, that the Party was ſeized at the Time; yet it is ſaid, That the Want of ſuch an expreſs finding may be ſupplied by ſuch Words as neceſſarily imply, that the Party was ſeized at the Time of the Force; as where it is expreſly laid that the Defendant diſſeiſed *J S. &c.* which is impoſſible, unleſs he had been ſeized of the Freehold at the ſame Time; and it hath been ſaid, That it is ſufficient in ſuch an Indictment to ſay that the Party was *Poſſeſſionatus pro termino Vitæ*, without uſing the word *Seiſitus*, *&c.* for the ſame Propriety of Expreſſion is not required in Indictments as in Pleadings; *ſed Quære.* Alſo it is ſaid, That if it do appear either in ſuch an expreſs or implicit Manner, that the Party injured had the Freehold of the Land at the Time of the Force, it is not neceſſary to ſhew farther what Eſtate in particular he had therein, or by what Title he claims the ſame; for it is not the Title, but the Poſſeſſion, which is in Queſtion. And upon the like Ground it hath been adjudged, That an Indictment on the ſaid Statute for entering on my Farmer, and forcibly expelling him, and diſſeiſing me, is good, without ſhewing what Eſtate ſuch Farmer had; for it is ſufficient to ſhew that he had the Poſſeſſion, and the Injury complained of is the forcible Diſſeiſin done to me, which, being the main Point of the Indictment, if it be ſufficiently ſet forth in Subſtance, the Indictment is good; yet in this very Caſe the Want of ſhewing that ſuch Farmer was ouſted, would have been an incurable Fault; becauſe his Poſſeſſion being my Poſſeſſion, unleſs he were ouſted, I could not be diſſeiſed. Alſo it hath been holden, That as an Indictment on 8 *H.* 6. muſt ſhew that the Party who is put out of Poſſeſſion was ſeized of a Freehold, in order to bring him within the Purview of that Statute, ſo alſo an Indictment on 21 *Jac.* 1. 15. muſt ſhew, That the Party injured was poſſeſſed of ſuch an Eſtate as will bring him within the Proviſion of that Act; and upon this Ground it hath been reſolved. That ſuch an Indictment, ſetting forth in general, that the Party was poſſeſſed, or that he was poſſeſſed for a certain Term, without adding, that it was for Years, is not good; for in the firſt Caſe it may be intended, That he was poſſeſſed only by Vertue of a Leaſe at Will; and in the ſecond,

2 Keb. 495. 3 Bulſ. 71. 2 Keb. 495. Hetley 73. Latch. 109. 2 Keb. 477, 499 1 Keb. 191. Cro El 754. Noy 131. 2 Rol Re. 65. Palm. 426. 1 Sid. 102. Con Yelv. 28. 1 Bulſ. 177. 3 Leon. 102. Allen. 49. Palm. 277. Con. 2 Rol. A. 80. Pl. 9. 2 Keb. 477. Palm. 277. Cro Ja. 633, 634. 2 Rol. A. 80 Pl. 3. Yelv. 165. 1 Sid 102. 1 Mod. 73. 2 Keb. 709.

That he was possessed of a Term for Life, in neither of which Cases he is within the Benefit of 21 *Jac.* 1. 15. Yet it hath been said, That the Possession of such an Estate as is within that Statute, is sufficiently set forth in the reciting Part of an Indictment, as thus, *Quod cum J. S.* was possessed for a certain Term of Years, and being so possessed, was by strong Hand, *&c.* put out of Possession, *&c.* without any direct Allegation of such a Possession. 1 Mod. 73.

Sect. 39. Fourthly, It hath been resolved, That a Repugnancy in setting forth the Offence in an Indictment upon any of these Statutes, is an incurable Fault; and upon this Foundation it hath been adjudged, That an Indictment on 8 *H.* 6. setting forth, that the Defendants *Pacifice intraverunt, &c. & eum adtunc & ibidem vi & armis disseisiverunt*, is void; and it hath also been adjudged, That an Indictment on 21 *Jac.* 1. setting forth, That the Party injured was possessed of a Term for Years, or of a Copyhold-Estate, and that the Defendants with strong Hand, ousted, and disseised him, is void, because it is absurd and contradictory to set forth a Disseisin of such an Estate whereof it is impossible that any Man can be disseised; also it hath been holden, That an Indictment on 8 *H.* 6. setting forth a Disseisin of Land, *adtunc & adhuc existens liberum Tenementum J. S.* is void for its Repugnancy, inasmuch as it implies, That *J. S.* always continued in Possession; which, if it be true, makes it impossible that he could be disseised at all; but some have said that this seeming Repugnancy may be reconciled, by intending that the Disseisee might re-enter after the Time of the Disseisin, and before the finding of the Indictment; however it seems clear, That if the words *Adhuc extratenet* be added, such a Repugnancy cannot be helped by any Intendment; and that no Restitution can be awarded on such an Indictment, whether those words *Adhuc extratenet* be in it or not, because the Party grieved appears by the Indictment it self to have had the Freehold at the Time of the finding thereof. Aleyn 50. Show. 272. Poph. 205. Raymond 67. 1 Keb. 423, 428, 435, 472. 2 Ro. Re. 311. Show. 272. 2 Bulf. 121. 1 Sid. 102.

Sect. 40. Fifthly, It hath been resolved, That an Indictment of a forcible Detainer, without shewing that the Defendant made an Entry into the same Lands, is not good, because the Statute doth not prohibit one who hath always been in Possession, to maintain the same with Force: And it seems clear, That a Conviction of a forcible Detainer upon View by Force of 15 *Rich.* 2. 2. cannot be good, unless it shew that the Defendant was also guilty of a forcible Entry, for the Words of that Statute are, *That at all Times that such forcible Entries are made, and Complaint thereof cometh to the Justices*, &c. *that the same Justices*, &c. *shall go*, &c. *and if they find any that hold such Place forcibly, after such Entry made*, &c. by which it is plain, That the Justices have no Jurisdiction by Force of this Statute, but where the Entry, as well as Detainer, was forcible: Yet in *Leighton*'s Case it was resolved, That such a forcible Entry is sufficiently set forth in the Complaint recited in such a Conviction; and it is plain, That the Statute could not intend that the forcible Entry should be viewed, because it is to precede the Proceedings of the Justices; but perhaps it is the better Opinion, That an Indictment upon 8 *H.* 6. setting forth an Entry and forcible Detainer, without shewing whether the Entry were forcible or peaceable, is good; for there is no *Medium* between a forcible and peaceable Entry, and an Entry not alledged to have been forcible, shall be intended to have been peaceable, or, if not so, yet it seems to be no Way material, whether it shall be taken to have been forcible or peaceable, because in either Case it is equally within the Statute, the Words whereof as to this purpose are, *Where any doth make forcible Entry in Lands and Tenements, or* 2 Rol. A. 82. Pl. 10. Palm. 195, 196, 197. Cro. Ja. 19, 20. 32. Cro. El. 915. B. R. Hil. 1708.

other Possessions, or them hold forcibly; by which it appears, That a forcible Detainer is a distinct Offence from that of a forcible Entry, and no Way depending on it; and my Lord Chief Justice *Holt* seemed to be of this Opinion in *Leighton*'s Case above mentioned. However it seems to be certain, That if an Indictment both for a forcible Entry and forcible Detainer be preferred to a Grand Jury, and found *Ignoramus* as to the Entry with Force, and *Billa vera* as to the Detainer, it will not warrant an Award of Restitution, but may be quashed, because a Grand Jury cannot find a Bill true for Part, and false for Part, as a Petit Jury may.

1 Rol. Ab. 80 Pl. 11. Yelv. 99. Cro. Ja. 151. 1 Sid. 97, 99. 414 2 Keb 505. Vide infra, Sect. 59.

Sect. 41. Sixthly, It hath been resolved, That no Indictment can warrant an Award of Restitution, unless it find that the Wrong-doer both ousted the Party grieved, and also continueth his Possession at the Time of the finding of the Indictment, for it is a Repugnancy to award Restitution of Possession to one who never was in Possession, and it is vain to award it to one who doth not appear to have lost it.

Bro. Force. 13. Lamb. 153. Dal. ch. 81.

Sect. 42. Seventhly, It hath been resolved, That the Time and Place of the Disseisin are sufficiently set forth in an Indictment, alledging, That the Defendant *Tali die intravit, &c. & ipsum A. B. manu forti disseisivit*, without adding the words *Adtunc & Ibidem*; for inasmuch as the Entry and Disseisin are both of them of the same Nature, and the one of them naturally tends to cause the other, it is implied, that they both happened at the same Time; and the forcible Entry being the principal Offence within the Purview of these Statutes, and the Disseisin being only added to shew that the Party grieved hath a Right to a Restitution, as to which the Day of the Disseisin is no Way material, it seemeth to be over-nice to require a precise Exactness in setting it forth; neither can it be to any Purpose to alledge that the Disseisin was at the same Place with the Entry, since it appears from the Nature of the Thing, that it could not but be so; yet in an Indictment of Murther, it is a fatal Mistake, not expresly to shew the Day and Place of the Stroke, as well as of the Assault, because these Offences are of different Kinds, the one being only a Trespass, and the other a Felony, and may well be intended to have happened at different Times and Places, and the giving of the Stroke being the principal Offence, ought to be set forth with the most exact Certainty.

Cro. Ja. 41. Dy 68. Pl. 28.

Sect. 43. Eighthly, It hath been resolved, That a Disseisin is sufficiently set forth, by alledging, That the Defendant entered, *&c.* into such a Tenement and disseised the Party, without adding, either the words [a] *Illicitè*, or [b] *Expulit*, or [c] *Inde*, for the word *Disseisivit* implies as much.

[a] Noy 125. [b] Cro Ja. 32. [c] Cro. El 186. Con. Noy 120.

Sect. 44. Ninthly, It hath been resolved, That an Indictment which pursues the Words of the Statute in alledging an Entry, *&c.* to have been made *Manu forti*, needs not expresly also say, That it was made *Vi & Armis*, because that is implied; also it is said, That as the Want of those Words will not vitiate an Indictment which pursues the Statute, so neither will the using of them make good an Indictment which does not pursue it; yet it hath been resolved, That such an Indictment may be good without mentioning any Complaint, tho' the Statute seems to require it; for it is said, That those Words in the Statute are put in *causâ abundanti*, and that if a Justice of Peace have by any Means whatsoever Notice of a forcible Entry or Detainer, he may and ought to proceed against the same according to the said Statute, as being a Disturbance of the publick Peace, the Preservation whereof was the chief End of these Statutes.

Cro. El. 461. Latch 224. 2 Bulf 258. Con. 1 Keb. 572. 2 Keb 133, 135.

Sect. 45. As to the seventh Point, *viz.* Of what Kind of Possessions a Restitution is to be awarded; it seems that it ought only to be awarded for the Possession of such Tenements as are visible and corporeal, for no one who hath a Right to such as are invisible and incorporeal, as Rents, Commons, *&c.* can be put out of Possession thereof, but only at his own Election, by a Fiction of Law, in order to enable him to recover Damages against the Person who hath wrongfully disturbed him in the Enjoyment of them; for such Things being mere Creatures of the Law, and depending entirely upon the Construction thereof, are always in the Possession of those whom the Law adjudges to have a Right to such Possession, and consequently all the Remedy that can be desired against a Force offered to a Man in respect of such like Possessions, is to have the actual Force removed, and the Offenders punished for the same, which may be done by Force of 15 *Rich.* 2. *&c.* Dal. ch. 81. Lamb. 153. Co. Lit. 323.

Sect 46. As to the eighth Point, *viz.* To whom such Restitution ought to be made; it hath been holden, That it shall only be given to him who is found by the Indictment to have been put out of an actual Possession, and consequently that it shall not be awarded to one who was only seized in Law, as to an Heir upon whom a Stranger abateth upon the Death of the Ancestor, before any actual Entry made by such Heir; and from the same Ground it followeth, That it shall not be granted to an Heir upon an Indictment, finding a forcible Entry made upon his Ancestor. Dal. ch. 83. Lamb. 153. Lamb. 154. Dal. ch. 83.

Sect. 47. It hath been holden by some, That if a Disseisee re-enter peaceably upon the Disseisor, and continue for some Time peaceably upon the Tenements in dispute, and afterwards detain them with Force, the Disseisor shall not be restored upon an Indictment finding the said Force, because his Possession was at first peaceably defeated, and at the Time of the Force, he had, in the Judgment of Law, no Possession at all; but I cannot be persuaded that this Opinion is agreeable to the Intention of the said Statutes, the principal End whereof seems to be to oblige all Persons to refer themselves to the Courts of Justice, for the Decision of their Claims to the Possession of Land, and to restrain them from disturbing the publick Peace, by such Endeavours to right themselves; but if such a Practice as this should be allowed, it would be easy to evade the Effect thereof by refraining from Violence at first, and then forcing the Party to leave the Possession of the Premisses after a short Continuance thereon in Peace; neither do I see any difference between such a Continuance for the Space of three Days, and a Continuance for three Hours or Minutes, inasmuch as the subsequent Force is in each Case equally within the Mischief intended to be provided against by the Statutes; and seeing the Statutes of 8 *H.* 6. and 31 *El.* 11. have expresly provided, That those who have been in Possession for three Years, shall not be put out of Possession by an Indictment of forcible Entry or Detainer; it seems plainly to be implied, That no one shall have the like Advantage, in respect of a Possession for a shorter Time. Crom. 162. b. 163. a. b.

Sect. 48. It will be needless in this Place to shew of what Kind of Hereditaments, or of what Kind of Estate therein, the Party who is to be restored must be found to have been seized or possessed, because this may sufficiently appear by what hath been said in the foregoing Part of this Chapter.

Sect. 49. As to the ninth Point, *viz.* By whom and in what Manner such Restitution may be awarded and given, there is no doubt, but that the same Justice, before whom an Indictment of forcible Entry or De-

Dal. ca. 82. Dy. 187. tainer shall be found, may grant an Award of Restitution to the Party; and it is said, That he may execute the same either in his own proper Person, or make his Precept to the Sheriff to do it.

1 Sid. 156. 1 Keb. 88. *Sect.* 50. But it seems clear, That neither Justices of Peace, nor any other Court whatsoever, have Authority to grant a Restitution upon a Conviction of any Force taken by them upon View, unless the same be found by an Indictment, according to the Direction of 8 *H. 6.* Also it Dy. 187. Pl. 6. seems to be agreed, That no other Justices of Peace, except those before whom such an Indictment shall be found, have any Power, either at Sessions, or out of it, to make any Award of Restitution; and that no Dal. ca. 82. Lamb. 184. other Court whatsoever can personally restore the Party without a Precept to the Sheriff.

Sect. 51. Also it hath been resolved, That Justices of Oyer and Terminer have no Power, either to inquire of a forcible Entry or Detainer, Kellew. 159. Dalis. 25. 9 Co. 118. b. 11 Co. 65. a. or to award Restitution on any such Indictment; because, when a new Power is created by Statute, and certain Justices are assigned to execute it, it cannot regularly be executed by any other; and inasmuch as Justices of Oyer and Terminer have a Commission entirely distinct from that of Justices of Peace, they shall not, from the general Words of their Commission, *Ad inquirend' de omnibus transgr' & de omnibus aliis Articulis & Causis cont' formam quorumcunque Statutorum fact' sive perpetrat*, be construed to have any such Powers as are specially limited to Justices of Peace; yet it hath been resolved, That the Justices of the King's Bench may award Restitution upon an Indictment of forcible Entry or Detainer removed before them, because the said Justices having a supream and sove- 7 Ed. 4. 18. a. 4 H. 7. 11. b. Dalis. 25. 9 Co. 118. b. 11 Co. 65. a. Dal. ch. 82. reign Jurisdiction over all Matters of a criminal and publick Nature, have always been esteemed to have Power in all Causes of this Nature, being brought judicially before them, to give the Parties such Remedies in Relation thereto, as they shall appear to have a Right to demand, either by Common Law or by Statute.

Lamb. 157. Dal. ch. 82. *Sect.* 52. The Sheriff, if need be, may raise the Power of the County to assist him in the Execution of a Precept of Restitution, and therefore, if he make a Return thereto, that he could not make a Restitution by reason of Resistance, he shall be amerced.

Sect. 53. As to the tenth Point, *viz.* How such Restitution may be barred by the Continuance of a Possession for three Years, it appears from the above mentioned Proviso of 8 *H. 6.* and also by 31 *El.* 11. That any one indicted upon these Statutes, may alledge such Possession to stay the Award of Restitution; in the Construction whereof it hath been Dal. ca. 79. Crom. 71. H. P. C. 139. Dyer 141. Pl. 48. 22 H. 6. 18. b Bro. Force, 22, 29 Crom. 71. holden, That such Possession must have continued without Interruption during three whole Years next before the Indictment; and therefore, That he who having been in Possession of Land for three Years, or more, is forcibly ousted, and then restored by Force of the Statute of 8 *H. 6.* cannot justify a forcible Detainer, till he have been in Possession again for three Years after such Restitution; and also for the same Reason it hath Dal. ca. 79. 1 Inst. 256. H. P. C. 139. Bro. Force, 22. been said, That he who under a defeasible Title, hath been never so long in Possession of Land to which another hath a Right of Entry, cannot justify such a Detainer at any Time within three Years after a Claim made by him who hath such a Right, because all defeasible Estates in the Land are wholly defeated by such a Claim, and the subsequent Continuance in Possession amounted to a new Entry.

Dal. ca. 79. 22 H. 6. 18. b. Crom. 71. *Sect.* 53. There have been some Opinions, That the three Years Possession must be of a lawful Estate, and consequently, that a Disseisor's Continuance in quiet Possession for never so many Years, shall not justify a forcible Detainer; but it seems necessary to make a Distinction between a Detainer against him who has a Right of Entry, and a Detainer against a Stranger, or one who by his Laches has lost his Right of Entry; for I do not see why three Years Continuance of a defeasible Possession should not justify a Detainer by Force against a Stranger, inasmuch as he cannot take Advantage of another's Right, and bare Possession is a good Title against all Persons, except him who hath the Right, and cannot be lawfully defeated by any other. Also if one who has the mere Right to Lands, have so long neglected to recover the Possession thereof, till in Judgment of Law he hath no more Right to such Possession, till he have recovered it by Action, than a mere Stranger, there doth not seem to be any reason that he should have more Advantage against a forcible Detainer, than if he were a mere Stranger.

Sect. 54. Also it hath been holden, That a peaceable Continuance in Possession for three Years after a forcible Entry, under any Title whatsoever, will not justify a forcible Detainer, inasmuch as the Possession was at first gained by Force; but I cannot think this a reasonable Construction of the said Statutes, for the Force in the Detainer being after three Years quiet Possession, seems justifiable by the express Words of the Statute; and where the Force used in gaining a Possession is afterwards wholly laid aside, there seems to be no colour to say, That it makes the subsequent Possession less quiet or peaceable than it would have been, if there had been no Force at all used at the first.

Sect. 55. It seems clear from the express Purview of the said Statute of 31 *El.* 11. that where-ever the Defendant pleadeth such a Possession in Bar of Restitution upon such an Indictment, either before the Justices of Peace, or in the King's Bench, no Restitution ought to be awarded till the Truth of the Plea be tried; and it hath been holden, That the Plea of such a Possession is good, without shewing under what Title, or of what Estate such Possession was, because it is not the Title, but the Possession only, which is material in this Case.

1 Keb. 538. *the King and* Burges.

1 Sid. 149. 1 Keb. 538. Raymond 84.

Sect. 56. It seems that from the Wording of 31 *El.* 11. if one who has been in Possession for three Years, be ousted, and the same Day re-enter with Force, and also be indicted for such Re-entry on the very same Day, it may be questioned whether the Prosecutor ought to have Restitution, inasmuch as the Words of the Statute are, *That there shall be no Restitution,* &c. *if the Person indicted have been in quiet Possession for three Years next before the Day of the Indictment found*; and here the Defendant hath been in Possession three Years before the Day of the Indictment, tho' not three Years before the Indictment, inasmuch as he was ousted the same Day; but if it be considered, That the Circumstance of finding the Indictment on that Day no way affects the Merits of the Cause, or lessens the Offence any more than if it were found in any other Day; and that Restitution must have been awarded if it had been found on another Day; and that the Mischief complained of in the Preamble is, that Persons were by Colour of such Indictments often turned out of their Possessions which they had quietly enjoyed for three Years next before such Indictments found, which does not extend to the Defendant in the present Case, I rather incline to think that Restitution might be awarded to the Prosecutor in this Case, inasmuch as it clearly appears, That the Defendant's Possession hath not had three Years uninterrupted Continuance within the Intent of the Statute.

Sect. 57. As to the eleventh Point, *viz.* For what other Causes such Restitution may be stay'd, it seemeth to be settled at this Day, That if the Defendant tender a Traverse of the Force, which must be done in Writing, and not by a bare Denial of the Force by Parol, the Justice ought not to make any Restitution, till the Traverse be tried; in order whereunto, he must award a *venire Facias*, whereon a Jury must be returned, on whose Verdict the Award of Restitution ought to depend.

1 Keb. 343. 1 Keb. 49. 571. 1 Sid. 284.

Sect. 58. It hath been resolved, That if such a Jury find Part of the Indictment to be true, and Part of it to be false; yet if they find so much thereof to be true as will warrant a Restitution, the Justice ought to restore the Party; as where on an Indictment of Forcible Entry and Forcible Detainer, the Jury find that the Entry was peaceful, and the Detainer was only forcible.

1 Sid. 97, 99. 1 Keb. 427.

Sect. 59. As the Justice is bound to stay the Award of Restitution, upon the Defendant's tendering a Traverse of the Force, so it hath also been said, That he ought not to make such an Award in any Case in the Defendant's Absence, without calling him to answer for himself; for it is implied by natural Justice, in the Construction of all Laws, That no one ought to suffer any Prejudice thereby, without having first an Opportunity of defending himself.

Savil 68. Pl. 141.

Sect. 60. As to the twelfth Point, *viz.* How such a Restitution may be superseded before it is executed, there is no doubt but that the same Justices by whom a Restitution is awarded upon an Indictment of Forcible Entry or Detainer found before them, may also afterwards upon an Insufficiency of the Indictment appearing unto them, supersede the same before it is executed; and it hath also been said, That if such an Indictment be taken, and Restitution awarded by four or five Justices, that two or even one of the same Justices may supersede the Execution thereof as well as more or all of them. But it seems to be agreed, That no other Justices, or other Court whatsoever, have such Power, except the King's Bench.

Dyer 187. Pl. 6. H. P. C. 140. Crom. 165. Dalt. cap. 81. 84. Cro El. 915. Yelv. 32.

Sect. 61. However it is certain, that a *Certiorari* from the King's Bench is a *Supersedeas* to such Restitution; for every such *Certiorari* has these Words, *coram nobis terminari volumus & non alibi*, and consequently it wholly closes the Hands of the Justices of the Peace, and avoids any Restitution which is executed after the *Teste*, but does not bring the Justices of Peace, *&c.* into a Contempt, unless they proceed after the delivering thereof.

Cro. El. 915. Yelv. 32. Moore 677. Pl. 921. 1 Keb. 93.

Sect. 62. As to the thirteenth Point, *viz.* How such Restitution may be set aside after it is executed; it is certain, That the Justices of the King's Bench, having a general superintendent Power over all the Proceedings whatsoever of Justices of Peace, may set aside any such Restitution, if it shall appear to them to have been either awarded or executed against Law; as where the Indictment whereon it was grounded, being removed before them, appears to be Insufficient, and thereupon is quashed; or the Defendant traverses the Force and gets a Verdict in the King's Bench; or where-ever it sufficiently appears that the Justices of Peace have been irregular in their Proceedings, as by refusing to try a Traverse of Force tendered by the Defendant, *&c.*

Savil. 68. Pl. 141. H. P. C. 140, 141. Cro. El. 31. Supra S. 58.

Sect. 63. Yet if an Indictment on these Statutes be removed into the King's Bench, and the Defendant, having been turned out of Possession by the Grant of Restitution to the Prosecutor by the Justices of Peace, traverse the Force in the King's Bench, and then the Offence be pardoned by a general Pardon, the Court cannot proceed on the Trial, notwithstanding

Noy 119. Yelv. 99. Cro Ja. 148, 149.

the Defendant would wave the Benefit of the Pardon, because it appears judicially, That the King can have no Benefit of a Fine from the Defendant, if the Verdict pass against him; and the Court will never falsify an Indictment, which is found by the Oaths of twelve Men by bare Affidavits; and consequently in this Case the Defendant can have no Remedy to set aside the Restitution by controverting the Truth of the Indictment.

Sect. 65. Neither can a Defendant in any Case whatsoever, [a] *ex Rigore Juris*, demand a Restitution, either upon the quashing of the Indictment, or a Verdict found for him on a Traverse thereof, *&c.* for the Power of granting a Re-restitution is vested in the King's Bench, only by an equitable Construction of the general Words of the Statutes, and is not expresly given by those Statutes; and is never made use of by that Court, but when upon Consideration of the whole Circumstances of the Case, the Defendant shall appear to have some Right to the Tenements, the Possession whereof he lost by the Restitution granted to the Prosecutor.

[a] Raym. 85. 1 Keb. 343, 808. 2 Keb. 505. H. P. C. 141 Cro. El. 916. Dyer 123. Pl. 34. 2 Keb 571. Savil 68. Pl. 141.

Sect. 67. The Court of King's Bench hath been so favourable to one, who, upon his Traverse of an Indictment upon these Statutes being found for him, hath appeared to have been unjustly put out of his Possession, that they have awarded him a Re-restitution, notwithstanding it hath been shewn to the Court, That since the Restitution granted upon the Indictment, a Stranger hath recovered the Possession of the same Land in the Lord's Court.

Cro. El. 41.

CHAP. LXV.

Of Riots, Routs, and unlawful Assemblies.

IN treating of Riots, Routs, and unlawful Assemblies, I shall consider,

1. What shall be called a Riot, Rout, or unlawful Assembly.
2. How they may be suppressed and punished by the Common Law.
3. How by Statute.

Sect. 1. And first a Riot seems to be a tumultuous Disturbance of the Peace, by three Persons, or more, assembling together of their own Authority, with an Intent mutually to assist one another, against any who shall oppose them, in the Execution of some Enterprize of a private Nature, and afterwards actually executing the same in a violent and turbulent Manner, to the Terror of the People, whether the Act intended were of it self lawful or unlawful.

Dalt. cap. 85, 86, 87. Cromp. 61, &c. Pult. 25, &c. 3 Inst. 176. H. P. C. 137. 3 Mod. 141.

For the better Understanding whereof, I shall consider the following Particulars:

1. How far such an Assembly may become riotous through the want of legal Authority expressed or implied, or be excusable by Reason of such Authority.

2. How

2. How far the Intention with which the Parties assemble together must be unlawful.
3. With what kind of Violence or Terror the intended Enterprize must be executed.
4. How far the Grievance intended to be redressed, must be of a private Nature.
5. Whether the unlawful Execution of an Act in its own Nature lawful may not make an Assembly riotous.

Sect. 2. As to the first Point it seems, That where-ever more than three Persons use Force and Violence, in the Execution of any Design whatever wherein the Law does not allow the Use of such Force, all who are concerned therein are Rioters: But in some Cases wherein the Law authorizes Force, it is not only lawful, but also commendable to make use of it; as for a [a] Sheriff, or [b] Constable, or perhaps even for a private [c] Person, to assemble a competent Number of People, in Order with Force to suppress Rebels, or Enemies, or Rioters, and afterwards with such Force actually to suppress them; or for a Justice of Peace, who has a just Cause to fear a violent Resistance to raise the *Posse*, in order to remove a Force in making an Entry into, or detaining of Lands. Also it seems to be the Duty of a [d] Sheriff, or other Minister of Justice, having the Execution of the King's Writs, and being resisted in endeavouring to execute the same, to raise such a Power as may effectually enable them to over-power any such Resistance; yet it is said not [e] to be lawful for them to raise a Force for the Execution of a civil Process, unless they find a Resistance; and it is certain, That they are highly punishable for using any needless Outrage, or Violence therein.

[a] 2 And. 67. Poph. 121.
[b] 3 H. 7. 10. b.
[c] Poph. 121. Moore 656.
[d] 2 Inst. 193.
[e] 3 Inst. 161. 2 Inst. 193. Ho. 62, 264.

Lamb. 179, &c. Dalt. cap 86. Crom. 61, 62. 6 Mod 43.

Sect. 3. As to the second Point, *viz.* How far the Intention with which such Persons assemble together must be unlawful; it seems agreed, That if a Number of Persons being met together at a Fair, or Market, or Church-ale, or any other lawful and innocent Occasion, happen on a sudden Quarrel to fall together by the Ears, they are not guilty of a Riot, but of a sudden Affray only, because the Design of their Meeting was innocent and lawful, and the subsequent Breach of the Peace, happened unexpectedly without any previous Intention concerning it; yet it is said, That if Persons, innocently assembled together, do afterwards upon a Dispute happening to arise among them, form themselves into Parties, with Promises of mutual Assistance, and then make an Affray, they are guilty of a Riot, because upon their confederating together with an Intention to break the Peace, they may as properly be said to be assembled together for that Purpose from the Time of such Confederacy, as if their first coming together had been on such a Design: However it seems clear, That if in an Assembly of Persons met together on any lawful Occasion whatsoever, a sudden Proposal should be started of going together in a Body to pull down a House or Inclosure, or to do any other Act of Violence, to the Disturbance of the Publick Peace, and such Motion be agreed to, and executed accordingly, the Persons concerned cannot but be Rioters, because their associating themselves together for such a new Purpose, is no way extenuated by their having met at first upon another; also it seems to be certain, That if a Person seeing others actually engaged in a Riot, do join himself unto them and assist them therein, he is as much a Rioter, as if he had at first assembled with them for the same Purpose, inasmuch as he has no Pretence that he came innocently into the Company, but appears to have joined himself unto them, with an Intention to second them in the Execution of their unlawful Enterprize; and it would be endless, as well as superfluous, to examine whether every particular Person engaged in a Riot, were in Truth one of the first Assembly, or actually had a previous Knowledge of the Design thereof. 6 Mod. 43.

Sect. 4. As to the third Point, *viz.* With what kind of Violence or Terror, the intended Enterprize must be executed, it hath been holden, That it ought to be accompanied with some offer of Violence, either to the Person of a Man, or to his Possessions, as by beating him, or forcing him to quit the Possession of his Lands or Goods, *&c.* And from hence it seems to follow, That Persons riding together on the Road with unusual Weapons, or otherwise assembling together in such a Manner as is apt to raise a Terror in the People, without any offer of Violence to any one in Respect either of his Person or Possessions, are not properly guilty of a Riot, but only of an unlawful Assembly. Dalt. cap. 85. Lamb. 175. 3 Inst. 176.

Sect. 5. However it seems to be clearly agreed, That in every Riot there must be some such Circumstances, either of actual Force or Violence, or at least of an apparent Tendency thereto, as are naturally apt to strike a Terror into the People, as the Shew [a] of Armour, threatening Speeches or turbulent Gestures; for every such Offence must be laid to be done *in Terrorem Populi:* And from hence it clearly follows, That Assemblies at Wakes or other Festival Times, or Meetings for exercise of common Sports or Diversions, as Bull-bating, Wrestling, and such like, are not riotous. And from the same Ground also it seems to follow, That it is possible for more than three Persons to assemble together with an Intention to execute a wrongful Act, and also actually to perform their intended Enterprize, without being Rioters; as if a competent Number of People assemble together, in order to carry off a Piece of Timber to which one of the Company hath a pretended Right, and afterwards do carry it away without any threatening Words, or other Circumstances of Terror. And from the same Ground it seems also to follow, That Persons assembled together in a peaceful manner to do a Thing prohibited by Statute, as to celebrate Mass, *&c.* and afterwards peacefully performing the Thing intended, cannot be said to be Rioters; for there seems to be no Reason why an Assembly should become riotous barely for doing a Thing contrary to Statute, any more than for doing a Thing contrary to Common Law. [a] Lamb. 178. Dalt. cap. 87. 3 H. 7. 1. a. 6 Mod. 141. 2 Keb. 558. Con. 1 Rol. Rep. 109. [b] Lamb 179. Pulton 25. 3 Keb. 578. Lamb 178. Crom. 62. a. Quære. 6 Mod. 141. 2 Keb. 558. Con. 1 Mod. 13.

Sect. 6. As to the fourth Point, *viz.* How far the Grievance intended to be redressed must be of a private Nature; it seems agreed, That the Injury or Grievance complained of, and intended to be revenged or remedied by such an Assembly, must relate to some private Quarrel only; as the inclosing of Lands in which the Inhabitants of a Town claim a Right of Common, or gaining the Possession of Tenements, the Title whereof is in dispute, or such like Matters relating to the Interests or Disputes of particular Persons, and no way concerning the Publick; for where-ever the Intention of such an Assembly is to redress publick Grievances, as to pull down all Inclosures in general, or to reform Religion, or to remove evil Counsellors from the King, *&c.* if they attempt with Force to execute such their Intentions, they are in the Eye of the Law guilty of levying War against the King, and consequently of High Treason, as appears from Chap. 7. Sect. 25.

Sect. 7. As to the fifth Point, *viz.* Whether the Execution of an Act, in its own Nature lawful, may make an Assembly riotous, it seems agreed, That it is no way material whether the Act intended to be done by such an Assembly be of it self lawful or unlawful; from whence it follows, That if Crom. 64. b 66. a. Dalt. cap 87 more than three Persons assist a Man to make a Forcible Entry into Lands, to which one of them has a good Right of Entry, or if the like Number in a violent and tumultuous Manner join together in removing a Nusance, or other Thing which may lawfully be done in a peaceful Manner, they are as properly Rioters, as if the Act intended to be done by them were never so unlawful; for the Law will not suffer Persons to seek the Redress of their private Grievances, by such dangerous Disturbances of the Publick Peace: However the Justice of the Quarrel in which such an Assembly doth engage, is certainly a great Mitigation of the Offence.

Lamb. 175, 176. Cromp. 61. Dalt. cap. 85. Bro. Riots 4, 5. Pulton 25.

Sect. 8. A Rout seems to be, according to the general Opinion, a Disturbance of the Peace by Persons assembling together with an Intention to do a Thing, which if it be executed will make them Rioters, and actually making a Motion towards the Execution thereof: But by some Books, the Notion of a Rout is confined to such Assemblies only, as are occasioned by some Grievance common to all the Company; as the Inclosure of Land in which they all claim a Right of Common, *&c.* However inasmuch as it generally agrees with a Riot as to all the rest of the above mentioned Particulars, requisite to constitute a Riot, which have been already fully explained, except only in this, That it may be a compleat Offence without the Execution of the intended Enterprize, it seems not to require any farther Explication.

Crom. 61. a. Bro. Riots 4. Pulton 25. a. Dalt. cap. 95.

Sect. 9. An unlawful Assembly, according to the common Opinion, is a Disturbance of the Peace by Persons barely assembling together, with an Intention to do a Thing, which if it were executed would make them Rioters, but neither actually executing it, nor making a Motion toward the Execution of it; but this seems to be much too narrow a Definition; for any Meeting whatsoever of great Numbers of People with such Circumstances of Terror, as cannot but endanger the Publick Peace, and raise Fears and Jealousies among the King's Subjects, seems properly to be called an unlawful Assembly; as where great Numbers, complaining of a common Grievance, meet together, armed in a warlike Manner, in order to consult together concerning the most proper Means for the Recovery of their Interests; for no one can foresee what may be the Event of such an Assembly.

Hob. 92.

21 H. 7. 39. Lamb. 179, 180. H. P. C. 137. Cromp. 64. a. Bro. Riots 1. 5 Co. 91. b.

Sect. 10. Also an Assembly of a Man's Friends for the Defence of his Person, against those who threaten to beat him if he go to such a Market, *&c.* is unlawful; for he who is in Fear of such Insults, must provide for his Safety, by demanding the Surety of the Peace against the Persons by whom he is threatened, and not make use of such violent Methods, which cannot but be attended with the Danger of raising Tumults and Disorders to the Disturbance of the Publick Peace: Yet an Assembly of a Man's Friends in his own House, for the Defence of the Possession thereof, against those who threaten to make an unlawful Entry thereinto, or for the Defence of his Person against those who threaten to beat him therein, is indulged by Law; for a Man's House is looked upon as his Castle.

Poph. 121. 3 H. 7. 1. a. 10. b. Vide supra. Sect. 2.

Sect. 11. As to the second Point, *viz.* How far Offences of this Nature may be suppressed and punished by the Common Law; it seems clear, That every Sheriff and Under-Sheriff, and also every other Peace-Officer, as Constables, *&c.* may and ought to do all that in them lies towards the suppressing of a Riot, and may command all other Persons whatsoever to assist them therein; also it is certain, That any private Person may lawfully endeavour to appease all such Disturbances, by staying those whom he shall see engaged therein from executing their Purpose, and also by ſtopping others whom he ſhall ſee coming to join them; for if private Perſons may do thus much, as it is moſt certain that they may, towards the ſuppreſſing of a common Affray, ſurely *à fortiori* they may do it towards the ſuppreſſing of a Riot: Alſo it hath been holden, That private Perſons may arm themſelves in order to ſuppreſs a Riot; from whence it ſeems clearly to follow, that they may alſo make uſe of Arms in the ſuppreſſing of it, if there be a Neceſſity for their ſo doing. However it ſeems to be extreamly hazardous for private Perſons to proceed to theſe Extremities; and it ſeems no way ſafe for them to go ſo far in common Caſes, leaſt under the Pretence of keeping the Peace they cauſe a more enormous Breach of it, and therefore ſuch violent Methods ſeem only proper againſt ſuch Riots as ſavour of Rebellion, for the ſuppreſſing whereof no Remedies can be too ſharp or ſevere. However it is enacted by 1 *Georg.* 5. *That if Perſons being unlawfully, riotouſly and tumultuouſly aſſembled, or twelve or more of them, ſhall continue together, and not diſperſe themſelves within one Hour after Proclamation made in Purſuance of that Statute, that then every Peace-Officer of the Place where ſuch Aſſembly ſhall be, and all Perſons who ſhall be commanded to be aſſiſting to ſuch Officer, may and ought to apprehend all ſuch Rioters, and carry them before ſome Juſtice of Peace; and that if any ſuch Rioter ſhall happen to be killed, maimed, or hurt by Reaſon of their reſiſting ſuch Officer,* &c. *the Officer ſhall be diſcharged,* &c. But the Statute being wholly in the Affirmative, cannot be thought to take away any Part of the Authority in the ſuppreſſing of a Riot, which was before that Time given either to Officers or private Perſons by the Common Law or by Statute. Poph. 121. Keiynge 76.

Sect. 12. Generally Offences of this Nature are puniſhed at the Common Law, as Treſpaſſes, by Fine and Impriſonment only; yet ſometimes, where they have been very enormous, they have been puniſhed with the Pillory; and anciently, if they were undertaken in Contempt of the King's expreſs Prohibition of their Meeting, under Pain of Forfeiture of Lands, *&c.* they ſeem to have been puniſhable with ſuch Forfeiture. Crom. 61. Dalt. cap. 46. Cro. Ca. 507. 2 Rol. Ab. 208.

Sect. 13. It hath been holden, That the Perſons of whom a Corporation conſiſts being guilty of a Riot, are puniſhable in their Natural, but not in their Politick Capacity; for the Corporation it ſelf cannot be in Fault, becauſe it is inviſible, and exiſts only in Suppoſition of Law; yet there are ſome Precedents by which it appears, that Corporations have been amerced, and their Liberties ſeized into the King's Hands, for ſuffering a dangerous Riot to happen within their Juriſdiction without uſing their Endeavours to ſuppreſs it. 21 Ed. 4. 13 b. 14. a. Dalt. cap. 88. Cro. Ca. 252.

Sect. 14. Women are puniſhable as Rioters, but Infants under the Age of Diſcretion are not.

As to the third Point, *viz.* How far Offences of this Nature may be ſuppreſſed and puniſhed by Statute; I ſhall conſider,

1. How far they may be ſuppreſſed and puniſhed by one Juſtice of Peace.
2. How far by two or more.

Sect. 15. As to the firſt of theſe Points, it is enacted by 34 *Ed.* 3. 1. *That Juſtices of Peace ſhall have Power to reſtrain Offenders, Rioters, and all Barrators; and to purſue, arreſt, take and chaſtiſe them according to their Treſpaſs and Offence; and to cauſe them to be impriſoned, and duly puniſhed,* &c.

14 H. 7. 9 b. Crom. 62. a. 63 b. 65. a. Lamb. 181, &c. *Sect.* 16. And this Statute has been liberally construed for the Advancement of Justice; for it has been resolved, That if a Justice of Peace find Persons riotously assembled, he alone without staying for his Companions hath not only Power to arrest the Offenders, and bind them Dalt. cap. 46. to their good Behaviour, or imprison them if they do not offer good Bail, Bro. Peace 7. but that he may also authorize others to arrest them by a bare Parol Command without other Warrant, and that by Force thereof the Per- Dalt. cap 46. Pult. 28. sons so commanded, may pursue and arrest the Offenders in his Absence as well as Presence. It is also said, That if a Justice of Peace be sick, and hear that Persons are riotously assembled, he may send his Servants Dalt. cap. 46. to arrest them, and bring them before him; and that if he hear that Per- 14 H. 7. 9. b. Lamb. 181, &c. sons are riotously together in a certain Place, and go thither and find none there, he may leave his Servants behind him with a Command to arrest Cromp. 64. a. them, when they shall come. Also it is said, That after a Riot is over, Kellw. 41. any one Justice of Peace may send his Warrant to arrest any Person who Cromp. 195. b was concerned in it, and also that he may send him to Gaol, till he shall Dalt. cap. 46. find Sureties for his good Behaviour.

Sect. 17. But it seems to be agreed, That no one [a] Justice of Peace hath any Power by Force of this Statute, either to record a Riot upon his [a]Bro. Peace 7 own View, or to take an Inquisition thereof after it is over: Also if one Kellw. 41. a Justice of Peace proceeding upon this Statute, shall arrest an innocent Lamb. 181, &c. Person as a Rioter, it seemeth that he is liable to an Action of Trespass, Pult. 26. a. and that the Party arrested may justify the rescuing of himself, because no H. P. C. 137. single Justice of Peace is by this Statute made a Judge of the said Offence. Cromp. 61. b. 63. a. 65. [b]But if a Riot shall be committed by Persons armed in an unusual Manner, Dalt. cap. 46. contrary to the Statute of *Northampton*, and any one Justice of Peace Con. Bro. Judges 10. acting *ex Officio*, in Pursuance of the said Statute, seize the Armour and [b]8 Co. 121. a. imprison the Offender, and make a Record of the whole Matter, such a Dalt. cap 22. Record cannot be traversed, because it is made by one acting in a judi- Sect. 5. pa. 135 cial Capacity, as appears more at large in the Chapter of Affrays; and 8 Co. 121. a. for the same Reason, if a Justice of Peace proceeding on the Statute of Dalt. cap. 22. 15 *Rich.* 2. against Forcible Entries and Detainers, shall upon his own View record a Riot, which shall be committed in the making of any such Forcible Entry or Detainer, a Riot so recorded cannot be traversed, as hath been Sect. 4. pa. 142. shewn in the foregoing Chapter. Also if a Justice of Peace acting as a Crom. 65. a. Judge, by Vertue of any Statute whatsoever, impowering him so to do, Dalt. cap. 46. make a Record upon his View of a Riot committed in his Presence, such Lamb 317. Vide infra Sect. 25. Record shall not be traversed; for the Law gives such an uncontroulable Credit to all Matters of Record, made by any Judge of Record as such, that it will never admit of an Averment against the Truth thereof.

Pult. 25. a. 26. a. Lamb 314. *Sect.* 18. It hath been questioned, Whether a Justice of Peace be authorized by Vertue of the above mentioned Statute of 34 *Ed.* 3. 1. to Crom. 62. a. raise the Power of the County to suppress a Riot; but it seemeth, That by being made a Conservator of the Peace, he hath by implication of Law all such Powers in Relation thereto, as are incident to the Office of a Conservator of the Peace by the Common Law; and consequently, That he hath a Right of demanding the Assistance of others to enable him to preserve 3 H. 7. 10 b. the Peace in the same manner, as every Sheriff and Constable are impowered 2 Inst. 158 Vide supra. Sect. 11. to demand such Assistance by the Common Law: However there seems to be no Reason to doubt, but that every Justice of Peace is authorized by 17 *Rich.* 2. 8. to raise the Power of the County to repress a Riot; for Pult. 25, 26. Lamb 314. by the said Statute it is enacted, *That as soon as the Sheriffs, and other the King's Ministers,* (under which Words all Justices of Peace seem clearly to be included,) *shall hear of a Riot, Rout, or other Assembly against the Peace, they with the Power of the County where such Case shall happen, shall disturb such Malice with all their Power, and shall apprehend all such Offenders, and put them in Prison, until due Execution of the Law be made of them; and that the Lords and other liege People of the Realm shall attend with their whole Strength, and Power the Sheriffs and Ministers aforesaid.*

Sect. 19. As to the second Point, *viz.* How far Offences of this Nature may be suppressed and punished by two or more Justices of Peace, it is enacted by 13 *H.* 4. 7. *That if any Riot, Assembly, or Rout of People against the Law, be made in Parties of the Realm, that the Justices of Peace, three or two of them at the least, and the Sheriff or Under-Sheriff of the County where such Riot, Assembly or Rout shall be made hereafter, shall come with the Power of the County (if need be) to arrest them, and shall arrest them; and the same Justices and Sheriff, or Under-Sheriff, shall have Power to record that which they shall find so done in their Presence against the Law. And that by the Record of the same Justices and Sheriff, or Under-Sheriff, such Trespassers and Offenders shall be convict in the Manner and Form as is contained in the Statute of Forcible Entries.*

Sect. 20. In the Construction of this Statute, compared with the above mentioned Statute of 17 *Rich.* 2. 8. and also with the Statute of 2 *H.* 5. 8. it hath been holden, That all Persons whatsoever, and even Noblemen, and all others of what Condition or Degree soever they may be, except Women, Clergymen, Persons decrepit, and Infants under the Age of fifteen Years, are bound under Pain of Fine and Imprisonment upon reasonable Warning to attend the Justices and Sheriffs in the Execution of the said Statute, and not only to arrest the Rioters but also to conduct them to Prison. Pult. 29 a. Lamb. 315. Dalt. cap. 46. Cromp. 63 a. Lamb. 116.

Sect. 21. Also it hath been holden, That those who attend the Justices in order to suppress a Riot, may take with them such Weapons as shall be necessary to enable them effectually to do it, and that they may justify the beating, wounding, and even the killing of such Rioters as shall resist, or refuse to surrender themselves. Poph. 120, 121. Cromp. 62. Dalt. cap. 46. Lamb. 316.

Sect. 22. It is said, That the Justices of Peace are not only impowered by the said Statute, to raise the Power of the County to assist them, in suppressing a Riot which shall happen within their own View or Hearing, but also, that they may safely do it upon a credible Information given them of a notorious Riot happening at a Distance, whether there were any such Riot in Truth or not; for it may be dangerous for them to stay till they can get certain Information of the Fact: But they seem to be punishable for alarming the Country in this Manner, without some such probable Ground of their Proceeding, as would induce a reasonable Man to think it necessary and convenient. Lamb. 318, 319. Dalt. cap 46. Pult. 29. Pult. 29 a. Lamb. 315, 316. Cromp. 64 b. Dalt. cap. 46.

Sect. 23. It seems clear from the said Statute, That if the Justices, *&c.* in going towards the Place where they have heard that there is a Riot, shall meet Persons coming from thence riotously arrayed, they may arrest them for being assembled together in such an unlawful Manner, and also make a Record thereof, *&c.* for the Statute extends to all other unlawful Assemblies whatsoever as well as to Riots. Dalt. cap 46. Lamb. 316. Cromp. 63 a.

Sect. 24. Also it seems clear, That after the Justices have had a View of a Riot, they may make a Record thereof, whether the Offenders be in Custody at the same Time or have escaped: And it is said, That the Justices may lawfully, upon a fresh Pursuit, arrest such of the Offenders as shall have escaped, but that they cannot at another Time award any Process on such a Record, and therefore that they ought to send it into the King's Bench, if any of the Offenders escape from a fresh Lamb. 318. Dalt. cap. 46. Pult. 29. a. b. 8 Co. 121.

Vide infra Sect. 29. Vide supra, Sect. 15, 16. Pursuit, and that Process shall issue against them from thence: However there seems to be no doubt, but that any of the same Justices who have recorded a Riot, or any other Justice of Peace, may at any Time by vertue of the above mentioned Statute of 34 *Ed.* 3. 1. arrest those who have been notoriously guilty of a Riot, in order to compel them to find Sureties for their Good Behaviour.

Raym. 386. Cromp. 65. a. 63. a. Dalt. ca. 46. *Sect.* 25. It seemeth to be certain, That the Record of a Riot expresly mentioned to have happened within the View of the Justices by whom it is recorded, is a Conviction of so great Authority, that it can no way be traversed, however little Ground in Truth there might be to affirm that any Riot at all was committed, or however innocent the Parties may be of the Fact recorded against them. And it is said, That if Pult. 29 a, b. Lamb. 316, 317. one be bound by Recognizance to keep the Peace, and on a *Scire Facias* thereon such a Record of a Riot be produced against him, he shall not only be concluded thereby from pleading the general Issue, but also from pleading any Matter of Justification whatsoever.

Sect. 26. However it seemeth clear, That if in such a Record of a Lamb. 317. Dal. ca. 130. Riot it be contained, that the Party was guilty therein of a Felony, or Maihem, or Rescous, the Party shall be concluded thereby as to the Riot only, and not as to any of the other Matters, because the Justices of Peace have by this Statute a judicial Authority over no other Offences except Riots, Routs, and unlawful Assemblies.

Sect. 27. And inasmuch as such a Record is a final Conviction of the Parties as to all such Matters as are properly contained in it, it ought to Lamb. 316. Dalt. ca. 46. be certain both as to the Time and Place of the Offence, and the Number of Persons concerned therein, and the several Kinds of Weapons made use of by them, and all other Circumstances of the Fact; for since the Parties are concluded from denying the Truth of such a Record, and have no other Remedy to defend themselves against it, but only by taking Advantage of the Insufficiency of what is contained in it, they may justly demand the Benefit of excepting to it, if it do not expresly shew, both that they are guilty within the Meaning of the Statute, and also how far they are guilty, and that the Justices have pursued the Power Lamb. 319. Raym. 386. Con. Dal. ca. 46. given them by the said Statute; and from the same Ground it seems also to follow, That such a Record may be excepted against, if it do not appear to have been made by the Sheriff or Under-Sheriff in concurrence with the Justices.

Sect. 28. It is said that the Offenders being under the Arrest of the Lamb. 317. Dalt. ca. 46. said Justices, and also convicted by a Record of their Offence, ought immediately to be committed to Gaol by the same Justices, till they shall make Fine and Ransom to the King, which can be assessed by no other Justices of Peace, except those by whom the Record of the Offence was made; and by 2 *H.* 5. 8. such Fine ought to be larger than it was wont to be before that Statute, for the Support of the Charges of the said Justices, *&c.* whereof Payment ought to be made by the Sheriff, by Indenture thereof between him and them.

Sect. 29. It is farther enacted by the said Statute of 13 *H.* 4. 7. that if it shall happen, *That such Trespassers and Offenders be departed before the coming of the said Justices and Sheriff, and Under-Sheriff, that the same Justices, three, or two of them shall diligently inquire within a Month after such Riot, Assembly, or Rout of People so made, and thereof shall hear and determine according to the Law of the Land.*

Sect. 30. Also it is farther enacted by 19 *H.* 7. 13. *That the Sheriff having a Precept directed to him to return a Jury, in pursuance of* 13 H. 4. 7. *shall return twenty four Persons dwelling within the Shire where such Riot, Rout, or unlawful Assembly shall be so committed and done, whereof every of them shall have Lands and Tenements within the same Shire, to the yearly Value of twenty Shillings of Charter-Land or Freehold, or twenty-six Shillings and eight Pence of Copyhold, or of both, over and above all Charges, for to enquire of the said Riot, Rout, or unlawful Assembly. And that he shall return upon every Person so by him impanelled, in Issues at the first Day twenty Shillings, and at the second Day forty Shillings, if they appear not, and be sworn to inquire of the Premisses at the first Day. And that the Sheriff for every Default,* &c. *shall forfeit twenty Pounds,* &c.

Sect. 31. It is not clearly settled, whether the Month, within which the Justices of Peace are confined to take their Inquiry by Force of these Statutes, must be reckoned according to the Computation of a Lunar, or of a Solar Month; however it seems to be agreed, That if the Justices give their Charge to the Jury, and it is said, that if they do but award a Precept for the returning of the Jury, within a Lunar Month, they may take the Verdict afterwards, for the Cause being regularly attached in them within the Time prescribed by the Statute, shall be prosecuted as all other Causes ought, with such convenient Dispatch as to the Judges thereof shall seem proper; and the Statute by obliging the Justices to make so speedy an Inquiry, meant not to hurry them in the Execution of it.

1 Sid. 186. 1 Keb. 695. Vide supra. Lamb. 322. Dal. ca. 46. Pult. 29. 6 Mod. 141.

Sect. 32. It is generally said, That any Justices of the County may take such an Inquiry, whether they dwell near the Place where the Riot happened, or at a Distance, or whether they went to view the Riot or not; for the Statute ought to be construed as largely as the Words will bear, in Favour of the Justices Power in the suppressing of such Riots; and therefore those Words in the Statute, that the *same Justices,* &c. *shall inquire,* ought to be thus expounded, That the same Justices who were before impowered to raise the *Posse, &c.* shall inquire; and it is clear, That any Justices in the County are within that part of the Statute which gives that Power; neither is it any Way reasonable to construe the last Clause of the said Statute, whereby the Justices who dwell nighest, are bound to execute the Statute under Pain of one hundred Pounds, in such a Manner as to restrain the Jurisdiction of those who by the foregoing Part of the said Statute are authorised to execute it; for if such an Exposition should prevail, the Negligence of the Justices who happen to dwell nighest would make the Statute wholly ineffectual.

Lamb. 322, 327. Dal. ca. 46. Pult. 29. b. Cro. 62. b. 63. a. seems contrary.

Sect. 33. It seems clear from the Wording of the above mentioned Clause, that the Sheriff ought not to join with the Justices in taking of such an Inquiry, as he ought to do in making a Record of a Riot upon View.

Lamb. 321. Raym. 386.

Sect. 34. Also it seems clear from those Words in the Statute of 13 *H.* 4. 7. *That the same Justices shall hear and determine,* &c. that they may award Process under their own *Teste*, against those who shall be indicted before them of any of the Offences above mentioned, according to the Form of the said Statute; and also that they may award the like Process for the Trial of a Traverse of such an Inquisition, and do all other Things in relation thereunto, which are of Course incident to all Courts of Record.

Lamb. 323, 328. Dalt. cap. 46, & cap. 132. Pult. 26. b. Crom. 67.

Sect. 35. But it hath been questioned, whether the Justices can safely dismiss the Offenders upon their paying such a Fine as shall be imposed upon

Dalt. ca. 46. Crom. 61. b.

upon them without some Judgment, for their Imprisonment as well as Fine, inasmuch as the Statute of 2 *H.* 5. 8. is express, That all Rioters attainted of great and heinous Riots, shall have one whole Year's Imprisonment at the least, without bail, *&c.* and that Rioters attainted of Petit Riots, shall have Imprisonment, as best shall seem to the King or to his Council.

Crom. 63. a. Pult. 24. b. Dalt. ca. 46. See 1 Leon. 282.

Sect. 36. Formerly, if the Fine imposed upon Rioters by Justices of Peace had been too favourable, it was a common Practice for the Court of Star-Chamber afterwards to impose such other Fine as might, together with that which was assessed by the Justices of Peace, be proportionable to the Heinousness of the Offence; and this was said not to be a double Punishment for the same Offence, but only an Award of due Penalty at several Times.

Sect. 37. It is farther enacted by the said Statute of 13 *H.* 4. 7. *That if the Truth cannot be found in the Manner as is aforesaid, then within a Month then next following, the Justices, three, or two of them, and the Sheriff, or Under-Sheriff, shall certify before the King and his Council all the Deed and the Circumstances thereof: Which Certificate shall be of like Force as the Presentment of twelve Men; upon which Certificate the said Trespassers and Offenders shall be put to answer, and they which shall be found guilty, shall be punished according to the Discretion of the King and his Council. And if such Trespassers and Offenders do traverse the Matter so certified, the same Certificate and Traverse shall be sent into the King's Bench, there to be tried and determined, as the Law requireth; and if they appear not before the King and his Council, or in the King's Bench, upon such Process and Proclamation for their Appearance as are required by the said Statute, they shall be attainted of the Riot,* &c.

Sect. 38. And it is farther enacted by 19 *H.* 7. 13. *That if a Riot,* &c. *be not found by the Jury by reason of any Maintenance or Embracery of the Jurors, then the same Justices,* &c. *over and above such Certificate which they must and are bound to make by the said Statute of* 13 H. 4. 7. *shall in the same Certificate certify the Names and Misdemeanours of such Maintainers,* &c. *on Pain that every of the said Justices,* &c. *shall forfeit twenty Pounds, if they have no reasonable Excuse for not certifying the same; which Certificate so made, shall be of like Force as if the Matter were found by Verdict of twelve Men; and every Person duly proved to be such a Maintainer,* &c. *shall forfeit twenty Pounds,* &c.

Lamb 323, 326. Pult. 29 b. Dalt. ca. 46.

Sect. 39. In the Construction of these Statutes it hath been holden, That the Certificate required by the above mentioned Statutes may be made, either by the Justices, *&c.* who went to see the Riot, or by those who took the Inquiry; but it seems to be most proper, That where-ever such an Inquisition is taken, such Certificate should be made by such Justices who made the Inquiry, because they having had the Examination of the Fact, must needs be best able to judge of the Circumstances thereof, and in that Respect are the most proper Persons to supply the Defects of the Inquiry: However the said Statute of 19 *H.* 7. 13. which is grafted on 13 *H.* 4. 7. seems clearly to imply, That some Justices are bound in a more especial Manner to make such Certificate than any others, by imposing the Penalty of twenty Pounds on those who neglect to make it as they are bound by 13 *H.* 4. 7. which Part of the Statute seems to be most reasonably applied to those Justices who took the Inquiry, or in Case that no Inquiry was taken, to those Justices who endeavoured to take one, but by the Fault of others were hindred from taking it; for there was no Need of such an additional Penalty on the neighbouring Justices, who were bound before to do their Duty in executing 13 *H.* 4. 7.

under

3

under Pain of forfeiting one hundred Pounds, as will be ſhewn in the following Part of this Chapter.

Sect. 40. Alſo it is generally ſaid, That ſuch a Certificate muſt be made within a Month after the Inquiry; and this ſeems to be a very reaſonable Conſtruction where an Inquiry has actually been made; but it may happen that no Inquiry at all may be taken, either thro' the Default of the Sheriff in not returning a Jury, or the Obſtinacy of the Jurors in refuſing to appear, or the rebellious Humour of the People in not ſuffering the Juſtices to do their Duty; in all which caſes a Certificate ſeems to be required, both by the Intent and Letter of the Statute, the Words whereof as to this purpoſe are, *If the Truth cannot be found in the Manner as is aforeſaid, then within a Month then next following, the Juſtices,* &c. *ſhall certify,* &c. And therefore in theſe Caſes it ſeems proper to make a Certificate of the Obſtructions, which prevented the Taking of ſuch an Inquiry, within a Month after they happen.

Pult. 29. b. Lamb. 324. Dalt. ca. 46.

Sect. 41. It ſeemeth clear from the plain Words of the Statute, That the Certificate ought to be made to the Privy Council-board, which is clearly diſtinguiſhed, both from the Chancery, and alſo from the King's Bench, which, in ſome Statutes relating to judicial Proceedings, are taken for the King's Council.

Lamb. 324. Con Crompt. 63. b. Dalt. ca. 46, & 130. Bro. Pæm. 1.

Sect. 42. It is ſaid, That if there be a Variance between the Inquiſition and Certificate, that ſhall be taken which is moſt for the King's Advantage; and therefore if the Inquiſition be of a Riot by ten Perſons, and the Certificate of a Riot by twenty, or by ten in Harneis; or of a Battery join'd with the Riot, that the Certificate ſhall be preferred, becauſe the Fine to the King ſhall be the greater; but if they differ only as to the Time, it is ſaid that the Inquiſition ſhall be preferred.

Pul. 29. b. Cro. 63. b. Lamb 325. Dal. ca. 46.

Lamb. 326. Pul. 29. b.

Sect. 43. Alſo it ſeemeth certain, that ſuch a Certificate, being in Nature of an Indictment at Common Law, ought to comprehend the certainty of Time, Place, and Perſons, and other material Circumſtances, both of the Riots and Maintenance, *&c.* but perhaps it needs not expreſs the Additions of the Offenders.

Dal. ca. 46, & ca. 130. Lamb. 321, 322.

Sect. 44. It is farther enacted by the ſaid Statute of 13 *H.* 4. 7. *That the Juſtices of Peace dwelling nigheſt in every County where ſuch Riot, Aſſembly, or Rout of People ſhall be made hereafter, together with the Sheriff or Under-Sheriff of the ſame County, and alſo the Juſtices of Aſſiſes for the Time that they ſhall be there in their Seſſion, in caſe that any ſuch Riot, Aſſembly, or Rout be made in their Preſence, ſhall do Execution of this Statute, every one upon Pain of an hundred Pounds, to be paid to the King as often as they ſhall be found in default of the Execution of the ſame Statute.*

In the Conſtruction of this Clauſe the following Opinions have been holden,

Sect. 45. I. That no Juſtice of Peace is in danger of incurring the Penalty thereof, unleſs he dwell in the County wherein a Riot happens.

Lamb. 326. Crom. 63. b. Dal. ca. 46.

Sect. 46. II. That if any Juſtices of Peace, who do not dwell neareſt to the Place, do actually execute the Statute, they excuſe all the reſt.

Dal. ca. 46. Lamb. 326. Crom. 63. b. Pult. 30. a.

Sect. 47. III. That if the Juſtices whoſe dwelling was neareſt at the Time of the Riot, or one of them, happen to die within the Month, thoſe whoſe dwelling is thereby become the neareſt, are bound to execute the Statute in the ſame Manner as the others were.

Crom. 62. b.

Lamb. 327. Dal. ca. 46. Pult. 30. a. *Sect.* 48. IV. That notwithstanding those Justices only who dwell nearest are liable to the Penalty of the Statute, yet if any others on Notice neglect to supply their Default, they are fineable at Discretion.

Crom. 63. b. Lamb. 327. Dal. ca. 46. Pult. 30. a. *Sect.* 49. V. That if the two Justices, or one of them, do their Duty in executing, or endeavouring to execute the Statute, they shall not incur any Penalty thro' a Default of the Sheriff, *&c.* either in refusing to appear, or to return a Jury, *&c.*

Sect. 50. VI. That the said Justices, *&c.* shall not avoid the Penalty Crom. 61. b. by executing the Statute in Part only, as by recording a Riot without committing the Parties.

Sect. 51. VII. That no Justice, *&c.* is subject to the Penalty of the Dal. ca. 46. said Statute on account of a Petit Riot, but only of such as are notorious, and in nature of Insurrections and Rebellions.

Dy. 210. Pl. 25. Lamb. 328. Pult. 28. b. Crom. 62. b. Dal. ca. 46. *Sect.* 52. VIII. That if a Justice of Peace, *&c.* had no express Notice given him of the Riot, he shall be excused, unless it were so very flagrant, that by common Intendment, every one dwelling near it could not but have Notice thereof.

Crom. 62. b. Lamb. 322. Pult. 28. Dalt. ca. 46 Crom. 64. a. *Sect.* 53. IX. That the Acquiescence or Agreement of the Parties aggrieved is no excuse to the Justices, because they ought, *ex Officio*, to make the Inquiry, and make Proclamation whether any will give Evidence for the King, *&c.* and may bind such of the Parties grieved as shall refuse to prosecute their Complaint to their Good Behaviour.

Sect. 54. Also it is farther enacted by 2 *H.* 5. 8. *That upon any Default of the said Justices,* &c. *touching the Execution of* 13 H. 4. *a Commission shall be awarded at the Instance of the Party grieved, to enquire as well of the Truth of the Case, as of the Default of the said Justices,* &c. *and that the said Commissioners shall presently return into Chancery the Inquests before them taken; and that the Jurors, who shall make Inquiry, shall be worth* 10 l. per Annum, *and shall be returned by the Coroners, if the Sheriff, supposed to be in Default, continue in his Office,* &c. *See the Statute.*

Sect. 55. Also it is farther enacted by 2 *H.* 5. 9. and 8 *H.* 6. 14. *That the Lord Chancellor, upon Complaint made to him, that a dangerous Rioter is fled into Places unknown, and also upon a Suggestion under the Seals of two Justices of Peace and the Sheriff, that the common Fame and Voice runneth in the County of the Riot, may award a* Capias *against the Party returnable in Chancery upon a certain Day,* &c. *and afterwards a Writ of Proclamation returnable in the King's Bench,* &c.

Sect. 56. But all the Penalties of the above mentioned Statutes having been found by Experience not to be sufficient to restrain the Rage of the Populace from breaking out into dangerous Tumults, whenever they happen to be perswaded that they lie under any real or pretended Grievance, it was thought necessary to make a farther Provision against such insolent Disturbances of the Peace, by more severe Laws; and to this End it was enacted by 1 *George* 5. *That if any Persons to the Number of twelve, or more, being unlawfully, riotously, and tumultuously assembled together, to the Disturbance of the publick Peace, and being required or commanded by any Justice of Peace, Sheriff of the County, or Under-Sheriff, or by the Mayor, Bailiff, or Bailiffs, or other Head-Officer or Justice of the Peace of any City, or Town corporate, where such Assembly shall be, by Proclamation to be made in the King's Name, immediately to disperse themselves, and peaceably to depart to their Habitations, or to their lawful Business, under the Pains of the said Statute, shall afterwards unlawfully, riotously, and tumultuously continue together by the Space of one Hour after such Proclamation made, or after a willful Let or Hindrance of a Justice*

ſtice of Peace, &c. *from making the ſaid Proclamation, ſhall be adjudged Felons without Benefit of the Clergy.*

Sect. 57. And it is farther enacted by the ſaid Statute, *That if any Perſon or Perſons ſhall with Force and Arms wilfully and knowingly oppoſe, obſtruct, or in any Manner wilfully and knowingly, let, hinder, or hurt any Perſon,* &c. *who ſhall begin to proclaim, or go to proclaim, according to the Proclamation appointed by the ſaid Statute, whereby ſuch Proclamation ſhall not be made, they ſhall be adjudged Felons without Benefit of Clergy.*

Sect. 58. And it is farther enacted by the ſaid Statute, *That if any Perſons unlawfully, riotouſly, and tumultuouſly aſſembled together, to the Diſturbance of the publick Peace, ſhall unlawfully and with Force demoliſh or pull down, or begin to demoliſh or pull down, any Church or Chapel, or any Building for religious Worſhip, certified, and regiſtered according to* 1 Will. & Mar. 18. *which is commonly called* The Toleration Act, *or any Dwelling-houſe, Barn, Stable, or other Out-houſe, they ſhall be adjudged Felons without the Benefit of the Clergy.*

Sect. 59. And it is farther enacted by the ſaid Statute, *That when-ever any ſuch Church,* &c. *ſhall be demoliſhed,* &c. *by any ſuch Rioters,* &c. *the Inhabitants of the Town or Hundred wherein the Riot happened, ſhall be bound to make good the Damage,* &c.

CHAP. LXVI.

Of Offences by Officers in general.

OFfences under the Degree of capital, more immediately againſt the Subject, not amounting to an actual Diſturbance of the Peace, are either;

1. Such as are committed by Officers; or,
2. Such as are committed by common Perſons without any Relation to an Office.

Offences by Officers ſeem reducible to the following Heads:

1. Neglect, or Breach of Duty.
2. Bribery.
3. Extortion.

Sect. 1. As to the firſt of theſe Offences, I take it to be agreed, That in the Grant of every Office whatſoever, there is this Condition implied by common Reaſon, that the Grantee ought to execute it diligently and faithfully: For ſince every Office is inſtituted, not for the ſake of the Officer, but for the good of ſome other, nothing can be more juſt, than that he, who either neglects or refuſes to anſwer the End for which his Office was ordained, ſhould give Way to others who are both able and willing to take Care of it. And therefore it is certain, That an Officer is liable to a Forfeiture of his Office, not only for doing a Thing directly contrary to the Deſign of it, but alſo for neglecting to attend his Duty Co. Lit. 233, 234.

Duty at all usual, proper, and convenient Times and Places, whereby any Damage shall accrue to those, by or for whom he was made an Officer. And some have gone so far as to hold, That an Office concerning the Administration of Justice, or the Common Wealth, shall be forfeited for a bare Non-User, whether any special Damage be occasioned thereby or not: But this Opinion doth not appear to be warranted by any Resolution in Point, and the [a] Authorities which are cited to maintain it, do not seem to come up to it: However it cannot but be very reasonable, That he who so far neglects a publick Office, as plainly to appear to take no manner of Care of it, should rather be immediately displaced, than the publick be in danger of suffering that Damage, which cannot but be expected some Time or other from his Negligence.

9 Co. 50. Co. Lit. 233.

[a] 39 H. 6. 32. 20 Ed. 4. 5. b. 22 Aff. 34 2 H. 7 11. b. Plow. Com. 379. Long Quinto Ed. 4. 27. 11 Ed. 4. 1.

Sect. 2. But it would be endless to enumerate all the particular Instances, wherein an Officer may be discharged or fined; and it also seems needless to endeavour it, because they are generally so obvious to common Sense, as to need no Explication; for what can be more plain, than that a Gaoler deserves to be discharged and fined, for voluntarily [b] suffering his Prisoners to escape, or for [c] barbarously misusing them? What can be more evident, than that a [d] Sheriff is justly punishable for perswading a Jury to underprize Goods in the Execution of a *Fieri Facias, &c?* And therefore I shall leave the particular Cases of this Nature to every Man's own Judgment, which, from the Consideration of the general Rules above mentioned, and the various Circumstances of every Case, will easily discern how far each Offence of this Kind deserves to be punished.

[b] 9 Co. 50. a. [c] Raym. 216. [d] Cro. Ja. 42. b.

CHAP. LXVII.

Of Bribery.

IN treating of Bribery, I shall consider,

1. What it is.
2. How it is punishable.

3 Inst. 145. *Sect.* 1. And first, Bribery in a strict Sense is taken for a great Misprision of one in a judicial Place, taking any valuable Thing whatsoever, except Meat and Drink of small Value, of any one who has to do before him any Way, for doing his Office, or by Colour of his Office, but of the King only.

Sect. 2. But Bribery in a large Sense is sometimes taken for the receiving or offering of any undue Reward, by or to any Person whatsoever, whose ordinary Profession or Business relates to the Administration of publick Justice, in order to incline him to do a Thing against the known Rules of Honesty and Integrity; for the Law abhors any the least tendency to Corruption in those who are any Way concerned in its Administration, and will not endure their taking a Reward for the doing a Thing which deserves the severest of Punishments.

3 Inft. 149. Hob. 9. Cro. Ja. 65.

3 Inst. 148. *Sect.* 3. Also Bribery sometimes signifies the taking or giving of a Reward for Offices of a publick Nature; and surely nothing can be more

palpably prejudicial to the good of the Publick, than to have Places of the highest Concernment, on the due Execution whereof the Happiness of both King and People doth depend, disposed of not to those who are most able to execute them, but to those who are most able to pay for them; nor can any Thing be a greater Discouragement to industry and virtue, than to see those Places of Trust and Honour, which ought to be the Rewards of those who by their Industry and Diligence have qualified themselves for them, conferred on such who have no other Recommendation but that of being the highest Bidders; neither can any Thing be a greater Temptation to Officers to abuse their Power by Bribery and Extortion, and other Acts of Injustice, than the Consideration of the great Expence they were at in gaining their Places, and the Necessity of sometimes straining a Point to make their Bargain answer their Expectation; for which Reasons, among many others, it is expresly enacted by 12 *Rich.* 2. 2. *That the Chancellor, Treasurer, Keeper of the Privy Seal, Steward of the King's House, the King's Chamberlain, Clerk of the Rolls, the Justices of the one Bench and of the other, Barons of the Exchequer, and all other, that shall be called to ordain, name, or make Justices of Peace, Sheriffs, Escheators, Customers, Comptrollers, or any other Officer or Minister of the King, shall be firmly sworn that they shall not ordain, name, or make, any of the above mentioned Officers, for any Gift, or Brocage, Favour, or Affection, nor that none which sueth by himself or by others, privily, or openly, to be in any Manner of Office, shall be put in the same Office, or in any other, but that they make all such Officers and Ministers of the best and most lawful Men, and sufficient to their Estimation and Knowledge.* Also it is farther enacted by 4 *H.* 4. 5. *That no Sheriff shall let his Bailiwick to Farm to any Man, for the Time that he occupieth such Office,* &c. Also it is enacted by 5 & 6 *Ed.* 6. 16. *That if any Person shall bargain or sell, or take any Reward, or promise of any Reward for any Office, or the Deputation of any Office, any way concerning the King's Revenue, or the Keeping of his Castles, or the Administration or Execution of Justice, (unless it be such an Office as had been usually granted before the making of the said Act by the Justices of the King's Bench, or common Pleas, or by the Justices of Assize,) that then every such Person so bargaining or selling, or taking such Reward, or Promise,* &c. *shall not only forfeit his Right to such Office, or to the Nomination thereof, but also every Person who shall give any such Reward or Promise,* &c. *shall be adjudged a disabled Person in Law, to have or enjoy such Office,* &c.

Vide Noy 102. Moore 781.

Vide Noy 102. Moore 781.

In the Construction of this Statute of 5 & 6 *Ed.* 6. the following Points have been resolved;

Sect. 4. I. That the Offices of Chancellor, Register, and Commissary in Ecclesiastical Courts, are within the Meaning of the Statute, inasmuch as those Courts do not only determine Matters which are brought before them, merely *pro salute Animæ*, but also have the Decision of disputes concerning the Lawfulness of Matrimony and Legitimation of Children, which touch the Inheritance of the Subjects, and also hold Plea of Legacies and Tithes, &c. in which respects they are Courts of Justice. Cro. Ja. 269. 3 Inst. 148.

Sect. 5. II. That one who makes a Contract for an Office contrary to the Purport of the said Statute, is so far disabled to hold the same, that he cannot at any Time during his Life be restored to a Capacity of holding it by any Grant or Dispensation whatsoever. Hob. 75. Co. Lit. 234. Cro. Ca. 361. Cro. Ja. 386.

Sect. 6. As to the second Point, *viz.* How Bribery is punishable; it is said, That at Common Law, Bribery in a Judge, in relation to a Cause depending before him, was look'd upon as an Offence of so heinous a Nature, that it was sometimes punished as High Treason before the 25 *Ed.* 3. And at this Day it is certainly a very high Offence, and punishable 3 Inst. 145. 1 Leon. 295. Cro. Ja. 65.

Rushw. Collections, part 1. fol. 31. nishable, not only with the Forfeiture of the Offender's Office of Justice, but also with Fine and Imprisonment, *&c.*

Sect. 7. Also all the other above mentioned Kinds of Bribery taken in a large Sense, seem to be punishable with Fine and Imprisonment, *&c.* and in the Time of King *James* the First, the Earl of *M.* 3 Inst. 148. Lord High Treasurer of *England*, being impeached by the Commons for refusing to hear Petitions referred to him by the King, till he had received great Bribes, and for other such like Misdemeanours, was, by Sentence of the Lords, deprived of all his Offices, and disabled to have any for the Future, or to sit in the Parliament, and was fined fifty thousand Pounds, and imprisoned during the King's Pleasure.

CHAP. LXVIII.

Of Extortion.

IN treating of Extortion, I shall consider:

1. **What shall be called Extortion,**
2. **How it shall be punished.**

Co. Lit. 368. 10 Co. 102. a. *Sect.* 1. As to the first Point it is said, That Extortion in a large Sense signifies any Oppression under Colour of Right; but that in a strict Sense it signifies the Taking of Money by an Officer, by Colour of his Office, either where none at all is due, or not so much is due, or where it is not yet due.

2 Inst. 209. Co. Lit. 368. *Sect.* 2. It is said, that at the Common Law, which was affirmed by the Statute of *Westminster* 1. 26. It was Extortion for any Sheriff or other Minister of the King, whose Office did any Way concern the Administration or Execution of Justice, or the common Good of the Subject, to take any Reward whatsoever for doing his Office, except what he received from the King: And surely this was a most excellent Institution, highly tending to promote the Honour of the King, and 42 Ed. 3, 4, b. 5. a. 2 Rol. Ab. 266. H. 1. the Ease of the People, and hath been always thought to conduce so much to the publick Good, that all Prescriptions whatsoever which have been contrary to it have been holden to be void; and upon this Ground it hath been resolved, That the Prescription, by vertue 4 Inst. 274. Moore 523. 2 Inst. 209. whereof the Clerk of the Market claimed certain Fees for the View and Examination of all Weights and Measures, *&c.* was merely void.

21 H. 7. 17. 2 Inst. 210. 2 Inst. 176. S. P. C. 49. A. *Sect.* 3. But it hath been holden, That the Fee of twenty Pence, commonly called the Bar-Fee, which hath been taken, Time out of Mind, by the Sheriff, of every Prisoner who is acquitted, and also the Fee of one Penny, which was claimed by the Coroner of every Visne, when he came before the Justices in Eire, are not within the meaning of the said Statute, because they are not demanded by the Sheriff or Coroner for doing any Thing relating to their Offices, but claimed as Perquisites of Right belonging to them, whether they do any Thing or not. But there seemeth to be no Necessity for this Distinction, for it cannot be intended to be the meaning of the Statute

to restrain the Courts of Justice, in whose Integrity the Law always [21 H. 7. 17. Co Lit. 368.] reposes the highest Confidence, from allowing reasonable Fees for the Labour and Attendance of their Officers: For the chief Danger of Oppression is from Officers being left at their Liberty to set their own Rates on their Labour, and make their own Demands; but there cannot be so much fear of these Abuses, while they are restrained to known and stated Fees, settled by the Discretion of the Courts, which will not suffer them to be exceeded, without the highest Resentment.

Sect. 4. Also it having been found by Experience, That generally it is vain to expect that any Officers who depend upon a known fixed Salary, without having any immediate Benefit from any particular Instances of their Duty, should be so ready in Undertaking, or diligent in executing them as they would be, if they were to have a present Advantage from them; it hath been thought expedient to permit [3 Inst. 149. 2 Inst. 210. Co. Lit. 368.] them to take certain Fees in many Cases, but it is certain that they are guilty of Extortion, if they take any Thing more: Also it hath been resolved, That a Promise to pay them Money for the doing of a [1 Rol. A. 16. Pl. 2, 3, 5, 26, 41. 1 Rol. R. 313. Noy 76. 1 Jones 65. Cro. El. 654. Moore 468. Cro. Ja. 103.] Thing which the Law will not suffer them to take any Thing for, is merely void, however freely and voluntarily it may appear to have been made; for if once it should be allowed, That such Promises could maintain an Action, the People would quickly be given to understand how kindly they would be taken, and happy would that Man be who could have his Business well done without them.

Sect. 5. As to the second Point, *viz.* How Extortion shall be punished, there is no doubt, but that at Common Law it is severely punishable, at the King's Suit, by Fine and Imprisonment; and also by [2 Rol. A. 32, 33, 75. Pl. 1, 2. Raymond 315.] a Removal from the Office, in the Execution whereof it was committed. Also Extortion in Sheriffs, Escheators, Bailiffs, Gaolers, the King's Clerk of the Market, and other inferiour Ministers and Officers [2 Inst. 209.] of the King, whose Offices do any way concern the Administration or Execution of Justice, or the common Good of the Subject, or for the King's Service, have a farther additional Punishment by the above mentioned Statute of *Westminster* 1. 26. by which it is enacted, *That no Sheriff, nor other King's Officer, shall take any Reward to do his Office; but shall be paid of that which they take of the King, and that he who so doth, shall yield twice as much, and shall be punished at the King's Pleasure.*

CHAP. LXIX.

Of Perjury.

OFfences under the Degree of capital, more immediately against the Subject, not amounting to an actual Disturbance of the Peace, which may be committed by private Persons, without any Relation to an Office; are either,

1. Such as are infamous, and grosly scandalous, proceeding from Principles of downright Dishonesty, Malice, or Faction.
2. Such as are of an inferiour Nature, and neither infamous, nor grosly scandalous.

Those

Those of the first Kind seem to be reducible to the following Heads,

1. Perjury, and Subornation of Perjury.
2. Forgery.
3. Cheats.
4. Conspiracy.
5. Keeping of a Bawdy-house.
6. Libels.

And first of Perjury, and Subornation of Perjury, of both which there are two Kinds:

1. By the Common Law.
2. By Statute.

Sect. 1. Perjury, by the Common Law, seemeth to be a willful false Oath, by one who being lawfully required to depose the Truth in any Proceeding in a Course of Justice, swears absolutely, in a Matter of some Consequence to the Point in question, whether he be believed, or not?

For the better Understanding whereof, I shall consider the following particulars:

1. How far this Offence must be willful.
2. In what Kind of Proceedings it may be committed.
3. In what Cases an Oath may be said to be so far lawfully administred, that he who takes it may become guilty of Perjury.
4. In what Kind of Oaths Perjury may be committed.
5. Whether the Matter of the Oath must be false.
6. How far the Oath must be absolute.
7. How far the Things sworn ought to be material to the Point in Question.
8. How far the false Oath must be credited.

5 Mod. 350.

Sect. 2. As to the first Particular, *viz.* How far this Offence must be willful, it seemeth that no one ought to be found guilty thereof without clear Proof, That the false Oath alledged against him was taken with some Degree of Deliberation; for if upon the whole Circumstances of the Case it shall appear probable, That it was owing rather to the Weakness than Perverseness of the Party, as where it was occasioned by Surprize, or Inadvertency, or a Mistake of the true State of the Question, it cannot but be hard to make it amount to voluntary and corrupt Perjury, which is of all Crimes whatsoever the most Infamous and Detestable.

Cro. El. 168, 169. Noy 128. 2 Rol. Ab. 257. Hob. 62.

Sect. 3. As to the second Particular, *viz.* In what Kind of Proceedings this Offence may be committed, it seems to be clearly agreed, That all such false Oaths as are taken before those who are any Ways intrusted with the Administration of publick Justice, in relation to any Matter before them in Debate, are properly Perjuries; and it seems to have been holden by some, That all such false Oaths as are taken before Persons authorized by the King to examine Witnesses in relation to any Matter whatsoever, wherein his Honour or Interest are concerned, are also punishable as Perjuries. And surely there can be no Offence of this Nature which will not justly deserve a publick Prosecution, inasmuch as if it should once prevail, it would make it impossible to have any Law whatſoever duly executed, and expoſe the Lives, Liberties, and Properties, of the moſt Innocent, to the Mercy of the greateſt Villains: And therefore it hath been holden, That not only ſuch Perſons are indictable for Perjury, who take a falſe Oath in a Court of Record, upon an Iſſue therein joined, but alſo all thoſe who forſwear themſelves in a Matter judicially depending before any Court of [a] Equity, or Spiritual [b] Court, or any other [c] lawful Court, whether the Proceedings therein be of Record or not, [d] or whether they concern the Intereſt of the King or Subject: And it is ſaid to be no way material, whether ſuch falſe Oath be taken in the Face of a Court, or before Perſons authorized by it to examine a Matter, the Knowledge whereof is neceſſary for the right Determination of a Cauſe; and [e] therefore, That a falſe Oath before a Sheriff, upon a Writ of Inquiry of Damages, is as much puniſhable as if it were taken before the Court on a Trial of the Cauſe. Alſo it ſeemeth, That any falſe Oath is puniſhable, as Perjury, which tends to miſlead the Court in any of their Proceedings relating to a Matter judicially before them, tho' it no Way affect the principal Judgment which is to be given in the Cauſe; as where a [f] Perſon who offers himſelf to be Bail for another, knowingly, and willfully ſwears that his Subſtance is greater than it is. Alſo it hath been reſolved, That not only ſuch Oaths as are taken upon judicial Proceedings, but alſo all ſuch as any Way tend to abuſe the Adminiſtration of Juſtice, are properly Perjuries; as where one [g] takes a falſe Oath before a Juſtice of Peace, in order to induce him to compel another to find Sureties for the Peace, *&c.* or where a Perſon forſwears himſelf [h] before Commiſſioners appointed by the King to inquire of the Forfeitures of his Tenants Eſtates, *&c.* whereby he makes them liable to be ſeized by Exchequer-Proceſs: Alſo it hath been ſaid, That a falſe Oath is puniſhable as Perjury, in ſome Caſes, wherein the King's Honour or Intereſt is concerned, tho' it do not concern the Adminiſtration of Juſtice; as where one ſwears a falſe Oath concerning the Poſſeſſion of Lands, before Commiſſioners appointed by the King to inquire of ſuch Perſons whoſe Titles to the Lands in their Poſſeſſion are defective, and want the ſupply of the King's Patents: And this is certainly an Offence of a very heinous Nature, [i] tending not only to fruſtrate the King's gracious Purpoſe, but to abuſe his Goodneſs by inducing him to grant his Patents to thoſe who are out of Poſſeſſion, and no Way within the Intent of the Commiſſion; which, inſtead of quieting the Poſſeſſions of the Subjects, cannot but end in the greateſt Diſturbance of them. However it ſeemeth certain, That no Oath whatſoever in a mere private Matter, howſoever willful or malicious it may be, is puniſhable as Perjury in a criminal Proſecution; for private Injuries are left to be redreſſed by private Actions; and upon this Ground it hath been holden, That a falſe Oath taken by one upon the making of a Bargain, that the Thing ſold is his own, is not puniſhable as Perjury. Alſo from what hath been ſaid it appears, That the Notion of Perjury is confined to ſuch publick Oaths only as affirm or deny ſome Matter of Fact, contrary to the Knowledge of the Party; and therefore, That it doth not extend to any promiſſory Oaths whatſoever; from whence it clearly follows, That no Officer, publick or private, who neglects to execute his Office in purſuance of his Oath, or acts contrary to the Purport of it, is indictable for Perjury, in reſpect of ſuch Oath; yet it is certain, That his Offence is highly aggravated by being contrary to his Oath, and therefore, that he is liable to the ſeverer Fine on that Account.

[a] Cro. El. 907. 1 Sid. 418. 1 Rol. A. 40. Pl. 16, 17, 18, 20, 21.
[b] Cro El. 185. 609. 2 Rol. Re. 410. 1 Rol. A. 4b. Pl. 12. 1 Leon. 131. Con. Dy. 243. Pl. 53.
[c] 2 Rol. Ab. 257. Pl. 2. 1 Rol. Ab. 41. Pl. 19. 42, 30. Winch. 3. Hutton 34. 1 Mod. 55. Yelv. 27. Cro. El. 297, 342, 348, 905.
[d] 12 Co. 101. Cro. Ja. 212. Con. Cro. Ja. 120. Vide Sect. 18.
[e] 1 Rol. Ab. 39. Pl. 3. 42, 27.
[f] Cro. Ca. 146.
[g] 2 Rol. Re. 410. 2 Rol. Ab. 77. Pl 5.
[h] Noy 100. Moore 627.
[i] Hob, 62.

3 Rol. Ab. 257. Pl. 4.

2 Rol. Ab. 257. Pl. 5. 3 Inſt. 166.

Sect. 4. As to the third particular, *viz.* In what Cases an Oath may be said to be so far lawfully administred, that he who takes it may become guilty of Perjury by swearing falsly; it seemeth clear, That no Oath whatsoever taken before [a] Persons acting merely in a private [b] Capacity, or [b] before those who take upon them to administer Oaths of a publick Nature, without legal Authority for their so doing, or [c] before those who are legally authorized to administer some kinds of Oaths, but not those which happen to be taken before them, or even [d] before those who take upon them to administer Justice by Vertue of an Authority seemingly colourable, but in Truth unwarranted and merely void, can never amount to Perjuries in the Eye of the Law, because they are of no manner of Force, but are altogether idle: And from the same Ground it seemeth also clearly to follow, That no false Oath in an Affidavit, made before Persons falsly pretending to be authorized by a Court of Justice to take Affidavits in relation to Matters depending before such Court, can properly be called Perjury, because no Affidavit is any way regarded, unless it be made before Persons legally intrusted with a Power to take it, as being both of sufficient Ability to ask all proper Questions of the Party who shall make such Affidavit, and also of such Integrity as not to suffer any Thing to be inserted therein, to the Truth whereof the Party hath not sworn. And though it may be said, That an Affidavit taken before Persons falsly pretending to be commissioned for such Purpose by the Courts of Justice, doth directly tend to impose upon such Courts, and may possibly happen through Surprize to be read, and may also in its own Nature be altogether as heinous, as if it had been made before Persons regularly impowered to take it; yet inasmuch as it is of it self of no manner of Validity, and is no otherwise regarded, than as it hath the Appearance of being sworn before Persons legally commissioned, without which it would have no manner of Credit, it seemeth that Offences of this Nature are most properly punished, by severely chastising those who usurp such an Authority of administring Oaths without any legal Warrant. However it hath been adjudged, That a false Oath, taken before Persons who having been commissioned to examine Witnesses, happen to proceed after the Demise of the King who gave them their Commission, and before Notice thereof, may be punished as Perjury; for it would be of the utmost ill Consequence to make such Proceedings void; and therefore though all such Commissions be in Strictness legally determined by the Demise of the King who gave them, without any Notice; yet for the Necessity of the Case, whatever is done under them before such Notice, must be suffered to stand good; for otherwise the most innocent and most deserving Subjects would be unavoidably exposed to numberless Prosecutions for doing their Duties, without any Colour of a Fault.

[a] 2 Rol. Ab. 257. 3 Inst. 165. Yelv. 72. [b] Cro. El. 169. 3 Inst. 165. [c] 1 Sid. 274. 2 Rol. Ab. 257. Pl. 6. Latch. 38, 132. [d] Yelv. 111. 3 Inst. 166. See 4 Inst. 97, 98. 29 Ca. 2. 25. 2 Rol. Re. 427. 4 Inst. 278. 3 Inst. 165. Cro. Ca. 97, 98, 99.

Sect. 5. As to the fourth Particular, *viz.* In what kind of Oaths Perjury may be committed, it seemeth clear, That a Man may be in Danger of being guilty thereof, not only in respect of a false Oath, taken by him as a Witness for another, but also in respect of a false Oath taken by him in his own Cause, either in an Answer to Questions put to him in a Court of [a] Law or [b] Equity, having Power to purge him upon Oath concerning his Knowledge of the Matters in Dispute, or in his [c] Affidavit concerning some collateral Matter, wherein the Parties own Oaths are allowed to be taken. But it seems, That a Juror who gives a Verdict contrary to manifest Evidence, is not properly guilty of Perjury within the above mentioned Description, because he is not sworn to depose the Truth, but only to give a true Judgment upon the

[a] 1 Rol. Ab. 40. Pl. 15, 83. Pl. 9. Cro. El. 609. [b] 1 Leon. 127. Cro. El. 135, 905. 1 Rol. Ab. 40. Pl. 16, 17, 18, 69. Pl. 42. 1 Sid. 244. [c] 1 Rol. Re. 79. Noy 128. 5 Mod. 348. Moore 656. Pl. 900. 2 Keb. 452. 2 Rol. Ab. 77. Pl. 4, 5.

Deposition of others, and in many Cases is not punishable at all *in foro humano*, as shall be set forth more at large in the Chapter of Conspiracy.

Sect. 6. As to the fifth Particular, *viz.* How far the Matter of the Oath which may amount to Perjury, must be false, it is [d] said not to be material whether the Fact which is sworn, be in it self true or false; for howsoever the Thing sworn may happen to prove agreeable to the Truth, yet if it were not known to be so by him who swears to it, his Offence is altogether as great as if it had been false, inasmuch as he wilfully swears, That he knows a Thing to be true, which at the same Time he knows nothing of, and impudently endeavours to induce those before whom he swears to proceed upon the Credit of a Deposition, which any Stranger might make as well as he.

[d] Palm. 294. Hetley 97. 2 Rol. Ab. 77. Pl. 5. 3 Inst. 166. Con. 3 Mod. 122.

Sect. 7. As to the sixth Particular, *viz.* How far the Oath must be absolute, it is said, That no Oath shall amount to Perjury unless it be sworn absolutely and directly; and therefore, That he who swears a Thing according as he thinks, remembers or believes, cannot in respect of such an Oath be found guilty of Perjury.

3 Inst. 166

Sect. 8. As to the seventh Particular, *viz.* How far the Thing sworn ought to be material to the Point in Question, it seemeth clear, That if the Oath for which a Man is indicted of Perjury, be wholly foreign from that Purpose, or altogether immaterial, and neither any way pertinent to the Matter in question, nor tending to aggravate or extenuate the Damages, nor likely to induce the Jury to give a readier Credit to the substantial Part of the Evidence, it cannot amount to Perjury, because it is merely idle and insignificant; as if upon a Trial, in which the Question is, whether such a one was *Compos* or not, a Witness introduces his Evidence by giving a History of a Journey which he took to see the Party, and happens to swear falsly in Relation to some of the Circumstances of the Journey. Also it hath been adjudged, That where a Witness being asked by a Judge, whether *A.* brought a certain Number of Sheep from one Town to another all together? answered, That he did so; where in Truth *A.* did not bring them all together, but Part at one Time and Part at another, yet such Witness was not guilty of Perjury, because the Substance of the Question was, Whether *A.* did bring them at all or not, and that manner of bringing them was only a Circumstance. And upon the same Ground it is said to have been adjudged, That where a Witness being asked, whether such a Sum of Money were paid for two Things in Controversy between the Parties? answered, That it was, where in Truth it was paid only for one of them by Agreement, such Witness ought not to be punished for Perjury; because as the Case was, it was no way material whether it were paid for one or both. Also it is said to have been resolved, That a Witness who swore that one drew his Dagger and beat and wounded *J. S.* where in Truth he beat him with a Staff, was not guilty of Perjury, because the beating only was material. But perhaps in all these Cases it ought to be intended, That the Question was put in such a Manner, that the Witness might reasonably apprehend that the sole Design of putting it, was to be informed of the substantial Part of it, which might induce him through Inadvertency to take no Notice of the circumstantial Part, and give a general Answer to the substantial; for otherwise, if it appear plainly, That the Scope of the Question was to sift him as to his Knowledge of the Substance, by examining him strictly concerning the Circumstances, and he give a particular and distinct Account of the Circumstances, which afterwards appears to be false; surely he cannot but be guilty

Vide infra Sect. 22. 1 Rol. Ab. 41. Pl. 25, 78. Pl. 3. Cro. El. 500. Noy 36. 2 Rol. Re. 145. Cro. Ca. 321. Hob. 53.

5 Mod. 348.

2 Rol. Re 41.

2 Rol. Re 42.

Hetley 97.

guilty of Perjury, inasmuch as nothing can be more apt to incline a Jury to give Credit to the substantial Part of a Man's Evidence, than his appearing to have an exact and particular Knowledge of all the Circumstances relating to it, And upon these Grounds, I cannot but think the Opinion of those Judges very reasonable, who held, That a Witness was
2 Rol Re. 368. Palm. 382. guilty of Perjury, who in an Action of Trespass for breaking the Plaintiff's Close, and spoiling it with Sheep, deposed that he saw thirty or forty Sheep in the said Close, and that he knew them to be the Defendant's, because they were marked with such a Mark, which he knew to be the Defendant's Mark, where in Truth the Defendant never used such a Mark; for the giving such a special Reason for his Remembrance could not but make his Testimony more credible than it would have been without it; and though it signified nothing to the Merits of the Cause, whether the Sheep had any Mark at all or not, yet inasmuch as the assigning such a Circumstance in a Thing immaterial had such a direct Tendency to corroborate the Evidence concerning what was most material, and consequently was equally prejudicial to the Party, and equally criminal in its own Nature, and equally tending to abuse the Administration of Justice, as if the Matter sworn had been the very Point in Issue, doth not seem to be any Reason why it should not be equally punishable. But I cannot find this Matter any where throughly settled or debated, and therefore shall leave it to every Man's own Judgment, which from the Consideration of the Circumstances of each particular Case, may generally without any great Difficulty discern whether the Matter in which Perjury is assigned, were wholly impertinent, idle, and insignificant, or not, which seems to be the best Rule for determining whether it be punishable as Per-
1 Sid. 274. jury or not. But it is said in *Siderfin*, speaking as I suppose of an Answer in Chancery, that a Man may be guilty of Perjury at the Common Law by swearing a Thing not material; but surely this ought not to be understood in so great a Latitude, as if it were meant that every Falsity in such an Answer must needs be Perjury, howsoever foreign, circumstantial and trivial the Point wherein it is assigned may be, which is directly contrary to what seems to be clearly taken for granted in other Books. And therefore perhaps where it is said, That a Man may be guilty of Perjury in a Thing not material, no more may be meant, but that he may be as well guilty thereof, by answering to a Matter not charged in the Bill, as by answering to the Matters therein contained, which may alone be said to be material, because the Defendant is not obliged in his Answer to take Notice of any Thing else; or else perhaps the Meaning may be, That in a Prosecution for Perjury at Common Law, setting forth a false Oath in such an Answer, relating to the Thing said to be in Variance, the Falsity
1 Keb. 935, 941. shall be intended *primâ facie*, to have been some way material in the Cause, unless the contrary be proved by the other Side: Whereas in all Prosecutions upon the Statute, it is necessary expresly to shew in what
Vide infra Sect. 23. manner the false Oath is material to the Cause in Question, because that Statute extending only to such Perjuries whereby some Person is grieved, cannot maintain a Prosecution which does not bring the Case within the Purview of it, by shewing that some one was grieved by the Injury complained of, which he could not be, unless the Thing sworn were some
Cro Ja. 212. 12 Co. 101. 2 Leon 198. way material. However it seemeth to be clear, That a Man may as well be guilty of Perjury by a false Oath tending to extenuate or aggravate the Damages, as by an Oath which is direct to the Fact in Issue.

Sect. 9. As to the eighth Particular, *viz.* how far the false Oath must be credited, it hath been holden not to be material upon an Indictment of Perjury at Common Law, whether the false Oath were at all credited or whether the Party in whose Prejudice it was intended, were in the Event any way aggrieved by it or not, inasmuch as this is not a Prosecution grounded on the Damage to the Party, but on the Abuse of publick Justice. 3 Leon 230. 2 Leon 211.

Sect. 10. Subornation of Perjury by the Common Law, seems to be an Offence in procuring a Man to take a false Oath amounting to Perjury, who actually takes such Oath; but it seemeth clear, That if the Person incited to take such an Oath do not actually take it, the Person by whom he was so incited is not guilty of Subornation of Perjury; yet it is certain, That he is liable to be punished not only by Fine, but also by infamous corporal Punishment. 1 Rol. Ab. 41. Pl. 21. 57. Pl. 5. 79. Pl. 2. Yelv. 72. Cro. Ja. 158. Cro. Ca. 337. 2 Keb 399. 3 Mod. 122. 2. Show. 4.

Sect. 11. Thus far of Perjury and Subornation of Perjury by the Common Law, and now I shall proceed to examine in what Manner these Offences are restrained by Statute; as to which it is to be observed, that it is enacted by 5 *El.* 9. *That whoever shall unlawfully and corruptly procure any Witness or Witnesses by Letters, Rewards, Promises, or by any other sinister and unlawful Labour or Means whatsoever, to commit any wilful and corrupt Perjury, in any Matter or Cause whatsoever depending in Suit and Variance, by any Writ, Action, Bill, Complaint or Information, in any wise concerning any Lands, Tenements or Hereditaments, or Goods, Chattels, Debts or Damages, in any of the King's Courts of Chancery,* White-hall, *or elsewhere, within any of the King's Dominions of* England *or* Wales, *or the Marches of the same, where any Person or Persons shall have Authority by Vertue of the King's Commission, Patent or Writ, to hold Plea of Land, or to examine, hear, or determine, any Title of Lands, or any Matter or Witnesses concerning the Title, Right, or Interests of any Lands, or Tenements, or Hereditaments, or in any of the King's Courts of Record, or in any Leet, View of Frank-Pledge or Law-Day, Ancient Demesne-Court, Hundred-Court, Court-Baron, or in the Court or Courts of the Stannary in the Counties of* Devon *or* Cornwal, *or shall unlawfully and corruptly procure or suborn any Witness or Witnesses, who shall be sworn to testify in* perpetuam Rei Memoriam, *shall for such Offence, being thereof lawfully convicted or attainted, forfeit the Sum of Forty Pounds. And if any such Offender so being convicted or attainted, shall not have any Goods or Chattels, Lands, or Tenements, to the Value of forty Pounds, that then every such Person shall suffer Imprisonment by the space of one half Year without Bail or Mainprize, and stand upon the Pillory the space of one whole Hour, in some Market-Town, next adjoining to the Place where the Offence was committed, in open Market there, or in the Market-Town it self where the Offence was committed.*

Sect. 12. Also it is farther enacted by the said Statute, Par. 5. *That no Person being so convicted or attainted, shall from thenceforth be received as a Witness in any Court of Record, in any of the King's Dominions of* England, Wales, *or the Marches of the same, till such Judgment against him shall be reversed by attaint, or otherwise; and that upon every such Reversal, the Party grieved shall recover Damages against the Party who did procure the said Judgment so reversed to be first given,* &c. See 1 Sid. 216.

Sect. 13. And it is farther enacted Par. 6. *That if any Person or Persons shall either by the Subornation, unlawful Procurement, sinister Perswasion, or Means of any other, or by their own Act, Consent, or Agreement, wilfully, and corruptly commit any Manner of wilful Perjury, by his or their Deposition, in any of the Courts before mentioned, or being examined* ad perpertuam rei Memoriam, *That then every such Offender being duly convicted or attainted shall forfeit twenty*

Pounds, and have Imprisonment by the space of six Months without Bail or Mainprize; and the Oath of such Offender shall not from thenceforth be received in any Court of Record in England *or* Wales, *until such Judgment shall be reversed,* &c. *on which Reversal the Party grieved shall recover Damages in the Manner before mentioned.* And it is farther enacted Par. 7. *That if such Offender shall not have Goods or Chattels to the Value of twenty Pounds, That then such Person shall be set on the Pillory in some Market-Place within the Shire, City, or Borough, where the Offence shall be committed, by the Sheriff or his Ministers, if it shall fortune to be without any City or Town-Corporate; and if it happen to be within any such City or Town-Corporate, then by the head Officer of such City,* &c. *where he shall have both Ears nailed,* &c.

Sect. 14. And it was farther enacted Par. 8, 9. *That one Moiety of the said Forfeitures shall be to the King, and the other Moiety to such Person as shall be grieved, hindered, or molested, by Reason of any of the Offences before mentioned, that will sue for the same,* &c. *and that as well the Judge and Judges of every such of the said Courts where any such Suit shall be, and whereupon any such Perjury shall be committed, as also the Justices of Assize and Gaol-Delivery, and Justices of Peace at their Quarter-Sessions, both within the Liberties and without, may enquire of, hear, and determine all Offences against the said Act.*

Sect. 15. But it is provided Par. 11. *That the said Act shall no way extend to any Spiritual or Ecclesiastical Court, but that every such Offender as shall offend in Form, as aforesaid, shall be punished by such usual and ordinary Laws as are used in the said Courts.*

Sect. 16. Also it is provided Par. 13. *That the said Statute shall not restrain the Authority of any Judge, having absolute Power to punish Perjury before the Making thereof, but that every such Judge may proceed in the Punishment of all Offences, punishable before the making of the said Statute, in such wise as they might have done, and used to do, to all Purposes, so that they set not upon the Offender less Punishment than is contained in the said Act.* From whence it seemeth undoubtedly to follow, That the Court of King's Bench, *&c.* proceeding upon an Indictment, or Information of Perjury or Subornation of Perjury at Common Law, may not only set a discretionary Fine on the Offender, but also condemn him to the Pillory, without making any Inquiry concerning the Value of his Lands or Goods.

But for the better understanding of the other Parts of this Statute I shall consider the following Particulars:

1. How far the very Words of the Statute must be pursued in a Prosecution grounded thereon.
2. In what kind of Oaths one may incur the Danger thereof.
3. How far the false Oath must appear to have been prejudicial to some Person.

Sect. 17. As to the first of these Particulars it hath been holden, That in every Prosecution on this Statute the Words thereof must be exactly pursued, and therefore that an Indictment or Action on the said Statute, alledging that the Defendant deposed such a Matter [a] *falso & deceptivè*, or [b] *falsò & corruptè*, or [c] *falsò & voluntariè*, without expresly saying, that he did it *voluntariè & corruptè*, is not good; and that such a Defect cannot be [d] supplied by adding the Words *contra formam Statuti*, or concluding *& sic voluntarium & corruptum commisit Perjurium*: Also it hath been [e] holden, That it is necessary expresly to allege that the Defendant was sworn, and therefore that it is not sufficient to say, that *tacto per se sacro Evangelio falsò deposuit.*

[a] 1 Leon 211. 3 Leon 230. Shower 190.
[b] Het. 12. Cro. El. 147.
[c] Savil 43.
[d] 1 Leon 214. 3 Leon 230. Het. 12. Savil 43. Cro. El. 147.
[e] Cro. El. 105.

Sect.

Sect. 18. However it hath been resolved, That it is not necessary to shew whether the Party, who is accused of Perjury, did take the false Oath through the Subornation of another, or without any such Subornation, notwithstanding the Words of the Statute are, *if any Persons either by the Subornation, unlawful Procurement, sinister Perswasion, or Means of any other, or by their own Act, Consent or Agreement commit wilful Perjury*, &c. for inasmuch as there is no Medium between the two Branches of this Distinction, so that all Perjury whatsoever must needs come within one of them; and it is no way material under which of them it doth come, it is a reasonable Exposition to look on the said Words as put into the Statute *ex abundanti*, seeing they express no more than the Law must needs have implied without them; from whence it follows, That they operate no more than if they had not been expressed, and consequently shall not oblige the Prosecutor necessarily to pursue them, which would put him under the Difficulty not only of proving the Perjury, which alone is material, but also of shewing it to be within one of the Branches of the said Distinction, which is nothing to the Purpose. 3 Bulst. 147. Vide supra Ch. 10 Sect. 8.

Sect. 19. As to the second of the above mentioned Particulars, *viz.* In what kind of Oaths one may incur the Danger of this Statute, it hath been resolved, That no one can be guilty of Perjury within the Meaning thereof, in any Case wherein a Man may not possibly be guilty also of Subornation of Perjury within the same Statute; for it is very reasonable to give the whole Statute the same Construction; nor can it well be intended, that the Makers thereof, who expresly inflict a greater Penalty on Subornation of Perjury than on the Perjury it self, should mean to extend the Purview of the Law in relation to what they esteemed the lesser Crimes, farther than in relation to that which they esteemed the greater; from whence it hath been argued and determined, That because that Part of the Statute, which concerns Subornation of Perjury, extends only to Subornation of Perjury in *Matters depending in Suit by Writ, Action, Bill, Plaint, or Information, in any wise concerning Lands, Tenements, or Hereditaments, or Goods, Chattels, Debts, or Damages*, &c. therefore the following Clause concerning Perjury it self, though it be penned in more general Words, shall come under the same Restriction. 5 Co. 99. a. And from hence it clearly follows, That no Perjury upon an Indictment, or criminal Information, can bring a Man within the Danger of this Statute, because they are omitted in the above mentioned Clause. Also upon this Ground Cro. Ja. 120. it seems easy to account for the Judgment in *Price*'s Case, who being indicted for a Perjury supposed to be committed by him in an Information for the King, which as I suppose must be intended to have been a criminal one, was discharged upon an Exception taken to the Indictment; but if the Information whereon the said Perjury was supposed to have been commit- 3 Inst. 164. ed, had been of a civil Nature, I do not see any Reason why it should not be as well within the Meaning, as it seems to be expresly within the Words, of the Statute; for surely the Opinion, That the King cannot by Indictment, which is his own proper Suit, punish his own Witness, who swears for him, cannot be agreeable to Law, because however the Perjury of such a Witness may seem to tend to promote the King's Interest in Relation to the Cause which happens to be in Dispute; yet certainly it is as heinous a Crime in its own Nature, and as much an Abuse to Justice, and of the same ill Consequence to the Publick, and consequently as worthy of the King's Resentment, as if it had been taken against him.

Sect. 20. Also it hath been resolved, That this Statute extends to no other Perjury except that of a Witness, not only because the Clause con-

concerning Subornation, to which the subsequent Clause concerning Perjury hath a Reference, relates to Perjury by Witnesses only, but also because the Clause concerning Perjury mentions only Perjury committed by Persons in their Examinations, *ad perpetuam Rei memoriam*, or else in their Depositions in some of the Courts above mentioned, which in common Speech are taken for such Oaths only as are taken by a Witness; and from hence it follows, That no one can come within the Statute by Reason of any false Oath in an [a] Answer to a Bill in Chancery, or in [b] swearing the Peace against another, or in a [c] Presentment made by him as Homager of a Court-Baron or by Reason of a false [d] Wager of Law, or for taking a false Oath before [e] Commissioners appointed by the King to make an Inquiry concerning his Title to certain Lands.

[a] Cro. El. 148. 2 Leon 201. Dalis. 84. Yelv. 120. [b] 2 Rol. Ab. 77. Pl. 5. [c] 2 Leon 201. [d] 1 Noy 7. 108. Finch 450. [e] Moore 627.

2 Rol. Ab. 77. Pl. 4. 1 Rol. Re. 79. 3 Keble 345.

Sect. 21. Also it hath been said, That he who makes a false Affidavit against a Man in a Court of Justice, is not within this Statute; but perhaps the Books wherein this Opinion is holden, ought to be intended only of such Affidavits which no way relate to a Cause depending in Suit before such Court; for if they be of such a Nature, That either of the Parties in Variance be grieved, hindred, or molested in Respect of their Cause in such Court by Reason of the Perjury; as where a Trial is put off, or as a Judgment or Execution set aside upon a false Affidavit, the Offence seems to be not only within the Meaning of the Statute, but also within the very Letter of it, unless the Words, Witnesses and Depositions, are confined to so strict a Signification, as to bear no kind of Application to any other Persons or Oaths, except those which are made use of upon the Trial of the Issue in Question, for which I cannot find any good Authority. However partly perhaps from this Notion, and partly because the Statute speaks expresly only of Depositions in the Courts above mentioned, it hath been questioned, Whether a false Oath before a Sheriff upon a Writ of Inquiry of Damages, be within the Statute or not? But if it be considered, That the Party to whose Prejudice such a false Oath is taken, is as much grieved by it as if it had been taken in the very Court, and the principal Judgment of the Cause depends upon such an Inquiry; and the Depositions made before the Sheriff, may as properly be said to be Depositions in the Court, by which the Sheriff is commissioned to take the Inquiry, as Depositions taken before Justices of *Nisi Prius*, upon a Trial of an Issue joined in a superior Court, which are undoubtedly within the Meaning of the Statute; and also inasmuch as those who give Evidence before a Sheriff upon such an Inquiry may in the common Use of the Word, be as properly called Witnesses, as those who give Evidence before the Court in which an Issue is joined, it seemeth to be the more plausible Opinion, that such a Perjury is within the Statute: But since it is disputable, whether it be so or no, and it is certain that it is Perjury at Common Law, and that in all Cases whatsoever where a Man takes a false Oath, which is not Perjury within the Statute, but is looked on as Perjury at Common Law, he is still punishable for it by Indictment or Information at the Common Law, it is certainly most advisable to prosecute such an Offender at the Common Law, and not upon the Statute.

Vide 2 Leon 40.

1 Rol. Ab. 30. Pl. 3, 42. Pl. 27.

See the Authorities above cited.

Cro. Ja. 8.

Sect. 22. As to the third Particular, *viz.* How far the false Oath must appear to have been prejudicial to some Person, It hath been collected from the above mentioned Clause, which giveth an Action to the Party grieved by the Offences mentioned in the Statute, That no false Oath is within the Meaning thereof, which does not give some Person a just Cause of Complaint; and upon this Ground it hath been said, That he who ſwears a Thing which is true, but not known by him to be ſo, is not within the Statute, becauſe howſoever heinous his Offence may be in its own Nature; yet, when it proves in the Event to be in Maintenance of the Truth, it cannot be ſaid to give him a juſt Cauſe of Complaint, who would take Advantage againſt another from his Want of legal Evidence to make out the Juſtice of his Cauſe.

3 Inſt. 166. Vide ſupra, Sect. 6. Cro. Hetley 97.

Sect. 22. Alſo from the ſame Ground it ſeemeth clearly to follow, That no falſe Oath can be within the Statute, unleſs the Party againſt whom it was ſworn ſuffered ſome Kind of Diſadvantage by it, for otherwiſe it cannot be ſaid that any one was grieved, hindred, or moleſted by it; and therefore it is certain, That in every Proſecution upon the Statute, it is neceſſary to ſet forth the Record of the Cauſe wherein the Perjury complained of is ſuppoſed to have been committed; and alſo to prove at the Trial of the Cauſe, That there is actually ſuch a Record, by producing the Record it ſelf, or a true Copy thereof, which muſt agree with that which is ſet forth in the Pleadings, without any material Variance; for otherwiſe it cannot legally appear, That there ever was ſuch a Suit depending, wherein the Party might be prejudiced in the Manner ſuppoſed: Alſo it ſeems to be agreed, That it is neceſſary not only to ſet forth the Point wherein the falſe Oath was aſſigned, but alſo to ſhew in what Manner it conduced to the Proof or Diſproof of the Matter in debate between the Parties; and it hath been adjudged, That an Indictment ſetting forth a Suit concerning the Manor of *Dale*, and aſſigning a falſe Oath concerning the Manor (*Manerium prædictum innuendo*,) is not good, becauſe it no otherwiſe appears, That the falſe Oath did concern the Manor of *Dale*, but by the *Innuendo*, which is not a ſufficient Averment. Alſo upon the ſame Ground it ſeems to be ſafeſt in a Proſecution upon the Statute for a falſe Oath in Chancery, to ſet forth the Bill and Anſwer, That the Plaintiff may appear to have been aggrieved by it; and for the ſame Reaſon it ſeemeth alſo, That you ought in ſuch a Proſecution of a Witneſs in Chancery, to ſet forth the Interrogatory in particular, and ſhew how it was material: Alſo it hath been reſolved, That as in an Action on the Statute brought by one Perſon, it muſt appear, That the falſe Oath was prejudicial to the Plaintiff; ſo in an Action by more than one, it muſt appear to have been prejudicial to every one of the Plaintiffs: And it hath been ſaid, That it is not ſufficient to ſhew that the falſe Oath cauſed the Court to make an Award againſt the Plaintiff, unleſs it alſo appear that ſuch an Award was prejudicial to him, and therefore where the Plaintiff at a Trial in Ejectment challenged a Juror, and proved his Challenge by a falſe Oath, by reaſon whereof the Inqueſt was not taken, and conſequently the Poſſeſſion of the Defendant, who had a defeaſible Title, continued longer than it otherwiſe would have done; it hath been adjudged, That ſuch a Defendant cannot have an Action on the Statute againſt ſuch Witneſs, becauſe in Truth he gained an Advantage by the Perjury. Alſo it hath been holden, That it is not ſufficient to ſhew that the Perjury, for which an Action is brought upon the Statute, was actually prejudicial to the Plaintiff, unleſs it be alſo ſhewn to have been made in ſome Cauſe which may properly be ſaid to have been depending in Suit between him and the Perſon for whom the Witneſs was examined; and therefore it hath been holden, That where *A.* brought a Bill in Chancery againſt *B.* and the Lord Keeper, by an Order made *C.* to be as a Party to the Bill againſt *B.* and afterwards a Commiſſion went forth to examine Witneſſes between *B.* and *C.* upon which *D.* being produced as a Witneſs on the Part of *C.* ſwore directly

Vide ſupra, Sect. 8. & 3 Inſt. 167. Coke Ent. 164. 6 Mod. 168. 2 Rol. Re. 76. 1 Keb. 452, 935, 941. 2 Leon. 12. 2 Rol. Re. 427. Cro. Ca. 351, 352, 353. 1 Keb. 452. Cro. El. 428. 1 Keb. 935, 941. 1 Sid. 106. 2 Leon. 12. 3 Leon. 68. 2 Leon. 40.

Yelv. 22. for him against *B.* whereupon a Decree was made against *B.* yet *B.* cannot have an Action on the Statute, because *C.* was not a Party to the Suit, but came in *à Latere*, by an Order; and it is said, That the Words of the Statute are, *where one is grieved by a Deposition in a Suit between Party and Party*, but perhaps the Authority of this Opinion may justly be questioned, not only because the Words of the Statute whereon it is grounded are mistaken, but also because the Offence seems in Truth to be both within the Meaning and Letter of the Law, since thereby a Person is grieved in respect of a Cause depending in Suit in a Court mentioned in the Statute: However there seems to be no doubt, but that a Perjury which only 2 Leon. 198. tends to increase or lessen the Damages to be given to a Plaintiff, is as much within the Statute, as any Perjury which goes directly to the Point 1 Keb. 9. of the Issue: Also it seemeth to be settled, That Perjury in a Cause Raymond 74. 1 Sid. 148. wherein an erroneous Judgment is given, is a good Foundation of a Pro- 2 Keb. 718, 854. 1 Keb. 531. secution upon the Statute, while such Judgment stands unreversed.

CHAP. LXX.

Of Forgery.

Of Forgery there are two Kinds:

1. By the Common Law.
2. By the Statute.

Sect. 1. Forgery by the Common Law seemeth to be an Offence in falsly and fraudulently making or altering any Matter of Record, or any other authentick Matter of a publick Nature, or any Deed or Will.

For the better Understanding whereof, I shall endeavour to shew:

1. In what Cases the making or altering of a Writing, shall be said to be so far false and fraudulent, as to amount to Forgery.
2. That a Man may be guilty of Forgery in respect of all the above mentioned Writings, and of no other.

Sect. 2. As to the first Particular, it is said to be possible for a Man knowingly to make a Deed in his own Name, and also to sign and seal it himself, which yet in Judgment of Law may be no better than a down-right Forgery; as if a Man make a Feoffment of certain Lands to 3 Inst. 169. Pult. 46. b. 27 H. 6. 3. *J. S.* and afterwards make a Deed of Feoffment of the same Lands to *J. D.* of a Date prior to that of the Feoffment to *J. S.* in which Case he is said to be guilty of Forgery, because he knowingly falsifies the Date, in order to defraud his own Feoffee, by making a second Conveyance which at the Time he had no Power to make: Also it is said, That his Moore 655. Crime would have been no less, if by his first Conveyance he had passed only an equitable Interest for good Consideration, and had afterwards by Noy 101. Moore 759, 760. such a subsequent antedated Conveyance endeavoured to avoid it. Also in many other Cases a Writing may be said to be forged where neither 3 Inst. 170. Con. Dy. 288. b. the Hand nor Seal of any one are forged; as where one being directed to draw up a Will for a sick Person, doth insert some Legacies therein of his own Head; or where one finding another's Name at the Bottom of a Letter at a considerable Distance from the other Writing, causes the Letter to be cut off, and a general Release to be written above the Name, and then takes off the Seal, and fixes it under the Release; or where one inserts into an Indictment the Names of those against whom in Truth it was not found; or where one makes any fraudulent Alteration of the Form of a true Deed in a material Part of it; as by making a Lease of the Manor of *Dale* appear to be a Lease of the Manor of *Sale*, by changing the Letter *D.* into an *S.* or by making a Bond for five hundred Pounds, expressed in Figures, seem to have been made for five Thousand, by adding a new Cypher. But Sir *Edward Coke* seems to say, That a Deed so altered may more properly be called a false than a forged Writing, because it is not forged in the Name of another, nor his Seal nor Hand counterfeited. But I see no good Reason why such an Alteration of a Deed should not as properly be called Forgery, as the entire making of a new Deed in another's Name; for in both Cases not only the Fraud and Villany are the very same, but also a Man's Hand and Seal are falsly made Use of to testify his Assent to an Instrument, which after such an Alteration is no more his Deed than a Stranger's. Also the Notion of Forgery doth not seem so much to consist in the counterfeiting a Man's Hand and Seal, which may often be done innocently, but in the endeavouring to give an Appearance of Truth to a mere Deceit and Falsity, and either to impose that upon the World as the solemn Act of another which he is no Way privy to, or at least to make a Man's own Act appear to have been done at a Time when it was not done, and by Force of such a Falsity to give it an Operation, which in Truth and Justice it ought not to have, as appears by the foregoing Cases in this Section, to most of which Sir *Edward Coke* himself seems to agree.

3 Inst. 171. 3 Mod. 66. 3 Inst. 169. Moore 619. 3 Inst. 169. Vide Moore 619. 3 Mod. 66. Vide 2 Rol. Ab. 28, 29. 11 Co. 27.

Sect. 3. But it seemeth to be clear, That he who writes a Deed in another's Name, and seals it in his Presence, and by his Command, is not guilty of Forgery, because the Law looks on this as the other's own Sealing.

Pult. 46. 21 H. 6. 4. b. Moore 619. Noy 99.

Sect. 4. Also it hath been adjudged, That he shall not be punished for Forgery who razeth out the word *Libris*, out of a Bond made to himself, and putteth in *Marcis*, because here is no appearance of a fraudulent Design to cheat another, and the Alteration is prejudicial to none but to him who makes it, whose Security for his Money is wholly avoided by it; yet it is said, That it would be Forgery, if by the Circumstances of the Case it should any Way appear to have been done with an Eye of gaining an Advantage to the Party himself, or of prejudicing a third Person: Also it is holden, That such an Alteration, even without these Circumstances is a Misdemeanour, tho' it be no Forgery.

Sect. 5. It hath been resolved, That a Man shall not be adjudged guilty of Forgery for writing a Will for another without any Directions from him, who becomes *Non Compos* before it is brought to him; for it is not the bare writing an Instrument in another's Name without his Privity, but the giving it a false Appearance of having been executed by him, which makes a Man guilty of Forgery.

Moore 760.

Sect. 6. It is said, That regularly a Man cannot commit an Act of Forgery by a bare Nonfeasance, as by omitting a Legacy out of a Will, which he is directed to draw for another; yet it hath been holden by some, even in this very Case, That if the Omission of a Bequest to one cause a material Alteration in the Limitation of a Bequest to another, as where the Omission of a Devise of an Estate for Life to one Man causeth

Moore 760. Noy 101.

a

a Deviſe of the ſame Lands to another to paſs a preſent Eſtate, which otherwiſe would have paſſed a Remainder only, he who makes ſuch an Omiſſion is guilty of Forgery.

1 Sid. 142.

Sect. 7. It ſeemeth to be no Way material, whether a forged Inſtrument be made in ſuch a Manner, That if it were in Truth ſuch as it is counterfeited for, it would be of Validity, or not; and upon this Ground it hath been adjudged, That the Forgery of a Protection in the Name of *A. B.* as being a Member of Parliament, who in Truth at the Time was not a Member, is as much a Crime as if he were.

And now I am to ſhew in the ſecond Place, That a Man may be guilty of Forgery at Common Law, in Reſpect of any of the above mentioned Writings, and of no other.

1 Rol. Ab. 65. Pl. 1, 2. 76 Pl. 3. Yelv. 146. Cro. El. 178. 3 Mod. 66.

Sect. 8. And firſt it is clear, That one may be guilty thereof by the Common Law, by counterfeiting a Matter of Record; for, ſince the Law gives the higheſt Credit to all Records, it cannot but be of the utmoſt ill Conſequence to the Publick, to have them either forged or falſified.

[a] 1 Rol. Ab. 68. Pl. 33. Cro. Ca. 326. 1 Jon. 325. [b] 1 Rol. Ab. 65 Pl. 5. 2 Bulſ. 137. [c] 1 Levin. 138. [d] 1 Sid. 142. [e] 1 Rol. Ab. 66. Pl. 10. Raymond 81. Owen 47. 1 Sid. 278. 3 Leon. 170. [f] Moore 760. Noy 101. Dy. 302. b. [g] 1 Rol Re. 431. 1 Sid. 16, 155, 451. 1 Rol. Ab. 66. Pl. 8, 9. Winch 40, 90. 3 Leon. 231. 1 Leon. 101. Cro. El. 296. 853. 3 Bulſ. 265. [h] Cro El. 166. Yelv 146. 3 Bulſ 265. [i] Yelv. 146.

Sect. 9. Secondly, Alſo there ſeemeth to be no doubt, but that one may be guilty of this Crime by the Common Law, by forging any other authentick Matter of a publick Nature, as a [a] Privy Seal, or a [b] Licence from the Barons of the Exchequer to compound a Debt, or a [c] Certificate of Holy Orders, or a [d] Protection from a Parliament Man.

Sect. 10. Thirdly, It is alſo unqueſtionable, That a Man may be in like Manner guilty of Forgery at Common Law, by forging a [e] Deed, and ſurely there cannot be any Reaſon to doubt, but that one may be equally guilty by forging a [f] Will, which cannot be thought to be of leſs Conſequence than a Deed, but I do not find this Point any where directly holden.

Sect. 11. As to other Writings of an inferiour Nature, it ſeems to have been generally laid down as a [g] Rule, That the Counterfeiting of them is not properly Forgery; [h] and ſome have gone ſo far as to hold, That the forging another's Hand, and thereby receiving Rent due to him from his Tenants, is not puniſhable at all; and therefore it cannot but be more ſafe to proceed againſt Offences of this Nature, as Cheats than as Forgeries; but ſurely it cannot be proved by any good Authority, That ſuch baſe Crimes as there are wholly diſregarded by the Common Law, as not deſerving a publick Proſecution; for the Opinion in the Books above cited, That they are puniſhable by no Law, ſeems by no Means to be maintainable, ſince many of them are moſt certainly puniſhable by Force of 33 *H.* 8. 1. which is ſet forth at large in the following Chapter; neither can it be a convincing Argument, That they are not puniſhable at Common Law, [i] becauſe they are of a private Nature; ſince Deeds concerning private Matters are alſo of a private Nature, as much as other Writings concerning ſuch Matters; yet no one will ſay, That the making a falſe Deed concerning a private Matter is not puniſhable at Common Law; but perhaps it may be reaſonable to make this Diſtinction between the counterfeiting of ſuch Writings, the Forgery whereof hath been already ſhewn to be properly puniſhable as Forgery, and the counterfeiting of other Writings of an inferiour Nature, that the former is in it ſelf criminal, whether any third Perſon be actually injured thereby, or not, but that the latter is no Crime, unleſs ſome one receive a Prejudice from it.

Sect. 12. Thus far of Forgery by the Common Law, and now I am to conſider Forgery by the Statute, which depends upon 5 *El.* 14. by which it is enacted, *That if any Perſon or Perſons upon his or their own Head and Imagination, or by false Conspiracy and Fraud with others, shall wittingly, subtilly, and falsly forge or make, or subtilly cause, or wittingly assent to be forged or made, any false Deed, Charter, or Writing sealed, Court-Roll, or the Will of any Person or Persons in Writing, to the Intent that the State of Freehold or Inheritance of any Person or Persons, of, in, or to any Lands, Tenements, or Hereditaments, Freehold or Copyhold, or the Right, Title, or Interest, of any Person or Persons, of, in, or to the same, or any of them, shall, or may be molested, troubled, defeated, recovered or charged; or shall pronounce, publish, or shew forth in Evidence, any such false and forged Deed, Charter, Writing, Court-Roll, or Will, as true, knowing the same to be false and forged, as is aforesaid, to the Intent above remembred, (except being an Attorney, Lawyer, or Counsellor, he shall for his Client, plead, shew forth, or give in Evidence such false and forged Deed,* &c. *to the forging whereof he was not Party nor Privy) and shall be thereof convicted, either upon Action or Actions of Forgery of false Deeds, to be founded upon the said Statute, at the Suit of the Party grieved, or otherwise, according to the Order and due Course of the Laws of this Realm,* &c. *shall pay unto the Party grieved his double Costs and Damages, to be found or assessed in that Court where such Conviction shall be, and also shall be set upon the Pillory in some open Market-Town, or other open Place, and there have both his Ears cut off, and also his Nostrils slit and cut, and seared with a hot Iron,* &c. *and shall forfeit to the King the whole Issues and Profits of his Lands and Tenements, and suffer perpetual Imprisonment,* &c.

See Pult. 45, 46.

Par. 15.

Sect. 13. And it is farther enacted by the said Statute, Par. 3. *That if any Person or Persons, upon his or their own Head or Imagination, or by false Conspiration or Fraud had with any other, shall wittingly, subtilly, and falsly forge or make, or wittingly, subtilly and falsly cause or assent to be made and forged, any false Charter, Deed or Writing, to the Intent that any Person or Persons shall or may have or claim any Estate or Interest for Term of Years, of, in, or to any Manors, Lands, Tenements, or Hereditaments, not being Copyhold, or any Annuity in Fee-simple, Fee-tail, or for Term of Life, Lives or Years, or shall as is aforesaid, forge, make, or cause, or assent to be made or forged, any Obligation, or Bill obligatory, or any Acquittance, Release, or other Discharge of any Debt, Accompt, Action, Suit, Demand, or other Thing personal; or shall pronounce, publish, or give in Evidence, (except as is before excepted,) any such false or forged Charter, Deed, Writing, Obligation, Bill obligatory, Acquittance, Release, or Discharge, as true, knowing the same to be false and forged, and shall be thereof convicted by any of the Ways and Means aforesaid, he shall pay unto the Party grieved his double Costs and Damages, to be found and assessed in such Court where the said Conviction shall be had, and shall be also set upon the Pillory in some open Market Town or other open Place, and there have one of his Ears cut off, and also shall suffer Imprisonment for one Year,* &c.

Sect. 14. And it is farther enacted by the said Statute, Par. 7 & 8. *That if any Person or Persons being convicted or condemned of any of the Offences aforesaid by any the Ways or Means above limited, shall after any such his or their Conviction or Condemnation, eftsoons commit or perpetrate any of the said Offences in Form aforesaid, that then every such second Offence shall be adjudged Felony without Benefit of the Clergy, saving to all Persons other than the said Offenders, and such as Claim to their Uses, all such Rights,* &c. *which they shall have to any the Hereditaments of any such Person, so as is aforesaid convicted or attainted, at any Time before,* &c. *saving also the Dower of such Offender's Wife, and the Right of his Heir.*

Sect. 15. And it is farther enacted by the said Statute, Par. 10. *That all Justices of Oyer and Terminer, and Justices of Assize, shall have Power to inquire of, hear and determine the Offences aforesaid.*

Sect. 16. But it is provided, Par. 9, 12 & 16. *That this Act or any Thing therein contained, shall not extend to any Ordinary, or his Commissary,* &c. *for putting their Seal of Office to any Will to be exhibited unto them, not knowing the same to be false, or forged, or for writing of the said Will, or probiting of the same, nor to any Proctor,* &c. *of any Ecclesiastical Court, for the Writing, setting forth, or Pleading of any Proxy made according to the Ecclesiastical Law,* &c. *for the Appearance of any Person being cited to appear in such Court; nor to any Archdeacon, or Official, for putting their authentick Seal to the said Proxy or Proxies, nor to any Ecclesiastical Judge for admitting the same; nor to any Person who shall plead or shew forth any Deed or Writing exemplified under the great Seal of* England, *or under the Seal of any other authentick Court of this Realm; nor to any Person who shall cause any Seal of any Court to be set to any such Deed, Charter, or Writing enrolled, not knowing the same to be false or forged.*

In the Construction of this Statute, the following Points have been holden,

Sect. 17. I. That a false Customary of a Copyhold-Manor, made in Parchment under the Seals of several Tenants of the Manor, and containing in it divers false Customs, apparently tending to the Disherison of the Lord, and falsly pretending by its Title to be set forth by the Consent of all the Tenants, and Allowance of the Lord, is within the first Branch of Forgery mentioned in the Statute, as being a sealed Writing made to the Intent to molest the Inheritance of the Lord.

Dy. 322. Pl. 26.
3 Leon. 108.

Sect. 18. II. That the Forgery of a Lease for Years, or of a Grant of a Rent-Charge for Years, in the Name of one who is seized of a Freehold or Inheritance, is also within the said first Branch of the Statute, because the said Branch is penned in general Words extending to any Molestation whatsoever of such Estate, without mentioning any Estate or Interest in the Claim whereof such molestation shall consist; and from this Ground it follows, That those Words in the second Branch of Forgery mentioned in the Statute, *to the Intent that any Person shall claim any Estate or Interest for Term of Years,* &c. are meant only of such Forgeries which relate to such an Estate or Interest *in esse* before.

3 Inst. 170.
Noy 42.
3 Inst. 170.
Noy 42.

Sect. 19. III. That the Forgery of a Will in Writing of one possessed of such an Estate, mentioning a Bequest thereof, is within the said second Branch of the Statute, as being a false Writing, made to the Intent that some Person may Claim an Estate for Years; notwithstanding the said Branch make no express mention of a Will, as the first doth.

Dy. 302. Pl. 45.

Sect. 20. IV. That the Forgery of a Lease of Lands in *Ireland* is not within either of the Branches of the Statute.

3 Leon. 170.

Sect. 21. V. That the Forgery of a Deed containing a Gift of mere personal Chattels, is also no Way within the Statute, the Words whereof to this Purpose are, *If any Person shall forge any Obligation or Bill Obligatory, or any Acquittance, Release, or other Discharge of any Debt, Account, Action, Suit, Demand, or other Thing personal.*

3 Leon. 170.

Sect. 22. VI. That the Forgery of a Statute-Merchant, or of a Recognizance in the Nature of a Statute-Staple, by acknowledging them in the Name of another are within the Statute, as being Obligations, because they must have the Seal of the Party, by the express Words of the Statutes, which appoint in what Manner such Statute or Recognizance shall be taken: But that the Forgery of the Statute-Staple is no Way within the Statute, because it needeth not the Seal of the Party, but only the Seal of the Staple provided for it.

See Ch. 42, & 62.
15 H 7. 15. a.
2 Rol. A 466. Pl. 2, 3, 4, 5.
Con. 3 Inst. 171.

Sect. 23. VII. That he who is truly informed by another, that a Deed is forged, is in danger of the Statute if he afterwards publish the 3 Inst. 171. same to be true; notwithstanding the Words of the Statute be, *If any one shall publish,* &c. *such false and forged Deed,* &c. *knowing the same to be false or forged.*

Sect. 24. VIII. That the double Damages to be awarded to the 3 Inst. 172. Party grieved by a forged Release of an Obligation, *&c.* shall be governed by the Penalty, and not by the true Debt appearing in the Condition.

Sect. 25. IX. That one who hath been convicted of publishing a forged Deed, may become guilty of Felony by forging another Deed afterwards, as well as by publishing any such Deed, notwithstanding the second Offence be not of the very same Nature with the first; for the Words of the Statute are, *If any Person being convicted or condemned of any* 3 Inst. 172. *of the Offences aforesaid,* &c. *shall after any such Conviction or Condemnation, estsoons commit any of the said Offences.*

Sect. 26. X. That notwithstanding it be necessary in every Prosecution upon the Statute strictly to pursue the very Words of it, (for which Cause it hath been resolved, That an Indictment, setting forth the For- 3 Keb. 356, 367. gery of a Writing indented, without adding, that it was sealed, is in- 3 Inst. 169. sufficient;) yet there is no Necessity that the Translation of such Words See 1 Keb 849. be made in proper classical *Latin*, so that it be intelligible; and upon 2 Keb. 119. 2 Levin. 221. this Ground it hath been adjudged, That an Indictment, setting forth that the Defendant *super Caput suum proprium* did forge, *&c.* meaning thereby to express that he did it of his own Head, is sufficient.

Sect. 27. XI. That upon an Indictment of Trespass, Forgery and Publication of a Deed, a Verdict finding the Defendant guilty *de Trans-* 2 Levin. 111, *gressione & Forgeria praedictis prout superius in Indictamento supponitur,* is suffi- 221. cient, because those Words *de Transgressione praedict'* include the whole: 3 Keb. 353. Also perhaps such a Verdict may be sufficient for another Reason, because the Offence is equally within the Statute, and the Punishment the very same, whether the Party be guilty both of the Forgery and Publication, or of one of them only.

CHAP. LXXI.

Of Cheats.

OF Cheats punishable by publick Prosecution, there are two Kinds,

1. By the Common Law.
2. By the Statute.

Sect. 1. And first it seemeth, That those which are punishable at Common Law, may in general be described to be deceitful Practices, in [a] 2 Rol. Re. defrauding or endeavouring to defraud another of his known Right by 107. Means of some artful Device, contrary to the plain Rules of common Cro. Ja. 497, Honesty; as by [a] Playing with false Dice; or by [b] causing an illiterate 498. 2 Rol. Ab. 78. Person to execute a Deed to his Prejudice, by reading it over to him in H. 1, 2. 1 Keb. 849. Words [b] 1 Sid. 312.

[a] 1 Sid. 431. [b] Noy 103. [c] Noy 99. Moore 630. Cro. El. 531. 1 Mod. 46. 2 Jon. 64. [d] Noy 99. [e] See the Books above cited, but 2 Rol. A. 863. C. & 12 Co. 123. are contrary. [f] 6 Mod. 105.

Words different from those in which it was written; or by [a] perswading a Woman to execute Writings to another, as her Trustee upon an intended Marriage, which in Truth contained no such Thing, but only a Warrant of Attorney to confess a Judgment, *&c.* or by [b] suppressing a Will, or by [c] levying a Fine in another's Name, or [d] suing out an Execution upon a Judgment for him, or acknowledging an Action in his Name without his Privity, and against his Will; in which Cases, by some good [e] Opinions, the Record may be vacated.

Sect. 2. It [f] seemeth to be the better Opinion, That the deceitful receiving of Money from one Man to another's Use, upon a false Pretence of having a Message and Order to that Purpose, is not punishable by a criminal Prosecution, because it is accompanied with no manner of artful Contrivance, but wholly depends on a bare naked Lie; and it is said to be needless to provide severe Laws for such Mischiefs, against which common Prudence and Caution may be a sufficient Security.

See the Authorities cited in Sect. 1.

Sect. 3. Some of the above mentioned Offences are punishable, not only with Fine and Imprisonment, but also with farther infamous Punishment, (as cheating with false Dice, especially if the Offender be a common Gamester,) others are punishable with Fine and Imprisonment only, by the Discretion of the Judges, which is regulated by the Circumstances of each particular Case; and some of them are made Felonies by 21 *Jac.* 1. 26. as appeareth from Chapter 45.

Sect. 4. Offences of this Kind by Statute depend upon 33 *H.* 8. 1. by which it is enacted, *That if any Person or Persons shall falsly and deceitfully obtain or get into his or their Hands or Possession, any Money, Goods, Chattels, Jewels, or other Things of any other Person or Persons, by Colour and Means of any privy false Token, or counterfeit Letter made in another Man's Name, to a special Friend or Acquaintance, for the obtaining of Money,* &c. *from such Person, and shall be thereof convicted, by Witness taken before the Lord Chancellor, or before the Justices of Assize, or before the Justices of Peace of any County, City, Borough, Town, or Franchise in their general Sessions, or by Action in any of the King's Courts of Record, every such Offender shall suffer such Punishment, by Imprisonment, setting upon the Pillory, or otherwise by any corporal Pain, except Pains of Death, as shall be appointed by those before whom he shall be so convict.*

Sect. 5. And it is farther enacted by the said Statute, *That as well the Justices of Assize for the Time being, as also two Justices of Peace in the same County, whereof the one to be of the* Quorum, *may call and convene by Process, or otherwise, to the said Assizes, or general Sessions, any Person being suspected of any of the Offences aforesaid, and to commit or bail him till the next Assizes or general Sessions,* &c.

3 Inst. 123.

Sect. 6. Sir *Edward Coke* is of Opinion, That the Offender cannot be fined in a Prosecution upon this Statute, because it is expresly ordained, That some corporal Punishment shall be inflicted, and no other is mentioned; however, there is a Precedent in *Croke*'s Reports, by which it appears, That one convicted on such a Prosecution hath been adjudged not only to stand on the Pillory, but also to pay a Fine of five hundred Pounds, and to be bound with good Sureties to his good Behaviour.

Cro. Ca. 564.

CHAP. LXXII.

Of Conſpiracy.

FOR the better Underſtanding of the Nature of Conſpiracy, I ſhall conſider the following particulars:

1. Who may be ſaid to be guilty of it.
2. In what Manner ſuch Offenders are to be puniſhed.

Sect. 1. As to the firſt Point, there can be no better Rule than the Statute of 33, or rather 21 *Ed.* 1. the Intent whereof was to make a final Definition of Conſpirators, to which purpoſe it declareth, *That Conſpirators be they that do confeder or bind themſelves by Oath, Covenant, or other Alliance, that every of them ſhall aid and bear the other falſly and maliciouſly to indict, or cauſe to indict, or falſly to move and maintain Pleas, and alſo ſuch as cauſe Children within Age to appeal Men of Felony, whereby they are impriſoned and ſore grieved; and ſuch as retain Men in the Country with Liveries or Fees for to maintain their malitious Enterprizes: And this extendeth as well to the Takers as to the Givers. And Stewards and Bailiffs of great Lords, who by their Seigniory, Office, or Power, undertake to bear or maintain Quarrels, Pleas, or Debates that concern other Parties than ſuch as touch the Eſtate of their Lords or themſelves.* 2 Inſt. 562.

Sect. 2. From this Definition of Conſpirators it ſeems clearly to follow, That not only thoſe who actually cauſe an innocent Man to be indicted, and alſo to be tried upon the Indictment, whereupon he is lawfully acquitted, are properly Conſpirators, but that thoſe alſo are guilty of this Offence, who barely conſpire to indict a Man falſly and malitiouſly, whether they do any Act in Proſecution of ſuch Conſpiracy or not; for the Words of the Statute ſeem expreſly to include all ſuch Confederacies under the Notion of Conſpiracy, whether there be any Proſecution thereof or not; and if ſuch a Confederacy be within the Letter of the Statute, there ſeems to be no manner of Reaſon to ſay, That they are not alſo within the Meaning of it, ſince it is a high Contempt of the Law, barely to engage in ſuch an Aſſociation to abuſe it, to ſerve the purpoſes of Oppreſſion and Injuſtice; neither can it be a ſevere Conſtruction which will bring a Crime ſo evidently contrary to the firſt Principles of common Honeſty, within the Meaning of a Law, the Words whereof do plainly ſeem to extend to it. And therefore I cannot but queſtion the Accuracy of that Deſcription of Conſpiracy which is given in the third *Inſtitute*, whereby the lawful Acquittal of the Party grieved is required to make the Offenders guilty of this Crime. It is true indeed, That a bare Conſpiracy to indict a Man will not maintain a Writ of Conſpiracy at the Suit of the Party grieved, becauſe it doth not do him any actual Damage; alſo it muſt be confeſſed, That it is often laid down as a general Rule, and taken for granted, That no ſuch Conſpiracy is a good Foundation for ſuch a Writ, unleſs the Plaintiff be lawfully acquitted; and it is certain, That there is no formed Writ of Conſpiracy in the Regiſter for a malicious Indictment or Appeal; but what ſuppoſes ſuch Indictment or 3 Inſt. 143. F.N.B. 114 d. 1 Rol. Ab. 110. Pl. 2. 111 Pl. 5. 114 Pl. 3. 9 Co. 56, 57. Regiſt. 134. 1 Jon. 93, 94.

Appeal to have been actually brought, and the Party to have been legally discharged; from whence it follows, That no one can have the Benefit of any such Writ in the Register, who upon a false Accusation, is put to the Trouble and Vexation of being apprehended, examined, or committed, *&c.* without being ever indicted or appealed. However it is certain, That an Acquittal by Verdict is not always necessary to maintain such a Writ, for it appears by the Register it self, That where one brought such a Writ in the usual Form, having in it the Words *quousque acquietatus fuisset, &c.* against one who had been nonsuited in a malicious Appeal of Felony brought against him, his Writ was abated, because such a Nonsuit would not make good the Words *quousque acquietatus fuisset*, and yet he afterwards brought a new Writ, wherein he used the Words *quietus recessit*, instead of *acquietatus fuisset*, and recovered. And why may not a new Writ as well be formed in any other Case, which is as much within the Mischief of the Statute as this? Or what colour can there be to say, That the malicious putting of a Man to the unreasonable Charge, Scandal, and Trouble, of a criminal Prosecution, which is so palpably Groundless, as not to have Probability enough to induce a Grand Jury to find an Indictment, should not be as good a Foundation of Complaint, and a Grievance as much within the Meaning of the Statute, as the putting one to the Charge and Vexation of a groundless Action, either in a Temporal or Spiritual Court, for which it appears by the [a] Register, That a Writ of Conspiracy doth lie without making Use either of the Words *acquietatus fuisset*, or *quietus recessit*? Neither can it be said, That the Opinion I contend for is wholly unsupported by Authority, as appears from the *Poulter*'s Case in [b] *Coke*'s ninth Report. However, since it is certain, That an [c] Action on the Case in the Nature of such Writ doth lie for a false and malicious Prosecution, for any Crime, whether capital, or not capital, tho' it do not proceed to an actual Indictment, or Appeal, and that the same Damages may be recovered in such Action, as in a Writ of Conspiracy, it hath been thought needless to inquire, whether such Writ may be maintained for such a Prosecution, or not. But howsoever the Law may stand in relation to Writs of Conspiracy, there seems to be no manner of Reason that the stated Form of such Writs should any Way restrain a Proceeding by Way of Indictment or Information against Persons which are apparently within both the Letter and Meaning of the Statute. Also it seems certain, That a Man may not only be condemned to the Pillory, but also to be branded for a false and malicious Accusation; but since it doth not appear to have been solemnly resolved, that such an Offender is indictable upon the Statute, it seems to be more safe and adviseable to ground an Indictment of this Kind upon the Common Law, than upon the Statute, since there can be no doubt, but that all Confederacies whatsoever, wrongfully to prejudice a third Person, are highly criminal at Common Law, as where divers Persons confederate [d] together by indirect Means to impoverish a third Person, or [e] falsly and maliciously to charge a Man with being the reputed Father of a Bastard-Child, or to maintain one another in any Matter, whether it be true or false.

Regist. 134. b. See S. P. C. 174. D. Vide 2 Inst. 407, 562.

[a] Regist. 134. F.N.B. 116 B. Finch 306. 2 Inst. 562. 1 Keb. 254.

[b] 9 Co. 56. b.

[c] 1 Jon. 93, 94. 1 Leon. 107. Cro. El. 70, 134. Palm. 315. Cro. Ja. 130, 357. Latch. 79. Cro. Ca. 15. 2 Rol. Re. 236, 237. 2 Bulf. 270, 271. 1 Rol. Re. 109. 1 Rol. A. 112. Pl. 11, 12, 13. 113 Pl. 14. 213 Pl. 3. Ray 135, 180. Con. 1 Bulf. 185. Yelv. 116. Hutt. 49. Cro. El. 563. 9 Co. 57. a.

[d] 1 Levin. 62, 126. 1 Sid. 174. 1 Keb. 350.

[e] 1 Levin. 62. 1 Mod. 185, 186. 1 Sid. 68. 1 Keb. 254. [f] 27 Aff. 44. 9 Co. 56. b. 2 Rol. Ab. 77. Pl. 2, 3. See Moore 788.

Sect. 3. Neither doth it seem to be any Excuse of a Confederacy to carry on a false and malicious Prosecution, That the Indictment or Appeal, which was preferred, or intended to be preferred, in Pursuance of

 it,

it, was [a] Insufficient, or that the Court wherein the Prosecution was carried on, or designed to be carried on, had no Jurisdiction of the Cause, or that the Matter of the Indictment did import no Manner of [b] Scandal, so that the Party grieved was in Truth in no Danger of losing either his Life, Liberty, or Reputation; for notwithstanding the Injury intended to the Party against whom such a Confederacy is formed, may perhaps be inconsiderable; yet the Association to pervert the Law in order to procure it, seems to be a Crime of a very high Nature, and justly to deserve the Resentment of the Law.

[a] Yelv. 46. Palm 45. 3 Keb. 141. Stile 157. 1 Rol. Ab. 110. Pl. 2. 1 Rol. Ab. 111. Pl. 7. Yelv. 46, 117. Cro. El. 563. 2 Bulst. 270, 271. Cro. Jac. 357. 1 Rol. Rep. 109. [b] Regis. 134. F. N. B. 116. f. 3 Ass. Pl. 13. 11 H. 7. 25. b. 26. a. 1 Rol. Ab. 112. Pl. 10. 2 Mod. 52, 306. Con 2 Keb. 881.

Sect. 4. Neither [c] is it any Plea for one who is prosecuted for such an unlawful Confederacy, That nothing more was intended by him, but only to give his Testimony in a legal Course of Justice against the Party to whose Prejudice such Confederacy is supposed to have been formed; for notwithstanding it may be said, That it would be a great Discouragement to legal Proceedings to make Persons liable to a criminal Prosecution, for barely intending to give their Evidence, and it would be a prejudging of a Cause to try the Truth of the Testimony intended to be given in it before the Cause it self is determined; yet the Law will rather venture this Mischief, than suffer so flagrant a Villany to go unpunished. However if there be any Probability, That the principal Cause will ever be tried, it seems proper to apply to the Court to stay the Trial of the Confederacy till the Merits of the principal Cause be determined.

[c] 9 Co. 55. b. 56, 57. 12 Co. 23, 90. 91, 92. Cro. El. 70, 71, 134. 1 Leon 107. 1 Rol. Ab. 113. Pl. 5, 114. Pl. 4, 5, 115. Pl. 7. Winch. 28, 54. Latch. 79, 80. Con. 1 Rol. Ab. 110. Pl. 1. F. N. B. 115. e. 27 H. 8. 2. a b.

Sect. 5. Yet it [d] seems to be certain, That no one is liable to any Prosecution whatsoever, in Respect of any Verdict given by him in a criminal Matter, either upon a Grand or Petit Jury; for since the Safety of the Innocent, and Punishment of the Guilty, doth so much depend upon the fair and upright Proceeding of Jurors, it is of the utmost Consequence, that they should be as little as possible under the Influence of any Passion whatsoever. And therefore, lest they should be biassed with the Fear of being harassed by a vexatious Suit, for acting according to their Consciences, (the Danger of which might easily be insinuated, where powerful Men are warmly engaged in a Cause, and throughly prepossessed of the Justice of the Side which they espouse,) the Law will not leave any Possibility for a Prosecution of this kind. It is true indeed, the Jurors were formerly sometimes questioned in the Star-Chamber, for their Partiality in finding a manifest Offender not guilty, but this was always thought a very great Grievance; and surely as the Law is now settled by *Bushel's* Case, there is no kind of Proceeding against Jurors in Respect of their Verdicts in criminal Matters allowed of at this Day. As to the Objection, That an Attaint lies against a Jury for a false Verdict in a civil Cause, and that there is as much Reason to allow of it in a criminal one; it may be answered, That in an Attaint, a Man's Property only is brought into Question a second Time, and not his Liberty or Life; and also it may be generally presumed, That a Jury is likely to be equally influenced with the Fear of an Attaint from either of the contending Parties, whereas if any such Examinations of their Proceedings were allowed in criminal Causes, they might be often in great Danger of one Side, by incurring the Resentment of a powerful Prosecutor, and provoking him to call their Conduct into Question for their supposed Partiality; but they could have little to fear from an injured Criminal, who would seldom be in Circumstances to make his Prosecution formidable.

[d] 22 Ass. 77. 27 Ass. 12. 21 E. 3. 17 a. 47 E. 3. 17. a. 12 Co. 23, 24. Regis. 134. F. N. B. 115. c d. 27 H. 8. 2. S. P. C. 172, 173.

12 Co. 23, 24. Vaugh. 135.

F. N. B. 105, 106.

Sect.

12 Co. 24. *See* Vaughan 138, 139. 11 Ed. 4. 18. 21 Ed. 4. 67. a. S. P. C. 173.

Sect. 6. And as the Law has exempted Jurors from the Danger of incurring any Punishment in Respect of their Verdicts in criminal Causes, it hath also freed the Judges of all Courts of Record from all Prosecutions whatsoever, except in the Parliament, for any Thing done by them openly in such Courts as Judges. For the Authority of a Government cannot be maintained, unless the greatest Credit be given to those who are so highly intrusted with the Administration of Publick Justice; and it would be impossible for them to keep up in the People that Veneration of their Persons, and Submission to their Judgments, without which it is impossible to execute the Laws with Vigour and Success, if they should be continually exposed to the Prosecutions of those whose Partiality to their own Causes would induce them to think themselves injured. Yet
12 Co. 24. if a Judge will so far forget the Dignity and Honour of his Post, as to turn Sollicitor in a Cause which he is to judge, and privately and extrajudicially tamper with Witnesses, or labour Jurors, he hath no Reason to complain, if he be dealt with according to the same Capacity, to which he so basely degrades himself.

Sect. 7. It appears not only from the Words of the Statute, but also from the plain Reason of the Thing, That no Confederacy whatsoever to maintain a Suit can come within the Danger of the Statute, unless it be both false and malicious; for it would be a most dangerous Discourage-
1 Rol. Ab. 111 Pl 6. 112. Pl 8. 115. Pl. 7. ment of all legal Prosecutions, if those who engage in them upon a probable Ground, should be in Danger of being found guilty of so heinous a Crime upon their not being able to bring their Suits to their intended
Bro Coro 89. S P. C. 173. 22 Ass. 77. Effect; and from hence it clearly follows, that if the Defendants to an Indictment or Appeal in Murder be found guilty of Homicide *se defendendo*, or by Misadventure, or get off by pleading the King's Pardon, their Prosecutors are in no Danger of being punished as Conspirators: And from the same Ground it also follows, That if the Defendants in a Writ of Conspiracy can shew a probable Cause of Suspicion, they shall be discharged; as where being accused of a Conspiracy for indicting a Person
1 Leon 107. Cro. El. 134. of Larceny, they can shew that a Larceny was committed at such a Time and Place, and that the Party charged by them for such Larceny was found by them at the same Time and Place, with suspicious Circumstances; or where
Kellw. 81. b. 83. b. 20 H. 7. 11. Persons being charged with a Conspiracy for indicting another for feloniously carrying away a Woman, with great Violence and Numbers, are able to prove that they saw the Persons whom they so accused riding armed in a warlike manner, and following after those who in Truth actually did the Felony, and that it was the common Report of the Country that they were all
20 H. 7. 11. Kel w 81. b. Cro. El. 134. 1 Leon 107. of the Company. But some have said, That there is a Necessity to plead such Matter specially, and that it cannot be given in Evidence on the General Issue.

a 8 H 4. 6. b. 28 Ass. Pl. 12. S P. C. 173. C. D. E 174. A. Cro. El. 701. 1 Rol A 111. Pl. 5. 112. Pl. 9 b 38 Ed. 3. 3. a b. S P. C. 174. a. c 1 Rol Ab. 111. Pl. 5. 112. Pl. 9. Cro. El. 701.

Sect. 8. It plainly appears from the Words of the Statute, That one Person alone cannot be guilty of Conspiracy within the Purport of it; from whence it follows, That if all the Defendants who are prosecuted for such a Conspiracy be acquitted but one, the [a] Acquittal of the rest is the Acquittal of that one also; also upon the same Ground it hath been holden, That no such Prosecution is maintainable against a [b] Husband and Wife only, because they are esteemed but as one Person in Law, and are presumed to have but one Will. But it is certain, That an Action on the [c] Case in the Nature of a Conspiracy may be brought against one only; Also [d] it hath been resolved, That if such an Action be brought

F. N. B. 116. Cro. Ja. 194. Cro. Ca. 239. 3 Mod. 220. 6 Mod. 170. 1 Saund 228. Raymond 180 2 Keb. 497.

[d] 1 Rol. Ab. 111. Pl. 5. 112. Pl. 9.

againſt ſeveral Perſons, and all but one be acquitted, yet Judgment may be given againſt that one only.

Sect. 9. As to the ſecond Point, *viz.* In what manner Offenders of this Nature are to be puniſhed, it is clear, That thoſe who are convicted of Conſpiracy at the Suit of the [e] Party ſhall only have Judgment of Fine and Impriſonment, and to render to the Plaintiff his Damages. Alſo it is certain, That he who is convicted at the Suit of the [f] King, of a Conſpiracy to accuſe another of a Matter which may touch his Life, ſhall have Judgment that he ſhall loſe the Freedom and Franchiſe of the Law, (whereby he is diſabled to be put upon any Jury, or to be ſworn as a Witneſs, or even to appear in Perſon in any of the King's Courts;) and alſo that his Houſes, Lands, and Goods, ſhall be ſeized into the King's Hands, and his Houſes and Lands eſtreped and waſted, his Trees rooted up and arraſed, and his Body impriſoned. And this is commonly called a villainous Judgment, and is given by the Common Law, and not by any Statute, and is ſaid generally in ſome [g] Books, to be the proper Judgment upon every Conviction of Conſpiracy, at the Suit of the King, without any Reſtriction to ſuch as endangered the Life of the Party; but I do not find this Point any where ſettled.

[e] 24 Ed. 3. 34. b. 3 Inſt. 143. 2 Inſt. 562. S. P. C. 175.

[f] 24 Ed. 3. 34. b. 3 Inſt. 143. 2 Inſt. 562. S. P. C. 175. 27 Aſſ. Pl. 59.

[g] *See the Books above cited.* 27 Aſſ. Pl. 59. S. P. C. 175.

CHAP. LXXIII.

Of Libels.

In treating of Libels, I ſhall conſider,

1. What ſhall be ſaid to be a Libel.
2. Who are liable to be puniſhed for it.
3. In what Manner they are to be puniſhed.

Sect. 1. As to the firſt Point it ſeemeth, That a Libel in a ſtrict Senſe is taken for a malicious Defamation, expreſſed either in Printing or Writing, and tending either to blacken the Memory of one who is dead, or the Reputation of one who is alive, and to expoſe him to publick Hatred, Contempt or Ridicule. 5 Co. 121. 5 Mod. 165, 166.

Sect. 2. But it is ſaid, That in a larger Senſe the Notion of a Libel may be applied to any Defamation whatſoever, expreſſed either by Signs or Pictures, as by fixing up a Gallows againſt a Man's Door, or by painting him in a ſhameful and ignominious Manner. 5 Co. 121. b.

Sect. 3. And ſince the chief Cauſe for which the Law ſo ſeverely puniſhes all Offences of this Nature, is the direct Tendency of them to a Breach of Publick Peace, by provoking the Parties injured, and their Friends and Families to Acts of Revenge, which it would be impoſſible to reſtrain by the ſevereſt Laws, were there no Redreſs from Publick Juſtice for Injuries of this kind, which of all others are moſt ſenſibly felt; and ſince the plain Meaning of ſuch Scandal as is expreſſed by Signs or Pictures, is as obvious to common Senſe, and as eaſily underſtood by every common Capacity, and altogether as provoking, as that which is expreſſed by Writing or Printing, why ſhould it not be equally criminal? 5 Co. 121.

Sect. 4. And from the same Ground it seemeth also clearly to follow, That such Scandal as is expressed in a scoffing and ironical Manner, makes a Writing as properly a Libel, as that which is expressed in direct Terms; as where a Writing, in a taunting Manner reckoning up several Acts of publick Charity done by one, says, *You will not play the Jew, nor the Hypocrite*, and so goes on in a strain of Ridicule to insinuate, that what he did was owing to his Vain-Glory; or where a Writing, pretending to recommend to one the Characters of several great Men for his Imitation, instead of taking Notice of what they are generally esteemed famous for, pitches on such Qualities only which their Enemies charge them with the Want of, as by proposing such a one to be imitated for his Courage, who is known to be a great Statesman, but no Soldier, and another to be imitated for his Learning, who is known to be a great General, but no Scholar, *&c.* which kind of Writing is as well understood to mean only to upbraid the Parties with the Want of these Qualities, as if it had directly and expresly done so.

Hob. 215. Poph. 139. Brown's *Case.*

Sect. 5. And from the same Foundation it hath also been resolved, That a Defamatory Writing expressing only one or two Letters of a Name, in such a Manner, that from what goes before and follows after, it must needs be understood to signify such a particular Person, in the plain, obvious, and natural Construction of the whole, and would be perfect Nonsence if strained to any other Meaning, is as properly a Libel, as if it had expressed the whole Name at large; for it brings the utmost Contempt upon the Law, to suffer its Justice to be eluded by such trifling Evasions: And it is a ridiculous Absurdity to say, That a Writing which is understood by every the meanest Capacity, cannot possibly be understood by a Judge and Jury.

Hurt's *Case*, Trin. 12 Annæ.

Sect. 6. And from the same Ground it farther doth appear, That it is far from being a Justification of a Libel, that the Contents thereof are true, or that the Person upon whom it is made, has a bad Reputation, since the greater Appearance there is of Truth in any malicious Invective, so much the more provoking it is.

5 Co. 125. b. Hob. 253. Moore 627.

Sect. 7. Nor can there be any Doubt, but that a Writing which defames private Persons only, is as much a Libel as that which defames Persons intrusted with a Publick Capacity, inasmuch as it manifestly tends to create ill Blood, and to cause a Disturbance of the Publick Peace; However it is certain, That it is a very high Aggravation of a Libel that it tends to scandalize the Government, by reflecting on those who are intrusted with the Administration of Publick Affairs, which doth not only endanger the Publick Peace, as all other Libels do, by stirring up the Parties immediately concerned in it to Acts of Revenge, but also has a direct Tendency to breed in the People a dislike of their Governors, and incline them to Faction and Sedition.

5 Co. 125. 2 Rol. Re. 86.

Sect. 8. But it hath been resolved, That no false or scandalous Matter contained in a [a] Petition to a Committee of Parliament, or in [b] Articles of the Peace exhibited to Justices of Peace, or in any other [c] Proceeding in a regular Course of Justice, will make the Complaint amount to a Libel; for it would be a great Discouragment to Suitors to subject them to publick Prosecutions, in respect of their Applications to a Court of Justice. And the chief Intention of the Law in prohibiting Persons to revenge themselves by Libels, or any other private Manner, is to restrain them from endeavouring to make themselves their own Judges, and to oblige them to refer the Decision of their Grievances, to those whom the Law has appointed to determine them. Also [d] it seemeth to have been holden by some,

[a] 1 Levinz 240. 1 Sid 414, 415. 1 Saund. 131. 2 Keb. 832. [b] 4 Co. 14 b. [c] Dyer 285. Pl. 37.

[d] 2 Keb. 832. Con 4 Co. 14. b.

ſome, That no want of Juriſdiction in the Court, to which ſuch a Complaint ſhall be exhibited, will make it a Libel, becauſe the Miſtake of the proper Court is not imputable to the Party, but to his Counſel. Yet if it ſhall manifeſtly appear from the whole Circumſtances of the Caſe, That a Proſecution is entirely falſe, malicious, and groundleſs, and commenced, not with a Deſign to go through with it, but only to expoſe the Defendant's Character under the ſhew of a legal Proceeding; I cannot ſee any Reaſon why ſuch a Mockery of Publick Juſtice ſhould not rather aggravate the Offence, than make it ceaſe to be one, and make ſuch Scandal a good Ground of an Indictment at the Suit of the King, as it makes the Malice of their Proceeding a good Foundation of an Action on the Caſe at the Suit of the Party, whether the Court had a Juriſdiction of the Cauſe or not. But it is ſaid, That no Preſentment of a Grand Jury can be a Libel, not only becauſe Perſons who are ſuppoſed to be returned without their own ſeeking, and are ſworn to act impartially, ſhall be preſumed to have proper Evidence for what they do, but alſo becauſe it would be of the utmoſt ill Conſequence any Way to diſcourage them from making their Inquiries with that Freedom and Readineſs which the Publick Good requires. For which Conſiderations, it ſeems reaſonable to exempt them from the Fear of any kind of Proſecution in reſpect of their Inquiries, as hath been ſhewn more at large in the Chapter of Conſpiracy.

See 1 Danv. Ab. 208, 209, 210, 211, *and the foregoing Chapter of Conſpiracy.*

Moore 627.

Sect. 9. However it ſeems clear, That no Writing whatſoever is to be eſteemed a Libel, unleſs it reflect upon ſome particular Perſon; and it ſeems, That a Writing full of obſcene Ribaldry, without any kind of Reflection upon any one, is not puniſhable at all by any Proſecution at Common Law, as I have heard it agreed in the Court of King's Bench; yet it ſeems, That the Author may be bound to his good Behaviour, as a ſcandalous Perſon of evil Fame.

See the Chapter concerning Surety for the good Behaviour.

Sect. 10. As to the ſecond Point, *viz.* Who are liable to be puniſhed for a Libel, it is certain that not only he who compoſes, or procures another to compoſe it, but alſo that he who publiſhes, or procures another to publiſh it, are in Danger of being puniſhed for it; and it is ſaid, not to be material whether he who diſperſes a Libel knew any Thing of the Contents or Effect of it or not; for nothing could be more eaſy than to publiſh the moſt virulent Papers with the greateſt Security, if the concealing the Purport of them from an illiterate Publiſher would make him ſafe in diſperſing them. Alſo it hath been ſaid, That if he who hath either read a Libel himſelf, or hath heard it read by another, do afterwards maliciouſly read or repeat any Part of it, in the Preſence of others, or lend or ſhew it to another, he is guilty of an unlawful Publication of it. Alſo it hath been holden, That the copying of a Libel ſhall be a concluſive Evidence of the Publication of it, unleſs the Party can prove that he delivered it to a Magiſtrate to examine it, in which Caſe the Act ſubſequent is ſaid to explain the Intenrion precedent. But it ſeems to be the better Opinion, That he who firſt writes a Libel dictated by another, is thereby guilty of making it, and conſequently puniſhable for the bare Writing; for it was no Libel till it was reduced to Writing.

9 Co. 59 b. Moore 627, 813.

Moore 627. Con. 9 Co. 59. b.

Moore 627, 813.

9 Co. 59. b.

9 Co 59. b. Moore 813.

5 Mod. 167.

Sect. 11. Alſo it hath been reſolved, [a] That the ſending of a Letter full of provoking Language to another, without publiſhing it, is highly puniſhable; and if the bare making of a Libel be an Offence, whether it be publiſhed or not, as it ſeemeth to be holden in ſome [b] Books, ſurely the ſending of it to the Party reflected upon, muſt be a much greater Crime, inaſmuch as it ſo manifeſtly tends to a Diſturbance of the Peace.

[a] 1 Keb. 931. 1 Levinz 139. 12 Co. 34. Poph. 139. Ray. 201. 1 Sid 270. 1 Mod. 58. Hob. 62, [illegible]5. 3 Inſt. 174. 4 Inſt. 180, 181.

[b] 5 Mod. 167. 9 Co. 59 b.

Sect.

1 Keb. 832. 1 Saund. 133. 1 Levinz 240. 1 Sid. 414, 415.

Sect. 12. Also it seems to be agreed, That he who delivers a Paper full of Reflections on any Person, in Nature of a Petition to a Committee of Parliament, to any other Persons except the Members of Parliament, may be punished as the Publisher of a Libel, in respect of such a dispersing thereof among those who have nothing to do with it.

[a] 9 Co. 59. b. Moore 813. [b] 9 Co. 59. b. Moore 813. [c] Moore 627.

Sect. 13. But it hath been resolved, That he who barely reads a Libel in the Presence [a] of another, without knowing it before to be a Libel, or who hearing a Libel read by another, [b] laughs at it, or who [c] barely says, That such a Libel is made upon such a Person, whether he speak it with or without Malice, shall not in respect of any such Act be adjudged the Publisher of it.

Moore 627.

Sect. 14. Also it hath been holden, That he who repeats part of a Libel in Merriment without Malice, and with no purpose of Defamation, is no way punishable; but it seemeth, That the Reasonableness of this Opinion may justly be questioned; for Jests of this kind are not to be endured, and the Injury to the Reputation of the Party grieved is no way lessened by the Merriment of him who makes so light of it.

1 Keb. 832. 1 Saund. 133. 1 Levinz 240. 1 Sid. 414, 415.

Sect. 15. But it seemeth to be settled, That the bare printing of a Petition to a Committee of Parliament (which would be a Libel against the Party complained of, if it were made for any other Purpose, than as a Complaint in a Course of Justice,) and delivering Copies thereof to the Members of the Committee, shall not be look'd upon as the Publication of a Libel, inasmuch as it is justified by the Order and Course of Proceedings in Parliament, whereof the King's Courts will take judicial Notice.

Cro. Ca. 175. &c.

Sect. 16. As to the third Point, *viz.* In what manner Offenders of this kind are to be punished, there seemeth to be no Doubt, but that they may be condemned to pay such Fine, and also to suffer such corporal Punishment, as to the Court in Discretion shall seem proper, according to the heinousness of the Crime, and the Circumstances of the Offender.

CHAP. LXXIV.

Of the Offence of keeping a Bawdy-House.

THE Offence of keeping a Bawdy-House being of so gross a Nature, and there being also so few Questions relating to it worth considering, I shall pass it over with these following Observations:

Kitchen 11. a. 3 Inst. 205.

1. That it comes under the Cognizance of the Temporal Law, as a Common Nusance, not only in respect of its endangering the Publick Peace, by drawing together dissolute and debauched Persons, but also in respect of its apparent Tendency to corrupt the Manners of both Sexes, by such an open Profession of Lewdness.

2. That a Feme-Covert is punishable for this Offence as much as if she were sole, as more fully hath been shewn, Chap. 1. Sect. 12.

3. That Offenders of this kind are punishable not only with Fine and Imprisonment, but also with such infamous Punishment, as to the Court in Discretion shall seem proper.

CHAP. LXXV.

Of Common Nusances.

OFfences under the Degree of capital, more immediately against the Subject, not amounting to an actual Disturbance of the Peace, which may be committed by private Persons without any Relation to an Office, and which are of an inferiour Nature to the six kinds of Offences last treated of, being neither infamous nor grosly scandalous, seem to be reducible to the following Heads:

1. Such as more immediately affect the Publick.
2. Such as more immediately affect the Interests of particular Persons.

Offences of this kind more immediately affecting the Publick, are four-fold;

1. Common Nusances.
2. Monopolies.
3. Forestalling, Ingrossing, and Regrating.
4. Barratry.

And first of Common Nusances; for the better understanding whereof I shall first consider them in general, and then descend to those relating to Highways and Publick Houses, which seem to be the most remarkable general Heads of this Offence.

As to Common Nusances in general I shall consider:

1. What shall be said to be a Common Nusance.
2. How it may be removed.
3. How it may be punished.

Sect. 1. As to the first Point it seems, That a Common Nusance may be defined to be an Offence against the Publick, either by doing a Thing which tends to the Annoyance of all the King's Subjects, or by neglecting to do a Thing which the common Good requires. 2 Rol. Ab. 83.

Sect. 2. But Annoyances to the Interests of particular Persons are not punishable by a publick Prosecution as Common Nusances, but are left to be redressed by the private Actions of the Parties aggrieved by them. 2 Rol. Ab. 83.

Sect. 3. And from hence it clearly follows, That no Indictment for a Nusance can be good, which lays it to the Damage of private Persons only; as where it accuses a Man of [a] surcharging such a Common; or of [b] inclosing such a Piece of Ground, wherein the Inhabitants of such a Town have a Right of Common, to the Nusance of all the Inhabitants of such a Town; or of disturbing a [c] Water-course running to the Mill of *J. S. ad grave Damnum J. S. & Tenentium suorum*, without saying *omnium Ligeorum Domini Regis*; or of doing a Nusance to a Thing no way appearing to be of a Publick Nature, *ad grave* [d] *Damnum*, or [e] *Detrimentum*, or [f] *commune Nocumentum*

1 Sid. 209.

[a] 2 Rol. Ab. 83. Pl. 7.
[b] 27 Ass. Pl. 6. 2 Rol. Ab. 83. Pl. 7, 12, 13. Cro. El. 90.
[c] 2 Rol. Ab. 83. Pl 10.
[d] 2 Rol. Ab. 83. Pl. 11. Cro. El 148.
[e] 1 Mod. 107.
[f] 1 Rol. Re. 406. 3 Keb 284. Cro. El. 414. Cro Ja. 382. 1 Saund. 135. 2 Keb. 461.

2 Leon 183, 184.

cumentum omnium Ligeorum Domini Regis prope Inhabitantium; yet it hath been reſolved, That an Indictment for not repairing a Bridge, by Reaſon whereof it was ruinous, *ita quod Ligei Dominæ Reginæ per eam tranſire non poſſunt*, and concluding, *ad Nocumentum eorundem*, is good without uſing the Words *ad Nocumentum omnium Ligeorum, &c.* for by the King's liege People ſhall be underſtood, all his liege People.

27 Aſſ. Pl. 19, 20. 2 Rol. Ab. 83. Pl. 1, 2, 3. 2 Rol. Ab. 84, Pl. 14.

Sect. 4. Alſo it is ſaid, That the Law hath ſo tender a Regard for the Intereſts of the King and of Religion, That an Indictment for doing a Thing which plainly appears immediately to tend to the Prejudice of either of them, is good, though it do not expreſly complain of it as a common Grievance; and upon this Ground it hath been reſolved, That an Indictment for converting the King's Money to one's own Uſe is good, without more. And upon the ſame Foundation alſo it hath been holden, That an Indictment for breaking and digging up the Wall of the Church of ſuch a Town, *ad Nocumentum Burgi Ligeorum Domini Regis*, is good.

6 Mod. 11, 178, 213, 259. 311. Moore 847. 2 Keb. 410. 1 Keb. 161.

Sect. 5. Alſo it hath been ſaid, That an Indictment of a common Scold, by the Words *communis Rixatrix*, which ſeem to be preciſely neceſſary in every Indictment of this kind, is good, though it conclude *ad commune Nocumentum diverſorum* inſtead of *omnium, &c.* perhaps for this Reaſon, becauſe a common Scold cannot but be a common Nuſance. And upon the like Ground it ſeems that it may probably be argued, That an Indictment for laying Logs in the Stream of a navigable publick River, *ad Nocumentum J. S.* may be maintained, becauſe it cannot but be a common Nuſance. And if the Law be ſo in this Caſe, why ſhould not alſo an Indictment ſetting forth a Nuſance to a Way, and expreſly and unexceptionably ſhewing it to be a Highway, be good, notwithſtanding it conclude *in Nocumentum diverſorum Ligeorum, &c.* without ſaying *omnium*; for why ſhould ſuch a Concluſion be more neceſſary in an Indictment for one kind of Nuſance than for any other? And perhaps the [a] Authorities which ſeem to contradict this Opinion, might go upon this Reaſon, That in the Body of the Indictment, it did not appear with ſufficient Certainty, whether the Way, wherein the Nuſance was alledged, were a Highway, or only a private Way; and therefore that it ſhall be intended from the Concluſion of the Indictment, That it was a private Way.

[a] Cro. El. 148. 2 Keb. 461. Vid 2 Rol. Ab. 83. Pl. 11.

1 Mod. 76. 2 Keb. 846. 3 Keb. 464. 5 Mod. 142.

Sect. 6. There is no doubt but that common Bawdy-Houſes are indictable as common Nuſances, as hath been more fully ſhewn in the foregoing Chapter; alſo it hath been ſaid, That all common Stages for Rope-Dancers, and alſo all common Gaming Houſes, are Nuſances in the Eye of the Law, not only becauſe they are great Temptations to Idleneſs, but alſo becauſe they are apt to draw together great Numbers of diſorderly Perſons, which cannot but be very inconvenient to the Neighbourhood.

1 Rol. Re. 109. 5 Mod. 142. *See* Ruſhworth's Coll. Part 2. Vol. 1. fol. 220, 247.

Sect. 7. Alſo it hath been holden, That a common Play-houſe may be a Nuſance, if it draw together ſuch Numbers of Coaches or People, *&c.* as prove generally inconvenient to the Places adjacent; and it ſeems to be a proper Diſtinction between Play-houſes and the Nuſances mentioned in the foregoing Section, That Play-houſes having been originally inſtituted with a laudable Deſign of recommmending Virtue to the Imitation of the People, and expoſing Vice and Folly, are not Nuſances in their own Nature, but may only become ſuch by Accident, whereas the others cannot but be Nuſances.

Sect. 8. It hath been resolved, That neither an old nor a new Dove-cote, whether it were erected by the Lord of a Manor, or one of his Tenants, is a common Nusance; for if a Dove-cote were a common Nusance, it could never become lawful by any Licence or Prescription whatsoever, because every Nusance is a *Malum in se*; but it is certain, that a Dove-house may be justified by a Prescription, and that it is so far countenanced by the Law, as to be [b] demandable in a *Præcipe* before any Land whatsoever which is not built upon, and that the Owner may justify the taking another's [c] Hawk which he shall find at his Dove-house, flying at his Pigeons; and from hence it seems clearly to follow, That tho' a Tenant, who builds a Dove-house without the Licence of the Lord of the Manor, may perhaps be liable to an Action on the Case at the Suit of such Lord, whose Prerogative is said to be incroached upon by the erecting such a House without his Licence, yet he cannot be punished for it by a publick Prosecution.

[a] 2 Rol. Ab. 138. f. 139. f. 1, 2, 3. 265. E. 1. 2 Rol. Re. 4. 30. Cro. Ja. 382, 491. Moore 238. 1 Rol. Re. 136, 201. Popham 143. Con. 5 Co. 104. b. [b] F.N.B. 2. c. [c] 16 E. 4. 7. b.

Sect. 9. But perhaps it may be argued, That if this Reasoning be good, it will follow from the same Ground, That a Gate erected in a Highway will be also no Nusance; because, if it were, it could not be justified by any Prescription, as it is agreed that it may be; but to this it may be answered, That the erecting of such a Gate is therefore a Nusance, because it interrupts the People in that free and open Passage which they before enjoyed, and were lawfully intituled to; but where such a Gate has continued Time out of Mind, it shall be intended, That it was set up at first by Consent, on a Composition with the Owner of the Land on the laying out the Road, in which Case the People had never any Right to a freer Passage than what they still enjoy.

1 Jones 221. Cro. Ca. 184. 1 Bulf. 203. 2 Rol. Ab. 137. C.

Sect. 10. It hath been holden, That it is no common Nusance to make Candles in a Town, because the Needfulness of them shall dispense with the Noisomness of the Smell; but the reasonableness of this Opinion seems justly to be questionable, because whatever Necessity there may be that Candles be made, it cannot be pretended to be necessary to make them in a Town; and surely the Trade of a Brewer is as necessary as that of a Chandler; and yet it seems to be agreed, That a Brewhouse, erected in such an inconvenient Place, wherein the Business cannot be carried on without greatly incommoding the Neighbourhood, may be indicted as a common Nusance.

2 Rol. Ab. 139. Pl. 2. 2 Keb. 500. Vide 1 Danv. A. 173. 174.

Sect. 11. It seemeth certain, That it is a common Nusance to divert Part of a publick navigable River, whereby the Current of it is weakened, and made unable to carry Vessels of the same Burthen, as it could before. Also it hath been holden to be a common Nusance to divide a House in a Town for poor People to inhabit in, by reason whereof it will be more dangerous in the Time of Infection of the Plague.

Noy 103. 2 Rol. Ab. 139. Pl. 3.

Sect. 12. As to the second Point, *viz.* How a Nusance may be removed; it seemeth to be certain, That any one may pull down or otherwise destroy a common Nusance, as a new Gate, or even a new House erected in a Highway, *&c.* for if one whose Estate is, or may be, prejudic'd by a private Nusance actually erected, as a House hanging over his Ground, *&c.* may justify the pulling down and destroying such a Nusance, whether it were erected before or since he came to the Estate, surely it cannot but follow, *à fortiori*, That any one may lawfully destroy a common Nusance; yet it seems clear, That in either Case no one can justify the doing more Damage than is necessary, or removing the Materials.

2 Rol. Ab. 144. S. Cro. Ca. 184. 1 Jon. 221. 2 Rol. A. 145. U, W. 5 Co. 101. b. 9 Co. 54. b. 1 Rol. Rep. 9 E. 4. 35. Bro. Nusance 14. 1 Jon. 221.

Sect. 13. It hath been adjudged, That if a River be stopped, to the Nusance of the Country, and none appear bound by Prescription to clear it, those who have the Piscary, and the neighbouring Towns, who have a common Passage and Easement therein, may be compelled to do it.

37 Ass. 10. 2 Rol. Ab. 137. A.

Sect. 14. As to the third Point, *viz.* In what Manner common Nusances may be punished; it is said, That a common Scold is punishable by being put into the Ducking-Stool, and there is no doubt, but that whoever is convicted of another Nusance, may be fined and imprisoned; and it is said, That one convicted of a Nusance done to the King's Highway may be commanded by the Judgment to remove the Nusance at his own Costs; and it seemeth to be reasonable, That those who are convicted of any other common Nusance should also have the like Judgment.

6 Mod. 11. 178, 213.

2 Rol. Ab. 84. Pl. 15.

CHAP. LXXVI.

Of Nusances relating to Highways.

AND now I am particularly to consider such Nusances as relate to Highways, and publick Houses;

And first for the better Understanding of those which concern Highways, I shall consider:

1. Such as relate to Highways in general.
2. Such as relate to Bridges in particular.

For the better Understanding of Nusances relating to Highways in general, I shall examine the following particulars:

1. What shall be said to be a Highway.
2. At whose Charge and by whom it ought to be repaired.
3. In what Manner it is to be inlarged.
4. How the Surveyors thereof shall be appointed.
5. How such Surveyors ought to execute their Office.
6. What shall be said to be a Nusance to the Highway.
7. How such Nusances are to be removed and punished.
8. In what Manner those who are charged with any Offence relating to the Highway, are to be proceeded against.
9. How Persons so proceeded against may defend themselves.

As to the first Point, *viz.* What shall be said to be a Highway, it is said that there are three Kinds of Ways:

1. A Footway, which is called in *Latin*, *Iter*.
2. A Pack and Primeway, which is both a Horse and Footway, and called in *Latin*, *Actus*.

Co. Lit. 56. a.

3. A Cartway, which contains the other two; and alſo a Cartway, and is called in *Latin*, *Via* or *Aditus*, and this is either common to all Men, and then it is called, *Via Regia*, or belongs to ſome City or Town, or private Perſon, and then it is called *Communis Strata*.

Sect. 1. It ſeemeth that any one of the ſaid Ways, which is common to all the King's People, whether it lead directly to a Market-Town, or only from Town to Town, may properly be called a Highway, and that any ſuch Cartway may be called the King's Highway, and that a Nuſance in any of the ſaid Ways is puniſhable by Indictment in the Court-Leet; for Indictments for [a] ſtopping Horſeways, and [b] Footways, have often been allowed, and where others have been quaſhed, no other Reaſon has been given for it, but that the Way was not called a common Way or Highway; and in [c] Books of the beſt Authority, a River common to all Men, is called a Highway; and it is laid [d] down as a general Rule, That Nuſances to any Way common to all Men, are inquirable in the Leet, and Horſe-Cauſeys are taken Notice of by [e] Parliament; and therefore there ſeems to be no Reaſon why any Way leading from Village to Village, which does not terminate there, but is alſo a Thorough-fare to other Towns, may not properly be called a common or Highway, or why a Nuſance therein ſhould not be indictable, whether it directly lead to a Market-Town or not; for ſince ſuch a Way lies open to all the King's Subjects, a Nuſance therein [f] cannot but be a common Nuſance, and if it be not puniſhable by Indictment it would not be puniſhable at all, inaſmuch as it [g] ſeems to be certain, That it is not puniſhable by Action, becauſe if one Man might bring his Action in Reſpect of the Poſſibility of the Damage which he might receive from it, all other Men might do the like, which would introduce a Multiplicity of Actions; and therefore the Diſtinction which is taken in ſome [h] Books concerning this Matter, ſeems to be very reaſonable, That every Way from Town to Town may be called a Highway, becauſe it is common to all the King's Subjects, but that a Way to a Pariſh-Church, or to the common Fields of a Town, or to a private Houſe, or perhaps to a Village, which terminates there, and is for the Benefit of the particular Inhabitants of ſuch Pariſh, Houſe, or Village only, may be called a private Way, but not a Highway, becauſe it belongeth not to all the King's Subjects, but only to ſome particular Perſons, each of which, as it ſeems, may have an Action on the Caſe for a Nuſance therein.

Palm. 389.
6 Mod. 255.
[a] Cro. El 63.
[b] 1 Vent. 208.
2 Keb. 178.
6 Mod. 255.
[c] 27 Aſſ. 23.
[d] Co. Lit. 56. a.
5 Ed. 4. 2. b.
[e] 3 & 4 W. & M. 12.
[f] Kitchin 35. a.
Palm. 389.
2 Rol. Rep. 412.
[g] Moore 180. Pl. 321.
Cro. E. 664.
Co. Lit. 56. a.
27 H. 8. 27. a.
[h] 1 Vent. 189.
Kitch. 35. a.
Co. Lit. 56.

Sect. 2. It hath been holden, That if there be a Highway in an open Field, and the People have uſed, Time out of Mind, when the Ways are bad, to go by Outlets on the Land adjoining, ſuch Outlets are Parcel of the Way, for the King's Subjects ought to have a good Paſſage, and the good Paſſage is the Way, and not only the beaten Track; from whence it follows, That if ſuch Outlets be ſown with Corn, and the beaten Track be foundrous, the King's Subjects may juſtify going upon the Corn.

1 Rol A 390. Pl. 1.

Sect. 3. It ſeemeth to be agreed, That an ancient Highway cannot be changed without the King's Licence firſt obtained upon a Writ of *Ad quod damnum*, and an Inquiſition thereon found, That ſuch a Change will not be prejudicial to the Publick; and it is ſaid, That if one change a Highway without ſuch Authority, he may ſtop the new Way whenever he pleaſes; and it ſeemeth, That the King's Subjects have not ſuch an Intereſt in ſuch new Way as will make good a general Juſtification of their going in it as in a common Highway, but that in an Action of Treſ-

Cro. Ca. 266, 267.
Vaugh. 341.

Cro. Ca. 267. Yelv. 141, 142. Trespass brought by the Owner of the Land against those who shall go over it, they ought to shew specially, by Way of Excuse, how the old Way was obstructed, and the new one set out; also it is said, That the Inhabitants are not bound to keep Watch in such a new Way, or to make Amends for a Robbery therein committed, or to repair it. Cro. Ca. 267.

Sect. 4. However it is certain, That a Highway may be changed by the Act of God; and therefore it hath been holden, That if a Water which has been an ancient Highway, by Degrees changes its Course, and go over different Ground from that whereon it used to run, yet the Highway continues in the new Chanel, in the same Manner as in the old. 22 Ass. 93. 1 Rol. A. 390.

As to the second Point, *viz.* At whose Charge, and by whom the Highway ought to be repaired, I shall consider:

1. What Provision is made by the Common Law concerning this Matter.
2. What by Statute.

a 1 Rol. Ab. 890. b March. 26. 1 Vent. 183, 189. H. P. C. 144. 8 H. 7. 5.

Sect. 5. As to the first of these Particulars, it seems to be agreed, That of common Right, the general Charge of Repairing all Highways lies on the Occupiers of the Lands in the Parish wherein they are; but it is said, That the Tenants of the Lands adjoining are bound to scowr their Ditches, and there is no doubt but particular Persons may be burthened with the general Charge of Repairing a Highway, in two Cases:

1. In Respect of an Inclosure of the Land wherein it lies.
2. In Respect of a Prescription.

1 Rol. Ab. 390. B. Cro. Ca. 366. 1 Sid. 464.

Sect. 6. And first a particular Person may be bound to repair a Highway in Respect of an Inclosure, as where the Owner of Lands not inclosed, next adjoining to the Highway, incloses his Lands on both Sides thereof, in which Case he is bound to make a perfect good Way, and shall not be excused for making it as good as it was at the Time of the Inclosure, if it were then any way defective; because, before the Inclosure, the People used when the Way was bad, to go for their better Passage, over the Fields adjoining, out of the common Track, which Liberty is taken away by the Inclosure.

1 Sid. 464. *Sect.* 7. Also it hath been holden, That if one inclose Land on one Side, which hath been anciently inclosed of the other Side, he ought to repair all the Way, but that if there be not such an ancient Inclosure of the other Side, he ought to repair but half that Way: And it is said, That where-ever one is bound to repair a Highway in respect of an Inclosure, and lays it open again as it was before, he shall be freed from the Charge of repairing it.

2 Saund. 160. 27 Ass. 8. 21 Ed. 4. 38. b. Brook Prescription 49, 78.

Sect. 8. Secondly, A particular Person may be bound to repair a Highway in respect of a Prescription; and it is said, That a Corporation aggregate may be compelled to do it by Force of a general Prescription, That it ought and hath used to do it, without shewing, That it used to do so in respect of the Tenure of certain Lands, or for any other Consideration, because such a Corporation in Judgment of Law never dies, and therefore, if it were ever bound to such a Duty, it must needs continue to be always so; neither is it any Plea, That such Corporation have always done it out of Charity, for what it hath always done, it ſhall be preſumed to have been always bound to do; but it is ſaid, That a Perſon cannot be charged with ſuch a Duty by a general Preſcription from what his Anceſtors have done, becauſe no one is bound to do what his Anceſtors have done, unleſs it be for ſome ſpecial Reaſon, as the having Land deſcended from ſuch Anceſtors, which are holden by ſuch like Service, *&c.* yet it ſeems, That an Indictment charging a Tenant in Fee-ſimple with having uſed of Right to repair ſuch a Way, *ratione Tenuræ Terræ ſuæ*, is certain enough, without adding, That his Anceſtors, or thoſe whoſe Eſtate he hath, have always ſo done, for that is implied in ſaying, That he has always uſed to do it *ratione Tenuræ ſuæ*. 21 Ed. 4. 31. b. Kellew. 52. a. Latch. 206.

Sect. 9. However it ſeemeth certain, That whether a particular Perſon be bound to repair a Highway by Incloſure, or Preſcription, *&c.* yet the Pariſh cannot take Advantage of it upon the Plea of Not guilty to an Indictment againſt them for not repairing it, but ought to ſet forth their Diſcharge in a ſpecial Plea. 1 Mod. 112. 3 Keb. 301. 1 Ven. 256.

And now I am to conſider in the ſecond Place, at whoſe Charge, and by whom the Highway ought to be repaired by Force of the Statute, for the better Underſtanding whereof, I ſhall examine:

1. Who are by Statute compellable to work in the Repairs thereof in their own Perſons, or by others.
2. Who may be aſſeſſed to a Rate made for the defraying of the extraordinary Charges of ſuch Repairs.
3. What other Proviſions have been made to this Purpoſe.
4. In what manner the Profits of Lands ſettled in Truſt for the Repairs of the Highways, ſhall be employed.

Sect. 10. As to the firſt Point, it is enacted by 2 & 3 *Ph. & Mar.* 6. and 22 *Car.* 2. 12. *That the Pariſhioners of every Pariſh ſhall endeavour themſelves to the amending of the Highways therein, and ſhall be chargeable thereunto as followeth,* that is to ſay, *Every Perſon for every Ploughland in Tillage or Paſture, That he or ſhe ſhall occupy in the ſame Pariſh, and every other Perſon keeping there a Draught or Plough, ſhall find and ſend at every Day and Place to be appointed for the amending of the Ways in the Pariſh, one Wain or Cart, furniſhed after the Cuſtom of the Country, with Oxen, Horſes, or other Cattle, and all other neceſſaries meet to carry Things convenient for that purpoſe, and alſo two able Men with the ſame, upon Pain of every Draught making default, ten Shillings; and every Houſholder, and alſo every Cottager and Labourer of that Pariſh, able to labour, and being no hired Servant by the Year, ſhall by themſelves, or one ſufficient Labourer for every of them, upon every of the ſaid Days, work and travel in the Amendment of the ſaid Highways, upon Pain of every Perſon making default, to loſe for every Day, one Shilling and Six-pence: And if the ſaid Carriages of the Pariſh, or any of them, ſhall not be thought needful by the Surveyors, to be occupied upon any of the ſaid Days, that then every ſuch Perſon that ſhould have ſent any ſuch Carriage, ſhall ſend to the ſaid work, for every Carriage ſo ſpared, two able Men, there to labour for the Day, upon pain to loſe for every Man not ſo ſent to the ſaid Work, Twelve-pence; and every Perſon and Carriage abovesaid, ſhall have and bring with them ſuch Shovels, Spades, Picks, Mattocks, and other Tools and Inſtruments as they do make their own Ditches and Fences withal, and ſuch as be neceſſary for their ſaid Work: And all the ſaid Perſons and Carriages ſhall do and keep their Work, as they ſhall be appointed by the ſaid Supervisors, or one of them, eight Hours of every of the ſaid Days, unleſs they ſhall be otherwiſe licenced by the ſaid Supervisors, or one of them.* 22 Car. 2. 12. Par. 9.

Sect.

Sect. 11. And it is farther enacted by 18 *El.* 10. Par. 2. *That every Person or Persons (except such as dwell in the City of* London,) *that shall be assessed to the Payment of any Subsidy to Her Majesty, to five Pounds in Goods, or fourty Shillings in Lands, or above, during all such Time as he shall stand so assessed and not altered, and being none of the Parties chargeable for the Amendment of Highways by any former Law, but as a Cottager, shall find two able Men yearly to labour in the Highways, at the Times appointed.*

Sect. 12. And it is farther enacted by the said Statute, Par. 3. *That every other that shall occupy a Plough-land in Tillage or Pasture, lying in several Parishes, shall be chargeable to the making of the Ways within the Parish where he dwelleth, as far forth, and in such Manner and Form as any Person having a Plough-land in any one Parish, is or ought to be chargeable.*

Dal. ca. 26. 3 Keb. 568. 2 Keb. 617.

Sect. 13. It was made a great Doubt in the Construction of these Statutes, what should be accounted a Plough-land within the Purview of them, for the settling whereof it was enacted by 7 & 8 *W.* 3. 29. *That any Person that shall have in his or her Occupation, Wood-land, or other Land, to the Value of fifty Pounds* per Annum, *shall be adjudged and deemed to have a Plough-land, as to all, or any of the Purposes within any of the Statutes before that Time made, of or concerning the Highways, any Thing in them, or any Usage, or Custom to the contrary, in any wise notwithstanding.*

Sect. 14. Also it is farther enacted by the above mentioned Statute of 22 *Car.* 2. 12. Par. 8. *That in such Places where there is no use of Carts and Teams for the Amendment of the Highways, but the Usage and Practice is to carry Stones, Gravel, Earth, or other Materials for such Amendment, upon the backs of Horses, or by any other Kinds of Carriages; that in all such Places the Inhabitants using any such Horses, or other Carriages, shall send in such their Horses as are accustomed to that kind of Labour, and such their other Carriages, with able Persons to work with the same, in like manner, and under the like Directions, Forfeitures and Penalties, as by any former Statute for repairing of Highways, is appointed for Carts and Teams.*

In the Exposition of these Statutes the following Opinions have been holden,

[a] 3 Keb. 255, 476. 1 Ven. 273. Wats. c. 40. 2 Inst. 704.

Sect. 15. I. That [a] Persons in holy Orders are within the Purview of them, in respect of their spiritual Possessions, as much as any other Persons whatsoever, in respect of any other Possessions, for the Words are general, and there is no Kind of Intimation that any particular Persons shall be exempted more than others.

[b] Raym 186. 3 Keb 567, 568. Vide Dalt. ca. 26. 2 Keb 617.

Sect. 16. II. [b] That he who keeps several Draughts in a Parish is bound to send a Team for each Draught, whether he occupy any Land in the Parish, or not; and in like manner, That he who occupies several Plough-lands, ought to send a Team for each Plough-land, whether he keep any Draught, or not.

[c] Palm. 389. 2 Rol. Re. 412.

Sect. 17. III. That [c] notwithstanding the Words of the Statute extend only to the Occupiers of Lands, yet if the Owner neither occupy them, nor let them, but suffer them to lie fresh, he shall be charged as much as if he had occupied them, for there is no reason that the Publick shall suffer for his Negligence.

Dalt. ca. 26.

Sect. 18. IV. That it is no Excuse for the Inhabitants of a Parish, being indicted at Common Law for not repairing their Highways, That they have done the full Work required of them by Statute, for since these Statutes are wholly in the Affirmative, and made in Aid of the Common Law, and to supply the Defects thereof, they shall not be construed to abrogate any Provision thereby made for these Purposes.

Sect. 19. *Dalton* is of Opinion, That he who keeps a Draught and but two Horses, ought to attend therewith at the Times appointed, and that if he carry with them such Loads as they are able to draw, he shall be excused. Dalt. ca. 26.

Sect. 20. As to the second Point, *viz.* Who may be assessed to a Rate made for the defraying of the extraordinary Charges of such Repairs, it is enacted by the above mentioned Statute of 22 Car. 2. 12. Par. 10, 11. and 3 & 4 *W. & M.* 12. *That where the Justices of the Peace of any County, City, or other Place, or the major Part of them, at their General or Quarter-Sessions, shall be fully satisfied that the common Highways, Causeys, Bridges, Streets or Pavements, within any Parish, Township, or Hamlet,* &c. *within their respective Jurisdiction, cannot be sufficiently amended, repaired, and supported, by Means of the Laws then in Force, without the Help of the said Acts, in all such Cases one or more Assessment, or Assessments, upon all and every the Inhabitants, Owners, and Occupiers of Lands, Houses, Tenements, and Hereditaments, or any personal Estate, usually rateable to the Poor, within any such Parish, Township, or Hamlet,* &c. *shall be made, levied, collected, and allowed, by such Person and Persons, and in such Manner as the said Justices by their Order at such Sessions shall direct and appoint in that behalf: And the Money thereby raised shall be imployed and accounted for, according to the Order and Directions of the said Justices, for and towards the amending, repairing, paving, cleansing and supporting such Highways, Causeys, and Bridges, from Time to Time, as need shall require, and the said Assessments shall be levied by Distress and Sale of Goods on Non-Payment upon Demand,* &c. *Provided that no such Assessment or Assessments to be made in any one Year, shall exceed the Rate of Six-pence in the Pound of the yearly Value of any Lands, Houses, Tenements and Hereditaments, so assessed, nor the Rate of Six-pence for twenty Pounds in personal Estate.*

By 1. Geo. c. 52. Sect. 6. On application of the Surveyors to ye Justices of Peace at ye Quarter Sessions, ye sd Justices being satisfied yt ye Highway are so far out of Order, yt ye y can not be repaird as ye ought to be wthout farther power yn ye Laws have hitherto directed may, at ye Sessions, cause Assessment to be made & ye mony to be disposed of, tho ye six day's work be not performed. But ye raising mony by Assessmt not to excuse ye work of any Teams or Labourer by Law appointed to work at ye sd ways. —

Sect. 21. And it is farther enacted by the above mentioned Statute of 7 & 8 *W.* 3. 29. *That if any Inship, Liberty, Precinct, or Vill, that uses to repair their own Highways, shall have levied the Rate of Six-pence in the Pound, and imployed the same towards the Repair of the Highways, and yet the said Highways are not sufficiently repaired, in such Cases it shall be lawful for the Justices of the Peace at their special Sessions to be held every four Months, for the Consideration of the Highways, to order the whole Parish to contribute to the Repairing thereof.*

Sect. 22. It is recited by 3 & 4 *W. & M.* 12. *That divers Parishes and Townships, having not any Gravel-Stones, Quarries, nor any other Materials fitting or convenient for the amending or repairing of the Highways within the said Parishes and Townships, the Surveyors of the Highways of such Parishes and Townships, had been forced to lay out their own Money for the buying of such Materials as were necessary for that Purpose, and yet had no Remedy by any Law then in Force for a Re-imbursement of such Expences*; and thereupon it is enacted, *That upon Notice given by the Surveyor or Surveyors of the Highways to the Justices of the Peace at their special Sessions, and Oath made of what Sum or Sums of Money, he or they have or hath so laid out and expended, upon amending and repairing of the said Highways, the Justices of the Peace, or any two of them, at their special Sessions, may by Warrant under their Hands and Seals, cause an equal Rate to be made for the Re-imbursing the said Surveyor or Surveyors, the Moneys by him or them laid out as aforesaid, upon all the Inhabitants of such Parish or Township where such Moneys are expended, according to the Rules and Methods prescribed by* 43 El. 2. *which Rate being confirmed and allowed by the said Justices in their special Sessions, shall be collected and gathered by the said Surveyor or Surveyors of the Highways; and if any Person or Persons refuse to pay the Moneys so assessed on him or them, that then the same shall be levied by the said Surveyors, by Distress and Sale of the Goods and Chattels of the Persons so refusing, rendring to the Party the Overplus, reasonable Charges for making the said Distress first to be deducted.*

Sect. 23. As to the third Point, *viz.* What other Provisions have been made to this Purpose, it is enacted by the said Statute of 3 & 4 *W. & M.* 12. *That no Fine, Issue, Penalty, or Forfeiture, for not repairing any Highway, shall be returned into the Court of Exchequer, or other Court, but shall be levied and paid into the Hands of the Surveyors of the Parish, or Place, to be applied towards the Repair and Amendment of such Highway; and that if any Fine, Penalty, or Forfeiture, imposed on any Parish or Place, for not repairing the Highways, shall hereafter be levied on any one, or more, of the Inhabitants of such Parish or Place, that then such Inhabitant or Inhabitants shall make his or their Complaint to the Justices of the Peace at their special Sessions, and the said Justices, or any two of them, are by the said Statute impowered and authorized by Warrant under their Hands and Seals, to cause a Rate to be made, according to the Form and Manner* [a] *aforesaid, for the re-imbursing such Inhabitant or Inhabitants the Money so levied on him or them, as aforesaid, which Rate so made, and confirmed by two Justices, as aforesaid, shall be collected, and levied by the Surveyor or Surveyors of the Highways of such Parish or Place so presented or indicted, as aforesaid, and the said Surveyor or Surveyors shall within one Month next after the making and confirming the Rate aforesaid, pay unto the Inhabitant or Inhabitants, such Money so levied on him or them, as aforesaid.*

[a] See the precedent Section.

Sect. 24. Also the later Statutes which have imposed any Penalties on Surveyors of the Highways, or others, for any Offences relating to the Highways, have generally ordained that the whole, or Part thereof, shall be applied to the Repairs of the Highways of the Place wherein the Offence shall be committed, as will more fully appear in the subsequent Part of this Chapter.

Sect. 25. As to the fourth Point, *viz.* In what Manner the Profits of Lands settled in Trust for the Repairs of the Highways shall be employed, it is enacted by the above mentioned Statute of 22 *Car.* 2. 12. Par. 2. *That where any Lands have been, or shall be given for the Maintenance of Causeys, Pavements, Highways and Bridges, all such Persons that are, or shall be, enfeoffed, or trusted with any such Lands, shall let them to farm at the most improved yearly Value without Fine; and that the Justices of the Peace in their open Sessions shall enquire by such Ways and Means as they think fitting, into the Value of all such Lands so given, or to be given, and order the Improvement and Imployment of the Rents and Profits thereof, according to the Will and Direction of the Donor of such Lands, if they find that the Persons so intrusted, have been negligent or faulty in the Performance of their Trust, (except such Lands have been given to the Uses aforesaid, to any College or Hall in either of the Universities of this Kingdom, which have Visitors of their own,) Any Law, Statute, Usage, or Custom, to the contrary notwithstanding.*

Sect. 26. As to the third general Head of this Chapter, *viz.* In what Manner the Highway is to be enlarged, it is enacted by 13 *Ed.* 1. commonly called the Statute of *Winchester*, Chap. 5. *That Highways leading from one Market Town to another shall be enlarged, so that there be neither Dyke, Tree, nor Bush, whereby a Man may lurk to do Hurt, within two hundred Foot of the one Side, and two hundred Foot of the other Side of the Way: So that the Statute shall not extend to Ashes, nor unto great Trees,* &c. *and if by Default of the Lord that will not avoid the Dyke, Underwood, or Bushes, in the Manner aforesaid, any Robberies be done therein, the Lord shall be answerable for the Felony, and if Murder be done, the Lord shall make a Fine at the King's Pleasure: And if the Lord be not able to fell the Underwoods, the Country shall aid him there-*

therein. And the King willeth, that in his Demean Lands and Woods within his Forest, and without, the Ways shall be enlarged, as before is said. And if percase a Park be taken from the Highway, it is requisite that the Lord shall set his Park the space of two hundred Foot from the Highways, as before is said, or that he make such a Wall, Dyke, or Hedge, that Offenders may not pass nor return to do Evil.

Sect. 27. Also it is enacted by the above mentioned Statute of 3 & 4 *W. & M.* 12. *That the Surveyors of the Highways shall make every Cartway leading to any Market-Town, eight Foot wide at the least, and as near as may be even and level.*

Sect. 28. And it is farther enacted and declared by the same Statute, *That no Horse-Causey, or Causey for Horses, travelling upon, or in any publick Highway, be less or under three Foot in breadth.*

Sect. 29. Also it is enacted by 8 & 9 *W.* 3. 15. *That the Justices of the Peace of any County, City, Riding, Division, Liberty, or Place, or the major Part of them, being five at the least, at their Quarter-Sessions, shall have Power to enlarge or widen any Highways in their respective Countries, Ridings, Divisions, Liberties, or Places, so that the Ground to be taken into the said Highways do not exceed eight Yards in breadth, and that the said Power do not extend to pull down any House, or to take away the Ground of any Garden, Orchard, Court, or Yard: And for the Satisfaction of the Persons who are Owners of, or may be interested in, the said Ground that shall be laid into the said Highways, the said Justices are by the said Statute impowered to impanel a Jury before them, and to administer an Oath to the said Jury, That they will assess such Damages to be given, and recompence to be made to the Owners and others interested in the said Ground, for their respective Interests, as they shall think reasonable, not exceeding five and twenty Years purchase for Lands so laid out, and likewise such Recompence as they shall think reasonable for the making of a new Ditch and Fence to that side of the Highway that shall be so enlarged, and also Satisfaction to any Person that may be otherwise injured by the enlarging of the said Highways: And upon Payment of the said Money so awarded, or leaving it in the Hands of the Clerk of the Peace of the respective County, for the Use of the Owner, or of others interested in the said Ground, the Interest of the said Persons shall be for ever divested out of them, and the Ground that shall be laid into any Highway by vertue of the said Act, shall be esteemed a publick Highway to all Intents and Purposes whatsoever; and the said Justices shall have Power to order one or more Assessment or Assessments to be made, levied, or collected, upon all and every the Inhabitants, Owners, or Occupiers of Lands, Houses, Tenements or Hereditaments, in their respective Parishes or Places that ought to repair the same, to such Person or Persons, and in such Manner as the said Justices at such Sessions shall direct and appoint; and the Money thereby raised shall be employed and accounted for, according to the Order and Direction of the said Justices, for and towards the purchasing of the Land to enlarge the said Highways, and for the making the said Ditches and Fences: And the said Assessments shall, by Order of the said Justices, be levied by the Overseers of the Highways, by Distress and Sale of the Goods of Persons so assessed, not paying the same within ten Days after demand, rendring the Overplus of the Value of the Goods so distrained to the Owner and Owners thereof (the necessary Charges being first deducted.)*

Sect. 30. But it is provided by the said Statute, *That no such Assessment or Assessments made in any one Year, for enlarging of Highways, shall exceed the Rate of Six-pence in the Pound of the yearly Income of any Lands, Houses, Tenements, and Hereditaments, nor the Rate of Six pence in the Pound for personal Estates.*

Sect.

Sect. 31. Also it is farther enacted by the said Statute, *That the Justices of Peace at their Quarter-Sessions, at the Request of any Person, for the putting in Execution the Powers contained in the said Act for the enlarging of Highways, shall issue out their Precepts to the Owner or Owners of Ground, or others interested in the same, that are to be laid into the said Highways, to appear at the next Quarter-Sessions, or shew Cause why the said Highways should not be enlarged.*

Sect. 32. And it is farther enacted, *That if any Order or Decree shall be made by the said Justices for the laying out of Ground for the enlarging of Highways, the Owners or Proprietors of the said Ground shall have free Liberty, within eight Months after such Order, to cut down any Wood or Timber growing upon the said Ground, or upon the Neglect thereof, that the same shall be sold by Order of the said Justices, and the Owners of such Wood or Timber shall receive the full of what shall be made thereof, the Charges being first deducted.*

Sect. 33. And it is farther enacted, *That any Person aggrieved by the Order or Decree of the said Justices may appeal to the Judges of Assize at the next Assize only to be held for the County where such Decree or Order shall be made, and any of the said Judges are by the said Statute impowered to examine, affirm, or reverse the said former Order and Decree, as in Judgment they shall think fit, and if affirmed, to award Costs against such Appellants for their Vexation and Delay, and to cause the same to be levied by Distress and Sale of the Appellant's Goods, rendring the Overplus to the said Appellants.*

Sect. 34. And it is farther enacted by the said Statute, *That where any common Highway shall be inclosed after a Writ of* Ad quod damnum *issued, and Inquisition thereupon taken, any Person aggrieved by such Inclosure, may make his Appeal to the Quarter-Sessions of the County to be held next after such Inquisition taken, which shall finally hear and determine such Appeal; and if no such Appeal be made, then the said Inquisition and Return entred and recorded by the Clerk of the Peace of such County at the Quarter-Sessions, shall be for ever afterwards binding to all Persons whatsoever.*

Sect. 35. As to the fourth general Head of this Chapter, *viz.* In what manner the Surveyors of the Highways shall be appointed, it is enacted by 3 & 4 *Will. & Mar.* 12. *That upon the six and twentieth Day of* December *in every Year, unless that Day be Sunday, and then on the Seven and twentieth, the Constables, Headboroughs, Tithingmen, Church-wardens, Surveyor or Surveyors of the Highways, and Inhabitants in every Parish, shall assemble together, and the major Part of them as are so assembled, shall make a List of the Names of a competent Number of the Inhabitants in their Parish, who have an Estate in Lands, Tenements, or Hereditaments, in their own Right, or their Wives, of the Value of ten Pounds by the Year, or a personal Estate of the Value of one hundred Pounds, or are Occupiers or Tenants of Houses, Lands, Tenements, or Hereditaments, of the yearly Value of thirty Pounds, if any such there be; or if there be no such Persons in the Parish, then the said List to be of the most sufficient Inhabitants of such Parish, and shall return such List unto two or more of the Justices of the Peace in or near the Division of the County in which their Parish lies, at a special Sessions to be held for that Purpose within the said Division, on the third Day of* January *next following, unless it shall happen on a Sunday, and then to be the fourth of the same Month, or within fifteen Days after; for which purpose the said Justices are required to hold a special Sessions at some Place within that Division where the Parish lies, and to give Notice of the Time and Place where they intend to hold the same, to the Constables, Headboroughs, Tithingmen, Church-wardens, and Surveyors of the Highways of every Parish within the said Division, at least ten Days before the Holding of the said Sessions;*

Sessions; and the said Justices shall then and there, out of the said Lists, according to their Discretion, and the Largeness of the Parish, by Warrant under their Hands and Seals, nominate and appoint one, two, or more, as they shall think fit, and approve of, being of like sufficiency as aforesaid, to be Surveyor or Surveyors of the Highways of every Parish within the Division, or for any Hamlet, Precinct, Liberty, Tithing or Town, of and in the same Division, for the Year ensuing; which Nomination and Appointment shall by the Constables, Headboroughs, Tithingmen, or Surveyors of the Highways for the Time being, or some of them, be notified to the Person or Persons so nominated, chosen, and appointed, by the said Justices within six Days after such Nomination, by serving him or them with the said Warrant or Warrants, or by leaving the same, or a true Copy thereof, at his or their Houses or usual Places of Abode; and from thenceforth the Person or Persons so nominated and appointed, shall be Surveyor or Surveyors of the Highways, for the Parish, Town, Village, Hamlet, Precinct, or Tithing, for which he shall have been so nominated, chosen, and appointed for the Year ensuing, and shall take upon him and them respectively and duly execute the said Office according to the former Laws made concerning the Highways, and the said Act; and if the said Persons so nominated and served with the said Warrant shall refuse, or neglect so to do, he or they so refusing and neglecting, shall forfeit the Sum of five Pounds, to be levied on his or their Goods and Chattels, by Distress and Sale of the same, by Warrant under the Hand and Seal of two or more Justices of the Peace of the same Division, or in Default thereof any neighbouring Justices of the Peace for the said County, which Warrant the said Justices are required to make upon Information of any one credible Witness upon Oath; the one Moiety of which Forfeiture shall go to him that shall inform, and the other Moiety for and towards the Repair of the Highways of the same Parish, rendring the Overplus to the Party whose Goods shall be distrained, the Charges of the Distress and Sale being first deducted; and in Case of such Neglect or Refusal, the said Justices are impowered to nominate and appoint some other fit Person or Persons to perform the said Office, who upon like Notice of such Nomination and Appointment, shall take upon him or them, and duly execute the said Office, and if he or they neglect or refuse so to do, shall forfeit the like Sum of five Pounds, to be levied and disposed of as aforesaid; and if the Constables, Headboroughs, Tithingmen, Church-wardens, and Surveyor or Surveyors of the Highways of any Parish, Town, Liberty or Precinct, or some of them, shall not return the said List of Names in such Manner, as in this Act is directed, every of them so neglecting, shall forfeit the Sum of twenty Shillings, to be levied in the Manner, and imployed to the Uses aforesaid.

Sect. 36. And it is farther enacted by the said Statute of 3 & 4 *W.* & M. 12. *That if any Justice of the Peace shall neglect or refuse to do what is required of him by the said Act, he shall forfeit five Pounds, one Moiety whereof shall go to the Person that shall sue for the same, the other Moiety to be employed in the Repairs of the Highways of the Parish where the Person who shall sue for the same inhabits, to be recovered in any of the King's Courts of Record, by Action of Debt,* &c.

Sect. 37. As to the fifth general Head of this Chapter, *viz.* In what Manner the Surveyors of the Highways ought to execute their Office, it is enacted by the said Statute of 3 & 4 *W.* & *M.* 12 *That every Surveyor of the Highways, appointed as by the said Act is directed, shall within fourteen Days next after his first Acceptance of the said Office, and so from Time to Time every four Months, during his being Surveyor, take a View of all the Roads, common Highways, Water-Courses, Bridges, Causeys, and Pavements within the Parish, Town, Village, Hamlet, Precinct, or Tithing, for which he is appointed Surveyor, that are to be repaired by the said Parish,* &c. *and shall make a Pre-*

By 1 Geo. c. 52. Sect. 2. Surveyors shall take such View oftener if required by Warrant from two Justices of ye Peace. And shall also take a view of the Nusances & Encroachments made upon them.

They shall also give a true Acct. in writing upon Oath, of ye State & Condition of all such Highways and especially of such Defects as want to be repaired & of ye Neglects of Labourers & of those who are oblig'd to find Labourers or Teams, to ye Justices at ye next special Sessions.

sentment upon Oath, *in what State and Condition he finds the same, to some Justices of the Peace of the same Division, if then resident there, otherwise to some neighbouring Justice of the Peace for the said County, and in Default thereof shall incur the Penalty aforesaid, as if he or they had refused or neglected to accept and execute the said Office, unless he shall have some reasonable Excuse for omitting the same, to be allowed of by two Justices of the Peace of the same Division,* &c. *And what Defaults and Annoyances they shall find in any of the said Highways,* &c. *they shall from Time to Time the next Sunday immediately after Sermon, give publick Notice of the same in the Parish-Church, and if the same shall not be removed, repaired, and amended within thirty Days after such Notice given, that then the said Surveyor or Surveyors shall within thirty Days remove, repair, and amend the same, and dispose of the same Annoyances, to and for the Repair of the said Highways; and the said Surveyor or Surveyors shall be re-imbursed what Charges and Expences they shall be at in so doing, by the Parties who should have done the same; and in Case the said Parties shall upon Demand refuse or neglect to pay the said Surveyors their said Charges, then the said Surveyors shall apply themselves to any Justice of the Peace within the Division of the County wherein such Highway is, and in Default thereof to any neighbouring Justice for the said County, and upon his or their making Oath before such Justice of the Notice to the Defaulter in manner aforesaid, the said Surveyors shall be repaid all such their Charges as shall be allowed to be reasonable by the said Justice, to be levied in Manner aforesaid.*

Sect. 38. Also it is enacted by the above mentioned Statute of 22 *Car.* 2. 12. Par. 12. *That the Surveyors shall appoint six Days for the providing Stones, Gravel, and other Materials, for the Amendment of, and for working in, the Highways, having respect to the Season of the Year, and the Weather, and giving Notice publickly some convenient Time before the several Days; at which Days all Persons liable to the said Work, shall attend and work accordingly: And the said Surveyors,* &c. *shall make Return of the Defaulters, within one Month after every Default made, to some neighbouring Justice of the Peace of the same County; and the said Justice shall present the same at the Quarter-Sessions of the Peace held next after such Return made unto him; and the Offenders shall respectively incur the same Forfeiture, Pains, and Penalties, inflicted and appointed by the Laws then in Force for the Amending of the Highways.*

Sect. 39. It is enacted by 5 *El.* 13. *That it shall be lawful for the Surveyors of the Highways, for the better Reparation and Amendment of the Ways within their several Parishes and limits where they shall be Supervisors (if it shall be so to them thought necessary,) to take or carry away of the rubbish or smallest broken Stones of any Quarry or Quarries lying and being within the Parish where they shall be Surveyors, without Licence, Controlment, or Impeachment of the Owner, so much as by their Discretions shall be deemed necessary for the Amendment of the said Ways: And that for the Fault of any Quarry not being within their said Parish or Limits, or in Default of Rubbish not to be found in any such Quarry, it shall be lawful for every such Surveyor, for the Use aforesaid, in the several Grounds of any Person or Persons being within the Parish and Limits where they shall be Surveyors, and nigh adjoining to the Way wherein such Reparations shall be thought necessary to be made, and wherein Gravel, Sand, or Cinders is likely to be found, to dig or cause to be digged for Gravel, Sand, or Cinders, and likewise to gather Stones lying upon any Lands or Grounds within the Parish, and meet to be used to such Purpose, and thereof to take and carry away so much as by the Discretion of the said Surveyors shall be thought necessary to be employed in the Amendment of the said Highways.*

Sect. 40. But it is provided by the said Statute, Par. 6. *That it shall not be lawful to any such Supervisor by vertue of the said Act to cause any rubbish to be digged out of any Quarry or Quarries, but only shall extend to such Rubbish as shall be found there ready digged by the Owner or Owners of the said Quarry or Quarries, or otherwise by his or their Licence and Commandment; nor shall not extend or give Authority to any Supervisor to dig or cause to be digged any Gravel, Sand, or Cinders in the House, Garden, Orchard, or Meadow of any Person, nor that it shall be lawful to any such Supervisor to cause any more Pits to be digged for Gravel in any several and inclosed Ground than one only; and that the same Pit or Hole so digged for Gravel as is aforesaid, shall not by any Way be in breadth or length, above ten Yards over at the most: And that every such Supervisor as shall cause any such Pit to be made and digged for Gravel, Sand, or Cinders, as is abovesaid, shall within one Month next after such Digging or Pit made, cause the same to be filled and stopped up with Earth, at the Costs and Charges of the Parishioners, upon pain to forfeit to the Owner or Owners of the Soil wherein any such Pit shall be made and digged, for every Default five Marks, to be recovered by Action of Debt,* &c.

Sect. 41. And it is farther enacted by the same Statute, Par. 6. *That every Supervisor shall within the Limits where he shall be Supervisor, have Authority to turn a Water-Course, or Spring of Water, being in any Highway, into any Ditch of the several Ground of any Person whatsoever next adjoining to the said Ways, in such Manner as by the said Supervisors shall be thought meetest.*

Sect. 42. Also it is enacted by the above mentioned Statute of 18 *El.* 10. Par. 7. *That where any Soil hath been cast into the common Highway, or common faring Way, that there is a Bank between the said Way and the Ditch, it shall be lawful for the said Surveyors,* &c. *to make Sluices or other Devices by their Discretions, to convey the Water out of the said Way into the Ditch; any Law, Right, Interest, or Usage, to the contrary notwithstanding.*

Sect. 43. And it is farther enacted by the said Statute of 3 & 4 *W. & M.* 12. *That it shall be lawful for the said Surveyors, where the Ditches and Drains already made are not sufficient to carry off the Water that lies upon the Highways, to make new Ditches and Drains in and through the Lands next adjoining to the said Highways, and keep them scoured, cleansed, and open, and come upon any of the said Lands with their Workmen for so doing.*

Sect. 44. Also it is enacted by the above mentioned Statute of 5 *El.* 13. Par. 8. *That every Surveyor for the Time being, shall within one Month next after Default or Offence made by any Person contrary to the Provision and true Meaning of either of the said Statutes of* 2 & 3 Ph. & Mar. 8. *or* 5 El. 13. *present every such Default or Offence, to the next Justice of Peace for the Time being, under pain of fourty Shillings.*

Sect. 45. And it is enacted by the said Statute of 22 *Car.* 2. 12. Par. 1. *That all Constables and Surveyors of the Highways, from Time to Time during their Continuance in their Offices, shall cause the several Acts of Parliament then in Force, touching the Repairing the Highways, to be put in Execution, and the Penalties thereby imposed to be levied and disposed of, as by the said several Acts is directed: And every Constable or Surveyor of the Highways refusing or neglecting to put the said Acts in Execution, or wilfully suffering any Waggons or Carts to pass thro' their respective Limits with more Cattle, or in other Manner than by Law is allowed, shall incur the like Penalty of fourty Shillings,* &c.

Sect. 46. And it is farther enacted by the said Statute of 3 & 4 *W. & M.* 12. *That the Justices of the Peace of every County shall in their respective Divisions once in four Months, hold a special Sessions, and shall thereunto summon*

summon all the Surveyors of the Highways within that Division to come before them, and shall give them a Charge to do their Duty, and declare to them what they are obliged to do by vertue of that or any former Act; after which the said Surveyors shall make a Presentment unto them upon Oath, of the State and Condition of the Highways within their respective Parishes, Towns, Hamlets, &c. *and what Offences and Neglects any are guilty of, contrary to the Meaning of any Statute made concerning the Highways, or any Thing relating thereunto: And before any such Surveyor shall go out of, or be discharged from his Office, he shall at some such special Sessions, give an Accompt upon Oath of all Money that hath come to his Hands, which ought to be employed in amending of the Highways, and how he hath disposed of the same; and in case any Moneys shall remain in his Hands, he shall deliver the same to the Surveyors of the Highways, that shall serve for the same Parish, Town, or Hamlet,* &c. *for the Year ensuing, and in case of Failure, to forfeit the double Value of what shall be judged to be in his Hands by the said Justices,* &c.

By 1. Geo. c. 52. sect. 10. If any Surveyor neglect his Duty in any thing required of him by that Act he shall forfeit for every Offence 40s.

Sect. 47. And it is enacted by 6 *Annæ* 29. *That if any Surveyor shall neglect to put either that or any former Law for repairing Highways in Execution, he shall forfeit five Pounds, to be levied by Distress,* &c. *by Warrant of one Justice of the Peace.*

As to the sixth general Head of this Chapter, *viz.* What shall be said to be a Nusance to the Highway, I shall consider:

1. What shall be said to be such a Nusance at Common Law.
2. What by Statute.

Kitch. 34, 35. *Sect.* 48. As to the first Point, there is no Doubt but that all Injuries whatsoever to any Highway, as by digging a Ditch, or making a Hedge overthwart it, or laying Logs of Timber in it, or by doing any other Act, which will render it less commodious to the King's People, are publick Nusances at Common Law.

2 Rol. Ab. 137. B. 265. c. 2. *Sect.* 49. Also it seemeth to be clear, That it is no excuse for one who layeth such Logs in the Highway, that he laid them only here and there, so that the People might have a Passage by Windings and Turnings through the Logs: Yet it is said to be no Nusance for the Inhabitants of a Town to unlade Billets, *&c.* in the Street before their Houses, by reason of the Necessity of the Case, unless they suffer them to continue there an unreasonable Time, after they are unloaded. (2 Rol. Ab. 137. B. 2, 3.)

Sect. 50. There is no Doubt but that it is a Nusance at Common Law to erect a new Gate in a Highway, as hath been more fully shewn in the precedent Chapter; also it seemeth clear, That it is a like Nusance to suffer the Ditches adjoining to a Highway to be foul, by reason whereof it is impaired, or to suffer the Boughs of Trees growing near the Highway, to hang over the Road in such a Manner as thereby to incommode the Passage. (8 H. 7. 5. a. Kitch. 34, 35. 8 H. 7. 5. b.)

Sect. 51. As to the second Point, *viz.* What shall be said to be a Nusance to the Highway by Statute, not only all the above mentioned Nusances, which are such at Common Law, are esteemed also Nusances by Statute, but there is also one particular Nusance which is made such by Statute, and doth not seem to be taken Notice of by Common Law, and that is the Drawing of a travelling Carriage with more than five Horses in length, the permitting whereof hath occasioned the carrying of such excessive Loads in such Carriage, that the Weight thereof hath in many Places rendred the Roads unpassable.

As to the seventh general Head of this Chapter, *viz.* How such Nusances are to be removed and punished, I shall consider the following Particulars:

1. In what Order Hedges and Ditches, adjoining to the Highway, ought to be kept.
2. How far all Trees and Bushes are to be removed from the Highway.
3. In what Manner all other Annoyances obstructing the Highway are to be removed.
4. How far all Persons are punishable for taking away Things made use of for the Benefit of the Highway.
5. How far they may be punished for drawing a Carriage with more than five Horses in length.

Sect. 52. As to the first Particular, *viz.* In what Order Hedges and Ditches, adjoining to the Highway, ought to be kept; it is said, That he who hath Lands next adjoining to a Highway, is bound of common Right to scowr his Ditches; but it is said, That he who hath Lands next adjoining to such Lands, is not bound by the Common Law so to do, without some special Prescription for that purpose; and perhaps it is the better Opinion, That he who hath Trees next adjoining to the Highway, and hanging over it to the Annoyance of the People, is bound by the Common Law to lop the same; and it seems clear, That any Person may justify the Lopping such Trees, so far as to avoid the Nusance.

8 H. 7. 5. a, b. Kitch. 34, 35. Dal. ca. 26. H. P. C. 144.

8 H. 7. 5. a, b.

Sect. 53. However it is enacted by 5 *El.* 13. Par. 7. *That the Hays, Fences, Dikes, or Hedges, next adjoining on either Side, to any High or Common faring Way, shall from Time to Time be diked, scowred, repaired, and kept low, by the Owner or Owners of the Ground or Soil, which shall be inclosed with the said Hays, Fences, Dikes, or Hedges aforesaid,* &c.

Sect. 54. And it is farther enacted by 18 *El.* 10. Par. 5. *That whoever shall not repair, ditch, or scowr, any Hays, Fences, Ditches, or Hedges adjoining to any Highway, or Common faring Way, according to the true Intent of the above-mentioned Statute of 5 El. 13. shall forfeit for every such Offence ten Shillings, to be levied by the Surveyors,* &c.

Sect. 55. And it is farther enacted by 3 & 4 *W. & M.* 12. *If any Owner or Occupier of Lands next adjoining to any Highway, not twenty Foot broad, shall neglect to cleanse or scowr their Ditches, Gutters and Drains, adjoining to the said Highways, or cause the Earth taken out thereof to be carried away, and lay sufficient Trunks, Tunnels, or Bridges, where any Cartways are, into the said Grounds, for the space of ten Days after Notice thereof given by a Surveyor,* &c. *every such Offender shall forfeit five Shillings,* &c.

By 1. Geo. c. 52. Sect. 8. If ye Neglect be for 30 days after Notice, Oath thereof being made by ye Surveyor before the Justices at ye Special Sessions, such Offender for every 8 yards of Ditching shall forfeit 2s 6d to be levied by Distress & Sale.

Sect. 56. And it is farther enacted by the said Statute of 3 & 4 *W. & M.* 12. *That the Possessors of the Land next adjoining to any Highways, where they are not twenty Foot broad, shall from Time to Time, and at all Times, keep their Hedges plasht, cut, or pruned, so as no Tree, Bush, or Shard shall stand or grow in such Highway, nor Bough or Branch be suffered to hang over the same, or any Part thereof; but the said Hedges shall be kept cut and pared right up from the Roots, and not permitted in any sort to spread into or hang over the Highway, or any Part thereof, to the end that there may be a free and clear Passage for the Travellers, and all sorts of Carriages loaden, without being any Ways prejudiced or obstructed by any Hedges, Trees, Boughs, or Branches whatsoever,*

soever, and that the Sun may freely shine into the said Ways to dry and amend the same.

Sect. 57. Also it is farther enacted by the above mentioned Statute of 18 *El.* 10. Par. 6. *That every Occupier of Lands adjoining to the Grounds adjoining to any Highway, or Common-faring Way, where any Ditching or Scowring should or ought to be, as aforesaid, shall from Time to Time, as Need shall require, ditch and scour in his Grounds so adjoining, whereby the Water conveyed from the said Highway,* &c. *over the Ground next adjoining, may have Passage over such next Ground so adjoining, on pain of Forfeiture for every Time so offending for every Rod not so ditched and scowred, twelve Pence.*

Sect. 58. As to the second Particular, *viz.* How far all Trees and Bushes are to be removed from the Highway, it appears from the above mentioned Statute of *Winchester*, Chapter 5. *That no small Tree or Bush, whereby a Man may lurk to do hurt, ought to be suffered to stand within two hundred Foot of either Side of a Highway leading from one Market-Town to another.*

Sect. 59. And it is farther enacted by the said Statute of 5 *El.* 13. Par. 7. *That all Trees and Bushes growing in the Highways, shall be cut down by the Owner or Owners of the Ground or Soil,* &c. And it is also enacted by the said Statute of 18 *El.* 10. Par. 7. *That whoever shall not cut down, or keep low, all Trees and Bushes, growing in or next adjoining to any the said Ways, according to the Intent of the above mentioned Statute of* 5 El. 13. *shall forfeit ten Shillings.*

Sect. 60. Also it is enacted by the said Statute of 3 & 4 *W. & M.* 12. *That no Tree, Bush, or Shrub shall be permitted to stand or grow in any Highway not full twenty Foot broad, but the same shall be cut down, grubbed up, and carried away by the Owner or Owners of the Land or Soil where the same shall stand or grow, within ten Days after Notice to him or them given by the said Surveyors, or any of them, on pain to forfeit for every neglect, five Shillings,* &c.

Sect. 61. As to the third Particular, *viz.* In what Manner all other Annoyances obstructing the Highway are to be removed; it seems clear, That by the Common Law any one may abate a Nusance to a Highway, and remove the Materials, but not convert them to his own Use, as hath more fully been shewn in the precedent Chapter; also it seemeth, That an Heir may be indicted for continuing an Incroachment, or other Nusance to a Highway, begun by his Ancestor, because such a Continuance thereof amounts in the Judgment of Law to a new Nusance.

1 Jon. 222.

Vide 4 Aff. 3. 17 Ed. 3 9. b. 2 Rol. Ab. 137. B 4. 142. K, L.

Sect. 62. But the Common Law not having been thought sufficiently to have provided against Mischiefs of that Kind, it was enacted by the above mentioned Statute of 18 *El.* 10. Par. 7. *That no Person, having any Ground adjoining to any Highway, or Common-faring-way, leading to any Market-Town, shall cast or scowr any Ditch, and throw or lay the Soil thereof into the Highway, and suffer it to lie there by the space of six Months, to the Annoyance of the said Highway, or Common-faring-way, upon pain of Forfeiture for every Load of Soil so cast into the Highway, or Common-faring-way, in Ditching or Scowring, twelve Pence: And that the Surveyors may make Sluices thro' Banks occasioned by the casting such Soil into any Highway,* &c.

1. Geo. c. 52. sect. 8. confines ye time to 48 days after notice given by ye Surveyor to remove it, & for not-removing to forfeit any sum not exceeding 5 li., nor under 20 s.

Sect. 63. And it is farther enacted by the above mentioned Statute of 3 & 4 *W. & M.* 12. *That no Person shall lay in any Highway, not twenty Foot broad, any Stone, Timber, Straw, Dung, or other Matter, whereby the same shall be any Ways obstructed or annoyed, on Pain to forfeit for every such Offence, five Shillings,* &c. And it is farther enacted, *That if any Timber, Stone, Hay, Straw, Stubble, or other Matter for the making of Dung, or on any other Pretence*

By ye same Law it is also enacted yt persons not removing Annoyances wth in 30 days after notice given, shall be liable to ye like forfeiture.

tence whatsoever, shall be laid in any such Highway as aforesaid, whereby the same shall be any Ways obstructed or annoyed, the Owners or Possessors of the Lands next adjoining to the same, shall clear the said Way by removing the said Timber, Stone, Hay, Straw, Dung, or other Matter, and have, take, and dispose of the same to his and their own Use; and if any such Owner or Occupier of Lands next adjoining to the said Highways, shall neglect to clear the said Ways of the said Nusances, he shall forfeit five Shillings, &c.

Sect. 64. As to the fourth Particular, *viz.* How far all Persons are punishable for taking away Things made Use of for the Benefit of Highways, it is enacted by the above mentioned Statute of 7 & 8 *W.* 3. 29, *That every Person who shall pull up, cut down, or remove, any Post, Block, great Stone, Bank of Earth, or other Security, which was set up, placed, and made, for securing any Horse, or Foot Causey, in a publick Highway, from Waggons, Wains, and Carts, shall upon Complaint to any Justice of the Peace or Division where such Offence shall be proved by the Oath of one credible Witness,* &c. *forfeit twenty Shillings, one Moiety thereof to the Surveyors,* &c. *and the other Moiety to him that shall discover the same.*

Sect. 65. As to the fifth Particular, *viz.* How far Persons may be punished for drawing a Carriage with more than five Horses in length, it is enacted by the above mentioned Statutes of 22 *Car.* 2. 12. Par. 6, 7. and 7 & 8 *Will.* 3. 29. and also by 6 *Anne* 29. and 9 *Anne* 18. and 1 *Georgii* 11. *That no travelling Waggon, Wain, Cart, or Carriage, wherein any Burthens, Goods and Wares shall be carried and drawn, (other than such Carts and Carriages as shall be imployed in or about Husbandry and Manuring of Land, and in carrying of Hay, Straw, Corn* [a] *unthrashed, Chalk, Timber for Shipping, Materials for Building, Stones of all Sorts, or such Ammunition or Artillery as should be for the Service of his Majesty, his Heirs or Successors,) shall at any one Time be drawn, or go in any common or publick Highway or Road, with above five Horses, Oxen, or Beasts in length, (except* [b] *only where such five Horses shall not be sufficient to draw such Cart or Waggon up any steep Hill, or out of any foul Place, in which Case it shall be lawful to join any Horses from another Cart or Waggon then travelling that Road, with the Consent of the Owner or Driver of such Cart or Waggon, to help such insufficient Horses up such steep Hill, or out of such foul Place,) on Pain of* [c] *forfeiting five Pounds, one Moiety to the Surveyor of the Highways of the Place where such Offence shall be committed, for the Repairs of the said Highways, and the other Moiety to him who shall discover, and prosecute for the same, to be levied by Distress of all, or any of the Horses, Oxen, or Beasts of any Person offending against the said Statutes, which* [d] *Distress may be made by any Person whatsoever,* (without any Warrant, as it seemeth from 9 *Anne* 18.) *And the Beasts so distrained are to be delivered forthwith to the Surveyor of the Highways, or other Parish Officer, of the Place where the Offence shall be committed; and if the said Penalty be not paid within three Days, the said Surveyor or other Parish Officer, may, by Warrant of one Justice of the Peace, sell the said Distress, and deliver the Money raised thereby to the said Justice, who is to distribute the Penalties in the Manner above directed, rendring the Overplus to the Owner, the Charges being first deducted; or if the Offender shall immediately pay the said Penalty to the Person who shall make such Distress, or to the Surveyor, or other Parish Officer, where the Offence shall be committed; then the Person so receiving the same, shall deliver it to the next Justice of the Peace, to be by him distributed, as aforesaid. Provided that if any Person shall refuse or neglect to carry any of the said Beasts by him so distrained, to the Surveyor, or other Parish Officer, as aforesaid, he shall forfeit twenty Pounds, to be levied of his Goods by Warrant of one Justice of the Peace,* &c. *And if any Surveyor, or other Parish Officer, shall refuse or neglect*

[a] 1 Geo. 11.

[b] 6 Annæ 29. 9 Annæ 18.

[c] 6 Annæ 29.

[d] 9 Annæ 18.

By 5 George 1. 12. No Waggon travelling for hire shall be drawn with more y^n 6 horses, either at length, or in Pairs, or sideways. And no Cart travelling for hire by more than three. On forfeiture of all the Horses above six in a Waggon, above 3 in a Cart, with all their Geers, to ye benefit of him who seizes. vid. ye Act for ye Exceptions.

neglect to deliver any Sum of Money, or Penalty by him received, to the said Justice, he shall forfeit twenty Pounds, to be levied, &c. *as aforesaid.*

Sect. 66. And it is farther enacted by the said Statute of 9 *Anne* 18. *That if any Person employed by any Carrier, or other Person subject to the Penalties mentioned in the said Act, shall drive, or assist in the Driving of any travelling Waggon,* &c. *with more than six Horses,* &c. *the Person so offending shall forfeit five Pounds, to be levied and disposed of in like Manner as the Forfeitures before mentioned are directed and appointed.*

Sect. 67. As to the eighth general Head of this Chapter, *viz.* In what Manner those who are charged with any Offence relating to the Highway are to be proceeded against, it is enacted by the above mentioned Statute of 2 & 3 *Ph. & Mar.* 8. *That the Steward of every Leet may enquire by the Oaths of the Suitors, of all Offences which shall be committed within the Leet, against every Article of the said Statute, and to assess such Fines and Amerciaments for the same, as shall be thought meet by the said Steward: And in Default of such Inquiry or Presentment, the Quarter-Sessions of every Place may inquire of the same Offences which shall be committed within the Limits of their Commission, and to assess such Fines as they, or two of them, whereof one to be of the* Quorum, *shall think meet: And the Steward of every Leet shall make Estreats indented of all the Fines, Forfeitures, and Amerciaments, for the Defaults presented before him, and shall deliver the one Part thereof sealed and signed by him to the Bailiff, and High Constable of every Hundred, Rape, Lathe, or Wapentake, wherein the Default shall be presented, and the other Part to the Constable and Church-wardens of the Parish wherein the Defaults were made; the same to be yearly delivered within six Weeks after the Feast of* Michaelmas: *And the Clerk of the Peace shall make the like Estreats indented of the Fines,* &c. *for the Defaults presented before the Justices of the Peace,* &c. *The which Estreats shall be sufficient Warrant to the said Bailiff, or chief Constable, to levy the said Fines,* &c. *by Way of Distress: And if no sufficient Distress can be found by the said Bailiff or Chief Constable; or if the said Offender shall obstinately refuse to pay the said Fine,* &c. *and do not pay the same within twenty Days after a lawful Demand of the same by the said Officer, he shall forfeit the double Sum that he should before have paid.*

Sect. 68. And it is farther enacted by the said Statute, *That every of the said Bailiffs and Head Constables, shall at least once every Year, betwixt the first Day of* March *and the last Day of* April, *make a true Account and Payment of all such Sums of Money, (to the Constable and Church-wardens of every Parish wherein the Offences were committed, or to two of them,) as he shall have collected upon any of the said Estreats, on Pain of, to forfeit for every Time he shall not so do, fourty Shillings.*

Sect. 69. And it is farther enacted by the said Statute, *That all Fines,* &c. *which shall be due for any Offence against the Purview thereof, shall be to the Church-wardens of every Parish wherein the Offences shall be committed, to be bestowed of the Highways in the said Parishes: And the said Church-wardens shall have Authority to call the said Bailiff and Head Constable to account, before the Justices of Peace, or two of them, whereof one to be of the* Quorum, *by Bill, Information, or otherwise: The which Justices shall have Authority to take the said Account, and to commit the said Bailiff and Head Constable to Prison till he shall pay all such Arrearages as shall be adjudged by the said Justices; and every of the said Bailiffs and Head Constables upon their Accounts shall have allowed for every Pound he shall collect and pay, Eight-pence for his own Pains, and Twelve-pence for the Fees of the Clerk of the Peace, or Steward of the Leet, for the Estreats indented of every several Parish that they shall deliver as is aforesaid;*

And

And the Successors of every Church-warden shall have the like Action of Account against their Predecessors, as is before appointed against the Bailiff.

Sect. 70. And it is enacted by the above mentioned Statute of 5 *El.* 13. Par. 8. *That every Surveyor shall within one Month after any Default or Offence against the said Statute of* 2 & 3 Ph. & Mar. 8. *or the said Statute of* 5 El. 13. *present every such Offence to the next Justice of Peace, on Pain to forfeit for every such Offence in such Sort, not by him presented, forty Shillings: And that every such Justice of Peace to whom any such Offence shall be so presented, shall certify the same Presentment at the next general County Sessions, on Pain to forfeit for not certifying of every such Presentment of every such Offence, five Pounds; and that the Justices of Peace of every County, where the said Offences shall be committed, may inquire thereof at their Quarter-Sessions, and assess such Fines for the same, as they or two of them, whereof one to be of the* Quorum, *shall think meet.*

Sect. 71. And it is farther enacted by the said Statute, Par. 9. *That every Justice of Peace may of his own proper Knowledge, in the open General-Sessions, make Presentment of any Highway not well and sufficiently repaired and amended, or of any other Default or Offence, contrary to either of the said Statutes of* 2 & 3 Ph. & Mar. 8. *or* 5 El. 18. *And that every Presentment made by any such Justice of Peace, upon his own Knowledge, as is aforesaid, shall be as good, and of the same Force, Strength, and Effect in the Law, as if the same had been presented, found, and adjudged, by the Oath of twelve Men: And that for every such Default so presented, as is aforesaid, the Justices of Peace of the said County shall immediately, at the said General-Sessions, have Authority to assess such Fines, as to them, or two of them, whereof the one to be of the* Quorum, *shall be thought meet: Saving to every Person that shall be touched by any such Presentment his lawful Traverse to the same Presentment, as he might have upon any Indictment of Trespass, or forcible Entry, by the Laws of this Realm, before the making of this Statute.*

Sect. 72. It hath been holden in the Exposition of this Clause, That the Party against whom such a Presentment shall be made, cannot take any Traverse to the Want of Repair of such Highway; but it is agreed, That he may plead that some other Person ought to repair the same, and Traverse his own Obligation to do it. Neither can I see upon what reason the former Opinion is grounded, that he cannot traverse the Want of Repair of such Highway, for since the Statute expresly *saves to every Person who shall be touched by any such Presentment, his lawful Traverse to the same, as he might have to an Indictment of Trespass or forcible Entry*; and since it seems clear, That every Defendant to any such Indictment may traverse the whole Matter alledged against him, as hath been shewn more at large, Chap. 64. Sect. 57. why may he not as well have the same Benefit in the present Case? And tho' the Record of a Justice of Peace acting by Force of any Statute, as a Judge, be not traversable; yet it seems hard by such a general Rule, to make any Record not traversable, which by the express Words of the Statute, which authorizes the making of it, is allowed to be traversable: It is true indeed, That a Presentment in a Court-Leet is not traversable, unless it touch the Party's Freehold; but I do not see why such a Presentment in Pursuance of this Statute should have the like Privilege since the Statute hath no mention of such Presentments in Courts-Leet, but gives the like Traverse as is allowed by Law upon any Indictment of Trespass, *&c.*

Kellew 34. Crom. 131. Dal. ca. 26.

Supra, ch. 64. Sect. 18.

5 H. 7. 4. a. Dy. 13. b.

Sect. 73. It is farther enacted by the said Statute of 5 *El.* 13. Par. 10. *That all such Fines,* &c. *to be assessed by the said General-Sessions, shall be estreated ed and levied in such Manner, and imployed to such Uses and Intents, as in the said Statute of* 2 & 3 Ph. & Mar. *are appointed.*

Sect. 74. And it is farther enacted by the above mentioned Statute of 18 *El.* 10. Par. 8. *That all Justices of Assize, Justices of Oyer and Terminer, and Justices of the Peace in their Sessions, and Stewards of Leets in their Leets, shall hear and determine every Offence, Matter, and Cause, that shall grow, come, or rise, by Reason of the said Statute.*

Sect. 75. Also it is enacted by the above mentioned Statute of 22 *Car.* 2. 12. Par. 9. *That if any Person shall fail in his respective Days Labour in every Year towards the Repairing of the Highways, or neglect to send his respective* Carriages, &c. *required by Law; the Surveyors ought to make Complaint thereof to the next Justices of the Peace, who ought upon Proof by Oath of one credible Witness, to levy by Distress and Sale of Goods,* &c. *for every Day-Labourer failing, as is aforesaid, one Shilling and six Pence; and for every Man and Horse, that shall make Default three Shillings; and for every Cart with two Men, ten Shillings, for every respective Day wherein they shall make Default; which Penalties shall be imployed towards the Repairs of the Highways,* &c.

Sect. 76. And it is farther enacted by the same Statute, Par. 10. and 3 & 4 *Will. & Mar.* 12. *That the Assessments to be made in pursuance of these Statutes, for the Repairs of the Highways, shall be levied by Distress and Sale of the Goods of every Person so assessed, not paying the same within ten Days after Demand, rendring the Overplus to the Owner, the necessary Charges being first deducted.*

Sect. 77. It will be needless to shew in this Place in what Manner the several Penalties for other Offences against the above mentioned Statutes concerning the Highways, are to be recovered, because the same may appear from the foregoing Part of this Chapter, wherein the several Clauses of the said Statutes relating to the said Offences are set forth.

Sect. 77. It is enacted by the said Statute of 22 *Car.* 2. 12. Par. 4. *That all Defects of Repairs of Causeys, Pavements, Highways or Bridges, shall be presented in the County only where such Causeys,* &c. *lie, and not elsewhere; and that no such Presentment or Indictment shall be removed by* Certiorari, *or otherwise, out of the said County, till such Indictment or Presentment be traversed, and Judgment thereupon given.*

Sect. 79. And it is farther enacted by the said Statute of 3 & 4 *W. & M.* 12. *That all Matters concerning Highways, Causeys, Pavements, and Bridges, mentioned in the said Act, shall be determined in the County where the same do lie, and not elsewhere; and that no Presentment, Indictment, or Order, made by vertue of the said Act, shall be removed by* Certiorari *out of the said County into any other Court.*

Sect. 80. Yet it hath been resolved, That if the Quarter-Sessions, under Pretence of the Jurisdiction given them by these Statutes, take upon them to do a Thing manifestly exceeding their Authority, as to make an Order on Surveyors of the Highways to make up their Accounts before a special Sessions, their Proceedings may be removed by *Certiorari* into the King's Bench, and there quashed; for the Quarter-Sessions have no manner of Power given them to intermeddle originally with such Accounts, but only by Way of Appeal.

Queen and Bramby. Mic. 10 Ann.

Sect. 81. It is enacted by the said Statute of 3 & 4 *W. & M.* 12. *That no Person shall be punished for any Offence against the said Acts, unless such Offender be prosecuted for the same within six Months after the Offence committed, and that no Person who shall be punished for any Offence by vertue of the said Act, shall be punished for the same Offence by vertue of any other Act, or Law whatsoever.*

Sect. 82. As to the ninth general Head of this Chapter, *viz.* In what manner Persons proceeded against for any of the above mentioned Offences may defend themselves; it is enacted by the said Statute of 3 & 4 *W.* & *M.* 10. *That if any Person shall find himself aggrieved with any Assessment or Rate, or other Act by the said Justices of Peace, the general Quarter-Sessions of the Peace, may take such Order therein, as to them shall be thought convenient, and the same to conclude and bind all the said Parties.*

Sect. 83. Also it seems to be implied in the Construction of these as well as of all other Penal Statutes, That no one ought to be convicted of any Offence against them, without having Notice of the Accusation made against him, and an Opportunity of defending himself. And therefore I shall take it for granted, that generally no one ought to be punished for any of the above mentioned Offences, without being called upon to answer for himself, and having Liberty to traverse the Matters alledged against him; it is true indeed, that it is generally holden, That no Traverse can be taken against a Presentment by a Justice of Peace of his own Knowledge, as to the Want of Repair; yet this Opinion seems justly questionable for the Reasons alledged in the sixty-eighth Section of this Chapter. Seventy second

Vide supra, Ch. 64. Sect 57, 58, 59.

Sect. 84. However it is certain, That in all other Cases, whoever is indicted or presented in any Court, except a Court-Leet, for any Offence relating to the Highways, may traverse the whole Matter alledged against him in such Indictment or Presentment; but it seemeth to be agreed, That he who is presented for such an Offence in a Court-Leet, can only traverse it so far as it concerns his Freehold, as by charging him with being bound to such Repairs in respect of the Tenure of his Lands, &c. for which purpose it is certain, that he may remove it by *Certiorari* into the King's Bench, and there traverse it; also there is no Doubt, but that after Conviction, or upon a Demurrer, or Confession, any one may take Exceptions to any such Indictment or Presentment in any Court for the Want of legal Form; but the Court in Discretion will very rarely suffer a Man to take such Exceptions, before such Conviction or Confession, without a Certificate that the Ways are in good Repair.

5 H. 7. 4. a. Dy. 14. Pl. 64. Finch 386.

And. 234. 1 Keb. 256, 291, 829. 2 Keb. 715, 728.

Sect. 85. Therefore for the better Understanding in what Cases it may be safe to demur to, or confess an Indictment or Presentment of this Kind, I shall lay down the following Rules concerning them.

Sect. 86. I. That it is [a] safest in every such Indictment to shew both the Place from which, and also the Place to which the Way supposed to be out of Repair doth lead, yet Exceptions for Want of such Certainty, have sometimes been [b] disallowed; however it seems certain, That there is no Necessity to shew [c] that a Highway leads to a Market-Town, because every Highway leads from Town to Town.

[a] 2 Rol. Ab. 81. Pl. 18. Palm 420. [b] 2 Keb. 715, 728. 3 Keb. 89, 644. 1 Brown 6. [c] Palm 389.

Sect. 87. II. That it is necessary [d] in every such Indictment expresly to shew in what Place the Nusance complained of was done, for which [e] Cause an Indictment for stopping a Way at *D.*, leading from *D.* to *C.*, is not good, for it is impossible that a Way leading from *D.* should be in *D.* and no other Place is alleged.

2 Ro Re. 412. [d] 3 Keb. 644. [e] 2 Rol. Ab. 81. Pl. 18.

Sect. 88. III. That every such Indictment ought also certainly to shew to what Part of the Highway the Nusance did extend, as by shewing how many Foot in length, and how many Foot in breadth it contained, or otherwise the Defendant will neither know of the Certainty of the Charge, against which he is to make his Defence, neither will the Court be able from the Record to judge of the Greatness of the Offence, in order to assess a Fine answerable thereunto; and upon this Ground it hath

Cro. Ja. 324

2 Rol Ab 80, Pl. 14. 81 Pl. 18.

hath been adjudged, That an Indictment for stopping a certain Part of the King's Way at *K.* is naught, for the uncertainty thereof: Also it hath been resolved, That the Place wherein such a Nusance is alledged, is not sufficiently ascertained in such an Indictment, by shewing that it contained so many Foot in length, and so many in breadth, by Estimation.

2 Rol. Ab. 81. Pl. 17.

Sect. 89. IV. That every such Indictment must shew, That the Way wherein a Nusance is alledged, is a common Highway; for which cause it hath been resolved, That an Indictment for a Nusance to a [a] Horseway, without adding that it was a Highway, is naught; and upon the same Ground it seemeth also, That an Indictment for a Nusance to a common Footway to the Church of *D.* for [b] all the Parishioners of *D.* is not good; yet it [c] seems, That if those last Words, *viz. For all the Parishioners of* D. had been omitted, such an Indictment might be maintained.

[a] Cro. El. 63.
[b] See 2 R. A. 83. C. 1 Vent. 208. Poph 206. 2 Keb. 728.
[c] 1 Vent. 208. 3 Keb. 28.

Sect. 90. V. That it is not safe in an Indictment against a common Person for not repairing a Highway, which he ought to have done in respect of the Tenure of certain Lands, barely to say that he was bound to repair it, *ratione Tenuræ Terræ*, without adding [d] *suæ*; also it is said, That in an Indictment against a [e] Bishop, *&c.* for not repairing a Highway, in respect of certain Lands, it ought to be shewn in what Capacity he ought to repair it, because otherwise it cannot be known in what Capacity the Process is to be awarded against him.

[d] Noy 93. 3 Keb. 855.
[e] 3 Keb. 58.

Sect. 91. VI. That in every such Indictment the Fact alledged against the Defendant must be expressed in such proper Terms, that it may clearly appear to the Court to have been a Nusance; and for this cause it hath been resolved, That a Presentment for diverting a Highway is not good, because a Highway cannot be diverted, but must always continue in the same Place where it was, howsoever it be obstructed, and a new Way made in another Place.

1 And. 234.

Poph. 206.

Sect. 92. But it hath been resolved, That an Indictment against a Man for stopping a Highway in his own Land is good, without laying the Offence done *Vi & Armis*. Also it is said, That a Presentment that a Highway in such a Place is decayed by the Default of the Inhabitants of such a Town is good without naming any Person in Certainty. But it hath been adjudged, That an Indictment against particular Persons must specially Charge them every one; for which Cause it hath been resolved, That an Indictment against several for not repairing their Streets, that they *& eorum uterque*, did not repair them, is not good.

2 R. A. 79. L.

2 R. A 81. Pl. 6, 7.

CHAP. LXXVII.

Of Nusances relating to Bridges.

AND now I am in the second Place to consider Nusances relating to Bridges in particular; for the better Understanding whereof, I shall examine:

1. How publick Bridges are to be repaired by the Common Law.
2. How by the Statute.

As to the firſt Point, I ſhall conſider,

1. In what Manner, and by whom ſuch Bridges are to be repaired by Common Law.
2. In what manner Perſons bound to ſuch Repairs are to be proceeded againſt.

Sect. 1. As to the firſt of theſe particulars, it ſeemeth to be clear, That thoſe who are bound to repair ſuch Bridges, muſt make them of ſuch height and ſtrength, as ſhall be anſwerable to the Courſe of the Water, whether it continue in the old Chanel, or make a new one; and that they are not puniſhable as Treſpaſſers, for entring on any adjoining Land, for ſuch Purpoſe, or for laying thereon the Materials requiſite for ſuch Repairs. Alſo it ſeemeth to be clearly [a] ſettled, That of common Right the Charge of repairing all common Bridges, lies upon the County wherein they are, unleſs Part thereof be within a Franchiſe; in which Caſe it is ſaid, That ſo much as is within the Franchiſe ſhall be repaired by thoſe of the Franchiſe. 43 Aſſ. Pl. 43. Dalt. ca. 14. [a] 2 Inſt. 701. H. P. C. 143. Cro. Ca. 365. 6 Mod. 307.

Sect. 2. Alſo it ſeemeth to be [b] certain, That ſuch Charge may be caſt upon a Corporation-aggregate, either in reſpect of a ſpecial Tenure of certain Lands, or in reſpect of a ſpecial Preſcription, and that it may be caſt upon any other Perſons by reaſon of ſuch a ſpecial Tenure, as hath been ſhewn more at large under the ſecond general Head of the precedent Chapter. But it is [c] ſaid, That a Man ſhall not be bound to repair a new Bridge built by himſelf, for the common Good: But that the County ſhall be bound to repair it, if it become of publick Convenience. [b] 2 Inſt. 700, 701. H. P. C. 143. Dal. ca. 14. [c] 2 Inſt. 701. 6 Mod. 307. See Cro. Ca. 365.

Sect. 3. As to the ſecond particular, *viz.* In what manner Perſons bound to ſuch Repairs, are to be proceeded againſt; it ſeemeth to be clear, That any particular Inhabitant or Inhabitants of a County, or Tenant or Tenants of Land charged to the Repairs of ſuch a Bridge, may be made Defendants to an Indictment for not repairing it, and be liable to pay the whole Fine aſſeſſed by the Court for the Default of ſuch Repairs, and ſhall be put to their Remedy at Law for a Contribution from thoſe who are bound to bear a proportionable Share in the Charge, for the Neceſſity of the Caſe requires the greateſt Expedition in Caſes of this Nature. [d] 1 Jon. 273. Poph. 192. 6 Mod. 307.

Sect. 4. Alſo it hath been [e] reſolved, That it is not ſufficient for the Defendants to an Indictment for not repairing a Bridge, to excuſe themſelves, by ſhewing either that they are not bound to repair the whole, or any Part of the Bridge, without ſhewing what other Perſon is bound to repair the ſame; and it is ſaid, That in ſuch Caſe the whole Charge ſhall be laid upon ſuch Defendants, by reaſon of their ill Plea. [e] 2 Levin. 112. Poph. 192. 43 Aſſ. Pl. 37. [f] 43 Aſſ. Pl. 37. Bro. Preſentment 22 and 29.

Sect. 5. It is ſaid, That where ſuch Defendants plead, that *A. B.* ought to repair the Bridge mentioned in the Indictment, and take a Traverſe to the Charge againſt themſelves, the Attorney-General in this ſpecial Caſe may take a Traverſe upon a Traverſe, and inſiſt that the Defendants are bound to the Repairs, and traverſe the Charge alledged againſt *A. B.* and that an Iſſue ought to be taken on ſuch ſecond Traverſe; and that the Attorney-General may afterwards ſurmiſe, that the Defendants are bound to repair it, and that the whole Matter ſhall be tried by an indifferent Jury, *&c.* 2 Levin. 112.

6 Mod. 307. *Sect.* 6. It seems that no Inhabitant of a County ought to be a Juror for the Trial of an Issue, whether the County be bound to such Repairs or not, but it is said that he may be a good Witness.

Sect. 7. As to the second Point, *viz.* In what manner such Bridges are to be repaired by the Statute, it is enacted by 22 *H.* 8. 5. *That the Justices of Peace in every Shire of this Realm, Franchise, City, or Borough, or four of them at the least, whereof one to be of the* Quorum, *may inquire, hear, and determine, in their General Sessions, of all manner of Annoyances of Bridges broken in the Highways, to the Damage of the King's liege People, and to make such Process and Pains upon every Presentment afore them, for the Reformation of the same, against such as owen to be charged for the making or amending of such Bridges, as the King's Justices of his Bench use commonly to do; or as it shall seem by their Discretions to be necessary and convenient for the speedy Amendment of such Bridges.*

Sect. 8. And it is farther enacted, Par 2 & 3. *That where it cannot be known and proved what Hundred, Riding, Wapentake, City, Borough, Town or Parish, nor what Person certain, or Body Politick, ought of Right to make such Bridges decayed, by reason whereof such decayed Bridges, for Lack of Knowledge of such as owen to make them, for the most Part lie long without any Amendment, to the great Annoyance of the King's Subjects, in every such Case, the said Bridges, if they be without City or Town corporate, shall be made by the Inhabitants of the Shire or Riding, within which the said Bridge decayed shall happen to be: And if it be within any City or Town-corporate, then by the Inhabitants of every such City or Town-corporate wherein such Bridges shall be. And if Part of any such Bridges so decayed happen to be in one Shire, Riding, City, or Town-corporate, and the other Part thereof in another Shire, Riding, City, or Town-corporate, or if Part be within the Limits of any City or Town-corporate, and Part without, or Part within one Riding, and Part within another, that then in every such Case the Inhabitants of the Shires, Ridings, Cities, or Towns-corporate, shall be charged and chargeable to amend, make, and repair such Part and Portion of such Bridges so decayed, as shall lie and be within the Limits of the Shire, Riding, City, or Town-corporate, wherein they be inhabited at the Time of the same Decays.*

Sect. 9. And it is farther enacted, Par. 4. *That in every such Case where* Vide 1 Keb. 422. *it cannot be known and proved what Persons, Lands, Tenements, and Bodies-Politick owen to make and repair such Bridges, that for speedy Reformation and Amending of such Bridges, the Justices of Peace within the Shires or Ridings wherein such decayed Bridges been out of Cities and Towns-corporate; and if it be within Cities, or Towns-corporate, then the Justices of Peace within every such City or Town-corporate, or four of the said Justices at the least, whereof one to be of the* Quorum, *within the Limits of their several Commissions and Authorities, may call before them the Constables of every Town and Parish, being within the Shire, Riding, City, or Town-corporate, as well within Liberty as without, wherein such Bridges or any Parcel thereof shall happen to be, or else two of the most honest Inhabitants within every such Town or Parish in the said Shire, Riding, City or Town-corporate, by the Discretion of the said Justices of Peace,* &c. *And at and upon the Appearance of such Constables or Inhabitants, the said Justices of Peace,* &c. *with the Assent of the said Constables or Inhabitants, may tax, and set every Inhabitant in any such City, Town or Parish, within the Limits of their Commissions and Authorities, to such reasonable Aid and Sum of Money, as they shall think by their Discretions convenient and sufficient for the repairing, re-edifying, and amending of such Bridges, and after such Taxation made, the said Justices shall cause the Names and Sums of every particular Person so by them taxed, to be written in a Roll indented. And shall also have Power and Authority to make two Collectors of every Hundred, for Collection of all such Sums of Money by them set and taxed, which Collectors receiving the one Part of the said Roll indented, under the Seals of the said Justices, shall have Power and Authority to collect and receive all the particular Sums of Money therein contained, and to distrain every such Inhabitant as shall be taxed, and refuse Payment thereof, in his Lands, Goods and Chattels, and to sell such Distress, and of the Sale thereof retain and perceive all the Money taxed, and the residue, (if the Distress be better,) to deliver to the Owner thereof: And that the same Justices, or four of them, within the Limits of their Commissions and Authorities, may also name and appoint two Surveyors, which shall see every such decayed Bridge repaired, and amended from Time to Time, as often as need shall require, to whose Hands the said Collectors shall pay the said Sums of Money, taxed, and by them received: And that the Collectors and Surveyors, and every of them, and their Executors and Administrators, and the Executors and Administrators of them, and every of them, from Time to Time, shall make a true Declaration and Accompt to the Justices of Peace of the Shire, Riding, City, or Town-corporate, wherein they shall be appointed Collectors or Surveyors, or to four of the same Justices, whereof one to be of the* Quorum, *of the Receipts, Payments, and expences of the said Sums of Money: And if they, or any of them refuse that to do, that then the same Justices of Peace, or four of them, from Time to Time by their Discretions, shall have Power and Authority to make Process against the said Collectors and Surveyors, and every of them, their Executors and Administrators, and the Executors and Administrators of every of them, by Attachments under their Seals, returnable at the General-Sessions of Peace: And if they appear, then to compel them to accompt as is aforesaid; or else if they or any of them refuse that to do, then to commit such of them as shall refuse, to ward, there to remain without Bail or Mainprise, till the said Declaration and Accompt be truly made.*

Sect. 10. And it is farther enacted, Par. 5. *That where any Bridge or Bridges lien in one Shire or Riding, and such Persons Inhabitants, Bodies-Politick, Lands or Tenements, which owen to be charged to the making and amending of such Bridges, lien and abiden in another Shire or Riding, or where such Bridges been within any City, or Town-corporate, and the Persons Inhabitants, Bodies-Politick, Lands, or Tenements, that owen to make or repair any such Bridges, lien and been out of the said Cities, and Towns-corporate, in every such Case the Justices of Peace of the Shire, City, or Town-corporate, within which such decayed Bridges, or any Part thereof, shall happen to be, shall have Power to inquire, hear, and determine all such Annoyances, being within the Limits of their Commissions and Authorities. And if the Annoyance be presented, then to make Process into every Shire within this Realm, against such as owen to make, or amend any such Bridges so presented before them to be decayed, to the Annoyance, and Let of the Passage of the King's Subjects, and to do further in every Behalf in every such Case, as they might do by Authority of the said Act, in Case that the Persons,* &c. *which owen to be charged to the amending or making of such Bridges,* &c. *were in the same Shire,* &c. *where such Annoyance shall happen to be. And that all Sheriffs, and Bailiffs of Liberties and Franchises, shall truly serve and execute such Process as shall come to their Hands from the said Justices of Peace, afore whom any Presentment shall be had for any such Annoyance, according to the Tenor and Effect of the said Process to them directed,* &c. *on Pain to make such Fine as shall be set on them by the Discretion of the said Justices.*

Sect. 11. But it is provided. Par. 6. *That nothing in the said Act contained shall be prejudicial to the Liberties of the five Ports, or Members of the same: And for Reformation of Annoyance of Bridges within the said Ports and Mem-*

Members: It is farther enacted, Par. 7. *That the Warden, Majors, and Bailiffs elected, and Jurates of the same Ports, and every of them, have Power and Authority to inquire, hear, and determine all manner of common Annoyances of Bridges within the same Ports and Members, and to make such Process, Pains, Taxations, and all other Things within the same Ports and Members, as the Justices of Peace may do in other Shires or Places out of the same Ports, by vertue of the said Act in every Behalf.*

Sect. 12. And it is farther enacted, Par. 8. *That the said Justices,* &c. *may allow such reasonable Costs and Charges to the said Surveyors and Collectors, as by their Discretion shall be thought convenient.*

Sect. 13. And it is farther enacted, Par. 9. *That such Part and Portion of the Highways in every Part of this Realm, as well within Franchise as without, as lie next adjoining to any Ends of any Bridges within this Realm, distant from any of the said Ends by the Space of three hundred Foot, be made, repaired, and amended, as often as need shall require; and that the Justices of Peace in every Shire of this Realm, Franchise, City, or Borough, or four of them at the least, whereof one to be of the* Quorum, *within the Limits of their Commissions and Authorities, may inquire, hear, and determine in their General-Sessions, all manner of Annoyances of and in such Highways, so being and lying next adjoining to any Ends of Bridges within this Realm, distant from any one of the Ends of such Bridges three hundred Foot, and to do in every Thing concerning the making, repairing, and amending such Highways,* &c. *in as large and ample Manner as they might and may do to and for the making, repairing, and amending of Bridges, by vertue of the said Act.*

In the Construction of this Statute the following Opinions have been holden:

2 Inst. 701. *Sect.* 14. I. That no private Bridges are within the Purview thereof, but only such as are common in the Highways, where all the King's liege People have, or may have Passage.

2 Inst. 701, 702. *Sect.* 15. II. That unless the Justices of Peace of a County, or Town, *&c.* be four in Number, and one of them of the *Quorum,* they have no manner of Jurisdiction by vertue of this Statute; but it is said, That the Justices of Peace of the County, in which such Town, being not a County of it self, and wanting such a Number of Justices, shall lie, may by vertue of the first Clause of the Statute, determine all Annoyances of Bridges within such Town, *&c.* if it be known what Persons in certain are bound to repair the same: But if it be not known, it seems that such Annoyances are left to the Remedy of the Common Law, because the
2 Inst. 704. Clause which in such Case authorizes the Justices of Peace to tax all the Inhabitants, seems expresly to confine the Power of taxing the Inhabitants of such Towns to their own Justices, *&c.*

Sect. 16. III. That all Housholders dwelling in any County, or
2 Inst. 703. Town, *&c.* whether they occupy any Lands or not; and also all Persons who have Lands in their own Possession or Manurance, whether they dwell in the same County, *&c.* or not; and also all Bodies-Politick, either residing in, or having Lands in their own Hands in a County, *&c.* are liable to be taxed as Inhabitants, within the Meaning of the Statute.

2 Inst. 704. Vide 1 Keb. 91. *Sect.* 17. IV. That the Taxation to be made in pursuance of the Statute ought to be assessed distinctly on each Inhabitant, and not on a whole Hundred, Parish, or Town in general.

Sect. 18. V. That all Privileges of Exemptions and Diſcharges from Contribution to the Repairs of decayed Bridges, whether ſuch Exemptions were originally derived from Charter or Act of Parliament, or any other Foundation whatſoever, are taken away by the expreſs Words of the Statute, *That the Juſtices,* &c. *ſhall tax and ſet every Inhabitant.*

2 Inſt. 704.

Sect. 19. It hath been queſtioned whether a Borough which hath no Bridge within its own Limits, be not liable to contribute to the Repairs of a County-Bridge.

1 Keb. 68.

CHAP. LXXVIII.

Of Nuſances relating to publick Houſes.

FOR the better Underſtanding of Nuſances relating to publick Houſes, I ſhall conſider:

1. In what Manner they are prevented and reſtrained by the Common Law.
2. In what Manner by the Statute.

Sect. 1. As to the firſt Point it ſeems to be agreed, That the Keeper of an Inn may by the Common Law be indicted and fined, as being guilty of a publick Nuſance, [a] if he uſually harbour Thieves, or Perſons of ſcandalous Reputation, or [b] ſuffer frequent Diſorders in his Houſe, or ſet [c] up a new Inn in a Place, where there is no manner of Need of one, to the Hindrance of other ancient and well governed Inns, or [d] keep it in a Place in Reſpect of its Situation, wholly unfit for ſuch a Purpoſe.

[a] Palm. 374. 2 Ro.Re. 345. [b] H.P.C. 146. Dalt. ca. 7. [cd] H.P.C. 146. Dalt. ca. 7. Palm. 374. 2 Ro. Re. 345.

Sect. 2. And it ſeems alſo to be clear, That if one who keeps a common Inn, refuſe either to receive a Traveller as a Gueſt into his Houſe, or to find him Victuals or [e] Lodging, upon his tendring him a reaſonable [f] Price for the ſame, he is not only liable to render [g] Damages for the Injury in an Action on the Caſe at the Suit of the Party grieved, but may alſo be [h] indicted and fined, at the Suit of the King; alſo it is ſaid, That he may be compelled by the Conſtable [i] of the Town to receive, and entertain ſuch a Perſon as his Gueſt, and that it is no way [k] material whether he have any ſign before his Door or not, if he make it his common Buſineſs to entertain Paſſengers.

[e] Palm. 374. 2 Ro.Re. 345. [f] 10 H. 7. 8. a. 39 H. 6. 18. b. 19 a. 9 Co. 87. b. [g] Dy. 158. Pl. 33. Bro. Ac. ſur cas. 76, 92. [h] H.P.C. 146. Dalt. ca. 7. [i] 5 E. 4. 2. b. Dalt. ca. 7. [k] Palm. 374. 2 Ro.Re. 345, 346.

Sect. 3. It ſeems to have been always clearly [l] agreed, That he who has an Inn by Preſcription may lawfully enlarge it upon the ſame Land which has been uſed with it, either by erecting new Buildings thereon, or turning Stables into Chambers of Entertainment, and that he ſhall have the ſame Privilege in ſuch new Parts of his Houſe as in any of the old.

[l] 2 Rol. A. 84. Pl. 8. 85 Pl. 9.

Sect. 4. Alſo it ſeems to be [m] ſettled at this Day, That any Perſon may lawfully ſet up a new Inn, unleſs it be inconvenient to the Publick in ſome of the Reſpects taken Notice of in the firſt Section, and that he has no Need of any Licence from the King for this Purpoſe, for the Keeping of an Inn is no Franchiſe, but a lawful Trade, open to every Subject.

[m] 2 Rol. A. 84. A. 2 Rol. Re. 345. Palm. 367, 374. 2 Keb. 506. 1 Bulſ. 109.

Sect. 5. As to the second Point, *viz.* In what manner Nusances of this Kind are prevented and restrained by Statute, it is enacted by 12 *Ed.* 2. 6. *That no Officer in City or in Borough, that by reason of his Office ought to keep Assizes of Wines and Victual, so long as he is attendant to that Office, shall not Merchandize for Wines nor Victuals, neither in Gross nor by Retail; and if any be convict of such Offence, the Merchandize shall be forfeited to the King, and the third Part thereof delivered to the Party that sued for the same,* &c.

Vide F. N. B. 172. Regist. 184.

Sect. 6. And it is farther enacted by 6 *Rich.* 2. 9. *That no Victualler shall have, exercise, or occupy any judicial Office in any Town, but only where no other Person sufficient may be found to have the same Office. In which Case yet the same Judge for the Time that he shall continue in the said Office, shall utterly omit and abstain himself and his from the Exercise of Victualling, upon pain of forfeiting his Victuals so sold.*

Sect. 7. And it is farther enacted by 3 *H.* 8. 8. *That as often as any Victualler chosen to bear any Office within any City, Borough, or Town-corporate, which for the Time that he shall stand and be in such Office, should have the assessing and Correction for selling of Victuals, that then two discreet and honest Persons of the same City, Borough, or Town-corporate, not being Victuallers, ne any of them being a Victualler, shall be chosen by the Commonalty of the same City, Borough, or Town-corporate, in like Form as the said Officer shall be chosen: Which two Persons, with the said Officer, shall be sworn truly to sess and set the Prices and Assizes of Victual there, for the Time that any such Victualler shall abide in the same Office: And that then it shall be lawful to all and every of the said Officers, after the same Victuals be set and sessed by the same Officer, and the said two Persons, or one of the same two Persons, the other being absent, to merchant and sell Wines, and all other Victual in gross, and at retail, during the Time that he shall be in any such Office, without any Thing therefore to forfeit: The said Statute, Act, and Ordinance of* 12 E. 2. *or any other Act or Acts, Ordinance, or Statute to the contrary made in any wise notwithstanding.*

Vide Cro. Ja. 609, 610. 2 Rol. Re. 225, 226.

Sect. 8. Also it is enacted by 21 *Jac.* 1. 21. *That all Hostlers or Innholders shall sell their Horse-bread, and their Hay, Oats, Beans, Pease, Provender, and also all Kind of Victual, both for Man and Beast, for reasonable gain, having Respect to the Prices for which they shall be sold in the Markets adjoining, without taking any Thing for Litter.* And it is farther enacted by the said Statute, *That every Hostler and Innkeeper dwelling in any Town or Village, being a Thorough-fare, and no City, Town-corporate, or Market-Town, wherein any common Baker, having been an Apprentice to the Trade for seven Years, is dwelling, may make within his House, Horse-bread sufficient, lawful, and of due Assize, according to the Price of Grain or Corn, any Thing in the said Statute contained to the contrary notwithstanding.* And it is farther enacted, *That if the Horse-bread, which any of the said Hostlers or Innholders shall make, be not sufficient, lawful, and of due Assize, according to the Price of Grain and Corn, as abovesaid; or that if any of them shall offend in any Thing contrary to this Act, the Justices of Assize, Justices of Oyer and Terminer, Justices of Peace in every Shire, Liberty, or Franchise within this Realm, Sheriffs in their Turns, and Stewards in their Leets, may inquire, hear, and determine, the said Offences of the said Hostlers and Innholders, who shall be fined for the first Offence, according to the Quantity of the Offence, and for the second Offence shall be imprisoned for one Month, and for the third shall stand upon the Pillory,* &c.

Sect. 9. And it is enacted by 5 & 6 Ed. 6. 25. *That the Justices of Peace within every Shire, City, Borough, Town-corporate, Franchise, or Liberty within this Realm, or two of them at the least, whereof one to be of the* Quorum, *shall have full Power and Authority within every Shire, City, &c. to remove, discharge, and put away common selling of Ale and Beer in common Ale-houses and Tippling-houses.*

Sect. 10. And it seems to have been the general Opinion in the Construction of this Clause, That an Alehouse-keeper suppressed in pursuance of it, cannot be afterwards licenced again but in open Sessions. Dal ca. 7. H. P. C. 14.

Sect. 11. And it is farther enacted by the said Statute of 5 & 6 *Ed.* 6. 25. Par. 1 & 6. *That none shall be admitted or suffered to keep any common Alehouse or Tippling-house, except in Fairs, but such as shall be allowed in the open Sessions, or by two Justices of Peace, whereof one to be of the* Quorum: *And that the said Justices shall take Bonds and Surety from Time to Time, by Recognizance, of such as shall be allowed to keep any common Alehouse or Tippling-house, as well for and against the using of unlawful Games, as also for the Maintenance of good Order within the same, as by their Discretion shall be thought necessary and convenient; for making of every which Recognizance the Parties bound shall pay but twelve Pence.*

Sect. 12. And it is farther enacted, Par. 2. *That the said Justices shall certify the same Recognizance at the next Quarter-Sessions of the same Shire, City, or Borough,* &c. *there to remain of Record before the Justices of Peace of the Shire,* &c. *upon Pain of forfeiting for every such Recognizance taken, and not certified, three Pounds six Shillings eight Pence.*

Sect. 13. And it is farther enacted, Par. 3. *That the Justices of Peace of every Shire, City, Borough,* &c. *may at their Quarter-Sessions by Presentment, Information, or otherwise by their Discretion, inquire of all such Persons as shall be allowed to keep any Alehouse or Tippling-house, and that be bound by Recognizance as is abovesaid, if any of them have done any Act whereby they have forfeited the same Recognizance: And the said Justices shall upon every such Presentment or Information, award Process against every such Person so presented or complained upon before them, to shew why he should not forfeit his Recognizance, and may also hear and determine the same by all such Ways and Means, as by their Discretion shall be thought good.*

Sect. 14. And it is farther enacted, Par. 4. *That if any Person, other than such as shall be allowed by the said Justices, shall obstinately, and upon his own Authority, take upon him to keep a common Alehouse or Tippling-house, or shall contrary to the Commandment of the said Justices, or two of them, use commonly selling of Ale and Beer, except in Fairs; that then the said Justices, or two of them, whereof one to be of the* Quorum, *shall for every such Offence commit every such Person so offending, to the common Gaol within the said Shire, City, Borough,* &c. *there to remain without Bail or Mainprize by the Space of three Days; and before his Deliverance the said Justices shall take his Recognizance with two Sureties, That he shall not keep any common Alehouse, Tippling-house, or use commonly selling of Ale or Beer, as by the Discretion of the said Justices shall seem convenient.*

Sect. 15. And it is farther enacted, Par. 5. *That the said Justices shall make Certificate of every such Recognizance and Offence, at the next Quarter-Sessions for the same Shire, City, Borough,* &c. *which Certificate shall be a sufficient Conviction of the same Offence; and the said Justices upon the said Certificate made, shall in open Sessions assess the Fine for every such Offence, at twenty Shillings.*

Sect. 16. And it is farther enacted by 3 *Car.* 3. 1. *That if any Person shall upon his own Authority, not being thereunto lawfully licenced, take upon him to keep a common Alehouse or Tippling-house, or use commonly selling of Ale, or Beer, Cyder, or Perry, except in Fairs, every such Person shall for every such Offence, forfeit twenty Shillings to the use of the Poor of the Parish where such Offence*

Offence shall be committed, the same Offence being viewed by any Mayor, Bailiff, or Justice of Peace, or other Head-Officer within the several Limits, or confessed by the Party so offending, or proved by the Oath of two Witnesses, to be taken before any Mayor, Bailiff, or other Head-Officer, or any Justice of Peace, being within the Limits of their Commission; the said Penalty to be levied by the Constables or Church-wardens of the Parish, or Parishes where the said Offence shall be committed, who shall be accountable therefore to the use of the Poor of the said Parish, by Way of Distress, to be taken and detained by Warrant or Precept from the said Mayor, Bailiff, or Justice, &c. *by whom the said Offence shall be viewed,* &c. *And for Default of Satisfaction within three Days next ensuing, the said Distress to be by the said Constables, or Church-wardens, apprized and sold, and the Overplus to be delivered to the Party offending; and if such Offender shall not have sufficient Goods and Chattels whereby the said twenty Shillings may be levied by Way of Distress, as aforesaid, or shall not pay the said Sum of twenty Shillings within six Days after such Conviction, as aforesaid, the said Mayor, Bailiff, or Justice,* &c. *before whom the said Offender shall be so convicted, shall commit such Offender to some Constable, or other inferior Officer of the City, Borough, or Parish,* &c. *where the Offence shall be committed, to be openly whipped, as the said Justice shall limit or appoint. And if such Constable,* &c. *shall neglect to execute the said Precept or Warrant, or to execute by himself, or some other, upon the Offender, the Punishment limited by the said Statute, the said Mayor,* &c. *may commit him to the common Gaol of the said County, City, or Town,* &c. *there to remain till the said Offender shall be by him or some other punished and whipped; or until the Person so neglecting shall have paid forty Shillings to the use of the Poor of the Parish, for his said Contempt. And if any such unlicenced Alehouse-keeper shall offend in any the Premisses the second Time, and be thereof convicted in Manner and Form aforesaid, the said Mayor, Bailiff, or Justice,* &c. *shall commit him to the House of Correction, there to remain for one Month, and be dealt withal as an idle, lewd, and disorderly Person: And if such Person shall again offend, and be convict as aforesaid, he shall be committed to the said House of Correction as aforesaid, there to remain till by the Order of the General-Sessions for the County, City, or Borough,* &c. *he shall be delivered from thence. Provided that such Offender as shall be punished by vertue of this Act, shall not be punished again for the same Offence by the above mentioned Statute of* 5 & 6 Ed. 6. *And that such Offender as shall be punished by vertue of the said Statute of* 5 & 6 Ed. 6. *shall not be punished again by vertue of this Act.*

Sect. 17. Also it is enacted by 1 Jac. 1. 9. and 4 Jac. 15. and 21 Jac. 1. 7. and 1 Car. 1. 4. *That if any Inn-keeper, Victualler, or Alehouse-keeper, or any keeper of a Tavern, or one who sells Wine in his House, and also keeps an Inn, or Victualling in his House, do permit or suffer any Person, whether such Person be an Inhabitant of the Place where such Inn,* &c. *shall be, or not, to continue drinking or tippling in any Inn or Victualling-house,* &c. *other than such as shall be invited by any Traveller, and shall accompany him only during his necessary Abode there, and other than Labouring and Handicraftsmen in Cities, and Towns-corporate, and Market-Towns, upon the usual working Days, for one Hour at Dinner-Time, to take their Diet in an Alehouse; and other than Labourers and Workmen, who for the following of their Work by the Day, or by the Great, in any City, Town-corporate, Market-Town, or Village, shall for the Time of their said continuing in Work there, sojourn, lodge, or victual in any Inn, Alehouse, or other Victualling-house, or other than for urgent and necessary Occasions, to be allowed by two Justices of Peace, That then every such Inn-keeper,* &c. *shall forfeit ten Shillings to the use of the Poor of the Parish where such Offence shall be committed; the same Offence being viewed and seen by any Mayor, Bailiff,*

 or

or Justice of Peace within their several Limits, or found by Verdict on a Trial upon an Indictment at Assizes, Sessions, or Court-Leet, or proved by the Oath of [a] *one Witness to be taken before any Mayor or Bailiff,* &c. *or any one Justice of the Peace, or by the voluntary Confession of any Offender, after which Confession the Oath of such Offender shall be taken, and be a sufficient Proof against any other offending at the same Time.* 4 Jac. 1. 5. [a] 21 Jac. 1. 7

Sect. 18. And it is farther enacted by the said Statute of 1 *Jac.* 1. 9. Par. 3. *That the said Penalty of ten Shillings shall be levied by the Constables or Church-wardens of the Parishes where the Offence shall be committed, by Way of Distress, and for Default of Satisfaction within six Days, the same to be presently appraised and sold, and the Surplusage to be delivered to the Party of whom the Distress was taken, and for Want of sufficient Distress the Party offending to be by the said Mayor,* &c. *committed to the common Gaol, there to remain till the said Penalty be paid. And if the said Constables or Church-wardens do neglect their Duty in levying the said Penalties, or in Default of Distress, do neglect to certify the same within twenty Days to the said Mayor,* &c. *every Person so offending shall forfeit fourty Shillings, to the Use of the Poor of the Parish where such Offence shall be committed, to be levied by Distress of Goods, by Warrant from any one Justice of Peace,* &c. *to be taken and detained six Days; within which, if Payment be not made, the same Goods to be appraised and sold,* &c.

Sect. 19. But it is provided by the said Statute of 1 *Jac.* 1. 9. *That the Punishment of such as shall offend against the same, within either of the two Universities, or the Precincts or Liberties of the same, shall be done upon the Offenders, and Justice ministred in this Behalf, according to the Intent of the said Law, by the Governours, Magistrates, Justices of the Peace, or other principal Officers of either of the said Universities, to whom in other Cases the Administration of Justice, and Correction and punishment of Offenders by the Laws of this Realm and their several Charters doth belong; and that no other within their Liberties, for any Matter concerning the said Law contrary to their several Charters, do intermeddle, and that all Penalties to be forfeited by vertue of the said Act, within either of the Universities or the Liberties or Precincts of the same, shall be levied by the Officers or Ministers of either of the said Universities, to be from Time to Time in that behalf appointed by the Vice-Chancellors thereof for the Time being respectively, and that all Powers and Authorities given by the said Act, shall by the Governours, Magistrates, and principal Officers abovesaid, of either of the said Universities, be duly executed within either of the said Universities,* &c.

Sect. 20. And it is farther enacted by 4 *Jac.* 1. 5. and 21 *Jac.* 1. 7. *That whoever shall be drunk, and within* [a] *six Months after such Offence, shall be convict thereof, either on an Indictment at Assizes or Sessions, or Court-Leet, or before* [b] *any Justice of Peace in any County, or any Justice of Peace, or other Head-Officer in any City or Town-corporate, upon View or Confession, or by Oath of one Witness, shall forfeit five Shillings, to be paid within one Week after Conviction, to the Church-wardens of the Parish where the Offence shall be committed,* &c. *And if such Person shall refuse or neglect to pay the said Forfeitures, the same shall be levied of his Goods by Warrant or Precept from the said Court, or Judge before whom the same Conviction shall be: And if the Offender be not able to pay the said Sum of five Shillings, he shall be committed to the Stocks for every Offence, there to remain six Hours; and if he shall be convicted a second Time of the like Offence, he shall be bound to the* [c] *good Behaviour, with two Sureties in a Recognizance of ten Pounds. And if any Constable or other inferior Officer of the Place where the Offence shall be committed,* &c. *do neglect the due Correction of the said Offender, or the due levying of the said Penalties, he shall forfeit ten Shillings to the Use of the Poor,* &c. *to be levied by Way of Distress, by Warrant from any Mayor,* &c.

[a] 4 Jac. 1. 5. Par. 11.
[b] 21 Jac. 1. 7. 4 Jac. 1. 5
[c] Par. 6.

Sect. 21. And it is farther enacted by the said Statute of 4 *Jac.* 1. 5. and 21 *Jac.* 1. 7. and 1 *Car.* 1. 4. *That if any Person shall remain or continue drinking or tippling in any Inn, Victualling-house, Alehouse, or* [a] *Tavern,* &c. *whether he be an* [b] *Inhabitant of the Place at the Time of such drinking, or not; and the same be viewed by any Mayor, or other Head-Officer, or Justice of Peace, or confessed by the Offender, or proved by one Witness in the Manner prescribed for the above mentioned Offence of suffering tippling in publick Houses, unless it be in such Cases as are excepted in the above mentioned Act relating to the said Offence of suffering tippling,* &c. *Every Person so offending, and being convict* [c] *within six Months, shall forfeit three Shillings and four Pence, to the use of the Poor of the Parish where the Offence shall be committed, to be levied by Way of Distress in such Manner as the above mentioned Forfeitures for Drunkenness are to be levied: And if any such Offender be not able to pay the said Forfeiture, any Mayor, Head Officer, Justice of Peace, or Court where any such Conviction shall be, may set him in the Stocks for four Hours.*

[a] 1 Ca. 1. 4.
[b] 21 Jac. 1. 7.
Supra Sect. 17.
[c] 4 Jac. 1. 5. Par. 11.
Supra Sect. 20.

Sect. 22. And it is farther enacted by the said Statute of 4 *Jac.* 1. 5. Par. 7. *That all Constables, Church-wardens, Headboroughs, Tithingmen, Ale-conners and Sidemen, shall in their several Oaths incident to their several Offices, be charged in like Sort to present the Offences contrary to the said Statute.*

Sect. 23. But it is provided by the same Statute, Par. 8. *That nothing therein contained shall in any wise abridge the Ecclesiastical Jurisdiction.* And it is farther provided, Par. 9. *That no Offender who hath once been punished for his Offence against any Article of the said Act, by any the Ways or Means before limited, shall be eftsoons punished for the same Offence by any other Ways or Means.*

Sect. 24. And it is farther provided, Par. 10. *That nothing in the said Act contained shall be prejudicial to either of the Universities, but that the Chancellor, Master, and Scholars,* &c. *may as fully use and enjoy all their Jurisdictions, Rights, Privileges and Charters, as before the said Statute they had or might have done, any Thing in the said Act to the contrary notwithstanding.*

Sect. 25. And it is enacted by 7 *Jac.* 1. 10. *That if any Person being an Alehouse-keeper, shall be lawfully convicted for any Offence committed against any of the Branches of either of the said Acts of* 1 Jac. 1. 9. *or* 4 Jac. 1. 5. *he shall for the space of three Years next ensuing the said Conviction, be utterly disabled to keep any such Alehouse.*

CHAP. LXXIX.

Of Monopolies.

FOR the better Understanding the Nature of the Offence of procuring or making use of a Monopoly, I shall consider:

1. What shall be said to be a Monopoly.
2. In what Manner the procuring or making use thereof, are restrained by the Common Law.
3. In what Manner by the Statute.

1 *Sect.*

Sect. 1. As to the first Point, it seemeth that a Monopoly is an Allowance by the King, to any Person or Persons, of the sole buying, selling, making, working, or using of any Thing, whereby any Person is sought to be restrained from any Freedom which he had before, or hindered from his lawful Trade. 3 Inst. 181. Noy 182.

As to the second Point it seemeth, That the procuring or making use of such Monopolies, is restrained by the Common Law two Ways,

1. By declaring all Grants of this Kind to be void.
2. By making those who procure or make use of them, liable to be fined.

Sect. 2. And first it is said, That all Grants of this Kind relating to any known Trade, are made void by the Common Law, as being against the Freedom of Trade, and discouraging Labour and Industry, and restraining Persons from getting an honest Livelihood by a lawful Employment, and putting it in the Power of particular Persons to set what Prices they please on a Commodity; all which are manifest Inconveniences to the Publick.

Sect. 3. And upon this Ground it hath been [a] resolved, That the King's Grant to any particular Corporation of the sole Importation of any Merchandize is void, whether such Merchandize be prohibited by Statute or not. [a] 2 Rol. Ab. 214. 3 Inst. 182. 2 Inst. 61.

Sect. 4. And for the like Reasons also it hath been resolved, That the Grant of the sole [b] Ingrossing of Wills and Inventories in a spiritual Court, or of the sole [c] making of Bills, Pleas and Writs in a Court of Law, to any particular Person, is void. [b] 2 Rol. Ab. 214. Pl. 4. [c] 1 Jones 231. 2 Rol. Ab. 214. Pl. 5.

Sect. 5. Also it hath been adjudged, That the King's Grant of the sole making, importing, and selling of [d] Playing-Cards, is void, notwithstanding the Pretence, That the Playing with them is a Matter meerly of Pleasure and Recreation, and often much abused, and therefore proper to be restrained; for since the Playing with them is in it self lawful and innocent, and the making of them an honest and laborious Trade, there is no more Reason why any Subject should be hindred from getting his Livelihood by this than by any other Imployment. [d] 11 Co. 84, 85, &c. Mo. 671. Pl. 919. Noy 173, &c. 2 Inst. 47.

Sect. 6. But it seemeth clear, That the King may for a reasonable Time make a good Grant to any one of the sole Use of any Art invented or first brought into the Realm by the Grantee, as shall be shewn more at large in the 14th, 15th, and 16th Sections of this Chapter. Also it seems to be the better Opinion, That the King may grant to particular Persons the sole Use of some particular Imployments, (as of Printing the Holy Scriptures and Law Books, *&c.*) whereof an unrestrained Liberty might be of dangerous Consequence. Noy 182, 183. 1 Mod. 256. 3 Keb. 792. 3 Mod. 75.

Sect. 7. Secondly, Also it is holden, That the procuring or making use of an unlawful Monopoly is farther restrained by the Common Law, by subjecting those who are guilty thereof to a Fine and Imprisonment for the Offence, as being *Malum in se*, and contrary to the ancient and fundamental Laws of the Kingdom; and it is said, That there are precedents of Prosecutions of this Kind in former Days, but I cannot find any modern Instance thereof. 3 Inst. 181. 2 Inst. 47, 62.

Sect. 8. As to the third Point, *viz.* In what Manner the procuring and making use of a Monopoly are restrained by the Statute, it is declared and enacted by 21 *Jac.* 1. 3. *That all Monopolies, and all Commissions, Grants, Licences, Charters and Letters Patents to any Person or Persons, Bodies Politick*

Politick or Corporate whatsoever, of or for the sole buying, selling, making, working, or using of any Thing within this Realm, or Wales, *or of any other Monopolies, and all Proclamations, Inhibitions, Restraints, Warrants of Assistance, and all other Matters whatsoever any Way tending to the instituting, strengthening, furthering, or countenancing of the same, or any of them, are altogether contrary to the Laws of this Realm, and so are and shall be utterly void, and of none Effect, and in no wise to be put in Ure or Execution.*

Sect. 9. And it is farther enacted, Par. 3. *That all Persons, Bodies Politick and Corporate whatsoever, shall be disabled, and uncapable to have, use, exercise, or put in Ure, any Monopoly, or any such Commission, Grant, or Licence,* &c. *or other Thing tending as aforesaid, or any Liberty, Power, or Faculty, grounded, or pretended to be grounded, upon them, or any of them.*

Sect. 10. And it is farther declared and enacted, Par. 2. *That all Monopolies, and all such Commissions, Grants and Licences,* &c. *and all other Things tending as aforesaid, and the Force and Validity of them, ought to be, and shall be examined, heard, tried, and determined, by and according to the Common Laws of this Realm, and not otherwise.*

3 Inst. 182, 183. *Sect.* 11. In the Construction of this Clause it hath been holden, That all Matters of this Kind ought to be tried in the Courts of Common Law only, and not at the Council-Table, or in the Court of Chancery, or any other Court of like Nature.

Sect. 12. And it is farther enacted, Par. 4. *That if any Person shall be hindred, grieved, disturbed, or disquieted, or his Goods or Chattels any Way seized, attached, distrained, taken, carried away or detained, by occasion or pretext of any Monopoly, or of any such Commission, Grant or Licence,* &c. *or other Matter or Thing tending as aforesaid, and will sue to be relieved in any of the Premisses, he shall have his Remedy for the same at the Common Law, by Action grounded on the said Statute, to be heard and determined in the King's Bench, Common Pleas or Exchequer, against the Party by whom he shall be so hindred or grieved,* &c. *or by whom his Goods shall be so seized or attached,* &c. *wherein every such Person which shall be so hindred or grieved,* &c. *or whose Goods shall be so seized or attached,* &c. *shall recover three Times so much as the Damages which he sustained by Means of such Hindrance,* &c. *and double Costs; and in such Suits, or for the staying or delaying thereof, no Essoin, Protection, Wager of Law, Aid Prayer, Privilege, Injunction, or Order of Restraint, shall be in any wise prayed, granted, admitted, or allowed, nor any more than one Imparlance: And if any Person shall after Notice that the Action depending is grounded upon the said Statute, cause or procure any Action at the Common Law grounded thereon to be stayed or delayed before Judgment, by Colour or Means of any Order, Warrant, Power or Authority, save only of the Court wherein such Action shall be depending, or after Judgment shall cause or procure the Execution to be stayed or delayed by Colour or Means of any Order, Warrant, Power or Authority, save only by Writ of Error or Attaint, that then the said Person or Persons so offending, shall incur a* Præmunire.

3 Inst. 183. *Sect.* 13. It is said, That the first Branch of this last Clause relating to the delaying of Causes of this Kind before Judgment, not only extendeth to the Privy-Council, Chancery, Exchequer-Chamber, and the like, but also to those who shall procure any Warrant from the King for such Purpose; and it is said, That the latter Branch, relating to the delaying of Execution after Judgment, extendeth even to the Judges of the Court where the Cause is depending.

Sect. 14. But it is provided, Par. 6. *That no Declaration in the Statute mentioned shall extend to any Letters Patents and Grants of Privilege for the Term of fourteen Years or under, of the sole working or making of any manner of*

3 *new*

new Manufactures within this Realm, to the true and first Inventor and Inventors of such Manufactures, which others, at the Time of making such Letters Patents and Grants, shall not use, so as also they be not contrary to the Law, nor mischievous to the State, by raising Prices of Commodities at home, or hurt of Trade, or generally inconvenient: The said fourteen Years to be accempted from the Date of the first Letters Patents, or Grant of such Privilege, but that the same shall be of such Force as they should be, if the said Act had never been made, and of none other.

Sect. 15. It hath been resolved, That no new Invention concerning the working of any Manufacture, is within the Meaning of this Exception, unless it be substantially new, and not barely an additional Improvement of an old one. 3 Inst. 184.

Sect. 16. Also it hath been holden, That a new Invention to do as much Work in a Day by an Engine, as formerly used to imploy many Hands, is not within the said Exception, because it is inconvenient in turning so many labouring Men to idleness. 3 Inst. 184.

Sect. 17. Also it seems clear, That no old Manufacture in use before, can be prohibited in any Grant of the sole Use of any such new Invention. 3 Inst. 184.

Sect. 18. And it is farther provided, Par. 7. *That nothing in the said Act contained shall extend to any Grant or Privilege, Power, or Authority whatsoever before the said Act, made, granted, allowed, or confirmed by any Act of Parliament, so long as the same shall continue in Force.*

Sect. 19. And it is farther provided, Par. 9. *That nothing in the said Act contained shall be in any wise prejudicial to any City, Borough, or Town-corporate within this Realm, concerning any Grants, Charters, or Letters Patents to them made, or concerning any Custom used by or within them, or unto any Corporations, Companies, or Fellowships of any Art, Trade, Occupation, or Mystery, or to any Companies or Societies of Merchants within this Realm, erected for the Maintenance, Enlargement, or ordering of any Trade of Merchandize: But that the same Charters, Customs, Corporations, &c. and their Liberties and Immunities shall be of such Force and Effect as they were before the making of the said Act, and of none other; any Thing before in the said Act contained to the contrary in any wise notwithstanding.*

Sect. 20. And it is farther provided, Sect. 10. *That nothing in the said Act contained shall extend to any Letters Patents, or Grants of Privilege concerning Printing; nor to any Commission, Grant, or Letters Patents concerning the digging, making, or compounding of Salt-Peter, or Gun-Powder; or the casting or making of Ordnance, or Shot for Ordnance: Nor to any Grant or Letters Patents of any Office erected before the making of the said Statute, and then in Being, and put in Execution, other than such Offices as had been decried by Proclamation: But that all such Grants, &c. shall be of the like Force and Effect, and no other, as if the said Act had never been made.*

Sect. 21. But it is enacted by 16 Car. 1. 21. *That it shall be lawful for all Persons, as well Strangers as natural born Subjects, to import any Quantities of Gun-Powder whatsoever, paying such Customs and Duties for the same as by Parliament shall be limited: And that it shall be lawful for all his Majesty's Subjects of this his Realm of* England, *to make and sell any Quantities of Gun-Powder at his Pleasure, and also to bring into this Kingdom any Quantities of Salt-Peter, Brimstone, or any other Materials for the making of Gun-Powder: And that if any Person shall put in Execution any Letters Patents, Proclamation, Edict, Act, Order, Warrant, Restraint, or other Inhibition whatsoever, whereby the Importation of Gun-Powder, Salt-Peter, Brimstone, or other the Materials afore mentioned, shall be any Ways prohibited or restrained, he shall incur a* Præmunire.

Sect. 22. And it is farther provided by the said Statute of 21 *Jac.* 1. 3. Par 11, 12. *That nothing in the said Act contained shall extend to any Commission or Grant, concerning the digging, compounding, or making of Allum, or Allum Mines,* &c. *nor concerning the Licencing of the Keeping of any Tavern, or selling of Wines, to be spent in the Mansion-House, or other Place, in the Tenure or Occupation of the Party selling the same, and a farther Provision is made in the latter Part of the Statute, for some particular Grants to particular Corporations and Persons, as* Newcastle *upon* Tine, &c.

Sect. 23. But it is said, That the said Clause relating to Allum was needless, because all such Mines belong of Course to the Persons in whose Grounds they are, and therefore no Privilege concerning them can be granted, but in the King's own Ground.

3 Inst. 185.

CHAP. LXXX.

Of Forestalling, Ingrossing and Regrating, and other Offences of like Nature.

FOR the better understanding the Nature of Forestalling, Ingrossing and Regrating, and other such like Offences, I shall consider,

1. How such Offences are treated by the Common Law.
2. How by Statute.

As to the first Point, I shall consider:

1. What is esteemed an Offence of this Kind by the Common Law.
2. How such Offence is punishable by the Common Law.

Sect. 1. As to the first of these Particulars it is said, That all Endeavours whatsoever to inhance the common Price of any Merchandize, and all kinds of Practices which have an apparent tendency thereto, whether by spreading false [a] Rumours, or by [b] buying Things in a Market before the accustomed Hour, or by buying and selling again the same Thing in the same [c] Market, or by any other such like Devices, are highly criminal at Common Law, and that all such Offences anciently came under the general Notion of Forestalling, which included all kinds of Offences of this Nature.

[a] 43 Ass. 38. 3 Inst. 195, 196. Bro. Indictment 40. Presentment 12.
[b] Crom. 80. b.
[c] Crom. 80. b.

Sect. 2. And surely there can be no attempt of this Kind, but must be look'd upon as a high Offence against the Publick, inasmuch as it so apparently tends to put a Check upon Trade, to the general Inconvenience of the People, by putting it out of their Power to supply themselves with a Commodity, without an unreasonable Expence, which often proves extremely oppressive to the poorer Sort, and cannot but give just Cause of Complaint to the richest.

3 Inst. 196. H. P. C. 152.

Sect. 3. But it hath been resolved, That any Merchant, whether he be a Subject or a Foreigner, bringing Victuals, or any other Merchandize into the Realm, may sell the same in Gross, but that no Person can lawfully buy within the Realm any Merchandize in Gross, and sell the same in Grofs again, becaufe by fuch Means the Price will be inhanfed, for the more Hands any Merchandize paffeth thro', the dearer it muft grow, becaufe every one will make his Profit of it: And if fuch Practices were allowable,* a rich Man might ingrofs into his Hands a whole Commodity, and then fell it at what Price he fhould think fit; which is of fuch dangerous Confequence, that the bare Ingroffing of a whole Commodity with an Intent to fell it at an unreafonable Price, is an Offence indictable at the Common Law, whether any Part thereof be fold by the Ingroffer, or not. Cro. Ca. 231, 232.

Sect. 4. And fo jealous is the Common Law of all Practices of this Kind, that it will not fuffer Corn to be fold in the Sheaf, perhaps for this Reafon, becaufe by fuch Means the Market is in Effect foreftalled. 3 Inft. 197. H. P. C. 152.

Sect. 5. As to the fecond Particular, *viz.* In what manner Offences of this Kind are punifhable by the Common Law; it is faid, That by an ancient Statute the Offender was to be grievoufly amerced for the firft Offence; for the fecond, to be condemned to the Pillory; for the third, to be imprifoned; and for the fourth, to be compelled to abjure the Vill: And there feems to be no doubt, but that at this Day all Offenders of this Kind are liable to a Fine and Imprifonment, anfwerable to the Heinoufnefs of their Offence, upon an Indictment at Common Law. 3 Inft. 195.

As to the fecond Point, *viz.* In what manner thefe Offences are treated by Statute, I fhall confider,

1. What particular Provifions have been made relating to this Matter.
2. What Cafes have been excepted out of thofe Provifions.
3. In what Manner the Offenders are to be proceeded againft.

The particular Provifions of this Nature are five-fold,

1. The obliging all Victuallers to fell at a reafonable Price.
2. The allowing all Foreigners free Liberty of importing and felling Victuals.
3. The giving the great Officers of State a Power to tax the Price of Victuals.
4. The prohibiting Confpiracies to raife the Price of Victuals.
5. The prohibiting all Foreftalling, Ingroffing, and Regrating.

Sect. 6. The firft of the faid Provifions depends upon 23 *Ed.* 3. 6. by which it is enacted, *That Butchers, Fifhmongers, Regrators, Hoftelers, Brewers, Bakers, Poulterers, and other Sellers of all Manner of Victual, fhall be bound to fell the fame for a reafonable Price, having refpect to the Price that fuch Victual fhall be fold at in the Places adjoining; fo that fuch Sellers have moderate Gains, reafonably to be required, according to the Diftance of the Place from whence the faid Victuals be carried, on pain to forfeit double the Value,* &c. *And the chief Officers of Towns are required to fee this Statute executed, on pain of paying the treble Value of the Thing fold,* &c.

Sect. 7. The fecond of the above mentioned Provifions depends upon 6 *R.* 2. 10. and 11 *Ric.* 2. 7. and 1 *H.* 4 17. by which it is enacted, *That all Manner of Aliens, being of the Amity of the King, coming into any Town of the Realm with Fifh, or other Victual, fhall be under the King's efpecial Protection, and may cut their Fifhes and Victuals in Pieces, and in part, or in all, at Retail, or in Grofs, as to them beft fhall feem, to fell and make their Profit,* &c. And it is farther enacted by 14 *H.* 6. 6. *That if any Man difturb any Alien to fell his Fifh in Grofs, or at Retail, in part or in whole, contrary to the*

above

above mentioned Ordinances, and thereof be duly attainted at the Suit of the King, or of the Party, he shall forfeit ten Pounds, &c.

Sect. 8. The Third of the above mentioned Provisions depends upon 25 *H.* 8. 2. by which it is enacted, *That to remedy the frequent Rise of the Price of Cheese, Butter, Capons, Hens, Chickens, and other necessary Victuals for Man's Sustenance, by ingrossing and regrating the same; the Lord Chancellor and other high Officers of State,* &c. *may upon Complaint of any inhansing of the Prices of such Victuals without Ground or reasonable Cause, in any Part of the King's Dominions, set and tax reasonable Prices of such Victuals: And that after Proclamation made of such Prices, all Farmers, Owners, Broggers, and all other Victuallers whatsoever, having or keeping any such Victuals to the Intent to sell, shall sell the same to such of the King's Subjects as will buy them at such Prices as shall be taxed by such Proclamation, under the Pains to be limited in the said Proclamation.*

Sect. 9. But it is provided, *That the Officers of Cities, Boroughs, or Towns-Corporate, and all other Persons having Authority to set Prices of such Victuals, may set such Prices in such Manner as if the said Act had not been made.*

Sect. 10. The Fourth of the above mentioned Provisions depends upon 2 & 3 *E.* 6. 15. by which it is enacted, *That if any Butchers, Brewers, Bakers, Poulterers, Cooks, Coster-mongers or Fruiterers, shall conspire, covenant, promise, or make any Oaths, that they shall not sell their Victuals but at certain Prices; or if any Artificers, Workmen, or Labourers, do conspire, covenant, or promise together, or make any Oaths, that they shall not make or do their Works, but at a certain Price or Rate, or shall enterprise, or take upon them to finish what another hath begun, or shall do but a certain Work in a Day, or shall not work but at certain Hours and Times, every such Person so conspiring,* &c. *shall forfeit for the first Offence ten Pounds, and if he pay not the same within six Days, shall suffer twenty Days Imprisonment; and for the second Offence shall forfeit twenty Pounds,* &c. *and for the Third, forty Pounds,* &c. *And if any such Conspiracy, Covenant, or Promise be made by any Society, Brotherhood, or Company, of any Craft, Mystery or Occupation, of the Victuallers above mentioned, with the Presence or Consent of the more Part of them, that then immediately upon such Act of Conspiracy,* &c. *over and besides the particular Punishment before appointed, their Corporation shall be dissolved; and that the said Offences shall be determined at the Assizes, Sessions of the Peace, or Court-Leet. See* 22 & 23 Car. 2. 15.

Sect. 11. The Fifth of the abovementioned Provisions depends chiefly upon 3 & 4 *E* 6. 21. and 5 & 6 *E* 6. 14. By the first of which Statutes it is enacted, *That no Person, not being an Inn-holder, or Victualler, selling by Retail in his House, shall buy to sell again any Butter or Cheese, unless he sell the same again by Retail, in open Shop, Fair, or Market, not selling more than a Weight of Cheese, or a Barrel of Butter at one Time.*

Sect. 12. And it is farther enacted by the said Statute of 5 & 6 *E.* 6. 14. which is the principal Statute relating to this Matter, *That whosoever shall buy or cause to be bought, any Merchandize, Victual, or any other Thing whatsoever, coming by Land or by Water toward any Market or Fair to be sold in the same, or coming toward any City, Port, Haven, Creek or Road of this Realm, or* Wales, *from any Parts beyond the Sea, to be sold, or make any Bargain, Contract, or Promise for the having or buying of the same, or any Part thereof so coming as is aforesaid, before the same shall be in the Market, Fair, City, or Port,* &c. *ready to be sold, or shall make any Motion by Word, Letter, Message, or otherwise, to any Person or Persons, for the inhansing of the Price, or dearer selling of any Thing above mentioned, or else disswade, move, or stir any one coming to the Market or Fair, to abstain or forbear to bring or convey any of the Things above rehearsed, to any Market, Fair, City, or Port,* &c. *to be sold, shall be deemed a Forestaller.*

Sect. 13. It hath been resolved, That an Indictment upon this Clause, charging the Defendant with meeting *J. S.* at such a Place near a certain Town, and there buying of him certain Goods, which he was about to sell in the Market of such Town, is insufficient, because it is not expresly said, that the Goods so bought were coming to the Market to be sold. 1 Rol. Re. 421.

Sect. 14. And it is farther enacted by the said Statute 5 & 6 *Ed.* 6. 14. Par. 2. *That whosoever shall by any Means regrate, obtain, or get into his Hands or Possession, in any Fair or Market, any Corn, Wine, Fish, Butter, Cheese, Candles, Tallow, Sheep, Lambs, Calves, Swine, Pigs, Geese, Capons, Hens, Chickens, Pidgeons, Conies, or other dead Victual whatsoever, that shall be brought to any Fair or Market to be sold, and do sell the same again in any Fair or Market holden in the same Place, or within four Miles thereof, shall be taken for a Regrator.*

Sect. 15. And it is farther enacted, Par. 3. *That whosoever shall engross or get into his Hands by buying, contracting or promise taking, other than by Demise, Grant, or Lease of Land or Tithe, any Corn growing in the Fields, or any other Corn or Grain, Butter, Cheese, Fish, or other dead Victuals whatsoever, within the Realm of* England, *to the Intent to sell the same again, shall be reputed an unlawful Ingrosser.*

In the Construction of the last mentioned Clause, the following Opinions have been holden.

Sect. 16. I. That [a] Salt is a Victual within the Meaning of it, not only because it is of Necessity of it self for the Food and Health of Man, but also because it seasoneth and maketh wholesome Beef, Pork, and other Victuals, in which Respect it seemeth it self to come under the Notion of Victual, and seemeth to be so understood by the Makers of 13 *El.* 25. as appears from Par. 21 of that Statute. [a] 3 Inst. 195. H. P. C. 152. Cro. Ca. 231.

Sect. 17. II. That such [b] Victual only as is necessary for the Food of Man is within the Purview of it; and therefore that Apples, and Cherries, and such like Fruits, are not within the Intent of it; for the Words are, *Corn, or Grain, Butter, Cheese, Fish, or other dead Victuals,* which Words are said to import the same as if it had been said, or other dead Victuals of like Quality: Also it is said, That there is not any Thing prohibited within the Statute, but what hath a Proviso, how in some Kind it might be bought; and therefore, since there is not any such Proviso for Apples, that they never were intended to be restrained: And agreeably hereto it hath been holden, That neither [c] Hops nor [d] Malt are within the Meaning of the Statute. [b] 3 Inst. 195. H. P. C. 152. Cro. Ca. 231. Owen 135. Cro. Ja. 214. [c] Cro. Ca. 231. [d] 3 Inst. 196. H. P. C 152. Con. Owen 135. 1 Rol. Re. 12.

Sect. 18. III. That the buying of Corn, with an Intent to make [e] Starch of it, and then to sell it, is not within the said Clause, because it is not bought to be sold again in the same Nature in which it was bought, but to be first altered by a Trade or Science, and then sold again. And for the like Reason it seemeth to be the better [f] Opinion, That the buying of Corn in order to make Meal of it, and then to sell it, is no way within the said Clause; and that the buying of [g] Barley with an Intent to make into Malt, and then to sell it, had no need of the Exception made for it in the said Statute. [e] Bridg. 5, 6. Owen 135. [f] Moore 595. Pl 810. Cro. Ca, 231. Con. Owen 135. [g] Cro. Ca 231. 3 Inst. 196. See Chap. 33. Sect 15 18.

Sect. 19. IV. That there is no Necessity in an Information or Indictment grounded on the said Clause for ingrossing any Victual therein mentioned, to say, [h] That the Defendant did not come by it by a Demise of Con Owen. 135. [h] 1 Jon. 157.

 Land,

Land, *&c.* but that the Defendant, if he have any such Matter to alledge in his Defence, may give it in Evidence.

1 Leon. 39. *Sect.* 20. V. That in every such Information, *&c.* the Words of the Statute must be precisely pursued, and therefore that it is not sufficient to say, That the Defendant bought so much Corn, *&c,* because the Words are, *shall ingross, or get into his Hands, by buying,* &c.

Sect. 21. And it is farther enacted by the said Statute of 5 *&* 6 *E.* 6. 14. Par. 4, 5, 6. *That whoever shall offend in any of the Things before recited, and be thereof duly convicted, shall for the first Offence, suffer Imprisonment for two Months, and forfeit the Value of the Goods so by him bought or had; and for the second Offence, shall suffer Imprisonment for one half Year, and forfeit the double Value of the Goods,* &c. *and for the third Offence, shall be set on the Pillory, and forfeit all his Goods, and be committed to Prison during the King's Pleasure.*

Sect. 22. And from hence it seems clearly to follow, That no Information for any of the above mentioned Offences against the said Statute, can be good, without shewing in certain the Quantity of the Thing in Relation to which the Defendant is supposed to have incurred the Penalty, not only because otherwise the Judgment to be given on such an Information can never be pleaded in Bar of any other, because it cannot appear that both of them were brought for the same Thing, but also because it cannot appear to the Court what Forfeiture the Defendant ought to incur, unless the Extent of the Offence, which is to be the Measure of it, be specially set forth: And for these Reasons it hath been adjudged, That an Information for ingrossing Corn, the Quantity whereof is expressed by the Word *Cumulus* only, is not good. 2 Bulst. 317. Cro. Ca. 381.

Sect. 23. And it is farther enacted by the said Statute of 5 *&* 6 *E.* 6. 14. Par. 8. *That if any Person having sufficient Corn and Grain, for the Provision of his own House, and sowing of his Grounds for one Year, do buy any Corn in any Fair or Market, for the Change of his Seed, and do not bring to the same Fair or Market the same Day, so much Corn as he shall fortune to buy for his Seed, and sell the same if he can, as the Price of Corn then goeth in the said Market or Fair, that then every such Person shall forfeit the double Value of the Corn so bought.*

Sect. 24. And it is farther enacted, Par. 9. *That if any Person shall buy any manner of Oxen, Ronts, Steers, Kine, Heifers, Calves, Sheep, Lambs, Goats, or Kids living, and sell the same again alive, unless he keep and feed the same five Weeks, he shall lose the double Value of the Cattle so bought and sold, one Moiety whereof shall be to the King, and the other Moiety to him that will sue for the same.*

The principal Exceptions out of the above mentioned Statutes seem to be reducible to the following Heads:

1. Such as relate to Corn.
2. Such as relate to Butter and Cheese, and dead Cattle.
3. Such as relate to Beer, Cyder, and Mum.
4. Such as relate to Fish.
5. Such as relate to Wine, Oil, Sugar, Salt, *&c.*
6. Such as relate to Fishmongers, Victuallers, Butchers, Poulterers, *&c.*
7. Such as relate to Badgers and Drovers.
8. Such as relate to Lessors, *&c.*
9. Such as relate to Shipping and Castles.
10. Such as relate to Towns-Corporate.

Sect. 25. As to the first of these Exceptions relating to Corn, it is enacted by the said Statute of 5 & 6 *Ed.* 6. 14. Par. 7. *That the buying of any such Barley, Bigge, or Oats, as any Person (not forestalling) shall buy to convert into Malt or Oat-meal in his own House, and so shall be converted indeed, shall not be taken to be within the said Act.*

Sect. 26. It seemeth to be the better Opinion, That if there had been no such Exception, yet the buying of Corn for such Purpose should not be intended to have been within the Purview of the Statute, as hath been more fully shewn already *Sect.* 18. But upon the Supposition, that such an Exception was necessary, it hath been holden that the buying of Corn and turning it into Malt in another's House, because it was of so great a Quantity, that it could not be malted in the Buyer's own House, is not within the Benefit of it. Owen 135.

Sect. 26. And it is farther enacted by 1 *W. & M.* Sess. 1. Ch 12. *That when Malt or Barley,* Winchester *Measure, shall be at twenty-four Shillings a Quarter or under; Rye at thirty-two Shillings a Quarter or under; and Wheat at forty-eight Shillings a Quarter or under, in any Port of* England *or* Wales; *every Person who shall put on Ship-board in* English *Shipping, the Master and two Thirds of his Mariners being their Majesties Subjects, any Sorts of the Corn aforesaid, from any such Ports where the Rates shall not then be higher than as aforesaid, with Intent to export the said Corn to Parts beyond the Seas, shall bring a Certificate in Writing under his Hand, containing the Quantity and Quality of the Corn so shipped, to the Persons appointed to collect the Customs within any such Port; and upon Proof of such Certificate by one or more credible Persons upon Oath, and upon Bond given by every such Exporter of two hundred Pounds for every hundred Tun of Corn so shipped, and so proportionably, that the said Corn (Dangers of Seas excepted) shall be exported beyond the Seas, and not landed again in* England, Wales, Guernsey, Jersey, *or* Berwick *on* Tweed, *shall receive from the said Persons appointed to receive the Customs, for every Quarter of Barley or Malt ground or unground, two Shillings and Six-pence; for every Quarter of Rye ground or unground, three Shillings and Six-pence; for every Quarter of Wheat ground or unground, five Shillings, without any Custom, Fee, or Reward to be paid for the same. And upon Certificate returned under the common Seal of the chief Magistrate in any Place beyond Sea, or under the Hands and Seals of two known* English *Merchants upon the Place, that such Corn was there landed, or upon Proof by credible Persons that such Corn was taken by Enemies, or perished at Sea, the Examination and Proof thereof being left to the Receivers of the Customs, the Bond shall be delivered up to be cancelled; and the Monies so paid, shall be allowed as paid to their Majesties.*

Vide 5 & 6 Ed. 6. 14. Par. 12, 13. 5 El. 5 Par. 26. 1 Ja. 1. 25. Par. 26. 21 Ja. 1. 28. 3 Ca. 1. 4. 12 Ca. 2. 4.

Sect. 28. As to the Second of the above mentioned Exceptions, relating to Butter and Cheese, and dead Cattle, it is enacted by 21 *Ja.* 1. 22. *That neither of the abovementioned Statutes of* 3 & 4 Ed. 6. 21. *or* 5 & 6 Ed. 6. 14. *or any other Provision whatsoever before that Statute made, concerning the Sale of Butter and Cheese in open Shop, Fair or Market, or the providing or buying of any Butter or Cheese, shall in any wise extend to any Cheesemonger, or Tallow-Chandler, free of the City of* London, *and having been brought up as an Apprentice seven Years, trading in Butter and Cheese, for such Butter and Cheese, and either of them, as he shall sell in* London, Westminster, *or* Southwark; *for the victualling of any Ship of the King or Subject, or to any Butter and Cheese, which he shall sell by any Quantities at one Time, and to one Person, not exceeding four Wey of Cheese, or four Barrels of Butter, without Fraud, so as he sell the same in open Shop, Fair, or Market: Provided that if the Justices of Peace of any County at their Quarter-Sessions, shall declare that such Traders shall forbear to buy any Butter or Cheese, for any Time within such County; that* then

Vide supra Sect. 11, 14, 15, &c.

then during the Time of such Restraint, the said Traders in Butter and Cheese, that shall buy any such Butter or Cheese, and sell the same again by retail, contrary to any of the said Acts, shall not be freed from the Penalties thereof.

Sect. 29. And it is farther enacted by 3 & 4 *W. & M.* 8. *That it shall be lawful for every Person, native or foreign, at any Time, to ship, lade, carry, and transport, or export, from any Place within* England, Wales, *or* Berwick *on* Tweed, *into any Part of the World in Amity with their Majesties, all Sorts of Beef, Pork, or Hogs-flesh, Butter, Cheese, or Candles, free from any Custom or Imposition whatsoever.*

Sect. 30. As to the Third of the above mentioned Exceptions, relating to Beer, Cyder, and Mum, it is enacted by 1 *Will. & Mar.* Sess. 1. Ch. 22. *That any Person may export any strong Ale, strong Beer, Cyder or Mum to be spent beyond the Seas, paying Custom for the same, at the Rate of one Shilling for every Tun, in such manner as is set forth more at large in the said Statute.*

Sect. 31. As to the Fourth of the above mentioned Exceptions relating to Fish, it is enacted by the said Statute of 5 & 6 *Ed.* 6. 14. Par. 7. *That the buying of any dried or salted Fish, Herring, or Sprats (not forestalled) and sold for reasonable Prices, shall not be deemed any Offence contrary to the said Act.*

Sect. 32. And it is farther enacted by the said Statute, Par. 15. *That it shall be lawful for any Subject, dwelling within one Mile of the main Sea, to buy all manner of Fish fresh or salted (not forestalling the same,) and to sell the same again at reasonable Prices.*

Sect. 33. And it is farther enacted by 5 *El.* 5. Par. 13. *That so much of the said Statute of* 5 & 6 Ed. 6. 14. *and so much of all other Statutes against Regrators, Ingrossers, and Forestallers, as concerneth the buying of Sea-fish unsalted, or Mud-Fish, to be taken and brought in any* English *Subjects Ships, Crayers, or other Vessel, into any Place of this Realm, shall be utterly repealed for so much of the said Fish, as any Buyer upon the Sea by way of Forestalling or Regrating, shall bring and discharge in any Port or Haven within this Realm.*

Sect. 34. As to the Fifth of the above mentioned Exceptions relating to Wine, Oil, Sugar, Salt, *&c.* the same Exception is made in Relation to Wine, Oil, and Salt by the said Statute of 5 *El.* 5. Par. 13. as is set forth in the last Section concerning Fish unsalted, or Mud-fish.

Sect. 35. And it is farther enacted by 13 *El.* 25. Par. 21. *That the said Statute of* 5 & 6 E. 6. 14. *is not meant to extend, nor shall extend to any Wines, Oils, Sugars, Spices, Currants, nor other foreign Victuals, brought into this Realm from beyond the Seas, Fish and Salt only excepted.*

Sect. 36. As to the Sixth of the above mentioned Exceptions relating to Fishmongers, Victuallers, Butchers, and Poulterers, &c. it is enacted by the said Statute of 5 & 6 *E.* 6. 14. *That the Buying of any Victual by any Fishmonger, Butcher, or Poulterer, as concern his own Faculty, Craft, or Mystery, otherwise than by Forestalling, which shall sell the same again upon reasonable Prices by Retail; or the buying of any Wine or other dead Victual above mentioned, being meet for Man's Sustenance, by any Innholder, or other Victualler, to sell the same by Retail within his House, or to any of his Neighbours for their Sustenance, for reasonable Prices, shall not be deemed any Offence contrary to the said Act.*

Cro Ca. 314. 1 Rol. Rep. 11, 12. 1 Jon. 320.

Sect. 37. Notwithstanding this Exception it hath been resolved, That any of the Persons therein mentioned may be indicted for ingrossing Victuals, with an Intent to sell them again against the Form of the Statute; for it shall be intended that they ingrossed, and did not sell at reasonable Prices.

Sect. 38. As to the Seventh of the above mentioned Exceptions relating to Badgers and Drovers, it is enacted by the said Statute of 5 & 6. *E.* 6. 14. Par. 7. *That the Buying of any Corn, Fish, Butter, or Cheese, by any such Badger, Lader, Kidder, or Carrier, that shall be allowed to that Office by three Justices of Peace,* &c. *which shall sell or deliver in open Fair or Market, or to any other Victualler, or to any other Person for the Provision of his House, all such Corn, Grain, Butter and Cheese, as any such Person shall buy, or cause to be bought, and that within one Month next after he shall so buy any such Corn, Grain, Butter or Cheese, so that the same shall be bought without Forestalling, shall not be deemed any Offence contrary to the said Statute.*

Sect. 39. And it is farther enacted by the same Statute, Par 12. *That it shall be lawful to every Person who shall be allowed by three Justices of Peace, to buy (otherwise than by Forestalling,) Corn, Grain, or Cattle, to be carried by Water from any Place within this Realm, or* Wales, *unto any other Place within the said Realm, or Dominions, if he shall without Fraud embark within forty Days next after he shall have bought the same, or taken Covenant, or Promise for the buying thereof, and with all possible Expedition transport the same to such Place as his Cocket shall declare, and there unlade the same, and bring a Certificate thereof from a Justice of Peace of the County, or Head-Officer of the Town, and Customer of the Port where it shall be unladen,* &c. *to be directed to the Customer and Comptroller of the Port where it shall be embarked.*

Sect. 40. And is farther enacted by the same Statute, Par. 16, 17. *That it shall be lawful for any Person known for a common Drover, being licenced by three Justices of Peace,* &c. *to buy Cattle in such Shires where Drovers had been wont in Times past, accustomably to buy Cattle at their free Liberty and Pleasure, and to sell the same as is aforesaid, at reasonable Prices, in common Fairs or Markets, distant from the Place where he shall buy the same forty Miles, so that the same Cattle be not bought by Way of Forestalling.*

Sect. 41. And it is farther enacted by 5 *El.* 12. and 13 *El.* 25. Par. 20. *That no Drover of Cattle, Badger, Lader, Kidder, Carrier, Buyer or Transporter of Corn or Grain, Butter and Cheese, shall be licenced to any such Office or Doing, in any County except* Westmorland, Cumberland, Lancaster, Chester *or* York, *but only in the General open Quarter-Sessions of the Peace, to be holden in the Shire where such Person so to be allowed shall dwell, and shall have dwelled three Years next before the* Teste *of his Licence: And that no Person be admitted to any of the said Offices or Doings, but such only as be or have been married Men, and shall be at the Time of such Licence to be granted, Housholders, and not Houshold-Servants, nor Retainers to any Person, and of the Age of thirty Years: And that such Licences shall be good only for one Year next after the Date, and shall bear Date of the Day and Place where the said Sessions shall be holden, and shall be signed and sealed with the proper Hands and Seals of three Justices present at the same Sessions, whereof one to be of the* Quorum, *on Pain that every Person that shall take any Licence contrary to this Ordinance, shall forfeit five Pounds, and that all Licences made otherwise than is before expressed, shall be void; and that the Justices in the said Sessions shall by their Discretion, take Bond and Surety from Time to Time, by Recognizance of such as shall be allowed a common Drover of Cattle, Badger, or Lader,* &c. *that they nor any of them shall by Colour of such Licence forestall, or engross, or otherwise do any Thing contrary to the Meaning of the said Statute of* 5 & 6 E. 6. 14. *And that every such Licence and Recognizance shall be made and written by the Clerk of the Peace of every County, where such Licence shall be granted, or by his Deputy, and by no other Person; and that every Person that shall have any such Licence, shall pay to the Clerk of the Peace,* &c. *Twelve-pence only; and for every such Recognizance, eight Pence; and for registering the same Licence and Recognizance, four*

Pence; and that the said Clerk, &c. *for the said Fee, shall keep one Register-Book, and therein shall register and write all the Names, Sirnames, and Dwelling-Places of such as shall be so licenced, with a brief Entry of the said Licence, and of the Day, Time, and Place where it shall be granted; and that the said Clerk of the Peace shall bring the said Book to every Sessions, that it may appear what Number of Licences have been granted. And that no Person shall by Authority of any such Licence, buy any Corn or Grain out of open Fair or Market to sell again, unless he shall be thereunto licenced by special and express Words contained in such Licence, on Pain to forfeit five Pounds for every Time that he shall do to the contrary, and that one Moiety of the Forfeitures afore rehearsed, shall be to the Queen, and the other to him who will sue for the same,* &c.

Sect. 42. As to the Eighth of the above mentioned Exceptions relating to Lessors, it is enacted by the said Statute of 5 & 6 *E.*6. 14. Par. 7. *That the taking of any Cattle, Corn, Grain, Butter, Cheese, or any other Thing in the said Statute mentioned, reserved without Fraud or Covin, upon any Lease for Life or Years, shall not be deemed any Offence contrary to the said Statute.*

Sect. 43. As to the Ninth of the above mentioned Exceptions relating to Shipping and Castles, it is farther enacted by the same Paragraph of the said Statute, *That the same shall not extend to Provision made, without Fraud, by any Person, of any of the Things in the said Statute mentioned, for the victualling of any Ship, Castle, or Fort, within the King's Dominions, without Forestalling, which shall be employed only to that Use and Purpose,* &c.

Sect. 44. As to the Tenth of the above mentioned Exceptions relating to Towns-Corporate, it is farther enacted by the same Paragraph, *That the said Statute shall not extend to any common Provision to be made without Fraud by any Person, of any of the Things in the said Statute mentioned for any City, Borough, or Town-corporate.*

Sect. 45. Also it is enacted by the said Statute of 5 *El.* 12. Par. 9. concerning the licencing of Badgers, &c. *That nothing therein contained shall in any wise extend to the Prejudice of the Liberty of any City or Town-corporate, but that every of them may assign and licence Purveyors, for the Provision of the same, as they might have done before.*

Sect. 46. As to the third Point, *viz.* in what manner Offenders of this Kind are to be proceeded against, it is enacted by the said Statutes of 5 & 6 E. 6. 14. Par. 10, 11. and 5 *El.* 12. Par. 8. *That the Justices of Peace of every County at their Quarter-Sessions may enquire, hear, and determine, all the Offences contrary to either of the said Acts within the County where any such Sessions shall be kept, by Inquisition, Presentment, Bill, or Information before them exhibited; and by Examination of two lawful Witnesses, or by any of the same Ways or Means, by their Discretion, and make Process thereupon, as though they were indicted before them by Inquisition, or by Verdict of twelve Men or more; and upon the Conviction of the Offender, by Information or Suit of any other than the King, to make Extracts of the Moiety of the Forfeitures to be levied to the King's Use,* &c. *and to award Execution of the other Moiety for the Complainant,* &c. *by* Fieri facias, *or* Capias, *as the King's Justices at* Westminster *use to do,* &c.

Sect. 47. Also it is provided by 31 *El.* 5. which ordains that Informations for Offences against Penal Statutes, must be laid in the proper County, *That nothing in the said Statute contained, shall extend to any Information or Declaration, for any Offence comprised in any Statute made against Ingrossing, Regrating, or Forestalling, where the Penalty or Forfeiture shall appear to be to the Value of twenty Pounds, or above, but that every such Offence may be laid in any County at the Pleasure of the Informer.*

CHAP.

CHAP. LXXXI.

Of Barratry.

IN treating of Barratry, I shall consider;

1. Who shall be said to be a Barrator.
2. In what Manner such an Offender is to be proceeded against.
3. To what Punishment he is liable.

Sect. 1. As to the first Point it seems, That a Barrator is a common Mover, Exciter, or Maintainer of Suits or Quarrels, either in Courts, or in the Country. Co. Lit. 368. 8 Co. 36. b.

Sect. 2. And it is said not to be material, whether the Courts wherein such Suits are commenced, be of Record or not, or whether such Quarrels in the Country relate to a disputed Title of Possessions or not: But that all kinds of Disturbances of the Peace, and the spreading of false Rumors and Calumnies, whereby Discord and Disquiet may grow among Neighbours, are as proper Instances of Barratry, as the taking or keeping the Possession of Lands in Controversy. Co. Lit. 368. 8 Co. 36. b.

Sect. 3. But it hath been holden, That a Man shall not be adjudged a Barrator in Respect of any Number of false Actions brought by him in his own Right; however if such Actions be merely groundless and vexatious without any manner of Colour, and brought only with a Design to oppress the Defendants, I do not see why a Man may not as properly be called a Barrator for bringing such Actions himself, as for stirring up others to bring them. 1 Rol. Abr. 355. A. 3 Mod. 98. 8 Co. 36. b.

Sect. 4. But it seems, That an Attorney is in no Danger of being judged guilty of an Act of Barratry, in respect of his maintaining another in a groundless Action, to the commencing whereof he was no way privy. 3 Mod. 97, 98.

Sect. 5. Also it seems clear, That no one can be a Barrator in respect of one Act only; for every Indictment for such Crime must charge the Defendant with being *Communis Barractator*. 8 Co. 36. b.

Sect. 6. It seems to have been holden, That a Feme-Covert cannot be indicted as a common Barrator, but this Opinion seems justly questionable; for since a Feme-Covert is as capable of exciting Quarrels, in the frequent Repetition whereof the Notion of Barratry seems to consist, as if she were sole, why should she not as properly be indictable for it? 2 Rol. Re. 39. See Chap. 1. Sect. 13.

Sect. 7. As to the second Point, *viz.* In what manner Offenders of this Kind are to be proceeded against, it is enacted by 34 *E.* 3. 1. *That in every County shall be assigned for the Keeping of the Peace one Lord, and with him three or four of the most worthy of the County,* &c. *and that they shall have Power to restrain Offenders, Rioters, and all other Barrators, and to pursue, arrest, take, and chastise them, according to their Trespass or Offence; and so cause them to be imprisoned and duly punished according to the Law and Customs of the Realm, and according to that which to them shall seem best to do by their Discretions and good Advisement,* &c.

Sect.

Yelv. 46. 2 Rol. Re. 151.

Sect. 8. It seemeth from these Words, That Justices of Peace (as such) have Cognizance of Barratry without any other Commission, *sed Quære*; for the contrary Opinion seems to have been holden in *Rolle*'s Reports.

1 Mod. 288. 1 Sid. 282. Cro. Ja. 526.

Sect. 9. However it seems clear, That no general Indictment of this Kind, charging the Defendant with being a common Oppressor, and Disturber of the Peace, and Stirrer up of Strife among Neighbours, is good, without adding the Words *communis Barractator*, which is a Term of Art appropriated by the Law to this Purpose.

[a] 2 Rol. Abr. 79. Pl. 3. 82. Pl. 6. Cro. Ja. 527. Cro. Ca. 340. 2 Keb. 409. 410. Cro. El. 148.

Sect. 10. [a] Also it seemeth to be certain, That an Indictment of Barratry concluding *contra formam Statuti*, is good, though no Statute be made directly against it, but only for the Punishment of it, supposing it an Offence at Common Law.

[b] 2 Keb 410. Cro. El. 195. Con. Latch 194. Palm. 450. 1 Rol Re 295.

Sect. 11. [b] Also it hath been holden, That an Indictment of this Kind may be good, without alledging the Offence at any certain Place; because from the Nature of the Thing, consisting in the Repetition of several Acts, it must be intended to have happened in several Places; for which Cause it is said, That a Trial ought to be by a Jury from the Body of the County.

[c] Cro. Ja. 527.

Sect. 12. [c] But it hath been resolved, That such an Indictment is not good, without concluding *contra Pacem, &c.* for this is an essential Part of it.

[d] 5 Mod. 18.

Sect. 13. [d] Also it seemeth to be settled Practice, not to suffer the Prosecutor to go on in the Trial of an Indictment of this Kind, without giving the Defendant a Note of the particular Matters, which he intends to prove against him; for otherwise it will be impossible to prepare a Defence against so general, and uncertain a Charge, which may be proved by such a Multiplicity of different Instances.

Hutton 104.

Sect. 14. As to the third Point, *viz.* In what manner Offenders of this Kind are to be punished; it is said, That if they be common Persons, they are to be fined and imprisoned, and bound to their good Behaviour; and if they be of any Profession relating to the Law, that they ought also to be farther punished, by being disabled to practise for the Future.

Vide 1 Dan. Abr 111 Pl 6, 115, Pl. 1.

CHAP. LXXXII.

Of Usury.

OFfences under the Degree of Capital more immediately against the Subject, not amounting to an actual Disturbance of the Peace, which may be committed by private Persons without any Relation to an Office, and which are neither infamous nor grosly scandalous, and more immediately affect the Interests of particular Persons, seem to be reducible to the following Heads:

1. Usury.
2. Maintenance.
3. The Offence of buying or selling pretended Titles.

In treating of Usury, I shall consider:

1. What it is.
2. How it is restrained by Common Law.
3. How by Statute.

Sect. 1. And first it seems, that Usury, in a strict Sense, is a Contract upon the Loan of Money to give the Lender a certain Profit for the Use of it, upon all Events, whether the Borrower make any Advantage of it, or the Lender suffer any Prejudice for the Want of it, or whether it be repaid on the Day appointed, or not. Wood's Inst. 171. 3 Inst. 151. See Bro. Usury 12.

Sect. 2. And in a larger Sense it seemeth, That all undue Advantages taken by a Lender against a Borrower come under the Notion of Usury, whether there were any Contract in relation thereto, or not; as where one in Possession of Land, made over to him for the Security of a certain Debt, retains his Possession after he hath receiv'd all that is due from the Profits of the Land. Gibs. 1070.

Sect. 3. But it hath been resolved, That an Agreement to pay double the Sum borrowed, or other Penalty on the Non-payment of the principal Debt at a certain Day, is not usurious, because it is in the Power of the Borrower wholly to discharge himself, by repaying the Principal according to the Bargain. 2 Ro. A. 801. Pl. 2, 3. 802. Pl. 4. 26 E. 3 71. a. 2 Inst. 89.

Sect. 4. As to the second Point, *viz.* How Usury is restrained by the [a] Common Law; it is said, That anciently it was holden to be absolutely unlawful for a Christian to take any kind of Usury, and that whosoever was guilty of it was liable to be punished by the Censures of the Church in his Life-time; and that if after Death any one was found to have been an Usurer while living, all his Chattels were forfeited to the King, and his Lands escheated to the Lord of the Fee. [a] 3 Inst. 151. 2 Rol. A. 800, 801. 2 Inst. 506, 507. Palm. 293, 294.

Sect. 5. Also it seemeth to have been the Opinion of the Makers of some late Acts of Parliament, as 5 *Ed.* 6. 20. 13 *El.* 8. Par. 5. and 21 *Jac.* 1. 17. Par. 5. That all kinds of Usury are contrary to good Conscience.

Sect. 6. [b] And agreeably hereto it seemeth formerly to have been the general Opinion, That no Action could be maintained on any Promise to pay any Kind of Use for the Forbearance of Money, because that all such Contracts were thought to be unlawful, and consequently void. [b] 2 Ro A. 801. 26 Ed. 1. 71. a. 1 Rol. Ab. 18. Pl. 14, 15. 2 Rol. Re. 239, 240, 469. Palm. 293.

Sect. 7. But it seems to be generally agreed at this Day, [c] That the Taking of reasonable Interest for the Use of Money is in it self lawful, and consequently that a Covenant or Promise to pay it, in Consideration of the Forbearance of a Debt, will maintain an Action: For why should not one who has an Estate in Money be as well allowed to make a fair Profit of it, as another who has an Estate in Land? And what reason can there be, that the Lender of Money should not as well make an Advantage of it as the Borrower? Neither do the Passages in the *Mosaical* Law, which are generally urged against the Lawfulness of all Usury, if fully considered, so much prove the Unlawfulness, as the Lawfulness of it; for if all Usury were against the moral Law, why should it not be as much so in respect of Foreigners, of whom the *Jews* were expresly allowed to take it, as in respect of those of the same Nation, of whom alone they were forbidden to receive it? From whence it seems clearly to follow, That the Prohibition of it to that People was merely political, and consequently doth not extend to any other Nation. [c] 1 Rol. A. 15. Pl. 35. 2 Rol. A. 802. Pl. 4. Winch 114, 120. Cro. Ca. 273. 1 Vent. 198. Exod. 22. ver. 25. Levit. 25. ver. 36, 37. Deuter. 23. ver 19, 20.

Sect. 8. As to the Third Point, *viz.* How Usury is restrained by Statute, it is enacted by 12 *Anna* 16. *That no Person whatsoever, from and after the nine and twentieth Day of* September, *in the Year of our Lord*, 1714. *upon any Contract which shall be made from and after the said nine and twentieth Day of* September, *take, directly or indirectly, for Loan of any Money, Wares, Merchandize, or other Commodities whatsoever, above the Value of five Pounds, for the Forbearance of one hundred Pounds for a Year, and so after that Rate for a greater or lesser Sum, or for a longer or shorter Time; and that all Bonds, Contracts, and Assurances whatsoever, made after the Time aforesaid, for Payment of any Principal, or Money to be lent, or covenanted to be performed upon or for any Usury, whereupon or whereby there shall be reserved or taken above the Rate of five Pounds in the Hundred, as aforesaid, shall be utterly void, and that all and every Person or Persons whatsoever, which shall after the Time aforesaid, upon any Contract to be made after the said nine and twentieth Day of* September, *take, accept, and receive, by Way or Means of any corrupt Bargain, Loan, Exchange, Chevizance, Shift, or Interest of any Wares, Merchandize, or other Thing or Things whatsoever, or by any deceitful Way or Means, or by any Covin, Engine, or deceitful Conveyance, for the forbearing or giving Day of Payment for one whole Year, of and for their Money or other Thing, above the Sum of five Pounds for the forbearing of one hundred Pounds for a Year, and so after that Rate for a greater or lesser Sum, or for a* [a] *longer or shorter Term, shall forfeit and lose for every such Offence the treble Value of the Money, Wares, Merchandize, and other Things so lent, bargained, exchanged, or shifted.*

[a] Vide Cro. Ja. 25. Mo. 644. Pl. 819. Noy 41. Cro. Ca. 283.

Sect. 9. And it is farther enacted by the said Statute, *That every Scrivener, Broker, Solicitor, and Driver of Bargains for Contracts, who shall, after the said nine and twentieth Day of* September, *take or receive, directly or indirectly, any Sum or Sums of Money, or other Reward or Thing, for Brokage, Soliciting, Driving or Procuring the Loan, or forbearing of any Sum or Sums of Money, over and above the Rate or Value of five Shillings for the Loan, or forbearing of one hundred Pounds, for a Year, and so rateably; or above twelve Pence, over and above the Stamp-Duties, for making or renewing of the Bond or Bill for Loan, or forbearing thereof, or for any Counterbond or Bill concerning the same, shall forfeit for every such Offence twenty Pounds, with Costs of Suit, and suffer Imprisonment for half a Year, the one Moiety of all which Forfeitures shall be to the Queen, the other to him that will sue for the same, in the same County where the several Offences are committed*, &c.

The Expositions which were made of the former Statutes of Usury being equally applicable to this which is penned almost in the very same Words, I shall take Notice of the Principal of them; as,

Dalis. 12 Con. Raym. 197.

Sect 10. I. That a Contract made before the Statute is no Way within the Meaning of it, and therefore that it is still lawful to receive six *per Cent.* in respect of any such Contract.

Sect. 11. II. That a Bond made, *bonâ fide*, to secure a just Debt payable with lawful Interest, shall not be avoided by reason of a corrupt Agreement between others, to which the Obligee was no way Privy: As where *A.* being indebted to *B.* in 100 *l.* agrees to give him 30 *l.* for the Forbearance of that 100 *l.* for a Year, and gives him a Bond of 60 *l.* for Payment of the 30 *l.* and for the Payment of the 100 *l.* enters into a Bond of 200 *l.* together with *B.* for the Payment of a true Debt of 100 *l.* due from *B.* to C.

2 And. 121. Moore 752. Pl. 1035. Cro Ja. 32, 33. Yel. 47.

Sect. 12. III. That the Receipt of higher Interest than is allowed by the Statute, by vertue of an Agreement subsequent to the first Contract, does not avoid an Assurance fairly made, and agreeable to the Statute, but only subjects the Party to the Forfeiture of the treble Value, for the

1 Mod. 69. 3 Keb 142. 2 Mod. 307. 1 Saund. 294. Raym. 196. 2 Keb. 525, 690. 1 Bulf 17.

Words are, *That all Assurances for the Payment of any Principal, &c. whereupon or whereby there shall be reserved or taken above the Rate of 5 l. in the Hundred, &c shall be utterly void.*

Sect. 13. IV. That in an Assurance for the Payment of fifty Shillings for the Use of 100 *l.* for six Months, the Computation shall be by Kalendar and not by Lunar Months, because by the latter the Interest would exceed the Rate allowed by the Statute. Noy 37. 1 Leon. 96.

Sect. 14. V. That the Receipt of Interest before the Time when it is in strictness due, being voluntarily paid by the Debtor for the greater Convenience of the Creditor, or for any other such like Consideration, without any Manner of corrupt Practice, or any previous Agreement of this Kind at the making of the first Contract, does not make the Party liable to the Forfeiture of the treble Value. 1 Bulst. 17, 20. Noy 171. 2 Keb. 690. Con. 1 Leon. 96.

Sect. 15. VI. That the Grant of an Annuity for Lives not only exceeding the Rate allowed for Interest, but also exceeding the known Proportion for Contracts of this Kind, in consideration of a certain Sum of Money, is not within the Meaning of the Statute, unless there were some underhand Bargain for the Security of the Repayment of the Principal or Consideration-Money. Cro. Ja. 253. Noy 151. 2 Levinz 7, 8.

Sect. 16. VII. That no Contract is usurious, by which the Lender runs the Hazard of losing all his Money, both Principal and Interest: As where on the Loan of a certain Sum for a Year, for the Victualling of a Ship, it is agreed, That if the Ship return, the Lender shall have so many thousand Fishes at such a Rate, which exceeds the Interest allowed by the Statute, and if the Ship never return, or if it perish by unavoidable Casualties of Sea, Fire, or Enemies, that then he shall have nothing: Or where on the Loan of 30 *l.* a Bond is given for the Payment of 100 *l.* on the Marriage of a Daughter of one of the Parties; provided, That if either of them should die before, that then nothing should be paid: But it is clear, That if the Interest only be hazarded on such a Contract, and the whole Principal secured, the whole is usurious. Also it hath been resolved, That an Agreement to pay more than the lawful Interest for the Loan of a certain Sum at such a Day, if *A. B.* shall be then alive, and if he shall be dead, then to pay such a Sum which is less than the Principal, is void by the Statute; for if such a Contingency would exempt the Case out of the Statute, by the same Reason twenty Lives might be added, and the Statute wholly evaded. Cro. Ja. 208, 209, 508, 509. 1 Keb. 539, 711. 2 Ro. Re. 48. 1 Lev. 54. 1 Sid. 27. 3 Keb. 304. 2 Ro. Re. 48. Cro. Ja. 508. 5 Co. 70. Moore 397.

Sect. 17. VIII. That an Assurance made in Pursuance of a fair Agreement for such Interest as is allowed by the Statute, shall not be avoided by the Fault of the Scrivener, who draws it up in such a Manner as to bring it within the express Letter of the Statute: As where the Parties agree, That 5 *l.* shall be paid for the Loan of 100 *l.* for a Year, and the Scrivener in drawing the Bond for it, doth, without the Knowledge of the Parties, who are illiterate Persons, make the 5 *l.* payable at the End of half a Year: Or where on the fair Loan of 100 *l.* agreed to be paid with common Interest, a Mortgage is made for the 100 *l.* with a Proviso, That it shall be void on Payment of 105 *l.* at the End of one Year, without any Covenant for the Mortgagor to take the Profits till Default be made of Payment, so that in strictness the Mortgagee is intituled both to the Interest and Profits. Cro. Ja. 677, 678. 2 Ro. Re. 414, 415. Hetley 11. 1 Jon. 396. Cro. Ca. 501. 1 Mod. 307.

Sect. 18. IX. That the Loan of Money for lawful Interest allowed by the Statute, shall not be construed to be within the Purview of it, in respect of any Expectations which the Lender may have of a voluntary Gratuity 5 Co. 70. b.

Gratuity to be given him by the Borrower, if there be no Kind of Agreement relating to it.

5 Co. 69. Cro. Ja. 509.

Sect. 19. X. That the Reservation of a greater Sum than is allowed by the Statute for Interest, upon the Non-payment of the Principal at the End of the Year, is not usurious within the Statute, because it is in the Power of the Borrower to avoid the Payment of the Money so reserved, by paying the Principal at the Day appointed; yet it seemeth clear, That if it were originally agreed, that the principal Money should not be paid at the Time appointed, and that such Clause was inserted only with an Intent to evade the Statute, the whole Contract is void; for the Construction of Cases of this Nature must be governed by the Circumstances of the whole Matter, from which the Intention of the Parties will appear in the making of the Bargain, which, if it was in Truth usurious, is void, however it may be disguised by a specious Assurance.

5 Co. 69. b. See Mo. 397. 2 And. 16.

a 3 Co. 80. 9 Co. 36. b. 1 Jon. 203. 1 Ro. Re. 41, 42. 2 Leon. 166. Con. Cro. El. 25, 588.

Sect. 20. XI. That a [a] Fine levied, or Judgment suffered, in pursuance of an usurious Contract, may be avoided by an Averment of the corrupt Agreement, as well as any common Specialty, or parol Contract.

1 Sid. 182. b. [b] Cro. Ja. 252, 508. 2 Rol. Re. 48. 2 Lev. 7, 8.

Sect. 21. XII. That it is not [b] material whether the Payment both of the Principal and also of the usurious Interest be secured by the same or by different Conveyances, but that all Writings whatsoever for the strengthning such a Contract, are void.

Cro. Ja. 440.

Sect. 22. XIII. That a Contract reserving to the Lender a greater Advantage than is allowed by the Statute, is equally within the Meaning of it, whether the whole be reserved by Way of Interest, or in Part only under that Name, and in Part by Way of Rent for a House, let at a Rate plainly exceeding the known Value.

3 Keb. 142. Con. Noy 2.

Sect. 23. XIV. That a second Bond made after the Forfeiture of a former, and conditioned for the Receipt of Interest according to the Penalty of the forfeited Bond, is as much within the Statute as if it had been made before the Forfeiture; for if such a Practice should be allowed, nothing could be more easy than to elude the Statute; and tho' the whole Penalty be due in strictness to the Obligee, yet the true principal Debt is in Conscience no greater after the Forfeiture of the Bond than it was before.

1 And. 49. 1 Sid. 285. 3 Mod. 35. 1 Keb 629. Noy 143. Cro. Ja. 440. V. d. Cro. Ca. 501.

Sect. 24. XV. That in pleading an usurious Contract by Way of Bar to an Action, you must set forth the whole Matter specially, because it lay within your own Privity; but that in an Information on the Statute for making such a Contract, it is sufficient to set forth the corrupt Bargain generally, because Matters of this Kind are supposed to be privily transacted, and such Information may be brought by a Stranger.

1 Leon 96, 97.

Sect. 25. XVI. That in every such Information it is necessary expresly to set forth the Place where the corrupt Bargain was made.

1 Leon 148, 149.

Sect. 26. XVII. That if an usurious Contract in the County of *D.* be pleaded in bar to an Action on a Bond said to be made in the County of *E.* the Trial shall be in the County of *D.* because the Ground of the Matter is the usurious Contract, and the Bond is confessed by the Plea.

Co. Lit. 6 b. 2 Rol A 685. 2 Raymond 191.

Sect. 27. XVIII. That he who hath agreed to pay Money upon an usurious Contract, shall not be admitted to give Evidence upon an Information against the Usurer, unless he have paid off the whole Debt; for by such Means a Man might avoid his own Act and Deed.

1 Leon 95, 96.

Sect. 28. XIX. That an Information for an usurious Contract on a Loan of Money, cannot be supported by Evidence of such a Contract on a Bargain concerning Wares sold.

CHAP. LXXXIII.

Of Maintenance.

Sect. 1. MAintenance is commonly taken in an ill Sense, and in general, seemeth to signify an unlawful taking in Hand, or upholding of Quarrels or Sides, to the Disturbance or Hinderance of common Right, and is said to be twofold: Co. Li. 368. b. 2 Inst. 208, 212.

Sect. 2. I. *Ruralis*, or in the Country; as where one assists another in his Pretensions to certain Lands, by taking or holding the Possession of them for him by Force or Subtilty, or where one stirs up Quarrels, and Suits in the Country, in relation to Matters wherein he is no Way concerned: And this kind of Maintenance is punishable at the King's Suit by Fine and Imprisonment, whether the Matter in Dispute any way depended in Plea or not, but is said not to be actionable. Co. Lit. 368. b. 2 Inst. 213. 1 Ric. 1. ch. 4. 2 Rol. Abr. 115. F.

Sect. 3. II. *Curialis*, or in a Court of Justice, where one officiously intermeddles in a Suit depending in any such Court which no way belongs to him, by assisting either Party with Money or otherwise, in the Prosecution or Defence of any such Suit. Pult. 25. 2 Inst. 212. 2 Rol. A. 115. F.

Of this second kind of Maintenance there seem to be three Species:

1. Where one maintains another without any Contract to have Part of the Thing in Suit, which generally goes under the common Name of Maintenance.
2. Where one maintains one Side, to have Part of the Thing in Suit, which is called Champerty.
3. Where one laboureth a Jury, which is called Embracery.

For the better understanding of the first of the above mentioned Species, I shall examine;

1. What shall be said to amount to an Act of Maintenance.
2. In what Respects some such Acts may be justified.
3. How far Offences of this kind are restrained by the Common Law. [a] 28 H. 6. 7. b. 12 a. 34 H. 6. 25, 26. a. b.
4. How far by Statute.

Sect. 4. As to the first Point, it seemeth clear, That whoever assists another with Money to carry on his Cause, as by retaining one to be of Counsel for him, or otherwise bearing him out in the whole or part of the Expence of the Suit, may properly be said to be guilty of an Act of Maintenance, as it seems to be taken for granted in the [a] Books cited in the Margin. 9 E. 4. 32. a. 21 H. 7. 40. b. 6 E. 4. 5. b. 19 E. 4. 3. b. 31 H. 6. 9. Bro. Maintenance 7, 14, 17, 20, 24, 43, 44, 52. 2 Rol. A. 118. Pl. 5, 6.

Sect. 5. Also it is said, That not only he who lays out his Money to assist another in his Cause, but also that he who by his Friendship or Interest saves himself that Expence which he might otherwise be put to, or but endeavours so to do, is also guilty of Maintenance; as where [b] one perswades, or but endeavours to perswade a Man to be of Counsel for another *gratis*. [b] 28 H. 6. 7. b. 12. b. 34 H. 6. 25. b. 9 E. 4. 32. a. Bro. Maintenance 6, 7, 20

[a] 22 H. 6. 5. b. Bro. Maintenance 14. Cro. E. 735. [b] 28 H. 6. 6. a. 11 H. 6. 41. b. Bro Maintenance 5, 51. Fitz. Maintenance 10. 2 Rol. Abr. Pl. 118, Pl. 7, 8. [c] Hetley 78, 79. [d] 1 Rol. Ab. 593 Pl. 11. [e] 19 E. 4. 3. b. 12 E. 4. 14. b. Hetl. 79. [f] 22 H. 6. 5. b. Bro. Maintenance 14. Fitz. Maintenance 8. [g] 22 H. 6. 6 b. 11 H. 6. 39. b. 19 E. 4. 3. b. Bro. Maintenance. 51. [h] 9 H. 7. 18. b. Bro. Champerty 9. [i] Bro. Maintenance 40. 18 E. 4. 1 Pl. 6. 2 Pl. 8. 17 E. 4. 5. b. Bro. Maintenance 39. [k] 12 E. 4 14. b. 19 E. 4. 3. b. 22 H. 6. 35. a. Bro. Maintenance 17. 3 Rol Ab. 118. Pl. 2.

Sect. 6. Also it is said, That all such Persons may properly be called Maintainers, who give or but endeavour to give any other kind of Assistance to either of the Parties, in the management of the Suit depending between them, as by [a] opening the Evidence to the Jury, or by [b] giving Evidence officiously without being called upon to do it, or by speaking in the Cause as [c] one of Counsel with the Party, or by [d] retaining an Attorney for him, or [e] perhaps for barely going along with him to enquire for a Person Learned in the Law.

Sect. 7. Also it hath been said, That those shall come under the like Notion, who give any publick Countenance to another in Relation to any such Suit; as where one of great Power and Interest says [f] publickly, That he will spend twenty Pounds on one Side, or that he will give twenty Pounds to labour the Jury, whether in Truth he spend one Penny or not; or where such a Person [g] comes to the Bar with one of the Parties, and stands by him while his Cause is tried, whether he say any Thing or not; for such kinds of Practices do not only tend to discourage the other Party from going on in his Cause, but also to intimidate Juries from doing their Duty. But it seems, That a bare [h] Promise to maintain another, is not in it self Maintenance, unless it be either in respect of the publick Manner in which, or the Power of the Person by whom, it is made.

Sect. 8. Also it is said to be as much Maintenance for a [i] Juror, as for any other Person, to sollicit a Judge to give Judgment according to the Verdict, because after a Juror has given his Verdict, he has nothing more to do: But it is said to be no [i] Maintenance for a Juror to exhort his Companions to join with him in giving such a Verdict as seems to him to be right.

Sect. 9. However it seems clear, That a [k] Man is in no Danger of being judged guilty of an Act of Maintenance, for giving another friendly Advice, what Action is proper for him to bring for the Recovery of a certain Debt, or what Method is safest to take to free him from such an Arrest, or what Counsellor or Attorney is likely to do his Business most effectually; for it would be extremely hard to make such neighbourly Acts of Kindness, which seem rather commendable than blame-worthy, to come under the Notion of Maintenance, which always seems to imply a contentious, and over-busy intermeddling in other Mens Matters, in which respect it is so highly Criminal. Yet it is said, that a Man of great Power not learned in the Law, may be guilty of Maintenance, by telling another who asks his Advice, that he has a good Title.

Fitz. Maintenance 21

3 H. 6. 54 a. Fitz Maintenance 18. Bro. Maintenance 1.

Sect. 10. Also it hath been said, That no one can be guilty of Maintenance, in respect of any Money given by him to another before any Suit is actually commenced; yet if it plainly appear, That it was given merely with a Design to assist him in the Prosecution or Defence of an intended Suit, which afterwards is actually brought; surely it cannot but be as great a Misdemeanour in the Nature of the Thing, and equally criminal at common Law, as if the Money were given after the Commencement of the Suit, though perhaps it may not in Strictness come under the Notion of Maintenance.

47 Ed. 3. 10. a. Bro. Champerty 2.

Sect. 11. However it is certain, That one may as properly be said to be guilty of Maintenance, within the meaning of the Words *adhuc Manutenet*, in an Action of Maintenance, for supporting another after Judgment, as for doing it hanging the Plea; because the Party grieved may be discouraged thereby from bringing a Writ of Error or Attaint.

As to the ſecond Point, *viz.* In what Reſpects ſome Acts of this Kind may be juſtified, I ſhall conſider the following Particulars:

1. How far they are juſtifiable in Reſpect of an Intereſt in the Thing in Variance.
2. How far in Reſpect of Kindred or Affinity.
3. How far in Reſpect of other Relations.
4. How far in Reſpect of Charity.
5. How far in Reſpect of the Profeſſion of the Law,

Sect. 12. As to the firſt of theſe Particulars, *viz.* How far ſome Acts of this Kind are juſtifiable in Reſpect of an Intereſt in the Thing in Variance, it ſeemeth to be clearly agreed, That if a [a] Tenant in Tail, or for Life, be impleaded, he in Remainder or Reverſion may lawfully maintain the Defence of the Suit with his own Money: And upon the like Ground it ſeems to be clear, That if in an Action of Treſpaſs, *&c.* brought by or againſt a [b] Leſſee for Years, the Inheritance come into Queſtion, the Leſſor may lawfully maintain his Leſſee, and give [c] Evidence to prove the Inheritance in himſelf; for though the Judgment which may be given againſt the Leſſee cannot directly bind his Inheritance, yet the Verdict may be a Prejudice to his Title, being given on a Suppoſal of his not having a good one: Alſo it hath been [d] admitted as clear Law, That if one ſeized in Fee of certain Land, bring an Action of Treſpaſs, *quare Clauſum fregit*, and then alien the Land, and afterwards in the Trial of the Cauſe it be queſtioned whether the Inheritance at the Time of the ſuppoſed Treſpaſs belonged to the Plaintiff or Defendant, the Alienee may lawfully produce Evidence to prove that the Inheritance was in the Plaintiff, becauſe the Plaintiff's Title is now become his own.

[a] 19 E. 4. 3. b. 9 H. 6. 64. Bro. Maintenance 3, 53. 2 Rol. A. 117. O. 2.
[b] 6 E. 4. 2. b. 2 Rol. Ab. 117. O. 3. Bro. Maintenance 33.
[c] 39 H. 6. 20. a. Bro. Maintenance 28.
[d] 14 H. 6. 7. b. Bro. Maintenance 23. 2 Rol. Ab. 117. O. 4.

Sect. 13. Alſo it hath been ſaid, That not only thoſe who have a certain Intereſt, but alſo that thoſe who have a bare Contingency of ſuch an Intereſt in the Lands in Queſtion, which poſſibly may never come *in eſſe*, may in like manner lawfully maintain another in an Action concerning ſuch Lands; from whence it follows, That if I grant to *B.* that if my Leſſee for Life ſhall die during my Life, that then he ſhall have the Land for ten Years, and after my Leſſee be impleaded, *B.* may maintain him.

9 H. 6. 64. A, B. 2 Rol. Ab. 117, O. 5.

Sect. 14. And it hath been ſaid, That not only thoſe who have a Contingency of ſuch an Intereſt, which it is in no Man's Power to bar them of, if the Contingent happen, may juſtify ſuch Maintenance, but that thoſe alſo ſhall have the ſame Privilege, who by the Act of God have the immediate Poſſibility of ſuch an Intereſt, though it be in the Power of another to deprive them of it; and therefore that an Heir Apparent, or the Huſband of ſuch an Heir, may lawfully maintain the Anceſtor in an Action concerning the Inheritance of the Land whereof he is ſeized in Fee.

14 H. 7. 2. a. 19 Ed. 4. 3. b. 21 H. 6. 16 b. 2 Inſt. 564. 2 Rol. A. 115. H. I.

Sect. 15. But it is ſaid, That the Grantee of a Reverſion, before the late Statute for Amendment of the Law which made all Attornment needleſs, could not maintain the Tenant of the Land without Attornment, becauſe his Poſſibility was wholly created by the Act of the Party, and could not be executed but by the voluntary Attornment of the Tenant, which there was no Remedy to compel him to make by the Common Law; but perhaps the Authority of this Opinion may be queſtionable, eſpecially if ſuch Grant were made for good Conſideration: For ſince thoſe who have only an equitable Intereſt in Lands, may lawfully maintain others in Actions relating to thoſe Lands, as ſhall more fully be ſhewn in

9 H. 6. 64 a. 2 Rol. Ab. 117. Pl. 7.

in the seventeenth Section; and since the Grantor in Equity shall stand intrusted for the Grantee after the Grant, and the Tenant may be enforced by a Court of Equity to attorn to him, I do not see any good Reason why such Grantee should be esteemed such a Stranger to the Land, that he may not lawfully defend an Action concerning it, in the Event whereof he is so nearly concerned.

34 H. 6. 30. b.

11 H. 6. 41. Bro. Maintenance 51. 2 Rol. Ab. 118. Pl. 8.

Sect. 16. But it seems clear, That he who is bound to warrant Lands, may lawfully maintain the Tenant in the Defence of his Title, because he is bound by the Warranty to render other Lands to the Value of those which shall be evicted.

Sect. 17. Also it seems to be agreed, That he who hath an equitable Interest in Lands or Goods, or even in a Chose in Action, may lawfully maintain another in an Action relating thereto; and therefore it seemeth to be clear, That a Man may lawfully [a] maintain those who are infeoffed of Lands in Trust for him, in any Action concerning those Lands, and that if he sell them to another, the Vendee shall have the same Privilege; also it hath been [b] resolved, That where *A.* was bound as a Surety for *B.* and *B.* thereupon made a Deed of Gift of certain Sheep to *A.* in order to save him harmless from the said Bond, with an implied Trust that the Sheep should be returned to *B.* if *A.* should not be damnified, and afterwards an Action was brought against *A.* for the taking of the Sheep, *B.* might justify the maintaining of him in Respect of the said Trust: Also it seemeth to be [c] certain, That the Assignee of a Bond, or other Chose in Action, being made over to him for good Consideration, in Satisfaction of a precedent Debt due *bonâ fide* to him, and not merely in Consideration of the intended Maintenance, may either maintain the Obligee in an Action brought by him for the Debt, or commence an original Action in his Name, for he hath an equitable Interest in the Debt.

[a] 34 H. 6. 30. b. 15 H. 7. 2. a. 2 E. 4. 2. a. Bro. Maintenance 19, 30. [b] Noy 100. Moore, 620. Pl. 847. See 39 H. 6. 19 b. 20. a. Fitz. Maintenance 14. [c] 34 H. 6. 30. b. 15 H. 7. 2. a. Noy. 52. Cro. El. 552. 1 Sid. 217. Bro. Maintenance 19.

Sect. 18. Also it seemeth to be [d] agreed, That where-ever any Persons claim a common Interest in the same Thing, as in a Way, Church-yard, or Common, *&c.* by the same Title, they may maintain one another in a Suit relating to the same.

[d] 18 Ed. 4. 2. b. Bro. Maintenance 41. Hob. 92. 2 Rol. Ab. 118. Pl. 8.

Sect. 19. It is said, That he who is [e] Bail for another, may take Care to have his Appearance recorded, but that he ought not to intermeddle any farther.

Noy 99. Moore 562. Pl. 764, 788. Pl. 1088. 1 Rol Re. 57.

Sect. 20. As to the second of the said Particulars, *viz.* How far some Acts of this Kind are justifiable in Respect of Kindred or Affinity, it seems to be agreed, That whoever is any Way of Kin or Affinity to either of the Parties, so long as the same [f] continues, or but related to him by being his [g] Godfather, may lawfully [h] stand by him at the Bar, and counsel and assist him, and also pray another to be of Counsel to him, but that he cannot justify the laying out of any of his own [i] Money in the Cause, unless he be either [k] Father, or Son, or Heir Apparent to the Party, or the Husband of such an Heiress.

[e] 34 H. 6. 26. a. 14 H. 6. 6 b. 18 Ed. 4. 12. b. [f] 20 H. 6. 1. 6 Ed. 4. 5. b. 14 H. 7. 2. a. [g] 6 E. 4. 5 b. Fitz. Maintenace 16. [h] 21 H. 6. 15 b. 11 H. 6. 41. b. 42. a. 12 H. 6. 2. Pl. 7. 19 Ed. 4. 3 b. 9 H. 6. 64. a. 9 Ed. 4. 32. a. [i] 19 Ed. 4. 5. a. 2 Inst. 564. 6 Ed. 4. 5. [k] 21 H. 6. 16. b. 2 Inst. 564. Vide supra Section 14.

As to the third of the said Particulars, *viz.* How far some Acts of Maintenance are justifiable in respect of other Relations, I shall consider,

1. How far a Lord may maintain his Tenant.
2. How far a Tenant may maintain his Lord.
3. How far a Master may maintain his Servant.
4. How far a Servant may maintain his Master.
5. How far one Neighbour may maintain another.

Sect. 20. As to the first Point it seems certain, That not only the [a] Lord, but also the *Cestui que Use* of a Seigniory, may come with the Tenant to a Trial in an Assize against him, and stand by him and assist him, and also pray the Sheriff to return an indifferent Jury: Also it seemeth, That the [b] Lord of a Town in an Action brought against the Inhabitants, wherein a Right to a common Burying-place, claimed by them, is brought into Question, may maintain them in the Defence of their Right, by shewing authentick Evidence thereof to the Jury: And in some [c] Books it is said generally, That the Lord may maintain his Tenant, without saying, how far he may do it; and I do not find it any where expresly holden, That the Lord may justify laying out his own Money in Defence of his Tenant's Title; but it seemeth the better Opinion, That he may as well justify it as any other of the abovementioned Acts of Maintenance; for the Lord, by accepting a Man for his Tenant, seemeth to take him under his immediate [d] Protection; and inasmuch as the Lands were originally derived from the Lord, and he hath the continual Benefit of the Services due from them, the Law in many Cases of [e] Common Right, obliges him to warrant them unto his Tenant, and where it doth not oblige him, surely it will at least permit him to do it: But it [f] seems clear, That he cannot maintain him in Respect of any Lands not holden of him.

Sect. 21. As to the second Point, *viz.* How far a Tenant may maintain his Lord, it is said, That he may justify [g] coming with his Lord, and standing with him at a Trial; but I cannot find any Thing more relating to this Matter in any of the Books.

Sect. 22. As to the third Point, *viz.* How far a Master may maintain his Servant, it is said, That the Master may go along with his [h] Servant, or with his [i] Chaplain, being retained to live in his House with him, in order to [k] retain Counsel, and that he may pray one to be of Counsel for him, and also that he may go with him to the [l] Trial and stand with him and aid him while the Cause is tried, but ought not to speak in the Court in favour of his Cause. Also it is said, That if my Servant be arrested in an Action of [m] Debt, I may assist him with Money in order to keep him out of Prison, that I may have the Benefit of his Service: But it is said, That the Master, in real Actions, cannot justify laying out Money for his Servant, unless he hath some of his Wages in his Hands; which, if the Servant be willing, the Master may safely lay out in his Behalf.

Sect. 23. As to the fourth Point, *viz.* How far a Servant may maintain his Master, it seemeth clear, That a Person generally retained by another as his Servant to do all manner of Services, and not for a [n] particular Occasion only, may justify [o] riding about to speed his Business, and going to [p] Counsel in his Behalf, and shewing his Evidences to the Counsel or to the Jury, and [q] standing by him at a Trial between him and another; but it is certain, That he cannot lawfully lay out any of his own [r] Money to assist the Master in his Suit.

Sect. 24. As to the fifth Point, *viz.* How far one Neighbour may assist another, it seems clear, That a Man may lawfully go with his [s] Neighbour to inquire for a Person learned in the Law, but that he [t] ought not to give him any Money towards carrying on his Suit.

Sect. 25. As to the fourth Instance wherein some Acts of this Kind are justifiable, *viz.* That relating to Charity, it seems to be [u] agreed, That any one may lawfully give Money to a poor Man to enable him to carry on his Suit. Also it hath been adjudged, That any one may safely

[a] 11 H. 6. 39. b. 40. a. 2 Rol. Ab. 117. N. Bro. Maintenance 50.
[b] 18 Ed. 4. 2. b. Bro. Maintenance 41. 2 Rol. Ab. 116 G.
[c] 9 H. 6. 64. a. Bro. Maintenance 3.
[d] Co. Lit. 65. a.
[e] Co. Lit. 101, 384. 11 H. 6. 42. a. 2 Rol. A. 117.
[f] Fitz. Maintenance 25.
[g] 11 H. 6. 42. a. 2 Rol. Ab. 116. K.
[h] Hetly 79.
[i] 19 H. 6. 30. b.
[k] 28 H. 6. 7. b. 12. b. 13. b. 34 H. 6. 25. b. 26. a. b. Bro. Maintenance 6, 14. Fitz. Maintenance 20. Con. Fitz. Maintenance 13.
[l] 19 H. 6. 30. b. 11 H. 6. 42. a. 2 Rol. Ab. 116. K. Hetley 79.
[m] 21 H. 7. 40. b. Moore 814. Bro. Maintenance 24. 31 H. 6. 9. b. 19 Ed. 4. 3. b. 2 Rol. Ab. 116 K. Hetley 79. Bro. Maintenance 44, 52.
[n] 39 H. 6. 5. b. 6. a. Con. Keil. 50. b.
[o] 19 E. 4. 3. b.
[p] 19 H. 6. 31. b.
[q] 11 H. 6. 42. a.
[r] 3 H. 6. 53. b. 54. a. 11 H. 6. 10. b. 11. a.
[s] 19 E. 4. 3. b. 12 E. 4. 14 b.
[t] 19 E. 4. 3. b. 2 Rol. A. 118.
[u] 21 H. 6. 16. b. 9 H. 6 64. a. 22 H. 6. 35. a. Bro. Maintenance. 14.

go with a [a] Foreigner who cannot speak *English*, to a Counsellor, and inform him of his Case.

[a] 19 E. 4. 3. b. 34 H. 6. 25. b. 15 H. 7. 2. a. Bro. Maintenance 7.

As to the fifth Instance wherein some Acts of this Kind may be justified, *viz.* That relating to the Profession of the Law, I shall consider,

1. How far they are justifiable in a Counsellor.
2. How far in an Attorney.

Sect. 26. As to the first Point, there is no Doubt but that a [b] Counsellor, having received his Fee, may lawfully set forth his Client's Cause to the best Advantage; but it is certain, That he can no more justify [c] giving him Money to maintain his Suit, or threatening a Juror, than any other Person.

Sect. 27. As to the second Point, there is no Doubt but that an Attorney may [d] lawfully prosecute or defend an Action in the Court wherein he is an allowed Attorney, in the Behalf of any one by whom he shall be specially retained, and that he may assist his Client, by laying out his own Money for him to be repaid again, and also may maintain an Action against him for the same by Virtue of such a Retainer, without any special Promise; and it is said also, That Attorneys may justify such Maintenance in other Courts, wherein they are not [e] allowed Attorneys, but that they cannot have an Action for the Money so laid out without a special Promise, and that they are no more justified by a general [f] Retainer to prosecute for another all his Causes, than if they were not retained at all; and it is certain that they ought not to carry on a Cause for another at their own Expence, with a Promise never to expect a Repayment. And it [g] seems justly questionable, whether Sollicitors who are no Attorneys, can in any Case justify the laying out their Money in another's Suit.

Sect. 28. However it is certain, That no Counsellor or Attorney can justify the using any deceitful Practice, in Maintenance of a Client's Cause, and that they are liable to be severely punished for all Misdemeanours of this Kind, not only by the [h] Common Law, but also by Statute; for it is enacted by *Westminster*, 1. 28. *That if any Serjeant, Pleader or other, do any manner of Disceit or Collusion in the King's Court, or consent unto it, in disceit of the Court, or to beguile the Court or the Party, and thereof be attainted, he shall be imprisoned for a Year and a Day, and from thenceforth shall not be heard to plead in that Court for any Man. And if he be no Pleader, he shall be imprisoned in like manner by the Space of a Year and a Day at the least. And if the Trespass require greater Punishment, it shall be at the King's Pleasure.*

[b] 11 H. 6. 10. b. 11. a. 2 Rol. Ab. 116. M. 2 Inst. 564. [c] Fitz. Maintenance 8. 22 H. 6. 6. [d] 13. H. 4. 16. b Kellway 50. b. Hob. 117. 2 Inst. 564. 2 Rol. Ab. 116. M. Fitz Maintenance 21. [e] 3 Mod. 98. Winch. 52. 1 Jon. 208. Cro. Ca. 159, 194. Con. Cro. El. 425, 459, 760. Moore 366. Pl 500. 2 Rol Ab. 114. Pl 4. 115. Pl. 6. [f] 2 Rol. Ab. 114. Pl. 5. 2 Rol. Ab. 115. Pl. 6. Winch. 53. [h] 2 Inst. 214.

In the Construction of this Statute the following Points have been holden,

Sect. 29. I. That Counsellors, *&c.* who are not sworn, are as much within the Meaning of it as Serjeants, *&c.* who are sworn.

Sect. 30. II. That all Fraud and Falshood tending to impose upon or abuse the Justice of the King's Courts, are within the Purview of it, as in the following Instances:

Sect. 31. First, Where an Attorney sues out an *habere facias seisinam*, falsly reciting a Recovery in a real Action, where in Truth there

11 E. 4. 3 b. Bro. Disceit. 28. 2 Inst. 215, 216. Dyer 249. Pl. 84. 2 Inst. 215. F. N. B. 98.

was no Recovery at all, and by Colour thereof puts the supposed Tenant in the Action out of his Freehold.

Sect. 32. Secondly, Where one brings a *Præcipe* against a poor Man, knowing that he had nothing in the Land, on Purpose to get the Possession from the true Tenant. 2 Inst. 215.

Sect. 33. Thirdly, Where one procures an Attorney to appear for a Man, and confess Judgment without any Warrant. 41 E. 3. 1. b. 2 Inst. 215. Dy. 362. Pl. 13.

Sect. 34. Fourthly, Where one pleads a false Plea, known to be utterly groundless, and invented merely with a Design to delay Justice, and abuse the Court; and therefore it is said, That if a Client desire his Attorney to plead such a Plea, the Attorney ought to enter upon the Roll, *non sum veraciter informatus, ideo nihil dicit.* 10 E. 4. 9. b.

Sect. 35. As to the third general Point of this Chapter, How far Offences of this Kind are restrained by the Common Law, it seemeth, That all Maintenance is strictly prohibited by the Common Law, as having a manifest tendency to Oppression, by encouraging and assisting Persons to persist in Suits, which perhaps they would not venture to go on in upon their own Bottoms; and therefore it is said, That all Offenders of this Kind are not only liable to an [a] Action of Maintenance at the Suit of the Party grieved, wherein they shall render such Damages as shall be answerable to the Injury done to the Plaintiff, but also that they may be [b] indicted as Offenders against publick Justice, and adjudged thereupon to such Fine and Imprisonment, as shall be agreeable to the Circumstances of the Offence. Also it seemeth, That a Court of Record may commit a Man for an [c] Act of Maintenance done in the Face of the Court. 2 Inst. 208. 212. [a] 11 H. 6. 11. a. 2 Inst. 208. 2 Rol. Ab. 114. D. 8 H. 5. 8. a. [b] 2 Rol. Ab. 114. D. 2 Inst. 208, 212. [c] Hetley 79.

Sect. 36. As to the fourth general Point of this Chapter, How far Offences of this Kind are punished by the Statute, it is enacted by 1 *E.* 3. 14. which was farther enforced by 20 *Ed.* 3. 4. *That none of the King's Ministers, nor no Great Man of the Realm, by himself nor by other, by sending of Letters, nor otherwise, nor none other great nor small, shall take upon them to maintain Quarrels nor Parts in the Country, to the Let and Disturbance of the Common Law.*

Sect. 37. And it is farther enacted by 1 R. 2. 4. *That none of the King's Counsellors, Officers or Servants, nor any other Person within the Realm of* England, *of whatsoever Estate or Condition they be, shall take or sustain any Quarrel by Maintenance, in the Country or elsewhere, upon grievous Pain, that is to say, the said Counsellors and the King's Great Officers, upon a Pain which shall be ordained by the King himself, by the Advice of the Lords of his Realm, and other less Officers and Servants of the King's, as well in the Exchequer, and all his other Courts and Places, as of his own Meiny, upon Pain to lose their Offices and Services, and to be imprisoned, and then to be ransomed at the King's Will, every of them according to their Degree, Estate, and Desert: And all other Persons through the Realm, upon Pain of Imprisonment, and to be ransomed as aforesaid.*

In the Construction of these Statutes the following Points have been holden:

Sect. 38. I. That Maintenance of a Suit in a Court-Baron is as much within the Purview thereof as Maintenance in a Court of Record. Fitz. Maintenance 24.

Sect. 39. II. That *Nul tiel Record* is a good Plea to an Action of Maintenance brought on these Statutes; and therefore, That he who barely assists another in taking out an Original which never is returned, is not liable to any such Action. 3 H. 6. 53. b. 54. a. Bro. Maintenance 1. Fitz. Maintenance 18.

Sect.

Fitz. Maintenance 17, 26. *Sect.* 40. III. That it is not material, whether the Plaintiff in an Action on the said Statutes were nonsuited, or recovered in the Action wherein the Maintenance is supposed.

Reg. 182. b. *Sect.* 41. Also it is certain, That he who fears that another will maintain his Adversary, may by Way of Prevention have an original Writ grounded on the said Statutes prohibiting him so to do.

Sect. 42. Also all Persons are prohibited to give or receive any Liveries or Badges for Maintenance, under severe Penalties, by 1 *R.* 2. 7. 7 *H.* 4. 14. 13 *H.* 4. 3. 8 *H.* 6. 4. and 8 *E.* 4 2.

Sect. 43. And it is farther enacted by 32 *H.* 8. 9. *That no Person whatsoever shall unlawfully maintain, or cause or procure any unlawful Maintenance, in any Action, Demand, Suit, or Complaint in any of the King's Courts of the Chancery,* Whitehall, *or elsewhere, where any Person shall have Authority by Virtue of the King's Commission, Patent or Writ, to hold Plea of Lands, or to examine, hear, or determine any Title of Lands, or any Matter of Witnesses, concerning the Title, Right, or Interest of any Lands, Tenements, or Hereditaments; and also that no Person whatsoever do unlawfully retain, for Maintenance of any Suit or Plea, any Person or Persons, or embrace any Freeholders or Jurors, or suborn any Witness by Letters, Rewards, Promises, or any other sinister Labour or Means, for to maintain any Matter or Cause, or to the Disturbance or Hinderance of Justice, or to the Procurement, by occasion of any manner of Perjury by false Verdict or otherwise, in any manner of Courts aforesaid, upon Pain to forfeit for every such Offence ten Pounds, the one Moiety thereof unto the King, and the other Moiety to him that will sue for the same by Action of Debt,* &c.

Savil 41, 42. *Sect.* 44. It seemeth that in an Information on this Statute it is not sufficient to say, That the Defendant maintained the Party without adding that he did it unlawfully.

Noy 68. Cro. E. 594. *Sect.* 45. Also it is said to have been adjudged, That Maintenance of a Suit in a Spiritual Court, is neither within this nor any of the other above mentioned Statutes concerning Maintenance.

Savil 41, 42. *Sect.* 46. Also it hath been holden, That in an Information on this Statute, it is necessary to shew that a Plea was depending, and therefore that it is not sufficient to say that a Bill was exhibited.

CHAP. LXXXIV.

Of Champerty.

2 Inst. 208. Co. Lit. 368. b. *Sect.* 1. AND now we are come to the second Species of Maintenance, called Champerty, which is the unlawful Maintenance of a Suit in Consideration of some Bargain to have Part of the Thing in Dispute, or some Profit out of it.

Sect. 2. Having shewn in the precedent Chapter what shall amount to an Act of Maintenance, and how far all Maintenance in general, and consequently Champerty, is punishable by the Common Law; I shall only take Notice in this Place, how far this Offence in particular is restrained by Statute, and to that End shall set down in order the several Statutes relating to it, and shew in what Manner they have been expounded.

Sect.

Sect. 3. And first, it is enacted by the Statute of *Westminster* 1. 25. *That no Officer of the King by themselves nor by other, shall maintain Pleas, Suits, or Matters hanging in the King's Courts, for Lands, Tenements, or other Things, for to have Part or Profit thereof by Covenant made between them; and he that doth, shall be punished at the King's Pleasure.*

In the Construction of this Statute the following Opinions have been holden:

Sect. 4. I. That by the King's Courts therein mentioned, are intended only his Courts of Record.

2 Inst. 208.

Sect. 5. II. That under the Word Covenant, which in a strict Sense signifieth only an Agreement by Deed, all Kinds of Promises and Contracts of this Kind are included, whether they be made by Writing or Parol.

F.N.B. 172. L. 2 Inst. 209, 563.

Sect. 6. III. That Maintenance in personal Actions to have part of the Debt or Damages, is as much with in this Statute as Maintenance in real Actions for a Part of the Land.

47 Ass. Pl. 5. 47 Ed. 3. 9. b.

Sect. 7. IV. That Maintenance in Consideration of a Rent granted out of Land in Variance, is within this Statute, but that Rent granted out of other Lands is no way within the Purview of it.

F. N. B. 172. K. M. 2 Inst. 209.

Sect. 8. V. That it is not material whether he who bring, a Writ of Champerty, did in Truth suffer any Damage by it, or whether the Plea wherein it is alledged be determined or not.

47 Ed. 3. 9 b. 47 Ass. 5. Con. 9 H. 7. 18. b. Fitz. Champerty 4. Bro. Champerty 2.

Sect. 9. VI. That the [a] Maintenance of the Tenant or Defendant is as much within the Meaning of the Statute, as the Maintenance of a Demandant or Plaintiff.

[a] 21 E. 3. 52. a. 30 Ed. 3. 3 b. 4. a. 2 Rol. Ab. 113. Pl. 3.

Sect. 10. VII. That [b] such Grants only of Part of the Thing in Suit, which are made merely in Consideration of the Maintenance are within the Meaning of the Statute, and not such as are made in Consideration of a precedent honest Debt, which is agreed to be satisfied with the Thing in Demand when recovered.

[b] 15 H 7. 2. a. Bro. Champerty 6.

Sect. 11. And it is farther enacted by the Statute of *Westminster* 2. 49. *That the Chancellor, Treasurer, Justices, nor any of the King's Counsel, no Clerk of the Chancery, nor of the Exchequer, nor any Justice or other Officer, nor any of the King's House, Clerk nor Lay, shall not receive any Church, nor Advowson of a Church, Land, nor Tenement in Fee, by Gift, or by Purchase, or to Farm, nor by Champerty, nor otherwise, so long as the Thing is in Plea before the King, or before any of his Officers, nor shall take no Reward thereof. And that he that doth contrary to this Act, either himself or by an other, or make any Bargain, shall be punished at the King's Pleasure, as well he that purchaseth as he that doth sell.*

In the Construction of this Statute the following Opinions have been holden:

Sect. 12. I. That it extendeth only to the Officers therein named, and not to any other Persons.

2 Inst. 484, 485.

Sect. 13. II. That it so strictly restrains all such Officers from purchasing any Land hanging a Plea, that they cannot be excused by a Consideration of [a] Kindred or Affinity, and that they are within the Meaning of the Statute by barely making such a Purchase, whether [b] they maintain the Party in his Suit or not, [c] whereas such a Purchase for good Consideration, made by any other Person, of any Ter-tenant, is no Offence, unless it appear that he did it to maintain the Party.

[a] 2 Inst. 485. [b] 2 Inst. 484. 50 Ass. Pl. 3. Bro. Champerty 8. Fitz. Champerty 6. [c] 22 E. 3. 10. b. 52. a. 2 Inst. 484. F. N. B. 172. D. E.

Sect. 13. And it is farther enacted by 28 *E.* 1. 11. in the following Words, *because the King hath heretofore ordained by Statute, That none of his Ministers shall take no Plea for Maintenance, by which Statute other Officers were not bounden before this Time; the King will that no Officer, nor any other, (for to have Part of the Thing in Plea) shall not take upon him the Business that is in Suit; nor none upon any such Covenant shall give up his Right to another; and if any do and be attainted thereof, the Taker shall forfeit unto the King so much of his Lands and Goods, as doth amount to the Value of the Part that he hath purchased for such Maintenance. And to obtain this, whosoever will, shall be received to sue for the King before the Justices before whom the Plea hangeth, and the Judgment shall be given by them. But it may not be understood hereby, that any Person shall be prohibited to have Counsel of Pleaders, or of learned Men in Law, for his Fee, or of his Parents and next Friends.*

In the Construction of this Statute the following Points have been holden:

Sect. 14. I. That a [a]Conveyance executed, hanging a Plea, in Pursuance of a Bargain made before, is not within the Meaning of it.

Sect. 15. II. That Champerty in any Action at [b] Common Law, whether it be real, personal, or mixt, is within this Statute: Also it seems the better Opinion, That the Purchase of Land while a Suit of [c] Equity concerning it is depending, is within the Purview of it.

Sect. 16. III. That a [d]Lease for Life, or Years, or a voluntary Gift of Land, hanging a Plea, is as much within the Statute as a Purchase for Money.

Sect. 17. IV. That a Surrender made by a [e]Lessee to his Lessor is not within the Meaning of the Statute; for since the Lessor may lawfully maintain his Lessee without such a Surrender, as hath been more fully shewn in the precedent Chapter, surely *à fortiori*, he may do it after the Surrender.

Sect. 18. V. That no [f] Conveyance, or Promise thereof, relating to Lands in Suit, made by a Father to his Son, or by any Ancestor to his Heir Apparent, is within the Statute, since it only gives them the greater Encouragment to do what by Nature they are bound to do.

Sect. 19. VI. That the [g] giving of Part of the Land in Suit, after the End of it, to a Counsellor for his Wages, is not within the Meaning of it, if it evidently appear that there was no kind of precedent Bargain relating to such Gift; but it seems [h] dangerous to meddle with any such Gift, since it cannot but carry with it a strong Presumption of Champerty.

[a] 30 Ass. Pl. 15. 8 Ed. 4. 13. 2 Inst. 563. Fitz. Champerty 13. F.N.B 172.D.
[b] 47 Ed. 3. 9. b. 47 Ass. 5. 2 Inst. 563.
[c] Moore 655. Pl. 898. Con. 2 Rol. Ab. 113. Pl. 2.
[d] 8 E. 4. 13. b. Bro. Champerty 10. F.N.B. 172. C.
[e] F.N.B. 172. E. 2 Inst. 564.
[f] 2 Inst. 564. F. N. B. 172. H.
[g] 13 H. 7. 17. a. Bro. Champerty 3.
[h] 2 Inst. 564.

CHAP.

CHAP. LXXXV.

Of Embracery.

FOR the better Uuderſtanding of the Nature of Embracery, I ſhall conſider,

1. What Kind of Maintenance comes under the Notion of Embracery.
2. What Acts of this Nature are altogether unlawful.
3. In what Circumſtances ſome Kinds of them may be lawful.
4. How far this Offence is reſtrained by the Common Law.
5. How far by Statute.

Sect. 1. As to the firſt Point it ſeems clear, That [a] any Attempt whatſoever, to corrupt, or influence, or inſtruct a Jury, or any Way to incline them to be more favourable to the one Side than to the other, by Money, Promiſes, Letters, Treats, or Perſwaſions, except only by the Strength of the Evidence and the Arguments of the Counſel in open Court, at the Trial of the Cauſe, is a proper Act of Embracery, [b] whether the Jurors on whom ſuch Attempt is made give any Verdict or not, or whether the Verdict given be true or falſe.

Sect. 2. [c] And the Law ſo far abhors all Corruption of this Statute, that it prohibits every Thing which has the leaſt Tendency to it, what ſpecious Pretence ſoever it may be covered with, and therefore it will not ſuffer a mere Stranger, ſo much as to labour a Juror to appear and little act according to his Conſcience.

Sect. 3. Alſo it is ſaid, That generally the giving of Money to a Juror [d] after the Verdict, without any precedent Contract in Relation to it, is an Offence ſavouring of the Nature of Embracery; becauſe if ſuch Practices were allowable, it would be eaſy to evade the Law, by giving Jurors ſecret Intimations of ſuch an intended Reward for their Service, which might be of as bad Conſequence as the giving of Money beforehand. But it ſeems clear, That the giving of Jurors ſuch a reaſonable Recompence, as is uſually allowed them for their Expences in travelling, *&c.* and which may fairly be expected by them from either Side that ſhall prevail, is no way criminal, becauſe if no ſuch Allowance were to be expected, it would be often difficult to prevail with Perſons to ſerve on a Jury at their own Charge; and therefore by Experience it hath been found neceſſary to permit the Parties to give Jurors ſome Amends for their Charges.

Sect. 4. It hath been adjudged, That the bare [e] giving of Money to another to be diſtributed among Jurors, is an Offence of the Nature of Embracery, whether any of it be afterwards actually ſo diſtributed or not; alſo it is [f] clear, That it is as Criminal in a Juror, as in any other Perſon, to endeavour to prevail with his Companions to give a Verdict for one Side, by any Practices whatſoever, except only by Arguments from the Evidence which was produced, and Exhortations from the general Obligations

[a] F.N.B. 171. B. C. Co.Lit.369.a. Moore 815. Pl. 1104.

[b] 21 H.6.20.a. 22 H. 6. 5. b. 37 H.6.31.a. Bro. Decies tantum 10, 11, 13.

Co.Lit 369.a. Mo. 815. Pl. 1104. 13 H 4.16 b. Moor 806. Cro. El. 816. Co.Lit.159.b. 369. a.

[d] 39 Aſſ. 19. Bro. Decies 14.

[e] 22 H.6.5.b. 28 H. 6. 7. b. 12. b. 31 H. 6. 8. b. 9. Bro. Maintenance 6, 14.

[f] 17 Ed.4.5.b. 18 Ed. 4. 4.b. Bro. Maintenance 32, 39.

tions of Conſcience to give a true Verdict. And there can be no Doubt but that all fraudulent Contrivances whatſoever to ſecure a Verdict, are high Offences of this Nature; as where Perſons by [a] indirect Means procure themſelves or others, to be ſworn on a *Tales* in order to ſerve one Side.

Sect. 5. As to the ſecond Point, *viz.* What Acts of this Kind are altogether unlawful, it ſeems clear, That neither the Party himſelf, nor his Counſel, nor Attorney, nor any Perſon whatſoever, can juſtify any indirect Practices of influencing a Jury, either by giving [b] or promiſing them Money, or [c] menacing them, or [d] inſtructing them in the Cauſe before-hand, *&c.*

Sect. 6. As to the third Point, *viz.* In what Circumſtances ſome Acts of this Nature may be lawful, it ſeemeth clear, That any Perſon who may juſtify any other Act of Maintenance, may ſafely labour a Juror to [e] appear and give a Verdict according to his Conſcience, but that no other Perſon can juſtify intermeddling ſo far, and that no one whatſoever can juſtify the labouring a Juror [f] not to appear.

Sect. 7. As to the fourth Point, *viz.* How far Offences of this Kind are reſtrained by the Common Law, there can be no Doubt but that they ſubject the Offender either to an Indictment or Action, in the ſame Manner as all other Kinds of unlawful Maintenance do by the Common Law: Alſo it ſeemeth, That if an Act of Embracery were not known before the Trial of a Cauſe, ſo that the Party to whoſe Prejudice it was intended, had no Opportunity to prevent the ill Effects of it, by challenging the Juror who was practiſed upon, it will be a good Ground to move the Court to ſet aſide the Verdict.

Sect. 8. As to the fifth Point, *viz.* How far Offences of this Kind are reſtrained by Statute, it is enacted, by 5 *Ed.* 3. 10. *That if any Juror, in Aſſizes, Juries, or Inqueſts, take of the one Party or of the other, and be thereof duly attainted, that hereafter he ſhall not be put in any Aſſizes, Juries, or Inqueſts, and nevertheleſs he ſhall be commanded to Priſon, and further ranſomed at the King's Will. And the Juſtices before whom ſuch Aſſizes, Juries and Inqueſts ſhall paſs, ſhall have Power to enquire and determine according to this Statute.*

Sect. 9. And it is farther enacted by 34 *Ed.* 3. 8. *That in every Plea, whereof the Inqueſt or Aſſize doth paſs, if any of the Parties will ſue againſt any of the Jurors, that they have taken of his Adverſary or of him, for to give their Verdict, he ſhall be heard, and ſhall have his Plaint by Bill preſently before the Juſtices, before whom they did ſwear, and that the Juror be put to anſwer without any delay, and if they plead to the Country, the Inqueſt ſhall be taken* maintenant. *And if any Man other than the Party will ſue for the King againſt the Juror, it ſhall be heard and determined as afore is ſaid. And if the Juror be attainted at the Suit of other than the Party, and maketh Fine, the Party that ſueth ſhall have half the Fine; and that the Parties to the Plea ſhall recover their Damages by the Aſſeſſment of the Inqueſt. And that the Juror ſo attainted have the Priſon of one Year, which Impriſonment the King granteth, that it ſhall not be pardoned for any Fine; and if the Party will ſue by Writ, before other Juſtices, he ſhall have the Suit in the Form aforeſaid.*

Sect, 10. And it is farther enacted by 38 *E.* 3. 12. *That if any Jurors in Aſſizes ſworn, and other Inqueſts to be taken between the King and Party, or Party and Party, do any Thing take by them, or other of the Party, Plaintiff, or Defenandant, to give their Verdict, and thereof be attainted by Proceſs contained in the ſaid Statute of* 34 E. 3 *be it at the Suit of the Party that will ſue for himſelf, or for the King, or any other Perſon, every of the ſaid Jurors ſhall pay ten Times as much as he hath taken. And that he that will ſue,*

[a] 1 Saund. 301.

[b] 13 H. 4. 16 b. 17 a. 11 H. 6. 11. a. 2 Rol. A. 116. L. 6. M. 3.

[c] 19 H. 6. 31. b. 13 H. 4. 17. a.

[d] 2 Bulſt. 25. Noy 102. Co. Lit. 369 a. Moore 815. Pl. 1104.

[e] Dyer 48. Pl. 19. Co. Li. 157. b. 369. a. Moore 813. Pl. 1101. Hob. 294. Noy 102.

[f] Hob. 294.

I *ſhall*

ſhall have the one half, and the King the other half. And that all the Embraceors to bring or procure ſuch Inqueſt in the Country to take Gain or Profit, ſhall be puniſhed in the ſame Manner and Form as the Jurors. And if the Juror or Embraceor ſo attainted, have not whereof to make Gree in the manner aforeſaid, he ſhall have the Impriſonment of one Year: And the Intent of the King, of Great Men, and of the Commons is, That no Juſtice nor other Miniſter ſhall enquire of Office, upon any of the Points of this Article, but only at the Suit of the Party, or of other as afore is ſaid.

In the Conſtruction of theſe Statutes the following Points have been holden:

Sect. 11. I. That all Actions of *Decies tantum* being founded on an Offence ſuppoſed to have been committed in ſome former Action appearing upon Record, it will be a good Plea in Bar, either that there is no [a] ſuch Record at all, or that there is not any ſuch [b] Record by which it may appear that the Juror was ſworn, and that it is a good [c] Exception in Abatement of the Writ, that there is a Variance in the firſt Record from that in the Declaration in the preſent Action; yet it is ſaid, That it is not neceſſary to [d] ſhew the whole Record in certain, but only ſo much of it as conveys the Plaintiff to his Action.

Sect. 12. II. That it is not [e] ſufficient to ſhew that the Defendants took Money in order to embrace a Jury, without ſhewing alſo that they actually diſpoſed of it accordingly.

Sect. 13. III. That the [f] Plaintiff muſt ſhew in certain how much was received, for otherwiſe the Court will not know for what Sum to give Judgment.

Sect. 14. IV. That the giving of Money to a Juror [g] after the Verdict is not within the Statute, unleſs there were ſome precedent Contract relating to it.

Sect. 15. V. That it is not [h] material whether the Jurors gave any Verdict or not, or if they did give one, whether it were true or falſe.

Sect. 16. VI. That all the Jurors and Embraceors may be joined in one Action, notwithſtanding they ſeverally received different Sums, becauſe all was received in order to give the ſame Verdict, which could not but be the entire Act of all the Jurors. But it is ſaid, That all the Defendants ought to plead ſeverally, that neither they nor any of them took any Money in the Manner as the Plaintiff hath declared.

Sect. 17. VII. That the [i] Defendants ought not to plead generally Not guilty, but that they ought ſpecially to deny the taking of the Money, *&c.*

Sect. 18. VIII. [k] That the Plaintiff ſhall be paid the Moiety of the Money due to him on a Judgment in *Decies tantum* before the King, becauſe the King's Moiety is not due as a Debt but as a Fine; and whereever the King is intituled to a Fine from the Suit of a Subject, the Plaintiff ſhall firſt be ſatisfied.

Sect. 19. IX. That the Husband [l] alone may bring a *Decies tantum* for an Embracery in a former Action brought by him and his Wife, becauſe by a *Decies tantum* Money only is to be recovered wherein the Wife can claim no Share.

Sect. 20. X. That he who buys Land to maintain a Suit at a lower Price than it is known to be worth, is as much within the Statute, for ſo much as the [m] Land is worth more than he gave, as if he had received it in Money.

[a] 5 Ed. 4. 3. a. Bro. Decies tantum 2. 11.
[b] 37 H. 6. 31. a. Bro. Decies tantum 13.
[c] 9 H. 6. 1. Bro. Decies tantum 1.
[d] 34 H. 6. 4. b.
[e] 37 H. 6. 31. a. F.N.B. 171. C.
[f] Pl. Com. 85.
[g] 39 Aſſ. 19. Bro. Decies tantum 14.
[h] 21 H 6 31. a. 37 H. 6. 31. a. Bro. Decies tantum 10, 13. F. N. B. 171. C. B. Co Lit. 369. a. Dy 95. Pl. 39. 40 Ed. 3. 3. b. 36 H. 6 28 b. Bro. Decies tantum 3, 4. F.N.B. 171 a. Finch 255. 21 H. 6. 20.
[i] Bro. Decies tantum 1. 16 Savil 42.
[k] 41 E. 3. 15. a 44 E. 3. 36 b. Bro. Decies tantum 5, 7.
[l] 7 H. 4. 2. b. 2. a. 43 E. 3. 16. a. Bro. Decies tantum 9. 19.
[m] 41 Ed. 3. 9 b. Bro. Decies tantum 4. 1 Rol. Ab. 579. A.

a 5 E. 4. 2 b. 3. a. Bro. Decies tantum 15. Cro. El. 138, 583. 11 Co. 65. b. 3 Inst. 194. b 44 E 3 36 b. Bro. Decies tantum 7.

Sect. 21. XI. That this being a popular Action may be barred by the [a] King's Release, being made before any Action brought, but that it cannot be barred by the Release of the Party grieved; and from the same Ground also it follows, That the Party grieved needs not in such Action declare of any Damages done to him by the Embracery; but if he do it is said, That he [b]ought to lay them severally against each Defendant, or else that his Writ shall abate, unless he will release them: But perhaps there may be good Reason to question this Opinion, for why may not the Damages be as well recovered, as the Action jointly laid against all the Defendants?

c 44 E. 3. 12. a. 47 E. 3. 4. a. Bro. Decies, 6, 8. d 47 E 3 4 a. Vide 6 E. 4. 11. a. b. 2 Rol. Ab. 277. B.

Sect. 22. XII. That no [c] Process of Outlawry lies in this Action, but only a *Capias* or Distress infinite, upon a *Nihil* returned, and that such Distress ought to be of the Lands which the Defendants had at the Time of the Writ of *Decies tantum* purchased, and not of those which they had at the Time of the Inquest; and that no *Capias* [d] into a foreign County lies against the Jurors, because it shall be presumed that they are in the County wherein they were returned on the Jury; but clearly this Reason can no Way be extended to the Embraceors: And perhaps it may be over favourable to carry it so far in Relation to the Jurors, especially since the Distress infinite can only affect the Lands which they had at the Time of the *Decies tantum*, before which they may possibly have sold those which they had at the Return of the *Venire*; and why should not the Sheriff's present Return that the Defendants have nothing in the County, over-ballance the Presumption chiefly grounded on the former Return, with which the present is not inconsistent, being made at a subsequent Time.

CHAP. LXXXVI.

Of the Offence of buying or selling a pretended Title.

FOR the better understanding the Offence of buying or selling a pretended Title, I shall consider:

1. How it is restrained by the Common Law.
2. How by Statute.

Moor 751. Pl 1031. Hob. 115. Pl Com. 80. a. 88. a.

Sect. 1. As to the first Point, it seemeth to be a High Offence at Common Law to buy or sell any doubtful Title to Lands known to be disputed, to the Intent that the Buyer may carry on the Suit, which the Seller doth not think it worth his while to do, and on that Consideration sells his Pretensions at an under Rate; and it seemeth not to be material, whether the Title so sold be a good or bad one, or whether the Seller were in Possession or not, unless his Possession were lawful and uncontested; for all Practices of this Kind are by all Means to be discountenanced, as manifestly tending to Oppression, by giving Opportunities to

Great Men to purchase the disputed Titles of others, to the great Grievance of the adverse Parties, who may often be unable or discouraged to defend their Titles against such powerful Persons, which perhaps they might safely enough maintain against their proper Adversary.

Sect. 2. As to the second Point, *viz.* How far Offences of this Kind are restrained by Statute, it is recited by 1 R. 2. 9. *That many Persons having true Title to Lands, and also in Personal Actions were wrongfully delayed of their Rights and Actions, by Means that the Defendants did commonly make Gifts and Feoffments of their Lands in debate, and of their Goods, to Lords, and other Great Men, against whom the said Pursuants for Menace that was made to them, neither could nor durst make their Pursuits: And also that many Persons oftentimes used to disseize others, and anon after such Disseisin to make divers Feoffments, sometimes to Lords and other Great Men, to have Maintenance, and sometimes to Persons unknown, to the Intent to delay the said Disseisees,* &c. And it is thereupon enacted, *That from thenceforth no Gift, or Feoffment, of Lands, Tenements or Goods, be made by such Fraud or Maintenance; and that if any be in such wise made, they shall be holden for none and of no Value; and that the said Disseisees shall from thenceforth have their Recovery against the first Disseisor, as well of the Lands and Tenements, as of their double Damages, without having regard to such Alienations, so that the Disseisees commence their Suits within the Year next after the Disseisin done.*

In the Construction of the Statute it hath been holden:

Sect. 3. That Feoffments of this Kind are only void in Respect of the Disseisees, but that they are effectual between the Feoffor and Feoffee, *&c.* Bro. Feoffments de terres 1, 19. Co Lit. 369 a.

Sect. 4. And it is farther enacted by 32 *H.* 8. 9. *That no Person or Persons whatsoever shall bargain, buy, or sell, or by any Ways or Means, obtain, get, or have any pretended Rights or Titles, or take, promise, grant, or covenant to have any Right or Title, of any Person or Persons, in, or to any Manors, Lands, Tenements, or Hereditaments, but if such Person or Persons, which shall so bargain, sell, give, grant, covenant, or promise the same, their Ancestors, or they by whom he or they claim the same, have been in Possession of the same, or of the Reversion or Remainder thereof, or taken the Rents or Profits thereof, by the Space of one whole Year next before the said Bargain, Covenant, Grant, or Promise made, upon Pain that he that shall make any such Bargain, Sale, Promise, Covenant, or Grant, to forfeit the whole Value of the Lands, Tenements or Hereditaments so bargained, sold, promised, covenanted or granted, contrary to the Form of this Act. And the Buyer or Taker thereof, knowing the same, to forfeit also the Value of the said Lands, Tenements, or Hereditaments so by him bought, or taken as is abovesaid. The one half of the said Forfeitures to be to the King, and the other half to the Party that will sue for the same in any of the King's Courts of Record, by Action of Debt, Bill, Plaint, or Information. In which Action, Bill, Plaint or Information, no Essoin, Protection, Wager of Law, nor Injunction shall be allowed.*

Sect. 5. But it is provided by the said Statute, *That it shall be lawful to any Person, being in lawful Possession, by taking of the yearly Farm, Rents, or Profits, of, or for any Manors, Lands, Tenements, or Hereditaments, to buy, obtain, get, or have by any reasonable Way or Means, the pretensed Right or Title of any other Person or Persons, hereafter to be made to, of, or in such Manors, Lands, Tenements, or Hereditaments, whereof he or they shall so be* in *in lawful Poſſeſſion, any Thing in the ſaid Act contained to the contrary notwithſtanding.*

Sect. 6. And it is farther provided, *That the ſaid Statute ſhall not extend to charge any Perſon with any of the above mentioned Penalties, except ſuch Perſon be ſued for the Offence within one Year.*

In the Conſtruction of this Statute the following Opinions have been holden:

Pl.Com.83.b.

Sect. 7. I. That it is not material whether any Suit be depending concerning the Lands contracted for, or not, whereas the Statutes ſet forth in the precedent Chapters extended only to Contracts concerning Lands which were actually in Suit.

Lit.Rep.369. Pl.Com. 84. Cro. Ca. 233. Dy. 77. Pl. 19, 20. Contr. 1 And. 76.

Sect. 8. II. That in an Action on this Statute, the Plaintiff needs not recite it, becauſe the Judges are bound *ex Officio* to take Notice of it, being of a publick Nature; but that if he do recite it, he muſt at his Peril take Care to recite it certainly, becauſe it is the Ground of his Action; and the Court will not aid him by intending that there is another Statute to maintain his Action, different from that whereon he himſelf hath founded it.

1 Leon 167. Lit.Rep.369

Sect. 9. III. That in ſuch an Action againſt the Buyer of a pretended Title, it ought expreſly to appear, That the Defendant did know that the Seller had not been in Poſſeſſion the Year before; and *vice verſâ*, that in ſuch an Action by the Buyer the contrary ought to appear, for otherwiſe it may be intended, that he was *Particeps Criminis*, and therefore ought not to have any Share of the Penalty.

Dy. 77. Pl. 19, 20. Pl. Com. 87, 88. Cro. Ca. 233.

Sect. 10. IV. That it is not ſufficient to ſhew, That the Seller had not been in Poſſeſſion, *&c.* a Year before, without expreſly averring that he had a pretended Right or Title, becauſe that is the Point of the Action.

[a] Cro.Ca. 233. [b] 4 Co. 26. a. Co.Lit.369 b. Moore 655. Pl. 898.

Sect. 11. V. That it is not [a] ſufficient to ſet forth the Value of the Land at the Time of the Conveyance executed, without ſhewing the Value at the Time of the Bargain, becauſe the Forfeiture is governed by the later.

[c] Pl.Com. 87. Dy. 77. Pl. 19, 20, 374. Pl. 17. [d] Co. Lit. 369. a. b. Con. Moore 266, Pl. 414. Dy. 374. Pl. 17. [e] Co. Lit. 369. b.

Sect. 12. VI. That a Contract for a [b] cuſtomary Right to a Copyhold Eſtate, or for a Leaſe for [c] Years, is as much within the Statute as a Contract for the Fee-Simple; for the Words of the Statute are, *any Right or Title*, and ſuch Contracts are as much within the Miſchief intended to be redreſſed by the Statute as any others can be: But it is [d] ſaid, That a Leaſe for Years made with an Intent to try the Title in Ejectment, is not within the Meaning of the Statute, becauſe it is in a Kind of Courſe of Law, [e] unleſs it be made to a powerful Man to ſway the Cauſe.

Pl. Com. 85. Dy. 77. Pl. 19, 20.

Sect. 13. VII. That in an Action for the making ſuch a Leaſe for Years, it is not neceſſary preciſely to ſet forth the Commencement and End of it, becauſe the Plaintiff is ſuppoſed to be a Stranger to it.

1 Leon 166. 1 And.76,77.

Sect. 14. VIII. That a Leaſe for Years by one out of Poſſeſſion being made off the Land, is as much within the Statute as if it had been made upon the Land, though it be wholly void in Law; for it is a Leaſe in Reputation, and taken for ſuch among the Vulgar, and tends as much to diſquiet the Poſſeſſion as if it had been effectual in Law.

Sect. 15. IX. That no Conveyance made by one who hath the uncontested Possession, and undisputed absolute Propriety of Lands, is any Way within the Meaning of the Statute, because it no Way favours of Maintenance, and can be prejudicial to no one; from whence it follows, That a Disseisor obtaining the Release, of the Disseisee, or a Mortgagor redeeming his Land, are in no Danger of the Statute in Respect of any Contract by them made, concerning such Land after such Release or Redemption. Bro Maintenance 38. Pl. Com. 88, 89 Co Lit. 369.a.

Sect. 16. X. That one who gains the Possession of Lands, by Virtue of a Judgment at Law in Affirmance of an ancient Title, cannot come within the Meaning of this Statute in respect of any Lease made of such Lands; for it can never be imagined, That it was the Intent of the Statute, to oblige all Persons who should recover their Lands, to occupy them themselves, which would be generally inconvenient, and often wholly impracticable; and therefore it must be admitted from the Necessity of the Case, That such Persons may lawfully lease their Lands and Houses to proper Tenants, to be manured and occupied for the usual Rents: But if it shall appear, That the Title to such Lands is still contested notwithstanding such Recovery, and that such Lease was in Truth designed for the Maintenance of the Title, I can see no Reason why it should not be as much within the Statute as any Case whatsoever. However there seems to be no Doubt, but that if a Disseisee enter upon a Disseisor, being in Possession of the Land under a pretended Title, and immediately sell it to a Stranger, he is as much within the Statute as if he had been out of Possession at the Time of such Sale; for notwithstanding his Entry was lawful, and he had both the absolute Property and Possession of the Land, yet inasmuch as the Disseisor claims a Title to it, which is yet in Dispute, such a Sale by the Disseisee seems within the Intent of the Statute, which meant absolutely to restrain all Persons from transferring their disputed Titles to any Stranger whatsoever. But it is said, that such a Sale by a Father to his Son and Heir Apparent, is excepted out of the general Purview of the Statute, by common Reason, which by the Ties of Nature as well as of Interest, obliges such a Son to maintain his Father; yet it hath been holden, That such a Sale to a Brother of the half Blood is within the Statute. Pl. Com. 88, 89 Co Lit. 369.a. Moore 655. Pl. 898. 1 Leon 166, 167. Co.Lit. 369.a. *seems contrary.* Savil 95, 96. 1 Leon 167. Mo. 656. 1 Leon 167. Savil 95, 96.

Sect. 17. XI. It is said that the above mentioned Proviso, That one who is in lawful Possession by taking the yearly Rents or Profits of Lands, *&c.* may lawfully buy the pretensed Right of any other Person by reasonable Means, is no more than the Law would have implied, if it had not been expressed; for such a Contract cannot possibly be to the Wrong of any one, and tends rather to quiet Suits than to promote them. And from the like Reason also it is said, That a Disseisor may lawfully get the Release of the Disseisee, though his Possession was unlawful; and it seems clear, That such a Release cannot come within the Meaning of the Statute, if the Disseisee had the true Right, and no other had any Pretence of Title to the Land; for in such Case it is clear, That the End of the Release is not for Maintenance, but for the Settlement of all Disputes: But if such a Disseisee had had but a contested Title, and such Release were intended only to enable the Disseisor to defend himself with the dubious Title of his Disseisee, surely it cannot but be as much within the Meaning of the Statute, as any Conveyance to one wholly out of Possession. However it seems clear, That those Co.Lit. 369.b.

Inſtances in the ſaid Proviſo by which it is ſhewn how it ſhall appear, that the Perſons who are permitted to contract for pretended Titles are in Poſſeſſion, as by the receiving of Rent, *&c.* are only put for Examples, and that thoſe who are any Way whatſoever lawfully ſeized in Poſſeſſion, Reverſion, or Remainder, are within the Co.Li.369.b. Benefit of the Proviſo; but it ſeems clear, That they can only juſtify the taking ſuch a Conveyance as will ſtrengthen the Eſtate whereof they are ſeized, and that they cannot take a Covenant from a Stranger to convey the Land to them, when he ſhall have recovered it on a pretended Right, becauſe ſuch a Covenant ſeems clearly to ſavour as much of Maintenance, as if they had been Strangers to the Land.

FINIS.

An Alphabetical

INDEX

OF THE

Principal Matters

Contained in this

BOOK.

Haun-

And

INDEX.

I N D E X.

Such

May

I N D E X.

INDEX.

 You

INDEX.

Cccc The

INDEX.

INDEX.

I N D E X.

taking

INDEX.

I N D E X.

INDEX.

Mis-

INDEX.

Where

INDEX.

Nose.

I N D E X.

Nose.

Notice.

Nusance.

Oaths.

Obscene.

Occupiers.

Offence.

Office and Officer.

INDEX.

INDEX.

Petit

INDEX.

Hhhh

The

No

INDEX.

I N D E X.

INDEX.

INDEX.

Sup-

I N D E X.

How

INDEX.

4 Kkkk Justi-

INDEX.

Weapon

INDEX.

FINIS.